ESSENTIALS OF LEARNING

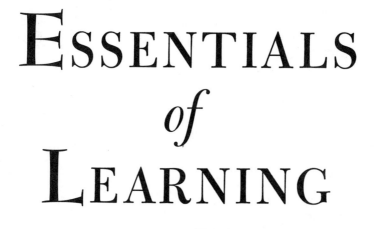

ESSENTIALS
of
LEARNING

AN OVERVIEW FOR STUDENTS OF EDUCATION

SECOND EDITION

Robert M. W. Travers

WESTERN MICHIGAN UNIVERSITY

THE MACMILLAN COMPANY

COLLIER-MACMILLAN LIMITED · *LONDON*

THE MACMILLAN COMPANY
COLLIER-MACMILLAN CANADA, LTD., Toronto, Ontario
PRINTED IN THE UNITED STATES OF AMERICA

PREFACE

TEXTS for students of education may be written to prepare the reader either for a profession or for a trade. In preparing for a profession, the student may be expected to master not only the tools he will need to practice it, but also knowledge in those related disciplines upon which future advances in the profession may be based. In contrast, trainees preparing to enter a trade may be expected to master only the practices of the trade, delving little into the body of knowledge upon which such practices are based. If teaching is the chosen profession, the student may be expected to include in his background a familiarity with those aspects of psychology that have the most direct bearing on problems of education. That aspect which impinges most directly is the psychology of learning.

The author hopes that this book will serve, for students of education, a function analogous to that served by textbooks on physiology for students of medicine. The latter texts generally attempt to provide a comprehensive overview of current knowledge, with some emphasis on the theoretical issues involved, the problems to be solved, and the relationship of body mechanisms to healthful functioning. Although this volume indicates some of the implications of research results for educational practice, it does not suggest specific classroom procedures. It attempts to provide a firm foundation on which the student can build in further studies in the areas of curriculum and teaching methods, for it is in these latter areas that the applications of psychological knowledge are to be found.

The problem of teaching graduate courses in learning to students in colleges of education is not too different from the problem of teaching undergraduate courses. The typical graduate student is ten or twenty years removed from any courses he had in psychology. The typical specialized textbook on learning, written for students of psychology, presupposes knowledge of recent developments in psychology with which the student of education may not have had contact. Also, such texts do little to relate results of research to problems of education. The author hopes that this book will leave the student of education not only with some knowledge of the important research that is being undertaken in the field of learning, but also with some understanding of the significant implications which the knowledge thus acquired may have for educational planning. Perhaps the reader will also come to the last page with a better understanding of the degree to which education is based on faith rather

v

than knowledge, and how great the need is for expanding knowledge of the learning process.

Both the instructor and the students should use this book much the same way that other instructors with other students use a mathematics textbook. Instructor and students should work through the book together, with the instructor spending time on those sections that give the students special difficulty. It is not the kind of book on which the student is turned loose while the instructor delivers an independent set of lectures or leads discussions on only indirectly related topics. A course in a college of education based on this text would never be criticized either as being too easy or as lacking in content. The writer believes that this book reflects a trend in the professional literature of education, for some excellent texts already exist in other parts of the teacher-training curriculum that are far outside the reach of either one of these common criticisms.

The writer will continue to be grateful for the help given by the many who reviewed and criticized the various versions of the first edition. This second edition owes much to many discussions held with Dr. Ian Reid over a period of several years. The preparation of the chapter on transfer of training was greatly facilitated through daily interactions on the topic with Dr. R. L. R. Overing during the spring of 1965. Dr. Overing also read a draft of the chapter and offered many helpful criticisms.

R. M. W. T.

CONTENTS

LIST OF ILLUSTRATIONS

LIST OF TABLES

ESSENTIALS OF LEARNING

1

Some Approaches to Learning

TWO DISTINCT approaches to research on learning can be clearly seen when one examines the history of the last century. One approach is based upon the point of view that research on learning is best conducted in schools and in realistic settings where education is actually in progress; the other is represented by those who have sought to study learning phenomena under simplified conditions in the laboratory. One cannot, on logical grounds alone, reject one of these research positions and embrace the other. The success achieved by one or the other will ultimately determine which one should be adopted, though the possibility exists that both may yield scientific knowledge. Perhaps time will show that both approaches have considerable merit. While more knowledge, to date, has been produced by laboratory studies of learning than by the study of learning in natural settings, this may merely mean that the time is not yet ripe for the direct study of classroom events related to learning. Keeping the latter possibility in mind, this chapter will attempt to review the major situations in which learning phenomena have been studied and attempt to indicate the problems as well as the advantages of each kind of situation for developing an organized body of knowledge about learning.

The Study of Learning in School Settings

Studies of learning in school situations have had a history of a little over half a century. Some of the earliest, if not *the* earliest, of such studies were conducted in the 1890–1900 period by Joseph Mayer Rice, a pioneer educational reformer who devoted the last half of his life to the reform of education. This task he pursued with almost fanatical vigor. Influenced by the German educational reformers, from whom he had acquired both his ideas and his enthusiasm, he believed that the American public would force educational reform on the schools if only the facts were placed before them. He observed the performance of hundreds of teachers scattered over the eastern half of the United States and published a summary of his observations in a book entitled *The Public School System of the United States* (1893). The public was little impressed with his opinions, but this did not curb his zeal for educational reform. If his opinions were to be discounted, then perhaps the public might be impressed with facts. What appeared to be needed were data concerning the relevancy of various aspects of the teaching process to the achievement of the academic objectives, and such data Rice set out to collect. He administered tests of achievement in arithmetic, spelling, and language, and attempted to relate scores on these tests to the practices of the teachers. He was able to demonstrate that the time devoted to spelling had little to do with the accomplishment of the pupils. Indeed, his results indicated that the time devoted to spelling could generally be at least halved without depressing the level of skill acquired by the pupils.

The knowledge that Rice developed as a result of his work could not be considered scientific knowledge, but, rather, it represented a number of isolated facts about education. Such collections of isolated facts are not the makings of an organized body of scientific knowledge, however valuable they may be. There is a possibility that they might ultimately lead to the development of scientific knowledge, just as the accumulation of knowledge about the stars by Tycho de Brahe led to Kepler's formulation of an astronomical theory. Rice's work did not produce any direct educational reform, though it might have over the years; nevertheless, his work did have an influence on the development of educational research, for it was the beginning of a long series of educational investigations of classroom practices which are still continuing today.

During the half century that followed Rice's efforts at educational reform, numerous studies were undertaken that were designed to find relationships between the amount of learning occurring in schools and the conditions under which learning took place. Many of these were concerned with finding relationships between ratings of the personality traits of teachers and rate of learning of pupils. Others related characteristics of teachers, such as are measured by tests, to the level of achievement of the pupils.[*] Such studies became popular sources of doctoral dissertations and also occupied the time of many directors of research in school systems. These inquiries, in their day, could certainly be justified. What could be more logical than to improve education by finding out about the conditions that make for rapid learning and then by planning education so that these conditions occur in every classroom.

[*] See, for example, the annotated bibliography of such studies by Tiedeman and Domas (1950).

This recipe for improving education was warmly and widely accepted. Surely by midcentury such studies would provide a sound basis for educational reform, but these hopes and expectations were not to be realized despite the widespread effort that was devoted to correlating various aspects of learning conditions with outcomes. By midcentury, the major conclusion that could be drawn from such studies was that only very small and inconsistent relationships were generally found between teacher characteristics and practices and other aspects of the learning situation on the one hand and amount of learning on the other. Perhaps the main value of such studies has been to show the great complexity of the learning process in the classroom and the multiplicity of factors that may influence pupil learning. The influence of any one factor, or even the influence of the combination of several factors, may be so small that it may not show up in research using the crude techniques of measurement that are available. Certainly, studies relating learning conditions in school to pupil achievement have provided little basis for the improvement of education. The reform they were expected to bring simply has not materialized.

During the years between the two world wars a related type of research in schools began to serve what may be termed a political purpose. The emergence after World War I of the progressive-education movement resulted in the appearance of new practices, which a conservative public promptly attacked. The newly developed techniques for conducting research in schools appeared to educators to offer a means of defending the newer practices, if not of demonstrating that they were superior to those they replaced. Thus, during the thirties there appeared a considerable number of studies that attempted to compare the achievement of pupils in progressive schools with the achievement of pupils exposed to a more traditional curriculum. The major purpose of such studies was to defend newer practices rather than to advance knowledge of the educational process.

Studies comparing older and newer practices varied in ambitiousness from minor researches conducted to fulfill the requirements of a master's degree up to very elaborate and costly programs of research financed by foundations. The most elaborately conceived of these was a study developed under the auspices of the Progressive Education Association and designed to study the effects of a progressive curriculum in a group of thirty schools. It was conducted as part of what was known as the *Eight Year Study*, a study of these thirty schools. Methods of appraisal of the outcomes of learning in a progressive curriculum, developed as a part of this study, formed an important landmark in educational research. These methods are reported in a volume by Smith and Tyler (1942). Later some of the students from the thirty schools were followed up in college to determine whether the progressive curriculum facilitated or interfered with intellectual and social development during the college years.

Excellent summaries have been made of such studies, which attempt to compare the effects of one teaching methodology with those of another; there would be little point in providing another review here. But the conclusions presented in such summaries do have considerable relevance to the present discussion, because they indicate the value and limitations of this approach to learning research. The main conclusions drawn from such studies have been summarized in a paper by Wallen and Travers (1963) as follows:

1. Differences in achievement of pupils exposed to different teaching methods are small and not generally consistent from study to study.

2. The method considered to be the experimental method in particular studies tends to show some slight superiority to the method described as the control method.

3. When teachers are asked to teach two classes by different methods, the teachers show only limited capacity for changing their pattern of behavior as they switch from method to method. This fact may account for the small differences between methods found in some of the studies.

4. Very few studies provide data indicating the way in which one method of teaching differs from another. Research workers usually report how the methods are *alleged* to differ, but few studies provide data indicating how the methods *actually* differ in terms of the recorded behavior of the teachers in the classroom.

5. Since information is generally lacking concerning the precise way in which teacher behavior differs in the two methods of teaching that are being compared, there is little basis for understanding any differences that may be found in the achievement of pupils exposed to the two methods. The situation is similar to that of an experiment in which some learning condition believed to be of vital consequence to the learning process is varied and the effects of this variation on learning noted, but in which the experimenter failed to record what was actually varied. Even if a typical study of the effects of various teaching methods turns up interesting differences, there is generally no way of finding out what such differences signify.

6. The results of the studies suggest that procedures for designing new teaching methods do not seem to take into account the major factors that influence learning. If they did, then the new teaching methods should produce markedly superior results to the older ones.

7. Even when two teaching methods differ markedly in the experiences that they provide for the children, the children exposed may still have many experiences in common. They may use the same textbook, consult

the same set of reference books, view the same visual and auditory aids. Such common experience in the two groups may produce learning that may well mask any differences produced by differences in method.

These conclusions lead to the position that the studies of teaching methods that have been undertaken have not resulted in anything resembling an organized body of knowledge, though some knowledge has been acquired. Here again, emphasis must be placed upon the fact that there is much knowledge available to humanity that is not scientific knowledge. The knowledge that such studies have yielded represents disconnected pieces of information. In addition, they have provided a certain understanding of some of the difficulties that face the person who wishes to acquire some insight into the learning process. Nowhere can be seen emerging the organized body of knowledge bound together by theoretical concepts of the kind that constitutes a science.

What has been said up to this point about the study of the learning process through direct study of the classroom fails to take note of a third type of classroom study, which has been highly productive, that came into being with the work of the great French psychologist Alfred Binet. In this approach an attempt is made to identify and measure characteristics of intellectual functioning that are of importance to the learning process. If the psychologist could measure capacities to perform intellectual functions, then the possibility is open of predicting the efficiency with which the individual can learn intellectual tasks. This Binet tried to do, and his famous test is an attempt to measure the child's capacity for performing those mental operations that must be performed successfully if the child is to learn at an adequate speed in school. For example, Binet and Simon (1905) postulated that the capacity to perform reasoning operations is important for success in schoolwork, and hence developed a series of problem situations through which the child's capacity to perform such operations could be tested. Research later demonstrated that the variable measured by such a test did appear to be related to the capacity to learn in school. Other research showed that, in the case of children of high-school age, there are a number of separate and distinct measurable characteristics that bear a clear relationship to the learning process and that show some stability over the years. Such variables, commonly referred to as aptitudes, have great significance for understanding the learning process. They have been discovered largely through the study of learning in school settings, and represent an area of application of psychology in which considerable success has been achieved. In addition, the knowledge produced by classroom studies in this area has come to acquire many of the characteristics of a scientific body of knowledge.

Laboratory Approaches to Learning

In many areas of scientific enquiry the scientist is limited to the study of phenomena as they occur in natural settings, but in other areas aspects of phenomena can be studied under simplified conditions in the laboratory. Great advantages accrue when this can be done, and history has shown that where laboratory approaches can be undertaken rapid advances are likely to be made. Of course, the word *rapid* must be interpreted conservatively. When the great physicist Cavendish obtained a numerical value of the gravitational constant, he concluded a phase of the work of Newton that had been begun a hundred years earlier. This may seem a long time, but this same century of experimentation in physics produced greater advances in knowledge of physics than the entire previous history of mankind.

The development of a laboratory science typically leaves the layman wondering what it is all about. It is a far cry from Faraday, working in his laboratory with wires and magnets, to the modern electric power station with its massive equipment serving the needs of mankind. (Indeed, there are stories of how visitors to the Faraday laboratory would chide him about the apparent uselessness of his work.) Even more obscure would be the relationship between the abstract mathematical work of Einstein and the development of the atomic bomb that fell on Hiroshima. Many in education today have a similar and understandable difficulty in seeing what laboratory studies of the eye-blink reflex or the learning of nonsense syllables can possibly have for the conduct of education in schools. Yet the fact is that most knowledge of learning has been derived from the study of learning situations which have little relevance on the surface to practical matters of education. The worth of laboratory studies must never be judged in terms of superficial appearance.

If the teacher is asked to divide learning situations into categories, he is likely to name such learning situations as English, mathematics, social studies, foreign languages, and so forth. If he has had some association with the progressive tradition, he may abandon subject-matter lines and suggest such categories as problem solving, information gathering, using reference sources, and many others which do not have much to do with the traditional curriculum. If the psychologist is asked to classify learning phenomena, he is likely to use an entirely different classification of learning, because he will think in terms of the situations in which learning has been systematically studied in the laboratory.

The experimental psychologist is likely to use an entirely different classification of learning phenomena from that used by the teacher.

Some experimental psychologists have favored a classification introduced by Skinner (1938) which divides all learning into classical conditioning and instrumental learning. Some recent writers prefer to sort learning phenomena into those in which the task of the learner emphasizes the acquisition of a muscular response and those in which the task involves mainly the organization of incoming information. We will have to look at both of these distinctions. In addition, some psychologists have tried to classify learning into a set of categories in which phenomena vary from the simple to the complex. Gagné (1964) provides such a classification in which the simplest learning is described as signal learning— learning to make a response when a particular signal is given—and in which the most complex learning is problem solving. Those who arrange learning phenomena in many categories from the simple to the complex have tended to imply that complex learning phenomena involve different laws of behavior than simple learning phenomena.

Our discussion of learning phenomena here will begin with the consideration of the distinction between classical and instrumental conditioning, since this twofold classification has had substantial impact on psychology as it has been applied to educational problems. This will be followed by a brief review of some of the main areas in which research on learning has been conducted and in which knowledge with important implications for education has been accumulated.

Classical Conditioning

A very large fraction of the work that has been undertaken in the study of learning has involved the study of phenomena that have come to be known as those of classical conditioning. The development of the concept of learning represented by classical conditioning must be attributed in its earlier stages to I. P. Pavlov (1849–1936) and V. M. Bechterev (1857–1957), two Russian physiologists of great stature who devoted much of their lives to the study of this aspect of learning. Some of the works of Pavlov (1927, 1928) have been translated and are available for English-speaking audiences.

Certain examples of classical conditioning had been noted for centuries before the Russian physiologists first developed experimental techniques for the study of the phenomena. Nearly a hundred and fifty years before Pavlov, Robert Whytt noted that salivation occurred not only in the presence of food, but also in the presence of objects associated with food and even when the idea of food flashed through the mind. In classical conditioning the starting point is always a response naturally elicited by some particular stimulus. These naturally occurring—that is, unlearned —forms of behavior are usually restricted to the few organs they involve. Such restricted relationships between stimuli and responses are commonly called reflexes and are illustrated by phenomena such as the response of salivation to the presence of food in the mouth, the jerk of the knee which results from a tap on the patellar tendon, the contraction of the pupil of the eye when a bright light falls upon it, and the withdrawal of the hand from the surface of a hot stove. They are restricted behaviors but are not clearly divided off from more complex behaviors, which may also occur with little learning being involved. The typical mammalian female cleans off the young shortly after birth, and this complex behavior occurs with little identifiable learning. It differs from what are ordinarily called reflexes mainly in the complexity of the behavior and in the number of organs involved in the response.

A typical example of conditioning, and one with which Pavlov worked extensively, is based on the salivation reflex in response to food. This reflex represents the unlearned, or unconditioned, response to the food stimulus. If food is presented on a number of successive occasions, and if before each presentation a bell is rung, the bell acquires the property of eliciting the salivary response. One way of describing this situation is that there has been "stimulus substitution": the bell becomes a substitute stimulus for producing a salivary response. The bell is referred to as the "conditioned stimulus."

Pavlov undertook extensive studies using this particular kind of technique. The animal used was a dog, and the first step was to operate on the dog, moving the opening of one of the salivary ducts so that it emptied the saliva to the outside of the cheek. Here it was collected in a small bottle so designed that the number of drops of saliva could be easily recorded. During the period of experimentation the dog was held loosely in position by a harness. The first step in any series of experiments was for the dog to become habituated to the harness; but this is no problem, for the dog is a docile and cooperative laboratory creature and becomes a very easily managed animal in experimental situations provided the experimenter has some knowledge of the conditions that are likely to upset it. Once the dog became used to the experimental situation, experiments were run. Pavlov attempted to develop a series of laws of learning based on his conditioning data, and went far to establish a scientific approach to problems of learning.

Bechterev used a rather different technique in most of his work. In his technique the unconditioned response consisted of the raising of a paw when the plate on which the paw rested was electrically charged. Other stimuli, such as a bell or a light, would then be introduced to become the conditioned stimuli in the training series. This type of learning, in which the animal comes to anticipate an unpleasant stimulus by lifting its paw to avoid it, is sometimes referred to as "avoidance learning." The fact that this type of learning phenomenon can be produced without resorting to surgery and the simplicity of the equipment required have made it a popular technique.

Pavlov and his contemporaries used these techniques for studying a wide range of behavioral phenomena. The techniques were particularly useful for determining the ability of animals to discriminate between different stimuli. They were also found useful for studying the effect of drugs on behavior.

The technique developed by Pavlov and his associates demonstrated itself to be highly productive in arriving at important discoveries about learning. Pavlov was able to demonstrate many important conditions related to learning that previous workers had not been able to identify. He was able to show the important part that inhibition plays in learning, and he discovered some of the conditions under which inhibition may develop. He was able to study intensively two aspects of behavior which will be considered in much greater detail later on, namely, discrimination and generalization. He also showed that the conditioning of the salivary reflex does not occur unless certain other conditions exist, such as hunger. A well-fed dog cannot be conditioned to salivate at the sound of a bell, and neither can a dog that is excited or under marked stress. Indeed, most of the more important learning phenomena which were demonstrated later to operate in much more complex learning situations were first demonstrated by Pavlov through the study of the conditioned reflex. Pavlov also demonstrated that even this relatively simple form of learning is complex.

A connection between mental disturbances and learning was noted by Pavlov, who observed that when animals were placed in some conditioning situations that taxed them to the limits of their ability, they showed signs of emotional disturbance. First learning stopped, and then the animals showed states of agitation which continued to recur in the testing situation over long periods of time. This observation of Pavlov proved to be an important one and stimulated considerable research during the years that followed, so that today there exists a large experimental literature in this field.

Some years later another important observation concerning the relationship between conditioning and emotionally disturbed behavior was made by an American psychologist, John B. Watson, who took the extreme position that all learning was an example of classical conditioning. Watson and Raynor (1920) carried out a famous experiment in which they demonstrated that a fear response could be acquired by a child in a situation very similar to that of the classical conditioning experiments.

In the Watson and Raynor experiment it was first established that an eleven-month-old child showed a "fear response" to the sound of a metal bar being struck a sharp blow. The bar was struck immediately behind the child's head. They also demonstrated that the child showed no fear of small furry animals such as cats, dogs, rabbits, and rats. Indeed, the response of the child to such creatures was one of approach rather than withdrawal, the latter being the typical response of young children.

In the experiment conducted by Watson and Raynor the child had brought to him a white rat, but just as he was about to touch the rat the metal bar was struck behind his head. Immediately he showed the fear response. This combination of the rat and the sound was presented to the child a number of times over a certain period. After the fifth presentation of the combination the rat was presented alone, whereupon the child showed the fear response.

This child, who had been conditioned to give a fear response to a white rat, which ordinarily would not have produced this response, later showed fear responses to other furry animals. The conditioned response showed what is termed *generalization*.

The demonstration suggests that the form of behavior elicited by classical conditioning may be sufficiently similar to many of the very important learning phenomena in humans that the understanding of the one may help in the understanding of the other.

Scientists of the last thirty years who have studied learning phenomena from the standpoint of the conditioned reflex have not been led to do this through the promise of making discoveries of immediate practical importance, but rather their choice has been determined by the fact that classical conditioning provides a learning situation in which a high degree of control can be exercised over the significant aspects of the learning situation. This viewpoint was taken by the late Clark L. Hull in a series of studies that he began to publish shortly after he went to Yale University as a professor in 1928. In these papers Hull took the position that the study of classical conditioning might lead to a set of theoretical formulations which might be useful in understanding learning in more complex situations. This Hull attempted to do in a classic volume entitled *Principles of Behavior* (1943). The principles of learning formulated in this work were reformulated in later volumes (1951, 1952).

Hull's formulation of a set of comprehensive learning principles represents one of the most ambitious attempts ever made to arrive at a set of laws from which behavior in learning situations could be predicted. It served as an inspiration to many of his associates and students who have continued to study learning through the classical-conditioning situation, of whom the most notable is K. W. Spence. Spence has summarized well (1956) his reason for basing much of his work on classical conditioning and the advantages that this involves. Certainly much that is

said in this book about learning is based on experiments involving classical conditioning, the results of which were later shown to apply to other
kinds of learning situations.

INTERPRETATIONS OF CLASSICAL CONDITIONING

Although the study of learning through the use of classical conditioning has yielded results of great significance, which also have some generality in their application, there is still considerable question concerning
the interpretation to be given to the phenomenon. It is perhaps odd that
so much has been learned through the study of the phenomenon and yet
there is doubt concerning its nature.

First, there is the problem whether classical conditioning represents a
model for describing all learning. Pavlov believed that the learning phenomena he studied were prototypes of learning occurring in other situations. John B. Watson, the founder of American behaviorism, took a
similar view. For him, behavior was built upon a foundation of reflexes
with which the organism was endowed through the structure it had inherited. Through conditioning, responses to new stimuli were built up
that ultimately came to constitute the adult organism's repertoire of
behavior. On the other hand, B. F. Skinner and some other modern
psychologists have taken the view that classical conditioning represents a
rather limited, and perhaps unimportant, category of learning.

Several interpretations of classical conditioning have been offered. The
first of these regards classical conditioning as simply a matter of "stimulus
substitution"—that is to say, a response comes to be elicited by a stimulus
that did not elicit it in the first place. In the Pavlov-type of experiment
a bell comes to produce salivation; the bell becomes a substitute for the
stimulus provided by food. In this interpretation of classical conditioning
the contrast is made between the "stimulus-substitution feature" which
it represents and other kinds of learning in which a new response is made
to a familiar stimulus and in which there is response substitution. Some
psychologists have attempted to classify all learning situations into those
that involve stimulus substitution and those that involve response substitution.

Another interpretation of classical conditioning is that developed by
Guthrie (1952), who took the position that it represents a special case of
a more general learning phenomenon. Guthrie's position will be briefly
outlined here in order to indicate how even a well-studied phenomenon
that has yielded much knowledge may, nevertheless, still be a source of
controversy concerning its nature. The Guthrie explanation offered is
known as a "stimulus-response contiguity" theory.

Guthrie notes that in classical conditioning the essential and, for him,
the only important feature of the process is that the experimenter arranges

for a response to occur in the presence of particular stimuli. Salivation is made to occur in the presence of the sound of a bell, or a withdrawal response is made to occur in the presence of a light. The reflex is used because this is a way to make a particular behavior occur. If one wishes to produce salivation in a dog, then the best way is to provide the dog with some food. Guthrie proposes that if a response occurs in the presence of a particular pattern of stimuli, then, in time, the pattern of stimuli comes to elicit the response. If a dog salivates frequently enough in the presence of a light, then the light will come to elicit the response of salivation. If we wish an individual to habitually smile in the presence of other individuals, then we must train him by arranging that on a number of occasions he does smile in the presence of others. He will then continue to show a smiling response in the presence of others until some other response becomes substituted for the smiling response.

Learning by this kind of mechanism is referred to as learning by contiguity: the stimulus and the response must occur approximately at the same time. This is the essential condition for learning to take place, from the viewpoint of the contiguity theorist. The word *contiguity* means a series of things or events that are connected in some way. In the case of contiguity learning, the stimulus and response are connected together in that they must occur approximately at the same time. Although there is considerable dispute whether learning can occur simply through the simultaneous occurrence of stimulus and the response to which it is to be attached, most teachers imply in their regular day-to-day teaching practice that learning will occur through such a procedure alone and without other factors operating. A teacher will commonly write a number of words on the board and ask pupils to first say each word aloud and then spell it aloud. The assumption is that the saying of the word aloud comes to be a sufficient stimulus to provoke the spelling of the word on appropriate occasions. Other teachers show maps of states and countries and ask the children to say aloud the proper names of these geographical areas. The hope is that this procedure will permit the child later to respond to a map of the country by indicating the correct names of places. Some foreign-language training follows a similar practice. The child is shown a number of objects, and emits the name of the object in the presence of the object. Later, when the object is shown, its name in the foreign language comes to mind. In all of these instances the procedure involves producing appropriate behavior in the presence of the particular object. The teacher attempts to control little except the contiguity of the stimulus and the response. In practice, the control of such contiguity does result in learning, though perhaps through the operation of other learning conditions that are not identified in the situation.

The theory that learning in a classroom situation is produced through the contiguity of stimulus and response is one that grossly oversimplifies matters. Classroom learning is probably much more complicated than this. However, when the teacher typically organizes learning so as to involve only contiguity, some learning does occur. Children do learn under conditions that are typically found in the classroom. This fact does not establish the general validity of the theory that the only condition necessary for learning is the establishment of contiguity between the stimulus and the desired response. Indeed, the opinion is commonly expressed that learning in school can be accomplished much more efficiently if factors other than contiguity are taken into account. If this is so, this does not, in turn, establish that contiguity learning does not occur. It may occur but be relatively inefficient as a means of producing learning. Nevertheless, classical conditioning may be interpreted as learning by contiguity of stimulus and response.

A third interpretation of classical conditioning is offered by Mowrer (1960; a, b) and is elaborated in two volumes. This interpretation, which does not separate classical conditioning from other forms of learning, forms a cornerstone for an attempt to build a comprehensive theory of learning. The total theory cannot be outlined here because it is fairly complex. Mowrer regards the classical-conditioning experiment of the type in which a dog learns to raise his paw at the signal of a bell to avoid an electric shock as an example of the more general phenomenon of avoidance learning. Mowrer's interpretation of the behavior of the dog is that the shock induces an internal state that can be described as fear. In the conditioning process the immediate learning that occurs is that the bell comes to trigger the internal response of fear. As conditioning proceeds, it is not, in Mowrer's interpretation, so much that the bell becomes associated with the avoidance response of lifting the foot as it is that the bell comes to trigger a fear response. This fear response may then become the drive that underlies the avoidance response. In this interpretation the classical-conditioning experiments that involve noxious stimuli, such as electric shocks, represent special cases of avoidance learning in general. Since all learning is not avoidance learning, Mowrer has to elaborate his theory to account for learning in which the response learned is one of approach rather than avoidance. In the case of approach learning, Mowrer considers that the conditioning stimulus comes to produce an internal state which may be described as hope or hopefulness, which again becomes the drive leading to the main observable response. Thus a dog, having learned that a bell signifies that food is in the offing, is said to manifest an internal-drive state described as hope when the bell is sounded. Here again the primary learning is the association between the new stimulus (bell) and the internal state (hope). Mowrer points out that a dog that has thus learned that a bell precedes food shows through its behavior much anticipation of food by wagging its tail, by a high level of activity, by barking, and so forth. Mowrer (1960, b) summarizes the learning phenomena in the following words:

> From this and related observations it was justifiably inferred that, in a situation of the kind described, a conditioned stimulus not only makes the subject salivate: it also makes him *hopeful,* just as surely as a stimulus which has been associated with onset of pain makes a subject *fearful.* And if a fear-arousing stimulus elicits the two forms of *avoidance* behavior previously discussed, it might be surmised that a hope-arousing stimulus would be capable, likewise, of producing either of two forms of "approach" behavior, one of which has already been alluded to and which, in ordinary life, is exemplified by the family dog coming "when called." Just as an organism wishes to get *less* of a stimulus that makes it afraid (cf. Holt's concept of *abience,* 1931) and may do so by fleeing, so will an organism try to get *more* of a stimulus that arouses hope (Holt's *adience*) and may do so by going toward the source of that stimulus.

Thus Mowrer arrives at the position that classical conditioning is a particular example of all learning phenomena, all of which involve either fear or hope. According to this view, classical-conditioning studies are valuable because they throw light on learning phenomena in general.

Instrumental Learning and Operant Conditioning

In current educational literature, instrumental learning is characteristically distinguished from learning during classical conditioning and set apart from it. It represents a broad class of learning phenomena of which the categories that follow really form subcategories. It seems appropriate here to give some general consideration to this area of instrumental learning before considering some of the areas into which it has been divided.

The concept of instrumental learning or instrumental conditioning has been developed mainly by B. F. Skinner (1938, 1953) and his associates. In the typical instrumental-learning situation with which Skinner worked in his early days, a hungry rat, placed in a box, learned to obtain food by pressing a bar. When the bar was pressed, either a pellet of food dropped down into the food cup, or a food trough containing powdered food was raised to within the animal's reach and it was allowed to feed for a controlled short period. The food-trough mechanism has the advantage of preventing the rat from engaging in minor hoarding operations. In his later research Skinner has worked very largely with pigeons, which learn to peck at a disc located on the wall of the box at about the height of the beak. The mechanism may be set so that a peck at the disc will raise a trough and permit the pigeon to feed for a few seconds. In both rat and pigeon studies, the animal learns to manipulate some object in its environment which in turn produces food. The central notion of instrumental conditioning (or instrumental learning, as it is sometimes called) is that the organism acts upon its environment and reaches a goal.

Although a person using common language might say that the rat presses the bar for the *purpose* of obtaining food, the scientist prefers to describe only the sequence of events (bar pressing and then food retrieval) and relate them to some inner state such as a lack of food. The concept of instrumental learning generally implies the existence of some inner state which is in a condition of disequilibrium and which is restored through the learned instrumental act. Instrumental learning also involves acts that occur when certain internal circumstances exist and terminate when the internal state that played a part in initiating them is terminated. In simple terms, a shivering man finds a warm place and stays there until his body temperature is restored to normal. In studying such a behavior sequence, and the conditions that led to the termination of the activity, little would be added by saying that the purpose of his searching behavior was that of finding a warm place. Indeed, by doing so we might easily miss the point that the behavior was one involved in the restoration of body equilibrium (body temperature).

Instrumental acts are characteristic of much of the educational process, and, indeed, learning in many subject-matter areas represents the acquisition of instrumental acts. The acquisition of skill in the writing of English represents the development of one such system of instrumental acts, for the writing of English is used mainly for the achievement of communication. Most problem solving of the kind that John Dewey described and believed should be the central focus of activity in the school represents instrumental learning.

The reader should not think that instrumental learning is a class of learning quite distinct from the other categories described here. Most of the research that has been undertaken on instrumental learning indicates that it represents a phenomenon quite similar to other kinds of learning. Almost all of the important characteristics of the learning process to be discussed later can be illustrated with examples from studies of instrumental learning as well as from classical conditioning. Nonetheless, there are close similarities among all of the learning phenomena discussed here.

Some of the most closely studied learning phenomena in the field of human behavior are represented by instrumental learnings. Examples of these are learning to drive a car, learning to fly an aircraft, and numerous industrial skills which industrial psychologists have now studied for nearly half a century in the hope that the learning process involved can be materially improved. The learning of language in the child appears to be largely an example of instrumental learning. Consider, for example, the acquisition of the magic word *please*. The child slowly learns that he can make certain changes in his environment through the use of this word. Just as the rat learns that the pressing of a lever results in the appearance of a pellet of food, so too does the young child learn that the surest way of obtaining some desired object held by an adult is to use the word *please*. Of course, while the early development of language may be nothing more than a simple case of the learning described in this section, the development of more complex linguistic skills may well involve other processes too.

Certain features of instrumental learning tend to differentiate it from classical conditioning. In the latter, the response remains the same throughout the learning series, but comes to be elicited by a new stimulus. In contrast, when a dog is conditioned to salivate at the sound of a whistle, the dog, throughout the learning period, responds with the same response of salivating. At the end of conditioning he is performing the same response as he did at the beginning of conditioning. There is little change in the response during any classical-conditioning experiment, but the response is manifested under new and changed circumstances as learning progresses. This is to be contrasted with instrumental learning, in which the response undergoes marked modification as learning progresses. In the process of learning to operate a typewriter the final response is markedly different after training than it was before training. Modification of response in this case is extensive, and much more than a matter of learning to hit the right keys. In addition to the latter skill, the typist learns to strike each key with a rapid flexion from the knuckle; the system of responses also become rhythmical. The accomplished typist's smooth and flowing behavior, with its high accuracy and speed, is in marked contrast to the clumsy, stumbling, slow, and inaccurate typing behavior of the novice. The responses to the situation have shown extensive modification as a result of learning. *A central feature of all instrumental conditioning is that the response undergoes modification during the conditioning process.* In the case of classical conditioning no such modification of response takes place. Most learning that takes place in educational settings involves the slow modification of responses, and in this respect closely resembles instrumental learning. In later chapters the reader will also see other reasons why the study of instrumental learning may have much greater significance than classical conditioning for the understanding of educational problems.

Instrumental learning also involves typically larger units of behavior than does classical conditioning, particularly when the skeletal muscles are involved. An animal learning to press a bar to obtain food uses far more of the muscles in his body than does the same animal learning to lift its left front foot to avoid a shock. This distinction cannot always be maintained because the classical conditioning of some emotional responses may produce widespread bodily involvement. The conditioning of fear responses has an effect on the entire body.

Another difference between classical conditioning and instrumental conditioning lies in the fact that in classical conditioning the experimenter determines *when* the particular response to be conditioned is to occur. In conditioning a dog to lift its paw at the sound of a bell, the experimenter produces the response at a particular instant by passing an electric current across a grid on which the paw rests. But when a rat learns to press a bar in instrumental conditioning, the experimenter cannot initiate bar pressing behavior at a particular instant. This distinction between classical and instrumental conditioning sometimes breaks down. In teaching a dog to shake hands with its owner at the command "Shake," the customary procedure is to lift and hold the dog's paw while the command is given. The desired response, even though it is inadvertent, is rewarded by a morsel of food. The point to note is that this familiar instrumental learning procedure requires the experimenter to initiate the response of the animal that is being trained.

Although the position was commonly taken a decade or more ago that classical and instrumental conditioning were very different learning phenomena, recent writers have expressed doubts that a rigid distinction can be made. Liu (1964) has pointed out that in most instrumental learning situations that have been studied, components of the learned behavior resemble classically conditioned responses. When a rat learns to press a bar that delivers food, many reflexes related to eating become conditioned to aspects of the situation. For example, the click that accompanies the release of food may come to produce salivation. Thus, in most instrumental learning, there are components of the learned behavior that are classically conditioned responses. A case of pure instrumental learning hardly seems to exist. Sometimes phenomena that look like instrumental learning also occur in attempts to produce classical conditioning. Thus, in a classical conditioning experiment in which a dog learns to raise its paw at a given signal and avoid a shock, the dog will also sometimes raise its paw at other times in the absence of the signal as if anticipating the shock. These unexpected avoidance responses represent an instrumental learning component of classical conditioning learning. The nearest one can find to a pure case of classical conditioning, uncontaminated by instrumental learning, is the conditioning of visceral responses and the conditioning of the heart to accelerate when certain stimuli are presented. The distinction between classical and instrumental conditioning is far less rigid than has commonly been assumed.

B. F. Skinner has introduced an expression to describe the gradual modification of behavior that takes place during instrumental learning. He speaks of the "shaping of behavior," which implies that behavior changes from a disorganized mass of responses to a response system with organization and form. The term *shaping of behavior* artistically describes the change that takes place, for example, as the novice at the violin proceeds from a stage where he makes scratching noises completely lacking in rhythm and beauty to the stage where he has mastered technique and can produce exquisitely executed music. It is equally elegant in its description of the change in behavior of the young child learning to make an oral presentation. The behavior of the child in front of the class changes, as the years go by, from that of either hesitant or explosive announcements to the smooth and organized performance of the mature speaker. In these cases, as in other examples of instrumental learning, learning results in the shaping of behavior.

In instrumental learning the behavior that occurs and is shaped is *operant behavior*. In typical experiments, operant behavior appears without any clear and identifiable stimulus. Some psychologists consider that this aspect of instrumental learning makes it unsatisfactory from the point of view of the experimentalist. For this reason some psychologists prefer to conduct their experiments in classical-conditioning situations, since these permit a rigid control over the significant stimuli affecting the situation. In contrast, psychologists who study instrumental learning generally take the position that this form of learning situation resembles much more closely most of the learning that takes place in daily life. Indeed, some of them take the position that classical conditioning represents a rare form of learning. Despite these differences of viewpoint, the fact remains that studies of both classical-conditioning phenomena and instrumental learning have produced discoveries of very general significance.

Some Situations in Which Learning Has Been Extensively Studied

Not all situations in which instrumental learning occurs have proved themselves to be equally valuable for studying the learning process. The scientist generally seeks out situations in which the phenomenon he wants to investigate can be conveniently studied. The behavioral scientist does this too, and for this reason much of the research on instrumental learning has been undertaken in a limited number of situations that permit the careful study of these phenomena. Some of the situations that have been widely used for the study of learning phenomena are discussed in the following paragraphs. Of course, these are not the only situations in which instrumental learning has been studied, but they represent common conditions under which the study of learning has been undertaken.

A list of the situations in which learning has been studied does not represent a comprehensive classification of learning phenomena. It indicates only some of the places where the scientist has been successful in making advances.

Selective response learning. Psychologists interested in learning have long studied the acquisition of responses in situations in which the subject must learn to make a particular response when a readily identified signal is given. The task that defines this kind of learning does not involve, to any extent, learning to discriminate the particular signal from other signals. Past experience permits the discrimination to be made easily.

Examples of selective learning with human subjects are found in many famous experiments by Edward L. Thorndike. An illustration of such a learning situation is provided by the directions given to the subjects of one such experiment (1935, p. 53):

This is an experiment in learning. I shall say a word. You will at once say a number from 1 to 5. Sometimes I will tell you whether you are right or wrong. Usually I will not. But I will tell you whenever you are doing especially well; and I will tell you every eight responses how well you did in those eight. You will be paid a bonus of one cent for every two that you get right more than you would get by chance. There will be forty words in each series, and the series will be repeated five times. The first time you will naturally get the right numbers only by chance, but the second time you will do a little better, and the third time still better, and so on. Remember you are always to respond by saying 1 or 2 or 3 or 4 or 5 just as soon as I say a word.

In this type of situation the human subject has no way of knowing which one of the five numbers is the correct number to go with any word until he has tried one or more of them. He cannot tell in advance which response to select, but as selective learning proceeds he identifies the correct selection and tends to eliminate selections that have proved to be incorrect.

On the surface this type of selective-learning experiment may seem to be a trivial affair with little practical implications, but this is not so. Such experiments can be designed to investigate phenomena of the utmost importance to education. Consider, for example, some of the possibilities of the type of Thorndike experiment described above. One possibility is to study the effect of punishment. What happens if wrong responses are punished by giving the subject an electric shock each time he makes a wrong response? Does the shock reduce more the tendency for the wrong response to occur than does the announcement of the word *wrong?* How do rewards help the retention of right responses? Does it make any difference whether the reward is large or small? Does the subject learn more rapidly when he is given a dime for each right response than when he is given a nickel? A great range of important problems of learning can be and have been investigated with this experimental procedure, and these are not problems of only academic interest.

Discrimination learning. A considerable part of the learning that takes place in schools involves the development of discriminations. The English teachers hope that the pupils will learn to discriminate between effective and ineffective or inappropriate forms of expression. Music teachers hope to develop pitch discrimination as well as the discrimination of beautiful from unmusical sounds. The essence of discrimination learning is that the learner acquires the ability to discriminate between stimuli that initially he cannot discriminate between. Oddly enough, surprisingly little is known about the capacity for human beings to learn discriminations. For example, to what extent are all pupils capable of making discriminations in the pitch of musical tones? Although the music curriculum of the elementary school is generally based on the supposition that this is a trainable skill, evidence is still lacking concerning the degree to which it is trainable.

In discrimination-learning tasks the subjects must learn to make discriminations between various cues present. When a rat learns to enter the box marked with a cross and to avoid the one marked with a circle, regardless of how the two boxes are located, the animal's first task is to learn to discriminate between the two markings. The difficulty of the task is dependent on the fact that the two cues are difficult to discriminate. In contrast, in the selective-response learning situation the task is that of linking a response with an easily identified stimulus. If a human subject had to say either "three" or "five" whenever the experimenter presented him with a word, and if "three" was correct when the word was a noun and "five" was correct when the word was a verb, the first task of the learner would be that of discriminating between the two classes of words. If he failed to note that some of the words were nouns and some were verbs, he would never learn when to say "three" and when to say "five." The latter task involves discrimination learning and is to be contrasted with the previously cited Thorndike experiment in which, for example, the word "three" was to be said by the subject whenever the experimenter said "house," and "five" when the experimenter said "chair." In the latter case the two stimuli can be readily distinguished, and the task of the subject is to associate a particular number with the word *house* and the word *chair*.

Tasks vary in the extent to which they require the learner to make perceptual discriminations and in the extent to which they require the learner to associate responses with readily identifiable stimuli. These are two characteristics of learning situations some of which emphasize the one and some the other.

An area in which the study of discrimination learning has been of vital importance is that of how people acquire concepts. Later in the book we will discuss in some detail important work on discrimination learning that indicates some of the factors that control the acquisition of ideas in children. It may not seem, at first sight, that the learning of an idea is that of learning a discrimination task. Consider, however, how a child comes to use the word *chair*. The child first comes to *discriminate* between objects to which the word *chair* can be appropriately applied and objects to which the word cannot properly be applied. As the child forms a more and more definite concept or idea of the nature of a chair, he comes to apply the word with fewer and fewer errors.

Studies of discrimination learning are also important for understanding the developmental process. An interesting example of such a study, which has important implications for human development, is described by Hebb (1958). It is also a study with important theoretical implications, which will be considered later in this book. The study involves the following facts: A patient who has been blind from birth is able to acquire vision as a young adult through a corneal-graft operation. On gaining vision, the patient quickly learns to recognize colors, but beyond that his immediate ability to use vision ends. Even after several months he shows almost no capacity for discriminating faces. Indeed, the task of discriminating one face from another seems to be beyond his abilities, although he is known to be a person of at least average intelligence. Such patients have been given relatively simple discrimination-learning tasks in order to study and determine the nature of their perceptual abilities. Surprisingly enough, it may require weeks of practice in discriminating triangles from squares before such a person is able to discriminate consistently, and even then he may be able to do it only by counting the corners. Such experiments provide information of the greatest importance for understanding the development of perceptual processes.

The conditions that result in the learning of complex discriminations have also been studied in the laboratory. The learning of complex discriminations constitutes an important aspect of education, as is evidenced by the stress placed in schools on learning to discriminate between good literature and trash, between correct and incorrect English usage, between the beautiful and the ugly, and so forth. Some attempts have been made by psychologists in the laboratory to study such complex discriminations, and, as was previously mentioned, some quite notable work has been undertaken in the area of concept formation.

Serial rote learning. The student who has taken courses in education may greet the heading of this section with surprise, for he may have heard it said that the schools of the last century were characterized by rote learning, while those of today, or at least those manned by qualified teachers emphasize meaningful learning. Actually, the contrast between the two kinds of learning is neither real nor reasonable; rote learning may be meaningful.

Serial rote learning means learning by the repetition of a sequence of responses in some kind of order. At one time the multiplication tables were learned by rote learning, with the pupil repeating to himself the sequence, twice one is two, twice two is four, twice three is six, and so forth. In recent times there has been some attempt to change this process and to require the pupil to count by twos—that is, he says to himself two, four, six, eight, and so forth. This also is a kind of rote learning, and the writer knows of no evidence showing that this method of learning is superior to the traditional one. The method was developed in order to make the learning process a more "meaningful" one. Both may or may not be meaningful depending on the particular conditions under which learning takes place. Research workers have found it necessary to define the word *meaningful* in precise ways in order to evade the confusion produced by the vague use of the term in current educational literature.

It would be ridiculous to suggest that rote learning should never be adopted as a procedure, for rote learning is widely used throughout early childhood for acquiring many skills. Counting is ordinarily learned by a process that can only be described as rote learning. Many nursery rhymes which the three-year-old delights to say are learned by rote. Nobody would want to eliminate these pleasant experiences from childhood merely because they are learned by a rote process. Incidentally, most young children who learn such rhymes do not know what they mean, and in a sense this actually represents relatively meaningless learning.

Rote learning, like all other learning phenomena, is complex. By this is meant that the laws of rote learning will be ultimately represented by complex equations. If any reader doubts the validity of this statement, he is referred to one of the basic works on the subject, entitled "Mathematico-Deductive Theory of Rote Learning," by Hull (1940). (However, this is probably one of the most difficult books that has ever been written in the area of psychology.)

Rote learning has also the distinction of being one of the first learning phenomena to be systematically studied, and many of the generalizations found in textbooks on educational psychology concerning the best methods of learning are derived from the early study of rote learning. One of the pioneers in this field was the German psychologist Ebbinghaus, who invented the use of nonsense syllables for the study of learning and memory. Ebbinghaus found that experiments involving memory for words were difficult to design, because subjects differed in the richness of their backgrounds of associations for particular words. Words themselves differ in the frequency with which they are associated with other words. Ebbinghaus (1885) saw that he could make up words never seen before by combining together two consonants and a vowel in such syllables as "taz," "reg," "mer," "sig," and so forth. With such materials he could then build lists of syllables for learning experiments that would be equally difficult for all subjects in terms of their previous experience with the materials. With these materials he was able to study the effect of varying the amount of material to be learned, the relationship of the number of repetitions to the retention of the material, and also the general characteristics of the forgetting phenomenon. The curve of forgetting, which appears in most introductory texts on educational psychology, was first found with data provided by Ebbinghaus' experiments. He was also able to demonstrate the relative strength of forward and backward associations and important matters in school learning, which will be discussed later in this book.

The pioneer work of Ebbinghaus led to a long sequence of studies which have turned out to have practical importance. Here again is an example of a technique by which a phenomenon is studied under greatly simplified conditions and which, despite its ivory-tower appearance, yields results of considerable significance. Oddly enough, although Ebbinghaus originally developed the nonsense-syllable technique in order to eliminate the factor of meaning in his research, the technique has been found in recent times to be a fruitful approach to the study of meaning in relation to learning. A long series of studies on meaning in relation to learning has been undertaken by Underwood and Schulz (1960) using nonsense syllables. These workers point out that so-called nonsense syllables vary in meaningfulness—that is, some have frequently appeared previously in meaningful contexts while others have not. For example, the syllable "sen" is frequently seen as a part of a word, but the syllable "bez" is only rarely seen. In terms of the number and strength of the previous associations formed, the one syllable differs substantially from the other. Lists of syllables can be built that differ in this respect.

An important technique for the study of learning that has evolved through the use of nonsense syllables is the paired-associates technique. This technique has proved to be highly valuable for the study of many learning processes. It is used in many variations. In one of these, the subject is presented with a series of pairs of words, one of which is a color and the other an adjective that may be descriptive of a color, as, for example, "yellow–bright," "red–warm," "blue–cold," etc. The subject learns to anticipate the second word when the first is presented. The technique for doing this generally involves the presentation of the first of each pair alone for about two seconds. The subject guesses what the second word might be, and then is shown both words together. Then the first word of the next pair appears alone, and so forth. Sometimes quite unrelated words may be used in the pairs, in which case the subject cannot anticipate the second word correctly until he has been through the list at least once. Sometimes nonsense syllables are used and pairs such as "bac–lub," "cre–mer," "gux–ked," and so forth are presented. One advantage of the latter technique is that it permits the control of meaning. For the present, it is sufficient to point out that syllables such as "juq," "kyh," "qyg," "wuq," and "zej," are much less meaningful in terms of many criteria than are syllables such as "bev," "giv," "hur," and "nov." We cannot consider at this point the techniques that are used for determining the meaningfulness of nonsense syllables; but it can be done, and such syllables can be rated on a scale from 1 to 100 in terms of meaningfulness.

With nonsense syllables, the paired-associate technique can be used to control the meaningfulness of the stimulus as well as the meaningfulness of the response. In the pairs of syllables thus presented, the first syllable represents the stimulus to which the second syllable, the response, is learned. One can thus conduct experiments in which the stimulus is a highly meaningful syllable but the response to be learned highly meaningless, or the reverse arrangement can be made. Additional possibilities are to study learning with both the stimulus and the response highly meaningless, or with the stimulus and the response highly meaningful. In this way one can study the effect of meaningfulness on learning and can sift out the effect of meaningfulness at the response end. This represents the development of a valuable experimental technique which can be used to explore problems of learning that could not be explored twenty years ago.

The study of rote learning of verbal materials has led to the study of more complex verbal behavior. Some of the research on the learning of simple associations between words has led to a better understanding of some of the processes underlying problem solving. In this, as in other areas of science, history fully endorses the procedure of starting by understanding simple phenomena, for such understanding has often led to the understanding of the complex.

Problem solving. A long history of research on problem solving can be found in the literature of psychology. Most of this research originated in Germany before the Nazis destroyed German psychology as a reputable science. Much of the work involved an attempt to identify mechanisms within the person that could account for problem-solving behavior as it was observed. Particularly important contributions were made by a group of psychologists known as the Gestalt psychologists, who studied problem-solving behavior both in men and in animals. Not all of the laboratory work of this group followed the lines of formal laboratory experimentation, but represented observation of problem-solving behavior within the laboratory. Generally, there was little attempt made to alter the conditions under which problems were solved and to determine the effects of the changed conditions on the problem-solving behavior. Some studies in this general category involved attempts to explore what is now commonly referred to as "creative thinking," in which the subject had to produce a novel solution to a problem.

The early work of the German psychologists in this area was not oriented toward the solution of any practical matters, but it laid a foundation for later workers who had a practical orientation. In the last decade there has been an upsurge of research interest in this area, but mainly among psychologists interested in the practical problem of improving the problem-solving ability of trouble shooters in the electronic and mechanical fields. One of the major difficulties in operating modern complex equipment is the maintenance of the equipment and the quick identification of the sources of trouble when malfunctions appear. For this reason, research on problem solving of a fairly complex nature has suddenly assumed a position of importance. Despite the need for results of practical importance, most of the research in problem solving that has yielded results of immediate value has been research conducted in the laboratory.

Transfer of training. Few areas of learning research have greater potential impact on education than transfer of training. The term *transfer of training* refers to the extent to which a learning activity facilitates or interferes with other activities. (A more detailed statement of the meaning of *transfer* will be given later in this book.) Nearly all learning in schools is planned on the supposition that it will influence behavior in other situations the child will encounter later in life. Research on transfer has been undertaken along two distinct lines. First, psychologists in the early part of the century conducted research mainly for the purpose of demonstrating that many of the then current educational doctrines were unsound. Second, programs of research were initiated that were designed to discover some of the conditions that facilitate transfer and some of those that tend to reduce it. Some of this research has been undertaken with the laboratory techniques for studying instrumental learning and classical conditioning, which involve the study of learning under simplified conditions. Others have preferred to study transfer under conditions that approach more nearly those found in the classroom. The phenomenon is complex and involves many variables.

Developmental studies of learning. In recent years the scientist's understanding of learning has been increased remarkably by studies of the long-term effects of environmental conditions on the learning process. Important centers for such studies have been the laboratories of Donald Hebb at McGill University and Harry Harlow at the University of Wisconsin. Particularly important results have been achieved in the under-standing of the effects of early learning experiences on later learning, and also knowledge concerning the way in which a living creature can learn how to learn. While some of these developmental studies have been undertaken with human subjects, the difficulty of controlling the environ-ment of such subjects over long periods has made it necessary to conduct much of the work at the subhuman level. Animals used in long-term studies have included chimpanzees, monkeys, dogs, and rats. Caution has to be exercised in the application of the results achieved with any one species to any other species, for sometimes the results of a study are unique to a species. However, when the same study is repeated and similar results are found over a wide range of species, there is then some basis for generalizing the results to man. Such studies involve what is known as the "comparative approach" to the study of behavior, an ap-proach that has fully justified itself in many areas of biological research. To some educators the thought that animal studies could contribute anything to education is repulsive if not ridiculous, but the fact is that such studies have produced an immense amount of important knowledge which has served as a basis for understanding human behavior.

Human and Subhuman Subjects in Experimental Research on Learning

Experiments are conducted with a wide range of living creatures. Much experimentation concerning learning is conducted with subhuman organisms because of their availability, but the experiments need to be replicated with human subjects before the results can be applied to the problem of managing human learning. This is the procedure followed in most of the other branches of science that seek significant findings that are to be applied directly to human problems. Were it not for the experi-mental work done on animals, advancements in knowledge concerning human behavior would be vastly hampered; but this does not mean that experiments involving human subjects are not of crucial importance, for they are. In order to indicate to the reader the kinds of important experi-mentation on children and adults that grow out of work on animals, a single experiment by Gewirtz and Baer (1958) will be discussed briefly.

Gewirtz and Baer base their study on a mass of experimental work, conducted on a wide range of living organisms, which shows that when animals are deprived of whatever is required to satisfy their needs, the satisfiers of these needs can be used to control and produce learning. A hungry animal—that is, an animal that has been purposely deprived of food—will learn all kinds of skills if it is rewarded appropriately with small quantities of food. Gewirtz and Baer point out that young children in the lower grades of elementary schools are commonly rewarded with social approval, a practice widely accepted by teachers as an important condition for promoting learning. These same research workers also point out that a child who has received substantial amounts of social approval should have had his need in this respect fully satisfied, and under such a condition social approval as a means of promoting learning would become less effective. They then sought to determine whether the latter position was sound.

As in most experimental studies, the task involving learning was much simpler than those ordinarily encountered in schools or, for that matter, in daily life. The children were given a game to play that involved inserting marbles in one of two holes in a box. The marbles fell down inside the equipment and then rolled out of the machine at the bottom. The children were free to decide into which hole to place the marble. However, whenever the child inserted the marble into a particular one of the two holes, the experimenter provided social approval by saying, "Fine," or "Good," or "Hm-hmmm." Other experiments have demonstrated that under such conditions the human subject will show an increasing tendency to perform the rewarded response—that is, in this case, children will show a tendency to insert the marble into the hole associated with approval. Now in this experiment the researchers took one further step. The children involved were divided into three groups. One group was isolated from all sources of social stimulation for twenty minutes before "playing the game." In this group each child was kept in a room by himself to produce social deprivation. The second group was taken from the regular class and started immediately on the game. The third group was exposed to a period of high social approval immediately prior to the game. The latter was accomplished by providing a period of play in which everything the child did was praised and admired by the experimenter. The purpose of the latter treatment was to provide a state of satiation with respect to social approval. The hypothesis was that a state of satiation would reduce the effectiveness of social approval in modifying behavior with respect to the game.

The results of the experiment, conducted with 102 children in the first and second grades, were in accordance with expectation. Those deprived of social approval showed a much greater tendency to put marbles in the hole associated with a comment of approval. The group satiated with social approval showed least modification of behavior as a result of the comments of the experimenter.

While the implications of this study are that social approval loses its effectiveness if used to excess, there are limits to the extent to which the results of a single experiment can be applied to the management of learning in the classroom. The study was conducted on first- and second-grade children, and the fact may be that social approval becomes a much less important reward in the higher grades. The usefulness of social approval in producing learning may also depend on the task involved. Questions such as these would have to be answered by further experiments, and the original experiment should also be repeated. Unfortunately, attempts to reproduce many promising experiments have often yielded results contrary to those originally found. However, the results of the Gewirtz and Baer experiment fit so well with other knowledge that the chances are high that they could be reproduced.

Summary

1. Research on learning has shown two main trends: Some research workers have preferred to study learning in a natural setting in the classroom; others have preferred to study learning under simplified conditions in the laboratory.

2. Studies of learning in classroom situations have had a long history. A primary purpose of such studies has been to discover relationships between particular teaching practices and the amount of learning. Another purpose has been to justify current practices or to compare one broad teaching methodology with another. Although extensive work has been devoted to such research, the results have hardly justified the effort. Such research presents difficulties in research methodology that have not been overcome at this time.

3. While laboratory approaches to learning have had little appeal to educators because of their remoteness from the classroom situation, the history of science justifies their use and so, too, does the knowledge they have already yielded in the area of learning itself.

4. Laboratory approaches to the study of learning are characterized by two essential features: First, in the laboratory, learning is studied under simplified conditions; second, conditions related to learning are systematically varied and the effects of this variation on the learning process are studied.

5. Classical conditioning is an important learning phenomenon studied in the laboratory. It involves a fixed form of behavior referred to as a reflex, which is characteristic of all members of the particular species, and which comes to be elicited by a new stimulus as a result of the conditioning procedure. Classical-conditioning studies have yielded many important principles of learning which have been found to apply and permit the prediction and control of learning phenomena in other situa-

tions. Despite the fact that studies of classical conditioning have yielded important results, the precise nature of the phenomenon itself is a matter of dispute. Several interpretations are possible, including those of stimulus substitution and contiguity of stimulus and response.

6. The study of classical conditioning resulted in the development of many concepts useful in the study and understanding of learning phenomena. These include the concepts of inhibition, generalization, discrimination, and others that refer to major aspects of the learning process.

7. The high degree of control that can be exercised over learning in the classical-conditioning situation has given it great appeal to the scientist. Some scientists, notably the late Clark L. Hull, considered that the laws thus derived might form a basic set of principles of behavior; but this optimism is not widely shared.

8. A second major category of learning phenomena that have been extensively studied are those classified in the category of instrumental learning. Instrumental learning is characterized by a shaping of responses and by the fact that the response learned cannot be considered a response to a well-identified stimulus. Also, instrumental learning generally involves rather large units of behavior and does not typically involve stimulus substitution. Despite attempts to draw rigid lines between classical conditioning and instrumental learning, the two classes of learning cannot always be rigidly distinguished.

9. Selective response learning represents one important class of learning situations within the general category of behavior known as instrumental conditioning. Selective learning results in the selection of correct responses or correct sequences of responses from an already existing repertoire of responses.

10. Another group of learning situations in which considerable research has been undertaken is that which requires the learner to make discriminations. Discrimination learning is involved in the learning of concepts as well as in other processes related to intellectual development.

11. Rote learning represents a third area in which considerable research has been undertaken. Although rote learning is popularly interpreted as involving learning without meaning, such is not necessarily the case. Substantial knowledge of the learning process has resulted from the study of learning in rote-learning situations.

12. Programs of research on learning have also been carried out in many other situations. Of particular importance to education are those in the areas of problem solving, transfer of training, and development in relation to learning.

2

Fundamental Concepts in Research on Learning

WHAT HAS been said up to this point assumes that the reader knows what is meant by learning. To be sure he does, but in a very general way. What we must do at this point is to try to sharpen the meaning of the term, recognizing that a full meaning evolves as research in the area is undertaken and as a more precise account of the process can be given. At this stage of the discussion we can only attempt to provide the reader with a broad account of what is meant by learning.

Learning is said to have occurred when a response undergoes modification on its recurrence as a result of conditions in the environment that have produced relatively permanent changes in the central nervous system. It will be noted that the definition excludes changes in behavior due to fatigue or other local conditions. Change in response due to fatigue may sometimes play a role in learning, but the changes are not a part of what we will here call the learning process. For example, a baby put down in his crib may cry loudly, and the only way to stop the crying response is by leaving him to cry. Eventually, he will become fatigued to the point where he will go to sleep. However, the modification of the response is quite temporary, for the next night he will perform in exactly the same way.

It is necessary at this time to make a distinction which many writers make between performance and learning. Performance represents the observable behavior of the individual. Performance is his response. Modifications in response indicate that learning has occurred, but scientists would say that the modifications in response are simply symptoms that learning is going on, and they do not constitute the learning as such. The fact that one has learned to be polite is identified by the fact that one is generally observed to be polite. Sometimes, however, one may be upset by the behavior of another and display rudeness. When this happens, it cannot be said that the learning of politeness has suddenly vanished nor that the learning will reappear, as if by magic, when the immediate frustration situation has passed by. For reasons such as this, one cannot identify the response of politeness with whatever is learned that makes one polite. The learning has not been erased merely because the consequences of it do not appear on a particular situation. Polite responses are, so to speak, peripheral. Learning is central. New responses occur as a result of learning because something has happened in the controlling centers in the brain. What is learned is some kind of modification of the way in which those centers in the brain control behavior. Thus it is customary to say that learning is a central phenomenon, but that performance is peripheral.

Despite this distinction, it is common, even in technical literature, to speak as if it were the response that is really learned. One commonly says that a student learned to type or that he learned to speak a foreign language. Here one is speaking as if it were the change in the response itself that constitutes the learning. This is almost necessary, because it is customary in our language to speak in this way. In the remainder of this book many statements will be made as though it is the response that is learned. Nevertheless, the reader will realize that there is a fundamental distinction to be made. This distinction is recognized here even though there is a certain amount of convenience in talking as if it were responses that are learned.

Responses can be modified in two ways. On the positive side there are those that occur more frequently or more strongly or more rapidly as a result of learning. They may occur more frequently on appropriate occasions, or they may require fewer cues for them to occur. Such changes and other related changes in behavior are usually referred to as the "acquisition" of behavior. Thus, learning to drive a car or learning a foreign language represents the acquisition of behavior, for the learner comes to manifest behavior that he did not manifest before. In contrast, on the negative side, learning may involve the elimination of behavior. We may want to eliminate a bad habit or perhaps the unpleasant emotional responses aroused by certain objects as a result of some unhappy experience with which they are associated. This kind of process, in contrast to the process of acquisition, is referred to as the process of "extinction." The term *extinction* also refers to a central process rather than to the observable decline in performance that accompanies it. One can observe the results of extinction, but not extinction itself. Unfortunately, much more is known at the present time concerning the process of acquisition than is known about the process of extinction. Teachers in the educational world, like psychologists in the laboratory, are much more effective in the production of new behavior than they are in the elimination of behavior that has already become established. Schools have disciplinary problems because there are not, at the present time, well-developed methods for the elimination of unwanted behavior. Every teacher knows that such problems are difficult to handle and that the behavior desired to be eliminated in the pupil is likely to persist long after the teacher has abandoned his efforts to eliminate it.

The problem of the elimination of behavior is also a matter of great importance outside the classroom. It is essentially the problem faced in much work with neurotic patients. The patient has unwanted behavior, such as anxiety responses, which troubles his life. The aid of the psychiatrist or clinical psychologist is sought in order to eliminate such behavior. Sometime in the future it is probable that the clinician will base his treatment on well-developed techniques for the elimination of behavior, which, in time, must be based on a theory of learning.

What is meant by a "response" in this discussion of learning? Any discharge of impulses within or from the nervous system constitutes the core element of a response. Sometimes this discharge results in activity of a set of muscles, as when a person runs a race. Sometimes it results in glandular activity, as when a discharge down a nerve activates the adrenal glands and many of the symptoms of excitement ensue. Discharges may also remain in closed circuits within the nervous system and provide many of the experiences that are commonly described as mental experiences. All of these activities represent responses, but the discharges of the nervous system to the muscles have consequences which can usually be perceived by other persons. When they constitute fairly large units of coordinated behavior, they are commonly referred to by such terms as skill in typing, language, escape behavior, laughter, and so forth. Most of the discussion of the problem of learning to be pursued in this book will refer to the modification of such large units of behavior.

Psychologists have found it convenient to distinguish between molar and molecular studies of behavior. Behavior studied at the molecular level is studied in minute detail. Studies of nerve impulses in individual nerve fibers or in small groups of nerve fibers or nerve cells constitute the essence of studies conducted at the molecular level and are characteristically undertaken by physiologists, though there are some psychologists who also work at this level. In contrast, most psychologists are much more interested in the study of much larger elements of behavior, such as are involved in the development of various skills. Such units of behavior that are commonly studied are illustrated by the solving of a problem, the writing of a sentence, the learning of a fact, the manifestation of neurotic behavior in a particular situation, and so forth. Behavior of this kind is referred to as molar behavior. Each unit of behavior studied within investigations of molar behavior involves the activity of probably millions, if not billions, of neurons. There is high probability that scientists are not going to be able to trace each nerve-impulse sequence. Hence it appears necessary to many psychologists to begin the study of behavior at the level of gross behavior, or the molar level, rather than at the level of detail, or the molecular level.

Even at the molar level there is some latitude of choice available concerning the level of detail at which behavior is to be studied. In much research on learning in the classroom, the unit of behavior studied is performance over a whole semester in a subject such as English. In many such studies pupils are given a test in the area of English both at the beginning and at the end of the semester. Half of the pupils are exposed to one method of teaching and half are exposed to another method, and the relationship between method of teaching and improvement in performance is sought. Many feel that these studies involve such large units of behavior that they provide very little information. In other studies much smaller units of behavior are studied, as when the psychologist in the laboratory studies the factors that influence a pupil's ability to recognize words flashed momentarily on a screen.

Measuring and Understanding Behavior

The scientist uses many approaches to his problems, but if there is a single thread that runs through all of his procedures, that thread is the utilization of measurement techniques. If physicists had not learned to measure the velocity of the electron, there would be no science of electronics today. A science of chemistry came into being when scientists began to measure the weights of the products of combustion. A science of behavior related to learning was born when Ebbinghaus first began to measure how many repetitions were required to learn materials presented under various conditions. Later came Thorndike, who developed further the infant science by placing animals, and later humans, in problem situations and measuring the time taken and counting the errors made in solving the problem. Slowly measurement techniques were developed and expanded into new realms, and they are now used to explore such matters as the learning of ideas, the role of anxiety in learning, the conditions under which attitudes can be changed, and numerous other learning phenomena. Through the introduction of measurement techniques, scientists have been able to provide in the course of a century greater understanding of how people learn than was provided by wise men through all previous centuries, who did not have such measurement techniques at their disposal.

The use of measurement in the development of knowledge forces the scientist to introduce precision into his thinking. The scientist is not prepared to conclude that a teaching method was successful because the children *appeared* to be learning. The scientist wants to know *how much* learning took place, how that learning was measured, and what aspect of the learning process was involved. He wants evidence that not only he, but others too, can see and understand. If he thinks he has demonstrated that a particular skill is learned, then he must be able to describe in precise terms how this was demonstrated so that others can reproduce the experiment. Experiments that can be reproduced almost always involve measurement. Indeed, it would be difficult to imagine an experiment that did not involve measurement and that could be described in such precise terms that another scientist could reproduce it.

Although measurement procedures constitute techniques of central importance in the conduct of scientific research, they have also acquired a position of increasing importance in the conduct of everyday affairs. To a limited extent this trend is seen in education, where there has been an increasing use of standardized measures of achievement and aptitude, given for the purpose of providing improved control over the learning process.

The writer looks forward to the day when the teacher will begin the school year by spending perhaps two days collecting information systematically about the pupils, feeding the data into an electronic computer, and receiving back from the computer conclusions about possible sources of difficulty the children may encounter in learning. It can be anticipated that the results of these two days of systematic inquiry, together with the work the electronic computer will perform on the data, will provide a much more thorough understanding of the individual child than the teacher can at present obtain during a full year of work with the same children. We are not saying that the information will be collected in the form of test scores, as it is commonly collected today, but only that data will be collected in some form that can be systematically analyzed, and that the data will be summarized and processed by a machine so the teacher will be provided with usable and relevant predictions. Neither are we saying that the teacher will give up using many current methods of diagnosing learning difficulties. There will obviously be times when it will be necessary to sit down with a pupil while he works a problem to see why he has difficulty in working it and to determine what can be done to remedy this difficulty. What is being pointed out is that there is no substitute for the systematic, careful collection of data and the processing of that data by up-to-date methods.

Phases of Activity Related to Learning

Information about the learning process is derived from a number of different sources, which can be classified in several different ways. There is no standard classification at this time used by all psychologists concerned with the study of learning. The classification presented here has a certain convenience for the discussion of educational problems, but other systems may be more convenient for discussing laboratory research or animal research.*

First, the classification presented here refers to the conditions under which learning actually takes place, as the training conditions or learning conditions. This represents a slight departure from current educational practice, since the word *training* is commonly taken to imply vocational training; but the terms *training* or *learning conditions* refer to all the conditions operating at the time learning takes place. If children are free to choose what they are to learn, then this represents a training condition as the term is used here. Whatever occurs during the learning process that influences the course of learning is a training or learning condition. Homework and help given by the teacher are training conditions, and so, too, are amount of help given by other pupils, techniques used to present material in the textbook, length of the study period, opportunity to practice whatever is to be learned, and so forth.

The course of learning is also influenced by what has gone on before learning is initiated. A child may have difficulty with long division because he has not been exposed previously to the learning of multiplication. Another child finds Spanish easy to learn because he lived at one time in a Spanish-speaking community and had acquired a vocabulary in that language. Science is easy for another child because he comes from a home in which there are frequent discussions around the dinner table on scientific topics. Any condition previous to the training period that facilitates or interferes with learning (here again *training* is used in a technical sense) is referred to as an "antecedent condition." It is difficult, if not impossible, to predict the course of learning unless something is known about antecedent conditions. Generally, curricula are designed in such a way that each stage of learning facilitates the next stage, but there are many antecedent conditions over which the teacher and curriculum specialist have no control. For example, conditions in the home may represent important antecedent conditions to the learning that takes place in school, but the school has little capacity to control such antecedent conditions.

In experimental studies of learning, great care often must be exercised

---

* The classification of conditions related to learning is contrasted with that used by Logan (1960), who classifies sources of information into *subject conditions, learning conditions,* and *performance conditions.* Subject conditions are such conditions as the species involved, level of drive, etc. Learning conditions include prior learning, number of trials, the nature of the learning task, and so forth. Performance conditions refer to the consequences of response in the learning situation, such as the nature of the rewards. For the design of the research in which Logan is engaged the classification is an excellent one, but it is inappropriate for much of the discussion in this book.

in the control of antecedent conditions. Unless this is done, it may not be possible to reproduce the results of experiments, as has been illustrated in at least one classic study by Kohler (1925). Kohler, a German psychologist, was isolated on the island of Tenerife during the first World War and devoted much of his time to the study of the behavior of chimpanzees. In one of his studies he observed that a chimpanzee was able to fit together two sticks by inserting the thin end of one into the broad end of the other; and once this task had been accomplished the chimpanzee was able to reach, with the combined sticks, for food that could not be reached by the use of either stick alone. Kohler concluded that this performance indicated the existence in the chimpanzee of a process known as insight and a capacity to learn to solve problems by processes other than those that involve the development of simple associations between stimulus and response. While nobody today would believe that problem solving is merely the product of past experience in connecting stimuli and responses (for it clearly involves much more complex processes), there has still been considerable interest in repeating the experiments of Kohler. The data from these repetitions indicates that naïve chimpanzees, who have had little experience in the manipulation of sticks, do not fit sticks together to form longer sticks in order to reach for objects. Before they will do this, they have to become educated chimpanzees and have to have had a very substantial amount of experience with the manipulation of sticks and with reaching for objects outside the cage using other objects as tools in the reaching process. Antecedent conditions—that is, past training—play a vital role in the phenomenon Kohler described.

We know that there are many antecedent conditions, over which the school has no control, that are of great influence on learning. Some of the basic skills that a child must acquire before he can even begin to learn to read are also largely acquired in the home and over a period of many years. These conditions antecedent to school learning are of greatest importance to the learning that goes on in schools.

Criterion performance conditions is a term that pertains to the conditions under which an attempt is made to observe the extent to which a particular skill, attitude, interest, belief, personality trait, or other characteristic has been learned. Variations in the performance conditions provide very different indications of the degree to which a particular response characteristic has been learned. For example, at the end of a course in American history pupils may be given a test, but this test may be one of several different types. If a recall test is given—that is, one in which the student has to recall what has been learned with very few cues provided —it will appear that he has learned less than when a recognition test is provided in which he has only to indicate that he can recognize the right answer to a series of questions. Performance may also be different when there are distractions present—that is to say, stimuli that are not the usual accompaniments of the performance. To measure a student's acquired attitude as it is manifested in the classroom is quite different from the measurement of the appearance of that attitude in situations outside the classroom.

The most appropriate criterion performance conditions to use for the appraisal of school learning are the conditions that exist in real life after the child leaves school and goes out, supposedly prepared to meet life's problems. Generally, little is known about how the school child behaves under these conditions and how his behavior is related to what he has learned in school. Most of those concerned with education realize that when the results of learning are measured under conditions as they exist in life after school, the results are likely to be quite disappointing. The hopes and dreams of teachers, like the hopes and dreams of many other members of our society, are not generally realized.

This section has been concerned with the environmental conditions that relate to learning, but this is not an exhaustive categorization of all the variables that must be taken into account in describing the learning process. The inner conditions the learner brings to the training situation are partly a product of the antecedent conditions to which he has been exposed and partly a product of the constitution he inherited. Species characteristics and differences in inherited structure within the species represent an additional class of variables which must be taken into account in understanding the learning process. Species differences are important in that they limit the extent to which knowledge about learning acquired through a study of one species can be applied to another species. Individual differences in the characteristics inherited by different members of the same species limit the extent to which studies undertaken on particular members of a species can be generalized to other members of the same species, unless the effects of these factors are taken into account. For example, studies of the learning of college sophomores cannot be applied directly to the management of the learning of mentally handicapped children unless the constitutional differences of these two groups are taken into account.

The Importance of Studying Learning under Well-Defined and Simplified Conditions

One must emphasize at this point that the scientist can rarely make a direct attack on problems, but must usually study the phenomena of the universe under much simpler conditions than those under which they ordinarily occur. The chemist cannot hope to study the laws of the combination of elements by studying anything so complex as a growing apple on a tree. The laws derived in the laboratory to describe the way in which elements combine in particular proportions are known to apply to such chemical processes as are found in the growing apple, but the scientist knows that they apply in this place because he has demonstrated that they apply in a wide range of situations. The behavioral scientist approaches many of his problems in a similar fashion. Rather than study the learning of literature by school children in classrooms, he may study the learning of sets of nonsense syllables in the laboratory or investigate how people solve problems he has devised. When he has completed his laboratory work, he is then, like ·the chemist, faced with the need for demonstrating that the generalizations he has discovered apply, at least to some extent, to the classroom situation. At least some of the generalizations concerning learning, which have been discovered by traditional scientific techniques using simplified situations, have been demonstrated to be widely applicable to learning in a wide range of situations. Many have also been shown to be applicable to both animal and to human learning. When a scientifically derived generalization has been demonstrated to apply to a wide range of situations, the chances are increased that the principle will be found to be applicable to some new but similar situation which may arise.

When teaching in a school situation, it is easy to acquire the habit of thinking of learning in terms of subject-matter boundaries. This may lead one to forget that aspects of remotely different subject-matter fields may involve similar learning processes. Reading English may involve learning processes very similar to those involved in the typing of a manuscript, but quite different from those involved in the learning of other aspects of English. Learning activities have been grouped by schools into subject-matter areas, but this grouping does not mean that the learning processes involved are similar within any subject-matter field. Laboratory studies may result in the classification of learning phenomena into categories very different from those used in classifying school learning.

The Control or Guidance of Learning

When the research worker refers to the "control of learning," he uses the term in much the same way as the educator uses the term *guidance of learning*. Unfortunately, through historical accidents the word *control* has become associated in educational literature with harsh and punitive educational practices. For this reason much literature makes reference to the *guidance of learning* rather than to the *control of learning*. However, since the term *control* is used as a technical term by research psychologists, it will be used in this volume to refer to all phenomena involved in guidance of the learning process. In no way does it necessarily imply the exercise of discipline.

The term *external control* is used by the behavioral scientist quite differently from the way it is commonly used. What the behavioral scientist means when he talks about the external control of the learning process is that some conditions are being provided that either facilitate or interfere with the learning process. A teacher who approaches a child who is having difficulties with an arithmetic problem and says, "Let's see if we can find out what your trouble is," is controlling the learning process just as much as one who says, "Everybody will now do problem six." In one case the control is subtle, in the other case direct. In both cases learning is to be achieved as a result of the teacher's behavior. The mere fact that a teacher attempts to help the child does not mean that the teacher is any less in control of the situation than if she issues a direct command. In both cases she may be equally certain about the consequences of her action.

External control means that there exists some condition in the environment that in some way has an effect on learning. The conditions commonly utilized by the teacher to exercise control are praise, recognition, demonstration, diagnosis of sources of difficulties, referral to sources of information, arrangement of social conditions, introduction of new materials and exhibits, the raising of questions, and so forth. Without the function of control, in the sense in which it is being used here, the teacher has no function in the learning process and is a doubtful asset.

Internal control of the learning process by the learner is an entirely different matter, but the various functions it can exercise have been far from fully recognized or understood at this time. On its simplest and most communicable level it involves the selection by the learner of the most favorable circumstances for learning. Skill in the identification of such efficient circumstances for learning has often been acquired through contact with teachers and guidance workers. Courses in study habits are given mainly in the hope that the pupil will be able to incorporate into his knowledge those methods that will guide his behavior in the future and thus result in more efficient learning. Often such courses produce little internal control over the learning process, but at least a few pupils seem to benefit from them.

There is another problem related to the internal control of learning processes that is less easily discussed because little is understood about it. It is a common experience that an individual may build up a capacity for studying in certain situations and not in others. A youngster may find that he can study only in his room, or at least has difficulty studying in other places. It seems that the stimuli provided by his room are all associated with studying and have acquired the capacity for eliciting study behavior. Stimuli associated with being in the library, on the other hand, are associated with social activity and do not arouse studying behavior. Some youngsters have never developed a studying situation in which the stimuli arouse studying behavior. Such students are academic problems. If a student can develop a situation in which all of the stimuli arouse studying, then he has control over his learning behavior, since he only has to take himself to that situation in order to study.

A rather similar form of internal control is manifested by many scientists who know that they can do creative work in certain situations and hence seek out these situations when they want to be creative. Some find that a corner of their home has this effect, others a special place in their laboratory. Still others may find, like the late Professor C. A. Spearman, that a local café provides ideal surroundings for creative work.

Unfortunately, most persons have not planned their habits of work so that the stimuli provided by certain situations tend to elicit certain behaviors such as studying, creative writing, or some other organized and useful activity. The result of this is that they have relatively little control over their own behavior. The acquisition of control requires, as most courses on studying habits indicate, living for a time a well-planned life in which certain activities take place on schedule and in an appropriate place. This appears to be a rather essential condition for the acquisition of what we have called here *internal control* over the learning process.

The Data from Which a Science of Behavior Is Built

The Characteristics of the Responses Modified in Learning

There is general agreement that the task of the behavioral scientist is to discover laws of behavior or generalizations about behavior. In the final analysis, this means the discovery of the conditions that lead living organisms to behave the way they do. If the behavioral scientist is one day able to establish equations for predicting behavior, then on one side of these equations will be the conditions that produce behavior, and on the other the characteristics of the behavior produced. The establishment of such equations is largely a dream of the future. The behavior in which most learning psychologists have been primarily interested consists of responses to particular situations, which may vary from a chimp's response to a feared object to a child's response to an arithmetic problem.

Performance is distinguished from learning, but the amount of learning that takes place is generally measured by observing some performance of the learner. The measurement of performance may seem to be a straightforward matter that really needs no discussion, but this is not so. In any event, one does not measure performance as such, but rather measures some *aspect* of performance; and there is considerable choice among the different aspects that can be measured. The major choices to be considered are as follows:

Accuracy of response. This is one of the most commonly measured aspects of performance. The teacher who assigns a number of arithmetic problems to a class is likely to score the degree of learning in terms of the number of problems that are answered correctly. Most school tests are scored in terms of accuracy of response. Accuracy of response is also an important learning objective in many fields of academic learning. Few teachers are satisfied when a pupil knows how to solve arithmetic problems. He must be able to solve them with accuracy. Even though the pupil can explain every step in the solution of the problem, unless he can actually arrive at a correct response the objective has not been achieved. No teacher can disregard accuracy of response as an important goal in most fields.

Accuracy of response is measured within education by two main techniques: the recall technique and the recognition technique. In the recall technique the learner must produce the entire response with few cues. The commonest application of the recall technique is the essay examination. In the latter method of appraising learning, the learner is provided with a question that indicates roughly the response that he is required to produce. The learner then attempts to produce the response. He may be asked to indicate the chemical formula for common baking soda, and he must attempt to write out the correct chemical formula. In the latter case the question clearly indicates the nature of the response required, but this becomes much more difficult when more complex responses are called for. If the student were asked to outline the causes of the War of 1812, he might have great difficulty in judging what to include and what to omit. This is the central difficulty in measuring learning by recall. The technique does not give the learner enough cues to indicate what is required of him without giving away the answer.

Recognition techniques of appraising learning do not have these disadvantages. A common example using the recognition technique is the familiar multiple-choice test, in which a problem is presented and then followed by four or five suggested answers only one of which is correct. The student must choose the correct answer from among those given. If the question and the alternative answers are clearly worded, then the person taking the test knows exactly what he is required to do. There is little ambiguity about the task. His response indicates whether he can or cannot do it, for he chooses either the correct answer or a wrong answer. The chief disadvantage of the recognition method of measuring learning is that it does not always indicate the kind of performance toward which learning is directed. In teaching writing skill, the goal is the ability to write clearly and understandably, not just to recognize good written expression in contrast to poor written expression. The goal is that of being able to produce.

Latency or speed of response. The time that elapses between the presentation of the problem situation and the occurrence of the response is referred to as *latency* of the response. In many of the historically important experiments on learning, latency has been the sole measure of learning. In a classical-conditioning type of experiment the time between the presentation of the stimulus and the response learned to that stimulus is taken as a measure of learning. The better the response is learned, the faster the response will occur. Speed of response is often an important indication of the extent to which the response has been learned, the latency of response is commonly measured in educational situations as a means of appraising learning.

An illustration of this is given by a teacher who mimeographed a list of one hundred simple arithmetic problems, such as $9 + 5$, 7×8, $24 \div 3$, and so forth. Then she administered the list as a test to a class, allowing only ten minutes in which to complete the entire list. Most of the pupils did not finish. The problems they completed were nearly all completed correctly, but there were great differences among pupils in the number of problems completed. The pupil who was able to produce a quick response to each problem was able to obtain a high score, but the pupil who required time to figure out each problem was not able to solve many problems. The score, consisting of the number of problems solved, can be considered a latency score.

Another example of such a score is found in the appraisal of progress in typing. This score is usually the number of words per minute or the number of strokes per minute. The longer the latency between seeing a word and typing it on the machine, the lower will be the score on the typing test. This score is often complicated by the usual practice of reducing the number of words per minute by an error score derived from the number of errors made.

The latency of a response may indicate the extent to which many educational objectives have been achieved. For example, in learning to type, it is not sufficient that the pupil be able to find the correct keys; he must be able to find them at a certain speed. Unless he achieves a minimum speed and accuracy, the goal of typing instruction has not been achieved.

The same is true of learning reading or learning to solve problems involving computation. It is not sufficient that the pupil be able to produce the response with some delay; he must be able to produce it almost immediately, if the response has been learned to the point where it can be usefully applied. In other areas latency may not be a particularly useful characteristic. If the task is to write a poem, there is little merit in determining whether it takes ten minutes, ten hours, or ten days to write it. Literary training does not usually attempt to train individuals to write poems *rapidly*. The important thing is to develop talent so that, given the conditions necessary for inspiration, a poem will emerge. The point to note is that skills learned in school vary in the extent to which latency is an important factor in what is learned. This is not commonly recognized, as when a teacher gives a speeded test at the end of the semester even though speed of response has not been emphasized as an attribute to be learned. If the object of learning has been to reduce latency of response, then it is appropriate to measure latency in an evaluation procedure. At other times it is inappropriate.

Amplitude of response. The term *amplitude of response* is not well chosen, but a few examples will clarify its meaning. In a sport such as baseball, the player must learn to hit the ball with accuracy, for there is no substitute for accuracy. He must also learn to hit the ball hard, or, as the saying goes, he must learn to take a good swing at it and follow through. The response of the player to the ball generally must be not a weak tap but a strong hit. His response must have good *amplitude*. The piano player who comes to a crescendo in the music must strike the keys with force. A large movement, then, rather than a small one, is referred to as a response that has amplitude. The reader may ask why the term *amplitude* is used and not *strength* of response. The reason is that the term *strength of response* has another, and quite distinct, meaning in the technical language of learning theory, which will be discussed at another place. The control of the amplitude of a response, as it has been defined here, represents an important objective in the learning of many skills.

Frequency of response. In many kinds of learning in school the teacher or the pupil or both may be concerned with changing the frequency with which certain responses occur. The English teacher may attempt to reduce the frequency of usage of such responses as "ain't" and to increase the frequency with which pupils use acceptable forms of speech. This same teacher will hope to bring about a reduction in the frequency of occurrence of the common spelling errors. Care in writing and speaking, and orderliness of work also, are behaviors that the teacher may wish to increase in frequency. Since changes in the frequency with which certain behaviors occur represent some of the more important objectives, the teacher can determine the extent to which learning in

these areas is being accomplished by measuring the frequency of occurrence of these behaviors. Social behavior is also seen to change as the
frequency of certain behaviors increases and that of others decreases.
Behaviors generally considered to be cooperative and constructive may
be expected to increase as the social education of the individual proceeds.
Behaviors involving hostility, rejection of the ideas of others, aggression,
and the like may be expected to decrease in frequency as the person
achieves important goals of social development.

Resistance to elimination (*resistance to extinction*).   Perhaps we should
use the technical term *resistance to extinction,* but this would involve
some explanation which is reserved for later in this volume, and we can
explain what we have in mind without going too deeply into problems
of learning at this stage. A bad habit such as smoking is one that is so
well and thoroughly learned that there may be no way in which the habit
can be displaced by some more healthy form of behavior. The strength
of the habit is seen in the fact that it generally resists all attempts to
inhibit it. The confirmed smoker smokes often in places where smoking
is expressly forbidden. As soon as the person stops smoking, he becomes
irritable and restless. A familiar strong habit seen in the classroom is
nail biting. The original function of nail biting is said to be tension
reduction—that is to say, the child finds that in time of crisis a bite at his
nails reduces some of his inner tension. When this has occurred frequently
enough, the habit becomes established and is carried on for its own sake.
The habit becomes so thoroughly learned that the person will tolerate no
interference with it. Nail biting will be pursued despite all of the typical
admonishments and threats with which adults meet this situation. The
amount of learning the habit undergoes after thousands of nail-biting
episodes establishes the habit with such strength that it is likely to
remain even when powerful forces are brought to play to inhibit it.
These inhibiting forces are often the pressure of the peer group when the
individual reaches his teens. However, in many cases the habit is then
only temporarily inhibited and reappears again later in life. Well-
practiced behaviors are extremely difficult to eliminate by techniques
ordinarily available to the teacher. Resistance to change can be used to
indicate the degree of learning.

Resistance to forgetting.   Sometimes the effectiveness of learning is
measured in terms of the amount retained after a given interval of time.
It is sometimes assumed that the more thorough the learning, the greater
will be the retention over time. At first sight this may seem to be a highly
satisfactory way of measuring the degree to which a given capability
was learned, but in practice this is not so. Forgetting is a complex
phenomenon, and the extent to which retention of learning occurs is
often determined by the activity that takes place following learning.

Much will depend on the extent to which the persons involved have opportunities for practicing the skill once learned. For example, we may measure the reading skill of young adults after they leave high school. In the case of most of these persons there is a gradual decline in reading skill through the twenties and thirties. However, there are some readers whose skill does not decline, and these are individuals who have extensive opportunities to read. In other areas skill may decline with the passage of time because other activities are learned that are incompatible with the original skill. A person may learn to play the violin with some skill, but if he then changes to the cello, the skill he learned on the cello may interfere with his ability to play the violin. If learning is measured by the resistance to forgetting, some control needs to be exercised over the activities of the individual during the period of forgetting, and this usually cannot be done. Under ideal conditions of education learning should be produced that is highly permanent. Indeed, if this does not happen, then education becomes a very inefficient process; but some forgetting processes are bound to occur, and only to a limited extent can one arrange the learning situation so that the effects of forgetting are minimized. The management of the learning situation to achieve this goal, insofar as it can be achieved, will be considered in later chapters of this book. While studies that measure the degree of original learning by measuring resistance to forgetting are of considerable interest, they do not stand out as presenting a particularly useful way of measuring the extent to which learning has occurred in school.

Transferability to new situations. Under some conditions of learning, responses become highly tied to the situations in which they have been learned and do not occur under other conditions. The speech therapist knows well that the child who has learned to speak without a lisp in speech therapy may still speak with a lisp in school and in the home. One of the problems of the speech therapist is that of arranging the learning of new speech habits so that they will occur under many different conditions. In other words, what is learned during speech therapy must transfer to other sets of conditions for the learning to have value. Responses and response systems vary in the extent to which they are tied to particular situations or are manifested under a wide range of conditions. The hope of every teacher is that whatever is learned in school will not be tied so closely to the school situation that it will fail to influence behavior outside of school.

Unusualness of response. This is a response characteristic that was widely emphasized by the progressive-education movement. This movement stressed that there should be a minimum of teacher control telling children what to do, and one of the alleged advantages of a lack of teacher control was that responses would then become more original or "more creative." Unusualness of response alone is obviously not a variable that reflects the value of education even by progressive standards. The behavior of the disturbed person is often highly unusual, but it is this aspect of his behavior that the clinician seeks to eliminate. An unusual response has merit insofar as it has aesthetic properties of its own, represents worthwhile invention, or provides some new and acceptable adaptation to some of life's problems.

Other scaled characteristics of responses. Responses may also be evaluated in terms of their location with respect to a scale. Attitudes and changes in attitudes are customarily measured in this way. In the measurement of attitudes the essential feature of the process is that a response is made and a value is assigned to the response by giving it a position on a scale. For example, a child in school may say, "I think Russians are mean," and the teacher concludes that the child has a very hostile attitude toward Russians and is at the opposite end of the attitude scale to a child who says, "I sure like Russian music; the Russians must be a lovely people." Such statements can be judged in terms of their position on a scale, which varies from a very unfavorable attitude toward Russia at one end to a very favorable one at the other. The usual variation of the evaluation procedure is for the individual to read a series of possible responses, which are all expressions of attitude, and then decide which of these expressions he could most easily endorse. This is really an indirect way of determining what his typical responses might be. Usually in such an attitude scale, values are assigned to the scale according to some rule that constitutes the particular scaling practices.

Typical studies in this field are those related to changes in attitude, which were done in great numbers during the thirties and, indeed, occupied the time of a large fraction of a generation of graduate students of education who were attempting to produce theses to satisfy the requirements of various graduate schools. An essential feature of such studies was that something was done to change an attitude and that the attitude was measured before and after the occurrence of this something, which might have been the showing of a film, the reading of a book, or a series of much more vague experiences in the curriculum. Such studies attempt to relate some educational practice to a change in response with respect to some attitude scale.

Learning Conditions

In seeking to understand the nature of the learning process, one would not make many discoveries if one were to limit his work to an examination of the responses (R-characteristics). True, the scientist would be able to establish the fact that learning occurs. He could establish the fact that as pupils have increased experience with typewriters and typewriting they increase both their speed and accuracy of reproducing material. He could also make observations concerning whether improvement of speed occurred before improvement in accuracy or whether the reverse was the case. He could note that progress was not made at a steady rate, but that the learner made much more rapid progress at certain times. Some of the facts he would discover would be matters of common knowledge, and a few might represent quite novel facts which are not generally observed, but despite all of these findings he could not progress far toward the development of a systematic knowledge of the learning process. His knowledge would be extremely limited because he failed to observe certain conditions (situational characteristics, or S-characteristics) that influence the learning process to a high degree. Whoever undertakes research on learning must not fail to study the conditions under which learning occurs, for the learning may be largely a product of the extent to which learning *conditions* are favorable.

A part of the problem of developing a comprehensive knowledge of the learning process is that many of the conditions that influence rate of learning have not yet been identified. Research is required to identify these conditions. Those that have been identified include the following:

Time distribution. Teachers have long recognized that the time distribution of learning is of great importance. No teacher of driver education would attempt to teach a high-school student to drive in a single day, but rather he would plan a series of lessons spaced over weeks. Each lesson might be only thirty minutes in duration. The school curriculum is also planned on the assumption that long periods of study in a particular area should be avoided. Research indicates that shorter periods of learning should be distributed over time.

Time is a factor in learning in another neglected respect. Some learning procedures are more efficient than others in that they require less time. When two methods of learning are compared, there must be information available concerning the time required for each of the methods; yet in most educational experiments such information is lacking. If, for example, a study claims to show that method *A* of teaching long division is superior to method *B* as demonstrated by the performance of pupils on a test taken later, there is always the possibility that method *A* produced superior results merely because it involved twice as much learning time. Only rarely have educational research workers reported the time involved in particular instructional procedures although such data may be crucial in deciding whether one method rather than another should be adopted. Poor methods of instruction may produce more learning than good methods if sufficient time is devoted to them.

Task characteristics. The characteristics of a learning task must be understood if learning is to be effectively planned, but only in recent years has research on learning placed any emphasis on identifying the features of tasks that make them easy or difficult to learn. A learning task that has been extensively analyzed in this respect is reading. It is recognized that, when a "look-and-say" method of learning reading is used, the task can be made easier for the learner if the words used have very different shapes and contours on the printed page. Since the task of the learner is partly one of shape discrimination, for this is how he first distinguishes one word from another, the difficulty of the task is partly dependent on the extent to which the shapes of the words differ. Other task characteristics involve the extent to which the words have meanings familiar to the learner. At a more advanced level of reading, the complexity of the sentence structure becomes an important task characteristic. Many of these task characteristics can be effectively measured.

Although a great amount is known about the characteristics of reading tasks, much less is known about the features of other tasks undertaken by school children. Little is known, for example, about the task of learning history. One characteristic of history, as it is taught in schools, is that it involves time relationships to some degree. At the lower elementary grades these time relationships are deemphasized because young children have difficulty comprehending them, but there is no readily available means for measuring the extent to which written history makes use of or ignores time relationships. As a matter of fact, rarely does anyone examine the subject matter involved in school learning to determine the characteristics of the task and to identify the factors that make the task difficult or easy.

The consequences of correct and incorrect behavior.   Among the most important conditions that are known to influence learning are the consequences of correct and incorrect behavior. A response, such as striking a key on the typewriter, may be followed by a number of conditions. The pupil may never find out whether or not he struck the right key. That is one possibility. Or he may find out, immediately or later, whether he was or was not right. He may be punished for striking the wrong key. The typewriter may be rigged so that whenever he strikes the wrong key a buzzer sounds or a light goes on. All these events may happen immediately or much later. The time relationships may represent important learning conditions. The consequences of responses are some of the most carefully studied events that occur in relation to the learning process. Long sections of this book will be concerned with these events, since they represent conditions under the control of the teacher through which the learning process can be facilitated.

The cues provided.   The course of learning is greatly influenced by the nature of the cues provided. Guidance in learning is a matter of providing cues that will help the learner. When these cues should be provided and what they should be are important aspects of learning research. Knowledge about such matters is necessary if learning is to be planned for efficiency. Although this is a matter of central importance to the classroom teacher, it is one that has not been investigated to any great degree. Traditional and newer outlooks on education differ a great deal on this point. Traditional methods of teaching gave many cues in the learning process; indeed, the pupil was to copy the teacher. Newer methods place greater emphasis on the pupil's solving his own problems with minimum cues. In imitative behavior rather complete cues are provided. In a problem-solving approach to learning the cues may be minimal.

The incentives. It is common knowledge that learning is most likely to move forward with efficiency if there are incentives provided. By this is meant that there should be goals established that will direct the pupil's behavior toward the attainment of those goals. Often, lack of learning is is a result of the fact that the goals established are not ones toward which the pupil directs his behavior. The classrooms described by J. M. Rice at the end of the last century were of this character. Children parroted their lessons with little enthusiasm and for the purpose of achieving rather unattractive goals. Later educators proposed that goals be attractive to the learner. Following this line of teaching, some suggested that the goals be established by the children and teachers working together in order to ensure that vigorous goal-directed behavior would occur. The latter point of view raises many psychological problems of great interest.

Other unidentified conditions. Many conditions of learning which are probably of great significance have not yet been identified. At the present stage of research it would be presumptuous to consider that they had. So long as these remain unknown, the teacher has only limited means of ensuring that the conditions for learning in the classroom are as favorable as they should be. There is at least a little evidence that the efficiency of learning could be greatly increased with properly designed equipment added to school facilities. There are also many obscure elements, such as social climate, which may well influence the learning process; but this is still a matter for speculation. Twenty years from now the list of learning conditions mentioned in a book such as this will probably be many times as long as it is today.

Mediating Processes and Intervening Variables

When a person is faced with a learning situation, the extent to which he will learn depends on his own personal characteristics. The characteristics of the learner that exert an influence on learning are referred to as *intervening variables,* because they intervene between the learning situation as it is presented and the response that occurs to that situation. Some of these intervening variables represent the capacity to perform certain internal processes, some of which are described as thinking processes. These internal processes are called "mediating responses" because they mediate between the stimuli (S) through which the learning situation is presented and the responses (R). Learners have an awareness of some of these mediating processes, but not all of them.

Probably all behavior involves a system of mediating responses. Of some of these responses the individual is aware; of others he is quite unconscious. When a disliked person enters his office, he may, without knowing it, frown and appear disgruntled. This behavior occurs because of the existence of certain mediating responses that lead to the production of the frown. Much behavior is generated in this way without deliberate effort.

Learning is associated with changes in the mediating processes that take place. A person presented with a novel problem involving arithmetic may sit in silence for ten minutes until he produces the answer. A long sequence of mediating responses occurs, which culminates in the discovery and announcement of the solution. When similar problems are then given to the same individual, he gives the answer to each with increasing rapidity. Some of the mediating processes that occurred on the first occasion are eliminated in later trials with similar problems, and thus the time taken to solve the problems is steadily reduced. Internal processes that are successful tend to be retained, and those that are unsuccessful tend to be eliminated. The mediating mechanisms also draw on the reservoir of past experience that may function in the solution of the problem. Often the existence of these mediating processes is dependent on past experience.

Although learning involves changes in these mediating responses, there is great obscurity concerning what these processes are, how they should be described, and how they change as a result of experience. For the most part, there is no direct way through which they can be observed, but rather they must be inferred from behavior. A person is faced with a difficult problem; then, after putting it out of his mind, the solution comes to him suddenly while he is digging in the garden. One may infer the existence of internal processes that enabled him to produce a solution; but there is no direct way of observing these processes, for even the problem solver was not aware of the fact that they were going on.

The mediating responses become modified by the consequences of behavior. When behavior results in the achievement of a goal, the mediating responses that led to that behavior are likely to take priority in similar situations over the other mediating responses that were not successful.

Feedback plays a vital role in the modification of mediating responses.

Perceptual processes. Some special mediating processes are referred to as perceptual processes. These involve the intake of information through the senses and the interpretation of the information at the higher levels of the nervous system. Although nobody denies the importance of these processes, psychologists of the twentieth century have tended to concentrate on the study of observable behavior rather than on the subtle internal events that permit a learner to acquire knowledge about the environment.

The psychologists of the last century generally took the position that perceptual processes could be explored by asking persons to describe their inner life. Some of these psychologists even maintained that this was a trainable skill and that individuals could learn to give accurate accounts of internal processes. Yet the fact is that research based on this procedure had not yielded knowledge of any great consequence for developing an understanding of learning. The failure of reports of personal experience to build a body of scientific knowledge has led psychologists to develop other experimental procedures from which the nature of perceptual processes may be inferred.

One laboratory procedure that psychologists have adopted is to study perception in situations in which the processes have been slowed down. One complicating factor in all such studies is that a perception always involves inputs from within the body as well as inputs from the outside. Those from inside often involve emotional responses that color perceptions of the outside world. Despite the immense difficulty of studying internal processes that the experimenter cannot directly observe, knowledge of them has been greatly advanced during the last decade. In recent years, substantial help in the development of a scientific knowledge of perception has been derived from the work of neurophysiologists who have studied the nerve structure of the body as an information handling and storing system. The psychologist and the physiologist working together have proven to be an effective team for the study of perceptual processes.

Relationship Between Stimulus, Mediating Process, and Response: Emitted and Respondent Behavior

The psychology of learning has multiple roots. On the one hand, it finds its beginnings in the doctrines of associationism, which developed through the work of philosophers. On the other, it is derived from the work of physiologists who, for one reason or another, became interested in problems of behavior. The physiologists of the late nineteenth and early twentieth centuries conceived of the nervous system as a mechanism similar to the telephone switchboard. Nervous impulses arriving in the central nervous system from the sense organs were switched through to the nerves leading to the muscles, which produced an appropriate response. Learning was a matter of connecting the inputs with the outputs in some appropriate manner. Just how such connections were brought about was a complete mystery. This type of model of the nervous system was the basis of the system of ideas about learning evolved by Edward L. Thorndike early in the present century. The analogy with the switchboard gave Thorndike's system the title of "connectionism," since learning was a matter of making these connections. In this system, for every output there was an input: every response was the result of some stimulus.

As the concept of mediating responses was introduced into psychology, the sequence of stimulus-response became lengthened to stimulus-mediating process-response, but thinking was still in terms of a chain of events. Learning involved modifications in that chain.

Psychologists did not have to look far to realize that many responses do not have any obvious stimulus. Some responses appear to be quite spontaneous, and though one may assume that there is some hidden stimulus which has not yet been identified, it is perhaps much more reasonable to assume that the individual is capable of actually generating responses without any external stimulus. The burden of proof for establishing the existence of stimuli for responses, when they are not evident, rests with those who believe that such stimuli can exist. One can reasonably assume that such stimuli do not exist, until the contrary is demonstrated.

One of the first psychologists who broke with the tradition that every response can be traced back to a stimulus was B. F. Skinner, who found it convenient to differentiate between two classes of responses. First, there are the responses that have traditionally played a central role in the development of behavioristic psychology, namely, respondent behavior that is initiated by some stimulus quite *identifiable* and usually external to the organism. In addition, Skinner classifies some behavior as "emitted" behavior. This type of behavior is emitted from the organism without any identifiable stimulus. Much of human behavior must be considered as manifesting examples of emitted behavior. In each one of these cases there is no identifiable stimulus associated with the behavior observed.

The concept of emitted behavior, which is becoming more and more accepted by modern psychologists, also finds some support from modern neurological research. Although most research on the physiology of the nervous system has not been based on any particular interest in problems of learning, it has produced information of the greatest value to the learning psychologist. The neurophysiologist today regards the nervous system as essentially an active mass of tissue, not one that remains passive until some impression from the outside world initiates activity. The central nervous system has the capacity for action in and of itself. Presumably such activity of the system is responsible for the behavior that we now describe as emitted behavior.

Scientific Understanding, Facts, and Laws

Learning theorists do not collect observations about learners and learning and expect that if enough facts are collected then scientific knowledge will necessarily result. The end product of a scientific inquiry is not a mass of factual material. Indeed, great collections of observations can be made without producing any notable result. Human beings have observed other human beings for countless generations without achieving any remarkable insight into human nature. The mere accumulation of observations alone does not result in scientific generalizations, which are the important product of scientific work.

The generalizations that the scientist derives from data are referred to as laws or principles. In a sense, they summarize the significant information derived from large quantities of data. They are like a refined crystalline product that is slowly evolved from a muddy and amorphous elixir. They differ from the generalizations that the layman expresses through his opinions in many important respects, for they are derived not from casually collected observations but through the painstaking efforts of the scientist to collect useful data. The general nature of scientific laws must be understood by the reader if he is to fully appreciate the difference between generalizations about learning based on carefully collected evidence and generalizations based on personal experience.

The Nature of the Laws Derived by the Scientist

This section will discuss the characteristics that scientific laws should manifest. Psychologists admit that much of the understanding they have achieved through research falls far short of presenting these characteristics. Psychology has a long way to go before it can provide a set of laws that can be stated with the same precision as, say, Newton's laws of motion. Some psychologists would even take the position that in the field of learning one should not refer to the products of research as laws of learning, but perhaps one might better describe them as broad generalizations about learning that leave much to be desired in the precision with which they are stated. The discussion of the nature of scientific laws that follows is designed to provide the reader with some insight into the goals the research psychologist sets for himself and his colleagues when he engages in research on learning. The psychologist realizes full well that such goals for research cannot be achieved in his lifetime, nor perhaps in the lifetimes of many generations to come. Nevertheless, some progress toward these goals has been and will be made.

The laws derived by the scientist are statements of relationships that have been established on the basis of evidence. For example, rewards are commonly used to facilitate the learning process, and the question may be asked whether the amount of learning produced is in any way related to the frequency of the reward. Evidence indicates that there is such a relationship, and that the establishment of this relationship has many of the essential features of the establishment of a law. Such a relationship constitutes part of a system of relationships between conditions of learning and the amount of learning produced. In this case the law, if it can be so called, represents a relationship between two variables, one of which is the amount of learning and the other the frequency of the reward. Scientific laws represent relationships between two or more measurable phenomena. Some complex laws may represent relationships among many measurable phenomena.

Although one may attempt to achieve precision in the statement of laws, difficulties encountered often limit precision. Under ideal conditions the scientist is able to arrive at laws that are stated in mathematical terms, but sometimes this ideal is not achieved and laws are formulated as general statements. Generalizations concerning learning are usually of the latter type, and fall short of the ideal that the scientist sets up for himself. Some would say that they do not have precision needed to be called laws. This is a matter of definition.

The Laws of Science Form Systems

The scientist attempts to develop systems of laws, and is not content to discover isolated relationships, though such relationships often form the beginning of systematic scientific knowledge. Many isolated oddments of information exist in almost every field before the scientist has any impact, but these oddments do not have the characteristics of scientific knowledge. Hippocrates realized that one of the best ways of lowering a fever was to give the patient large quantities of fluid, but this relationship between fluid intake and the control of fever can hardly be thought of as a law of physiology. The farmer who predicts the weather by attending to the aches in his joints and the color of the sky is not using scientific law, and neither is he the discoverer of one if he arrived at this system of predicting the weather. Even if the farmer's system of predicting the weather can be shown to be a good one, and even valid, one still cannot consider his system a scientific one, nor is it similar to one that the scientist attempts to develop. The task of the scientist is not merely the collection of items of knowledge, even if these items represent verifiable knowledge.

The scientist attempts to develop systems of laws that are interrelated— that is, he attempts to build an organized system of knowledge. In the field of learning, the psychologist *hopes* to build a system of laws that will permit a high degree of prediction and control in learning situations, much as Isaac Newton developed a set of laws of motion that permit a high degree of prediction of the behavior of matter in certain situations and therefore permit the development of means of exercising control over matter. The psychologist, in this respect, is attempting to do what the physicist has already done with so much success. He has not, as yet, produced as well organized a set of laws of learning; but considerable progress has been made.

Scientific Laws Have Boundary Conditions

Scientific laws are discovered within a certain context. For example, some of our knowledge of learning phenomena has been derived from a study of college sophomores. Other knowledge about learning has been derived from the study of laboratory rats. One cannot justifiably, without further inquiry, use the laws derived from the study of rats to plan the learning conditions for college sophomores, and what has been learned with college sophomores cannot be directly applied to the training of circus animals. Once a law has been discovered in a certain context, such as the behavior of college sophomores, one cannot rightfully assume that the same laws apply to the behavior of other living creatures. The discovery of a law in a limited situation must be followed by scientific explorations of the generality of the law. Sometimes scientists then find that the law has only limited application, perhaps limited to the original type of situation in which it was discovered. Sometimes laws are found to have wide generality. This process of exploration of the generality of a law establishes the boundary limits of the law.

This book is concerned mainly with generalizations about learning that have been shown to have applicability to a wide range of situations. In some cases the laws have been demonstrated to be valid for a great many different species behaving in a variety of situations. Some of the laws appear to have applicability mainly to the human species, and perhaps to only certain members of the human species.

Models, Theories, and Laws

The point has been made that scientists attempt to develop laws that form systems. In the field of physics Newton's law of motion form one such system of laws. The laws of thermodynamics form another such system. The advantage of developing a system, rather than a set of isolated laws, is greater and gives knowledge power that it would not otherwise have. Psychologists have also tried to follow this scientific tradition and have attempted to develop systems of generalizations about learning rather than isolated generalizations.

Laws or generalizations form systems because they are based on a common conception of what the phenomena involve. At an advanced stage of development they consist of systems of interrelated equations. A model is an analogy found useful in the understanding of phenomena. Research in learning, like research in any other field, makes extensive use of models. Just as the organic chemist found it convenient to think of the carbon atom as an object like a small billiard ball that could hook onto other little billiard-ball-like objects (an atom is certainly nothing like a billiard ball), so, too, does the psychologist attempt to develop simplified pictures of how the learning process takes place. These simplified pictures are referred to as models. Some of the sources from which these models are derived will now be considered.

Neurological models. Some psychologists find it convenient to base their conception of learning on knowledge of the general structure and physiology of the nervous system. In such a case one would say that the psychologist was using a neurological model. One of the earliest of these models, already mentioned, was developed as a result of the discovery that the nervous system includes a number of nerves conducting impulses into the major centers and a number conducting impulses from these centers to the muscles and glands. This led to the conception of the brain as a switchboard much like a telephone switchboard. This, in turn, led to the conception that learning involves the *connection* between stimuli and responses. Such a model, one has to point out, is based only partly on established fact, for a part of it is an imaginative elaboration of such fact. While the general structure of the nervous system had been established at the time this model was popular, there was still no evidence that the central portions of the nervous system functioned as a switchboard. Indeed, we know today that the central nervous system is not well described by this analogy.

No modern psychologist would use the analogy of the switchboard as a model for describing learning. Much more sophisticated models, based on neurological and physiological research, have been developed which are much more useful for scientific purposes. One such model, developed by Donald Hebb, will be discussed in later chapters, but in the discussion of Hebb's conception of learning the reader must remember that the model is not fully supported by established facts. The model is a convenient way of thinking about learning. It is retained only as long as it is found to be a useful aid. It is not meant to provide a comprehensive and precise description of how learning occurs.

Mechanical models. Some psychologists have found it useful to build mechanical models of the learning process. Some have attempted to imagine what kind of a machine would have to be built in order to stimulate the learning process. Some have thought in terms of the mechanisms provided by computers as possible analogy, and have considered how such computers would have to be modified or used to become machines that would learn. Computers can be made to perform many processes similar to those involved in learning, and can be so designed that they will modify their procedures as a result of experience. It is quite clear in this case that the mechanical model does not correspond to the machinery of the nervous system, and that it is only developed as a convenient crutch for the thinking of the scientists. This point must be emphasized, because the layman is all too prone to think that the model proposed by the scientist is a realistic and precise description of the learning process. It is clearly not.

Mathematical models. Some psychologists who devote their energies to the study of learning are concerned more with the development of mathematical functions that describe the process than they are with mechanics or analogies derived from neurology or mechanics. They point out that mathematical descriptions of events, which are here called mathematical models, have proved to be of importance in physics and chemistry as well as in other sciences, and hence there is at least a possibility that they might be of value also to the psychologist. While a few psychologists have given thought to the problem of developing mathematical models of learning—and some have attempted to obtain data to justify the models thus produced—little of the material has yet reached the point where it can be applied to practical situations.

Some attempts to develop mathematical models are also based to some extent on mechanical models. If learning involves certain mechanisms, then it follows that certain mathematical relationships should exist between the way in which the different parts of the learning process operate. Research can then be undertaken to determine whether such relationships do or do not occur.

Phenomenological models. Some scientists have tried to build models of the learning process, deriving from personal experience most of the ideas that they include. The late Kurt Lewin, a scientist of undoubted brilliance, attempted to build such a model. Since the world of personal experience was named by the German philosopher Emanual Kant the "world of phenomenal reality," models of learning based on personal experience have come to be known as "phenomenological" models. Such models of learning have been found to be particularly valuable by those who have studied perception in relation to learning. Although the reader may have the impression that there is little to the building of a learning model based on the phenomena of experience, such is far from the case. The model built by Lewin, which will be considered briefly in the chapter on perception, is both complex and highly sophisticated; but even the genius of Kurt Lewin was not successful in overcoming many of the difficulties inherent in the construction and use of such a model.

Later chapters will provide a more thorough discussion of the utilization of various models of the learning process. The important point to emphasize at this time is that a model is only an analogy. It is not a true representation of the learning process, and is discarded as soon as it no longer serves the purpose of helping understanding.

The concept of a scientific model and the concept of a scientific theory are closely interrelated. Unfortunately the word *theory* has had a number of distinct and separate meanings attached to it that may interfere with the concept of a scientific theory as it is used here. Among the popular meanings is the one implicit in the expression, "I have a theory," meaning that the person has a hypothesis. The term *theory*, as it is used here, refers to a set of related and established laws or generalizations. Generally a theory is based on a model of learning. Thus, reinforcement theory of learning, discussed at length in the next few chapters, is represented by a system of generalizations that have all been discovered through a study of certain classes of conditions related to learning. According to this model of learning, the process is guided to a great extent by the manipulation of certain environmental conditions. Later in the book some space will be devoted to perceptual theories of learning, which assume that the *way* the learner perceives the learning situation is a crucial factor. Such perceptual theories are very different from reinforcement theories of learning, and deal largely with very different learning phenomena. Perceptual theories and reinforcement theories are not necessarily in conflict, but they arrive at different generalizations because they are concerned with different phenomena. Ultimately, the generalizations included in perceptual theories and reinforcement theories will be brought together in a more comprehensive system.

The concept of the nature of scientific theory as presented here always implies that the theory includes a number of relationships that have been established on the basis of systematically collected evidence. If this definition is accepted, the student does not have to choose between theories of learning when he comes to apply learning theory in the classroom. On the contrary, the student's problem, when confronted with a particular classroom situation, is that of selecting the particular set of generalizations that has greatest applicability. On one occasion he may well find that a reinforcement theory of learning and the knowledge it has evolved will serve him best. In other situations he may turn to perceptual theories of learning because they provide him with established relationships directly applicable to the problem at hand.

Generalizations about Behavior Are Probabilistic

The scientist who studies the learning process seeks to discover relationships that will ultimately permit him to predict and control the course of learning. The relationships that he discovers are "probabilistic." By this is meant that the propositions describing these relationships will state that there is a certain probability that a certain event will occur. If an attempt is made to predict whether an individual entering a course in French will pass the final examination, the prediction is likely to be made in terms of a probability. One may predict that he has a 90-per-cent chance of passing the final examination, or that he has only a 50-per-cent chance. The prediction is made in this form because most of the generalizations that have been discovered permit only this kind of prediction. Many psychologists believe that all laws of behavior will be stated ultimately as probabilistic laws. Indeed, in a sense, even the laws of physics are probabilistic laws, but the probabilities are very high that the events will occur as predicted.

A Classification of Laws of Learning

Generalizations about learning, like other generalizations about behavior, may also be grouped in terms of the variables they involve. Some of these relationships are more powerful and useful than others, and hence this grouping is convenient when one comes to study discovered relationships and to examine them in terms of whether they are to be considered as strong or weak relationships. The following categories are commonly considered:

Relationships between responses. These may be represented as $\Delta R_1 = f(R_2)$—that is, a change in one response (ΔR_1) is a function of another response (R_2). Many generalizations about learning that are utilized by the guidance worker are of this kind. The guidance worker may look at a test score derived from a language aptitude test and conclude that the examinee would do well to avoid courses in the foreign-language area. The guidance worker comes to this conclusion because previous data have demonstrated that a relationship exists between scores on the aptitude test (R_2) and grades in foreign-language courses (ΔR_1).

This represents a response-response relationship and relates one set of responses, those of the aptitude tests, to another set of responses, which are those made on examinations in the foreign-language course. Both sets of responses are complexly determined from within the individuals involved. Indeed, the relationship between the one set of responses and the other are not only complex, but also obscure. In most response-response relationships little is known about the reason for the underlying relationship. However, one can often be fairly confident that the relationship will occur in new populations. For example, a test of language aptitude may have been shown to be a good predictor of grades in foreign languages in schools in New York City, and one knows from experience with other tests that a test that is valid in New York City is likely to be valid in other cities of the country.

However, sometimes one is quite unjustified in assuming that a test that is valid in one situation will also be valid in another situation. In other words, relationships of the response-response type have their limitations.

Relationships between a response (R) and a set of conditions (S). These are important relationships, since they indicate how to change a particular situation (S) in order to arrange for a response (R) to occur. Such relationships can be represented symbolically by the equation $\Delta R = f(S)$, which states that a change in response is a function of a particular situation. For many practical purposes this equation is much too simple, for the occurrence of a response is dependent also on the characteristics of the responding organism.

Relationships in this category are important and powerful, since they indicate characteristics of the situation in which the individual must be placed in order to produce certain kinds of behavior. If a classroom is to be a place in which learning behavior is to proceed efficiently, then the classroom must manifest certain characteristics that favor learning behavior. Research suggests a number of conditions in the environment that are both favorable and unfavorable to the eliciting of learning behavior. Insofar as such conditions have been identified, they are invaluable to the teacher in arranging effective learning situations. In such cases the teacher would be making use of relationships in the category under consideration.

Relationships between behavior and organic conditions. These are represented by the equation $\Delta R = f(O)$—that is, the change in response is a function of an organic condition. Some relationships in this category have been established. For example, the child with a brain injury emits a large quantity of behavior supposedly as a result of his internal condition. The typical picture of this child in the classroom is of one who wriggles and squirms and cannot keep still. In addition he tends to be over-reactive to all stimuli, most of which would be disregarded by other children. Another example is that of children who are hungry and who, under such conditions, are likely to be restless. The restlessness is generated by the internal condition of hunger. These relationships are not very powerful in their implications for classroom practice because they do not permit the accomplishment of many useful goals in the classroom. The child who is overactive because of some internal condition has to be tolerated. The chances are that not too much can be done about the situation. Perhaps a physician may prescribe tranquilizers, but these may possibly have the harmful effect of limiting learning capacity. Relationships in this category may help in the understanding of the causes of behavior, but they do not lead to the useful control of behavior.

Relationships between the development of organic conditions and the occurrence of particular stimuli. This kind of law may be represented by the equation $\Delta O = f(S)$. Relatively few research workers have been concerned with the establishment of relationships in this category, though they could be of considerable importance. Those involved in research on problems related to psychosomatic medicine are particularly concerned with the discovery of relationships between organic conditions and the occurrence of particular circumstances to which the person is exposed. The finding by Brady and his associates at the Walter Reed Hospital, that gastric ulcers will occur in primates placed in particular situations, represents an attempt to state a relationship in this class. Relatively little is known about the organic effects of persistent conditions, except through their ultimate effects on behavior. While some knowledge is available concerning the conditions that produce deep-seated anxieties and the ways in which these influence behavior, little is known about the relatively permanent organic changes which are involved in this process. In time, much will have to be found out about the organic effects of the conditions existing in the school, including such matters as the effect of various degrees of heat and light, the effect of demanding or relaxed teachers, the effect of long periods of sedentary activity, the effect of prolonged pleasant, as contrasted with prolonged unpleasant, learning activities, and so forth. Before the ultimate effects of such conditions on behavior can be fully understood, some understanding must be achieved of some of the organic changes involved.

In a case in this category, controversies sometimes arise concerning whether a phenomenon does or does not belong in it. An example of such a controversial case is found in a series of studies by Gibson and Walk (1959), Gibson, Walk, Pick, and Tighe (1958), Gibson, Walk, and Tighe (1959), and Walk, Gibson, Pick, and Tighe (1959). The first of these studies demonstrated that rats learned to discriminate a circle and a triangle more readily if they had been previously exposed to the presence of such figures on the wall of their cages during the time they were reared. The later studies have shown that the figure displayed, in order to be effective, had to be three dimensional cutouts rather than flat figures painted on a flat surface. If one accepts the conclusion that learning was facilitated by mere exposure to the appropriate figures, then the law of behavior involved would fall into the general category of an internal change in the organism occurring as a function of a stimulus. The phenomena involved are generally weak, appearing in some experiments but not in others. Mere exposure to stimuli would seem to be an inefficient way to learn, though some learning theorists, notably Hebb (1949), have maintained that such exposure plays a vital part in development.

If one accepts the conclusion that exposure to the figures (S) produced a subsequent change in response (Δ R) in a discrimination learning task, then the relationship involved falls in the category $\Delta R = f (S)$. However, if one infers from the later behavior of the rats that exposure to the stimuli during rearing produced some relatively permanent internal change that later modified behavior, then laws in the category $\Delta O = f (S)$ are also involved.

Summary

1. Evidence for learning is supplied by the modification of a response that is both relatively permanent and a consequence of environmental conditions. Although the evidence for learning is found in the modification of performance, a distinction must be made between performance and learning. Although performance is a peripheral activity, learning is a change in the central nervous system.

2. Positive modifications in behavior that result in the development of new behavior are referred to as the process of *acquisition*. This is to be distinguished from that aspect of learning involved in the elimination of behavior. The latter is referred to as the process of *extinction*. Considerably more knowledge is available about the acquisition of behavior than about the extinction of behavior.

3. Psychologists have found it convenient to distinguish between "molar" and "molecular" studies of behavior. Molecular studies involve research at a highly detailed level. Molar studies, which are typical of those reported in this volume, are studies involving a gross level of behavior. Even at the molar level, the level of detail examined may vary from study to study. Research in education generally involves a study

of a less detailed level of behavior than does laboratory research in learning.

4. The systematic study of learning involves careful measurement and (first through the attempts of Ebbinghaus) the measuring of retention and the conditions that affect it. The increased emphasis on the measurement of aptitude and achievement in schools represents a similar need for precision in the practical conduct of learning programs.

5. The learning process can be conveniently divided into a number of separate phases. Conditions that occur before learning is initiated, but that contribute or interfere with learning, are referred to as "antecedent conditions." These are to be contrasted with the actual conditions of learning, which are referred to as *learning conditions* or *training conditions*. The word *training* is used here to refer to any procedure designed to produce learning, and does not imply a distinction between training and education, as is implied by some current educational writing. *Performance conditions* are the conditions existing at the time a skill that has been learned is demonstrated. There is much evidence to show that the extent to which learning is manifested is often highly dependent upon performance conditions.

6. If learning is to be studied systematically, then there are advantages in studying learning phenomena under simplified conditions in the laboratory. Traditional scientific techniques have been very successful when they have taken this approach.

7. When the research worker refers to the "control" of learning, the concept he has in mind is similar to that of the teacher who refers to the "guidance" of learning. While the word *control* in education has come to mean the exercise of harshness and punitive methods for directing the learning process, the research worker uses the word in a much broader sense to refer to any condition that influences learning. In this sense all good teaching is "controlling," because it influences the learning process. One cannot imagine good teaching that does not have this influence.

8. Control of learning may be external or internal. The teacher exercises external control, but the pupil can exercise internal control, as, for example, when he finds for himself the best environment for undertaking the learning that he desires. Internal control is also exercised in such matters as the choice of learning goals and of means of reaching those goals.

9. Learning becomes apparent in the modification of responses. Rarely does learning result in the complete and overall modification of responses, but rather it appears in the modification of particular aspects of response. The aspects of response that most commonly undergo modification through learning are accuracy, latency or speed, amplitude, frequency,

resistance to change, resistance to forgetting, unusualness, and other scaled characteristics.

10. The systematic study of the learning process requires more than the measurement of changes in response characteristics. It requires also the measurement of the conditions that exist during the learning process. A satisfactory inventory of the learning conditions that exercise control over learning cannot be given at this time. Such an inventory would include, among other conditions, the time distribution of training, task characteristics, the consequences of correct and incorrect behavior, the cues provided, and the incentives. Any prediction of the outcomes of learning must take into account such characteristics of the learning situation.

11. A systematic account of learning must take into account much more than the characteristics of the learning situation (S-characteristics) and the characteristics of the responses (R-characteristics). It must also take into account the characteristics of the learner and the mediating processes that occur during learning. No progress may occur in some learning situations, because the learner is not able to perform the mediating processes needed for effective learning.

12. A special class of mediating processes is referred to as perceptual processes. Although many works on education place special stress on the importance of these processes in relation to learning, they represent only one of several categories of mediating processes. Although no one would deny the importance of perceptual processes in learning, there are great difficulties involved in the study of perception and the processes related to it. At one time, most students of learning took the position that stimuli, mediating processes, and responses always occurred in this sequence, but today the view is widely held that responses may be generated by the nervous system without any identifiable initiating stimulus. The nervous system appears to have the capacity of generating behavior. Such behavior is referred to as *emitted behavior*.

13. Research on learning is not just concerned with the accumulation of facts. The end product of research on learning is a set of generalizations. Such generalizations represent relationships among variables. Once knowledge has reached a well-developed state, the generalizations form systems. All generalizations and laws have limits and boundary conditions that must be known before they can be applied to new situations.

14. In advanced sciences, systems of laws are represented by systems of interrelated equations. In less advanced sciences, such as the psychology of learning, generalizations form systems because they are all based on a particular concept or model of learning. These models or concepts of learning may be derived from knowledge of the nervous system, may be mechanical models or mathematical models, or may be based on personal experience, in which case they are referred to as

phenomenological models. These models are analogies that help the scientist in his exploration of learning.

15. The generalizations derived from research concerning learning are probabilistic in the predictions they make. They do not indicate exactly what will happen if a subject with particular characteristics is exposed to a particular learning situation. They indicate only what probably will happen.

16. Generalizations concerning learning may be categorized. Some categories have far more important implications for education than others. Particularly important for the educator are those that state that a change in a response is a function of some set of environmental conditions. The latter type of generalization indicates to the educator the environmental conditions that must be provided in order to facilitate learning.

3

Reinforcement and Learning

T HE PURPOSE of this chapter is to describe some of the well-established phenomena related to learning and to show how knowledge of these phenomena on the part of the teacher provides a basis for the management of learning in the classroom. The chapter is oriented toward the presentation of findings rather than toward the development of a theory of learning. Although a review of what is known always provides a tempting occasion for theory building, an effort will be made to resist this temptation. The discussion of research findings necessarily involves some cautious generalization, but this should not be interpreted to mean that the author is endorsing a particular comprehensive theoretical position.

Emitted Behavior and Respondent Behavior

Older conceptions of learning regarded the learning process as a matter of building up connections between stimuli and responses. In such theories all behavior was considered to be a response to some form of stimulation, and since often no external stimulation could be found to account for behavior, then internal stimuli were thought to exist that might produce such behavior. This point of view made many scientists feel uncomfortable, for it really amounts to imagining the existence of stimuli in order to make the behavior theory acceptable. B. F. Skinner (1938) was the first to take the position that only some behavior is the result of specific and identifiable stimulation, and that there is other behavior that simply does not stem from any identifiable source of stimulation. This was an important step forward in thinking, and one the student must understand because it has many implications for thinking about educational problems.

Skinner classifies behavior either as *respondent* or *emitted. Respondent behavior is that which follows some identifiable stimulus and which is produced by it.*

A reflex such as the eyeblink that occurs immediately after a loud and sudden sound would be classified as a respondent behavior, as would any behavior about which it can be clearly demonstrated that the stimulus has a clear-cut function in eliciting the response. A fear response in a frightening situation would be another respondent behavior. For reasons that will be apparent later, it is not always easy to determine whether or not a response is the immediate consequence of a particular stimulus.

Skinner points out that much behavior is not respondent behavior, for it is not preceded by any identifiable stimulus. Although one can imagine the existence of internal stimuli, this is not very useful. Skinner prefers to make no such assumption. *Behavior that occurs without any identifiable stimuli he refers to as "emitted behavior." The behaviors so emitted are referred to as "operants"* (1953).

The distinction between emitted and respondent behavior is not so clear as it might seem at first glance. When Skinner talks about a behavior that has an identifiable stimulus, he is referring to behavior very closely tied to a particular stimulus. The response of the leg to a tap below the knee satisfies the definition of a respondent behavior. Reflexes fall into the classification of respondent behavior, but few other behaviors do. A pupil who pays attention to the teacher and takes occasional notes is not manifesting respondent behavior, and neither is a pupil who applauds at the end of a lecture. Skinner would not classify most of such behavior in the respondent class, for he would say that the relationship of the stimulus to the response is complex and not of the direct nature found in respondent behavior. In the cases of some children in the classroom there will be virtually no relationship between the stimuli that can be observed and the behavior manifested. The child who doodles, the child who talks to himself, the child who wiggles restlessly in his seat, are all examples of behavior that has little relationship to immediate stimuli. Such cases present rather clear examples of what is meant by emitted behavior, but Skinner does not limit his definition of emitted behavior to these cases alone.

Skinner takes the position that most behavior falls into the category of emitted behavior. He also considers respondent behavior generally rather trivial in character, and hence has directed his research to the study of emitted behavior and the way it develops and changes as a result of learning. Some behavior that one might think at first sight to be respondent behavior is much more plausibly described as operant. Consider, for example, typical conversation. Two individuals meet in the street and each emits a certain amount of conversation related to his recent doings. What the one says can hardly be described as a direct response of the other; at least, it is not respondent behavior in the same way that a reflex is respondent behavior. One person does not cause another to say what he does say, although the presence of the other person produces the kind of situation in which such things are said.

For the young child, the conditions existing in the environment have very little to do with the kind or amount of behavior he emits. A baby will lie quietly and then begin to show some general activity, which may vary from slight movements of the arms and legs to violent movements accompanied by crying. In the first few weeks of life this behavior is not the result of any identifiable stimulus, but rather it is strictly a function of internal conditions. When the state of activity is high, it can be reduced by mild stimulation, as when the mother picks up the crying baby and calms it. As the child grows and develops, the activity manifested becomes less and less a sequence of random movements and more and more a behavior that is the instrument for satisfying the needs of the child. The operant behavior becomes, as it is said in technical terms, *shaped*. Much of this book has to do with the shaping of behavior, particularly those aspects of behavior that are shaped in the classroom.

As behavior is shaped, an important change occurs. Certain behaviors tend to occur only on certain occasions. For example, vocal behavior occurs with greater frequency when the child is with other children and less frequently when he is alone. His talking behavior is not the direct result of the presence of other persons in the same way in which the pupillary reflex is a direct response to light. Indeed, the child may talk when there are others present, but he may not be talking in response to what they are saying. One can say that the presence of other people comes to produce the kind of situation in which talking behavior occurs. Playful and recreational behavior occurs particularly on weekends. It is not the presence of the weekend that causes the recreational behavior, but rather the weekend is just one of the conditions under which it occurs.

Children of school age typically show the linking of certain behaviors to certain occasions. A typical third-grade child conforms in the classroom and accepts the authority of the teacher. However, as soon as the school bell rings, the child enters a world in which other behaviors emerge. The same child who is docile in the schoolroom may be aggressive and hostile to the adults in his home environment. The school and the home are linked to different patterns of behavior. This is important in the understanding of personality, and should make the teacher cautious about generalizing from observations made on children in the classroom.

When an operant appears only in the presence of certain stimuli, it is referred to as a *discriminative operant*. Much of the behavior of the adult can be usefully described as consisting of discriminative operants; this is in contrast to the behavior of the child, which is much less closely tied to specific situations. The tendency for children to speak out of turn, to embarrass adults, to do the unexpected, is a result of the fact that much of their behavior does not yet consist of discriminative operants but is emitted behavior, equally likely to occur under a wide range of conditions.

Response Probability

In any learning situation the learner starts with an inability to make the correct responses to the relevant stimuli. If this were not so, learning would not be attempted, for learning would already have taken place. A child who is starting to learn to read cannot name words correctly when the printed symbols for them are presented. As learning proceeds, the learner becomes more and more capable of producing the correct response. After a day's practice with fifteen words he may be able to name them correctly in 80 per cent of the cases. At this stage of learning it would be said that he has an 80-per-cent probability of naming them correctly, or, more commonly, a correct response probability of 0.8. When the learning series was started, the response probability was 0.0, for the learner had no capability of making the correct response. The response probability is a measure of learning that is commonly used both in experimental studies of learning and in appraisal of pupil progress. The teacher may give a test at the end of the day and find that one pupil recognizes the words in 60 per cent of the cases and that another recognizes the words in 90 per cent of the cases. These would represent response probabilities of 0.6 and 0.9 respectively, although the teacher would probably enter the grades as 60 and 90. The response probability is considered a measure of the strength of the response, and is a convenient term for discussing the extent to which learning has occurred.

The term *response probability* can be used to describe the progress of learning in all areas. A youngster comes to school with a strong tendency to become aggressive toward his classmates. He has a high probability of manifesting aggressive behavior toward his classmates, and his teachers are concerned with lowering this response probability. The chances are that the teacher will not be able to make any very permanent change in the probability, though it may be possible to arrange the classroom situation so that the stimuli that initiate hostile behavior are reduced. This might be done by arranging classroom groupings so that the child spends little time with equally aggressive children. This does not really change the response probability, for when we refer to response probability we refer to the probability that a response will occur given certain circumstances known to elicit the response. A child's capacity to read can be measured by his response probability *when confronted with reading materials.* If, after the child has learned to read, he is not exposed to reading materials, so that he shows no reading behavior, we would not then say that he has forgotten to read or that we have eliminated the reading related to learning. The response probability remains unchanged *in the particular situations that evoke the response.* Although a learned response does not occur under particular circumstances, this does not mean that the capacity for making the response has been lost. Indeed, learning must be thought of as some internal change that remains fairly stable despite changes in surface behavior.

The internal part of the learning process is often thought of as representing a factor H, which is strengthened or weakened as learning proceeds. This designation was originally introduced by C. L. Hull, and was extensively discussed by him (1943). In much of the literature on learning, H is referred to as *habit strength,* but the word *habit* is not used in the sense in which it is commonly used in everyday language. As learning progresses, there is a greater and greater tendency to make the response to be learned and a decreasing tendency to make other responses. H represents the strength of the internal tendency. Thus, if H has a high value, then there is a high probability that the corresponding response will occur if situations are presented in which this particular response is appropriate. If habit strength is low, the corresponding response is said to be a weak response, and it has a low probability of occurrence under appropriate stimulus situations.

Many interpretations of the central process involved in learning are possible. Only one of these interpretations involves habit strength. One of several other interpretations is offered by Mowrer (1960, a), who points out that when a rat is placed in a box equipped with a small lever or bar which, when pressed, causes the release of a small quantity of food, the common description of what happens involves the statement that the rat "learns to press the bar." Mowrer suggests that this statement is nonsense. Rats in such a situation do not have to learn to press the bar, for they will sooner or later press it in their explorations of the box. According to Mowrer, the rat does not learn to press the bar, but learns to *want* to press the bar when hungry. What he is suggesting is that learning in such a situation does not involve the learning of a habit, but the learning of a motive.

Another interpretation of the internal process involved in learning is that which involves a change in perceptual processes. The bar may at first be undiscriminated from other stimuli by the rat. Through experience, the rat learns not only to discriminate the bar from other objects in its environment, but to recognize it as a food-obtaining object. This is the position that some learning theorists have taken, notably Tolman (1948).

This does not mean that such theorists can demonstrate that such internal processes actually occur any more than Mowrer can demonstrate that rats learn to want to push a bar. Such internal processes are always inferred from behavior and are in the position of being theoretical constructs or ideas. The survival of one of these conceptions over other conceptions of the internal process involved in learning depends entirely on the extent to which it proves itself useful in research and in predicting behavior. Such theoretical constructions are not retained simply because they have plausibility in terms of personal experience.

Reinforcement of Operants

Generations of psychologists have made the observation that certain kinds of events that follow particular behaviors increase the probability that the behaviors will occur. If a hungry rat is placed in a box equipped with a lever, the depression of which releases a pellet of food, the animal will soon learn to press the lever. The event that follows the pressing of the lever, namely the release of food, is an event that increases the probability that the rat will press the lever. Other behaviors that occur in the box and that are not followed by this particular event will decrease in the frequency with which they occur. The delivery of the food is described as a reinforcing event or as a reinforcer. The behavior of the rat in the box is shaped by the reinforcing event, and soon the hungry rat directs most of its energies to the pressing of the lever to the exclusion of other forms of behavior. Many other events besides the delivery of food have been demonstrated to reinforce the behavior of the laboratory rat.

In the case of human behavior a large number of different events can be identified as having reinforcing properties. Skinner has pointed out that one of the most common reinforcers used in civilized societies is money, but not all members of such a society are reinforced by money. Young children are not generally reinforced with money since other events are generally found to have better reinforcing properties. The preschool child is typically reinforced for appropriate behavior with adult approval. Adolescent behavior is highly reinforced by the approval shown by other adolescents. The effectiveness of such reinforcing events is not only generally known but is also extensively used within the human community when one member attempts to control the behavior of another member.

The term *reinforcer* is used here rather than the older term *reward*, though an examination of the research literature shows that the two terms are used as if they were interchangeable. The term *reward* generally carries with it the implication that the event is a pleasureable one, and the term *reinforcer* is neutral and is commonly used to indicate only that the event increases the probability of occurrence of the behavior it follows.

Learning is typically produced in animals through the control of reinforcing events. Rats will learn a maze by being deprived of food for 22 hours before being placed in the starting box of the maze. They then rapidly learn to find the goal box that contains, on each trial, a small amount of food. Hungry pigeons will learn a number of skills through the manipulation of reinforcing events involving the delivery of food. Although consumables represent the core element of reinforcing events used to produce learning in laboratory animals, human learning can be produced and controlled through the manipulation of a great range of other events, including money, approval, and the occurrence of words such as *right*. The teacher who has knowledge of the events that reinforce may be able to exercise control over the learning of pupils.

The impressive part that reinforcing events play in the control of learning in laboratory situations has led some psychologists to take the position that all learning involves reinforcing events and that, conversely, no learning will take place without the occurrence of reinforcing events. Such a generalization extends far beyond the limited laboratory data on which it is based, but the position it represents gains considerable strength from the fact that even if learning does take place in the absence of reinforcements, there would be difficulties in keeping the pupils in the learning context since reinforcements have this maintaining function.

Those who maintain that all learning is dependent upon the occurrence of reinforcers refer to this generalization as the *law of reinforcement*. The position taken here is that reinforcing events play an important role in learning, but that there is no advantage in taking the extreme position that reinforcement is a necessary condition for learning.

The basic concept of reinforcement has had a long history, although the central idea involved has masqueraded at times under other names. The central idea goes back to Edward L. Thorndike (1911), who proposed that when a satisfying condition followed a response, then the bond between the stimulus and response was strengthened, increasing the probability that the response would occur in the future when the same stimulus was presented. The reverse was to happen when an annoying condition was presented. Later Thorndike (1932) modified his position, since his data seemed to indicate that annoyers did not have the opposite effect of satisfiers. While the terms *satisfiers* and *annoyers* may appear to have a subjective flavor, they do not have it in the work of Thorndike, who defines them with all the objectivity needed to satisfy even the most ardent behaviorist. A satisfier simply represents a condition the organism seeks to perpetuate, and an annoyer is one it seeks to terminate.

In recent times psychologists have dropped the terms *satisfiers* and *annoyers.* In the place of the word *satisfier* they use the word *reinforcement,* which has been already defined as a condition that increases the probability that the response reinforced will occur. Reinforcers are sometimes pleasant, but not necessarily so. One can imagine an experiment in which a child is learning addition, and each time he adds correctly he is given a small electric shock. He may find the shock unpleasant, but since it indicates that he is right in his answer, it will increase the probability that he will give right answers in the future. A reinforcer may be an unpleasant experience, though more often it is probably a pleasant one. The term *reinforcement* is a neutral one in this respect and has nothing to do with whether an experience is pleasant or unpleasant.

Reinforcement theory generally assumes that certain conditions or events have the property of acting as reinforcers without any learning process intervening. Thus, food and water in a hungry and thirsty animal may be assumed to function as reinforcers as soon as the nervous system is capable of producing learning behavior. Other stimuli may presumably have the same effect. Such stimuli might include, in the case of a child, a soft touch on the skin, a bright and shiny object, moving objects, and so forth. A list of such primary reinforcers has never been made up for man or for any other living creature, but it is generally assumed that one could be produced as a result of experimentation. Such a list is needed, if this type of reinforcement theory is to be applied to the shaping of human behavior.

A wide range of other phenomena may function as reinforcers. For a child, the process of exploring his environment may, in itself, reinforce the activity. Money represents a generalized reinforcer for most people, although there are some whose behavior would not be reinforced by the offering of money. Skinner (1953) implies in his writing that there is no real problem in finding reinforcers of human behavior, that the commonest and most effective way in a learning situation is to tell the learner that the response made was the correct one. Some doubt may be felt concerning the soundness of this position. There are certainly some children who may be much more concerned with obtaining the social approval of their classmates than with knowing that their response is in some way approved by society. Skinner's attempt to build teaching machines is based to a great extent on the premise that knowledge of a response being right is a powerful reinforcing factor. It most certainly is with many pupils, but there are those for whom such a condition may have very little reinforcing value at all. Perhaps in a class of the future the teacher will spend the first day of school in determining the conditions that are effective for reinforcing the behavior of each child.

Some books assume that the reinforcers of behavior are known and can be identified. One common statement is that all children need social approval, implying that social approval is a major condition leading to reinforcement. There is little or no evidence to support this point of view. Another common statement is that the experience of accomplishment is of particular importance because it will, in and of itself, promote development. In some it may, but here again there is little or no evidence to support this point of view.

A special case of reinforcement is seen in the phenomenon known as *knowledge of results*. It has been known for a long time that performance will not improve unless the individual knows whether what he does is right or wrong and what errors he makes. In a classic experiment, E. L. Thorndike asked individuals to draw lines three inches long. As they continued to draw lines they *believed* to be three inches long, they showed no improvement in their performance. Practice alone did not provide improvement, for they did not know whether the lines they were drawing were of the right length. Improvement would occur only if they were told after each line whether it was too short or too long. This information provides *knowledge of results*. Another way of saying this, which is becoming more and more commonly seen in technical literature, is to say that the information provided concerning the length of the line is *feedback*. As feedback or knowledge of results produces improvement, it functions as a reinforcer for whatever behavior resulted in the improvement.

Sometimes knowledge of results does not have to be provided by an independent agent such as an experimenter, but the feedback may be provided by the person's own manipulations. In solving a puzzle, such as the familiar Japanese wire puzzles that have to be disassembled without forcing, the problem solver can see easily when he is solving the problem and when he is failing. The feedback is quite automatic and serves to reinforce whatever manipulations led to the solution of the puzzle. This kind of feedback does not occur when the problem is a mathematical one of the type "What does a dozen oranges cost if five oranges cost thirty-five cents?" In the latter case the pupil who works the problem cannot know whether or not his solution is correct until the teacher tells him. The exception to this is when the pupil arrives at an answer that is completely ridiculous, such as two cents.

Primary and Secondary Reinforcers

A distinction is commonly made between primary and secondary reinforcers. Certain conditions appear to function as reinforcers without any learning taking place. Food will reinforce the behavior of any hungry animal, and from the earliest age. Every professional animal trainer, as well as the amateur training his dog, knows that food can be used to shape behavior. Water will do the same thing in a thirsty animal, and so will any condition that satisfies a basic physiological need. Such a reinforcer is known as a primary reinforcer.

Scientists are not able at this time to make a complete list of the primary reinforcers, but they are almost certainly not limited to food, water, proper temperature conditions, and the like. It is possible that most forms of mild stimulation will have reinforcing properties. A child may continue to play with an object for long hours because the object stimulates him in a reinforcing way. The neighbor's child who beats a drum all day long may be demonstrating that the noise produced in banging the drum reinforces him to beat the drum further. In popular language one would say that he likes the sound of the drum and hence goes on beating it. The scientist states that the noise of the drum reinforces the drum-beating behavior.

Stimulation may be reinforcing, and this reinforcement may be a primary one—not dependent on prior learning. Of this one cannot be sure at the present time. From the point of view of the educator, the important point is that stimulation may be reinforcing.

Secondary reinforcers are those that derive their properties from having been associated with primary reinforcers. *A stimulus that was not originally a reinforcing one can become so through being associated with one that is reinforcing.* The basic phenomenon was first described by Pavlov (1927), and has had a long history in psychology.

There is experimental evidence to show that new conditions can acquire the properties of reinforcers that they did not originally possess. An example of such a reinforcer is money. For the very young child, money has little meaning beyond that of being a plaything that is shiny and fun to play with. As the child grows older it becomes a more and more powerful way of controlling behavior, and, ultimately, much of a person's performance on a job is controlled by the way in which he is offered monetary rewards for behaving in one way but not in another. How money has come to acquire this property of being a highly generalized reinforcer is a complex problem and one about which we can only speculate at this time. We do, however, know something about the way in which stimuli can acquire new reinforcement properties in much simpler situations that have been extensively studied.

If a pigeon is fed at ten-second intervals and if a buzzer is sounded during each of the intervals, then the buzzer comes to acquire the same reinforcing properties as the food. It is then possible to use the buzzer as a reinforcer—that is, the buzzer can be used to provide some modifications in the pigeon's behavior. If each time the pigeon stands on one leg the buzzer sounds, then the pigeon will more and more frequently stand on one leg. In technical language it may be said that the sound of the buzzer has become a secondary reinforcer for the particular pigeon, a property that the sound ordinarily does not possess. Secondary reinforcers lose their power after they have been used for some time without being paired with the original reinforcer through which it acquired its reinforcing properties. It is possible that some conditions of reinforcement may result in much greater permanence of secondary reinforcing properties than is ordinarily found in typical laboratory experiments, but the failure of secondary reinforcers to continue to function as such is one of the difficulties encountered in using this type of mechanism to account for the fact that many different kinds of objects come to have reinforcing properties that remain stable over long periods of time. Money comes to have the property of being a rather general reinforcer, and even small amounts of money, too small to be of real economic significance to the individual, may still reinforce behavior.

Another example of the development of a secondary reinforcer is provided in a study by Wolfe (1936), who trained chimpanzees to work for chips which they were then able to insert into a slot machine to obtain grapes. The chimpanzees would even show some hoarding behavior, but difficulty was experienced in arranging conditions so that the animals would hoard as many as twenty chips.

After some training, the chips acquire some properties as secondary reinforcers. They remain weak and transitory reinforcers and do not retain this property without reconditioning. Nothing comparable to the extraordinary power that money acquires for many human beings as a shaper of behavior is seen in the property that the chips acquire for the chimpanzees.

If the mechanism of secondary reinforcement described in the previous paragraphs were the only one of which anything were known that provided an account of the expanding numbers of objects and conditions that come to have reinforcement functions as the individual grows, there would be the greatest difficulty in accounting for most adult behavior. Other mechanisms also seem to be at work.

A strong case can be made to support the proposition that the reinforcers of behavior are those conditions that satisfy the needs operating in the particular situation in which behavior is to be reinforced. In teaching a rat to run a maze, the experimenter uses a hungry one; and when the rat reaches the end of the maze, a small amount of food is provided. The food is the reinforcer of the correct decisions made in running the maze and satisfies the need of the animal for food. If the animal were well fed prior to entering the maze, then food would not be very effective as a reinforcer. It works best as a reinforcer when the need for food is at a relatively high level. In children, too, there appears to be some relationship between reinforcement and the needs that are operating in the child. While this is a matter that will be discussed at much greater length under the topic of motivation, some brief discussion of the matter is appropriate here. If a child is quite unconcerned about his academic performance and has no need to excel, then praise from the teacher for his accomplishments is likely to have little reinforcement value. In contrast, a child who has a high need for recognition may have his desirable behavior highly reinforced by being held up to the class as a model of good behavior. For many years the slogan used as a basis for curriculum design was that the curriculum should be related to the needs of the child. It is perhaps more precise to say that if learning is to occur, the reinforcers provided should be related to the needs of the child.

Just how many distinct needs are commonly operating in classroom behavior is not known at this time, and the problem of identifying them is a complex one. It is not simply a matter of determining a need structure that presumably can be considered to encompass the needs of all pupils. Clearly, the need structure that determines much of behavior in the adult is a product of development and not a structure with which the person is originally born. In our present state of knowledge, there are strong reasons for believing that the human infant first displays through his behavior a need for stimulation. Many writers have referred to this need as a curiosity drive or an exploratory drive. These latter concepts have had a long and reputable history in the literature of experimental psychology and were first introduced to account for the fact that a well-fed and well-watered rat, placed in a maze, will show characteristic activity such as wandering about the maze, sniffing the corners, standing up on its hind legs, sniffing the chicken wire that covers the top, and so forth. Children show similar behavior, and this points to the possible conclusion that some kind of tendency to explore is a basic characteristic of all higher organisms.

Self-Reinforcing Activities

Those psychologists who regard reinforcement as a necessary condition for human learning have long had difficulty in accounting for the fact that some human learning occurs in the absence of observable reinforcers. Certainly, a person can read a book and learn much from the process, but where are the reinforcing events? Such apparent exceptions to the notion that reinforcement is necessary for learning permit two courses of action. One of these is to take the position that not all learning requires reinforcing events; the other is to assert that hidden reinforcers are operating. The second of these two positions has generally been preferred by researchers in the field of reinforcement phenomena, perhaps because they tend to think of these phenomena as representing a general principle underlying all learning. Let us examine this position.

If reinforcement is a necessary condition for learning, then activities that do not involve observable reinforcers must involve reinforcers that cannot be observed. Thus, an activity such as reading is said to involve reinforcing events internal to the reader and the activity is said to be self-reinforcing. The purpose of invoking such unobservable reinforcers is to sustain reinforcement as a necessary condition for all learning; but the possibility exists that some learning may take place without the occurrence of such events, in which case the scientist would be guilty of imagining events that had no real existence at all.

The safest position at the present time is to stay close to the facts. Since there are some learning tasks in which the acquisition of a skill is closely tied to the presence of reinforcers occurring at the appropriate time in relation to the response, one can say that such events are sometimes necessary for learning; but to say that these are necessary for all learning goes far beyond the facts. When learning occurs without the occurrence of observable reinforcing events one can conservatively say that reinforcers *may* be operating, but one does not really know.

Negative Reinforcement and Punishment

In the presence of some stimuli, organisms tend to try to escape from them. Such stimuli were referred to by Thorndike as *annoyers*. In recent times a more common practice has been to refer to these stimuli as *aversive stimuli*. Some stimuli are fairly universally aversive for living organisms. Stimuli that produce tissue damage are generally in this category. Most very strong stimuli fall into the category of aversive stimuli.

Certain stimuli are more restricted in their aversive properties. Hebb (1958), for example, has found that young chimpanzees are typically fearful of some strange objects but not of others. Humans also show certain aversive responses that are typical of their species. At a certain stage of development the human child will seek to avoid people who are strange to him. Other stimuli undoubtedly produce avoidance responses in nearly all members of the human species, but few of these have as yet been identified.

There are also considerable individual differences in the stimuli that are responded to as aversive. This is summed up in the well-known phrase, "One man's meat is another man's poison." One person may love to perform before a crowded audience, but another will go to extraordinary measures to avoid such a performance. One person enjoys camping in the wilds, but another is terrified by the thought of it. One seeks fellowship, yet another avoids human contacts. Individual differences in the aversive properties of stimuli are extensive.

In the presence of an aversive stimulus, the organism typically shows escape behavior. When an escape behavior is successful, it reduces or removes the aversive stimulus. When this happens, the effective response is reinforced by the reduction or removal of the stimulus. The reinforcement thus operating is often referred to as *negative reinforcement* to distinguish it from positive reinforcement (previously considered in this chapter), but there are some psychologists who use the term *reinforcement* without qualifying it as positive or negative. *A negative reinforcer is a stimulus the removal of which increases the strength of a response.*

A child in school, or even before entering school, learns that if he threatens or insults an older or larger child, unpleasant consequences may occur. On his first few ventures of this nature, he probably escapes from the aversive stimuli produced by the older child by running away. This is escape behavior, which, if successful, is reinforced. However, he soon learns to *avoid* aversive stimuli produced by older and larger children by developing caution in what he says to them. Thus, *escape* behavior gives way to *avoidance* behavior. Aversive stimuli that originally reinforced the escape behavior come to reinforce avoidance behavior.

Negative-reinforcement phenomena were first explored with classical-conditioning phenomena. In the typical demonstration a dog is placed in a harness, a bell is sounded, and, shortly after the bell, an electric shock is applied to one of his paws. The dog then raises his paw. After several repetitions of this sequence, the bell is sounded and the dog anticipates the shock by raising his paw. Learning has occurred, and the character of the learning is such that it is commonly called *avoidance learning*. The central characteristic of negative reinforcement is that once the organism has learned what to anticipate, he can avoid *aversive* circumstances simply by performing in the way in which he has learned. The student who enrolls in a university is told that unless he pays his fee by a certain time, he will have to pay an additional fee. For most students this is a successful way of ensuring that fees will be paid.

Most aversive stimuli are administered in the anticipation that they will lead to and strengthen behavior that avoids the situation in which such stimuli are provided. Teachers expect children to walk in the halls in school and not run. If a child runs, then he is punished, sometimes by having to go back to the end of the hall and begin again. After a few incidents of this kind, walking behavior may become established. The teacher may hope to accomplish two goals by making the running situation aversive. On the one hand, she may wish to weaken the tendency to run and, on the other, she may hope to strengthen the tendency to walk in

FIGURE 1. The illustration shows an apparatus developed by Foringer and Company for the study of certain reinforcement phenomena in Rhesus monkeys. The animal is restrained from moving away from the apparatus by a Findley low-restraint harness which permits considerable freedom of movement within a limited range. The apparatus illustrated is designed for studying vigilance behavior—that is, behavior involving prolonged alertness. By responding appropriately to the stimuli presented, the monkey can prevent itself from being subjected to an electric shock every two seconds. An error in performance results in the monkey receiving a shock. The apparatus is very flexible and permits experimenters to study a wide range of behavioral phenomena in addition to vigilance behavior. (Courtesy of Foringer and Company, Inc., P.O. Box 5882, Bethesda, Md.)

the particular situation. A child might learn always to walk in this situation, not because the tendency to run is any less strong, but that the tendency to walk is relatively stronger. The term *punishment,* as it is used here, refers to application of an aversive stimulus for the purpose of reducing the strength of a response. Punishment may have other effects and may provide negative reinforcement for other behaviors, but the criterion of the effectiveness of punishment is whether it reduces the actual strength of a response (not the relative strength of the response in comparison with competing responses).

Negative reinforcement is extensively used for producing desired behavior and has every semblance of being effective. When some rule is introduced into a school, it may be quite plain to the pupils that infringement of the rule may result in aversive consequences. Thus, behavior that complies with the school rule may be reinforced by negative means. However, for the school faculty this is generally not enough. They will probably try to make it clear that the pupil should be a good citizen and should contribute to his community by obeying the laws that have been established. This is an attempt to provide positive motivation to conform to the school rules. Efforts may be made to enhance this motive on the part of the pupil by providing him with opportunities to participate in the formulation of the rules. What is being done in such a case is to provide a certain social orderliness within the school community and to achieve this by manipulating as many learning conditions as possible. These include negative reinforcement, among others. The establishment of a school rule, with the corresponding modification in the conduct of the individuals involved, is an extremely complicated matter from the point of view of the psychologist, and many different learning conditions must be manipulated to produce the desired conduct.

At this point punishment must be distinguished from negative reinforcement. Punishment is an attempt to obliterate a response. Negative reinforcement operates when an avoidance response occurs and is thereby reinforced. The two concepts are confusing, because in practice they are often used together as guides. A child is punished for running out in the road (punishment), but the parent hopes that this will lead him to an avoidance response that is negatively reinforced. In this case the hope is that the punishment will stamp out the response of dashing out into the street and that when the child begins to do this impulsively, he will immediately show avoidance behavior. Mowrer (1960a, p. 28) distinguishes punishment learning from avoidance learning, as it has been discussed here, in this way: "It is proposed that so-called punishment be termed passive avoidance learning (learning to avoid by not doing something) and that the contrasting form of avoidance learning (learning to do some-

thing as a means of avoidance) be termed active avoidance learning."
The distinction is a convenient one.

Not always does society provide punishment under conditions in which
there is some clear and feasible set of avoidance responses to the act
punished. The person who is punished as a habitual criminal may have
no other course open to him than a career of crime, for nobody will give
him honest employment. A child who is punished for nail biting or thumb
sucking may have no other outlet for whatever may be the underlying
impulses. In such cases, punishment is directed toward the very temporary suppression of behavior, but it cannot provide a negative reinforcement for more desirable behavior.

Although the effects of negative reinforcement may produce effective
learning, particularly when guidance is given in finding a suitable avoidance response, the effects of punishment in eliminating behavior are at
this time largely unpredictable. The main difficulty in discussing the
effects of punishment is that the effects are different under different
conditions. Learning theories of past centuries generally took the position
that praise and punishment had opposite effects. Praise insured that learning took place, and punishment was believed to be effective in unlearning
undesirable behavior. Edward L. Thorndike considered that this was
probably so, and early in his career designed experiments to verify this
popular belief. His early results seemed to support the hypotheses. Responses that were rewarded occurred with greater frequency; those that
were punished appeared to occur less frequently. Later work by Thorndike cast some doubt on this early finding and led him to conclude that he
had been wrong—that punishment did not weaken the tendency to respond in a particular way. What he did not realize at that time was that
there were certain technical difficulties in the interpretation of his data,
and that some corrections had to be introduced in order to produce a
sound interpretation. Since that time similar data have been reworked,
taking into account the correction factors that must be applied. When
this is done, the Thorndike type of experiment indicates that punishment
does have some weakening effect on a response, both in animals and men
in the type of learning situation which Thorndike studied; but the picture
is greatly complicated by the fact that experimental work on the effects of
punishment using different situations has often come up with different
conclusions, some of them showing that punishment has no effect on the
strength of a response.

In the case of the Thorndike experiments (1932, 1935) the punishment was of a mild nature, sometimes a matter of merely being told that
a response was wrong. It is perhaps surprising that merely being told
that a response is wrong does not have a marked tendency to depress

the response. The point is a significant one, because this type of correction is commonly used by teachers in the classroom.

The relationship of severity of punishment to the extent to which a response is suppressed by punishment has been extensively studied using animal subjects. Estes (1944) devised a simple experiment for the study of punishment, in which a rat that had learned to press a lever to obtain a small pellet of food was punished by means of an electric shock when it touched the lever. This lever-pressing response can be extinguished by allowing the rat to press the lever without receiving any food. When pressing the lever is not reinforced with food, it becomes a progressively weaker form of behavior and eventually disappears—that is, it becomes extinguished. If punishment weakens a response, then the administration of an electric shock on a few occasions when the animal touches the lever should weaken the response, and it should be more easily extinguished. Estes found that, for this to happen, punishment had to be rather severe or prolonged. Even so, the response was never completely eliminated by punishment.

How does punishment work? This has been a subject of much discussion for a long time. The most promising explanation at this time is that punishment arouses a response of anxiety, which becomes attached to the stimulus occurring at the time of punishment. When this anxiety is later aroused, it then allegedly produces an inhibition of the response. In the case of the rat, the lever would be the stimulus to which the anxiety becomes attached. Strong punishment, with the resulting high level of anxiety it may engender, may produce a more permanent inhibition, for it is known that high anxiety responses are often highly stable and do not fade in the way in which most other responses fade. When sufficient anxiety is aroused, there may be a disturbance of behavior not only with respect to the specific response in connection with which it is generated, but with respect to a whole range of unrelated behaviors.

Some years ago Hull (1943) described an interesting demonstration. A rat is placed in a box divided into two compartments. The compartment in which the rat is placed has a grill floor through which an electric shock can be applied to the paw. When the shock is applied, the rat will scramble over the partition into the other compartment. If the process is repeated a few times at suitable intervals, the rat will establish a permanent habit of scrambling over the partition even after the electric current is turned off. The habit will persist and show a high degree of permanence. The reason why the habit is not extinguished has been a matter for considerable speculation. The most plausible explanation seems to be that the act of escape from the compartment associated with shock reduces anxiety, which in turn serves to reinforce the escape response. This continued reinforcement gives the habit a high degree of permanence and counteracts any tendency for the habit to extinguish itself. Analogous behaviors may be observed in human subjects. This type of demonstration has been undertaken with a number of different species, and, although not all studies are in complete agreement, the results generally indicate that a relatively stable avoidance response is produced.

The relative efficiency of negative and positive reinforcement for producing learning is a matter of interest. In a classic experiment Warden and Aylesworth (1927), using rats in a discrimination task, found that rats that were both rewarded for correct responses and punished for incorrect responses (electric shock) learned about nine times as fast as rats that received only rewards. However, the results provide an important lesson in the caution that should be exercised in the generalization of the results to human learners. In a study by Travers, Reid, and Nelson (1964) groups of children were administered rote learning tasks and knowledge of results was provided either by the announcement of right or wrong, or by an electric shock. In no case did the groups receiving the electric shock outperform the other groups. As a matter of fact no significant differences were found between the average acquisition rates of the different groups. Certainly the effect of introducing a rather strong and unpleasant punishment for the making of wrong responses did not have the dramatic effect on the children that it had for rats. The data suggest that, in the case of the children, learning is dependent upon the amount of information transmitted by the signal, and that the aversive or rewarding properties of the stimulus have little consequence for immediate learning. However, aversive stimuli introduced into a learning situation may have long-term consequences with human subjects, such as that of slowly building up an avoidance response to the particular learning situation that may become generalized to all learning situations.

Evaluation of Negative Reinforcement as an Educational Practice

While negative reinforcement may produce efficient learning, there are reasons, in addition to those already considered, why it should not be used unless no other learning procedure is possible. The most important reason is that negative reinforcement involves anxiety as the motive that redirects behavior, and anxiety often has many uncontrolled and undesirable effects. Anxiety, once aroused, becomes attached easily to stimuli that happen to be present even though they have no relationship to the anxiety state. These stimuli then become capable of arousing anxiety. The teacher who utilizes extensive negative reinforcement may arouse anxiety in the pupils even on those occasions when positive reinforcement is being applied. The anxiety aroused by the teacher may also generalize to other teachers, until the pupil is fearful in most teaching situations.

The fact that irrational and unreasonable anxieties are likely to be generated by the use of negative reinforcement is only one reason why this practice is not recommended. A second problem is that once such anxieties have been developed and have become attached to objects, they are not easily dissipated. Thus, a person in whom anxiety is frequently aroused in childhood is likely to grow up to be an adult in whom anxiety is aroused by numerous stimuli. For this reason, there is strong argument for avoiding arousal of anxiety in the school except at a relatively low level. Some anxiety, at a low level, is unavoidable, and may be harmless; but persistent anxiety at a relatively high level is probably damaging to the personality.

A third reason is that aversive stimuli generally indicate failure, and a long series of studies show that failure experiences reduce both the level of performance and general intellectual functioning. A review of such studies by Lazarus *et al.* (1952) shows a remarkable uniformity in the results of research related to this problem.

Indirect Consequences of Punishment

The direct effects of punishment on the learner are becoming understood, but little work has been done on the effects of punishment on the behavior of other pupils who are present but not punished. A number of studies of this problem have been undertaken, and they have been brought together by Kounin, Gump, and Ryan (1961). In the studies reviewed by these writers the typical situation was one in which a student misbehaved and the teacher became involved in some reaction to the misbehavior. For example, one of the situations involved the late arrival of a pupil to class (the pupil knew that he was engaging in an experiment). Teachers responded in various ways to the pupil, depending on the requirements set up by the experimenter. In one case the teacher was supportive of the late pupil, helping him to catch up on what he had missed. In another case the teacher was punitive. These techniques used by the teachers are referred to as *desist techniques*. The general conclusions are that such incidents generally have little effect on the motivation of other pupils, though there were occasional groups in which some minor effect was noted. There were, however, considerable differences in how the pupils interpreted the behavior of the teacher. If the teacher was disliked, then there was a tendency to exaggerate the punitiveness and to take sides against the teacher; but when the teacher was liked, the reverse was more likely to occur.

A particularly compelling argument against the use of aversive stimuli in the control of behavior emerges from the research of R. E. Ulrich, N. H. Azrin, R. Hutchinson, and others. These workers (1965) report that in a wide variety of species, pain produces aggressive behavior, which may be directed toward inanimate objects or against other living organisms that happen to be present. They have shown, for example, that laboratory rats that do not ordinarily attack one another will do so when given an electric shock. The attack behavior can be maintained over long periods by the repetition of the electric shocks. Animals that had learned to press a bar to stop the shock would fail to do so in the presence of another member of their species, but would engage in fighting behavior despite the fact that this resulted in the continuation of the shock. Although, at the time of writing, electric shock has not been used with children, milder aversive stimuli produce aggressive behavior in children toward children. In one situation children were rewarded for building columns of blocks on a table, which the experimenter would shake and knock down before the columns reached the required height. The child was also told that a pushbutton on the table could be pressed to shake the table of another unseen child. The children showed a tendency to push the button after their own table had been shaken, an irrational act of aggression that contributed in no way to the completion of their own task. These and other data present overwhelming arguments against the use of aversive stimuli in the control of human behavior.

The Effect of Delay in Reinforcement

Studies on Subhuman Organisms

What happens if there is a delay in the appearance of the reinforcement? This is an important problem for education, because sometimes the classroom situation provides immediate reinforcements, but sometimes the reinforcements are delayed minutes and even days. The child who struggles with an English composition, then has to wait several days before the teacher returns his paper, provides an example of extreme delay in reinforcement. The latter situation is contrasted with the typical recitation situation in which reinforcements are immediate. Should the child be able to look up the answer to a problem as soon as he has arrived at a solution, or are there advantages in the alternative procedure whereby the solution is later checked by the teacher? On the surface, the problem of the effect of delay in reinforcement on learning appears to be a simple one to which there should be a straightforward answer, but the problem has proved to be complex and difficult to study.

The effect of delay in reinforcement was first studied indirectly by

Thorndike (1935), who was concerned with a problem known as the *spread of effect*. Thorndike thought that he discerned in his data a phenomenon that had not been noted before, namely, that a reward not only strengthened a response which it immediately followed, but that it also seemed to strengthen other responses that preceded or followed the reinforced response. In terms of an educational situation, this would mean that in reinforcing a child for the correct spelling of a word, one might also be reinforcing all other responses occurring close in time to the reinforced response. If this were so, it would have many important educational implications. However, further work by Sheffield and Jenkins (1952) cast considerable doubt on the validity of the Thorndike results and suggested that they might be the result of an artifact in the experimental situation. This is the position most widely taken with respect to the Thorndike concept of spread of effect, but some results support the Thorndike position.

Another approach to the problem is to study directly the effect of delay in reinforcement in such situations as maze learning with rats. They may be rewarded at the end of the maze by receiving a pellet of food either immediately or after an interval of time. Usually the interval is not more than ten seconds. Another situation is one in which a rat is placed in a modified type of Skinner box in which the pressing of a lever is reinforced some time after pressure is applied. Spence (1956), who has reviewed a number of such studies, points out that many of the results give the impression of inconsistency, since (at least in the earlier studies) some of the important factors connected with the effect of delay in reinforcement had not been controlled. For example, in a study by Ramond (1954) the learning curve for a one-second delay group appeared to flatten out at a lower level than the curve for a five-second delay group. In the Ramond study an apparatus was used in which hooded rats ran down a one-foot alley from a starting box and were required to touch a lever at the far end. Learning was measured in terms of the time taken from the starting box to the touching of the lever. In contrast, Spence reports data collected in his own laboratory by Harker (1950) as a part of a doctoral dissertation in which rats in a similar apparatus were run with a one-second delay and with a ten-second delay. In the Harker data the group with the ten-second delay in reinforcement might well have attained the same level of proficiency as the one-second delay group, but they would have taken more trials to do so. Spence attempts to bring order into this situation by bringing in some observations made by Shilling (1951), who had observed that with a five-second delay in reinforcement the rats remained in position at the food cup making anticipatory movements related to feeding, while those with a delay of ten seconds in reinforcement moved away from the food box and engaged in unrelated activities. Spence suggests that reinforcement will remain effective despite delay, if the subject maintains an orientation both toward the objects that constitute the task and toward the reinforcing agency. In the case of the rat, the animal is incapable of maintaining such an orientation for as long as ten seconds, but is able to do so for five seconds. A further experiment by Carlton (1945) tested this hypothesis. In the Carlton experiment a situation was used in which contact with a bar by a rat resulted in the withdrawal of the bar and the delivery of a food pellet after an interval of time. In the case of one group of rats, the alley confined them so that they could not turn away from the food trough after pressing the bar. In another group of rats freedom of movement was possible, so that the animals could turn away from the food trough and lose their orientation to the situation. The results were according to expectation. The rats whose movements were confined learned more rapidly as a result of the delayed reinforcement than did the rats that were free to move. The data supported the position that the maintenance of an orientation is of importance in making a delayed reinforcement effective.

What is the explanation for the need for an orientation to be maintained if delayed reinforcement is to be effective? On the negative side, one can see that if an animal begins to engage in other activities and is then reinforced, the reinforcement is likely to operate on these new activities. On the other hand, an orientation toward the stimulus situation may inhibit other activities from taking place prior to the incidence of reinforcement. One can be sure that this is not the entire picture. Another mechanism that may operate involves secondary reinforcement. When the animal maintains a posture anticipating the reinforcement, the tensions in his muscles produce sensations. These sensations become associated with the reinforcement and hence, in turn, acquire reinforcing properties. This is simply an application of the generalization previously stated that a stimulus associated with a primary reinforcer acquires reinforcing properties referred to as secondary reinforcing properties. If such were the case, then the secondary reinforcers developed during the delay period might serve to reinforce previous activity. This is a very tentative explanation.

Studies on human subjects. The effects of changing time conditions such as is involved in introducing a delay in the occurrence of a reinforcing event may be expected to be less in the case of human learners than when subhuman organisms are involved. The reason for this is that the human is able to obtain information from a reinforcing event and utilize it in relation to behavior that occurred some time before the reinforcing event. Another fact to be taken into account is that the reinforcers of human learning are largely pieces of information about the appropriateness or correctness of behavior, and the information provided by the

reinforcing event can sometimes be given before the behavior has occurred. For example, Annett (1959) trained subjects to estimate the
number of dots flashed on a screen by two procedures. In the one procedure the dots were presented briefly, the subject guessed how many
there were, and then the experimenter announced the actual number. In
the second procedure the subjects were told how many dots there were
before they appeared on the screen. Both procedures produced equal
amounts of learning for a given number of trials. The information following the guess made by the subject would be classified as a reinforcing
event, but the same information given before the trial would not come
under most definitions of reinforcement. Yet both events were equally
effective in producing learning. The human learners were able to store
the information when it was given in advance and use it later in checking
their own behavior when confronted with a display. Such a performance
could not occur with subhuman learners whose behavior conforms closely
to the response-reinforcement paradigm and for whom the reinforcement
must generally follow closely on the response. A number of other studies,
including those of von Wright (1957), have demonstrated how information given prior to a learning trial may sometimes be more effective than
the same information given as a reinforcing event following a learning
trial.

Although the designers of teaching machines have emphasized the
importance of reinforcing events following immediately on the events
they are to reinforce, studies of the reinforcement of human behavior
have not demonstrated the importance of immediacy of reinforcement.
Auble and Mech (1956) assigned children a routine computational task
similar to that which might be undertaken in a classroom, and varied
the time of incidence of reinforcement from immediately to a delay of
one and one-half hours. The delay did not produce less improvement
than was produced by immediate reinforcement. However, the results
are equivocal, since the experimenters failed to include a group with no
reinforcement provided by the teacher. There is a possibility that such
a nonreinforced group might have shown as much improvement as the
reinforced groups.

The studies discussed by Spence do suggest some ideas that may be
of value in understanding some aspects of delayed reinforcements with
human subjects. The behavior of the human is vastly complicated by the
use of language, which permits the reinstatement of ideas related to
previous learning situations. There is a possibility that language may
play the same role in humans that the orienting response plays in the rat
in the lever-pressing situation. Consider how this might work. Suppose
that a group of pupils were asked to work a problem in long division
at the end of their afternoon of work. Since there was no time to correct

the work in the classroom, the teacher took home the papers and corrected them that evening. While doing this, she noticed that a number
of the pupils had all made the same error, but that others, more by luck
than anything else, had avoided this particular error. First thing next
morning, after the class was assembled, she decided to discuss this error
and to work the problem on the blackboard. Some of the pupils who,
by luck, had worked the problem correctly were *attending* to the teacher
and thinking about the problem, and hence were reinforced for working
the problem the way they did. Other pupils, who had also obtained the
right answer, were neither attending to the teacher nor thinking about
the problem, and hence were not reinforced. It is difficult to imagine that
the reinforcement provided by the teacher's demonstration could be
effective unless the children were attending and also thinking about the
problem. The situation suggests that the process of attending, and
the process of thinking about the problem, function in the same way as the
orienting activity of the rat awaiting its reinforcement. The situation also
suggests that in humans, as well as in lower animals, some orienting
activity is necessary if a delayed reinforcement is to be effective. Too
often, no attempt is made to ensure that the pupils engage in such an
orienting activity prior to the provision of reinforcement.

Studies of Praise and Reproof with Human Subjects

Although many studies of praise and reproof have been undertaken in
laboratory settings, similar studies undertaken in classroom settings are
few. A study by Silberman (1957) throws some light on the effect of
praise and reproof on the learning of reading in the elementary school.
Silberman observed the behavior of teachers in 40 classes and counted
the number of instances in which statements of each one of the following
types were made:

1. Supportive statements ("right," "good," "fine work").
2. Problem-structuring statements ("Your difficulty is . . .").
3. Neutral statements.
4. Directive statements ("Pass the papers forward," "Read this").
5. Reproving statements ("You're all wrong," "Won't you ever learn?").

The data indicated that the number of teacher behaviors in each one
of these categories had little relation to pupil growth in reading. Perhaps
this is hardly surprising. The number of reinforcements the teacher can
supply in the reading process in relation to the number of reinforcements

needed is small, perhaps so small that it is quite inconsequential. The teacher may be far less important than other sources of reinforcement. These other sources include parents and the pupils themselves, providing reinforcements for one another. Also, once reading skill has developed to the point where the child can read materials of intrinsic interest to him, then the process of reading becomes self-reinforcing. Unfortunately there are many pupils who do not reach the latter level of skill. Many students arrive in college never having reached the point where they can sit down and enjoy a book. As a matter of fact, there are even some freshman college students who have never in their entire lives read through to completion even a brief piece of material such as a short story. For such individuals, reinforcements must come from without, for the process has not reached the point where it is self-reinforcing.

The fact that, in many studies of verbal learning, learning occurs without awareness on the part of the learner substantiates the position taken in this book that a vast amount of important learning takes place at an unconscious level. The immediate implication of these studies is that important changes in the speech habits of children can be made without the learner even being aware that he is acquiring new speech habits. If the teacher and the other people who come into contact with the child systematically reinforce appropriate, precise, and correct speech, then much can be accomplished to build up sound speaking habits. Unfortunately, this is not at all what is done. On the contrary, a child is very unlikely to be positively reinforced for speaking correctly. When he speaks incorrectly, he is likely to encounter aversive action on the part of the teacher or other adults, but this is not an efficient way to develop effective speech habits. What is needed is positive reinforcement for effective speech, for it is this practice that in the long run will make for desirable speaking habits. Many teachers also insist that pupils have to be made aware of their speech errors in order to correct themselves. This does not seem to be necessary at all. Positive reinforcement alone will change speech habits, even though the learner is unaware of the fact that his behavior is being modified. It may well be that such unconscious learning is much more effective in changing speech habits than is the process of language analysis that is characteristically pursued by teachers in English classes. There is at least evidence that systematic reinforcement changes the language behavior of individuals, but there is no evidence at all that the teaching of grammar and the kind of language analysis that goes along with grammar has any influence on the language habits of pupils. The writer never learned any English grammar and has never found the lack any particular disadvantage, except when he has been faced with the task of helping his youngsters solve problems of grammar such as are discussed in the eighth grade. Perhaps some children benefit by such a pedantic approach to the learning of language, but there is little or no evidence to support this claim.

The Chaining of Behavior

Psychologists have long been impressed with what appears to be the tendency for behavior to run off in chains of activities. A person who ties a knot performs a sequence of activities that must take place in proper order. Chaining theory of behavior has generally taken the position that chains of behavior may be internal or external or may involve both elements. Theory of the chaining of behavior was first stated by Watson (1924) in a systematic form. He took the position that the chain started with a stimulus that led to a response. The response, in turn, led to a new stimulus situation that produced the second response in the sequence, and so forth. Thus, when I see the front door before me, I take out the key from my pocket. The touch of the key in my hand is an important stimulus that leads to inserting the key in the lock. Each act leads to a stimulus that triggers the next response in the sequence. This old concept of the chaining of behavior has recently been revived by Gagné (1965), who gives it a major role in his description of learning. However, a simple chain theory of complex sequences of behavior does not fit all the facts as well as it may seem to on the surface.

One bothersome fact pointed out by Hebb (1948), which suggests that in a sequence of behavior the occurrence of a response may not provide the stimulus for the next response, is that many sequences occur so quickly that the person would not have time to respond to each new stimulus. For example, a violinist will run off a fast passage with the notes following one another at the rate of five to eight per second. At this speed it is physiologically impossible for the sound of the one note, or the tensions in the muscles while playing the note, to be the stimulus for the playing of the next note. There simply isn't enough time for these to be fed back into the brain to initiate the next act of behavior. Thus, in such a case the chaining theory of behavior breaks down. Hebb suggests that the brain is capable of emitting, in proper order, a long sequence of messages to the muscles without each message having to be initiated by some event that excites the senses.

One attempt to understand how the nervous system may run off whole sequences of behavior is to introduce the concept of *expectancy*. When this concept is introduced, the implication is that the expectation of the achievement of some goal ties together the various behaviors involved in the sequence and gives them characteristic unity. However, the concept of expectancy is difficult to handle and does not lend itself readily to experimental study.

Those who have emphasized the role of reinforcement in learning have also developed a theory concerning the way in which chains of behavior may be established.

In discussions of reinforcement, the implication is generally made that reinforcement operates first and foremost on the end response, or consummatory response. A child who is asked to spell a word is reinforced for spelling it correctly, but the child is slow in starting to spell it and then enunciates each letter with hesitation. The act of spelling is the end product of a sequence of events that begins with the teacher asking the question, and is then followed by internal processes operating in the student, finally leading to the response of spelling the word, which, in turn, leads to the reinforcement. A pupil answering an examination question may spend a considerable period thinking and making notes before he finally writes out the answer to the question. The relationship of reinforcement to those responses that precede the final response has long been a subject for speculation among psychologists.

An attempt to relate reinforcement concepts of learning to the chaining of behavior is found in the concept of the fractional anticipatory goal response originally introduced by Hull (1943) and later developed by Spence (1956). The idea involved is that most learning occurs in situations in which a chain of responses leads up to the final or consummatory response. These elements in the chain, prior to the final response, are referred to as *fractional anticipatory responses.*

Any particular fractional anticipatory goal response has two main consequences. First, it changes the situation originally confronted. A rat in a maze that makes the fractional anticipatory response of turning left is immediately confronted with a new situation and a new set of external stimuli. Second, the movement itself stimulates sense organs within the body, and these send impulses to the nervous system to produce sensations. The fact that each partial response is followed by two new sources of stimulation, the one external and the other internal, suggests a theory of how chains of behavior may be established.

The theory that has been most commonly stated is that the stimuli produced at each stage become conditioned to the next fractional anticipatory goal response. Written in symbolic terms, a response, r_{g1}, occurs, and this leads to a stimulation, S_1, which in turn becomes conditioned to r_{g2}, which produces stimulation S_2, and so forth. The reinforcement producing this conditioning is that which occurs during and after the consummatory response; at least this is the essence of the theory as it was originally produced by Hull (1943). Another point of view expressed by Spence (1956) is that such anticipatory responses become linked in some way to incentives, and hence also have arousal value and raise the activity level of the organism. How the latter can come about is not clear to the present writer.

There are, of course, many difficulties with such a chain-reaction interpretation of behavior in addition to those already considered. Although it has some adequacy for understanding a chain of responses such as may occur when a rat runs a maze, it has much less adequacy in understanding sequences of responses that lead up to the solution of a problem by a human. In the case of the rat, there is some uniformity to the sequence of responses that must be performed to reach the goal, and hence the conditioning of this sequence of responses suggests a reasonable mechanism. However, in the more typical problem situation faced by the human problem solver, considerable variation in behavior is shown from occasion to occasion, and the concept of a sequence of responses conditioned in a chain hardly seems to apply. As a matter of fact, even a rat running a maze may show variation in the procedure adopted for reaching the goal box. If a maze is so designed that more than one route may be used to reach the goal box, a rat may be observed to pursue one path to the goal on many successive occasions and then suddenly begin to pursue a different path. Although the concept of a chain of fractional anticipatory goal responses can be stretched to cover the latter case, the argument is not too convincing.

Quantity of Reinforcement and Learning

The reader might well expect that a clear-cut answer could be given to the question concerning the relationship of the quantity of reinforcement to rate of learning, but such is not the case. The problem is clearly an important one, for in many learning situations rewards can be graded, and the teacher may have to decide whether a reward has to be large for learning to occur with efficiency.

The concept of quantity of reinforcement is a complex one. Reinforcements can be varied in two fairly distinct respects. The same reinforcement can be given in greater or lesser amounts, as when a rat is reinforced with larger or smaller pellets of the same food. Or the rat can be reinforced with some preferred food, rather than with a standard diet pellet. The latter is sometimes referred to as varying the *quality* of the reinforcement. In the one case the variation involves merely providing a greater *amount* of the same reinforcer; in the other case, the *nature* of the reinforcing agent is varied. In the two cases the quantity of reinforcement is evaluated in terms of different scales.

The earliest experiments on the effect of varying the magnitude of a reward on learning produced inconsistent results, and subsequent work has not resolved all of the inconsistencies thus revealed. In the early thirties a series of laboratory experiments on this problem were conducted in the laboratory of E. L. Thorndike at Columbia University, and were brought together and analyzed by Thorndike himself in a single chapter of a book (1935). The experiments utilized a typical Thorndike format for the conduct of experiments. Connections had to be learned between particular situations and particular responses. In a study conducted by R. T. Rock (1935) in this series, subjects had to learn a connection between a word in code and a corresponding English meaning. The subjects were required to guess which of four English words represented the correct translation of each one of a set of code words. In another situation, subjects learned that they were given the best rating for a ball-tossing skill when they sat on a particular stool. In another experiment, Thorndike himself undertook in cooperation with Forlano (1936), subjects learned to match English words with Spanish words they did not know. For each Spanish word, the subject had to choose one of five English words. In each one of these two experiments a correct choice was followed by the announcement "Right," plus a small reward of money which varied from one cent up to eight cents. In interpreting the results of the experiment, one must keep in mind that they were conducted in the depths of the depression years, when money represented an important and meaningful reward. The differences in the rewards offered were of real consequence to those who received them.

In the case of the Rock experiment, no significant differences were found between the different levels of reward in their effect on learning. On the other hand, in the case of the Thorndike and Forlano results, a distinct relationship was found between the amount of monetary reward and the amount of learning. An increase in reward resulted in an increase in the rate of learning, except that the highest level of the reward resulted in a slight decline instead of a further increase. Thorndike interprets the latter results as being due to the excitement of the subject in the high-reward situation.

How did Thorndike explain the differences in the results of the two experiments? The tasks involved are sufficiently similar that the results are not likely to reflect task differences. Thorndike suggested that the differences are attributable to a slight difference in the experimental procedure. In the case of the Thorndike and Forlano experiment, each subject went through a number of experimental runs, and the reward was varied from run to run. Subjects were thus in a position to compare one reward level with another and perhaps modify their behavior accordingly. In the case of the Rock experiment, such a comparison could not be made by the subjects. There is a possibility that a contrast effect is necessary before much differential reaction to different levels of reward becomes apparent.

In passing, the reader may be interested to note that Tuckman (see Thorndike, 1935), also working in Thorndike's laboratory, undertook a series of experiments in which he studied the effects of variation in the amount of punishment administered. A small amount of punishment was found to have about the same inhibiting effect as a punishment four times as great. The punishment administered was an electric shock.

In the last twenty years experiments have been undertaken largely on animals. In well-known studies by Crespi (1942, 1944) and Zeaman (1949), in which rats were given various amounts of the same reinforcement for running down a straight-alley maze, an increase in reward was found to be associated with an increase in speed of performance, and a decline in reward resulted in reduced speed of running. These experiments were not directly concerned with the effects of the magnitude of reinforcement on skill learning, but with the relationship of one aspect of the response, namely, running speed, to the magnitude of the reinforcement. Spence (1956) reports that these results were not completely duplicated in his own laboratory.

While many of the early studies of the effect of magnitude of reward on learning utilized rats running a straight-alley maze, much of the more recent work has involved discrimination learning situations. In such studies with rats the results are equivocal. Sometimes the larger magnitudes are associated with improved learning, but sometimes they are not. On the other hand, work with primates indicates that the rate at which a discrimination learning skill is acquired is directly related to the magnitude and quality of the reward. The differences in the results with primates and the work with rats may reflect the fact that for a differential reward to have differential effects the organism must be able to discriminate between the different magnitudes. A rat that is unable to discriminate between a small pellet and a large pellet cannot be expected to behave differently in the presence of the one than the other. Thus, for there to be a differential effect the animal must have the opportunity of being exposed to both large and small rewards under conditions that will bring out the contrast.

Not enough information is available at this time to resolve the results of animal experiments with those on human subjects. Perhaps the variation in the amount of reinforcement has an effect on the rate of human learning only when the subject can make comparisons between one level of reinforcement and another, as was the case in the Thorndike and Forlano study. On one point there does seem to be general agreement; regardless of whether the subjects are human or subhuman, an increase in reinforcement results in a more vigorous response on the part of the learner.

Pending the outcome of further research, the wisest classroom policy would seem to be to avoid providing extremely large reinforcements, which are often difficult to handle and which can usually be given only on rare occasions. A costly prize can be provided only rarely by a school, and there is little assurance that it will have any more effect on behavior, as a reinforcer, than perhaps even a word of praise or commendation. Small and frequent reinforcements are administratively the most useable, and at the same time they are likely to be just as effective as much larger reinforcements that are more difficult to administer.

Correlated Reinforcement

A condition of reinforcement widely used in teaching practice is that of *correlated reinforcement*. This condition requires that the quantity of reinforcement be related in some way to performance. The assignment of a grade so that the grade reflects the quality of performance is an example of correlated reinforcement. This phenomenon has not been widely studied by experimental psychologists, though it was mentioned by Skinner (1938) many years ago. More recently it has been examined within a program of experimental studies by Logan (1960), who has conducted his research with rats in a maze-learning situation. The limited data related to this problem and the fact that studies have been restricted to a single species—the rat—means that few generalizations can be made that apply to the human learner. However, several advantages of correlated reinforcement can be pointed out.

First, correlated reinforcement provides the learner with considerably more information than can be supplied through a reinforcement that does not vary in magnitude. If the learner is reinforced, he finds out not only that his response is generally in the right direction, but also the degree to which it is in the right direction. The reinforcement has more information embedded in it when it is correlated with performance than when it is not so correlated.

Second, the learner may modify his behavior and obtain definitive information concerning the value of the modification when the reinforcement is correlated with performance. Thus, correlated reinforcement enables the learner to have some degree of control over the learning situation which he would not have with uncorrelated reinforcement.

Third, although the evils of a quantitative grading system can be suppressed, the advantages of quantitative grades may still remain. A numerical grading system provides one form of correlated reinforcement that may have advantages if the competitive aspects of the system are suppressed.

Extinction and Elimination of Behavior

The central theme of the chapter has been the formation of behavior—that is, the positive shaping of behavior as a result of learning. The emphasis has been on the acquisition of behavior and not on the elimination of unwanted behavior. Although reinforcement was indicated to be the major condition through which behavior is built, punishment was shown to be largely a useless effort to eliminate unwanted behavior. Yet learning has two important aspects. On the one hand, it is a positive process that results in the acquisition and emergence of new behavior. On the other, learning may proceed by the elimination of undesirable and unwanted behavior. Both the positive and negative aspects of the formation of behavior involve learning. Both are learning processes.

Teachers often think of learning only in a positive sense, emphasizing the skills that are slowly acquired through contact with the school. They forget that an important problem in school learning is also the getting rid of undesirable behavior acquired elsewhere. The child who is a so-called disciplinary problem in school is one who displays certain unwanted aspects of behavior that interfere with positive learning. The pupil may show high needs to interact with other pupils in ways that are not particularly constructive, and may devote little of his energies to the pursuit of learning as it is done by other children. He may be hostile to the teacher. He may be a bully. He may be interested in affairs outside the school and absent himself frequently. All of these are well-learned habits of behaving that the teacher may wish to see eliminated and may have to eliminate before constructive learning within the school situation can take place. Every teacher knows that this is a difficult task, for attempts to eliminate well-established patterns of behavior are likely to be quite fruitless.

The mental-health worker is faced with even more serious problems of eliminating behavior. The person who comes to the clinic with serious neurotic disturbances is often one who has learned a whole host of worthless responses. Perhaps the problem of the individual who reports at the clinic is that he responds to most of life's situations with anxiety. In other words, he has learned inappropriate anxiety responses to life which the clinician must help him to unlearn; but, as everyone knows, unlearning is a difficult matter. The best-established way of eliminating learned responses is through what is known as *extinction,* a phenomenon also first noted by Pavlov.

Next to the concept of reinforcement, no single concept has so much to offer the person involved in the guidance of learning as the concept of extinction. The fact that extinction phenomena are found in almost every type of learning situation yet studied gives ample support for its generality, and provides a strong argument for applying what has been discovered in the laboratory to the handling of problems within the classroom situation.

A response that has been previously learned through reinforcement may be extinguished if it is permitted to occur and recur without reinforcement. If a child has learned through reinforcement that he can obtain the attention of the teacher by raising his hand, then this same hand-raising behavior can be extinguished if the teacher ignores it when it occurs. Mere lack of reinforcement does not, by itself, produce extinction. The eye-blink reflex, which can be observed in any human, continues to occur throughout life although no reinforcement is provided for it. The absence of any reinforcement does not extinguish the eye-blink reflex. Extinction will occur only when a particular aspect of behavior has been previously learned through reinforcement. Since most behavior is learned through reinforcement, it follows that most of it can be extinguished if proper conditions for extinction can be provided.

Examples of the extinction of responses are many and obvious. The teacher who fails to give help to the pupil who asks for it will eventually extinguish the response that may be entitled "coming for help." A salesman who fails to sell a single item of his product after ringing many doorbells is likely to give up for the day; even the most determined salesman requires the occasional reinforcement provided by a sale. The teacher who repeats monotonously, "Now please be quiet, kids," and obtains no response at all is likely to eventually give up this method and try another.

A second phenomenon associated with extinction is *spontaneous recovery.* A pupil's hand-raising response may be extinguished on one day due to the inattention of the teacher; but next day the response appears again, even though it is a shorter lease this time. This may occur day after day with the tendency each time for the response to be weaker. Ultimately, the response will be totally extinguished.

Extinction stands at the present time as the best-established mechanism for the elimination of a response. It is possible by other techniques to suppress a response rather temporarily. Punishment seems to do this in most cases. But it is not generally considered to be a successful method of eliminating a response. Extinction, on the other hand, when repeated several times after spontaneous regeneration has occurred, is likely to be most effective in weakening and ultimately eliminating a response from the person's repertoire.

The process of extinction is rarely used deliberately as a means of eliminating an unwanted response. On the other hand, paradoxical though this may seem, it is still one of the major mechanisms that can be observed to operate in the classroom; but the teacher brings this mechanism into play usually without knowing that she has taken any such action. For example, the writer once visited a classroom in which the teacher disregarded any of the intellectual accomplishments of the youngsters. It was not that she failed to provide reinforcements, for she did, but these were all quite unrelated to any of the intellectual achievements of the pupils. She would pass by a group that was struggling to produce a graph to represent some data that had been collected. Her comment to the group was, "You are certainly working together nicely." What she was doing with this comment was reinforcing the social behavior of the children toward one another. The teacher did, however, disregard the intellectual accomplishment of the pupils rather than reinforce it, and thus took a first step toward extinguishing intellectual achievement. The teacher was not aware of the fact that this was happening, and neither were the pupils. The whole direction of the life of a group of thirty pupils was being modified without any thought being given to the modification. Extinction, as it operates in the classroom, is often of this nature.

Schedules of Reinforcement

Research has clearly shown that the permanence of behavior that has been acquired is closely related to the way in which reinforcement has been administered. Reinforcement can be administered on every occasion on which a response occurs, or only on some of the occasions. If it occurs on every occasion, it is referred to as continuous reinforcement, but if it is administered only on certain occasions and not on others it is customary to speak of it as partial reinforcement. In the case of partial reinforcement, the rule that determines whether a particular instance of the behavior is or is not reinforced is known as the *schedule*. Substantial work has been undertaken to determine how the particular schedule adopted influences the permanence of the behavior thus acquired. A single outstanding work on this subject by Ferster and Skinner (1957) summarizes data based on half a billion observations. While it is true that these observations were all mechanically recorded, the book is nevertheless the result of long, hard years of work.

Three kinds of schedules of reinforcement have been most systematically studied. The first of these is known as fixed-ratio reinforcement, whereby the behavior to be reinforced is reinforced, for example, the first time in every six times it occurs, or the first time in every ten. The second is known as fixed-interval reinforcement, whereby the behavior to be reinforced is reinforced every time a given interval has elapsed. Thus one may reinforce a child's efforts to spell once at the end of every five-minute period. The third type of schedule is that of variable-interval reinforcement, whereby reinforcements are provided at varying intervals.

First, let us discuss how the pecking behavior of the pigeon is studied in the laboratory. A pigeon may be placed in a box that has been specially designed for the purpose of studying schedules of reinforcement. The pigeon is hungry, not having eaten for twenty-four or more hours, and the weight of the pigeon has been lowered until it is 80 per cent of its maximum body weight by putting the bird on a reducing diet over a period of several days. The first task of the pigeon in the box is to learn where the food trough is to be found. The food trough can be in two positions. When it is raised, the pigeon can easily reach the food contained in it. When it is lowered, it cannot be reached by the pigeon. As soon as it is raised, a light goes on above it and a buzzer sounds. The pigeon soon learns to go to the opening in the side of the box and obtain food as soon as it hears the buzzer or sees the light. The buzzer and the light become stimuli that produce this response in the pigeon under these conditions of training. The next task in this experimental situation is to train the pigeon to peck at a small round illuminated disc located on the side of the wall at the same level as the pigeon's head. This is done by first reinforcing any movement the pigeon makes in the right direction. As soon as he moves toward the disc, the food trough is raised, the buzzer sounds, and the light goes on. Soon the pigeon consistently moves towards the disc, but from then on it is necessary to reinforce only those movements that involve the beak coming close to the disc. In the final stages, the pigeon is reinforced only for those movements that actually bring the beak of the bird into actual contact with the disc. *This training procedure illustrates a general principle of training, which is that one may begin by reinforcing at first those responses that are in the right general direction.* Slowly the reinforcer becomes more and more discriminating in what is reinforced. If one waited for a child to perform an entire act correctly before providing reinforcement, the act might never be produced and hence nothing might ever be reinforced. Reinforcement whenever behavior in the right direction occurs will eventually lead the child to produce the behavior desired.

Once the pigeon has reached the stage of pecking at the disc in order to obtain the food, the effects of various schedules of reinforcement can be studied. First, consider fixed-ratio reinforcement. In this type of

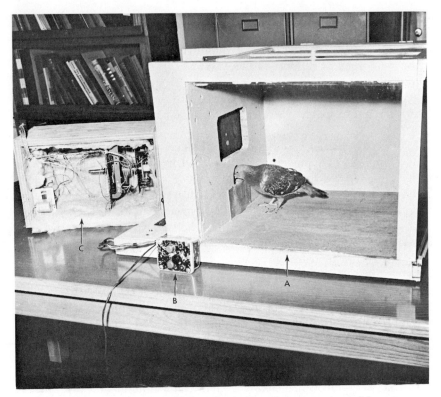

FIGURE 2. A box designed for the public demonstration of learning phenomena in the pigeon is illustrated above. Compartment A houses the pigeon. With the feeding trough in the up position, the grain becomes available to the bird. In a recessed area, directly above the pigeon, a button is located. The pigeon may be taught to peck the button, thereby actuating the feeding trough and the secondary reinforcers of buzzer and light. Box B contains a switch and cable through which all controls may be operated at a distance of about ten feet from the training box. Box C contains automatic programming devices that may be switched into operation through switch B. Box C is ordinarily closed and its interior is lined with soundproofing material. It, too, may be operated remotely. (Courtesy of the University of Utah Photographic Service.)

schedule the pigeon is reinforcd with food every so many pecks. One might, for example, arrange the apparatus so that the food trough appeared after every ten pecks. The pigeon would then be allowed to feed for, say, ten seconds, and then the trough would disappear. After another ten pecks at the disc, the trough would reappear again. The bird will show a steady and continuous work output under these circumstances and will keep up a rapid pecking of the disc between feedings. This is comparable to the teacher who tells the pupils to finish a page of work in the workbook and then take a ten-minute break, each pupil doing whatever he wants before he goes on to the next page. The ten-minute period of free activity for the pupil corresponds to the reinforcement. Under these conditions one may expect work output to be high and continuous so long as the reinforcement is provided. In the case of the pigeon, if the reinforcement is eliminated from the schedule, extinction of the work habit is rapid. Sustained work on this schedule is maintained only so long as the reinforcement comes when expected. Much the same would be expected to be true of children. Cut out the reinforcement, and it is hardly to be expected that the children will, of their own choice, go on working page after page at the same high rate of output. Fixed-ratio reinforcement is characterized by high rate of output, which rapidly vanishes when the reinforcement is removed. It does not result in a continuation of the work habit after the reinforcing agent is withdrawn; and yet this is what one wants to do in the case of children: One wants the work habits to persist beyond the immediate learning experiences.

The second type of reinforcement schedule that has been extensively studied is known as the fixed-interval schedule. In this schedule the reinforcement comes only after a fixed interval of time regardless of the amount of work accomplished during the interval. This is illustrated when the pigeon is reinforced for pecking once every minute on the minute. The bird thus reinforced shows a characteristic program of behavior. Immediately after reinforcement the bird ceases to peck at the disc, but as the end of the minute approaches, pecking behavior reappears and becomes more and more rapid. Most of the work output occurs just before the reinforcement. A parallel situation is found with children who are given a time-limit task. Almost every parent has seen a child whose teacher has given him a project to be completed in a semester. The typical pattern of behavior of the child is to put off doing the project week after week. Without the intervention of the parent, it is quite probable that the project will be undertaken in the few hectic days before it is due. On the other hand, if the teacher is prepared to vary the schedule of reinforcement and offers to provide help and criticism that the project requires at each one of the various stages, he will have changed the schedule of reinforcement to one of fixed ratio, and a relatively well-distributed pattern of work over the semester may be expected. Fixed-interval reinforcement is a poor teaching procedure by any standards, and yet it is one that is widely used. Fixed-interval reinforcement also has the disadvantage that the response that is reinforced rapidly fades once the reinforcing agent is removed. The pupil, given a project that he has to hand in at the end of the term, is unlikely to acquire (by means of this activity) habits of work that have any permanence. Whatever work habits are acquired are likely to be rapidly extinguished.

The third type of reinforcement schedule, known as variable-interval reinforcement, must now be considered. In this case the pigeon has no way of knowing when the reinforcement is to be expected. Reinforcements are distributed at random. The bird works hard and continuously, and after the reinforcement is withdrawn, pecking will continue at a high rate for long periods. This is the schedule that produces behavior most resistant to extinction, and therefore it has substantial merit in producing behavior of great permanence. It is manifested by the informal teacher who moves around an informally run classroom helping children here and there and complimenting one or another of the children on his work or work habits or on his social relation with other children. It is rarely seen in the teacher who conducts a class along rigid and formal lines. The latter type of classroom procedure almost requires that all children start and finish together, and hence predisposes itself to the use of a fixed-interval type of reinforcement with the consequently high rate of extinction of the behavior reinforced. Although the variable-interval reinforcement found in the informal classroom does have the advantages that have been discussed, it also has its limitations. One of these is that it may not occur with sufficient frequency to be of much value for any particular child. Indeed, this is the central problem in the use of teacher reinforcements for learning in the classroom. To some extent this problem has been recognized, and teachers have used such devices as that of organizing children into groups so that they will reinforce one another. Little knowledge is available concerning the effectiveness of the reinforcement thus provided. It seems quite unlikely that this procedure will solve the problem of providing an adequate frequency of reinforcements. An alternative suggested by B. F. Skinner is that machines be provided to take over much of the teaching process; this radical suggestion will be considered later.

Schedules of reinforcement have application in the development of behavior that one wants to see repeated—that is, behavior that is to come to represent an enduring characteristic of the individual. Behavior related to work habits one would expect to develop best with a variable-interval schedule of reinforcement. The same might be true in the development of typical behavior related to interpersonal relations and all characteristics that are commonly referred to as personality traits. In all of these cases, what one wants to develop is a characteristic that will keep on reappearing and that involves repetitive behavior. The stability of behavior that has been exposed to variable-interval reinforcement has been demonstrated in the case of behavior that comes to represent a stable trait of the organism that is reinforced.

Some Studies of the Reinforcement
of Human Behavior

In laboratory animals, a great number of different circumstances are used to reinforce behavior—food, water, some novel object, avoidance of light, the opportunity to explore an open area, and many others. In the case of pupil behavior in the classroom, reinforcers are generally limited to approval, disapproval, information given in statements such as "right" and "wrong," and occasionally rewards such as are provided by prizes and awards. Even though the range of reinforcers used with human behavior is limited, there is still considerable interest in asking which of these reinforcers is the most effective. The opinion is commonly held that approval or telling a child that he is right is much more effective than disapproval or telling him that he is wrong, but opinion in such matters is often far from being correct.

A number of studies have been undertaken to compare the effectiveness of various reinforcing conditions on children of school age and preschool age. Some of these studies involve button-pushing tasks, which are quite different from those that humans typically undertake. Others have used learning tasks similar to those undertaken in schools. Both throw some light on the general problem of what reinforces. Let us consider the button-pushing task first.

Nickell and Travers (1963) undertook a study to compare the effectiveness of approval as a reinforcer with the delivery of a small physical object (a marble). The equipment that provided the task consisted of a panel, about 2 feet square, with four knobs equally spaced in a horizontal line. The boy or girl was told to push the knobs one at a time and that he would be told when he was pushing the right knob either by being told "that's good" or by the delivery of a marble by the machine itself. The task was so arranged that the pushing of one knob was reinforced with the words "that's good," the pushing of another was reinforced with the delivery of a marble, the third was reinforced with both the delivery of a marble and also "that's good," while pushing the fourth was never reinforced at all. However, even a knob that was reinforced was not reinforced all the time, but only on 50 percent of the occasions. The subjects were boys and girls who ranged in age from prekindergarten to ninth grade. When the data were examined as a whole, the delivery of the marble was found to be a reinforcer superior to the words of approval. The only group that responded better to approval was prekindergarten girls. Just why the delivery of a marble should have had such a reinforcing effect is not clear, for the children were told that they could not keep the marbles. Perhaps the novelty of the event may account for the effect, for novel events have been demonstrated to have reinforcing properties with a wide range of higher organisms. Another explanation may be that when a knob was depressed that delivered a marble, the subject had the experience of performing an act that resulted in the delivery of a marble without the experimenter being involved (the delivery was automatic). Such an experience of producing directly a particular effect may produce a satisfaction that the approval of the experimenter may not have.

The tasks involved in such studies are not ones to which the human subject readily adapts. To many children the pushing of buttons is pointless, and there is difficulty in persuading them to complete the series of trials. Differences in the reinforcing conditions used could be interpreted as being a result of the attitude of the boys and girls toward the whole experimental situation. Perhaps the dropping of a marble is a more interesting event than a comment by the experimenter. For this reason, one may speculate that the use of different reinforcers in learning situations that involve tasks more similar to those typically undertaken by humans might well result in differential effects.

A study involving rote learning in children, that used extreme differences in classes of reinforcers, was undertaken by Nelson, Reid, and Travers (1964) in an attempt to answer this question. In this latter study, children were exposed to a paired-associate learning task. In one of the tasks the children were to read a list of words and were told to respond with either the word *long* or the word *short*. After the pupil had selected one of these two answers he was given a signal (reinforcement) to indicate whether his answer was right or wrong. Three different signals were used with different groups of subjects. These signals were the words *right* and *wrong*, an electric shock, and a tone of 400 cycles per second. The shock was strong enough to bring tears to some of the children, though none left the situation presumably because they had been offered a dollar to complete the task. (All the children were volunteers and were free to leave the laboratory at any time they wished.) The tone as a form of reinforcement had none of the unpleasant characteristics of the shock, but also none of the immediate social qualities of the verbal reinforcements. In addition, half of the subjects received the reinforcing signal when they responded correctly and half when they responded incorrectly. Despite the dramatic differences in the reinforcing events used, and despite the fact that substantial numbers of fifth- and sixth-grade subjects were used (180), no significant differences were found between the groups exposed to the different reinforcing conditions. Although some of the children who received electric shock were in tears or near to tears before the set number of trials had been completed, this group did not perform differently from the other groups.

The conclusion from both of the latter studies is that the characteristic of an event that determines, above all, its reinforcing properties for human subjects is the amount of information it carries. In the case of the latter experiment, all three reinforcing conditions carried equal amounts of information for the learner. If a child is motivated to solve a problem, then the condition in his environment most likely to influence the course of learning is that which provides useful information. The other characteristics of the information source are trivial.

Few studies are available that compare the effectiveness of one source of reinforcing pupils with other sources, yet the learning situation in the classroom can be arranged with many different sources of reinforcement. Common sources of reinforcement in the form of knowledge of results are provided by teachers reinforcing pupils. The typical recitation situation illustrates the operation of this form of reinforcement. Another source of reinforcement is found in situations in which pupils work together and in which one pupil checks and corrects the responses of another pupil. The history of education presents many plans for organizing classrooms in a form in which much of the teaching was undertaken by pupils who taught other pupils. One of the most famous of these was the Lancastrian plan, which attempted to overcome the shortage of teachers in the early days of public education by having the more advanced pupils teach the less advanced. The improvement in the teacher-pupil ratio slowly eliminated such a plan. The contribution to learning that can be made from pupils interacting with pupils was lost to view until the progressive education movement revived interest in it during the period between the world wars. However, the revived interest in this technique did not bring with it any notable research program to evaluate its worth.

Myers and Travers (1964) undertook a study in which pupils learned under various reinforcing conditions, one of which involved one pupil teaching (reinforcing) another pupil. The task was to learn the English equivalents of 60 German words. Learning sessions were scheduled on Monday, Tuesday, and Wednesday, and a multiple-choice test of the learning was administered on Friday. In the pupil-teaching-pupil situation, the pupil playing the role of teacher held up a small filing card to the pupil. On the one side of the card was a German word and two English words one of which was the equivalent of the German word. The "teacher" also had the same information printed on his side of the card and this he read to the pupil. The pupil then made a guess at the right answer. When he was right he was told so by the teacher, who had the right answer marked on his side of the card. When he was wrong the next card was presented to him.

Under these conditions of learning, the pupil in the pupil role learned about as much as other pupils who were interacting with a teacher in

a typical class recitation. The pupil in the teacher role learned significantly less. Another interesting finding was that pupils working with
pupils showed less decline in performance over the three days than did
pupils who worked on the same task alone.

This learning situation has been explored at grade levels from 4 to 8.
Pupils working in pairs seem to provide an efficient learning situation,
which could well be a substitute for the more commonly observed classroom recitation. (Delegating the work of teaching and learning also has
the advantage that it releases the teacher's time for other activities.)

Reinforcement and Level of Complexity of the Behavior Reinforced

Behavior may be reinforced at all levels of complexity. At the lower
levels of education, reinforcement is usually applied to specific small
units of behavior. For example, in learning to read, the pupil is at first
reinforced for correct responses either to words or to short sentences or
exclamations. He is not at first reinforced for apparent understanding of
principles related to phonics. Much the same is true of mathematics.
He learns that the sum of $\frac{1}{2}$ and $\frac{1}{4}$ is $\frac{3}{4}$, possibly with some understanding
of the basic idea that $\frac{1}{2}$ is equal to $\frac{1}{4} + \frac{1}{4}$. When pupils work other
mathematical problems of this kind, the teacher reinforces right answers
and provides no reinforcement of wrong answers.

The limited time that the teacher has available makes it desirable that
he reinforce broader categories of behavior than those that have been
considered up to this time in this chapter, and this is what is actually
done. What most teachers do for a rather large fraction of their time is
to reinforce what may be termed general work habits. A pupil is praised
for doing his work quickly or systematically or neatly or imaginatively.
He may be complimented for having drawn material from a number of
sources or from unusual sources, or the teacher may remark on how well
he organized his work. In a similar vein his social habits may be reinforced on a broad base. He may be told that he is showing cooperation
or good leadership or organizing ability. In all of these cases it is reinforcement of a broad category of behavior that is sought, and this is
sound.

Other aspects of behavior reinforced by teachers are related to the
development of attitudes. This process must be distinguished from those
that have been previously considered, in that it appears to be carried on
largely at an unconscious level by teachers, and pupils are largely unaware of the learning that is taking place. Sometimes this type of indoctrination, or reinforcement as it is called here, takes place at a conscious
level, but this does not necessarily make it more effective. The writer can

recall the many instances when his own children returned from school expressing such attitudes as "All Russians are wicked" or "Most Russians would overthrow their system if they had the opportunity." These attitudes were not the result of deliberate efforts made by the teacher, but part of the complicated reinforcement system taking place in the classroom. Probably if the teachers were questioned about this they would say that they could not even recall mentioning the topic of Russia.

Pupil Reinforcement of Teacher Behavior

Nearly all documents on the training of teachers are based on the assumption that teacher behavior in a classroom is determined largely by previous training conditions plus the characteristics the teacher brought with him to the teacher-education program. Rarely is it recognized that teacher behavior may be to some extent, and in some cases to a considerable extent, a result of on-going conditions in the classroom. Although studies by Anderson, *et al.* (1945, 1946) suggest that a considerable fraction of the variance of pupil behavior may be a result of teacher behavior, it is also possible that a considerable fraction of the variance of teacher behavior may be a product of pupil behavior. The neglect of this problem by teachers and by those responsible for teacher education probably stems from the fact that it is highly anxiety-producing for a teacher to consider the possibility that his behavior may not be under his control, and still worse that this behavior may be under the control of his pupils. Whatever feelings of security he may have may well vanish when he realizes that he may be the one who is really being controlled, and by those who, by tradition in education, he is supposed to control.

Relationship of Motivation to Reinforcement

Common observation suggests that there is some relationship between motivation and reinforcement. What reinforces one child may not reinforce another, and such differences are presumably due to the differences in the motives operating in the two children. A child who responds with hostility to the teacher is not likely to be reinforced when the teacher pats him on the head. Speculation suggests that his motives require other kinds of reinforcement. The best-developed theory of the relationship of motivation to reinforcement is what is known as drive-reduction theory, developed by psychologists at Yale University, and particularly by the late Clark Hull. Let us consider some simple examples of learning from the field of animal psychology that illustrate the main points of this theory. Although there is much data that runs counter to the theory, it has had sufficient success in predicting behavior in some spheres to assume an important position in current psychology.

A rat is placed at the starting point in a maze. The rat has been deprived of food for twelve hours and is extremely active, as is typical of a hungry rat. The rat moves around the maze and eventually arrives at the end, where a small amount of food has been provided, which it eats. The quantity of food is much too small to satisfy the rat's appetite. The rat is then placed once again at the starting point of the maze where he continues to be active, and ultimately he finds the food dish again, which by this time has been refurnished with food. The cycle is then repeated until the rat runs directly to the food box without hesitation and without making any wrong turns. The rat has learned the maze, which means that it has acquired a new and complex sequence of responses it did not possess before the training period. The classical way to interpret this situation would be to say that a drive was operating that resulted in activity on the part of the rat. We know a hunger drive is operating, not because the rat looks hungry or is active, but because the rat has been deprived of food. The extent of hunger would be characteristically measured in terms of the number of hours of deprivation from food. This is an objective way of doing it, and, as a matter of fact, little would be accomplished if we did what we commonly do in the case of a child—arrive at some evaluation of the state of motivation merely by observing. The latter is not a very satisfactory way of determining the degree of motivation existing, for there are no clear-cut cues to be derived directly from behavior that would indicate the motive and the level of the motive operating.

The rat learns to run the maze problem, and eventually reaches the point where it runs like a streak from the point of departure to the food box. A theory to account for this learning is that each time the rat reaches the food box and consumes the food, drive reduction occurs—that is, there is a reduction in the hunger drive as a result of the ingestion of food. This drive reduction is postulated to strengthen or reinforce the responses that led to the reaching of the food box and the food. This conception of learning, which is commonly referred to as a drive-reduction theory, as it is presented in this particular illustration, is obviously a gross oversimplification of what is going on. Consider this matter for a minute.

The case of the rat running the maze is, on the surface, data that can be interpreted in terms of a drive-reduction theory. The theory may be stated in general terms, in the form of the proposition that "a reinforcer is a condition that reduces a drive." Sometimes the proposition is stated in more general terms, so that it incorporates within it behavior related to the complex motives that are presumed to underlie human behavior.

Drive-reduction theorists have generally taken the position that any response occurring at the time a drive is reduced will be reinforced. Thus, if a hungry chimpanzee happens to be scratching its head when food is given, then the incidental scratching behavior will be reinforced. Although at first sight this may seem to be far-fetched, the position is supported by a large body of experimental evidence, which also provides a good explanation for some behavior appearing in humans. Accounts of superstitious behavior provide a rich source of examples of the apparent reinforcement of irrelevant behavior. The member of the primitive tribe who has a series of successful days of hunting just after he has picked up an odd-shaped stone may well continue to carry the stone as a good-luck charm. From then on, when hunting is poor, he may pull out the stone from his clothing and handle it, and from time to time, by chance, this action is followed by the appearance of game, which further reinforces the behavior. B. F. Skinner was the first to note a similar behavior manifestation in animals, which he has also termed superstitious behavior. Skinner noted, for example, that a pigeon that happened to be hopping on one foot when the food trough became available might begin at that point an unusual tendency to hop.

Anxiety functions in many individuals as a powerful motive in some of the situations they encounter in daily life. It is not uncommon for the response to anxiety to be one of escape, a response that reduces the anxiety. A typical example of this is seen in the case of many young people who enter jobs and then find that the working situation generates high anxiety, perhaps because they do not know whether they are being successful or unsuccessful, and perhaps because their supervisor makes comments about their work which they interpret as indications that they are failures. A frequent response to such an anxiety-producing situation is to seek escape, and the common escape found by such a young worker is to leave the job and find another one. Now there is considerable evidence to show that such individuals who have once escaped from a job situation in this way continue to act in the same way in other job situations. The escape pattern is reinforced by the reduction in anxiety that it produces. This pattern is quite typical of many maladjusted individuals; they become job jumpers. According to the drive-reduction hypothesis, the reduction of anxiety that occurs in escape strengthens the tendency to escape, and thus one would expect that escape behavior would become characteristic of such individuals when anxiety is aroused by other job situations. This, of course, is what is found to happen. Indeed, one is tempted to generalize and say that any behavior that has the property of reducing anxiety tends to become fixed as a part of the repertoire of the individual and becomes a characteristic behavior. At the present time this appears to be the only satisfactory explanation of much neurotic behavior that generally has the characteristic of great permanency.

Although the drive-reduction theory is an attractive one, there is much evidence that goes against it; but the mere fact that there is contradictory evidence is not sufficient to destroy a theory. For almost any scientific theory ever built there has been evidence that runs counter to it; but theories are often retained, despite such conflicting evidence, because they are still more useful than alternative theories. Let us consider some of the facts that run counter to a drive-reduction theory of reinforcement.

When the rat ingests food, it is quite clear that drive reduction cannot take place for some time. The food must first be digested and then absorbed into the blood before it can result in any decrease in the hunger state that characterizes the rat. Direct reduction of the hunger drive cannot possibly occur soon enough for it to operate directly on the learning process and to provide reinforcement. If drive reduction is the operating mechanism, then it must be some secondary drive that is being reduced by the taking of the food. Some have suggested that what are called operating secondary drives may be related to the taking of the food into the mouth and that these are reduced when food is brought into the mouth. It is difficult to demonstrate that this is not so. The taking of food into the mouth must be a secondary reinforcer, but this does not necessarily imply that the mechanism is one of drive reduction.

Another argument that has been advanced against a drive-reduction theory of reinforcement is that organisms often learn behavior that heightens, rather than decreases, drive states. Meals are commonly begun with appetizers, which are designed to raise rather than reduce appetite. Many activities are learned that deliberately raise drive states rather than reduce them. Much of the behavior involved in love play is of this nature. It has, among other complex functions, that of increasing drives related to sex. The object of learning such behavior is to more effectively raise drives related to sex to a high level, and the learning occurs in relation to the increase of a drive rather than in relation to drive reduction.

Information Given before Responding versus Information Given after Responding: Two Methods of Teaching

Although this chapter has emphasized that the response-reinforcement model of learning produces efficient results in many learning situations, the reader must not lose sight of the fact that man differs from lower organisms in that he is able to use information provided in advance of action. Lower organisms are much less capable of either obtaining or using such advance information. Only man can be told in advance of attempting to solve a problem how he should go about solving it. This is because man can obtain through verbal communication more information than lower organisms can and he has a vastly greater capacity for storing information for later use. How much information should be given to a human learner prior to his attempt to solve a problem is a controversial issue in education. Traditional teaching procedures generally advocated giving the pupil substantial information before he, the pupil, attempted to solve the problem. In recent times effort has been devoted to the development of teaching methods in which the pupil himself attempts to discover the principle involved in the solution of particular classes of problems. This is the discovery method of learning, which in many respects follows the response-reinforcement model in that a minimum amount of information is given in advance and the pupil has to make some kind of response before he finds out whether he is right or wrong. Discovery methods provide the pupil with little advance information concerning how he should go about solving a problem in contrast with more traditional methods that guide the pupil with little advance information. Information given before responding can influence behavior only when the information can be stored until needed. Information given after responding can influence behavior only if a knowledge of the response can be stored long enough so that it can be evaluated in terms of the information given.

Instances are certainly accumulating in which information given before the subject makes a response produces learning superior to the learning condition that requires the subjects to respond and then to find out whether his response was appropriate. In order to compare the effect of giving information before a response is made with the effect of providing information subsequent to the response, von Wright devised an ingenious situation (1955, 1957). The essential feature of the von Wright situation was that the subject had to follow his path through a paper maze presented on a moving band of paper. The apparatus could be arranged so that the subject could see far enough ahead so that he could take the correct turn each time the pathway split. The apparatus could also be arranged so that the subject could see only a small part of the pathway ahead and hence had to make a decision, each time the path split, without knowing whether the choice was correct or not. In the latter case, the subject had to wait until the paper had moved a certain distance before he could find out whether he was on the right path or had chosen a blind alley. It required from three to five times as much time to learn the maze when information followed the making of a choice than when it preceded it. When information is given after the choice has been made the subject must retain information about the choice he has made, then evaluate that choice in the light of the information later provided, and finally store in his memory the information about what he should have done. The latter is a complicated process in contrast to that of storing advance information concerning a correct response.

A number of studies have been conducted by Annett (1959, 1961) in which a comparison has been made between subjects given information in advance of the task and subjects who were given knowledge of results after they had made a response. An important point to note is that the Annett tasks were perceptual rather than motor. In one experiment the task of the subjects was to estimate the number of dots presented on a screen for a very brief exposure. One group was told the correct number in advance of each presentation; the other group saw the dots presented, guessed the number, and then was told the correct number. (A control group was given no information at all.) Both groups improved, but they did not differ from one another significantly; it made no difference whether information was given before exposure to the stimuli or after responding.

In a second study by Annett (1959, 1961) the task of the subjects was to identify the occurrence of a tone that was so faint that it could barely be heard (this is referred to as a *near-threshold tone*). One group received a short flash a half second before each signal (tone) occurred; another group received a flash after the signal to indicate to the subject that he had responded correctly or that he had missed the signal. The group that received the advance information showed a significantly greater gain than the group that received information after responding.

The tasks that have shown some advantage for information given before rather than after responding have been tasks in which the learning involved is better described as perceptual learning rather than motor learning. The central focus of the task is on perceiving rather than on other forms of action. However, the research that has been done on this problem is so limited that one cannot present the latter statement as a well-established generalization.

Reception Learning and Learning with a Feedback Loop

The preceding section implies that two learning processes can be distinguished. All of the learning processes considered in this chapter involve some form of reinforcement, often in the form of information. Under such conditions, learning may be viewed as involving a *feedback loop*. The person performs, he obtains information concerning his performance, and that information modifies his performance. Such a cycle involves a behavior-reinforcement-behavior *loop*. In contrast, most of the learning that takes place in school does not involve such a loop, for the pupil simply receives information from a book, from the voice of the teacher, or from some other source. This latter kind of learning has been conveniently named by Ausubel (1963) *reception learning*. Sometimes the same subject matter may be learned either by means of reception or by feedback-loop learning.

Reception learning appears to occur even during early childhood. There is an accumulation of evidence that indicates that some learning about the environment will occur merely from the fact that the child lives there. Such learning is commonly referred to as *perceptual learning*. (However, this early learning takes place through direct contact with the environment and not through verbal communication.) There also seems agreement that children in the preschool years and elementary school grades also require the manipulation of concrete situations for the *efficient* acquisition of much of the important information they manage to acquire, for learning by passive observation is relatively slow. The manipulation of concrete situations involves feedback loops and is clearly essential for developing understanding of the ways in which the environment can be influenced by the individual. It is valuable also for the acquisition of other forms of knowledge about the environment during the early years of life when reception learning through the use of language cannot yet take place effectively.

The reception learning that occurs in childhood—from infancy through the elementary grades—shows a progressive shift in the extent to which information can be transmitted through the use of words and other symbolic forms of communication. In infancy, reception learning is accomplished through the direct impact of the environment on the developing child. The child receives and stores information about the environment merely by being there. At a much later age, a teacher may transmit information to a pupil through verbal communication; but even with bright children at the sixth grade, only a limited amount of reception learning can occur through verbal communications.

The capability of children to learn through verbal communication is probably overestimated by adults who learn effectively in this way. The emphasis of the progressive education movement on learning through concrete manipulations was a reaction against this adult prejudice, but the movement failed to recognize that older children may learn successfully through the reception of verbal communications.

Summary

1. The study of classical conditioning is the study of respondent behavior—that is, the study of behavior in which the stimulus that elicits it is clearly defined. Research workers have often preferred to study

learning in this type of situation, because it permits control over the relevant stimuli.

2. Some psychologists, notably B. F. Skinner, have taken the position that respondent behavior does not represent a significant category of behavior. In contrast, such psychologists consider behavior to be more typically emitted behavior which is not the consequence of specific and identifiable stimuli.

3. Behaviors that are emitted are referred to as operants, a term that carries the implication that they operate on the environment. Instrumental learning represents the selection and modification of operants that result in the achievement of a particular goal.

4. As learning occurs, behavior is shaped and certain responses are retained while others are discarded. In the development of a skill, the early stages are characterized by much excessive movement and unnecessary action. As the skill is developed, the surplus movement tends to disappear, and the smooth and apparently effortless performance of the accomplished person results.

5. As learning proceeds, behavior occurs more and more frequently in the presence of certain stimuli. These stimuli are known as discriminative stimuli, and the behaviors that occur in their presence are known as discriminative operants. Most of the behavior of the adult consists of discriminative operants.

6. Learning is accompanied by a change in the probability that particular behaviors will occur. Indeed, the course of learning may be represented by a record of the change in such probabilities.

7. The term *habit strength* refers to an internal condition that is modified as learning takes place. The probability that a particular response will take place is related to habit strength.

8. A reinforcer is a condition that, if it follows a response, increases the probability that that response will occur on subsequent occasions. The concept of a reinforcer is a refinement of Thorndike's concept of a satisfier. Little has been done to provide an inventory of the reinforcers that may be used to shape the behavior of children, despite the fact that such an inventory is sorely needed by teachers. There are probably wide individual differences in the reinforcers that are effective with different children. A particularly important category of reinforcement is that known as knowledge of results, or *feedback*.

9. Psychologists have considered that reinforcers can be classified into primary and secondary categories. A primary reinforcer is a condition that has reinforcing consequences without any learning taking place. Secondary reinforcers are believed to acquire their properties by having occurred in the presence of primary reinforcers. Since learning is involved in the development of secondary reinforcers and since learning conditions differ

among children, the end result is the appearance of individual differences in the conditions that reinforce. Unfortunately, scientists have not been able at this time to agree on a list of conditions that represent primary reinforcers. Some psychologists would list as secondary reinforcers conditions that other psychologists would consider to be primary reinforcers.

10. Negative reinforcers are those conditions which, if removed, result in an increased probability that a behavior will occur. Negative reinforcers are all aversive conditions, that is, conditions that the learner attempts to avoid. Such aversive conditions are commonly used in a situation known as punishment. In the latter situation, an aversive condition is provided in an attempt to eliminate a response.

11. Punishment is a socially approved practice, rather than one endorsed by scientific research. The results of punishment are not generally those the punisher wishes to produce. At best, the punished response is repressed, that is, inhibited, but it is likely to reappear when the possibility of punishment is removed. For this reason, the results of punishment are likely to be variable and rather unpredictable. If it is at all possible, methods other than punishment should be used for preventing the appearance of unwanted behavior.

12. The effect of delay in reinforcement is a complex one. Under some conditions, reinforcements may be delayed and still be effective. For this to happen, the learner must maintain an orienting activity toward the stimulus complex at the time the reinforcement is applied. In the case of human subjects, verbal behavior may be used to orient the subject toward a task for which reinforcement is later provided. The human may rehearse later to himself what he did in a task, and reinforcements provided at the time of this rehearsal may be effective.

13. Research has not provided final answers concerning the effect of varying the magnitude of the reinforcement provided. Under some conditions an increase in the magnitude of a reinforcement may result in a more vigorous response. Under other conditions the increase may also result in improved efficiency of learning.

14. More is known about the process of the acquisition of behavior than the elimination of behavior. This is one of the reasons why the treatment of mental disorders is so difficult. The most extensively studied process for the elimination of behavior is that described as extinction, which occurs when a response that has been learned through reinforcement occurs without reinforcement. An extinction series is generally followed by spontaneous recovery, which must be followed by a further extinction series if the process is to be effective. Each time spontaneous recovery occurs, the response is more easily extinguished than on the previous occasion. Some psychologists interpret much of the treatment given to disturbed persons as a process of extinction.

15. The permanence of acquired behavior depends to some extent on the schedule of reinforcement provided. Fixed-ratio reinforcement results in continuous behavior, and the behavior resulting from this schedule of reinforcement is rapidly extinguished. Fixed-interval reinforcement results in intermittent behavior with a build-up of activity just before each reinforcement is to occur. The best schedule for assuring that sustained behavior will occur as a result of reinforcement is to provide variable-interval reinforcement. Despite these findings, there are occasions when learning should be planned with 100-per-cent reinforcement.

16. The reinforcement of verbal behavior constitutes an important educational activity, and hence any research on the reinforcement of such behavior may have important educational implications. Scientists have demonstrated that verbal behavior may be shaped through the occurrence of a range of reinforcers. The person whose verbal behavior is shaped may or may not be aware of the fact that his behavior is undergoing modification. Studies of verbal conditioning may also have important implications for clinical psychology, since one task of the clinician is to alter the way in which the patient talks about himself.

17. A number of studies have attempted to compare the reinforcing value of various events for children. In verbal learning tasks, the reinforcing value of an event appears to depend more on the information carried by the event than on whether the child regards it as pleasant or unpleasant. A single study suggests that pupils may be as effective reinforcers of other pupils as teachers when the task is well arranged for this kind of learning.

18. Reinforcements may be applied to strengthen simple responses or develop complex skills. In either case the principles involved are the same. The teacher cannot afford to spend her time reinforcing minute aspects of behavior. In order to function effectively, the teacher must reinforce broad categories of behavior, such as work skills.

19. Although the teacher shapes the behavior of the children through the use of reinforcements, the pupils also reinforce the teacher, and may, over the years, produce changes in the general behavior pattern of the teacher. Such reinforcement may produce a deterioration in the effectiveness of the teacher. Relatively little data exists with respect to this problem, though what is known about the reinforcement process indicates that teacher behavior may be thus modified.

20. The relationship of reinforcement to motivation has long been a subject for both speculation and study. The most widely held position at the present time is that represented by drive-reduction theory. The position taken by this theory is that reinforcements function as they do because they result in the reduction of a drive. While many criticisms can be made of this position, it is widely held mainly because there is, at

present, no alternative and equally plausible theory. The proposal put forward by Mowrer represents an alternative theory that may prove to be acceptable.

21. While subhuman organisms must receive reinforcements after a response is made, the human can sometimes profit from receiving before the response the same information that might be given as a reinforcer following the response. In some situations learning occurs more readily when the information is provided before responding. The tasks in which this is so appear to be mainly perceptual tasks rather than those involving some overt muscular response. Time conditions related to reinforcement are much more crucial in the case of simpler organisms than in the case of man.

4

Generalization, Discrimination, and the Development of Stimulus Control

A DESCRIPTION of the learning process would be weak if it were limited to the effect of reinforcement and punishment on the strength or frequency of responses. Other events also occur, and learning produces certain effects on behavior other than those we have considered up to this point.

Stimulus Generalization

One of the most important of these phenomena is stimulus generalization, which probably plays a central role in behavior at all times. The intimate connection that exists between stimulus generalization and the course of learning is such that any account of learning in either human or subhuman species requires that this phenomenon be adequately described before other learning phenomena that are dependent on it are introduced.

Generalization, as a phenomenon, is shown in experiments with relatively simple animals as well as in the study of complex processes with human beings. It is clearly seen in the case of Pavlov's dogs, trained to raise a front paw each time a tone is sounded. Once training to this stimulus has been established, the dog will almost certainly make the same response when a different tone is sounded. Generalization has taken place, and the animal responds to related tones much as he would to the one to which he originally learned to respond.

Much the same is true of the child who is learning to talk. He learns to call his own dog a "dog," and will not only call all other neighborhood dogs "dogs," but will use the same word to designate cats and perhaps even horses, cows, goats, and other animals. Here again generalization has occurred, and a range of stimuli are capable of eliciting the one response "dog." Here also, as in all generalization phenomena, the generalization may be limited. The child may not respond to very large animals, such as elephants, nor to very small ones, such as mice, with the word *dog*.

Objects most similar to that to which the response has been learned are more likely to elicit the response than those that are very different. Objects that are greatly different do not elicit the response. A child who has learned the appropriate verbal response to the printed word "BOY" may make the same response to words that have similarity of form, such as "TOY," but will not so respond to a word that is greatly different in shape and contour, such as "HOUSE."

The concept of stimulus generalization is closely related to the concept of *equivalent stimuli*. Stimuli are said to be equivalent for an organism if they generate a similar response. In a young child all moving and living creatures encountered on the same block may arouse the response "cat." The creatures represent equivalent stimuli for him, because he has not learned to discriminate one from the other. This child's lack of discrimination is a social disadvantage in attempting to tell others about his experiences. In other situations, advantage may be gained by responding to a set of stimuli as if they were equivalent. For the child to show an avoidance response to all moving objects on the street, regardless of their shape and size, even has survival value. Learning when to generalize and when not to generalize is an important part of education.

Without stimulus generalization, the living creature would learn to respond only to the specific situations in which learning occurred. If the child learned to say "boy" when the printed word "BOY" was written on the blackboard, then, without stimulus generalization, he would not be able to make the same response if the word were written smaller or in different type. Stimulus generalization permits the learner to respond to a wide range of stimuli as though they were all the same. Thus, what is learned in one situation can be applied in other situations even though they may differ.

In order that a child may learn to respond by saying "boy" only to the printed word "BOY," it is necessary that a period of discrimination learning be planned during which he learns to discriminate the word *boy* from other words. In this period of discrimination learning, if it is well planned, the child will first learn to make easy discriminations among words and will be exposed to successively harder discriminations. Despite training, some generalization will still occur, particularly under circumstances in which the stimulus is exposed only briefly. The famous case is that of the errors the proofreader lets by. In such cases, he responds by the correct word even though the incorrect one is printed. Years of experience in proofreading will reduce this error of stimulus generalization, but probably never to the point where it does not occur at all.

Stimulus generalization not only accounts for what one may term stupid behavior, as when a child points to a cat and calls it a dog, but it also accounts for, or is believed to account for, some of the more creative aspects of child behavior. A child who insists that his small backyard is a vast ranch is manifesting behavior similar to that manifested in stimulus generalization experiments. Substitution of one article for another, as occurs in much creative activity, also appears to be a similar phenomenon and is the very essence of invention.

The fact that the stimulus generalization seems to underlie not only stupid behavior but also creative behavior makes it particularly difficult to handle. The tendency in classrooms is to stress the building up of discriminative behavior and to suppress generalization behavior. The prosaic development of precise discriminations generally takes precedence as an objective over free, creative, and often undisciplined expression.

Although generalization is a clean-cut phenomenon in the case of simple stimuli, experiments with complex events sometimes produce results that are difficult or impossible to explain in terms of any simple theory of conditioning. More than a decade ago Razran (1951) conducted an experiment with some disturbing results. What he did was to condition a salivary response of a human subject to words. This was done by the straightforward procedure of saying the words while the subject was eating. After this procedure has been followed a number of times, the saying of the words alone will produce a flow of saliva. One of the words used in the conditioning trials was *freeze*. Once the salivary response had been well conditioned to this word, Razran determined whether the response would generalize to similar words. What he found was that he obtained generalization to words similar in meaning such as *chill*, but not words similar in form such as *frieze* but which differed in meaning. Generalization was in terms of a dimension of meaning and not in terms of the objective properties of the stimulus. The educational implications of this are that responses learned in a particular situation may not generalize to a new situation because the learner fails to understand the meaning of the new situation or misinterprets it.

Gradient of Generalization

If a response has been established to a stimulus (S_1), then the response will occur with varying degrees of strength to stimuli S_2, S_3, S_4, and so forth that resemble S_1 in varying degrees. The greater the degree to which the new stimulus resembles S_1, the greater is the likelihood that the response will occur or that it will occur in full strength. The relationship between the response R and the stimulus S, as S is varied from the original stimulus with which learning took place, is known as the *gradient of generalization.*

The phenomenon of the gradient of generalization was well illustrated in Pavlov's original work with salivation in dogs. A dog trained to salivate at the sound of a tone pitched at 440 vibrations per second will also salivate to a sound one octave lower (220 vibrations per second), but it will salivate to a lesser degree. Drop the pitch of the sound still further and the dog will salivate even less. The closer the note is to the original note, the more the amount of salivation approximates that produced by the original note.

Gradient of generalization is known to occur in a great range of situations, though the exact form of the generalization curve is not known. It occurs not only in the case of positive responses that have been acquired, but also in the case of avoidance responses. A person who, through having been seriously injured by a power saw, develops a fear of power saws and withdraws from them may also show a similar but lesser withdrawal from other power tools. Although the whine of a power saw may produce in him intense fear and a need to escape from it, the noise of a power drill may merely give him the feeling that he does not want to touch the device. The drill induces an avoidance response, but it is milder than that induced by the saw.

Avoidance responses tend to show less generalization to new stimuli than do approach responses. This means that when one learns to avoid an object, there is less generalization to the avoidance of similar objects than there is in the case of approach responses. Avoidance responses have a high degree of specificity that approach responses do not have.

An example of a gradient of stimulus generalization is found in a classic study by Yum (1931). Yum gave his subjects the task of learning to associate pairs of words. For example, they would learn that the word *breeze* was to be said as the correct response when the word *house* was presented. The words were learned until the subject was able to give a correct answer to each of the words. Twenty-four hours later the subjects were presented the task again but under three different conditions. Under

one condition precisely the same words were presented. In the second
condition, a word that is approximately a synonym was substituted for
the original stimulus word: One of the original words was *house;* it now
was replaced by the word *cottage;* but the correct answer for the subject
was still *breeze.* In the third condition, a more remotely related word was
substituted for the original stimulus word. For example, the word *house*
was replaced by the word *barn.* Now one would expect that the original
learning of the association *house–breeze* would have tended also to
strengthen not only the association between *breeze* and *house,* but also
the association between *breeze* and words that have meanings related to
the word *house.* The more closely they were related to the word *house*
the greater would be the strengthening of the association. Thus, on the
recall task undertaken 24 hours later, one would expect that those given
the word *house* would be most likely to respond with the word *breeze,*
those given the word *cottage* would be less likely to respond with *breeze*
and those given the word *barn* would be even less likely to recall the
word *breeze.* This is what Yum found. In response to the original word,
50 per cent gave the correct answer, but in response to the next most
related word only 33 per cent gave the correct answer; and to the even
more unrelated words only 11 per cent of the responses were correct. The
original learning had also produced some ability to produce the same
responses to related stimuli but to a lesser degree.

In another experiment, Yum asked subjects to learn an association
between a diagram and a word, and then later presented diagrams
modified from the original in various degrees. He found that the capability of the diagram to elicit the particular word depended upon the
degree to which it resembled the original diagram. This relationship is
shown in Figure 3.

Stimulus Discrimination

The learning of discriminations is a process that operates in a direction
opposite to that of generalization. The child learns to say "Dad" to the
large male of the household, and at first addresses all male newcomers
to the house as "Dad." Soon he learns that the word can be used appropriately only when one of the many persons he encounters is thus ad-
dressed. He will probably still make many mistakes and continue to
address as "Dad" anyone who is about the same size as his father and who
is clad in a similar way. Discrimination develops slowly and probably
never reaches the ultimate state of perfection. Throughout life he may

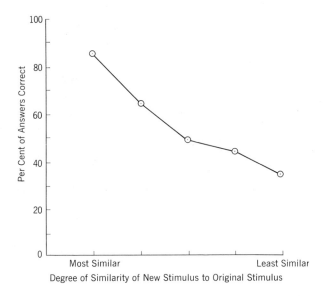

FIGURE 3. Data showing stimulus generalization derived from Yum (1931).

occasionally mistake at a distance other people for his father, and particularly on occasions when he is expecting to meet his father.

The learning of discriminations is one of the commonest learning tasks and represents a process that operates in a direction opposite to that of generalization. In discrimination learning, the subject learns to respond only to a narrow range of stimuli and to ignore other related stimuli that lie outside that range. Pavlov trained dogs to respond by salivating to a given note, say middle C, by providing food following the sound of this note. The dogs then learned *not* to salivate when other notes were sounded. The latter was done by sounding another note and then not providing food—an extinction process. In this way he was able to discover the capacity of dogs to discriminate various notes. By a similar process children learn to respond positively to the family and friends but to avoid a similar response to strangers. Most of the social responses a child learns toward his family and friends must be inhibited when manifested to strangers. Discrimination learning involves the acquisition of inhibitions.

Since discrimination learning in man has been closely studied in relation to the learning of ideas and concepts, it is in this latter area that we will continue the discussion of the topic.

Response Generalization

Just as a living creature is capable of responding with the same response to a range of stimuli as though they were the same, so too does a single stimulus have the capacity of evoking a range of responses. The fact that a stimulus may evoke not only the response with which it has been characteristically associated, but other related responses as well, is referred to as *response generalization*. This phenomenon accounts for at least some of the variability of behavior commonly observed. The note of middle C, as printed on a sheet of music, generally evokes in the piano player the response that produces on the piano the tone of middle C, but sometimes it evokes related response, as when the notes B or D are struck instead. Another familiar example is often seen when a person encounters an old friend he has not seen for years. The friend's name happens to be Mr. East, but all the person can think of are such related names as Mr. West, Mr. Coast, Mr. Orient, and so forth. The stimulus, namely the friend, was able to evoke a range of related responses, but for some unknown reason the correct response was inhibited.

The capacity for a stimulus to evoke a range of answers is an important phenomenon that may account for some of the transfer of training that takes place.

When the typical response to a stimulus is blocked and the organism generally produces another response, this alternative response may also be blocked. If this happens, the organism may cease to respond, or a third response may be produced. Thus a person writing down a telephone number may begin to write it with his pen; when the pen does not work he picks up another from the table; when the new pen does not work, he borrows a pencil. The responses thus emerge in a certain order that is sometimes referred to as the *response hierarchy*, a term originally used to describe the ordering of the clergy within a church from the highest official to the lowliest. Responses in relation to any particular stimulus can be regarded as being ordered from those most likely to occur to those least likely.

Stimulus Control

As the individual develops, behaviors of particular kinds tend to occur more and more in the presence of certain stimuli. These behaviors are known as *"discriminative operants."* For example, talking behavior is elicited largely in the presence of other human beings; and, indeed, an adult who talks to himself when he is alone is considered peculiar. Laughing behavior occurs mainly on social occasions, not in work situations; washing behavior occurs in the bathroom and not in the kitchen; drinking coffee becomes associated with the coffee break; newspaper-reading behavior is likely to accompany breakfast; and so forth. Behaviors come to occur on particular occasions. It is not that these behaviors are the direct responses to the situations. In my case, I begin to read the paper as soon as I sit down to breakfast. This is not because my response to the breakfast on the table is that of reading, but rather that this is the occasion when newspaper reading is elicited. It is also not just a response to the presence of the newspaper, for there are many other times in the day when there is a newspaper present and I do not begin to read. The breakfast is the situation in which this particular behavior occurs. The situation triggers the behavior, rather than causes it.

Much of our behavior becomes triggered by particular situations. We rise and dress at the sound of the alarm. We eat our breakfast, and the amount we eat does not have too much to do with how hungry we are. In the office our manner and bearing is appropriate to that situation and quite different from what it would be if we were in our own home or at a party. If we are studying for an examination, we are likely to reserve a time and place for studying; for if we do not, then studying is not likely to happen. What we are doing in the latter case is tying studying to a certain situation which, in time, comes to elicit it. The latter is most important in the development of good study habits.

The tendency for certain stimuli to elicit certain classes of behavior is referred to as the phenomenon of stimulus control. The process of development is characterized by an increasing tendency for behavior to come under stimulus control. Indeed, one major difference between the young child and the adult lies in the extent to which behavior manifests stimulus control. Popular language states that the sophisticated adult is one who knows what is the appropriate thing to do on every occasion. The scientist turns this statement around and states that the situations themselves *elicit* appropriate behaviors.

Imprinting

In the newborn baby relatively few external stimuli will initiate and maintain behavior. Pain-producing stimuli fall into one category of controlling stimuli, but pain only initiates a generalized activity and does not result in withdrawal until considerable learning has been undertaken. Stimulation of the mouth or cheek will also initiate activity in the newborn, but this activity is of a much more specific nature and is generally limited to the muscles involved in sucking action. As development proceeds, a few stimuli emerge as producing activity in themselves, though it is difficult to say how much previous learning is involved. The doctrine of instinct was originally involved to account for such stimulus-initiated activity. The tendency for organisms to respond to certain classes of stimuli was attributed to instincts, and for each class of stimuli to which a response emerged there was postulated to be a corresponding instinct. There were two central weaknesses that ultimately resulted in the abandonment of this doctrine. One was that the list of instincts became longer and longer, and there seemed to be no end to the number that could be postulated. The other was that an instinct remained a poorly-defined entity, and was often no more than a mystical inner machination concocted to account for some behavior that was poorly understood. Yet the doctrine had a kernel of truth. Some of the objects that initiate and sustain activity in a living creature appear to have this property the first time they are presented. Learning may be involved, but learning is not the whole story.

During the last few years, there has been a revived interest in the phenomena that some of the early psychologists studied and which they referred to as instinctive behavior. Interest in these phenomena is found largely in biologists rather than psychologists, and studies have been directed mainly toward those aspects that have come to be known as *imprinting*.

The phenomenon of imprinting was first discussed in technical literature in a publication by Lorenz (1935). Lorenz noted that in certain species of bird, notably ducks or geese, the newly hatched young will follow a moving object after brief exposure to it and will continue to follow this moving object in preference to other objects throughout its period of growth. Uusally the moving object is the mother bird, but a moving block of wood will elicit the same response, and the young bird will stubbornly persist in following the block. The young bird that follows a particular object is said to be imprinted, because the learning is believed to be to a great extent irreversible. The response occurs with a minimum of experience. The behavior becomes stimulus-controlled on the first exposure, and the control is also relatively permanent and a uniform characteristic of the species. Such is the essential nature of imprinting. Numerous related phenomena have been observed in other animals that present a rather similar pattern of emergence. The scientists who have studied these phenomena call themselves ethologists and are particularly concerned with the study of the behavior of animals in their natural habitat; but many psychologists who study behavior under carefully controlled experimental conditions believe that the phenomena observed in animals in their natural habitat resembles rather closely that displayed under artificial conditions. For example, Hinde (1954) has shown that hatched chicks of the herring gull show fear responses to certain moving objects in the sky, but that objects that resemble the owl produced much greater fear responses than other objects.

Somewhat related to the phenomenon of imprinting are the fear responses that primates show to certain strange objects introduced into their familiar surroundings. Perhaps it is unwise to refer to these responses as fear responses and much safer to describe them as an increase in the level of arousal.

Ethologists, in discussing these responses that occur with little or no practice, divide them into three categories. First there are *reflexes*. These are responses that occur the first time a critical stimulus is applied. Reflexes are illustrated in man by the salivary reflex and the knee-jerk reflex which the doctor elicits in order to test the state of the nervous system. These responses are typical of all members of a species and appear with little variation. They appear when the critical stimulus is provided. Secondly, there are *taxic movements,* which are similar to reflexes except that they are more complex. These are illustrated by the feeding behavior of the newborn mammal. Third, there are *instinctive responses* which have been illustrated by the response of the herring gull to the silhouette of the bird in the sky. In these instinctive responses it may be necessary that the animal have had a particular life history in order for them to emerge at the appropriate time. For example, the behavior of male rats toward receptive females would be classed as an instinctive rat behavior, and yet it is influenced by the previous life history of the rat. Hayward (1957), for example, has shown that if male rats are trained during infancy to avoid a female rat, they are inhibited in all sexual behavior toward a receptive female when they are adults. Although the component responses of the sexual act in the mature rat appear to be reflex in character, the general nature of the response toward the receptive female seems dependent on a history of previous relations with the female.

Familiar examples of imprinting and instinctive acts are found in the bird-catching and mice-catching activities of cats. Cats do not have a built-in tendency to destroy birds and mice specifically. They do have a tendency to follow and grasp small moving objects, and it happens that mice and birds are the commonest of small moving objects in their environment. Following and grasping a bird or a mouse leads to eating, and this in turn leads to the reinforcement of the activity.

The rapid learning phenomena associated with imprinting probably have important implications for human learning and human development, but techniques have not yet been devised that permit the study of these phenomena in an organism as complicated as the human being. The scientist would be particularly interested in knowing whether some objects have the property of inducing fear responses in young children the first time they are presented, what those objects are, and what are the previous learning conditions, if any, that result in the appearance of these fears. Some of the common fears of young children have many of the same characteristics as the instinctive acts of other animals. For example, around the age of three to six months the majority of infants come to manifest a fear of strange faces. Crying and generally disorganized behavior will appear when a stranger gives attention to the infant. Later, the response becomes less and less pronounced and is characteristically manifested in shyness when an unfamiliar person appears. In the presence of a stranger the three-year-old may well run to his mother and clutch her around the legs, but this response also wanes with the passage of time.

In contrast, fear of the dark is probably a different kind of phenomenon. It is found in only a minority of children and does not emerge at any uniform age. It may, in some cases, be a conditioned response involving a fear-producing incident that was associated with darkness. Another plausible explanation is that a child placed in the dark is deprived of most of the stimuli that normally guide behavior. In the absence of such stimuli, the cues that lead to ordinary adaptive behavior are absent, and the child's behavior becomes more and more disorganized and nonadaptive. Crying follows, and this in turn generally leads to escape from the situation by the action of the parent.

Inhibition

That some events result in action is a familiar daily experience, but not so obvious is the fact that some events have the opposite effect and prevent action from occurring. Such events are said to be inhibiting events, and they may occur externally to the body or internally. If, while we are walking along the street, someone shouts "Stop!" our walking is likely to be inhibited and we will come to an abrupt halt. In the latter case this inhibiting event is external to the body. On the other hand, a passing thought of doing violence to another who has wronged us may produce guilt feelings that in turn inhibit further hostile thoughts. In the latter case the guilt feelings are internal events that have inhibiting effects on behavior. Inhibition is not just a case of something not happening, but rather is it a case of one event actively preventing another from happening.

Diamond et al. (1963), who have reviewed the history of the concept of inhibition, point out that the concept arrived relatively late in the history of psychology. In the last century, the philosopher Herbart and the psychiatrist Freud both suggested that all thinking involves inhibitory processes. Freud's position was that thinking, in relation to a real world, involved the repression of the basic needs that demand immediate gratification. Both repression and suppression are inhibitory processes within the psychoanalytic system. If the child is to learn to handle the real world, then appropriate inhibitions of primitive impulses must be learned. While the psychology of Freud included the idea that inhibitions play an important role in normal development, his concern for the treatment of disturbed persons led him to focus discussions of inhibitory processes on instances in which they have damaging effects. This emphasis, together with the implications that inhibiting processes are damaging, found a receptive audience among those groups of educators who, in the tradition of Rousseau, had taken the position that repressive and inhibiting influences in education were necessarily evil influences.

Education has long neglected the problem of what inhibitions should be developed and how they should be developed. The question is not whether one should or should not develop inhibitions in the growing youngster; the question is what inhibitions should be developed. Aggressive tendencies need to be inhibited, but not to the point where the individual becomes incapable of expressing them through acceptable channels. A person incapable of expressing aggression develops many social difficulties. In his intellectual life he must know what questions to ask and what not to ask in order to obtain the information needed to solve his problems. He must often learn not to ask the first question that comes into his head, but wait until he sees what are the crucial issues. Again he must learn *not* to investigate every trivial phenomenon that comes his way, but must exercise discrimination in what he investigates and what he does not investigate.

This phenomenon was very clearly illustrated some years back in Hebb's laboratory (Hebb, 1958) at McGill University. Two Scottish terriers from the same litter were raised under fundamentally different conditions. One was raised in the home of one of the staff members, while the other was raised under conditions that provided little stimulation. The latter dog was, in fact, raised in a large box, and the only time it had any contact with humans was when it was fed or when the box was cleaned out. When the two dogs reached full growth they were compared on various tests in the laboratory. One of the most striking differences between these two dogs was in their performance in relation to visitors, who were often asked to guess which one of the dogs had been raised with the impoverished curriculum and which with the enriched curriculum. The visitors were invariably wrong in their guesses, for the dog that had been raised under impoverished conditions was the one that was thoroughly friendly to visitors. The home-raised dog knew too much about life to bother with visitors. It knew what to attend to and what to ignore. It had learned a set of useful inhibitions. The other dog, in contrast, tended to explore everything and showed no discrimination in the objects to which it directed its attention. Perhaps the spontaneity of the child may be understood largely in terms of the idea that he has not learned to be discriminating in the direction of his attention, and hence attends to anything novel. Although such spontaneity is an excellent characteristic in a child, it may merely indicate lack of education in an adult. Once the environment has become filled with discriminative stimuli, then behavior becomes oriented with respect to those stimuli.

Inhibitions can be acquired in a number of ways, although the full range of conditions that produce inhibition have not yet been discovered. This statement is made because many of the inhibitions of the adult cannot at this time be understood in terms of known mechanisms.

There are several mechanisms related to the production of inhibition. One of these is extinction. If a response is systematically extinguished, the conditioned stimulus that originally elicited that response not only ceases to produce it but becomes an effective means of inhibiting it. A child whose questions are systematically ignored may be expected to ask adults fewer and fewer questions, and ultimately may be expected to be inhibited in this respect in the presence of those who have ignored his questions. Extinguishing bad behavior by ignoring it is a common technique used by adults when the child seeks the kind of reinforcement afforded by adult attention.

A second method of producing inhibition is to provide the stimulus necessary for eliciting a response and then prevent the response from occurring. This phenomenon was first discovered in connection with classical conditioning, but is probably reproducible under other circumstances. An example of the kind of condition likely to produce inhibitions of an undesirable nature is illustrated by the teacher who asks a pupil a question, but who passes on to other matters before the student has had time to give an answer.

A third type of condition, previously mentioned, that produces temporary inhibition is punishment. In textbooks on education of twenty years ago it was commonly stated that punishment should be avoided because this tended to produce inhibited children. This is probably not true, for the characteristic effect of punishment is to produce inhibitions of a temporary nature which rapidly wear off. If the inhibitions were at all permanent, there would be no problem in handling the criminal. Here experience conforms closely to theory, for it is well established that prison has a temporary inhibiting effect and that the criminal soon re-engages in crime after he is released. There is no evidence that mild punishment produces either a permanent or general inhibiting effect.

Two exceptions must be noted to the latter statement concerning the effects of punishment. Estes (1945) has shown that if punishment is sufficiently severe, almost to the point of being brutal, it may have a much stronger inhibiting effect on the behavior against which it is directed. This may be the result of the generation of a quite permanent anxiety state, which may also inhibit behavior in a range of related situations as well as in the one in which punishment has occurred. A person who has seriously and painfully injured himself while operating a machine may never have the courage to go near that machine for the rest of his life. The inhibition of behavior related to the use of that machine may be complete and permanent. It is doubtful whether punishment of this severity, with its relatively permanent effects, occurs today in schools.

Summary

1. An important mechanism in learning is that known as stimulus generalization. This mechanism manifests itself when a response which, through training, occurs in the presence of a particular stimulus also occurs in the presence of related stimuli that did not originally elicit the response. Stimulus generalization accounts for the appearance of many inappropriate responses in children, but it also makes an important positive contribution to the learning process. If it were not for stimulus generalization, the learner would have to learn appropriate responses to every new stimulus complex that he might encounter.

2. A response that has been learned in relation to a stimulus (S) will occur in the presence of related stimuli. The probability that it will occur depends on the relationship of the new stimulus to the original stimulus S. The relationship between the probability of occurrence and the resemblance of the new stimulus to the original stimulus S produces the gradient of generalization.

3. The process of generalization must generally be accompanied by the learning of discriminations. The learner must learn to discriminate between when a response previously learned can be applied to a new situation and when it cannot. This is a matter of learning to discriminate situations.

4. Imprinting is an interesting example of stimulus control acquired through what may be termed "one-trial learning." The possibility exists that this phenomenon or a similar one may occur in human subjects, but little is known as yet concerning its occurrence at this level.

5. Inhibition plays an important role in behavior. It represents one psychological or physiological event preventing another from happening. Although clinical psychologists have tended to consider and emphasize

those aspects of inhibition that produce behavior problems, acquired inhibitions are essential for effective living. Inhibitions serve many purposes including those of conserving the energies of the organism so that responses are made only to worthwhile stimuli.

6. Although some inhibitions must be learned for effective adjustment, attempts to produce inhibitions through punishment are generally ineffective. Only in the case of very severe punishment are inhibitions produced that have any extended duration.

5

Concept Learning and Verbal Learning

Nature of Concepts

Living organisms show by their behavior that they do not discriminate every stimulus from every other with which they are confronted. Some stimuli they treat as equivalent, but some they differentiate. A child in the second grade may respond to all of the school's teachers in much the same way, treating them with deference, seeking them out as sources of information and support. In the latter case the child has *categorized* teachers as a class and behaves toward one much as he behaves toward another. Teachers are also discriminated from nonteachers: A second-grade child can discriminate between teachers and such persons as janitors, principals, supervisors, and visitors. Teachers stand out as a category of events in the environment and are distinguished from other events. This instance of categorization by the second-grade child is typical of his behavior with respect to his environment in general. He does not perceive and respond to the millions of objects and events in his environment as if each one were separate and distinct, for he has already categorized them to a great extent. Many of the words he uses refer to the categories. A word such as *table* refers to a category of objects he has widely seen and used, but categorizing behavior can go on without the use of language. Animals behave as if they categorize the objects and events in their environment into such groups as the edible and the nonedible, the friendly creature and the hostile one, the situation that should be approached and the situation that should be avoided, and so forth.

The concept of categorizing behavior has been developed by Bruner, Goodnow, and Austin (1956), and the presentation here follows to a great extent that put forth by these three scientists. What is the function of such categorizing behavior? Bruner *et al.* suggest that it serves to simplify the environment for the organism. The organism no longer has to respond to millions of situations, but only to a much smaller number

of categories of situations. Categorizing also reduces the need for learning. New situations are perceived as falling into the same categories as
old situations and hence are responded to in the same way. Categorization
also permits the identification of events or objects, and the category can
be communicated to another person by means of language. When one
person says to another, "Be careful of John; he is a crook," the statement
shows that John is to be placed in a certain category. The example leads
to a further function of categorization—that once an object has been
placed in a certain category, the classification leads to a certain class of
action with respect to that object. If a person knows that John falls into
the classification of "crook," then his behavior toward John will be different from what it would be if he knows that John falls into the classification "honest."

Bruner *et al.* suggest that one can consider organisms as endowed with
a basic motive to categorize, but there is no need at this time to postulate
such a motive. At present, relatively little value has been derived from
such a hypothesis, and alternative hypotheses have to be considered.
Perhaps organisms are reinforced for manifesting categorizing behavior
and hence develop at an early age a marked tendency to categorize experiences.

Objects are categorized in terms of attributes. The class of objects
known as "table" is characterized by the attributes that include a flat
horizontal surface, one or more legs to support it, a height such that the
surface can be reached by adults and so that objects can be placed on it
and removed from it, and others. The process of identifying the attributes
that characterize a particular category is referred to as the process of
concept attainment, which is distinguished from the process of *concept
formation.*

The distinction between concept formation and concept attainment
is illustrated by the example that follows. A child is learning to distinguish
between the categories of dangerous and harmless snakes. He does not
know the attributes that distinguish one from the other, but he has
already *formed* the concept of a harmless snake and the concept of a
dangerous snake. His task is to find the attributes that distinguish the
one from the other, and this is the process known as concept attainment.
The child will probably *attain* the concept of a dangerous snake by asking
questions, visiting the zoo, and perhaps also by searching in books and
encyclopedias. In practice the processes of concept formation and concept attainment move forward together. The combined processes are
referred to here as *concept learning.*

Let us consider now the process of concept attainment by discussing
a specific example. A child uses the word *dog* and indicates by this usage
that he has *formed* a concept of a dog. The child also shows through his

behavior that he has not yet identified the attributes of dogs by which he can discriminate them from other animals. The process of concept attainment has to be undertaken; in this case, it might proceed along the following lines:

1. Suppose the child is taken for a walk in the park by his mother. On this walk he encounters a number of animals, including dogs, cats, horses, squirrels, and others. These are "exemplars" of the category *dog* and exemplars of the category other than dog. As each exemplar is encountered, the child might make a decision; and, if the decision is that the animal is a dog, then the child might say "dog." The decision of the child in each case would be either endorsed or corrected by his mother.

2. Through the making of such decisions and through the information provided the child by his mother, the child learns to respond to certain attributes rather than to others in deciding whether an animal is or is not a dog. Early in the process of concept attainment he may be reacting mainly to the size of the animal. Small animals are called dogs; larger animals are called something else. As learning proceeds, the child shows through his decisions that he is responding more and more precisely to the attributes that discriminate the category dog from the category non-dog.

3. The decisions that the child makes as he is faced with a series of exemplars in the attainment of a concept provide information concerning the *strategy* the child is following. A strategy is defined as an observed regularity in the decision-making process. In attaining his concept of a dog, the child may respond to all animals by saying either "dog" or "not dog," or he may select certain animals for making these decisions. These two sets of behavior represent different strategies. Strategies in the attainment of concepts have considerable significance for education.

Classification of Concepts

One useful classification of concepts is into the categories of conjunctive, disjunctive, and relational. Let us examine these classes of concepts, pointing out some of the difficulties of attainment that they present.

Let us consider first the conjunctive class of concept. Suppose that a child is learning about the various musical instruments. The trombone he eventually identifies as being (1) a wind instrument, (2) made of brass, and (3) played by extending it. If an instrument is not characterized by *all* of these properties or attributes, then it is not a trombone. The concept of a trombone is a conjunctive concept. In a conjunctive concept all of the attributes must be there at the same time. If one of them is lacking, then the object belongs in a different category. Conjunctive concepts are some of the simplest concepts to acquire and retain.

More difficult to acquire are disjunctive concepts. A simple illustration of a disjunctive concept that most children acquire is a strike in baseball. Most children and adults know that a strike is *either* a ball that is above the plate and between the batter's knee and shoulder levels *or* a ball that the batter attempts to hit or does hit. In a disjunctive concept there is always an *either-or* element in the situation. An "out" in baseball is an even more complicated disjunctive concept, since it may occur under each one of a number of different conditions. In comparison with conjunctive concepts, disjunctive concepts are harder to learn and may present difficulties both from the point of view of learning and from the point of view of teaching.

A third type of concept is the related type, also often difficult to acquire. The relational concept is illustrated by the phrase "to the south of." Many children have difficulty in mastering the notion that, for example, South America is north of the South Pole. The concept involves the relationship of two positions on a map and also the relationship of the positions of those objects to the orientation of the map itself. Such relational concepts may be difficult to master even when they are concerned with fairly concrete matters such as geography. Even more difficult are they when they involve abstract material such as that found in geometry or algebra. It is hardly surprising that many students never do master the concepts involved in the idea of the similarity of two triangles. Even more difficult relational concepts are found in calculus and are mastered by very few. No doubt a certain effectiveness in brain functioning is necessary before such concepts can be mastered. Some never have the necessary machinery in their nervous systems for doing this.

Classroom Management of Concept Learning

The teacher can exert considerable control over concept learning. This can be done in a number of ways some, of which are described in the following paragraphs.

Reducing the number of irrelevant attributes. Hunt (1962) has reviewed the research literature on this problem and concludes that learning a concept is facilitated by reducing the number of irrelevant dimensions. A teacher attempting to develop the concept of *Gothic arch* would do well, on this account, to provide a simple sketch of a *Gothic arch* rather than the picture of the interior of a beautiful cathedral where such arches provide the setting for stained glass windows. A complicated presentation means that the student has to begin by discriminating from the vast medley of material the attributes that have some relevance for understanding the problem and he may be blocked from progress by failing to make these discriminations. Studies of perceptual learning generally provide an argument in favor of simplicity of materials for cognitive learning.

Improving the identifiability of the relevant attributes. Many concepts are difficult to learn because the defining attributes are vague. For example, one of the difficulties of teaching writing skills is that the attribute "good style" is not characterized by easily identifiable attributes. On the other hand, the attributes of a chemical element are relatively clear and recognizable. Sometimes the attributes that define a concept can be made clearer and more recognizable by being taken out of context and by being represented by simplified representations. Many of the attributes of a living cell can be more readily communicated when represented by a drawing than when photographs of the cell are shown. The photographs may not show clearly such attributes as the presence of nucleoli, but a drawing can do this. After such a drawing has been examined, the pupil may then turn to a photograph or to a cell presented by means of a microscope and will then be able to identify the structure he has easily identified in the drawing. Archer (1962) conducted an experiment that showed quite strikingly one of the factors involved in identifiability of attributes. Subjects, both men and women, were presented with various shapes including squares, trapezoids, and parallelograms. He found that men responded more readily to form rather than size in an attribute and that women did the reverse. He also noted that women had difficulty in naming the forms that may have been a factor in producing the difference.

Providing sufficient time for viewing material after feedback is given. A learner can be shown an exemplar, spend time in studying it, make a guess whether it is or is not illustrative of a particular concept, and then be informed of the correctness of his response. This is the usual concept-learning procedure. However, there is a variation that can be added to the procedure. After the learner is told whether he is right or wrong, *either* the display can be removed *or* time can be given for a further examination of the display. Bourne and Bunderson (1962) found that a concept was more readily learned if the subject was given time to examine the exemplar after being given information about the correctness of his response. The data suggest that when the subject is allowed to review the material in the light of the information provided that he is then in a better position to form hypotheses. Bourne and Bunderson also noted that the advantage of providing time for viewing the display after feedback had a particularly significant effect when the display was a complex one. The moral of all this is that the learner must be given time to utilize the information provided by the teacher and in the light of the materials that are being considered.

Facilitating the coding of information. Available knowledge suggests that when visual information can be coded verbally, then information related to the concept can be more readily retained. In the example previously discussed of the student learning the characteristic of a Gothic arch, the learning and retention of the concept is probably improved by student learning that this kind of arch is pointed. What the student is doing in such an instance is to code the visual information in the words "pointed arch." A study by Chan (1964) not only reviews studies related to this problem but also adds evidence indicating the importance of meaningful verbal labels in the retention of visual materials.

Arranging for concepts to be learned in an order consistent with their structure. The position in this matter, which is commonly taken today, has its roots in the work of the German philosopher Johann Friedrich Herbart who was also the eighteenth century's most distinguished thinker about educational problems. Herbart was the first to develop the modern definition of a concept, but he also understood that concepts cannot be learned readily in any order. Herbart proposed that, as knowledge is acquired, it is organized into what he called an *apperceptive mass.* New ideas could be added easily to this mass provided they were related to what was already there. The essence of this conception of cognitive learning is that a new idea can be acquired without difficulty provided it can be fitted in memory storage in relation to previously acquired ideas.

Herbart's apperceptive mass is similar to the ideas of several modern thinkers on the subject. Both Woodruff (1964) and Gagné (1964) have voiced the opinion that efficient concept learning will take place when the concepts of an area of knowledge are learned in a particular order. The illustrations generally given are derived from mathematics where it is fairly evident that the concept of addition should precede that of multiplication and the addition of integers should precede the addition of fractions. In mathematics, concepts can be arranged in the order they have to be introduced for the logical development of the subject matter. In other disciplines, the ordering of concepts is a much more difficult task—if it can be undertaken at all.

Ausubel attempts to overcome the difficulty that has just been mentioned by embracing a solution that originally came from Herbart. Ausubel (1963) proposes that for an idea to be efficiently learned it must be *subsumed* under an idea that is more general and all inclusive.

For example, before one can learn concepts related to addition or subtraction, one must first have acquired the concept of number. Addition, when it is learned, is subsumed under the concept of number. Another example is that the child first learns that objects are differentiated in terms of color without being able to identify the colors. Later colors are learned in a few broad categories such as red and blue. Finally, the more subtle tones become identified. As learning progresses, the ideas and propositions that are learned provide less and less inclusiveness and provide more detailed knowledge of the features of the environment that have been previously responded to in gross terms.,

This position concerning the nature of cognitive learning has some implications for the organizing of subject matter for teaching school children. Ideas that have high generality and are closely tied to experience and hence have a low level of abstraction should come first. For example, the idea that all plants grow would have high priority on this basis, and so, too, would the idea that food is necessary for growth and for keeping warm. Later come the less readily observable facts, such as that growth involves cell division.

The fact that ideas are generally learned in a context of other, more general ideas leads to another important observation. Everyone has had the experience of acquiring some mastery of an area of knowledge and of then not using the knowledge for some years. What typically happens is that the details tend to disappear while the more general and inclusive concepts remain. Ausubel refers to this as a process of *obliterative subsumption,* meaning that ideas are obliterated by becoming absorbed in the more general ideas under which they are subsumed.

Arranging for sequences of positive and negative instances. Although many years ago Hovland and Weiss (1953) demonstrated that human learners acquired information with greater facility from positive instances than from negative instances, a more recent study by Huttenlocher (1962) has shown that the most effective teaching technique is to arrange sequences of instances that include both positive and negative instances. The implication is that in teaching botany, for example, it is not enough to show some examples of an oak tree, but it is also necessary to provide opportunities for contrasting the oak with other trees.

Clearly, how concepts are learned in the classroom depends on the teaching method pursued by the teacher. In the case of teaching in the tradition of the progressive-education movement, the pupil is free to explore his environment and to discover classifications of objects and events. Through interactions with other pupils and with the teacher, some degree of conformity is assured between his system of categories and those used by the rest of the community. In such a situation the strategy adopted by the pupil is his choice alone. If he wishes to attain the concept of, say, "a half," because a task involves the use of this concept, he may clarify the meaning of this concept in many ways. One way is to equip himself with a set of cues concerning the attributes to look for by turning to a dictionary in which the definition lists such attributes. Dictionaries are essentially sources of cues that may be used in attaining concepts. Usually a dictionary definition is not sufficient to provide a well-developed concept, and the child must also have some practical use of the concept before he can use it effectively, and successfully classify exemplars that are presented to him.

In a more traditional educational framework a somewhat different procedure is involved. In such a framework the teacher controls to a great extent the strategy that the pupil is to follow in the attainment of a concept. She is likely to be in the position of deciding what exemplars to provide. If she is teaching the concept of "a half," she may decide to provide a set of exemplars using the midmorning cookies, dividing some in half and others in different fractions. Each exemplar might be presented to the class with the instructions that each child is to decide whether a cookie is or is not divided into halves. If the pupils do not catch on after the first few exemplars, the teacher may decide to give the children cues concerning the attribute to look for. She might, for example, point to the equal sections of a cookie that the children know is divided in half and ask them, "What can you tell me about these two pieces?" If this does not produce the desired effect, she may ask, "Are these pieces alike?"

This same teacher may also decide to press the pupils into adopting another strategy. She may have a number of different objects divided in various ways. By this procedure she is able to vary a number of different attributes of objects, as well as the attribute that is involved in the concept of a half. If a more complex concept is involved, requiring the identification of several attributes, the teacher must make some decision concerning the advisability of varying several attributes from exemplar to exemplar or of varying only one of the attributes so that the pupil can learn to distinguish between the critical and the noncritical attributes.

Second, a teacher can adjust the strategy of concept attainment to the ability level of the child. Clearly, some strategies require greater ability than others. If a teacher were to present materials in such a way and with such directions that a complex scanning strategy were called for, the duller children in a typical class might be quite baffled by the procedure. Learning situations that require the application of simple and straightforward strategies are obviously those that are suitable for children of limited ability. Teachers of the mentally handicapped have long had sufficient awareness of this problem to plan learning in such a way that only very simple strategies are pursued.

Concepts and Language Usage

The relationship of language to the development of concepts and to other aspects of behavior is extremely complex. No full account can be given of this relationship at the present time because it is still in the stage of early exploration. Two main attacks are evident on problems of language. On the one hand, there are the linguists who are evolving knowledge of the structure of language and the relationship of this structure to the communication of meaning. On the other, there are psychologists who are attempting to understand language as an aspect of behavior that, like other aspects of behavior, can be described as presenting some degree of lawfulness. The brief discussion here of language does not even touch on the work that the linguists have undertaken and makes only a brief and passing contact with psychological research on language.

That a close relationship exists between conceptual development and the development of language seems clear. There is considerable agreement that man's intellectual superiority over other animals is associated with the fact that he has capability in the use of language, but this does not mean that the development of concepts requires the use of language. First, primates and other animals show evidence of the development of concepts but do not show any linguistic skills. Even the chimpanzee, who shows considerable concept development by the time he reaches adult life, does not seem capable of acquiring more than a few words. Chimps in captivity have, after extended training, been able to learn to say "papa" and "mama" and a few other words which they learn to use with some appropriateness. The learning of a language for them presents much the same difficulties presented to a few humans, known as aphasics, who have lost the ability to use language. Here again is a relevant piece of evidence. Although the aphasic has lost the ability to use words, he may still show evidence of good utilization of concepts.

Another source of evidence is that a person in an experimental situation may attain a concept without knowing that he has attained it, let alone given it a name. Attaching a word to a concept so that it is conveniently labeled is not an essential part of the concept-attainment process.

Nonetheless, language is an important element in the use and manipulation of concepts and especially when the use involves a social setting. Language ensures that there will be a certain degree of uniformity of the concepts manifested by a community using the same language. Skinner (1958) refers to a verbal community, meaning a community that uses a common classification system in referring to events. If each person formed his own classification system, it would be as confusing as if each were to use his own language.

The relationship between concepts and language is a complicated one.

Although there is a correspondence between words used and the categories into which objects and events are classified, there is not a precise relationship of this kind. Words can exist that do not refer to any real category of objects or events that have ever been experienced. A person may speak, for example, of ghosts even though he has never seen a ghost and never expects to. On the other hand, the words that are used to denote colors quite clearly refer to categories of experience. The word *blue* refers to the category in which are included a great many of the several million distinct hues that have been separately catalogued. Although the belief is popularly held that nouns refer to "objects, places, or things," this is a naive conception of language. Words refer to internal conditions, which in turn are related to the external world.

Language also serves another important function in relation to the development of concepts. A child often brings to the teacher a new word he has encountered and seeks to find out its meaning. What has happened here is that the child has used a word as a cue to indicate to him that others have a concept he does not have. Many of the concepts that a child acquires are initiated through encountering new words that have meaning for others and for which the child then seeks to acquire meaning.

Language also permits the expression of the relationship among concepts. Education has to do far more than equip the pupil with the knowledge represented by each of a large number of concepts, for the pupil must also acquire a knowledge of certain concept relationships. Scientific knowledge, for example, is presented in books as a series of statements that express relationships between concepts. Thus the statement that "at constant volume the pressure of a gas is proportional to its absolute temperature" represents a relationship involving a number of different concepts that are linked together to form the statement of a scientific principle. The rules that determine how the words representing the various concepts can be linked together are referred to as the rules of syntax. However, the rules of syntax are not a sufficient basis for linking together words to produce propositions representing important truths. It is easy to string together words into a sentence which is perfectly correct in terms of the rules of syntax but which contains no truth whatsoever. Consider for example the statement: "Man is a blue bug eating fresh grass in a factory." No grammarian could find fault with it.

The Development of Cognitive Structures

The word *cognition* is derived from a Latin word meaning "knowing" and, hence, cognitive psychology is the psychology of knowing or the psychology of those processes by which an organism acquires knowledge of the environment. The term *cognitive structure* is widely used by psychologists, but does not seem to have any uniform meaning in current literature. In this book, an attempt will be made to define the term *cognitive structure*, though the definition must be reached by an indirect route.

Most knowledge, and particularly that included in a curriculum, has structure. It is not merely a collection of isolated facts or disconnected pieces of information. The information included in a body of knowledge is generally tied together in many different ways. Consider, for example, the knowledge represented by a limited area of history. The elements of such knowledge form a time sequence and are structured within a time dimension. They are also structured in other ways. The facts of history can be geographically structured, particularly in ages past when events occuring in one place did not influence events occuring in other places. Historical events can also be structured in terms of the way in which one historical event exerted an influence on subsequent historical events. There are many other structures that can be invoked to give form to historical knowledge. Thus, historical knowledge can be regarded as structured knowledge. The historian who has such knowledge must have within him some kind of structure that corresponds to the structure of the knowledge he possesses. Such an internal structure representing knowledge is referred to as a cognitive structure.

Such cognitive structures can be thought of as being strictly physiological structures that are assumed to exist even though one cannot directly observe their presence; but some psychologists prefer to think of cognitive structures as psychological events and processes of which one can have some direct awareness.

A cognitive structure may involve all kinds of relationships. The knowledge one may have of the location of various objects in one's environment has to be represented by a cognitive structure involving spatial relationships; but it may also involve time relationships, for the person knows that on an exploration he will encounter one object before he comes to another. School learning involves the development of cognitive structures, for knowledge must be acquired as an organized system of ideas (although teaching is sometimes more like a process of tossing a miscellaneous group of objects into a box). The acquisition of a concept involves the development of a cognitive structure in that it involves the acquisition of knowledge concerning the attributes that define the concept.

The difference between rote learning and meaningful learning resides largely in the extent to which they involve the development of a cognitive structure. Rote learning involves little or no development of a cognitive structure, but what is commonly referred to as meaningful learning does.

Reinforcement Approaches to a Theory of Verbal Behavior

A reinforcement view of learning, such as has been presented in the previous pages, appears to provide an adequate description of many of the simpler forms of learning such as are involved in the acquisition of many of the important manipulative skills, the use of language at its simpler levels, skills such as reading as it is learned in the lower grades, rote learning tasks such as are involved in the learning of spelling and number combinations, and a host of other achievements that are products of the school program. Many psychologists would take the position that although reinforcement plays a central role in learning at the simpler levels, it does not seem to provide an adequate foundation for understanding complex learning and, particularly, the more complex academic learnings that are basically verbal in form.

A few psychologists are optimistic that the simple principles of learning, such as have been presented in previous chapters, could well form a basis for understanding the acquisition of complex verbal learning. Skinner (1958) is one who has taken this point of view.

Skinner's interpretation of verbal behavior is that it is a form of instrumental behavior that results in the manipulation of the environment. It is shaped, he claims, by the same laws of learning that shape all other forms of instrumental behavior. The child who learns to say "please" to obtain a cookie has learned an instrumental act that has been promptly reinforced in the past by his being given the desired cookie. Skinner does not introduce the notion that the word *please* has meaning for the child, but rather, it is an effective form of goal-directed behavior. The word *please* then is a verbal operant. A thirsty two-year-old who says "water" expects that this word will produce the desired substance and, according to Skinner, is functioning in much the same way as a rat that presses a lever in order to obtain food. That the environment is rich in the reinforcements it provides for the linguistic efforts of the child cannot be denied. Within limits, a reinforcement concept of the development of language has high plausibility, particularly in the early stages.

Skinner classifies usage of speech not in terms of categories used by grammarians, such as nouns, adjectives, and so forth, but into categories representing the behavioral function that the particular usage serves. A brief discussion of two of the major categories of speech introduced by Skinner will serve to illustrate the kind of analysis of language he is attempting to make. These two categories he names the *mand* and the *tact*.

The term *mand* is derived from such words as *demand* or *command*

and represents a form of speech designed to produce a change in the environment. A young child who says to his mother, "Come," is using a mand that may have the effect of bringing his mother closer to him. "Give it to me," "Take it away," and "Put that down" are all mands. Sometimes the mand may be quite subtle in the way in which it manipulates the behavior of others. The student who comes to the counselor and says, "I am just not good at anything," is probably angling for the answer, "But that is not true; you are good at quite a few things." In this case the behavior of the student would be wrongly interpreted if the bare meanings of the words were taken at their face value. The student is almost certainly not attempting to inform the counselor of his incompetence. His statement is, rather, a verbal operant likely to produce a reassuring response from the counselor.

The *tact* is another major category of behavior within Skinner's classification system. The tact is a verbal behavior that directs attention toward an object in the environment. "What is this?", "What is happening here?", "I wonder how this works?", "Could this be fixed if this part were replaced?" are all tacts. The term *tact* is derived from the word *contact* and refers to a contact with the environment.

Skinner also assumes that there are a number of classes of subvocal behavior that are controlled by external stimuli. He assumes, for example, that a person reading a book makes subvocal responses that correspond to the words of the text. Skinner refers to these as *textual responses*. He makes a similar assumption about the behavior of the person who is listening to a lecture, and implies that there is some internal echo of the words that are heard. The subvocal responses in the latter case are referred to as *echoic responses*. However, these are behaviors that are assumed to occur and he has little or no evidence to support his position in this respect. As a matter of fact what little evidence there is suggests that the muscular responses involved in reading silently are quite different from those involved in talking aloud.

Skinner's book on verbal behavior is filled with delightful anecdotes told in a style that reflects his own habits of thinking. He has done little to follow up on any of his speculations with research, though some work has been begun by others. Although lack of research and supporting evidence is always damaging to a position, the main argument against his theory of behavior is that it is much too simple to account for verbal behavior.

Research on verbal behavior within the framework of reinforcement theory came, not from those most concerned with the development of reinforcement theory, but from those interested in the verbal processes involved in the treatment of disturbed and maladjusted persons.

Clinical psychology, and to a great extent psychiatry, is a verbal process whereby the therapist interacts with the client. Some schools of clinical thought hold that the person treating the patient should play a passive role and merely provide a congenial environment in which the patient can express his thoughts and ultimately achieve some reorganization of his thinking. Such a therapist might at times grunt or give a noncommittal "ummmmm" to indicate that he is aware of the client's problem, and he may also reflect back the client's thoughts, as when he says, "You feel, then, that your father does not understand you."

For a long time many clinicians have had the suspicion that the "noncommittal" comments of therapists are not as noncommittal as they may seem at first sight. There is the distinct possibility that they may function as reinforcers, and hence play a part in the shaping of the client's behavior in a way of which both the client and the therapist are quite unaware. The study of the effect of consistent patterns of such reinforcements is hence an extremely important area of study, and the results of such study could have profound effects on the practice of therapy in the future and on the practice of teachers who also attempt to influence verbal behavior with verbal reinforcements. The studies could also have profound effects on educational practice because they could indicate how the use of verbal reinforcements may have important effects on the shaping of pupil behavior, and even indicate the existence of effects of which the teacher may be quite unaware at the time.

Experimentation in this general area follows a definite pattern of techniques that have been developed over the years. Subjects on whom experiments are to be conducted are placed in the experimental situation, and given some task that requires them to speak. Many different tasks have been used. Sometimes the subjects are asked to tell a story, sometimes they are told that this is a counseling situation in which they can freely discuss their problems, and sometimes much more artificial situations are used. An example of the latter is an experiment in which the individuals involved are given a series of cards with verbs printed on them. In addition to the verbs are a series of pronouns: I, he, we, you, and they. These pronouns appear in a different order on each card. The subject must read the verb and then make a sentence that uses the verb and begins with one of the pronouns. In these tasks the experimenter reinforces a particular class of word whenever it is used by the subject. In the storytelling task he may reinforce all plural nouns. In the task involving the verbs and pronouns he may reinforce certain pronouns, such as *I* and *we*, but not any others. The expectation, according to reinforcement theory, is that the class of words reinforced will be used with increasing frequency.

The reinforcers used in such experiments have been many and diverse. Many use the familiar educational reinforcer "good." Others use variations such as "all right," "fine," and "right." Some use common expressions such as "mmm-hmm" or "uh-ha." Sometimes, in common with these strictly verbal reinforcers, they use such expressive acts as smiling, nodding the head, and leaning forward toward the speaker. The sounding of a buzzer or the flashing of a light, without the subject being given any instructions concerning the meaning of these, is also sometimes introduced as a reinforcer, though why these should function as reinforcers is hard to understand.

An excellent review of studies of verbal reinforcement is provided by Krasner (1958), whose interest, it should be noted, was primarily that of a clinical psychologist concerned with finding out the effect of the comments and gestures of the clinician on the verbal behavior of the patient. Our purpose here is to provide a much briefer overview of these studies, indicating the general nature of the conclusions to which they point. The reader must realize that in any group of studies in the behavioral sciences one does not find complete consistency. Some studies will stand out from the others because they lead to conclusions that are different from those drawn by the majority of investigators. Nevertheless, in the group of studies under consideration there is considerable consistency of results, though some of the later research has failed to demonstrate the phenomenon.

The results indicate that when subjects are given some verbal task to perform and are reinforced whenever they use a particular class of word (such as plural nouns), they tend to increase the frequency with which they use that class of word. When the experimenter switches to the reinforcement of a new class of words, then it is the new class of words the subject begins to use more frequently. For example, Verplanck (1955, a) was able to produce an increase in the rate at which his subjects used plural nouns by reinforcing these behaviors either by agreeing with the subject about his statement or by paraphrasing his statement. Later Wilson and Verplanck (1955, b) performed another experiment in which they reinforced plural nouns, travel words, adverbs, or words standing for living things. In this latter experiment the reinforcements were "mmm-hmm," "good," and the experimenter writing the word down. Incidentally, Verplanck has found in these studies that experienced experimenters must be used to administer the reinforcements, since inexperienced experimenters do not seem to produce changes in the frequency with which subjects use particular classes of words.

What happens when the experimenter stops reinforcing the particular class of words? The subjects behave according to expectation. When the reinforcement of particular classes of words ceases, extinction becomes apparent; and the words which were reinforced are used less and less frequently. One presumes that the speed of extinction will depend on the particular schedule of reinforcement used. With some schedules of reinforcement one would expect a slow rate of extinction, and the change in verbal behavior produced by reinforcement might be a permanent one.

The phenomenon is not so simple as might appear from the description of the over-all results given here. Ulrich (1962), for example, was unable to replicate the findings reported here, but his results may have been due to the fact that he used students as experimenters. One complicating factor that has important implications for education is that the prestige of the person giving the reinforcement has much to do with the results obtained. In one study by Verplanck (1955, b), the experimenters most successful in modifying the verbal behavior of the subjects were those who had prestige and were socially adept, while the least successful had the opposite characteristics. A similar finding is reported by Marion (1956), whose data indicated that subjects did not change their verbal behavior in response to reinforcement unless the experimenter was a person of relatively high status to the subject. Saying the word "good" is not enough. The word must be said by a person who has enough prestige to give the word some value as a reinforcer.

A point of interest is whether the individuals involved in such studies are aware of what is happening to them and of how their behavior is being changed. In most of the studies that have been undertaken in this area, the period of acquisition and extinction, if an extinction series is run, is followed by a brief question period. Often some kind of questionnaire is used. Questions commonly included, are "What do you think it was all about?" and "What do you think was the purpose of saying 'good'?" Care has to be used in asking such questions to ensure that the question itself does not suggest the answer.

The typical finding is that subjects are not aware of the purpose of the experiment. Although subjects may notice the reinforcer, they do not identify the relationship between the reinforcer and the class of words that are reinforced, and neither are they aware of any tendencies to increase the use of some words over others. A few subjects do recognize the relationship. Krasner (1958), in his review of the literature, comes to the conclusion that if all studies are taken together, then roughly 5 per cent of the subjects acquired some awareness of what was happening. Some subjects do not recognize the presence of the reinforcing stimulus. Oddly enough, there is little difference between the behavior of the subjects who notice the reinforcer and those who do not. Those who give no indication of having noticed it modify their verbal habits just as much as those who are apparently aware of it. Of course, nearly all the subjects have no idea that the reinforcer is provided *as* a reinforcer; to most it is just a peculiar whim of the experimenter. When asked about the possible purpose of the experiment, the subjects generally provide many suggestions, but these are typically remote from the actual purpose.

In at least one study by Verplanck (1955, a) the conditioning was carried out as part of a conversation in which the subjects had no idea that an experiment was being undertaken at all. In such a situation the subjects showed just the same conditioning as that manifested by persons who are the subjects of a similar experiment in the laboratory.

Psycholinguistics and Verbal Learning

Up to a point a reinforcement theory of development of verbal behavior accounts for observation and even has applications. Patients in mental hospitals who have long refused to engage in verbal behavior have reportedly, on occasion, been led to slowly increase the frequency of their verbal utterances through the judicious application of reinforcing events. However, conditions controlling the incidence of rather trivial communications may be far different from those that control verbal behavior in activities such as problem solving. Psychologists generally agree that more complicated theories are necessary. They point out that although the words *pink* and *rink* are physically very similar, they do, in fact, produce entirely different responses. A simple reinforcement theory would lead one to expect that similar stimuli would produce similar internal responses, but such is obviously not the case. The internal responses aroused by the stimuli and the subsequent actions have little to do with the physical characteristics of the words. What this means is that some internal process has to be assumed to occur that provides an analysis of the verbal stimuli. What the psychologist then tries to do is to invent the simplest internal mechanism he can that will account for the way in which individuals make an analysis of verbal stimuli. Osgood (1963) has reviewed attempts to suggest mechanisms that will account for our understanding of verbal stimuli, and has made suggestions of his own. He points out that psychologists have attempted to understand verbal behavior by introducing one more stage into the stimulus-response model of Skinner. The two-stage model assumes that a word can acquire meaning by being associated with a particular situation. For example, a little child falls and skins his knee. His mother says "hurt." Now the word will probably become associated with pain-producing situations. Osgood would describe events in this way: The child falls and receives a painful wound. The wound produces a set of responses in the child including visceral responses that are emotional in nature. Tears come to his eyes and he probably yells. At the same time he hears the word "hurt." The word has acquired the property of arousing these various reactions to a slight degree. On a subsequent occasion, when the word alone is heard, the various bodily reactions that are aroused by real bodily damage are aroused to a mild degree. The word may not make the child actually cry, but some reaction will occur. If he hears the word in the context of a story about somebody being seriously injured he may actually experience sinking feelings in his stomach, for the words have come to produce some of the responses the actual situation produces. The word becomes the *sign* for the particular situation it denotes. The internal responses produced by the sign are *mediating responses*.

In technical terms one can say that when the sign-to-be (the word *hurt*) occurs at the same time as another stimulus (the pain-producing situation which is called the *significate*) then the sign-to-be acquires the property of arousing a portion of the responses that the significate produces. Thus the word *hurt* acquires one form of meaning as it comes to arouse a part of the internal responses produced by an event that actually does hurt. Meaning, in this sense, is referred to as representational meaning. This concept of meaning is essentially similar to that of the fractional anticipatory goal response discussed earlier.

What the theory does is to introduce a stage between the incidence of the stimulus and the occurrence of some observable response in which the stimulus produces an internal response giving it *representational meaning*. In this way, words that are very different in their physical appearance on paper (words such as *hurt, pain,* and *injury*) can produce similar internal responses and hence similar representational meanings. Very different stimuli that occur at the time of a particular event can then acquire the same meaning by producing the same mediating processes.

Now the mediating processes produced by a particular word generally lead to some action. A child who has learned the meaning of the word *hurt* will respond appropriately when he hears the word directed at him. When he puts his hand out toward the hot stove, his mother says "hurt" and he withdraws his hand. The theory discussed here would interpret the events in this way.

The mother says "hurt." The sound of this word, through past learning, produces in the child internal responses similar to those that would occur in the presence of an actual injury, but to a lesser degree. These internal mediating processes lead to action on the part of the child, and he withdraws from the hot stove. Just as the internal mediating responses that occur when the child is hurt lead to withdrawal from the cause of injury, so too does the word *hurt* lead to similar mediating responses and similar withdrawal behavior.

Although the argument is convincing in terms of personal experience, there are difficulties in following it up through research. The mediating processes involved are obscure, and even the best laboratory instrument available does not permit them to be recorded. Research utilizing this two-stage model has used very indirect ways of studying the processes believed to be involved. The research methods cannot be described here, but some of the results seem to indicate that the model has value. A series of studies that make an indirect attack on the problem of the nature of representational meaning are found in Osgood *et al.* (1957).

Osgood also points out that the two-stage model that has just been described is still too simple to account for many important aspects of verbal behavior. For this reason he proposes a three-stage model that introduces an additional stage between the partial responses to the stimuli and the actions that result.

Alternative Approaches to the Problem of Meaning

Up to this point, consideration has been given to what has been referred to as representational meaning; but there is another sense in which a sign or word may be said to have meaning. Ask most people what they associate with the word *serendipity,* and they are likely to say that their mind is a blank; but give them the word *party,* and they can give all kinds of associations. The more meaningful the word, the more ideas are associated with it. Meaning that is reflected in the number of associations that are aroused is referred to as associational meaning to distinguish it from representational meaning. It is conceivable that a word could have a strongly developed representational meaning but a poorly developed associational meaning. For example, suppose that a person became involved in a serious accident and, just at the time of the accident, he heard somebody say the word *balou.* After the accident the sound of this word might well produce a sinking feeling in his stomach, a fact that would indicate that it had representational meaning; but the only idea that he might be able to associate with the word might be that of the accident.

The meaningfulness of a word or a single syllable in terms of association can be measured by a number of techniques that have been reviewed in a volume by Underwood and Schulz (1960). The initial work in this area was conducted with nonsense syllables, since psychologists had long used such syllables in experimental studies because they allegedly eliminated differences in familiarity, such as would characterize words. The typical syllable used is a three-letter combination consisting of a consonant-vowel-consonant, though syllables consisting of all consonants have been used. In Glaze's initial study (1928), subjects were presented syllables and were asked to indicate what they meant, if they meant anything at all. The percentage of subjects who had an association with the syllable was taken as a measure of the meaningfulness of the syllable. In a later study Hull (1933) asked subjects to indicate what each one of a number of syllables made them think of. Similar techniques have been used by other investigators. One variation of this technique is to ask the subject to write down all of the words a particular syllable brings to mind. Another approach is to find out the speed with which subjects obtain an association with a syllable. Another measure is the pronunciability of the syllable. Finally, Underwood points out that all of these measures are highly related and that they in turn are related to the frequency with which the syllables appear in the English language. His thesis is that the meaningfulness of a syllable is a product of the frequency with which the syllable has been experienced in the past. Hence, meaningfulness is considered to be a function of the extent to which the syllable has entered into association with words and concepts.

Once the meaningfulness of syllables had been measured, the way was opened for a series of experimental studies of the effect of meaningfulness on learning. Syllables can be used in a paired-associates technique, which has already been described (see page 23). Through the use of this technique the experimenter can find out the effect on learning of varying the meaningfulness of the stimulus and also of the meaningfulness of the response. This is much more than one is able to do in the study of learning situations in the classroom.

Underwood and Schulz distinguish two stages in the learning of paired associates. The first is the *response-learning* or the *response-recall* stage. The second is the *associative* or the *hook-up* stage. These can be illustrated by the behavior of the visitor to Mexico who is slowly learning a little Spanish. At first, when he goes to a restaurant, he knows what he wants but has no Spanish words (or responses) with which he can communicate to the waitress. As he acquires a Spanish vocabulary, he acquires many responses (Spanish words) that can be appropriately used in a restaurant. His problem then is to use suitable ones. He may want to order boiled eggs but is not sure which of several words to use. The responses have been acquired or learned, but they have not yet been hooked up or associated with appropriate situations.

In the response-learning stage, the responses emitted are, of course, those that are available, but the frequency of output depends on the frequency with which they have been presented to the learner. This statement is best explained by way of illustration. If a person is asked to re-spond to each one of a list of words with a single letter of the alphabet, he is more likely to give the commonly occurring letters of the alphabet than those that occur less frequently. Likewise, he is more likely to give common words than rare words if the task calls for giving words.

In the hook-up stage of learning, words and other components of complex learning come to be associated one with another. A new word may be learned on a single exposure, but long experience with its use in different contexts is necessary before it acquires any fullness of meaning. This additional learning, which goes on when the word is related to other words and the idea it represents is related to other ideas, represents the hook-up stage of learning.

The work of Underwood brings back into focus the importance of frequency (that is, amount of practice in terms of the number of repeti-tions) as a factor in learning. Frequency with which a response is re-peated has fallen into disrepute as a factor in learning since Edward L. Thorndike took the position that frequency was merely a condition that permitted other learning factors to operate. The work of Underwood indicates that the more frequently a response is made, the more likely it is to be an available response, and hence, the more likely it is to become attached to a new stimulus.

The Level of Difficulty of Verbal Material

One approach to the study of verbal learning is to measure the prop-erties of printed materials and to relate these to learning processes in-volving the materials.

The earliest measure of the difficulty of printed verbal material was derived from estimating the difficulty level of the words it contained. This sounds a simple matter but actually it is not. The usual practice has been to establish vocabulary difficulty by consulting a word count. The latter is a list of words, with a measure opposite each indicating how frequently the word occurs in certain printed sources. The basic data for a word count is derived by counting the number of times that different words appear in a selected sample of reading material. Such material commonly includes a sample from a widely read magazine, newspaper articles, best sellers, and other materials that are widely read. The use of measures of the difficulty of vocabulary is a reasonable procedure for establishing the difficulty level of reading material for adults. One can assume that adults will be most familiar with those words that appear most often in print and that, hence, reading material that contains these commonly occurring words will be easy reading material. However, vocabulary is not the only factor involved. The length of the sentences and the complexity of their structure is also important. Material may contain only simple words, but the sentence structure may be of such complexity that it is difficult to comprehend. Hence, a measure of reading difficulty has to include more than a measure of vocabulary level. That factors other than vocabulary are important is indicated in a study of Coleman (1962), who altered the sentence length of material. The original version and the repunctuated versions had average sentence lengths of 39, 23, and 15 words. The versions of the passages having shorter sentences were significantly more comprehensible than the version with the longest sentences.

Numerous different formulae have been developed for estimating the difficulty of reading material. A reading-difficulty formula usually combines a measure of the difficulty level of the vocabulary with a measure of the difficulty level of the sentence structure. A review of the area by Klare (1963) lists 21 different formulae, although probably only four or five of these are extensively used. The same review also provides evidence that the measure of reading difficulty is highly related to the judgments of experts concerning the difficulty of the passages. The formulae also provide a good prediction of the extent to which children of a particular age can read a set of passages and derive information from them. The evidence, taken as a whole, indicates that the formulae provide measures related to the ease or difficulty with which learners can master the passages.

Measures of reading difficulty based on word counts have limitations when the materials are to be read by children. The level of difficulty of a word, estimated by determining how frequently it occurs in print, is not a good estimate of the likelihood that the child will know its meaning. A better estimate of vocabulary difficulty is derived by determining what words children actually know.

Edgar Dale was the first to recognize that a word count is not a suitable measure of vocabulary difficulty in the case of children's reading materials. In order to remedy deficiencies in reading difficult formulae he obtained direct estimates of what words children knew or did not know and used these in the development of the Dale-Chall (1948) reading formula. Although Dale's early determination of the difficulty level of words for children was derived by presenting the words to 4th grade children and by asking which ones they recognized, some of his later work has involved more precise methods of measuring the familiarity of children with particular words.

Incidental Learning

A phenomenon of considerable interest and probably one of considerable importance is denoted by the term *incidental learning*. The phenomenon is generally defined in terms of the situations in which it occurs. In the typical defining situation, subjects are assigned a task to perform that may be anything from learning a set of nonsense syllables to solving a problem or playing a game of chess. The same persons are then later tested on the knowledge they have acquired about some aspect of the materials that were not relevant to undertaking the main task. For example, in a task involving the learning of nonsense syllables, the subjects may be tested later on the color of the ink used for printing particular syllables. They could also be tested on matters such as the size or color of the paper used or on any other incidental features. The number of different incidental and intentional learning tasks involved in such studies is large. Some psychologists have added confusion to the situation by defining incidental learning as learning occurring in a situation where there are *no* instructions to learn. Leo Postman does this in a long series of studies in which one subject is assigned the task of reading a set of nonsense syllables to another subject, who is instructed to learn them. The one who reads the syllables does not have a learner role. Later he is tested for his learning of the syllables. In the Postman studies, the person who reads the syllables is described as the incidental learner.

The results of research in this area show, as perhaps one might expect, that some incidental learning occurs in most situations. If one makes the assumption that the human learner has a limited capacity for receiving and storing information, then one would expect that the more rapidly the learning task is undertaken the more the learner will be occupied by the central task and the less will be the incidental learning. This is exactly what was found in a study by Fisher and Cook (1962) in which doubling the speed of presentation of the task the subjects were instructed to learn reduced the amount of incidental learning. Another interesting finding reported by Johnson and Thompson (1962) is that the higher the motivation of the subject to perform the assigned task, the less is the incidental learning. Perhaps again, this may reflect the fact that when the information-processing capacity of the learner is fully utilized by the task he is assigned, he is simply not capable of processing incidental information.

An interesting situation in which incidental learning may play an important role is found where children are working together on a problem in school. If a child is learning to perform a task by watching another, does he also tend to acquire some of the personality characteristics of the other child? Bandura and Huston (1961) undertook an experimental study of this problem. The characteristics of the child that was observed did, to some degree, rub off on the observer child, even though these characteristics had nothing to do with the task that was to be learned.

Complex Verbal Learning

The difficulties of studying problems of verbal learning are evident from the fact that the nonsense syllable was introduced into the laboratory by Ebbinghaus in order to avoid some of these difficulties. During the century that followed the appearance of Ebbinghaus' classic research, those who have studied human learning have generally preferred the nonsense syllable to meaningful words or connected discourse. Only in the last decade has research involving the latter class of material begun to thrive, though the nonsense syllable still remains one of the major tools of the laboratory psychologist. This means that research on complex verbal processes is still limited in quantity, primitive in technique, and lacking in results likely to have any great impact on education.

Although the learning of principles is one of the most important verbal learnings undertaken in schools, one can only speculate on how a learned principle may influence behavior.

Consider, for example, the classic demonstration by Judd (1908) that the learning of the principle of refraction enabled pupils throwing darts at an underwater object to adapt to changes in depth of the water. The pupils in the experimental group in such a demonstration learn a principle that later influences behavior. The principle involved may be learned in a number of different ways. It may be learned (1) as a rote learning task, (2) as a generalized description of the phenomenon of the apparent displacement of an underwater object viewed at an angle to the surface of the water, or (3) as a generalized description of a large number of different phenomena, all of which involve refraction. In the first case, no generalization from the learning of the principle to situations involving refraction may be expected. In the second case, the learning may be expected to influence behavior in situations involving objects below the surface of water. In the third case, the learning of the principle may be expected to influence behavior in a range of situations involving refraction. In the second case, what is learned becomes a mediating response influencing behavior in a limited class of situations; and in the third case, a great number of situations call forth the mediating mechanism.

In the third case, learning is likely to require that the individual have extensive contact with a wide range of situations involving the principle. Some learners may be capable of generalizing from a few instances but the majority will probably not. One presumes that the more capable learners in terms of intelligence-test scores will be those most capable of generalizing, but there is little evidence to support that contention.

Summary

1. Organisms have a limited capacity to utilize the vast amount of information provided by the environment. Through categorizing behavior they are able to reduce large numbers of objects or events to a relatively small number of categories.

2. Concept learning is a process of learning to group objects or events into categories. The pupil also learns to assign names to the categories that have been learned.

3. Concepts are commonly classified as conjunctive, disjunctive, and relational. Conjunctive concepts are generally the most easily learned; disjunctive concepts are typically the most difficult.

4. Laboratory research on concept learning has produced knowledge that can be used as a guide in planning concept learning in the classroom. The teacher would do well to present simplified examples of the category she is trying to teach the children to understand. In technical terms, this means that she should reduce the number of irrelevant attributes in the early stages of learning. She should also try to make the defining attributes as identifiable as possible. Generally, concepts are learned most easily in an order consistent with the structure of the subject-matter. In addition, suitable sequences of positive and negative instances can contribute to the efficiency of the learning situation.

5. The learning of concepts is closely tied to the acquisition of language skills, although concepts can be acquired without the learning of language. However, as language is mastered, the child acquires the means of expressing relationships among concepts. Syntax is a set of rules applied in stating relationships among concepts.

6. The acquisition of knowledge, and the concepts that knowledge implies, results in the development of internal structures corresponding to the structure of knowledge. Such internal structures are referred to as cognitive structures. Meaningful learning is learning that results in the development of cognitive structures.

7. Several different accounts have been given of the development of language and language usage in young children. Skinner has taken the position that language development and usage can be considered to be the result of reinforcement learning. For Skinner, language is an instrument for manipulating the environment. Some research on the reinforcement of verbal responses gives some support to the Skinner position.

Other psychologists regard the concept of reinforcement as inadequate for understanding the development of language. In particular, they note that Skinner does not need any concept corresponding to meaning in his concept of language. Osgood has proposed a model of language in which words acquire what he terms representational meaning. Another concept of meaning that has had a long history is associational meaning. A word has associational meaning insofar as it is associated with other words or ideas.

6

Motivation

M EN HAVE long believed that a concept such as motivation has to be introduced in order to understand behavior. Philosophers, psychologists and biologists have reflected on this problem and have conducted related experiments; but the results of their labors have not led to a single accepted conception of the nature of motivation. This area of inquiry still remains a center for controversy and one from which several competing theories of motivation have emerged. In the area of motivation, none of the major issues have been settled, despite the existence of a vast body of experimental information. To explore in greater detail the research that has been undertaken the reader is referred to Cofer and Appley (1964), a comprehensive review based on nearly three thousand references.

First, consider some of the observations of behavior that have led to the development of the concept of motivation. One is that organisms differ in the vigor with which they approach particular situations, and the same organism approaches the same situation with a different degree of vigor on different occasions. Some children will play baseball with all the energy they can muster; others can hardly be induced to come near the diamond. A child who usually plays the game energetically may, when he is tired, be listless and slow during practice. Another observation of importance is that behavior has direction. Behavior is not just a series of unrelated items, but rather it forms sequences that terminate when particular events happen. A hungry animal goes foraging for food and continues to forage until food is found. Such sequences of behavior suggest that direction is provided by the needs of the organism. Certainly the particular sequences manifested are often related to bodily needs for food and water. Another observation is that certain objects have the property, under some circumstances, of arousing behavior. Food objects produce behavior in most animals, but a much wider range of objects can arouse the behavior of humans. Some objects are fairly specific to particular humans or groups of humans. A work of art will produce great excitement in one individual but will hardly attract the attention of another.

From observations such as these has sprung the concept of motivation—a somewhat vague concept, but one that is generally implied to have two components. On the one hand, motives are said to be energizing; and on the other, they are said to have the property of giving behavior direction. By way of illustration, hunger generally produces restless behavior in the adult human, but hunger also gives some direction to behavior in that it becomes directed toward food objects or the behavior shows a heightened sensitivity to food objects. Energizing behavior can sometimes take place without the behavior showing any directional properties. The infant that cries when a diaper pin is sticking him has been energized, but the behavior lacks any clear directional properties.

Motivation as Arousal

Although the concept of arousal will be defined in greater detail in the chapter on the nervous system, a brief discussion of the concept is appropriate in a chapter on motivation. An organism is in a state of arousal if it shows a relatively high degree of activity and a high level of responsiveness to outside stimuli. In sleep, the level of arousal is at a minimum. During periods of excitement the level of arousal is high. Excessively high levels of arousal and excessively low levels are unfavorable for learning. Moderate levels seem necessary for effective learning to take place. A similar concept of an optimum level of motivation is implicit in other theories of motivation. Excessive hunger in a rat may interfere with its ability to learn a task, such as running a maze. In a series of studies by Spence (1956) and his associates, the data has tended to show that, as the level of anxiety increases, the rate of learning with complex tasks declines; the learning of simple tasks is much less affected by the change. High levels of motivation make available a large number of alternative responses to a problem situation, and these in turn interfere with the learning of the correct response. Although most such studies have been undertaken in laboratory situations with learning tasks that appear to be only remotely related to learning in everyday situations, the facts do fit common observation fairly well. Everyone is familiar with the person who fails primarily because he is too strongly motivated to succeed. Such a person is exemplified by many new persons on the job whose bursting enthusiasm results in a bull-in-a-china-shop performance. The child who is overconcerned with success in school may plunge ahead in his work before he fully understands what to do, and may complete an assignment before he realizes that he has done it incorrectly. The overenthusiastic teacher, determined to show that he is the best teacher in the school, may expect so much of his pupils that they are overwhelmed and fail to accomplish as much as they would have accomplished under calmer and better-organized learning conditions. An extreme case of high arousal, in which the resulting effect is shown in thoroughly disorganized behavior, is seen in the case of the mental patient known as a manic. Such a patient shows extremely high activity and produces wild plans, none of which are ever brought to fulfillment. The arousal level of the manic is too high for effective action.

Similar problems, produced by a high state of arousal, are presented by children who are commonly referred to as brain-damaged children. The supposition is that such children have suffered middle brain damage at birth through the rupture of small blood vessels in that region. There is considerable difficulty involved in demonstrating that children who show this high state of arousal together with a number of other symptoms are brain-damaged children, but this is a supposition held by many authorities in the field.

These so-called brain-damaged children are typified by high distractibility, which makes it difficult for them to undertake any systematic learning. Such a child who is working with a teacher may rush to the window the first time a vehicle passes down the street. Almost anything else may distract him from the learning task that the teacher presents him. Learning is further impeded by the fact that many such children also have difficulty with perception. For example, they may have the greatest difficulty in perceiving the number 6 as a definite shape that differentiates it from other numbers.

One way of handling such children, so that conditions become more favorable to learning, is to attempt to lower the level of arousal by lowering the amount of stimulation provided by the environment. This is the opposite of what is done in the case of the normal child, who is generally placed in a highly stimulating environment in order to raise the arousal level. Thus it is common in a modern classroom for many objects of interest to be laid out on tables for the children to examine. A science table is one of the common exhibits in a modern well-run classroom. One purpose of such materials is to raise the level of arousal and to keep the children actively learning about a variety of objects in their surroundings. Group activities may also serve the same purpose.

In the case of the child suspected of brain damage, the reverse procedure is undertaken. The problem here is not to raise the level of arousal, but to lower it. This is done by reducing the stimulation provided by the environment.

Epps, McCammon, and Simmons (1958), who have attempted to bring together current knowledge concerning the education of children who have had various kinds of brain damage, discuss the education of such children in the following terms:

The brain-injured child who enters a school program for the first time may be very distractable, hyperactive and destructive. Even if he is not physically active, it is likely that he has trouble in attending to one thing for very long. In order to focus the child's attention on one thing at a time, it is necessary to reduce drastically the stimuli from the room. The glass in the lower window sashes may be painted white to make them opaque. Only materials in use at the moment should be in sight; all others should be out of reach if not out of sight. For the young mentally deficient child it might be necessary to have the room bare, including the walls, with the exception of a chair for each child and a large table around which the children can sit. This may seem odd to those that are accustomed to thinking of much individual space for the brain-injured child, but the separate work space is a later step for older or better socialized children who are motivated to learn. In the earliest stage, the main object is to give the children a group feeling of relatedness to others.

There are also many children who do not have other symptoms of brain damage, but who show excessive activity and are classroom problems on this account. No rigid rules can be set up concerning the way in which these children should be handled. Most of the problems of some of them can be solved by providing freedom of movement and not expecting long periods of concentration. Although medication may solve the learning difficulties that they produce in others by keeping them quiet, such treatment probably may not facilitate their own learning.

The Drive Concept of Motivation

Most of the research that has been undertaken on motivation has involved studies with subhuman organisms and with behavior related to eating and drinking. In recent years a concentrated effort has also been made to study mating behavior. The pattern of research has been vastly influenced by the basic observation that deprivation of food or water generally results in an increased level of activity which persists until food or water are reached. Such a phenomenon, familiar to the owner of almost any pet, cannot necessarily be accounted for in terms of a simple mechanism. Indeed, there has long been controversy concerning what the basic underlying mechanism can be. The popular account of the phenomenon is that the animal deprived of food becomes hungry and is thus motivated to search for consumable objects, but such an explanation presents many difficulties. One obvious flaw is presented by the familiar fact that a caged animal that has no opportunity for searching for consumables still shows heightened activity as it becomes more food-deprived. Psychologists who have long studied this sequence of behavior under laboratory conditions have evolved other accounts of the mechanism. The most widely held of these is that deprivation produces an imbalance in the body chemistry which, in turn, leads to an energizing condition referred to as *drive*, which results in activity until the imbalance is restored through the ingestion of food. This statement introduces the theoretical concept of *drive*. It is called a theoretical concept because there is no direct way of observing a drive; all that can be done is to observe the condition that precedes it—namely, deprivation—and what is believed to be the consequence of it—namely, activity. Some psychologists have taken the position that deprivations have the effect of providing strong sources of internal stimulation and that it is these strong stimuli that function as drives. This is the stimulus conception of drive.

The theory as it has been stated does not assume that the drive directs behavior, but only that it energizes behavior. One can, of course, devise experiments to determine whether the drive condition resulting from food deprivation directs the behavior of the rat more toward food than toward water and hence to establish whether the drive only energizes behavior or whether it also gives direction to behavior.

Such a theory of motivation has been extended to cover other conditions in which the equilibrium of the body is disturbed. Such a theory is based on the concept of motivation.

Homeostatic Theory of Drives

The drive theory developed up to this point involves the concept of homeostasis, which is simply the idea that an organism will act in such a way that its normal physiological balance is maintained or restored. Any event within or without the organism that disturbs normal physiological conditions results in activity of the organism that continues until the physiological balance is restored. If the temperature of the environment falls, the normal temperature of the warm-blooded organism tends to fall also. The organism will become active in various ways. It may shiver, which is an activity that is effective in raising body temperature. It may become restless and remain so until it finds shelter in which the normal body temperature can be restored. Hunger produces a similar restlessness in both infant and adult. The adult has learned to go to the refrigerator when this occurs, but the young child may merely appear to be restless and irritable. Sometimes the adult may not recognize that his restlessness is a result of physiological disturbance stemming from deprivation of food. He may wake in the middle of the night and toss on his bed for hours wondering why he cannot sleep. Then, in the early hours of the morning, he may suddenly recall that he had only the most meager dinner the night before. He rises, satisfies his hunger, and then falls into a deep sleep which is not disturbed even by the sound of the alarm clock.

Chemical imbalances do not generally produce unlearned "goal-directed" activities that restore normal tissue conditions. A baby in the first few weeks of life does not cry for its bottle (though its mother insists that this is so). The baby goes through a cycle of activity-inactivity and only slowly learns that certain discomforts are removed by the intake of food. Such learning is never complete. Restlessness resulting from hunger is generally recognized only if it occurs when feeding is to be normally expected. At other times the reasons for the restlessness remain unrecognized.

Directional Properties of Drives

Although most people assume that an animal knows whether it is hungry or whether it is thirsty, experimental findings do not support this common-sense belief. In one of the earliest studies of the capability of an animal to discriminate hunger from thirst, Hull (1943) had considerable difficulty in teaching animals to make such a discrimination. The animals did eventually learn, but only after a prolonged series of learning trials that must have involved both a frustrated experimenter and frustrated rats. Later studies involving improved training techniques, resulted in the animals learning the discrimination much more rapidly. A more recent study by Bailey (1955) has also shown that rats cannot only learn to discriminate hunger from thirst but can, in each case, learn to discriminate satiation from deprivation. Research also shows that, consistent with human experience, extreme states of hunger and thirst are much more readily identified than those involving smaller amounts of deprivation. Perhaps it is hardly surprising that animals do not learn the discriminations readily for, in their natural state, survival depends on eating when food is available and on drinking when water is available. Something is known about the physiological mechanism involved. Midbrain centers are activated by the conditions of hunger and thirst. If the thirst center is stimulated in an animal eating food, the animal will go to the water trough. If the same animal is stimulated in the hunger-arousing area, it continues to eat.

Psychologists who have studied the complex motivations of human subjects have long been impressed with the inability of the individual to identify the factors that are energizing his behavior. This is hardly surprising when even the simpler sources of drive are not readily identified.

The mechanism involved in the raised level of activity that accompanies food deprivation is complex. Although the older theories took the position that the contractions of the stomach that accompany hunger were the main sources of the activity, possibly through the contractions producing pain-like sensations, Cofer and Appley (1964) cite evidence that there are at least two centers in the brain that respond to deprivation of food and satiation following feeding. The mechanism is undoubtedly complex.

One can speak of deprivation producing a generalized state of drive regardless of whether it involves deprivation of food or water, or warmth, or whatever else. Such a statement does not imply that the mechanism involved in each case is the same, for clearly it is not; and the mechanisms that lead to an increased level of activity are numerous. Although there is diversity of mechanisms, Hebb (1956), Bindra (1959), and many other psychologists take the position that there is little point in discussing separate and distinct energizing effects such as a hunger drive, a thirst drive, and so forth. At any time, the activity level of a complex living creature is influenced by many different sources, and it is meaningful to talk only of the general level or drive that is operating.

The common sources of chemical imbalance in the body are those related to deprivation from food or water, excessively high or excessively low temperatures, and pain. The latter condition, pain, may not fall into quite the same category, but many consider it a similar kind of tissue disturbance. When any of these conditions arouse activity, it is common to say that a drive is operating; but this is only a shorthand way of saying that there is some disturbed tissue condition and that it is resulting in activity.

At one time it was thought that the inborn responses to painful stimuli were withdrawal responses, but this does not seem to be the case at all. A particularly interesting study in this connection has been run by Melzack and Scott (1957), who raised dogs from a very young age to maturity in cages that were so constructed that the dogs were prevented from having any painful or unpleasant experiences. When these dogs were fully grown, their behavior was compared with that of twelve control dogs which had been derived from the same litters as the experimental dogs but which had been reared in a normal environment. The experimental dogs showed little tendency to withdraw from pain-producing objects and, indeed, might come into contact with them again and again without showing the development of an avoidance response at all. Apparently, avoidance responses develop very slowly and seem to require *learning* for their development; and this in turn requires a large number of exposures. Pain-producing stimuli generate activity, but this is the limit to which they can be said to produce or maintain activity, at least in the first stages.

The relationship of the external factors to the internal factors in motivation is complex. Hull (1952) and later Spence (1956) pointed out that a goal object, such as food, acquires motivational value if an animal comes to anticipate its presence in a particular location. The mechanism involved is the fractional anticipatory goal response. In the case of an animal that has learned that food is awaiting at the end of a straight-alley maze, the various features of the alley have acquired the property of arousing responses related to feeding such as salivation, licking the lips, and so forth. These responses are, themselves, sources of internal stimulation. The running response becomes conditioned to these internal stimuli and, thus, the stimuli associated with the alley acquire the property of indirectly energizing the running response. The fact that physical characteristics of the environment can acquire the property of energizing behavior must be kept in mind in reading the following section. When one finds that some particular characteristic of the environment has energizing properties, one is tempted to assume that this is *not* a consequence of learning. Such an assumption is dangerous unless it can be substantiated.

Primary and Secondary Drives

Those whose thinking about motivation began with the homeostatic concept recognized that human motivation could not be described in terms of basic drives alone. Indeed, even the behavior of the lower organisms is of such complex nature that motivational concepts other than those provided by the concept of basic homeostatic drives had to be introduced. The latter were described as "primary drives"; the additional elements that had to be introduced were described as "secondary drives" or motives. These secondary drives or motives were assumed to be learned in much the same way as the various skills that constitute the repertoire of the mature organism.

In drive-reduction learning theory the basic source of motivation has been internal stimuli associated with deprivation. Deprivation of food is postulated to result in stimuli which in turn result in activity. When food is ingested, the primary source of stimulation is reduced or eliminated, and the activity of the organism ceases. Through conditioning, it is claimed, stimuli other than those that originally aroused activity come to function as initiators and maintainers of activity. These are referred to as secondary drives. The smell of food is thus believed to function as a substitute for the internal stimulation resulting from deprivation. The taking of food into the mouth may be sufficient to reduce this secondary drive. According to this type of theory, whatever stimulus happens to be operating at the time the primary drive is operating acquires the property of functioning as a drive. Repetition is necessary if the drive is to acquire any strength. Secondary drives can also be extinguished.

The difficulties of maintaining a theory of primary and secondary reinforcement, with the latter derived from the former by conditioning, must be discussed. The phenomenon is the well-established one of stimulus substitution, but this does not seem to assist in any way in overcoming the difficulties involved.

First there is a real question as to whether situations in which primary drives are directly and clearly operating can be actually identified. Suppose that a hungry animal is learning to escape from a puzzle box. The animal is motivated by food deprivation and, on escaping, consumes the small quantity of food provided, which functions as a reinforcer. If the food is to function as a primary reinforcer, drive-reduction theory suggests that it must reduce the strength of the primary drive. This it can do only after it has been swallowed and begins to enter the blood stream, but this takes time. Since reinforcers appear to function effectively if they have a close temporal proximity to the movement that is to be reinforced, it is highly doubtful whether the reduction of the primary drive can occur in a sufficiently short time after the movement to be reinforced to be in any way effective. In order to overcome this difficulty, it is commonly proposed that in most, if not all, experiments involving hunger, only secondary reinforcers are operating. The smell of the food or the sensations produced by the food in the mouth have secondary reinforcing effects. These secondary reinforcers form a link in a chain of events that ultimately leads to the satisfaction of the primary drive through the ingestion of the food. Each one of the links in this chain may be postulated to be a secondary reinforcer through its relationship to the events that follow. A gradient of reinforcement is thus set up, with those events nearest to the primary drive reduction providing the greatest reinforcement and those farthest away, in general, providing the weakest reinforcement. Unless such a gradient of reinforcement is postulated, it hardly seems possible to account for the reinforcing effect of food in typical animal experiments.

Second, there is the obstinate fact that laboratory attempts to develop secondary drives have not generally been able to produce secondary drives that simulate closely those that operate in daily life. Many experiments have been undertaken to demonstrate that stimuli can acquire motivating properties; two of the most colorful and well-known of these were published over a quarter of a century ago. In the mid-thirties, Wolfe (1936) and Cowles (1937) demonstrated that poker chips could acquire much the same reinforcing value for chimpanzees as money has for man.

In these studies the first step was to teach a chimpanzee to place a chip in a slot in order to obtain a grape. Once this had been done, the tokens could be used to reinforce other aspects of the behavior of the chimpanzees. The chimps would learn ways in which the tokens could be obtained and would, to some extent, hoard the tokens for later use. Insofar as they showed hoarding behavior and the capacity to work for the tokens, one can speak of the development of a secondary drive. Secondary drives thus produced appear to be weak and transient in character. The development of secondary drives may account for the fact that eating behavior will result in the reinforcement of responses in learning situations with animals; even though the food reduces the primary drive too late to function directly as a reinforcer of the response to be learned, the secondary reinforcers in the situation perform this important function. These secondary reinforcers continue to be effective, because they are frequently strengthened by their association with the reduction of the primary drive through a continuous chain of events. Without such strengthening of the secondary reinforcer, it would, presumably, become rapidly extinguished, just as laboratory-produced secondary reinforcers are rapidly extinguished. The theory of the operation of secondary drives supposes that there is frequent reinforcement of the secondary drives, but we do not know at this time whether this is so.

Most attempts to produce stable secondary drives, and hence secondary reinforcers, have not been particularly successful; the reason may be primarily the lack of adequate experimental technique. This point is brought out by Mowrer (1960, a), who reports that through the use of procedures similar to those used in partial-reinforcement schedules, advanced students in his laboratory have been able to develop secondary reinforcers that are virtually inextinguishable. In the cases cited by Mowrer the secondary reinforcer was the sound of a buzzer, which had been associated in rats with the satisfaction of thirst. Such a reinforcer could then be used to produce and maintain bar-pressing behavior in the rats, and it continued to function as a reinforcer after long periods during which it was never paired with thirst satisfaction.

The homeostatic theory of primary drives, which has been considered in the previous paragraphs, had certain merits that must not be overlooked. One of these is the fact that drives were considered as initiators of action, and that in this respect they functioned as stimuli that produced activity in the nervous system, which in turn resulted in muscular activity. This conceptual formulation of the operation of primary drives, with the drive operating as a special stimulus, was a considerable advance over earlier theories of motivation, which contained within them a strong element of mysticism.

External Components of Drives

Although homeostatic drives have the effect of increasing activity, the phenomenon is not a simple one. Campbell and Sheffield (1953) shattered all illusions that the phenomenon might be a simple one when they placed rats in a box in a darkened soundproofed room, and first allowed them to eat freely for four days and then starved them for three. A fan provided a noise to mask any other noise that might occur. The box was so arranged that any movement of the rat could be automatically recorded. Once a day the light was turned on and the masking fan turned off. Campbell and Sheffield noted little increase in activity during the period of food deprivation. However, the turning on of the light and the turning off of the fan, resulted in an increase in activity both during the period when the rats were being fed and while they were being starved; but during starvation the increase in level of activity resulting from external stimulation was greater.

The results of the latter experiment imply that the rats during food deprivation do not show an increase in level of activity when the level of external stimulation is low, but they do show an increased sensitivity to respond to external stimuli. This is why, when the light goes on, the animals show more activity if they are hungry than if they are satiated. The experiment points to the importance of environmental factors in the operation of drives. It also raises questions concerning the role of external stimuli in energizing behavior. If homeostatic drives are simply strong stimuli that raise the level of activity, then some external stimuli may be expected to have similar properties. To this problem we now turn our attention.

Motivating Effects of External Stimuli

The layman's conception of motivation is that it is a force internal to the organism, and the drive conception of motivation which has been considered here is generally consistent with that point of view. However, much evidence suggests that external factors as well as internal are responsible for motivating behavior. The evidence that a drive state resulting from hunger does not raise the level of activity, but raises sensitivity to stimuli, is one such item of evidence suggesting that external as well as internal factors are contributors; but there are many other sources of evidence that also indicate that external factors can play a crucial role.

Psychologists have long reported the observation that animals show exploratory and watchful behavior, particularly when the circumstances in the environment are novel. As far back as 1930, Nissen made the observation that rats would even cross an electrified grid if the other side contained a novel environment. This kind of behavior in animals received passing reference in the literature that was published during the twenty years following his observation. During these years, emphasis was placed on the development of a drive theory involving mainly internal factors; and with the desirability of maintaining theory as simple as possible, external factors were neglected. But in the early fifties, voices were raised against the narrowness of a doctrine that proposed that all motives were based on a very limited number of basic drives that were related to physiological needs. Harlow was one of the first to rebel against such a narrow concept of motivation, pointing out that animals after having had their basic needs satisfied do not typically lie down and go to sleep when placed in a maze; but rather they move around, stand on their hind legs and sniff the top cover, and perform innumerable behaviors that can be collectively described as exploration behaviors. In order to account for such behaviors, an exploratory drive has been postulated; but the important and verifiable fact is that the behavior can be controlled by the nature of the stimuli presented. In a classic experiment, Berlyne (1950) was able to demonstrate that, when various objects were introduced into a box in which the rats spent time, the rats spent more time in the vicinity of the novel objects than in the vicinity of objects with which they were familiar. The novel objects aroused attentive behavior and, to some extent, approach behavior. The biologist would certainly expect such behavior, for survival in the wild state is highly dependent on the organism responding to novel objects, though not necessarily by approaching them. In this connection an interesting observation was made by Barnett (1958) to the effect that wild rats, unlike laboratory albino rats, did not explore novel objects that were introduced into their regular habitat, but showed fear responses. Despite this evidence there seems no doubt that both wild and albino rats are highly attentive to novel objects, even though the result is approach behavior in the one and avoidance behavior in the other.

Although research has established a considerable amount of empirical information related to the effects of novelty on behavior, the mechanism involved remains relatively obscure. Writers of a decade or more ago took the position that complex organisms had a tendency to explore their environment, a tendency commonly referred to as an exploratory drive. Such a tendency would have survival value in that the organism that explored would be more likely to learn the location of food and water than the one that remained immobile except when hungry or thirsty. Such an explanation has a certain attractiveness to it, but it has little scientific value. To propose an exploratory drive adds little to the empirically established fact that animals explore their environment and pay special attention to novel objects and events.

Another explanation is that when the input of stimulation or the amount of environmental change is reduced, equilibrium of the organism is disturbed. The resulting activity—exploratory behavior—restores equilibrium by increasing the input of stimulation. Berlyne (1960), elaborating on this theory, and suggested that lack of a changing environment is energizing. The internal unbalancing effect of reducing external sources of stimulation is dramatically demonstrated in studies in which severe reductions are made in the input of sensory information. When this happens to a human subject, severe disorganization results.

The matter is of such central interest to our knowledge of motivation that we will consider the general nature of the research techniques used to deprive a person of sensory experience. One technique has been to place him in a soundproof room so that most auditory stimuli, except those produced by his own body, are eliminated. Visual stimuli are then eliminated by blindfolding him. His arms are then placed inside cylinders, which are so constructed that he cannot touch any object. Deprivation is, of course, not complete. The person is still able to produce some tactile and pressure sensations simply by moving his body, but what remains is small compared with the ordinary sensory inputs of the body. Under such conditions, a person rapidly becomes very confused, and some even begin to have hallucinations. Subjects exposed to this kind of a situation rapidly find it quite intolerable and insist on being withdrawn from it. Much of the reputed discomforts of solitary confinement are presumably derived from the decrease in sensory input and the resulting disturbing effect on the nervous system. The latter seems to be a reasonable speculation.

A way in which even greater deprivation of sensory inputs can be achieved is by immersing the person in a tank of water after he has been placed in a diving suit. The uniform pressure of the water on the outside of the diving suit will cause the sense organs in the skin to adapt and eventually reach the point where they no longer transmit sensory impulses to the central nervous system. Here again, it is found that the situation rapidly becomes intolerable, and the subject has great need to escape.

Bexton, Heron, and Scott (1954) paid college students to lie on a bed in a lighted cubicle for twenty-four hours a day, except for time spent in the ingestion of food or the excretion of waste. Sounds were kept at a minimum. Visual inputs were controlled by goggles. Cardboard tubes on the arms partially prevented inputs through the sense of touch. Under such conditions problem-solving skills and perceptual skills deteriorated, and emotional disturbances appeared. Whether this impairment is a result of a lack of sensory input or a lack of variation in the input is difficult to determine. There can be no doubt that real and deep-seated changes are produced by such situations, however one may interpret them. This is well brought out in a further study by Heron (1957), who demonstrated that similar conditions produced changes in the pattern of electrical currents in the brain.

Another approach to the study of this problem is to investigate the extent to which living organisms can be reinforced by stimulation of various kinds. In a series of studies Olds (1958, 1959) has shown that rats will learn many of the tasks that rats are commonly trained to do in the laboratory when the only reward is that of having the opportunity to press a lever. In another approach to this problem, Butler (1953) was successful in training rhesus monkeys to discriminate colored cards when the only reinforcement was the opportunity to look out of the box through a window for thirty seconds. The box, which has since been named a Butler box, is constructed so that the monkey can see outside only when a small door is opened. In a further experiment, Montgomery and Segall (1956) showed that the opportunity to explore a large maze could be an effective reinforcer.

An interesting interpretation of the relationship between behavior and environmental factors which does not introduce the concept of restoring equilibrium has been proposed by Woodworth (1958) in what he refers to as his behavior primacy theory. This theory, in Woodworth's own words, is that "the direction of receptive and motor activity towards the environment is the fundamental tendency of animal and human behavior and that it is the all-pervasive primary motivation of behavior" (pp. 124–125). Woodworth points out that behavior shows a continuous tendency to act on the environment. Some of this behavior is playful, such as is engaged in by young animals. Other behavior is highly organized and directed toward a definite goal that will establish a new relationship between the behaving organism and its environment. Woodworth points out that it is hardly reasonable to assume that all incidental behavior represents the primary drive to deal with the environment but that large-scale purposive activities are based on this primary drive.

Complex Motivation Involving Both Internal and External Energizing and Direction-Giving Events

It has long been recognized that individuals differ in the situations that arouse in them activity and in the situations they seek out for themselves. One person becomes highly active when given the opportunity to engage in athletics; another is aroused by the opportunity to engage in commerce or trade; still others are sparked by the chance to engage in social leadership. Generally, those who are energized by particular conditions or events seek out those same conditions or events when the environment does not provide them. The person who is energized by social activities calling for leadership, and who moves to a new community, will rapidly find clubs or other organizations where leadership can be exercised. That the energizing and direction-giving properties of such situations is learned cannot be denied, although the learning mechanism is not clearly understood at this time. One theory has already been considered: that the energizing properties of these situations is acquired through having been coupled with primary drives. Another theory, the affect theory, will be considered in the next section.

Another fact that must be introduced at this time is that individuals tend to seek out those situations to which they have been typically exposed. For most people there exists a set of environmental circumstances that they have typically encountered in the past and which they will tend to seek out when they are withdrawn. The person who spends most of his day reading becomes restless when placed in a situation where ordinary reading materials are absent. Under such circumstances he may begin to read an old newspaper spread on the floor, material he would never attend to in the course of his ordinary activities. The man who has spent a lifetime in business retires; but when he is no longer confronted with all of the activities that have engaged him for a lifetime, only misery results.

Observations such as these lead again to an equilibrium type of motivation theory. This concept of motivation has been elaborated upon by Helson (1964), whose position is that although stimuli in general are likely to have energizing properties, the extent to which they do depends on the extent to which they are above or below the usual level encountered under the particular circumstances. Thus, for a man typically earning two dollars an hour, an offer of three dollars an hour to do a particular job is highly motivating. He may also be highly energized to find another job if his employer tells him that his pay is to be cut to a dollar and a half an hour. In the latter case he will probably be sufficiently energized to go out and look for another job where the original level will be restored. This level, in terms of which such events are judged, is referred to by Helson as the *adaptation level* (he defines it in more precise terms than these). In fairness to Helson, one must say at this point that his theory of motivation is much more complex than is indicated in this paragraph. The theory does imply that external stimuli that have energizing effects on behavior may operate in much the same way as internal conditions; both may activate behavior through the existence of a disequilibrium with the activity continuing until equilibrium is restored.

Observation supports the contention that as the individual grows, behavior becomes activated by only certain kinds of situations or sources of stimulation. Observation also supports the contention that individuals differ greatly in the nature of the situations that arouse them and which they seek out in order to be aroused. One person is challenged by a mountain; another is challenged by an argument. Why such differences exist in the characteristics of the situation that produce arousal is not clear at this time

When behavior is aroused by a particular class of situations, it is customary to say that the individual is characterized by a need with respect to some aspect of those situations. Thus, if a person is aroused by situations that require a high degree of skill for their mastery, through custom we would say that the individual is characterized by a high need for achievement. The person will not only be aroused by such situations, but will also seek out such situations because of the value they have for him.

Individuals differ in the situations that arouse them—that is, they differ in their need structure. Many different classifications of need have been offered, but none are entirely satisfactory.

Various scientists have suggested ways in which the needs of adult man may be classified. Any classification is more a matter of convenience than the result of theorizing. Also, almost any classification can include only the more common needs. For example, a few individuals have a highly developed need for timepieces—covering their walls with clocks, and generally carrying more than one watch in their pockets. A need of this kind is rare, so rare that it is hardly worthwhile including in any classification system that is developed. The same would be true of a need for raising Arabian horses or any of the other fads and fancies which are so commonly encountered among human beings. A classification of needs that is to be of any use must cover the common needs that frequently play a part in the behavior of man. Such a classification will not be complete; indeed, a complete classification hardly seems to be possible at this time.

A classification of needs is justified by its usefulness. It cannot be justified on theoretical grounds alone. Indeed, theory hardly seems to have evolved to the point where it can provide a basis for a classification of needs. Such a classification must be based largely on observation of the kinds of objects and events that appear to have the property of arousing action

The classification of needs presented here is just one of many that have been developed. This particular classification was developed by H. A.

Murray at Harvard (1938) during the thirties. It is presented because it is one of the few that have as yet resulted in much research, and hence has become more than a matter of pure speculation.

Murray postulated that the individual was motivated by certain psychogenic needs, which he listed and which included such categories as a need for achievement, a need for status, and a need for play. In general, his list of needs includes complex motives but does not include those that are derived from simple deprivations such as hunger and thirst. The latter are termed *viscerogenic needs*, that is, needs that are related to the periodic bodily events such as lack of water and food, distension of the bladder and bowel, and so forth. The psychogenic needs, as listed by Murray, are considered by him to be learned-reaction systems, but possibly built in some way on the foundation laid by the viscerogenic needs. Murray's classification of needs is not based on a theoretical foundation, but is derived from general observation. It was advanced to provide a basis for research and is not suggested as any final system. The classification of psychogenic needs proposed by Murray is as follows. Most of his terms are self-explanatory; a few, which are either used in an unusual sense or are terms rarely encountered, have a brief explanation added.

Acquisition (the need to gain possession)
Conservance
Order (the need to arrange, to be precise, to be orderly)
Retention
Construction
Superiority
Achievement (the need to achieve a standard of excellence)
Recognition
Exhibition
Inviolacy (the need to protect oneself from situations derogatory to the ego)
Infavoidance (the need to avoid failure and to avoid attempts to do things beyond one's powers)
Defendance
Counteraction (overcoming defeat by retaliating or making a comeback)
Dominance
Deference (a need to show respect to a superior)
Similance (a need to empathize or imitate)
Autonomy
Contrarience (a need to be different from others)
Aggression
Abasement (a need to abase oneself before some person or persons)
Blamavoidance (avoidance of blame)
Affiliation (a need to be accepted by others, to feel that one belongs)
Rejection
Nurturance (a need to take care of others and help them)

Succorance (a need to be helped and aided by others)
Play
Cognizance (a need to explore, to find out, to ask questions)
Exposition (a need to demonstrate facts, to give information, to interpret)

This classification of needs is not claimed to be a final one, and neither is it comprehensive. The list refers to what are supposed to be the common needs of man, but this does not mean that all individuals manifest these needs. For example, a person may have such a low affiliation need that he may be utterly unconcerned about whether he does or does not interact with others. Many persons show, for all practical purposes, zero amounts of some of the needs listed above.

In Murray's original presentation of the need system his attitude was that this was the basis of a program of research, and this it has been over the years that followed. Workers who have pursued research in the area over the years have concentrated on the study of only a few of these needs, for the Murray program is an immense one and has to be cut down to a suitable size if research is to be undertaken. Most of the research that has been undertaken has concentrated on the measurement and study of achievement need and affiliation need.

A need is assumed to be latent in a personality, and at times when it has been adequately satisfied it may have no effect on behavior. The situation is supposed to be analogous to that found in the case of the viscerogenic needs. A person who has fully satisfied his thirst does not think about drinking, and his behavior is not directed in any way toward obtaining water. Much the same supposedly occurs in the case of a need such as the need for affiliation. A person who has engaged in extensive activities that satisfy this need might be expected to show little behavior related to its satisfaction. A person who has spent a week entertaining house guests may show little inclination for company and may even say, "It's good to be alone again."

The latent need is aroused by deprivation, but also by any stimulus related to its satisfaction. If a person taking a test is told that the test measures a rather unimportant ability, then his need for achievement is unlikely to be aroused in the situation. On the other hand, if he is told that the test measures an ability that is closely related to success in life, then whatever achievement need he has may be aroused. When a need is aroused, it means that it shows increased power as a motivating force. Individuals may differ in the degree to which a need is aroused at a particular time. Thus, a person who has a low latent need for achievement may still manifest a much greater achievement need in a particular situation than another person who has a high latent achievement need but whose need is not aroused. The fact that need level depends both on the strength of the latent need and the degree of arousal makes experimentation extremely difficult in this area, for there are no standardized techniques for producing a particular level of arousal.

Needs such as those described by Murray are generally measured through a phenomenon related to them. The phenomenon is illustrated by the famous story of Buddha, who starved in order to free his mind of earthly matters so that he could think about means of attaining values of fundamental importance. Things did not work out in the way he expected, for he soon found that the more he deprived himself of food, the more his thoughts tended to dwell on matters of food. The story illustrates the fact that failure to satisfy a need results in increased imagery related to that need. The same also appears true in the case of arousal. The person whose need is aroused shows an increased imagery related to that need. Strength of need is determined by measuring the amount of imagery an individual displays related to the need in a standardized situation.

A presentation of the research developments derived from Murray's need system must be preceded by a discussion of a further concept that has had substantial influences on current theory of motivation. This is the concept of affect.

Affect and Motivation

For more than two thousand years there have been scholars who have proposed that men are motivated primarily by a quest for pleasure and an avoidance of unpleasant circumstances. The argument is persuasive because it fits so well with personal experience, but it is just this feature of the theory that puts the scientist on his guard. He is reminded of the fact that the theory of the Earth being flat also fitted personal experience. Nevertheless, the theory has been sufficiently attractive to win support from schools of philosophy such as the British Empiricist school. Substantial support from psychologists has come only very recently, though over the last hundred years one can point to psychologists who have endorsed such a theory of motivation. Freud regarded the behavior of the young child to be dominated by the "pleasure principle" and elaborated at great length the difficulties the child has in reconciling the demands of the environment with the quest for personal gratification. Among contemporary psychologists the terms *pleasure* and *pleasure principle* and the related term *feeling* have fallen into disuse; preference has been shown for the term *affect*. Why this shift in terms has taken place one cannot be sure, for the evidence that is accepted for the existence of affect is generally the same as that which past generations of psychologists accepted for demonstrating the existence of states of *pleasure* or *unpleasure*.

A major difficulty in undertaking a discussion of the term *affect* is the unsatisfactory nature of the definitions that are typically proposed. Obviously there are internal responses that correspond in a rough general way with the term, and ordinary language provides numerous attempts to describe such internal states. One often hears such expressions as "I enjoyed that," "I feel very upset," "I am having fun," or "This is what I love to do." But such expressions convey only a very general description of the inner states that collectively fall within the definition of *affect*. Humans also show certain expressive behaviors indicative of affect, such as smiling or crying. Many animals show characteristic behaviors indicative of strong positive or negative affect, as when a cat purrs or hisses, or a dog wags its tail, or a bird puffs up its feathers. Such behaviors are generally indicative of the occurrence of states of affairs significant to the behavior of the organism—conditions to which the organism shows either strong approach or strong avoidance tendencies. The problem of definition is complicated further by the fact that psychologists themselves do not have an agreed upon definition of the term. A quarter of a century ago, most psychologists would have taken the position that emotion was not a necessary component of affect, but some today would consider emotional processes to be those that give affect its particular qualities. Often the term is introduced to denote a "something" that has to be introduced to account for observations. This is the position of P. T. Young, who has championed the concept for nearly half a century. Young (1961) points out that food preferences clearly indicate that factors other than bodily need exert control over them. Animals eat even when they have no immediate need for food, particularly when the food contains such substances as saccharin. Suitable additives may make needed foods rejected and toxic substances accepted. Young suggests that food ordinarily ingested by animals in their natural states stimulates receptors in the mouth that result in an immediate state of enjoyment—this is the affect component—and that laboratory experiments that result in the ingestion of substances with no food value are accomplished by the introduction of substances that influence affective states. Such a substance, saccharin, has also been shown by Sheffield *et al.* (1954) to function as a reinforcer, again suggesting that affective states may play a crucial role in at least some reinforcing events. Young takes the position that responses become organized in relation to the removal or avoidance of distress or the continuation or cessation of enjoyment. Affect, for Young, gives direction to behavior and also provides conditions that favor the making of organized responses.

Although Young's conclusions were drawn largely from studies of food preferences in rats, there are other psychologists concerned primarily with human behavior who have been led to a similar theory of motivation in which affect plays a central role. McClelland, a student of H. A. Murray at Harvard, and Atkinson, a student of McClelland, have long collaborated on the development of such a theory. Although McClelland first proposed such a theory in papers published during the immediate postwar period, the version of the theory to which reference is generally made is that appearing in a volume by McClelland *et al.,* (1953). The general nature of this theory is that if a situation produces an affective response, then, at some later time, the occurrence of some part of that situation may produce a part of the affective state. This state is said to have motivating properties. If the affective state has been one of enjoyment, then it is motivating in a positive direction; but if the affective state has been unpleasant, then it produces avoidance or escape behavior. McClelland also makes another point similar to that made by Helson—that it is a change in affect from the prevailing state that has motivating power, not just the affect itself. Central to this conception of motivation is the idea that affect is of primary importance in giving direction to behavior and little is said about any energizing effect it may have.

McClelland began by directing his attention to the achievement motive, and for many years he devoted his efforts to the development of methods of measuring this motive and discovering its properties. The essential procedure followed in the measurement of achievement motivation was that of showing the subject an ambiguous picture and then requiring the subject to write a story about it. The story is then scored for *achievement imagery.* The latter concept has been quite precisely defined in McClelland (1953) as well as in other sources—for example, Atkinson (1958). In order to illustrate what this might involve, a statement from a story which said, "The boy in the picture is worried about whether he can get a high score on the examination tomorrow," would be scored high for achievement imagery. On the other hand, a statement that would receive a low score would be one like, "The boy likes reading the book, which is fun."

McClelland and his associates were able to demonstrate that conditions calculated to increase the level of achievement motivation produce an increase in the amount of achievement imagery. For example, if the subjects were told that some task they had performed measured a very important skill, or that they had just performed miserably on some assigned task, then the subsequent performance on the test of achievement motivation would show an increase in achievement imagery. Such instructions are designed to arouse achievement motivation. Similar relationships have been demonstrated between conditions that raise the level of motivation and the appearance of imagery in a storytelling test situation. For example, Atkinson and McClelland (1948) demonstrated that an increase in hunger through starvation over periods up to sixteen hours produced an increase in the references to food found in such story-writing tasks. In another study, Shipley and Veroff (1952) were able to demonstrate that students in a fraternity whose affiliation needs were supposedly aroused showed a greater amount of imagery related to affiliation than did those in whom such a need had not been so aroused. In most of the studies that have been undertaken, men appear to show increments in score as a result of arousal, but relatively little success has been achieved in demonstrating the arousal phenomenon with women.

The interpretation of the results of such studies is not entirely clear. Some have suggested that the appearance of imagery represents an unsatisfied motive rather than a high level of the motive as such. If this is so, then a person with a high achievement motive that was well satisfied by actual accomplishment might show little achievement imagery on a test of the kind used in these studies.

Studies have been undertaken that demonstrate that performance on simple tasks may, under some conditions, be related to measures of achievement motivation. French (1955), who uses a strictly verbal device for measuring achievement motivation, found a significant relationship between the motivation measure and performance on simple tasks when the subjects were aroused by being told that the performance measured a very important ability. Similar relationships have been found between such measures of motivation and grades in college. In one such study, Jorgenson found a correlation of 0.26 between such variables in the case of sixty-one college students (unpublished study). In a further study of considerable educational significance, French (in Atkinson, 1958) showed that subjects with high achievement needs improved their output most when they were encouraged by information related to their performance, such as "You are working very efficiently." In contrast, a group high in affiliation motivation showed the greatest output when it was reinforced with such statements as "This group works very well together." The French data give support to the contention that the reinforcement given to a student should be related to the motives that are operating in the particular situation.

Some data exist concerning the conditions that result in the development of the achievement motive. A study was conducted by Winterbottom (see Atkinson, 1958) in which the child-rearing practices of mothers were studied and the results related to the achievement motivation of the children. The conclusions drawn by Winterbottom were that the mothers of the high-achievement-motivated children, in contrast with the low-achievement-motivated children, (1) were more demanding before the age of eight, (2) evaluated their children's accomplishments higher and were more rewarding, and (3) were more likely to impose restrictions on their child before the age of ten, but less likely to impose restrictions later.

Other studies indicate a relationship between class origin and pattern of motivation. A study by Douvan (1956) showed that children from a lower class demonstrated much greater variation in achievement motivation, depending on the particular situation in which they were placed. The middle-class children, on the other hand, tended to show a relatively high level of achievement motivation, regardless of the situation in which they were placed. The results of this study conform well to the experience of many teachers who find that the middle-class children work hard at their school work even when it is dull. In contrast, the children from lower socio-economic groups must be aroused by one means or another before they will immerse themselves in schoolwork.

Of the various motives postulated by Murray, the achievement motive is the one that has been most carefully studied and concerning which the greatest amount of information has been collected. However, other studies have been undertaken with measures of affiliation and measures of status. French (1956), for example, found that people with high affiliation motivation tended to choose as work partners people they liked. In contrast, the achievement-oriented person tended to choose as a work partner a person who was good at performing the task to be done. This study raises the possibility, often disregarded in educational practice, that work groups may help to satisfy the social needs of some children but not of others. The highly achievement-motivated child may feel frustrated when assigned to a work group, unless it happens that the group includes other children who are similarly motivated and who are also eager to perform the task required.

The work that has been pursued in the general area discussed in this section appears to open the way to the understanding of many of the motives that underlie the behavior of the child in school, and is also highly suggestive of the range of reinforcements that may have to be used by the teacher.

The Doctrine of Interests as Motives

While experimental psychologists such as P. T. Young and David McClelland were conducting experiments that led to the concept that affect plays a central role in motivation, psychologists concerned with the development of tests were attempting to produce measures of the affect that individuals experience when they engage in each of a variety of activities. These measures of affective response are referred to as measures of interest.

The doctrine that interests are major motives has had a long history in education. It is implicit in the doctrine of Rousseau that self-directing forces emerge from within and direct behavior in ways that will benefit the individual. Thus, it is assumed by such a doctrine that, were it not for the evil influences of the environment, the individual would grow to become a fine and noble and productive citizen. Furthermore, it was believed that the punishing and misguided behavior of the adults the child encounters during his development results in the warping of his personality and failure to realize his maximum potentialities. The progressive-education movement revived the essentials of this doctrine and especially its emphasis that a 'curriculum should be designed around the interests of children. It was assumed that interests were more or less fixed structures within the individual, and that, functioning as motives, they would direct the behavior of the child along those lines where learning could be most successfully accomplished and where the individual would derive a feeling of self-fulfillment. Unfortunately, this version of the development and function of motives as interests lacked the most important element in a behavioral theory—namely, a factual basis. In order to provide a proper basis for a theory of this kind, it would be necessary to establish the existence of characteristics called interests in children and to demonstrate that they were relatively permanent structures of personality. There would be little value in basing a curriculum on interests if it were found that the interests of children in Miss Jones' class changed radically when Miss Smith took over the class for a few weeks.

The word *interest* is a rather vague one. Psychologists who have realized the need for clarity in the use of concepts have tended to define interests more and more precisely, but a number of different meanings are still current. Some of these meanings are as follows:

1. Interests may be defined in terms of the activities in which the individual chooses to engage. These are interests as they are manifested in day-to-day behavior. Sometimes these are referred to as *manifest interests*. This is not generally considered to be a useful concept of interest, since few persons are ever free to pursue whatever activities they desire.

2. Interests may be defined in terms of expressed preferences for particular activities. These may be casual statements in the course of an interview concerning what the individual would like to do Such expressions of preference may also be carefully collected and systematically analyzed. Interests that are appraised through the individual's *expression* of what he likes or dislikes are referred to as *expressed interests*.

3. Interests may be assessed through the reaction of the individual to a number of questions generally organized in the form of an inventory.

When the assessment is made systematically through the use of an inventory and the responses are scored, the resulting scores are said to measure *inventoried interests.* In most of the inventories available today, the questions are so arranged that the person answering them must decide which of two or more activities he prefers or likes least. The scores derived from such an instrument are designed to indicate the relative strength of interests within the individual. One such widely used instrument, built along these lines, is the Kuder Preference Record.

There is another type of measure, commonly referred to as a measure of inventoried interest. Instead of deriving scores directly from expressions of preference for particular activities, the responses given in the test may be matched with those of particular groups of individuals. Thus, it may be possible to conclude that the preferences of a particular person resemble more the preferences of one group than of another. Usually the groups with which comparisons are made are occupational groups, and hence one may perhaps infer that the preferences of a person are more like the preferences of musicians than they are of chemists. The Strong Vocational Interest Inventory provides such comparisons, and the preferences of a person can be compared with the preferences of people in numerous different occupational groups. To give to such scores, which indicate the degree of resemblance to various occupational groups, the name of *interest* is to use this word in a new and different sense from that in which it has been used previously in this section. Edward K. Strong, who developed the technique, emphasizes that his instrument indicates only the degree to which the person's responses on the test resemble those of people in particular occupational groups. To refer to these scores as measures of vocational interests goes far beyond the data available. Perhaps the device can be used to indicate the extent to which the individual has a cultural background similar to that of individuals in particular groups.

Manifest interests, expressed interests, and inventoried interests all represent variables that can be to some extent measured. A study by Berdie (1955) shows on a relatively large population what has been demonstrated in many smaller studies, that expressed interests and inventoried interests represent different variables and cannot be equated. What a person says interests him in a free response to a question may be different from the interests indicated through the checking of an inventory.

Although the assumption is generally made in education that interests represent motives, the psychologist has had great difficulty in testing this hypothesis, which must remain just a hypothesis until research has demonstrated it to be true. The obvious way of attempting to demonstrate that interests function as motives would be to show that level of interest in a particular activity is related to speed of learning in that same area. The argument is that if interests function as motives, then a high level of interest means a high level of motivation, which in turn results in a higher level of learning. At least there can be no dispute about the fact that increases in level of motivation generally increase rate of learning, except where very high levels of motivation are reached. Nevertheless, if a research worker were to find a relationship between a student's interest in a course in mathematics and a measure of the student's achievement in mathematics, he should not conclude that this demonstrated that interest in mathematics functioned as a motive in courses in mathematics. Another explanation might be that students with aptitude for mathematics might have had, in the past, favorable experiences in mathematics classes which had developed in them a positive liking for the class. If the latter explanation were true, it would imply that success in mathematics produced interest, rather than that interest led to success. Thus, the possibility exists that interest may be either cause or effect—either caused by success or a contributor to success. A third possibility is that both phenomena may occur.

Many studies have been undertaken to try to relate scores on interest tests with measures of achievement. The earliest of these was undertaken by Thorndike (1917), who studied the relationship between expressed interest and the person's rating of his ability to perform in corresponding areas. Thorndike found an almost perfect relationship between the two. The Thorndike results have never been duplicated, and were probably artifacts produced by the tendency for people to say that they like doing the things they do well. A few studies have used more modern techniques, which avoid some of the pitfalls of rating, and have found very different results. Gowan (1957) and Berdie (1950) studied the relationship between inventory measures of interest and achievement in subject-matter fields at the college level and found very small but statistically significant correlations between interest and achievement. Generally these correlations were of the order of 0.2.

In keeping with the previous findings are those of Gordon and Alf (1962) who studied the usefulness of an interest inventory for predicting grades in 57 Navy training schools. The interest inventory was administered to over 100,000 recruits, about half of whom subsequently entered the schools. The interest measures showed small but positive correlations with grades in related training situations of the order of 0.2. Also, when a combination of aptitude scores and interest scores were used to predict grades, a slight improvement did occur. The addition of an interest factor changed the general order of the correlation between predictors and grades from 0.59 to 0.62. The increment is small but statistically significant. Whether it is large enough to be of any real consequence in a practical situation is an open question. Cattell (1961) has found that measures of interest in children add to the prediction of school achievement to about the same extent as they did in the Gordon and Alf study conducted with young adults.

Not all studies show even this small glimmer of optimism. When interest tests were tried out by the U.S. Air Force, neither Brokaw (1956) nor later Schweiker (1959) could find that they had any value for predicting performance in technical training over the predictions that could be made from aptitude tests. Working with civilian populations, Merritt (1950) found no relationship between interest and achievement in corresponding areas.

An interesting and unusual study is that of Collins (1955), who found a small relationship represented by a correlation of 0.20 between breadth of interest and academic achievement.

Since many of the studies relating achievement to interest use a device such as the Kuder Preference Record, which virtually ranks a person's interests from those that are strongest within him to those that are weakest, Frandsen (1953) suggests that a person's ranked interests should be compared with his ranked achievement. Frandsen was able to obtain for each of 137 high-school students the rank order of their success in each of their school subjects and also the rank order of their interests. An average correlation of 0.27 was found between these rankings. Frandsen found also that students' expressed interests were more highly related to achievement than were inventoried interests.

Scores from interest inventories do differentiate students in different college curricula (Berdie, 1955). What this means is not quite clear. It may be a matter of verbal custom. A person may feel considerable pressure to say that he likes activities related to those he has selected for a career. This evidence has nothing to do with whether interests are or are not aspects of motivation. Another source of evidence indicates that interests do not appear in some situations to operate as motives. Samuelson and Pearson (1956) found that the Kuder Preference Record could not be used to differentiate drop-outs from graduates of a trade-school program. If interest had any strength as a motivating factor, one would expect that the graduates would show a higher interest pattern on scales related to the course than would the drop-outs, but such was not the case.

In summary, data generally demonstrates a very small relationship between interest measures and measures of learning, and these relationships tend to be too small to be of practical significance. If interests function as motives, then they appear to function as very weak motives, for individuals learn almost as rapidly in areas for which they express little interest as in areas for which they express high interest. The small relationship commonly found between interest scores and achievement-test scores may also reflect only the fact that a person who has a high score on, say, mechanical activities is also the person who probably has had some mechanical experience in his background. This background experience may, in turn, facilitate his learning in a course involving mechanical learnings. This, in turn, may generate a relationship between interest scores and achievement scores. At the present time one may conclude that a high interest score should not be taken to indicate that the person may be expected to be a relatively rapid learner in related areas.

There appear to be some exceptions to the general conclusions drawn in the previous paragraph. One of these is that extremely low interest levels, which amount to an aversion for a particular activity, may be very significantly related to learning. Persons with actual aversion for flying were found to be very poor risks in the U.S. Air Force flight-training program (Personal communication, Eli Flyer). This one can understand, for such individuals not only have a low measured interest in flying, but may be expected, in addition, to have anxieties related to flying. A low negative interest probably derives its characteristics from the anxiety to which it is related. The permanent and durable aspects of anxiety make it a characteristic likely to remain unchanged by training. Also, the anxiety is likely to be at a high enough level to produce some disorganization of behavior.

Fear or Anxiety and Hope as Motives

In the jigsaw puzzle that constitutes the total picture of the field of motivation, a few pieces at this time seem to fit together; but the main area is still a blank. A few of the pieces that apparently form only a small but consistent picture have been discussed in the previous pages, but these pieces occupy only a fraction of the total area. In another part of the picture a few more pieces are beginning to fit together. These are the aspects of the field that have to do with anxiety.

The traditional view of anxiety or fear was that it was basically an unpleasant type of experience that most people would do well to be without. Furthermore, it has been known since at least the middle of the last century that anxiety is a common accompaniment of many forms of mental disease, and that it sometimes may even be the major symptom that brings the patient to the office of the specialist. In most theories of mental disorder it is not the anxiety itself that is the cause of the disease, for the anxiety is considered to be only the symptom of an unresolved conflict of which the person is largely unaware.

Anxiety is usually defined in subjective terms as a state rather similar to fear, with the exception that fear is generally directed toward some object, and anxiety does not point to any particular catastrophe that is anticipated. On the objective side, the clinical worker hardly expects his patients to come to him and state that they are suffering from anxieties. Rather, they make such statements as, "I feel guilty about the way I treat my brother," "I feel upset in my present job," I worry a great deal," "I feel disturbed if anything in the house is out of place," "I guess I will never amount to much," "I wonder whether things will go all right today," "I have a feeling that something dreadful is going to happen," and so forth. Fortunately, most of these expressed anxieties have no objective basis. The implied catastrophe never really happens.

The tendency in modern psychology is to avoid the subjective type of definition of anxiety and to define anxiety in objective terms such as, for example, by the statements the individual makes about himself. Another objective approach to the definition of anxiety defines it in terms of the kinds of situations the individual has encountered. For example, a rat that has been severely shocked may be said to develop anxiety if placed again in the box in which it received the shock and if it manifests escape behavior, cringing behavior, high level of activity, or certain other symptoms. Sometimes a similar procedure is used in human subjects in order to generate anxiety. Severe electrical shocks are given. Later anticipations of severe shocks in the same situation are considered to correspond to the existence of anxiety states.

Anxiety is *not* an all-or-none affair; rather it is a condition that may exist in varying amounts. Most of our knowledge of anxiety is derived from the clinical study of patients who manifest extremely high anxiety, and also certain types of clinical cases who are believed to be without anxiety. The high-anxiety cases are typical of many groups of neurotic and psychotic individuals. The damaging effect that high anxiety may play in the life of a disturbed person has done much to give anxiety the bad name that it has in education. Much of therapy is an attempt to rid the individual of the anxiety that makes his life so miserable. However, most theories of therapy consider the state of anxiety to be a symptom rather than a cause, and efforts are directed primarily toward resolving the underlying conflict.

No program of therapy is designed to eliminate all anxiety in a person's make-up. Such a goal would not be a feasible one, for even the mere reduction of anxiety to manageable levels is often a task well beyond the ability of the therapist. Even if anxiety were a matter easily handled by a well-set therapeutic routine, it is most unlikely that therapy would be pursued until all anxiety had been eliminated, for psychopathic personalities are generally considered to be persons whose behavior difficulties are a result of a deficiency in anxiety. Although this conclusion is somewhat speculative, it is certainly one that is widely held. Extremes of anxiety, both at the high and the low end of the scale, seem to result in behavior difficulties, which suggests that anxiety in moderate degrees is a constituent of the efficiently operating personality.

The undesirable effects of extreme anxiety have resulted in the failure of many clinicians to recognize the possibility that mild anxiety, as it operates in the so-called normal personality, may not be at all an unpleasant phenomenon. Indeed, there are some reasons for believing that it may actually be a pleasurable experience. The psychologist cannot disregard the fact that many people go to great pains to experience mild states of anxiety. The adventurer is typically a person who places himself in positions of which anxiety is bound to be the consequence. To a lesser extent, amusement parks have various pieces of equipment that are designed to produce fear and anxiety. Many individuals, it is well known, will actually pay money in order to have these experiences. Mild anxiety might even be described as an exhilarating condition. It is sought after, and also becomes a means of driving the individual along his path. The problem solver experiences mild tensions that serve both to keep him working at a problem and to make him later seek out other problems to solve in order to regain this state of tension.

Experimentation with anxiety as a drive is difficult, because it is impossible at this time to determine the amount of anxiety that the experimental situation itself produces. What has been done generally in work in this field is to measure what is termed the "general level" of anxiety of the person involved in the experiment. This has been customarily done with a questionnaire that lists a large number of symptoms of anxiety and in which the number of the symptoms that the individual claims to manifest anxiety is counted. The score is commonly described as a measure of manifest anxiety. A scale that has been used for this purpose is the "Taylor Manifest Anxiety Scale."

Taylor (1951), after developing this scale, studied the conditioning of the eyelid response in subjects who had either very high or very low scores on the anxiety scale. She found that the high-anxiety group conditioned more readily, which suggested that manifest anxiety had drive properties. Montague (1953) undertook another study, shortly after Taylor had undertaken hers; it showed that, on simple rote-learning tasks, subjects classed as anxious performed better than those classed as nonanxious. However, he also produced the interesting finding that the anxious subjects, although performing better on the simple task, performed more poorly than the nonanxious subjects on a more difficult rote learning task. One interpretation of the latter data is found in an old principle known as the Yerkes-Dodson law, which states that there is an optimum level of motivation for all tasks and that the more difficult the task the lower is the optimum level of motivation. If one were to apply this law to the interpretation of the Montague data, one would infer that the anxious subjects were too highly motivated on the difficult task for them to perform optimally; but that on the simpler task, for which the optimum level of motivation would be higher, they were nearer to performing at their most effective level.

Other interpretations of the relationship between task difficulty and optimum level of motivation (as measured by anxiety scales) are possible. Taylor and Spence (1952) attempted to interpret Montague's results in terms of Hull's (1943) theory of learning in which the effect of drive is to increase the availability of a response. In a simple task, involving a single dominant response, a high drive level would make this response more available and hence improve performance. However, on a complex task, where many different responses could be made at a particular choice point, all of these would show an increased tendency to occur and tend to disrupt performance. Taylor and Spence (1952) and later Farber and Spence (1953) devised experiments in which they sought to test out this explanation. They devised tasks in which strong competing responses were likely to occur. In such situations the high-anxious subjects would be expected to perform at a lower level than the low-anxious subjects, assuming that the high drive level of the former would make the competing responses more available. The data generally fitted well the proposed explanation.

Although the Taylor, Farber, and Spence studies have been undertaken on college students, rather similar findings have been reported in experiments with elementary school children. Casteneda, McCandless, and Palmero (1956) developed a form of the *Taylor Manifest Anxiety Scale* for administration to children. High-anxious and low-anxious children were selected on the basis of the scale and then given a series of problems in which the child had to find the combination of buttons to press to turn off a particular combination of lights. They found that the high-anxious group performed better than the low-anxious group on the easy combinations, but that the high-anxious group performed more poorly on the more difficult combinations.

Grimes and Allinsmith (1961) investigated the relationship of achievement to anxiety in children learning to read by two different methods. The children in twelve classrooms were taught by a phonetic method in which the teaching situation was considered to be highly structured. Children in another twelve classrooms in a different school system were taught by a look-and-say method that involved much less structured teaching and far more informal activity. They found that, in the unstructured setting, high anxiety was related to poor performance in reading, but that in the structured setting there was no relationship between anxiety and reading achievement.

The latter finding helps to explain why research attempting to relate measures of anxiety to learning has not produced uniformly consistent results. Attempts to reproduce the classic study of Taylor and the other research undertaken in the Spence laboratory have sometimes produced the same results, but sometimes they have not. Just as Grimes and Allinsmith found the expected negative relationship between anxiety and achievement on a complex task in one set of classes and not in another (because another variable was affecting the results) so, too, have some research workers produced consistent replications of the early work, but others have not. Small differences in the experimental procedure or in the way in which the subjects are recruited may account for differences in results. For example, in eyelid conditioning of human subjects, Prokasy and Whaley (1962) have shown that it makes a difference whether subjects are, or are not, given a signal "ready" before each trial. Even such a small difference in experimental procedure could determine whether the results of the studies in the Spence laboratories could, or could not be, reproduced.

Research on anxiety as a motive should not be taken as a basis for inferring that anxiety is necessarily an undesirable motive. Very mild anxiety, as may occur in solving a problem, may be a valuable condition for learning and may represent much of the spice in life. The evidence that goes against the use of anxiety as a motive is derived from studies in which rather high levels of anxiety are involved. Any motive may operate at such a high level that its effects are those of disorganization. A child may have such a high need for recognition that it may make him behave with foolishness on many occasions, but this does not mean that all recognition motivation is undesirable.

The problem in the case of anxiety is, however, a special one, for it is one of the few motives over which the teacher has at least partial control. Teachers, through their behavior, can raise and lower the level of anxiety in children. This fact makes the manipulation of anxiety a matter that the teacher is tempted to undertake.

Mowrer (1960), who uses the term fear in much the same way as others use the term anxiety, has made an interesting suggestion. Mowrer suggests that, just as fear is a broad and general state related to the learning of avoidance responses, so too there is a similar state related to approach responses. This state, which is the counterpart to anxiety or fear, is named by Mowrer as *hope*. This does not mean that when hope is aroused in a person, he says to himself, "I certainly feel hopeful in this situation." Indeed, he may not recognize it as having any relationship to what is commonly described as hope. He may not even be aware of the operation of hope. In fact, Mowrer writes about the operation of hope in rats and lower animals, who cannot possibly have formulated such a complex concept. In the case of the rat, the operation of hope is seen in consistent approaching and exploratory behavior related to positive reinforcement.

For Mowrer, all motivation is incorporated in these two concepts of *fear* and *hope*. The one is closely tied to avoidance behavior and the other to approach behavior. Both fear and hope are complex internal responses of a kind that would be described by most other psychologists as emotional responses involving the smooth muscles and viscera. Both are regarded as responses to stimuli, which may be either internal or external, and, hence, Mowrer assigns an important role to stimuli in the motivation of behavior. One might expect that Mowrer's theory might involve the concept of affect, for it is easy to jump to the conclusion that both fear and hope generally involve affective experiences in our own personal life. However, Mowrer does not do this; he prefers, in this respect, to avoid introducing concepts that he considers do not have to be introduced in order to account for the facts that experiments have revealed.

Level of Aspiration as a Measure of Motivation

Related to the concepts of anxiety and hope in the field of motivation is the concept of *level of aspiration*. This concept was first developed by Lewin when he was still in Germany. The term was coined by Dembo (1931), a student of Lewin. American investigators have generally adopted an operational definition of level of aspiration, which states that it is the level of future performance on a familiar task that an individual expects to reach. The expectation is defined in terms of the level the individual says he will perform on the task. Success then may be defined in terms of whether the individual surpasses the level he expects to reach; failure is the reverse. Insofar as success and failure are to be considered as reinforcing conditions, then success and failure must be evaluated in terms of level of aspiration.

The basic studies in the area undertaken by early workers were reviewed by Frank (1941). Measures of level of aspiration have some consistency over periods of a week. They also show some consistency from task to task. These early studies are also consistent with some modern studies on a related phenomenon, namely that of overachievement or the tendency to achieve beyond that expected in term of measured aptitudes. No clear relationships have been found between personality characteristics and tendencies to have a high or low level of aspiration, which tends to be influenced more by the person's previous history of success or failure than by any other condition. The many research studies tend to show that level of aspiration tends to follow the level of performance—that is, as performance declines, so too does level of aspiration, and vice versa. However, level of aspiration is much more susceptible to change by success than by failure.

The extent to which level of aspiration must be taken into account in estimating the reinforcing value of a particular performance is a matter that still needs to be investigated. It seems probable that an important relationship of this kind exists.

The level of aspiration set by a person with respect to a particular task can be considered to be a consequence of the operation of motives, such as anxiety. If a task has been previously associated with failure, it may be expected to be one for which the person is likely to have a relatively low level of aspiration. The reverse might be expected to be true in the case of goals that arouse a high degree of hopefulness.

An article by Child and Whiting (1949) brings together some interesting experimental evidence concerning the conditions that result in the raising or lowering of the level of aspiration of students in a learning situation. The results of this study fit in well with those of other investigators, and also with the ideas presented on the subject by Lewin *et al.* (1944) in a famous article on the subject.

In the Child and Whiting study the subjects involved were 151 men attending an Eastern university. The results of the study are organized around a number of conclusions:

1. *Success generally leads to a raising of the level of aspiration, and failure to a lowering.* Students who had met with frustration in the attainment of a goal, and who had not attained the goal set for themselves, showed a marked tendency to lower their level of aspiration in subsequent situations. Even if frustration was involved in the successful achievement of a goal, the tendency was for the subsequent level of aspiration to be raised. The data suggests that success provides some kind of reinforcement that results in the raising of the level of aspiration. Perhaps what is reinforced is "hope," and this in turn results in the raising of the level of aspiration. On the other hand, when failure is the result of effort, then anxiety generated by the situation is increased, and this in turn may result in a lowering of the level of aspiration and perhaps even a complete rejection of the goal.

2. *The effects of failure on level of aspiration are more variable than those of success.* This conclusion reminds one of the conclusion drawn with respect to the effects of punishment. Punishment has rather unpredictable results. Perhaps failure in some task raises the level of anxiety, which may be dissipated by approaching the task with renewed vigor and hence with renewed anticipation of success, or perhaps it produces a higher expectation of failure. Nevertheless, despite the variability of the effects of failure, the general conclusion still holds that failure generally results in a lowered level of aspiration.

3. *The stronger the success, the greater is the probability of a rise in the level of aspiration; the stronger the failure, the greater is the probability of a lowering.* This conclusion surely has important implications for the teacher. In an age when the emphasis in education is on the striving for excellence, whatever produces a gross lowering of the level of aspiration does not have a place in education, except under unusual circumstances. Any dramatic failure may have this effect, and hence such failures should surely be avoided, unless there is some really significant reason why the level of aspiration should be lowered. Sometimes a student who has set his sights too high needs to have this happen to him. A student who has decided to become a doctor, despite the fact that his counselor has told him that he does not have the ability required for success in medicine, may have to experience failure before he will accept realistic goals.

A number of research workers have noted that the level of aspiration in some persons with respect to a task is much more realistic than with others. Some set a level of aspiration in keeping with their past performances; others set a level of aspiration either much higher than they are ever likely to attain or so low that success in terms of their goals is assured. In other words, persons differ in the extent to which they are realistic in their expectations. This difference in what are called *reality levels* indicates that the level of aspiration is complexly determined, and its relation to motivation is also certainly complex.

Worell (1959) studied level of aspiration with respect to academic work for college students. His hypothesis was that the student who set a reasonable level of aspiration for himself in line with his previous performance had a sound contact with reality and hence should be successful in grade achievement. This was found to be the case. Students whose levels of aspiration were considerably above their previous record were found to have relatively low scholastic standing.

Walter (1952) studied the relationship of level of aspiration in fourth- to twelfth-grade children to some of the characteristics of the children. Boys showed a higher level of aspiration than did girls. The discrepancy between level of aspiration and actual achievement was unrelated to actual achievement.

In more recent research, an attempt has been made to relate measures of level of aspiration to achievement motivation. The two concepts have such a marked superficial resemblance that one is tempted to assume that a measure of one might be highly related to a measure of the other. The results of research indicate that two distinct psychological functions are involved. In a study of this problem by Martire (1956, a, b) no direct correlation was apparent between level of aspiration and achievement need, but subjects who had a strong generalized achievement motivation and who were understood to be anxious about failure in a stressful achievement situation had a significantly lower level of aspiration than other subjects. The relationship involved is obviously complex. The complexity of the relationship was also brought out in another study by Clark *et al.* (1956), in which students were assessed along a dimension of hope of success versus fear of failure on a regular course examination. They found that students at the extremes on this measure of level of aspiration obtained lower need-achievement scores than other students. Wylie (1961), who has reviewed the research available concerning the relationship between achievement need and level of aspiration, has concluded (pp. 248–249) that the results of the various studies cannot be fitted together in any meaningful way.

A Critique of Some Current Doctrines Concerning Needs

Doctrines held by some educators concerning needs stem from an oft-quoted experiment by Davis (1939) on the self-selection of diets by young children. Although the experiment is an interesting one and also the source of many ideas, it was poorly designed by modern standards and yielded results that are controversial. The subjects of the study were infants of six to eleven months of age at the beginning of the experiment, which was continued for six years. The experimenters claim that these infants had never had "supplements of the ordinary foods of adult life," though how the experimenter could be sure of this is not clear, since not all of them had been under their supervision prior to the experiment. The infants were provided with a tray on which were a large number of dishes containing a great range of foods. The nurse sat holding a spoon until a child indicated that he wanted a particular dish. It is claimed that only when the infant pointed to or reached for a particular dish did the nurse offer the food in a spoon. The tray was removed only when the child stopped eating, which was generally twenty to twenty-five minutes after starting. The experimenter claimed that at the end of the period the children showed a satisfactory state of nutrition, despite the fact that some of them had begun the experiment with nutritional deficiencies. A check of the foods consumed by the children showed that the diets selected by the children represented an adequate diet by modern nutritional standards.

Although the inference often drawn from this experiment is that the child knows what is good for him, such a conclusion is in no way justified. In order to arrive at a more reasonable inference from the data, certain additional facts must be understood. First, the infants were not presented with thirty-four foods at one time, but rather, the foods were grouped into fifteen different diets. Also, the behavior of the infants indicated that in the early stages of the experiment the infants selected foods at random. The result of this random selection and the variation of the diet from meal to meal means that each infant was required to sample a great range of foods during the early part of the experimental procedure. This fact must be kept in mind in the interpretation of the results of the experiment; but before an interpretation can be made, certain additional items of experimental data must be considered.

Let us consider what happens in the case of the typical laboratory rat that is given freedom to choose its own diet. It performs very much like the child, and over a period obtains a diet that provides all of the necessary foods in adequate quantities for healthy living. On the surface this appears to confirm the conclusion that living organisms adjust their behavior so that their needs are satisfied in a way that is healthy, but this is not so. Young (1944) and Young and Chaplin (1945) have carried out an additional experiment that changes this interpretation radically. In their experiments rats are raised on a diet that has an excess of certain kinds of foods. What happens to such rats when they are allowed to choose their own diet? They adjust their diet so that they continue to consume an excess of the food they had previously consumed in excess. What they do under a free-choice situation is to continue to consume the same balance of foods in their diets to which they were accustomed. The rat on a bad diet, when given a free choice, continues to consume a diet that manifests the same imbalance.

In such experiments with rats, the explanation for the continued choices of the organism is that reinforcement related to the original choice of food established a food-choosing habit that continued to guide the animal's eating behavior. Further consumption of the same food further strengthens the habit, which may be such that the animal may ultimately die from a dietary deficiency, even in a situation where foods necessary for correcting the deficiency are available.

Just what happened in the case of the Davis experiment on self-selection in infant feeding is hard to say. As far as one can determine, the food-selection procedure was such that the infants were forced from the start into selecting a variety of foods. The fact that they were each exposed to fifteen different diets means that they could hardly avoid developing a habit of choosing a variety of foods. Just as Young showed that an animal habituated to a particular food will continue to choose the same food, so too, presumably, will a creature that is exposed to a variety of foods continue to choose a variety of foods. If this were not so, species would rapidly die out in their natural habitats. One cannot conclude that the self-selection procedure necessarily results in a healthful selection of foods, for the foods presented were such that a variety of them selected at random would be very likely to satisfy the physical needs of a child. If a small dish of alcohol solution had been provided, would the infants have learned to avoid this dish or would they have become alcoholics? The writer's suspicion is that they would have become alcoholics, particularly if the solution had been well-flavored and sweetened. The situation seems to have been organized so that the infants would obtain a healthy diet, and the process of self-selection may have had very little to do with the matter.

Despite the fact that the scientific evidence does not support the contention that children free to choose a diet will select foods in proper amounts and balance to produce good health, there is a little evidence that animals will in a few instances seek out foods that will remedy a deficiency. For example, Bare (1942) showed that rats that had had the adrenal gland removed and, as a result, had a great physiological need for salt, showed a preference for fluids with a high concentration of salt rather than a low concentration. A similar study conducted by Epstein and Stellar (1955) gave similar results. These studies suggest that something other than reinforcement may sometimes be at work, though the phenomenon has been demonstrated only with a case of extreme deprivation.

The Davis study and the criticisms that have been leveled against it are mentioned here because the results have been generalized as if they applied to complex motivations such as probably operate in classrooms. One school of educators has even taken the position that if self-selection is effective in the case of diet then it must work too in the selection of curricular materials. On this basis the child is offered a wide range of materials to explore in the classroom and the supposition is that somehow he will select those that will benefit him the most. Even if the Davis experiment had been a well-designed one in the first place, such broad generalization from it would hardly be acceptable; and to generalize broadly from a basically poor experiment is absolutely inexcusable.

Summary

1. The concept of motivation is introduced by psychologists to account for aspects of behavior that cannot easily be accounted for otherwise. Two distinct aspects are generally considered: the energizing aspect and the directing aspect. Some psychologists stress the energizing aspect of motivation but consider the direction-giving aspect as unimportant.

2. One simple concept of motivation is that it is the level of arousal of the organism, a matter also considered in the chapter on the nervous

system. For any particular task there appears to be a level of arousal that is optimum for performing the particular task. If the general level of arousal of the organism is excessively high, as it is in the case of children suffering from the brain-damage syndrome, new skills may be difficult to acquire.

3. Another concept of motivation is the drive concept, which is derived largely from physiology. The basic drives, according to this concept, are related to tissue needs. When the organism is deprived of certain needs, such as the availability of food, an imbalance is produced in the body chemistry, which in turn raises the level of activity. This is a homeostatic theory of motivation in which drive serves as a regulating mechanism keeping the chemistry of the body at a particular level. The state of imbalance is referred to as a need; the resulting activation of behavior is referred to as a drive.

4. The directional properties of the basic drives—at least those that have been most commonly studied—do not appear to be as marked as is commonly supposed. Animals can *learn* to discriminate hunger states from thirst states, particularly when considerable deprivation is involved; but the training requires care and persistence on the part of the experimenter. Even the high level of drive produced by pain does not appear to produce avoidance behavior without some learning being involved.

5. Drive theory could not account for all motivation in terms of the direct operation of primary drives; and, hence, a series of learned secondary drives had to be introduced. Such secondary drives, since they were learned responses, could be extinguished. Attempts to develop in the laboratory secondary drives that have some stability has proved to be a difficult problem. Secondary drives that have been developed have tended to be weak and transitory. However, Mowrer (1960a) claims that work in his laboratory has demonstrated the development of a stable secondary drive that was virtually inextinguishable.

6. Although early workers claimed that deprivations produced activity directly as if they were strong internal stimuli, more recent research has shown that the matter is not so simple. Deprivation of food appears to sensitize the organism to external stimuli so that it becomes more responsive to them. Such research indicates the importance of external factors as well as internal in motivation.

7. The effect of novelty seems well established as a condition that both energizes and directs behavior. However, the matter is not simple; for although novelty attracts attention, it sometimes produces approach behavior and sometimes avoidance behavior. The attentiveness produced by novel stimuli obviously has survival value.

8. Deprivation from normal sources of stimulation has important effects on behavior. When such deprivations are extreme, the situation

rapidly becomes intolerable. In situations where there is considerable uniformity of the environment, the opportunity to produce some change can function as a reinforcer. Woodworth has proposed that the fundamental motivation is that of acting on the environment. This is referred to as behavior primacy theory.

9. Different individuals are energized by being confronted with different external situations. To some extent an individual will seek out those situations he has typically encountered, and he may be uneasy when confronted with conditions very different from those anticipated. Attempts have been made to classify situation-related needs. The particular classification developed by Murray was presented as one such classification in view of the influence it has had on psychology for over a quarter of a century.

10. Although a few psychologists and philosophers have long held the position that affect is an important component of motivation, it is only recently that an influential group of psychologists have come to recognize the possibility that this may be so. The difficulty of handling the concept is at least partly owing to the fact that it eludes effective definition.

11. Both the public at large and people engaged in developing psychological tests have long believed that interests are important motives. With this in mind, many tests of interest have been developed and research has been undertaken to determine the extent to which these measure motives relating to learning. Small but consistent positive relationships have been found between such measures and performance in educational and training situations. If interests function as motives, they function as weak motives.

12. Some educators have held the opinion that children, if given an opportunity to exercise choice, will select those curricular materials from which they can benefit most. This doctrine appears to be based mainly on an experiment by Davis (1939), which has been largely misinterpreted. An interpretation in the light of recent knowledge does not give support to the notion that self-selection results in desirable choices.

13. Mowrer has proposed that anxiety and hope represent the two basic motives underlying behavior.

14. A measure of motivation that has been extensively explored is level of aspiration. This is the expected performance level on a familiar task. Although the study of level of aspiration has produced many interesting findings, it has not proved to be particularly useful as a measure of motivation.

7

The Nervous System and Learning

THE MATERIAL discussed up to this point has involved mainly psychological conceptions of learning. Concepts such as reinforcement have evolved through research studies of behavior, and these have not depended in any way on a knowledge of anatomy or physiology. Many psychologists have taken the position that orderliness can be found in behavior and that these orderlinesses can be discovered without first discovering the underlying laws of physiology. For example, one can demonstrate that the pecking behavior of a pigeon, placed in a box so designed that this behavior can be recorded, is related to the schedule of reinforcement to which the bird has been exposed. This relationship could have been discovered without the scientist ever knowing much about the anatomy and physiology of the pigeon. This orderliness of behavior relates a condition of learning to subsequent behavior, and was established after much study of the behavior of the birds had demonstrated that such a law probably existed. Many laws of behavior are established in this way.

Another approach to the study of behavior is to begin by examining the anatomy and physiology of the nervous system and to see what this knowledge suggests concerning the nature of behavior. This approach to the discovery of the mechanisms of behavior has had a long history and has produced many influential ideas.

Early studies of the general anatomy of the brain and nervous system provided little information concerning the relationship of these gross structures to behavior. Indeed, that the nervous system had anything much to do with behavior was a relatively late discovery. The learned man of the middle ages had no understanding that the nervous system had any function at all in this respect. It was only with the development of techniques for studying the function of nerves and the detailed anatomy of the nervous system that any understanding of the function of the nervous system became possible. Physiologists early in the nineteenth century were able to show that when a nerve was pinched, or touched with acid, or electrically stimulated, the muscle to which it was attached showed a twitch and sometimes even a spasm of contraction. Even relatively low-powered microscopes were able to show that a single nerve leading to a muscle consisted of a large number of fine strands which came to be known as nerve fibers. Just how such fibers functioned was not known until further electrical and chemical techniques permitting such study had been developed near the beginning of the present century.

Early in the present century Thorndike seized upon the newly developed knowledge of the structure of the nervous system and attempted to correlate it with his theory of learning. Behavior was to be considered a result of connections between stimuli and responses, and learning was a matter of developing new stimulus-response connections. In terms of the anatomy of the nervous system, the development of these connections was to be considered a matter of establishing connections between the nerves transmitting sensory information into the nervous system and those transmitting impulses to the muscles and glands. The viewpoint of Thorndike became known as a "connectionist" viewpoint. The nervous system was to be conceived as a mechanism much like that of a telephone switchboard which somehow managed to make the right connections if learning had been successful.

We now know that the nervous system is vastly different from a telephone switchboard. The learning of behavior is much more than the switching of incoming nervous impulses to nerves that produce the appropriate responses. Knowledge of the anatomy and physiology of the nervous system indicates that the switchboard concept of the nervous system is quite inappropriate. Even the production of a relatively simple response, such as that of saying "four" in answer to the stimulus "two times two," may involve very complex processes in the brain. Learning is much more than a matter of connecting the stimulus to the response.

With advancing knowledge of the nervous system, psychologists have had to reconsider their conception of the nature of learning. Although some psychologists have believed that a psychological theory of learning can be developed without reference to what is known about the nervous system, others have considered that a psychological picture of learning can be better developed if it is based on, and closely linked with, current knowledge of the nervous system. Some psychologists would go so far as to take the position that psychological theory, if it takes into account other biological knowledge, may eventually help the neurologist to make discoveries in his own field.

Concepts of learning related to neurology have acquired considerable significance during the last ten years and have represented an approach productive of knowledge. For this reason the student of education can no longer ignore the anatomical structure and physiological functioning of the child if he is to acquire some understanding of the learning process as it takes place in schools. Since the teacher-education curriculum typically ignores the fact the child has a body the workings of which determine what he can and cannot learn, this chapter begins by attempting to provide a sketchy outline of knowledge in this area. Later in the chapter we will consider some of the important concepts related to learning that have been built on this knowledge.

The Nerve Cell

The earliest theories of learning were developed by philosophers who lived in an age when little was known about the structure of the body, and few thought that there could be a close relationship between bodily structure and the way in which the organism learns. Anatomical discoveries that occurred at the end of the last century were the first to influence the scientist's conception of how learning occurs, and these discoveries formed the basis for the connectionist theories of learning produced by a whole generation of psychologists.

Much of our present knowledge of the relationship between learning and the anatomy of the nervous system has been made possible through the development of techniques that permit the inspection of the actual cellular structure of this part of the human anatomy. If a thin slice of the cortex of the human brain is viewed through a microscope, very little can be seen except a gray mass of varying density. Unless some technique is used for staining the individual cells in the nervous tissue, they will never be seen; and herein lies a great difficulty: nerve cells cannot be dyed with any of the pigments commonly used for coloring cells to facilitate their inspection. Rather late in the study of microanatomy it was found that osmic acid and silver salts had the important property of rendering the colorless cells visible by staining them black, and the osmic-acid technique is still used to this day for the microscopic study of nervous tissue. It is through such techniques that knowledge of the minute structure of the human nervous tissue has slowly developed.

In structure, the nerve cells of which the nervous system is composed are similar to the other cells in the body. Like the other cells, the nerve cells consist of a mass of protoplasm bounded by a membrane that defines the limit of the cell and separates it from other cells. Within the protoplasm of the cell lies a slightly denser mass of material known as the nucleus. It is known that the nucleus plays an important part in the development of the cell and in maintaining its normal functions.

Unlike other cells, the nerve cell may extend through the protrusion of fine processes to points that are even several feet from the cell body itself. These fiber-like processes represent the means whereby nerve impulses are transmitted from one location in the body to another. A drawing of a nerve cell and the processes that extend from it are shown in Figure 4.

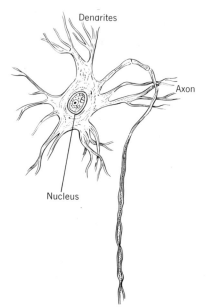

FIGURE 4. Diagram of a nerve cell body, axon, dendrites, and other commonly observed features.

In the typical nerve cell the extension at one end is single and long, and is known as the *axon.* The axon may have branches at its extremities. A number of branching fibers spring from the other end and are known as the *dendrites.* Nerve impulses *may* pass either way within the nerve cell and its extensions, but the ordinary direction is from the dendrite end of the cell to the axon end.

The cells that constitute the central agents in the sense organs that respond to stimulation from the outside world and send impulses to the central nervous system, informing it of the presence of a particular stimulus, are simply highly specialized nerve cells.

A nerve cell is either in a state of passivity, during which time it continues a vegetative type of existence, or it is in a state of activity, when it is transmitting an impulse from one end to the other. When the cell becomes thus active, it is said to have been *fired.* After a nerve cell has been fired, it enters into a period of recovery known as the *refractory* phase. In the early part of this phase it simply cannot be fired, but in later stages it can be fired when stimulated with more than the energy ordinarily required. However, recovery is not a slow process, ordinarily taking something less than a tenth of a second.

When a nerve impulse arrives at the end of an axon, it reaches a gap that separates it from the dendrites of the nearest nerve cell. The impulse may activate the dendrites of the next nerve cell or it may not. Much depends on the particular chemical condition that happens to be in existence at the gap. It may also happen that the neighboring nerve cell has entered into a refractory phase and may not be capable of being activated at that time. Much in the nervous system depends on the particular instant at which a particular impulse reaches a particular point. If it arrives at one time, it may set off a whole chain of activity. If it arrives a fraction of a second later, further activity may be blocked. Time sequences are of the greatest importance in determining what happens in the nervous system.

At one time it was thought that the nerve impulse traveled with the speed of light. Only less than a century ago was it demonstrated that nerve impulses are rather slow-moving phenomena—at least they are slow in comparison with light. Nerve impulses vary considerably in the speed with which they are transmitted, and, as we shall see, this has some important consequences. The speed of the impulses along an axon varies from a walking speed to the speed of an aircraft, that is, somewhere between three feet per second and 400 feet per second.

The Synapse

One nerve cell does not actually join another nerve cell. The membranes of one nerve cell isolate it from the next. There are, however, places where the axon of one cell comes into contact with the dendrites of another cell or with the other cell body itself. This point of contact is known as a *synapse*. At this place the axon or branches of the axon grow tiny knobs, which can be seen under high-powered microscopes. It is believed that these knobs play an important role in the transmission of nerve impulses from one cell to another. Scientists concerned with problems of learning have speculated that when learning occurs, these knobs may show development and hence facilitate the transmission of an impulse across to the next cell. Certainly, changes in conditions at the synapse seem to be the most likely ones to explore if a physiological basis of learning is to be found.

Transmission at the synapse may be from the axon of one cell to the dendrites of another, or it may be from the axon of the one cell to the cell body of another. Axon-to-cell-body represents the most direct form of transmission and probably the most rapid. Transmission from the axon of one cell to the dendrites of another is a slower and more uncertain process. There is always the possibility that the impulse started in the dendrites may fade out before it reaches the cell body, and hence may fail to fire the cell.

The synapses permit only one-way traffic. An impulse arriving at the end of an axon may activate the dendrites of a neighboring cell, but the reverse process cannot occur. Just how the impulse is transmitted across the synapse is not properly understood at this time; neither is the reason for the synapse's one-way operation. An impulse may arrive at a synapse and be insufficient to activate the dendrites of another nerve cell. However, if two impulses from two different axons of two nerve cells were to arrive at this same synapse at approximately the same time, they might be able to arouse activity in the dendrites that the one impulse could not do. This illustrates the process known as *summation*. Nerve impulses may summate to produce activity that one of them alone would not be able to produce.

The places where groups of nerve fibers within the nervous system end in synapses and a new set of nerve fibers begins are referred to as *nuclei*. Nuclei are rather like a relay system within a telephone network. Groups of nerve-cell bodies are referred to as *ganglia*. Nerve tracts may be seen to leave some ganglia. These nerve tracts are bunches of axons closely grouped together. When such clusters of nerve fibers are found outside of the nervous system, they are commonly referred to as *nerves*. Thus the sciatic nerve, famous as the source of sciatica, is a bundle of such nerve fibers serving the leg. In living tissue such nerves appear as white, glistening cords, from which it is possible to tease out, with a needle, individual fibers.

The all-or-none principle.   In the axon of nerve cells, firing takes place on an all-or-none principle. This means that if a nerve impulse is transmitted down the axon, then a full-size impulse is always transmitted. It is impossible to transmit half-size impulses by providing some rather weak stimulus to the nerve cell. This is known as the all-or-none principle, which has certain important implications for the way the nervous system operates. If a sense organ is stimulated first with a weak stimulus and then with a strong one, the weak one does not produce smaller impulses than the strong one. Both produce nerve impulses of equal size. However, the stronger source of stimulation produces a greater number of impulses per second than does the weaker one. Intensity of stimulation is translated in the nervous system into frequency of nerve impulse. A strong stimulus, in contrast to a weak stimulus, also has another effect. It may excite more nerve cells and thus produce a greater volley of nerve impulses.

The dendrites do not function in quite the same way, for different amounts of stimulation may produce impulses of different size, and the impulses tend to fade as they pass along the dendrite. They may, in fact, entirely fade out before they reach the cell body itself, and hence may fail to initiate an impulse in the axon. If the electrical disturbance does reach the cell body, it is likely to fire the cell and discharge an impulse down the axon.

General Structure of the Central Nervous System

The gross anatomy of the nervous system is fairly familiar to most students who have had a course in general psychology. The central nervous system consists of the brain and a long extension, known as the spinal cord, which passes all the way down through the middle of the backbone. The brain and spinal cord develop in the young embryo as a hollow tube running the length of the head and trunk. As development proceeds, three enlargements appear toward the front end; these eventually form the brain. The central nervous system is sometimes referred to as the CNS.

The foremost of the three enlargements that emerge early in the development of the brain eventually form the cerebral hemispheres, which are the two large masses popularly referred to as the brain. Somewhat to the rear of the cerebral hemispheres is another large outgrowth, the cerebellum. Right beneath the cerebral hemispheres and connecting them with the spiral cord is the thalamus, the lower half of which is the hypothalamus. The thalamus, because of its position, is an important relay station for all nerves that are transmitting impulses originating in the sense organs. The thalamus and the hypothalamus appear also to have some control function, in that they regulate many important processes in the body, such as rate of breathing, some processes that are related to the control of body temperature, and so forth. These functions occur quite automatically and are not in any way dependent on the intervention of higher mental processes.

Within the central nervous system are bundles of nerves that constitute the so-called white matter. The so-called gray matter consists of masses of nerve cells and areas through which an impulse arriving along one nerve fiber is transmitted to another nerve fiber.

Nerves enter and leave the brain and spinal cord at regular intervals along its length. These form the major portion of the peripheral nervous system, which has ramifications in every section of the body. A somewhat distinct system of nerves, which is also peripheral to the central nervous system, is the autonomic nervous system. The latter consists of a rather diffuse set of nerve cells and their extensions, which, as will be seen later, can be well thought of as a component of the effector nerves of the body.

Nerve tracts, whether they lie within or outside the central nervous system, can be classified as afferent, efferent, or internuncial. In the peripheral nervous system, those bundles of nerve fibers transmitting impulses from the sense organs toward the central nervous system are referred to as afferent nerves. Those transmitting impulses to the effector mechanisms, the muscles and glands, are referred to as efferent nerves. Much the same classification is used for the nerve tracts within the central nervous system. Those that conduct impulses derived from sensory stimulation, and usually those that conduct impulses from lower to higher levels in the nervous system, are referred to as afferent tracts. Those that conduct impulses destined to activate the effectors of the body are referred to as efferent tracts. The latter tracts usually conduct impulses from the higher levels in the nervous system to the lower levels.

The axons of the sensory cells terminate shortly after entering the brain or spinal cord. Nerve impulses they may transmit may then be carried further by new nerve cells. The peripheral efferent nerves also terminate a short distance within the spinal cord or brain, and at that point they may be activated by nerve impulses from other sets of nerves, which in turn may have been activated at some quite remote point in the central nervous system.

The internuncial system of fibers conducts impulses from one point to another within the nervous system without specifically being conductors of impulses originating in the sense organs or impulses destined to arouse an effector. It is possible that some internuncial fibers may sometimes function as a part of the efferent system and sometimes as a part of the afferent system. At this time we have no way of knowing which fibers function in which way and when. This is purely a matter of speculation, but it seems highly likely that this is sound speculation.

Internuncial fibers are found at all levels of the central nervous system, from the lowest section of the spinal cord to the cerebral hemispheres. However, there are no internuncial fibers in the peripheral nerves. It is possible that sometimes the simplest forms of behavior will occur without the operation of internuncial fibers, as in the case of the simplest of reflexes, but such may not be the case. Even the simplest form of behavior may be extremely complex, in terms of the number of nerve cells and their processes that may be involved.

Internuncial fibers may represent a diffuse network, or they may be located in large bundles. One such large bundle connects the one hemisphere with the other and is known as the *corpus callosum*. This bundle is so large that it is easily seen by the student who is dissecting a brain.

By custom it is usual to refer to activity in the cerebral hemispheres as "activity in the higher levels" of the nervous system. In contrast, activity in the spinal cord is referred to as "activity in the lower levels."

Connections of the Afferent and Efferent Nerve Tracts with the Cerebral Hemispheres

Some specialization of function exists within the cerebral hemispheres. Consider first the sensory inputs. The input from a sense organ such as the eye tends to go directly to a specific area of the cortex that is located at the rear of the head. This localization occurs in the case of sensations derived from the eye, the ear, the skin, and the muscles. However, this statement needs qualification, for the sensory nerves, or the afferent nerves as they are called, do not go directly to the corresponding sensory area in the cerebral hemisphere. First they go to one or more relay points, the most important of which is the thalamus. Second, they tend to be conducted to the side of the brain on the opposite side of the body to that from which they originated. The latter point is sometimes made without the student realizing that this tendency to cross over is only partial, and that each sensory system also sends impulses to the same side as well as to the opposite side of the brain.

The areas on the surface of the cerebral hemisphere, which have specialized functions as terminations of the sensory tracts, are known as the *sensory-projection areas*. They are the areas on which the impulses derived from the sense organs are projected. The specialization of function that these areas represent is likely to be misinterpreted by the student who encounters it for the first time, for he is likely to jump to the conclusion that these areas are the ones that produce the phenomena of perception. The student is likely to conclude erroneously that since the occipital (rear) lobe of the brain functions mainly in connection with vision, visual perception is a function that occurs in the occipital area alone. Such is not the case. Although the occipital lobe plays an essential role in visual perception, there is ample evidence that visual perception is dependent for its functioning on extended areas of the brain and that perceptual functions cannot be completely localized within one particular area of the cerebral cortex.

Figure 5 shows the approximate location of some of the sensory-projection areas in the brain of man. Some are hidden from view in such a diagram. From the viewpoint from which the drawing has been made, the visual area is scarcely visible because it is tucked away between the two hemispheres at the back of the brain. The auditory area is also largely hidden because it is tucked away down in the deep fissure it borders, known as the *Sylvian fissure*. The large sensory area across the

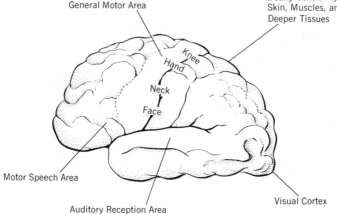

FIGURE 5. Some of the areas in the human cerebral cortex that show specialization of function.

top of the brain carries sensations from the toes at the top and from the head at the bottom.

The afferent conduction system from the sense organs has a fairly direct path of conduction to the sensory projection areas on the surface of the brain. However, this is not the only path through which the sense organs transmit information to the brain. In addition, there are afferent nerve paths that run to parts of the cortex other than those specifically designated as the sensory-projection areas. These are described as forming the nonspecific projection system, and are considered to play an important part in the coordination of information reaching the brain concerning the outside world. Here again it may be pointed out that the sensory inputs to the brain are in many respects highly diffuse, and that perception is dependent on the collective effect of these inputs.

The efferent system is built along a plan similar to that presented by the afferent system. In the cortex, just to the fore of the main sensory area, is the source of the major tracts that transmit impulses to the muscles and glands. This area is commonly known as the motor-projection area. The part at the top controls the activity of the toes, and that farther down and to the side of the head controls the muscles of the upper trunk and neck. That this is so has been demonstrated on patients during operations. Stimulation of a particular part of the motor-projection area of the cortex results in a movement of the corresponding muscle.

The cells that lie in the motor-projection area of the cortex send out axons through which impulses are transmitted to the effector system, but these same axons do not extend right to the muscles themselves. They go as far as certain relay points just below the cerebral hemispheres, where a second set of nerve cells relays them further.

Just as some of the sensory nerves do not go directly to the sensory areas in the cortex but spread their information diffusely through the cortex, so too do some of the efferent nerves rise from diffuse locations in the cortex. It is believed, at present, that the direct efferent tracts exercise direct control over behavior, and that those tracts that have diffuse origins serve a function of coordination and adjustment. Although the nature and location of the main afferent and efferent tracts in the central nervous system are well established, problems of how behavior is controlled are much less understood.

Just as the sensory nerves tend to cross over to the opposite side of the brain before the impulses they transmit terminate in the cortex, so too do the efferent, or motor, tracts cross over to the other side of the body before they reach the effector mechanisms. For this reason, if a person suffers a stroke that damages the right motor cortex, he is likely to be paralyzed on the left side of the body. How the nervous system came to evolve with this complicated crossover system is not known at the present time, and what biological survival value it serves is also a mystery.

The Information Transmission Process

The sensory nerves and the related higher centers serve the function of transmitting information about the outside world and thus providing the organism with a basis for effective action. The transmission process is much more complex than that of simply transmitting faithfully an impression of the outside world to the higher centers. Although a sense organ, such as the eye, has an immense capacity for receiving information from the outside world, the transmission process does not result in this information in its entirety being sent to those centers that engage in the complex processes of perception. Only a very small fraction of the total input can be handled by the higher centers—probably much less than one per cent of the input.

Three main physiological processes determine what information is transmitted: *lateral inhibition,* the *Hernandez-Peon effect,* and *habituation.* Each one of these must be considered separately.

Lateral inhibition. The neighboring fibers of a nerve tract such as the optic nerve do not function as independent conductors. When one fiber is conducting information to the higher centers, the tendency is for activity in neighboring fibers to be lowered. This phenomenon has been studied mainly in creatures much simpler than man, in which it is possible to record the impulses in single nerve fibers. An example of such a study is that by Hartline and Ratliff (1956), who studied the transmission of visual information in Limulus, a crab. There are reasons for believing that the nerve processes of the crab are closely similar to those that occur in the nerves of higher organisms, because the nerve structures are very similar. In the case of the optic nerve, the effect of lateral inhibition would be to accentuate information derived from the boundaries of objects where there are generally contrasts in illumination and to depress transmissions of information from the areas within the boundary lines. What this means in terms of visual perception is that the information about the external world that is transmitted resembles in many ways that derived from a line drawing.

Psychological information fits very well with the physiological information about lateral inhibition. Psychological studies indicate that the boundaries of objects transmit more useful information than do the areas between the boundaries. When one is asked to describe an object to another person, one is likely to draw an outline of the object, for such an outline emphasizes the important features. For a similar reason, black-and-white sketches or line drawings are highly effective means of communicating information; studies have also shown that such drawings can often communicate information much more effectively than can photographs that provide a much more realistic representation of the environment. The effectiveness of the black-and-white line drawing or sketch stems from the fact that it emphasizes the important information and eliminates the trivial. In technical terms one would say that the line drawing represents compressed information of the kind that the receiver can use efficiently.

The nervous system compresses information that is taken in through the sense organs. This process has the general effect of accentuating those aspects of the information that have particular value to the receiver and of de-emphasizing those aspects that have less value. This is a simplification process and enables the receiver to deal with a complex environment without attending to all the vast detail.

Although information is compressed as it is transmitted to the higher centers, it may be compressed before it is ever received. The teacher who provides simplified representations of objects on the blackboard is compressing the information in order to facilitate transmission to the learner. Effective teaching is, to some extent, a matter of compressing information in a way that facilitates transmission within the nervous system.

Although the compression process that has been discussed in this section occurs in the nerve tracts themselves, there are undoubtedly compression processes that occur at all levels of the nervous system. The utilization of concepts, which permit the classification of objects and events in the environment into categories, represents a method of compressing information at the higher levels of the nervous system. These processes also, by simplifying complex information about the environment, protect the higher centers from becoming overloaded.

The Hernandez-Peon effect. A particularly important experiment was carried out in 1956 by Hernandez-Peon, Scherrer, and Jouvet (1956). In this study, tiny stainless steel electrodes were inserted into the cochlear nucleus of the cat. This nucleus is a relay point for information transmitted by the auditory nerve; all the information that the cat receives through the ear must pass through this relay station. After the cat had recovered from the operation it was placed in a room where it was exposed to a series of click-like sounds. With each click, a burst of activity was shown to occur in the cochlear nucleus. This activity could be picked up by means of the implanted electrodes. While the clicks were thus being recorded, the cat was exposed to a number of stimuli judged to be important to cats. These were two mice enclosed in a bottle, fish odors delivered through a tube, and an electric shock delivered to the paw. Any of these stimuli was shown to have the effect of depressing the transmission of the sound of the clicks as they were recorded in the cochlear nucleus.

A subsequent series of experiments from the same laboratory all lead toward the conclusion that when highly significant information is transmitted through one of the senses, then less significant information coming in through the other senses tends to be blocked. Such a mechanism also protects the higher centers from becoming overloaded.

Habituation. One of the ways in which the nervous system is protected from being overloaded with trivial or useless information is through habituation. An example of habituation is seen in the case of the person who is in a room with a loudly ticking clock. At first he is fully conscious of the incessant ticking but, after a short while, he ceases to be aware of the noise at all. He has become habituated to the sound. One must assume that some information about the ticking is transmitted, but in a weakened form, because the sudden stopping of the ticking is likely to command attention. Hernandez-Peon and Scherrer (1957) have shown at the physiological level that the habituation is accompanied by a blocking of the transmission of information. An electrode inserted into the cochlear nucleus (a relay point for auditory information) of a cat shows a weakening of the transmission of a repetitive sound as time passes by.

Habituation protects the organism from becoming overloaded with trivial information. Each tick of the clock provides no new information that was not provided by the previous tick and hence does not have to be transmitted to the higher centers.

Any frequently repeated stimulus can produce blocking and, hence, habituation. Related phenomena are commonly observed in the class-room. One teacher, observed by the present writer, tinkled a small bell a dozen times each hour whenever she wanted to gain the attention of the pupils. The pupils were observed to show no response to the bell. Teachers who say every few minutes "Less noise, please" are generally ineffective in reducing the noise level, for the pupils become habituated to the signal.

The Handling of Information by
the Higher Centers

The youngest of humans responds selectively to some parts of the environment but not to others. Effective transactions between an organ-ism and its surroundings are dependent on this selectivity for a number of reasons. First, the environment is overwhelmingly complex, and organ-isms do not have the capacity for taking in all the information that the world supplies. Second, the response mechanisms are limited and also capable of performing only limited tasks at any given time. Preoccupa-tion with many different aspects of the environment could lead to futile attempts to handle simultaneously many different problems that would be far beyond the response capacity of any human of any age. That aspect of the environment to which the person responds is referred to here as the *information channel,* though other terms are sometimes used. Glaser (1965) refers to the *interface* between the pupil and the environ-ment in discussing the contact between the pupil and his environment in the school setting. Our preference is for the term *information channel* since we are concerned with the aspect of the environment that is trans-mitting information having some impact on the individual. Those aspects of the environment that at any time constitute the information channel are determined through establishing what information is being received by the learner.

At a particular instant in a classroom, the teacher may be addressing the class, but one pupil may be watching a cat stalk a bird on the grass outside. For the latter pupil the information channel at that particular time is the cat-and-bird situation. If another child is attentively examin-ing a butterfly in a bottle, the butterfly is the information channel.

Sometimes the information channel is internal. A person suffering deep pain may be able to think of nothing except the pain and may be quite out-of-touch with external events.

An information channel is always a very limited set of events because the human is capable of handling only a limited amount of information at a time. If the teacher attempts to arrange a learning situation so that the pupil must derive information simultaneously from many different sources, the learner may become confused and acquire no information at all.

The higher centers of the nervous system have a limited capacity for utilizing information, and generally handle information from one source at a time. Credit for reaching this point of view and for gathering together the research on which it is based must go to Broadbent (1958), but other scientists who have approached the problem from an entirely different position have also arrived at the same conclusion. (See, for example, the work of Feigenbaum and Simon on rote learning [1963].)

The most familiar example of data that support the one channel model of the higher centers is that illustrated by what is known as the "cocktail party problem." Colin Cherry, a communications engineer, was the first to point out that in a situation in which there are many speakers a person typically listens to one while blocking the voices of the others. In a number of studies (1963) he has shown that when different messages are communicated simultaneously to a listener, then the behavior of the listener has several important characteristics.*

If the listener is asked to follow one source, he will do so to the exclusion of the other sources. Such a listener will not be able to identify at the end of the session the messages derived from the sources other than that to which he was instructed to listen. As a matter of fact, if messages from the other source were transmitted in a foreign tongue, the listener might not even be aware of that fact.

Broadbent (1958) has conducted a series of experiments that also support the finding that the higher centers can utilize information from only one source at a time. Thus, if information is being received from an auditory source, not only will information from other auditory sources be blocked but so too will information from visual sources and tactile sources, and from all other sensory sources. It is as if the incoming messages have to feed through a bottleneck that can accommodate only one message at a time.

Sometimes one may have the illusion of being able to attend to more than one message at a time. This will occur when each one of the messages has a high degree of redundancy, by which is meant that only a part of the message has to be heard in order to understand the entire message. Most messages communicated in English have a high degree of redundancy. Thus, the content of two messages may sometimes be under-

---

* The single-channel concept applies only when the quantity of information to be processed from a single source is equal to or greater than the information processing capacity of the system.

stood by attending to one for a part of the time and to the other for a part of the time.

One may also *experience* inputs from the different senses simultaneously provided that no particular attempt is made to utilize or store the incoming information. The higher centers function as a single channel only with respect to the processing and utilization of information.

This current model of the perceptual processes, based as it is on substantial information, has important implications for education. First, it is contradictory to the doctrine long preached by textbooks on audiovisual aids that the more senses through which information is transmitted simultaneously the more effective will be the learning. The central idea expressed in the latter doctrine is that two senses can pump in more information than can one. This does not seem to be the case, and a study by Van Mondfrans and Travers (1964) provides corroborating evidence. Another matter also suggests that little advantage is to be achieved by transmitting the same information through several senses simultaneously: An increasing body of evidence points in the direction that the amount of information that can be processed by the higher centers is probably the same regardless of the modality from which it is derived, and this amount is probably fairly small. If this is the case, one might expect that a single message, such as a narrative, might provide at least as much information as the higher centers could process.

Although only information from a single source is processed, other sources of information are continuously monitored. As soon as information is present with higher priority than that in the source to which attention is directed, attention is switched to this new high-priority source. An example of information of high priority is a person's name. Whatever a person is doing, if his name is mentioned even in a faint voice, he will turn his attention to the source that mentioned his name. The peripheral awareness that one has of the world around him represents, in a sense, the monitoring process.

The transmission system is also readily overloaded, and when this occurs the person is typically left in a state of confusion. Confront a person with a task that is novel to him and then fire at him the directions at high speed. Bewilderment is almost certainly the outcome. What has happened is that the information transmission process has become jammed through overloading.

Level of Arousal and the Arousal System

Common observation indicates that a person varies from time to time in his likelihood of producing a response. When one is waiting for a visitor, the slightest sound of footsteps on the sidewalk outside the house will alert him in readiness to greet the visitor; but when one is relaxing on a Sunday afternoon, similar sounds may go unnoticed. In the one case the nervous system is in a higher state of arousal than in the other. During sleep, the arousal level is at a minimum.

One must suppose that built into the brain is some system that can initiate and maintain arousal. One possible system would be a circular activity between the cortex of the brain and some of the lower centers. If this were so, then the lower centers could stimulate the cortex, and the cortex could in turn stimulate the lower centers. The arousal system may be to some extent dependent on external stimulation for its activity, but it must have some capacity for initiating activity; otherwise arousal would stop as soon as stimulation stopped, and the individual would fall asleep. Clearly this is not so, for we may remain at a high level of arousal even when outside stimulation falls to a very low level. Early physiologists thought of the nervous system as a passive system of telephone lines and a central switchboard, but modern workers conceive of it more and more as a system capable of initiating activity and an organization of cells that is fundamentally active.

A center of particular importance in the nervous system, in relation to the arousal process, is the reticular formation, a mass of cells that extends from the midbrain for some distance down the stem. It has now been demonstrated that this body sends a bombardment of impulses to the cortex when it is operating normally, and that this bombardment is necessary for the normal operation of the cortex. Some of the tranquilizer drugs depress the activity of this body, with a resulting diminution of activity of the cortex. When sufficient doses are administered to produce this effect, another interesting phenomenon occurs: The animal ceases to be able to learn, although it is quite capable of moving around and performing all of the other functions it normally performs. This is some slight evidence to support the point of view that the arousal system plays a vital part in learning. The relationship of the reticular body to other parts of the nervous system is shown in a diagrammatic form after Bindra (1959) in Figure 6.

On the basis of the available evidence, Bindra (1959) proposes two generalizations that summarize much that is known about the operation of the arousal system in relation to learning. His first generalization is as follows:

There is an optimum range of level of arousal within which a given measure of performance will reach its highest (or lowest) value; the greater the deviation in either direction from the optimum arousal level, the greater will be the decrease (or increase) in the performance measure.

Bindra cites a number of studies to support this generalization, which is already well supported by everyday observation. If a person is drowsy

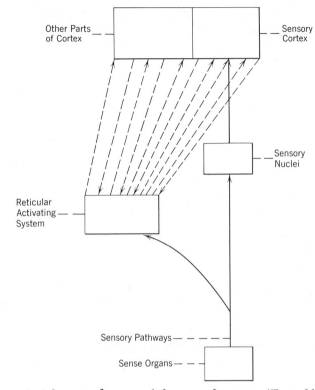

FIGURE 6. Schematic diagram of the arousal system. (From *Motiva-tion—A Systematic Interpretation*, by Dalbir Bindra. Copyright © 1959, The Ronald Press Company.) Reproduced by permission of the Ronald Press.

and near to sleep, he will be unlikely to show anything near maximum performance on any skill that he has already learned. If he is driving a car, he may well land in the ditch. When drowsy, he may be quite in-capable of performing many thinking skills and problem-solving skills that he performs with great facility when he is wide awake. As the arousal level increases, the person becomes more and more capable of performing his various skills, but the improvement does not increase in-definitely. A certain point will be reached for a particular skill (such as driving a car) where an increase in the arousal level results in a decrease in the skill. If the driver of a car is highly excited by some event, he may drive carelessly and not observe the red lights and other signs. If the state of excitement reaches a really high pitch, he may reach the point where he becomes incapable of driving a car. A high level of ex-citement or arousal may incapacitate a person for thinking through a problem to a logical conclusion. In common language we would say that the person is too excited to concentrate.

Bindra's second generalization is as follows:

With increased practice at performing an activity or task (i.e., with increased habit strength of a response), there is an increase in the range of the optimal level of arousal, as well as the range within which the activity occurs at all.

This generalization also fits many common observations. In the training of a soldier or a pilot who is to operate later under high-arousal conditions, it is necessary that he develop the skill to the point where, as the saying goes, he can do it in his sleep. Normally, slight increases in the level of arousal may improve performance, but larger increases may be disruptive unless the skill is a highly practiced one. This, of course, is what the concert artist does. He practices to the point where the high-arousal state involved in playing before an audience does not disrupt the activity. Indeed, he may play slightly better before the audience than he has played in his studio. This is to be contrasted with the school child who has learned his lesson to the point where he can demonstrate in the quiet of his home that he has learned it, but who is quite unable to perform with equal skill in the relatively high-arousal situation of the classroom.

Of considerable interest in this connection is the problem of training many brain-injured children who show excessively high levels of arousal and hence have difficulty in learning.

Considerable knowledge concerning the operation of the brain has been derived by a study of electrical changes in the scalp that result from brain activity. These electrical changes are very small. They were first noticed by the German physiologist Berger. Later workers used an amplifier similar to that found in most record players in order to increase the amplitude of the electrical changes. Such improved equipment today is standard in most neurological clinics, and provides a permanent record in ink of the electrical waves observed in the scalps of patients. This kind of record is known as an electroencephalograph, commonly abbreviated EEG. Popular usage refers to these recordings as the recordings of brain waves.

Berger discovered that when an individual is in a waking state but relaxed and not attending to anything in particular, his brain produces changes in electrical potential at about the rate of ten cycles per second. This rhythm, which rapidly disappears when he becomes active and starts to solve a problem, is known as the *alpha rhythm,* and its presence or absence is of considerable importance in the diagnosis of brain disorders.

The firing of a single cell or the firing of one cell after another could not produce this phenomenon, for the electrical discharge of a single cell is a very small disturbance and could not be recorded easily through the scalp or skin, if it could be recorded at all. The alpha rhythm must be the result of a large number of nerve cells firing together in the same rhythm. The presence of the alpha rhythm indicates that *some* cells of the brain are firing synchronously. Of interest is the fact that when *very large numbers* of cells fire synchronously, the result is an epileptic fit.

When the person ceases to be passive but, say, is asked to solve some simple arithmetical problem, the rhythm tends to disappear. In technical terms it can be said that the higher the state of arousal of the individual, the less marked is the alpha rhythm. In its place there appears a new, but less marked, rhythm with faster frequencies, known as the *beta rhythm.*

What this means in behavioral terms is that when the brain is relatively inactive, insofar as the production of behavior is concerned, the cells work together synchronously. In contrast, during activity they tend to work on an individual basis and to fire asynchronously—that is, groups of cells containing considerable numbers cease to be active together. When this happens, the electrical effects tend to cancel one another out, and the typical alpha rhythm disappears. Asynchronous firing is characteristic of mental activity, and the significance of this fact will be shown as this presentation proceeds.

Another interesting fact that has considerable implications for the educator is that during sleep a very strong and slow rhythm appears, known as the *delta rhythm.* Delta waves are also found under two other sets of conditions. First, they are found in some seriously disturbed patients during a waking state, and they are found in those patients who have some serious disturbance of their perceptual and thought processes. Delta waves also appear in young infants and are, in fact, the main manifestation of activity of the brain during the first few months of life. The implication is that the newborn infant does not have any experience corresponding to the conscious awareness of the adult.

The Nervous System as an Initiator of Activity

Early conceptions of learning described the learner as a passive organism on which the environment left impressions. Such a conception of the learner is not in keeping with present-day knowledge of the physiology of the nervous system, which can be demonstrated to be an organ that generates activity. Thus, behavior is much more than a matter of stimuli generating responses, for responses may be generated by the nervous system itself. Although the old stimulus-response conceptions of learning implied that learning was a matter of connecting stimuli with responses, such a connectionist viewpoint does not receive much support from present knowledge of physiology.

Clear demonstration of the nervous system as an initiator of activity has done much to encourage learning theories that are based on such an assumption. This conception of the nervous system fits well with Skinner's conception of emitted behavior and variability of behavior, which permits the reinforcement of certain aspects and the extinction of others.

Self-initiated activity within the nervous system is also a basis for understanding the continued mental activity that takes place in day-dreaming, thinking behavior related to problem solving, and all of the spontaneous internal activity that characterizes the typical mental life. Learning clearly comes to involve the direction of such internal activity and the relating it to the solution of the problems of living. The conception of the nervous system as a source of self-initiated activity has done much to reformulate our whole conception of the learning process.

Delays in the Nervous System and Mediating Processes

When the professor asks the student, "What is the numerical value of sine 45°?" the student pauses and then, after a few seconds' delay, gives his answer. Thinking processes produce delays, and we may well ask what kind of neural processes could account for such delays. It is clear that some kind of processes must occur between the afferent inputs into the central nervous system and the occurrence of the efferent outputs, and these processes are known as *mediating processes*. In these processes, holding mechanisms are involved. Let us consider at this point some of the mechanisms that produce delay in the nervous system.

First there is the fact that different nerve fibers conduct impulses at different speeds. This has one important consequence. If the foot is given a sharp tap, the nerve endings in the skin send a volley of impulses up to the spinal cord and thence to the brain. The impulses may start together, but since they move at different speeds, they do not all arrive at the same time. The sensations derived from the sudden tap are much more prolonged than is the stimulus. This is one type of delay that tends to distort experience and to make stimuli seem to be somewhat different from what they really are.

Second, some delay occurs each time an impulse traveling down one nerve cell arrives at a synapse and activates another nerve cell. In the typical knee-jerk reflex, which the physician tries to elicit by tapping the tendon just below the kneecap, there is a characteristic delay between the tapping of the tendon and the appearance of the knee jerk. Much of this delay is due to delays at the synapses in the spinal cord, though some of it is due to the time it takes for the impulse to reach the spinal cord and return to the muscle that heaves up the leg.

Hebb (1948) suggests that there is a third delaying process that we have not as yet considered and which is of greatest importance to the operation of what are termed the higher mental processes. If an incoming impulse were to activate a loop like that shown in Figure 7, it would

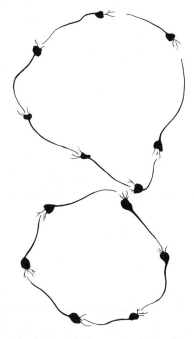

FIGURE 7. Schematic diagram of a part of a cell assembly that may permit continued activity within the nervous system after the stimulus initiating activity has ceased to operate.

be possible for the impulse to travel around that loop and thus delay the initiation of action. Since impulses travel at a high speed, it is probable that the impulse would return to the point from which it started before that section of the loop had had time to recover and was able to transmit the impulse again around the loop. If at that point a second loop were available, the impulse might then travel around this second loop. Thus, an impulse could for some time continue to activate the central nervous system. This provides some basis to account for the fact that when we see an object, we can and do continue to think about that object for some time after it has been removed from our field of vision.

Such a system of loops is known as a *cell assembly*. What we have referred to as mediating processes in the nervous system *may* consist of activities of cell assemblies of this type. One cannot at this time take a preserved brain and follow by careful dissection the path of such a cell assembly. A part of the difficulty in doing this is that the cell assemblies are believed to be extremely diffuse, straggling systems with paths that perhaps run all over the cortex. To separate such a path from the paths of the billion or more other cells does not seem to be feasible.

Hebb (1949) also relates the theory of the cell assembly to the process of learning in another way. He suggests that the establishment of the cell assemblies corresponds to the early learning process. The difficulty of the blind adult who gains vision for the first time is that he has no cell assemblies related to visual perception to enable him to interpret his percepts. His first task in learning to use visual cues involves the establishment of cell assemblies that permit him to recognize elements in his visual field. Hebb suggests that the establishment of these assemblies is a slow process, which accounts for the fact that early learning take place at such a slow speed. However, once the assemblies have been established, learning of complex functions dependent on them moves ahead at a rapid pace. These more advanced, or late, learning activities involve the development of connections between assemblies so that a whole series of assemblies may become activated in sequence. Although this theory has considerable elegance and fits the facts quite well, the evidence that supports it is indirect.

It is possible for the adult to perceive the shape of a square as a square because cell assemblies have been laid down that become active when a square is presented in the field of view. When the square is removed from the field of view, the individual still continues to think about the square, because the cell assemblies involved continue to be active.

According to the theory developed by Hebb (1958, p. 105), each cell assembly "corresponds to a relatively simple input, such as a particular vowel sound or syllable instead of a whole word, an increase of brightness, a simple odor, pressure on a particular area of the skin, a line of a particular slope in the visual field, and so on. Thus the perception of an actual object will involve not one but a number of assemblies. Activity of assemblies ABCDE is the perception of one object, of ABCDX a different object." This is theory, not fact; but it is a theory that fits well the evidence available at the present time and that has also permitted the scientist to make some predictions that have turned out to be valid.

According to this picture of the functioning of the nervous system, thinking consists of the successive activity of a series of cell assemblies. Such a sequence of cell-assembly activities is known as a *phase sequence*. Such a phase sequence constitutes an important type of mediating process. The particular sequence that is run off, given an initial starting point with a particular set of assemblies active, may vary from time to time and according to the particular activities with which the brain is engaged. One sequence may be much more compatible with activity in the brain than another, and hence tends to be run off.

Although it has been demonstrated that a piece of isolated brain tissue may continue for as long as an hour to manifest activity that has been initiated in it, there are good reasons for supposing that a cell-assembly mechanism is not the only means whereby the nervous system maintains activity that has been aroused in it. Another kind of activity that may maintain internal thought processes is derived from a theory of thinking of many decades ago known as the *motor theory* of thinking.

In the motor theory of thinking it was postulated that thinking was simply a matter of quietly talking to oneself or making some slight movements of the muscles. Thus, the person thinking about running a race would be making very slight movements of the muscles involved in actually running a race. Certainly it could be demonstrated that the theory had an element of truth to it. Thought is almost invariably accompanied by slight movements of the vocal cords, not enough to result in audible speech, but enough to be recorded by sensitive devices that amplify the electrical phenomena that accompany muscle movements. Another interesting fact is that the deaf and dumb do not show movements of the vocal cords during periods of thought, but rather show very slight movements of the fingers, which have in the past been the means of communication among them. Undoubtedly, the well-trained deaf of today who were born that way and who have learned to speak would tend to show movements of the vocal cords rather than movements of the fingers during thought processes.

The original movement theory of thinking, or the motor theory as it was called, failed to take into account one important fact—that any muscle activity immediately stimulates sense organs in the muscles, which in turn send impulses to the brain. Thus, a cycle is set up: efferent nerve impulses, muscle activity, sensory activity in the muscle, afferent impulses to the higher centers of the nervous system, efferent nerve impulses, muscle activity, and so forth.

Teachers of physical education have long maintained that training in motor skills such as are involved in sports involves the person's becoming more aware of the kinesthetic cues from muscles that provide him with much of the information available concerning the position of the parts of his body. Research has clearly established that a person deprived of such kinesthetic cues has difficulty in performing tasks involving posture and movement, and the theory that training in sports involves training in sensitivity to such cues is credible. How far sensitivity to such cues is trainable has still to be demonstrated.

Other cycles also exist. Sometimes, in writing, the written message perceived through the eye may in turn stimulate thought, which in turn results in the production of more writing. Doodling may also serve a similar function. The doodler presents certain ideas in a sign language which in turn stimulates ideas. Individuals differ enormously in the kinds of cycles they establish. One person familiar to the present writer spends a great deal of time during any conference writing, for this is the way in which he organizes his thinking. The notes he makes stimulate further thinking about the problems at hand, and this leads to the production of original contributions to the conference. Other individuals the writer knows cannot get along very well merely through the use of implicit speech at such a low level that it cannot be heard; some find it necessary to talk aloud in order to carry on an effective thought process. Unfortunately, their habits interfere rather considerably with the thinking habits of others, since they talk incessantly and usually monopolize the conversation.

Little is known about the relative value of the various cycles that can be set up for the facilitation of the thinking process, and neither is it known why some adults adopt one type of activity during thinking and others adopt a different one. Probably chance factors enter greatly into their establishment. If the child solves a problem while he happens to be doodling, then doodling is likely to be repeated as a part of the process for solving problems. Teachers often discourage some of these activities that are related to the thinking process, and commonly expect all children to do their thinking through the use of subvocal speech. This may or may not be desirable; we do not know at this time.

Inhibitory Processes

Up to this point, stress has been placed on the self-energizing properties of the nervous system, but important functions are also played by inhibition processes. The phenomenon discovered by Hernandez-Peon and his associates, which has already been discussed, represents an important inhibitory process involving the higher centers; but inhibitory processes may occur at all levels of the system. Over half a century ago Charles Sherrington (1906) pointed out that even simple muscular movements involve inhibitory processes. For example, when the biceps muscle in the upper arm contracts to raise the forearm, the triceps muscle at the rear of the upper arm must slowly relax to permit a smooth and even over-all movement. The relaxation of the triceps muscle involves inhibitory processes. Thus, in the movement of the limb, when the nerves leading to the muscle producing one form of movement are excited, those leading to the muscle that would produce the opposite movement are inhibited. This is the principle of reciprocal innervation.

Although the nature of sleep has long been considered controversial, many have taken the position, first proposed by Pavlov, that sleep is a state of general inhibition. Apart from the familiar ways of producing sleep, it can also be produced by rhythmical stimulation of the nervous system with mild electric currents. The latter is somewhat reminiscent of the way in which a mild rhythmical patting will often put a baby to sleep. For reasons unknown, these stimuli have the properties of producing states of general inhibition. The picture is complicated by the fact that sleep is not merely a state of inhibition, but clearly has important functions to perform which are clearly necessary even though they are not understood.

Most of the experiences that are attributed to "nervous fatigue" are inhibitory phenomena. To investigate this theory we should consider certain related facts:

First, nerves do not become fatigued through prolonged and repeated stimulation. Each time a nerve is stimulated and transmits an impulse, there is a very brief period that follows, known as the refractory period, during which another impulse cannot be transmitted. At the end of this very short period, recovery is complete, and the nerve is ready to transmit another impulse. Repeated stimulation does not produce a state of fatigue in which the nerve is unable to transmit an impulse for several seconds, minutes, or hours. Nervous fatigue, as a condition of depressed nervous activity resulting from excessive activity and the accumulation of by-products, does not occur.

Second, muscles can show fatigue. After a muscle has been frequently and strongly stimulated through the nerve, a time will come when further stimulation shows only a very weak level of activity. Try doing push-ups, and the time will soon come when one cannot raise oneself off the floor. In such a situation one would commonly say that the muscles were tired. Actually the difficulty is not muscular fatigue, but fatigue at the point where the nerve joins the muscle. Nervous impulses become blocked at that point and fail to activate the muscle.

Third, inhibitory processes in the nervous system tend to set in after a given activity has been pursued for a time. After a person has studied a book, say on history, for a long period of time, the point is reached where a change of activity is sought. It is largely for this reason that vacations are taken—to break the monotony of the daily routine. People whose jobs include a diversity of activities and little monotony do not feel the same need to "get away from things." When monotonous activity is prolonged, the boredom felt is the result of this kind of inhibitory process.

Related to the latter type of inhibitory process is the type of inhibition that may occur when an activity is repeated without reinforcement. The process of extinction sets in. Pavlov referred to this process as *reactive inhibition,* indicating by this that extinction is not just a fading process, but one that involves the building up of an inhibition. Not all psychologists would agree with this interpretation. A person who makes continued efforts to achieve a goal may manifest this phenomenon if he is faced with repeated failure, which amounts to performance without reinforcement. For example, a child beginning the violin may attempt to play the scale of C major in front of his teacher, who tells him each time that he is out of tune. If this goes on for a time, he may not only give up in his attempt to play a scale in tune, but he may also look upon the task with the greatest aversion. In such a case, reactive inhibition has set in, and it may become a relatively permanent characteristic of his behavior toward scale playing. A similar phenomenon is noted in children who have little success in learning to read at the time when most children do learn to read. Such children may not only grow up to be poor readers or nonreaders, but they may even grow up to be individuals who have an aversion for reading in any form. Much of what is called boredom is the result of performance without reinforcement, but boredom is also sometimes the immediate result of lack of stimulation.

When a person says that he is too tired to work any more, he may be referring to any of the phenomena just discussed. His muscles may be fatigued to the point where he cannot work any further, much as the person doing push-ups reaches the point where he cannot raise his body off the floor. Even when a person says that he is too tired to think, the cause may lie in the inability of his muscles to operate effectively. If certain muscles do not operate effectively the whole thinking mechanism may fail to operate.

Not all tiredness is of this kind. A person may close his book and say that he is too tired to study, and then settle down to play a brilliant game of bridge. In this case the primary problem is almost certainly not fatigue in the muscle area, but a general state of inhibition in the nervous system produced by pursuing a single course of activity over too long a period. This is often what one means by mental fatigue, and its main characteristic is that it is quickly dissipated by turning to another activity. It is characteristically seen in pupils toward the end of a day in school, when they become restless and have difficulty in concentrating on their work. Once the schoolbell sounds, most of this fatigue is dissipated.

The Autonomic Nervous System

An important division of the nervous system is a complex of nerves and ganglia that constitutes what is known as the *autonomic,* or *sympathetic,* nervous system. Since many significant aspects of behavior are associated with the activity of this system, some consideration to its function in relation to behavior must be given here.

The most recognizable components of this system are two cordlike structures that extend through the length of the body cavity. These are known as the sympathetic trunks. Each one of these has a number of bulges along its length consisting of masses of nerve cells. From the trunks, nerves can be seen to go to the viscera. It is also known that this system has nerves connected to all of the smooth muscles of the body, which are the muscles that are both slow-acting and not under voluntary control. The system also can activate certain glands, such as the adrenal glands.

The system derives its name from the fact that most of the functions it serves are not under voluntary control, and the system gives the superficial appearance of being an independent one, functioning on it own. The appearance here is deceptive, because it has been established that there are centers in the central nervous system that can induce activity in the autonomic system. The relationship to the central nervous system is highly complex.

The autonomic nervous system has built into it a complex series of reflex mechanisms. The pupil of the eye contracts automatically in the presence of bright light. Peristalsis occurs in the intestines when they are stretched by the presence of food, and by this means food is moved along the length of the tract.

The autonomic nervous system can be properly considered a part of the effector mechanism—that is, the efferent system that results in activity. That it does produce action is beyond question, but the action it produces is highly generalized and is not confined to specific muscles, as it is when an efferent nerve from the spinal cord is involved.

The autonomic nervous system also shows the effects of learning, and many visceral and other responses are acquired through a learning process that has not been clearly described as yet. The person who develops severe migraine headaches whenever he is placed in a stressful situation is manifesting an acquired response of the autonomic nervous system. The headaches are due to the activity of the small smooth muscles found in the walls of the blood vessels that supply the brain. A person's digestive system may not function properly in many situations that have been associated with stress. The blushing mechanism, in the case of a particular individual, may be triggered by numerous stimuli that do not ordinarily set it into action. Some of these learnings are relatively harmless, but others could conceivably have serious consequences and proceed to the point where the health of a person is damaged. Psychosomatic medicine is that branch of medicine that attempts to help people whose natural reflexes of the autonomic nervous system have been modified so that they are fired by inappropriate stimuli. One is tempted to suggest that the mechanism of classical conditioning might well account for disturbances of behavior occurring through the activity of the autonomic nervous system, but convincing evidence will have to be presented to prove that this is so. What can be demonstrated at the present time is that some of the reflexes associated with the autonomic nervous system can be conditioned, but there is a long step from such a demonstration to the position that psychosomatic disorders are a result of a process similar to classical conditioning.

Time Involved in Complex Operations

The time involved in various complex operations involving the higher centers of the nervous system can, in some cases, be roughly estimated. Information arriving from the senses leaves a trace that lasts for a short time and does not vanish as soon as the source of the information is removed. We can look at an object and then turn away, but our examination of the object leaves a trace that permits us to recall for a short time much about what we have seen; but the trace rapidly vanishes, and, even after a few seconds, little of it remains. Thus, one can glance at a telephone number and retain it long enough for dialing, but a few seconds later he might not be able to recall the number. Such a short-term retention of inputs of information is described by Hull (1957) as involving a *stimulus trace*. The stimulus trace is an internal phenomenon, the residue of the impact of the stimulus. The duration of such traces is brief, and current estimates suggest that they fade within a period of two or three seconds. If the material is committed to permanent memory, then the matter is different; but most stimuli are of only temporary significance, and the information they provide is held only in very temporary storage.

Perceptions of objects are not immediate, but only a rough estimate can be made of time taken for a full perception to develop after an object is presented to the senses. Flash a slide on a screen, and some time will elapse before the viewer will fully appreciate to the limit of his capacity what he is seeing. The time taken for perception to develop will depend on the complexity of what is presented; but Solley and Murphy (1962) suggest that the time is somewhere between 0.2 and 0.5 seconds and imply that the time may not differ too much from one mammalian species to another. An important point brought out by the same two authors is that any distracting event that occurs while a perception is developing may prevent the perception from emerging. This suggests that when, in a teaching situation, the pupil is confronted with the task of perceiving some novel object, time should be given for him to develop a full perception.

The rate at which reading can take place is obviously related to perception time. When the eyes of the reader are fixated at a particular place on a line of print, information is taken in that has to be interpreted by the nervous system. Gilbert (1959) has shown that, when a short line of printed material is flashed on a screen, a person can read it provided that the flash of print is followed by a blank display. However, if some other material is flashed on the screen immediately after the printed message, the line of print cannot be read. Gilbert takes this to mean that it takes time to interpret the line of print; he refers to this as *perception time*. If another message arrives on the screen during this perception time, then the perception is disrupted. The fixation of the eyes on particular parts of the page during reading serves the purpose of ensuring that only a particular part of the printed message is transmitted at one time and that enough time is allowed for the processing (perception) of this information before other information is allowed to enter the visual system. Thus, the fixations have to be of at least a certain minimum duration to permit the higher centers to handle effectively the information transmitted.

Another important constant that has not been properly established is the time it takes to switch from attending to an auditory input to attending to a visual input. One cannot switch from eye to ear instantaneously, and evidence suggests that some time is lost when the switch is made. During the time thus lost there is probably no intake of information from the outside. Broadbent (1958) suggests that the time lost in switching from attending to visual information to attending to auditory information may be as much as a half second. One can at least say that the time lost is not negligible, and that teaching films that involve a great deal of switching of this kind should be so designed that they provide the learner with the time intervals needed to make the switches. There is another odd and interesting fact in this matter of switching from one input to another. Reid (1964) observed in a study of the phenomenon that frequent switching requires effort and produces a great deal of frustration. In this respect the nervous system appears to work at a rather leisurely pace and is not readily pushed into making rapid shifts.

Another time consideration is the effect on learning of the length of time for which a particular stimulus or source of information is presented.

Here is a simple illustration: Suppose that children are learning French vocabulary by reading on the screen a French word, presented along with a picture of the object it represents. Suppose the teacher inserts a slide, allows it to remain five seconds for the children to read the word, and then withdraws it; and then nothing is shown on the screen for another five seconds (while the next slide is being inserted). From the child's point of view, the procedure involves a five-second exposure of the slide followed by five seconds with nothing on the screen. Thus the words are given at a rate of one every ten seconds. A significant question to ask about this learning situation is whether the children would learn more if the slide with the French word and the object were exposed for ten seconds rather than for only five. A number of studies have been undertaken of this kind of problem, though the learning task has generally involved nonsense syllables rather than foreign vocabulary. These studies include those by Murdock (1960), Bugelski (1962), and Bugelski and Rickwood (1963). The general finding of these studies is that exposure time is not a matter of any great importance, provided that the learner has time to read and understand what is presented. One may infer that it makes little difference whether the French words and objects are presented for five or for ten seconds; what is important is the ten seconds from one word to the next word.

Summary

1. The typical approach taken by the psychologist in the study of learning is to work with data concerning behavior. From such data he hopes to arrive at a theory of learning that will predict the conditions under which learning will occur most effectively.

2. Another approach is to begin by studying the structure and function of the human organism, and particularly those that are most closely related to the learning process. The hope has also been held that the study of the anatomy and physiology of the nervous system might also help to develop a more powerful theory of learning than could otherwise be developed.

3. An early tie was established between the biologists and psychologists when the traditional associationistic theory of learning appeared to match well with the concept of the nervous system as a complex switchboard that could establish relationships between stimuli and responses. The psychology of Edward L. Thorndike, of the early part of the century, was of this character. The conception of learning that this involved and the conception of physiology was soon found to be much too simple to account for the facts.

4. The nerve cell is the functional unit of the nervous system, and has been carefully studied by microanatomists since techniques were developed for making it clearly visible under the microscope. The nerve cell consists of a cell body and nucleus and an extensive system of hair-like processes that play an important role in the transmission of impulses. The longest of these is the axon, which may extend many feet to remote parts of the nervous system. Large numbers of other extensions of the nerve cell are referred to as the dendrites. Within the axon the transmission is an all-or-none affair, but this does not apply to the dendrites, where an impulse may fade out before it reaches the cell body.

5. The place where the axon of one nerve cell comes into proximity with the dendrites of another is referred to as the synapse. Under certain conditions the nerve impulse transmitted down the axon may result in the excitation of the dendrites of another cell at the synapse.

6. Axons fire and then enter a refractory phase during which a new impulse cannot be transmitted. At the end of the refractory phase, recovery is complete.

7. Major relay stations within the nervous system are referred to as nuclei. Groups of nerve-cell bodies are referred to as ganglia.

8. The central nervous system develops in the embryo as a tube running the length of the organism. Three swellings in the forepart of this tube eventually become that portion generally known as the brain. Nerves enter and leave the central nervous system along its length. The main nerve tracts within the system are referred to as the efferent, the afferent, and the internuncial. Those transmitting impulses away from the central nervous system to the muscles and glands are referred to as the efferent nerves. Those transmitting information from the sense organs are referred to as the afferent nerves. Internuncial fibers connect one part of the nervous system with another.

9. The impulse arriving along the afferent tracts may be relayed to the cerebral cortex, where they terminate in areas known as the sensory-projection areas. Although these areas have some specificity of function, they are not the only areas involved in perception related to these functions. The efferent system also has specific areas from which the efferent tracts originate.

10. The information that is transmitted from the senses to the higher centers undergoes compression during the process of transmission. Lateral inhibition, which has been studied in relation to the visual sense, appears to have the effect of compressing information by accentuating that which has greatest significance and suppressing that which has least. Additional information is discarded through two other mechanisms involved in the Hernandez-Peon effect and habituation.

11. Particularly important for the understanding of learning is the arousal system.

12. Studies of the Berger rhythm clearly demonstrate the activity that is inherent in the nervous system. Level of arousal depends on many factors, including the amount of sensory stimulation. The latter may in turn increase the activity of the arousal center in the midbrain. There appears to be an optimum level of arousal for effective learning. If the arousal level drops below or is raised above this level, then the efficiency of learning declines.

13. Inhibitory processes play an important role in the functioning of the nervous system. What is ordinarily called fatigue is an inhibitory process.

14. There is rarely, if ever, a direct path within the nervous system from the stimulus to the response. Most stimuli are reacted to after a delay. Although there are minor delays when the nerve impulse is being conducted along a nerve fiber, and other delays at synapses, these do not account for the relatively long delays that generally occur before a response occurs to a situation. An important mechanism postulated to account for such delays is the cell assembly. This idea was first made popular through the work of Hebb. If such cell assemblies exist, then the earliest stages of learning involve the establishment of such assemblies.

15. The nervous system cannot be fatigued in the ordinary sense of the term. The refractory phase represents a brief period of physiological fatigue, but recovery is rapid and complete. What is ordinarily referred to as mental fatigue may involve fatigue at the point of junction of muscle and nerve. In addition, so-called mental fatigue may involve the onset of states of inhibition in the central nervous system.

16. The autonomic nervous system performs important efferent functions. Disturbances of these functions may lead to illness. Such disturbances may be the result of conditioning through which the natural reflexes of the system come to be triggered by inappropriate stimuli.

17. Some knowledge has been obtained concerning the time involved in certain operations related to the handling of information. After there has been an input of information, the input leaves a stimulus trace for about two or three seconds. The time taken to structure information and to achieve a clear perception is about 0.2 to 0.5 second. In much learning, the time of exposure of each stimulus is much less important than the time from the exposure of one stimulus to the exposure of the next.

8

The Transfer of Training

ALL TEACHING is based on the assumption that the immediate skills, understandings, attitudes, appreciations, and other learned functions influence behavior in a diversity of subsequent situations. Skill in the writing of English is not taught so that the pupil may write better themes in school, but so that he will be able to prepare all kinds of effective written communications in his daily life. It is assumed that there will be *transfer of training* from whatever is learned in the field of writing in school to whatever has to be written in outside situations. For a similar reason, many schools today insist that problems within the school be handled according to democratic procedure, and the hope is expressed that such democratic practices will transfer to situations outside of the school. The concept of transfer of training is not a new one in education; it finds expression in the old educational doctrine of formal discipline.

The doctrine of formal discipline was based on the idea that certain mental activities exercise the mind and produce general mental agility. In order to produce the maximum amount of exercise, the most difficult subjects were advocated; clearly, the more difficult the exercise, the more agile the brain would become by its mastery. For this reason, mathematics and Latin often formed the core of the curriculum because of the difficulty pupils had in mastering these subjects. The fact that many pupils failed in a curriculum based on this concept of education was considered as a further argument that this was the way that education should proceed. Failure indicated that the school subjects were tough, and toughness meant that the subjects provided an excellent basis for training the mind. Mastery of these subjects was alleged to make for a sharp intellect that could master all kinds of problems.

The doctrine of formal discipline was attractive on the surface. It was based on a persuasive analogy from physical training—that exercise of muscles in rather artificial situations ultimately develops strength that can be utilized in all kinds of organized sports. Such analogies give plausibility to the doctrine, but they do not provide data to indicate that it is a sound one. The concept of formal discipline is really an educational theory, and, like all other theories, must stand or fall on the basis of rather carefully collected evidence.

The study of the effectiveness of formal discipline as a procedure for developing the mind led educators and psychologists to realize that this was part of a more general problem—namely, the extent to which the learning of any response facilitates or inhibits the learning or retention of other responses. This has become known as transfer of training. The term *transfer* is used because it implies that what is learned with respect to one task is transferred to the learning of future tasks. McGeogh and Irion (1958) define transfer of training a little more broadly: "Transfer of training occurs whenever the existence of a previously established habit has an influence upon the acquisition, performance, or relearning of a second habit." All learning takes place within the context of previous learning and hence involves transfer. In the learning of a simple skill, what is learned at one stage facilitates progress at the next stage—thus, what is learned at one stage transfers to learning at the next. The familiar learning curve is a product of transfer. In the McGeogh and Irion definition, the second habit may be learned after or before the first habit; the influence of the first habit on the second may be either forward or backward in time.

Transfer may be positive or negative. When it is positive, the acquisition of one skill facilitates the acquisition or retention of another skill. When it is negative, the acquisition of one skill interferes with the acquisition of another skill. An example of positive transfer is found in the teaching of arithmetic. The teaching of children to add two-digit numbers facilitates the learning of the addition of three- and four-digit numbers. This illustration is prosaic rather than dramatic, but it refers to the kind of transfer that most teachers must work toward. Examples of negative transfer are much more difficult to find, but one example is when the student of music arrives for his weekly lesson having spent the week practicing his assignment incorrectly; what has been learned incorrectly interferes with the subsequent learning of the correct version.

Transfer is not limited to intellectual responses alone; many emotional responses demonstrate transfer phenomena. One of the most transferable types of responses is the anxiety response. A child who is made highly anxious by the treatment accorded him by a teacher may show similar anxiety responses in the presence of other teachers. The anxiety may then spread to the entire school situation and may even transfer to the doing of homework and to all activities related to the school.

During the acquisition of a skill, some events occur that are not learning phenomena as such, but that may affect the acquisition of subsequent skills. For example, sometimes fatigue may depress the further acquisition of learning; in such a case, one would not speak of negative transfer.

Another phenomenon that resembles transfer but is not a true learning phenomenon is that of the "warm-up period." When a person begins a new activity, he does not function at maximum efficiency until some time has elapsed; this may be a matter of seconds or minutes, depending on the activity. In many activities this is a recognized phenomenon. The pitcher always goes through a warm-up workout before he is sent to the mound. The musician, even when practicing in his own home, goes through a warm-up activity such as playing scales before he undertakes more complicated exercises. The concert artist may practice behind the scenes right up to the minute of going on to the platform. The lecturer may spend some time right before his lecture reviewing ideas in his mind before he starts speaking, and he may do this even when he is to give a lecture he has given many times before. These are practices that have been arrived at through practical experience with the daily problems of living.

To a limited extent, one may expect that one activity may serve as a warm-up for a related activity, and there is some evidence that this is so. There also appear to be individual differences in the length of the warm-up period necessary. Some persons require little; others require an extended period. This characteristic of behavior has some implications for the planning and scheduling of the periods in the school; but not enough is known about it to be able to predict with any confidence that one arrangement of classes is better than another. Individual differences suggest that no one schedule can be arranged that will be effective for all children. Here, as elsewhere, mass education requires some compromises; and even then some children may be placed on schedules that are not the best for them.

The Design of Studies of Transfer

Let us suppose that a teacher is firmly convinced that the best way to give high-school youngsters a sound education is to train them in Latin because of the supposed value that this field of content has for the training of the mind. This teacher, having a scientific turn of mind, decides to collect some evidence that would either substantiate or reject her point of view. The problem seems to be a simple one with a straightforward solution. If Latin trains the mind, then those who take courses in Latin should become better problem solvers and better reasoners than those who do not. All that has to be done is to administer a test of reasoning at the end of high school and determine whether those who took Latin obtained higher scores than the others. Suppose a teacher does this and finds that the Latin scholars obtained much higher scores than those who took other subjects, and his conclusion is that the study of Latin has a general beneficial effect on the thinking processes of the students.

The conclusion of this teacher does not follow from the data. True, the pupils who had been exposed to Latin obtained higher scores on the reasoning test, but her conclusion overlooks the fact that these pupils might have also obtained higher scores if the test had been administered prior to the learning of Latin. As a matter of fact, there is considerable evidence that those who choose Latin as an elective in high school are likely to be the brighter students, and will obtain better scores on almost any test administered to them. This is a major difficulty in planning any study designed to throw light on the problem of formal discipline.

Studies that test the extent to which there is transfer from one field of learning to another within the school curriculum are difficult to design. Also, there are likely to be practical difficulties in carrying them out. One way to test the particular educational theory about the learning of Latin would be to identify a group of youngsters, say at the beginning of their junior year in high school, and assign half of them at random to Latin courses and the other half to some other subject such as shop, for which there are no special claims concerning its value as mental gymnastics. Students could be assigned to the one group or to the other either by such a process as tossing a coin or by the more refined process of using intelligence-test scores, which would then be used to match the two groups of students. The students would be tested on their ability to perform some task which, it was agreed, would indicate the mind-training value of the Latin courses. Studies to determine the influence of a particular aspect of a curriculum on intellectual ability should generally follow the plan outlined below:

Group I (*Experimental*)	Test of initial level of skill A	Training in B hypothesized to transfer to skill A	Test of final level of skill A
Group II (*Control*)	Test of initial level of skill A	An unrelated activity	Test of final level of skill A

The value of Latin for facilitating learning in other fields of study has been investigated, though it has not been possible to carry out the clear-cut experimental design outlined above. There are various statistical devices that permit estimation of what the results would have been in the experimental plan discussed had it been carried out. One of the earliest studies in this area was undertaken by Hamblen (1925) as a doctoral study. In the Hamblen study an effort was made to find out whether the teaching of Latin increased knowledge of English vocabulary when emphasis was placed on the teaching of the derivation of English words from the Latin forms. The control group consisted of children who were taught Latin, but with whom the derivation of English words was not stressed. The children in both groups were given a vocabulary test at the beginning and at the end of the school year. The group that studied Latin with an emphasis on the Latin derivations of English words showed a greater gain in vocabulary than did the control group. However, an important outcome of this study is that the gain was almost entirely in words that are Latin in origin. In all probability, an even greater increase in the scores of pupils in English vocabulary would have been made if the time devoted to the study of Latin had been devoted to the study of English.

Later studies raised questions about the modest effect of learning Latin on English vocabulary. When Douglass and Kittleson (1935) later studied the effect of learning Latin on the pupils' knowledge of English grammar, spelling, and vocabulary, no significant differences were found between those who had learned Latin and those who had not. Pond (1938) conducted a similar study, but could find no effect of the teaching of Latin on growth in English vocabulary.

If the teaching of Latin has little effect on the acquisition of related English vocabulary, it is even less likely to have an effect on the development of complicated learning skills that are even more remotely related to the activities involved in the learning of Latin.

The classical design for the study of transfer of training has since been replaced by a more complicated system of designs as scientists' concepts related to these phenomena have become more sophisticated. Two main designs are commonly found today. One is called the *proaction* design and the other the *retroaction* design. The word *proaction* means that the effect occurs on some condition in the future. The term *retroaction* means that the effect of a condition is manifested backward in time on some previous condition. Now consider each one of these designs separately.

The proaction design takes the following form:

Experimental group:	Learn Task 1	Test on Task 2
Control group:	Rest or unrelated activity	Test on Task 2

In this design a determination is made of the effect of learning Task 1 on the *subsequent* performance of Task 2.

Contrast the above design with the retroaction design, which can be schematically represented as follows:

Experimental group:	Learn Task 1	Learn Task 2	Test on Task 1
Control group:	Learn Task 1	Rest or unrelated activity	Test on Task 1

In this design the implication is that the learning of Task 2 acts back on the learning that has occurred in Task 1, and hence produces either an increase or decrease in performance when the test on Task 1 is subsequently given. In this design the effect of the learning of Task 2 on the retention of Task 1 is studied. Although this is referred to as the retro-action design, implying that there is a backward effect, the impact of Task 2 is an immediate one on the *memory trace* of Task 1. This is to be contrasted with the so-called proaction design, in which the effect of one task is on the *learning* of another task.

A serious problem in the design of all experiments in transfer is that of deciding what the control group is to do while the experimental group is active. A state of rest has much to be said in its favor, but this provides the human subject with opportunities to rehearse what they have already learned. True rest also provides the control-group students with some advantages, for they may come refreshed to the final testing, while the experimental group may by that time be tired of being tested. Another approach is to provide the control group with some irrelevant task, though one cannot be sure that any task is completely irrelevant to the learning situations.

Why have psychologists differentiated between the proactive and the retroactive transfer of learning situations? The answer is that transfer of training appears to operate differently in these two situations. Transfer may be positive in one of these situations and negative in the other, a fact that indicates the tremendous complexity of the problem of transfer.

Early Laboratory Approaches to the Study of Transfer

Thorndike was the first to attempt to formulate a systematic theory of transfer. Although his theory would be considered today a gross over-simplification of the phenomenon, it is necessary to outline it here because such an outline will facilitate the understanding of later-developed theories. You may remember that learning, for Thorndike, involves the development of bonds between stimuli and responses. According to him, what is learned is a bond that may be considered a connection in the nervous system between an input on the stimulus end and an output on the response end. In Thorndike's (1923) theory, transfer of training will occur from an activity involving certain bonds, say XYZ, to another activity, if that activity involves also the bonds XYZ. This is the famous theory of *identical elements*. But Thorndike is actually vague concerning what he means by identical elements. In one sentence he speaks of identical elements as "mental processes which have the same cell action in the brain as their physical correlates [p. 359]." However, he does add, "It is of course often not possible to tell just what features of two mental abilities are thus identical."

Thorndike sought experimental evidence to support his position on transfer, and attempted to impose the theory of identical elements in the interpretation of the data. He quoted studies by Woodworth (1899), Swift (1903), and Starch (1910) that showed that skills learned with one side of the body, such as the left hand, were readily transferred to the symmetrically opposite side of the body, in this case to the right hand. This, he said, was because there were identical elements involved in the two skills, and these were believed to be perceptual skills. To perform any task of dexterity with the hands requires that the person be able to see what has to be done and to make use of cues when he sees that things are going wrong. These visual skills appeared to Thorndike to represent the identical elements involved in the transfer of training from one side of the body to the other. The massive transfer of training found in these studies was to be expected in terms of Thorndike's theory.

Thorndike himself had conducted studies on transfer of training, some of them with a young man who was also destined to become a famous psychologist—Robert S. Woodworth. These experiments involved the results of training, in estimating areas, lengths, and weights of particular sizes and shapes, on the ability to estimate other areas, sizes, shapes, and weights. The conclusions to this series of studies are given here in Thorndike's own words (1923):

> Improvement in any single mental function need not improve the ability in functions commonly called by the same name. It may injure it.
> Improvement in any single mental function rarely brings about equal improvement in any other function, no matter how similar, for the working of every mental function-group is conditioned by the nature of the data in each particular case. . . .
> The general consideration of the cases of retention or of loss of practice effect seems to make it likely that spread of practice occurs only where identical elements are concerned in the influencing and influenced functions. [Vol. 1, p. 250]

At the time when Thorndike conducted his review of the literature on transfer, a number of studies had been undertaken to determine the effect of learning poetry by rote on both the further learning of poetry and the learning of other materials. The position taken by the advocates of the doctrine of mental discipline would be that the learning of poetry would provide mental drill that should produce a widespread improvement in the mind. The empirical evidence provided by these studies showed that there was little transfer from the learning of one poem to the learning of another, let alone to the improvement of other memory functions.

There was another valuable outcome of this work, of less immediate practical value but of long-term consequence: attempts to reformulate the problem of transfer. Thorndike considered the common elements that produced transfer to be identical elements in the internal processes. There is also another way of looking at the matter. Transfer may be related to the extent to which the tasks involved resemble one another. Task similarity is surely a factor. Then, too, there may be transfer because there are similarities in the responses involved. In modern terms one may say that two tasks may resemble one another on the stimulus side or they may resemble one another on the response side. The resemblance may also be on both sides.

Two examples will now be considered of changing tasks on the stimulus end and changing them on the response end. In learning a foreign language, new verbal responses are learned to all the common situations encountered in life. In learning French, the person learns to say "*bon jour*" instead of "good morning," when he encounters someone in the morning. The stimulus situations remain the same, but new responses are learned to them. At a more advanced stage of learning French, the student replies in French to questions asked in French, and in such a case both the stimulus situation and the responses are different from those he has previously learned in his native culture. Now for an example in which the familiar responses must be made to new situations: A student entering a course in psychology is likely to find that many familiar terms are used in the discussion of human behavior, but he is confused by the fact that these are used with new meanings—that is to say, they are applied to new situations. The new uses he must learn to the familiar terms represent learnings that are often difficult to undertake, because previous learning has already produced a well-established set of uses.

A Model for Transfer of Training

A model that incorporates the idea that the amount of transfer from Task 1 to Task 2 depends on the similarity of the tasks (stimulus similarity) and the similarity of the responses to the tasks (response similarity) has been developed by Osgood (1949). The model is based on data derived from the retroaction design, previously discussed, and summarizes research in which Task 1 is learned, then Task 2, and finally Task 1 is relearned. The effect of Task 2 on Task 1 is studied in this design. Maximum positive transfer is achieved when Task 1 and Task 2 are identical, for then the learning of Task 2 is the same as additional learning on Task 1.

Osgood claimed that when he reviewed the literature, no exceptions could be found to his model. In the same article he also attempted to formulate a general model for transfer of training involving the use of a retroaction design as well as the proaction design previously considered. The model he provided is represented by a simple three-dimensional graph which has provided some success in predicting when positive transfer and when negative transfer is to be expected. This graph is reproduced in Figure 8.

In this graph, response similarity between what we have called Task 1 and Task 2 is shown along one dimension. Stimulus similarity is shown along a second dimension. Response similarity and stimulus similarity

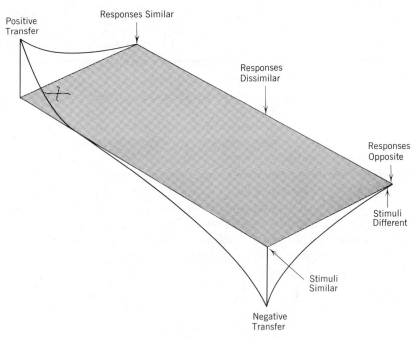

FIGURE 8. Diagram showing the relationship between response similarity and stimulus similarity of two tasks and the amount of transfer expected from one task to the other. The diagram is an attempt by Osgood (1949) to bring together the findings available at the time. (Reproduced by permission of the American Psychological Association)

are together represented by a plane. The third dimension represents a dimension varying from positive transfer to negative transfer. The curved surface represented in the diagram is used to indicate whether positive or negative transfer is to be expected. Any point in the rectangular plane indicates a particular degree of stimulus similarity and a particular degree of response similarity between two tasks. In order to find out how much transfer there will be from the first task to the second, a perpendicular line is drawn from the plane to the point where it cuts the curved surface. If it cuts it above the plane, then the transfer is positive. If it cuts it below the plane, then the transfer is negative.

As an example, consider the point X. This point represents two tasks that involve almost the same stimuli and almost the same responses. The perpendicular from that point cuts the curved surface above the plane, indicating that positive transfer is to be expected. This is to be expected because the performance of the same task again and again with minor variations is the process by which most skills are acquired

The Osgood model appears to be based partly on the mechanism of stimulus generalization that may underlie transfer phenomena. If two tasks present similar stimuli and require the same responses, then what is learned in relation to the stimuli presented with one task will generalize to the related stimuli provided by the second task. Thus, what is learned in relation to the one task is to some degree transferred to performance on the second task. This represents the operation of stimulus generalization. On the other hand, consider the case of two tasks that call for different responses to similar stimuli. In such a case, two sets of responses are learned to the same stimuli. These responses come to compete with each other and, hence, negative transfer is produced.

The Osgood model takes advantage of the fact that the learning of one set of responses to stimuli can also strengthen related responses. The darkened area in the diagram is the area in which such phenomena are represented. Thus, the child studying French who learns to associate rue–"road" also learns at the same time to associate rue–"street" even though the latter association is never deliberately practiced. The association that is directly learned, in this case the association rue–road, will be strengthened more than other related responses that are strengthened by generalization. Thus, when a list of French words and their English equivalents have been learned, it is easy for the student to learn the same French words and the synonyms of the English words. However, the learning of the original list of French and English equivalents would not help the student to learn a new list in which the original French words had to be associated with nonsense syllables, as for example in the association rue–"tek." Indeed, the chances are that the learning of the original French-English associations might interfere with the learning of the new list, because when the student was presented with the word *rue,* he might immediately begin to say the word *road,* which might block him from recalling the syllable *tek,* which he was now attempting to learn.

Thus, when learning a new set of associations to a particular set of stimuli, the associations previously learned will facilitate learning if the new responses are similar to the original responses; but if the new responses are very different, then interference is likely to be produced. The phenomenon of facilitation can be interpreted as response generalization; negative transfer is probably a blocking effect produced by the fact that there are responses that compete with the new responses to be learned. These are very different phenomena, but sometimes both may operate at the same time.

Data fit the Osgood model well when positive transfer is involved. In classic investigations by Yum (1931) and Gibson (1941), transfer was studied when the responses were the same but the stimuli varied. As the stimuli became less similar to those involved in the original learning, less and less transfer was found. This fits well a common-sense view of transfer and also the Osgood model. Some research supports the predictions of negative transfer made by the Osgood model, but some does not.

The Osgood position is also supported to some extent, but not entirely, by data in a study by Deese and Hardman (1954). In this study, subjects learned in Task 1 to complete short sentences with single-word responses. In Task 2 they learned new completions that were either synonyms or entirely different words. Positive transfer occurred in the case of the synonyms, but negative transfer occurred when the new words learned were unrelated to the word previously learned. However, not all of the results of this study gave support to the Osgood model. Hartman and Deese carried their study one step further by asking their subjects to relearn Task 1 after they had finished with Task 2. It was then that they found the surprising result that both lists used in Task 2 produced negative transfer. This finding would not have been predicted by Osgood.

Simple perceptual-motor learning tasks have demonstrated positive transfer when the stimuli remain the same but the responses are altered, although the Osgood model predicts negative transfer. Duncan (1953) developed an apparatus that permits the study of this kind of learning and the transfer that it involves. The apparatus involves a series of six lights that could be turned on or off by the experimenter. The subject responded by taking hold of a lever, which he could move into one of six slots. The subject was instructed at the beginning of Task 1 that a colored light would appear on the screen in front of him and that he was to move the lever into one of the slots. For each colored light there was one slot that was correct; the others were wrong. In Task 1 the learning task was to discover which slot was associated with each light. In Task 2 the subject was told that a new system of relationships between the lights and the slots had been established and that he was to learn the new system. The experimenter found positive transfer that depended on the extent to which the first task was learned and the degree of similarity of the two tasks. The better the learning of the first task, the greater was the amount of transfer. The more closely similar the responses were in the two tasks, the greater also was the transfer.

Experiments on transfer involving the building of associations between words or between words and nonsense syllables involve all kinds of un-controlled variables that may well account for the some of the incon-sistencies found from experimenter to experimenter. Deese (1958) has pointed out, in this connection, that some experimenters using word-association tasks have found positive transfer where negative transfer was fully expected. He suggests that this may sometimes be a result of using in the experiments students unfamiliar with word-association tasks. What is transferred in such cases is a general skill in performing these tasks, which they learn with the first task presented.

Some recent writers have found that their data fit better an earlier model known as the Skaggs-Robinson model, which was first published in 1927 (Robinson, 1927). The Skaggs-Robinson hypothesis stated that both the amount and the nature of the transfer depended on the similarity of the two tasks involved. If the two tasks were either identical or entirely dissimilar there was little negative transfer to be expected, but if the tasks show a particular degree of similarity then maximum negative transfer or interference would occur. Robinson (1927), whose paper contains the hypothesis, did not distinguish between stimulus similarity and response similarity as does Osgood. The relationship between the amount of transfer and the similarity of the two tasks would be repre-sented graphically by the relationship shown in Figure 9. Bugelski and Cadwallader (1956) found that less interference was produced when Task 2 in the retroaction design was one involving opposite responses rather than similar responses. The Osgood model predicts that the learn-ing of opposite responses will produce maximum interference or negative transfer with Task 1, but this is not what the data showed. On the con-trary, maximum interference was produced when the responses called for in Task 2 were similar but not identical with those in Task 1, a finding that fits well the Skaags-Robinson hypothesis.

Learning How to Learn: Learning Sets

That people can learn how to learn has long been demonstrated in experimental situations. This phenomenon has been well established in laboratory studies of the learning of meaningless nonsense syllables, chosen because such material is supposedly equally unfamiliar to all

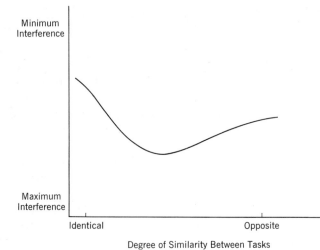

FIGURE 9. Graph representing the Skaags-Robinson hypothesis.

subjects. Ward (1937) showed that as subjects learned lists of syllables, their speed of learning became more and more rapid with each new list. Later Melton and VonLackum (1941) demonstrated that such a phenomenon could still be demonstrated after considerable amounts of practice. This learning-how-to-learn phenomenon represents a rather permanent kind of learning, and is manifest for long periods after practice has stopped.

Somewhat earlier Woodrow (1927) had demonstrated that even in such familiar classroom activities as learning poetry, facts, dates, and foreign vocabulary, pupils could be taught learning techniques that would improve their learning efficiency.

A similar phenomenon has been demonstrated by Harlow (1949), who has developed a program of research in this general area, first working with monkeys and later extending the studies to human subjects. In the typical Harlow type of experiment, a monkey is trained on simple discrimination problems. The monkey may be presented with two objects, a cube and a solid triangle; under one of them there is a raisin. Soon the monkey learns that the raisin is under the cube and not under the triangle. Having mastered this problem, he is presented with the next one. This time the two objects are both cubes, but one is black and one is white. He must learn a new discrimination, and it takes time to master this problem. When the monkey has mastered it, another new problem is presented, and so forth. After a long series of such problems, the monkey is able to master new problems with great speed and requires very few trials compared with the trials required to master the first problems. It is said that the monkey has learned how to solve problems of this kind. He has learned, so to speak, what to look for. He also has learned to switch as soon as the rules are switched. He has learned how to learn new problems. Harlow, in referring to this phenomenon, states that the monkey has acquired a *learning set* for solving the problems. A similar phenomenon has been shown to occur with young children. As problems of a particular class are solved, new problems in the same class are solved with increasing speed and facility.

When Harlow talks about a learning sequence that produces the development of a learning set, he is generally referring to a long series of problems that are presented to the subject. It is not uncommon in his work for there to be several hundred problems in a single sequence designed to build a learning set. These problems are generally distributed over many sessions, which take place on successive days. The learning sets he develops both in primates and in young children are rather slowly acquired. Older children and adults might develop learning sets much more rapidly, but data on such subjects is at present hard to find, perhaps because it is much easier to find young children who will participate day after day than it is to find older people who are equally available.

Harlow maintains that the development of learning sets represents a very generalized type of learning phenomenon. He suggests that most concepts, such as triangularity, redness, number, and so forth, are attained by a process similar to that involved in the development of learning sets. He also considers that his data throws light on the phenomenon known as insight. He believes also that he is dealing with the basic phenomena involved in the transfer of complex skills to new situations.

An interesting phenomenon in the development of learning sets occurs when the problems present reversals in the cues provided. For example, a child learns, when he is presented with two dishes turned upside down, that a piece of candy is to be found under the black dish and that there is nothing under the white dish. The problem conditions are then reversed, and the candy is placed under the white dish instead of the black dish. In terms of the Osgood model of transfer, negative transfer would be expected, and the child would be expected to have difficulty in learning the new solution because it conflicts with what he has previously learned. This is found to be the case. However, the rules can be switched again and the problem reversed, and, after this has happened many times, the negative-transfer effect disappears and the subject switches rapidly as the problem is switched. The subject becomes flexible in his approach to the problems presented and learns to change his pattern of response readily as the problem changes. The possibility of using such training in order to develop flexibility in problem solvers needs further exploration because of its important implications for education.

Harlow (1959) has attempted to answer the question "How can the acquisition of learning sets be planned so that they are learned with maximum rapidity?" The answer to this problem is also clearly important for education. In attempting to find an answer, Harlow points out that the amount transferred from any problem to the next problem in the series depends on the amount learned with the particular problem. If learning with a particular type of problem is discontinued before much is learned, then little transfer to the next problem can be expected. On the other hand, one should not give practice with a particular problem beyond the point where learning shows diminishing returns. Harlow, after reviewing the evidence, suggests that in the early problems in a series considerable time should be spent on them, since the learning curve on these problems continues to rise even after many trials. In the later stages of the acquisition of a learning set, little is learned, for by this stage the learner has reached the point where he solves new problems with great rapidity. Evidence has come from Harlow's laboratory to show that if training on problems in the early stage is too brief, then a learning set may never develop. On the other hand, after the early stages of learning have been passed and the subject is learning with rapidity, only two or three trials with each new problem may be needed to produce further development of a learning set.

In recent years Harlow has attempted to link the concept of a learning set to what he has called *error-factor theory.* According to this theory, in any learning situation the subject brings to it certain responses that turn out to be wrong responses. For example, consider the case in which a young child is learning to choose the black inverted dish that covers a piece of candy and to avoid the white dish that has nothing underneath. In such a case, the experimenter would arrange the experimental situation so that the black dish was sometimes to the right and sometimes to the left. However, a subject might have a tendency to choose the right-hand dish, a tendency that would result in the subject's making errors during the learning process. If the subject had a tendency to choose the white dish rather than the black one, then learning would become a difficult task, indeed, and, in fact, might never occur.

Harlow has attempted to list some of the error factors involved in learning. Some subjects, he notes, have a preference for particular stimuli rather than others. Such tendencies account for the behavior seen in some subjects who continue to make the same error time after time. Another error factor is due to what is called the differential cue. Many cues are present on each trial, and the subject may learn to respond to the wrong cue. For example, in demonstrating addition of two-digit numbers, the teacher may have, by accident, selected problems so that the right-hand digit of the sum is always 4. A child may note this and, in the next problem he attempts, write down 4 for the first digit of the sum. The demonstration of the teacher gave him a false cue, which introduced an error factor into his behavior.

Harlow's results are important also because they throw light on a psychological phenomenon called *insight*, which at one time intrigued many psychologists and about which a substantial amount of technical literature has been written. The word *insight* has many meanings, but in psychological literature it generally refers to the sudden solution to a problem. In much psychological writing, a solution to a problem is said to be insightful if it occurs suddenly and if the animal or person can from that point on solve the problem immediately every time it is presented. If the solution occurs slowly with the gradual elimination of wrong moves, it is said that the solution is occurring by trial and error. For a long time there was doubt whether animals did make sudden solutions to problems.

Data of considerable interest in this connection was collected by Karl Kohler, a German psychologist who, during much of World War I, was a prisoner of war on the island of Teneriffe. During his internment there, he was able to experiment with the problem-solving ability of chimpanzees. In one classic study he was able to show that one of his chimpanzees was able to put together two sticks, fitting one inside the other, in order to reach a banana outside the cage, which he could not reach with either stick alone. The solution came suddenly, and was discussed by Kohler in his book on the subject (1926) as an illustration of insightful behavior. Our present interest in the data is not really in the matter of whether the chimp did or did not have the psychological experience of insight, but rests on the fact that only under exceptional conditions does the sudden solution to a problem occur. This became apparent when later workers tried to reproduce the results but were unable to do so. It had to be discovered that animals will show such sudden insightful solutions to problems only after they have had extensive training with the same general class of problems. What happens is that as the animal develops a learning set that facilitates the solution to a particular class of problems, solutions come quicker and quicker. Eventually some solutions come almost immediately. Probably much the same is true with humans who solve problems with great rapidity once they have had extensive experience with similar problems. What is generally termed insightful behavior in the human problem solver is behavior that is dependent on a background of wide experience.

The discussion of insightful behavior and its relation to experience raises a problem that has often been discussed in educational circles— namely, whether thinking skills should be taught first and then knowledge of facts, or whether the reverse should occur. A third alternative is that they be taught simultaneously. Knowledge and experience appear to be a prerequisite to adequate thinking. Before one can think, he must have had extensive experience in the area in which thinking is to occur. The experience constitutes the early learning process that must occur before the complex operation of thinking is possible. This does not mean, of course, that curriculum should begin with a process of rote learning of facts; but rather, it means that there must be a progression of problems faced by the pupils. The earliest of these problems must be very simple and must eventually lead to more and more complex problems. Some information may be learned with each problem, so that the sum total of information is steadily increased. This is precisely what a learning program designed for use in a teaching machine attempts to do.

The phenomenon of learning sets also accounts for the tendency for both knowledge and thinking to be compartmentalized. The eminent scientist may appear stupid when he tries to think about social and political problems. The compartmentalization of knowledge and thinking is a well-established phenomenon, which has been clearly demonstrated in studies by Furst (1950).

Learning to learn, the phenomenon of learning sets, represents an example of transfer in which general methods of attack on problems that are learned during the training period are transferred to new problems at a later time. A person who has had experience with problems of a certain class has a whole repertoire of approaches to those problems. A teacher of reading who finds a pupil having difficulty knows about a great many different sources of difficulty that she can explore with the child. A less experienced teacher might find the same problem completely baffling. To a great extent this is why an experienced teacher who has taken a problem-solving approach to her work over the years becomes highly skilled at solving the problems presented by the classroom.

Although the experiments on learning sets have found comparable results with chimpanzees and with young children, one must exercise some caution before generalizing the results to older children and adults. The results of the experiments reported by Kendler and Kendler (1962) suggest that, with the development of language, some of the long and slow training processes involved in the traditional experiments on learning sets may be short-circuited. Through the use of language, approaches to the solution of problems may be learned without prolonged training, though some practice in the application of the rules thus learned would appear to be necessary.

Variability of Training and Transfer

Is more transfer to be expected by giving concentrated training with a single type of task, or by providing training with tasks that show variability? The answer to this question has important implications for curriculum design. A study by Duncan (1958) attempts to answer it. But the answer may well be inferred from studies of learning sets undertaken by Harlow, though the latter has never made a direct experimental comparison of equal amounts of training given under different amounts of task variability. In the Duncan study the number of different tasks given to different groups varied from one to ten, and different amounts of training were given at each level of task variation. The results were quite clear. Among groups trained with different sets of tasks, the amount of transfer increased as a direct function of the degree of variability in the tasks. The latter conclusion was true regardless of whether a small or large amount of training was involved.

A special case of the development of a learning set is seen in the acquisition of a mode of attack on a problem that can then be transferred to the solution of new problems. In a significant experiment undertaken many years ago by Woodrow (1927) it was demonstrated that a group that had considerable training in the techniques most effective for the memorizing of poetry was able to memorize poetry more rapidly than one that had had only practice in memorizing without instruction in techniques of memorizing. What the one group had learned was an effective way of going about this particular task. The individuals in this particular group knew how to go about the task that was presented to them. Most courses in study habits, commonly run by departments of educational psychology, help the student to develop modes of attack; and there is a little evidence to show that students become a little more effective as learners once they have mastered efficient modes of attack.

Should the student learn modes of attack through his own efforts, or should he be shown? This is an educational issue of great importance. Some have taken the extreme viewpoint that the pupil himself should discover efficient modes of attack on problems by solving them himself; but most of the studies that have been undertaken in this area do not support this point of view. A number of studies have shown that some guidance early in learning may develop modes of attack, which can then be used efficiently in solving problems encountered in the future. These modes of attack correspond to what have been described as successful strategies.

There is some question whether guidance should be given right at the time a problem is first presented, or whether the learner should be allowed first to become somewhat familiar with the situation. In learning to use a tool, it may be desirable for the learner to begin by handling and examining the tool and perhaps even making certain minor attempts to use it before he is actually shown how the tool should be used. Learners need to make these preliminary adjustments to the learning situation before they are ready for any instruction.

Transfer Involving Complex Mediating Processes Including Verbal Processes

The Osgood model appears to apply most effectively to those situations in which the task undertaken is a perceptual-motor task, such as is involved in learning to operate a piece of equipment. It also appears to apply, but with considerably less adequacy, to simple paired-associate learning such as is involved in learning new names for familiar objects in foreign language learning. The main limitation of applying the model is that there are no well-established techniques for measuring either stimulus similarity or response similarity. Consider, for example, the problem of predicting whether the experience of learning to drive a car will later facilitate learning to operate an airplane. A car is steered with the hands but to change direction in an airplane, you also use your feet. The throttle of a car is controlled with the foot, but that of the aircraft is manual. A car needs no control for elevation, but an airplane does. Should one consider the stimulus elements on these two tasks to be positively or negatively related? It would appear that they call for neither similar nor opposite responses, but different responses. Should one infer from the latter statement that no transfer would take place? Probably not.

The model becomes less applicable when one enters the field of complex verbal learning such as takes place in many school subjects. A student learns Archimedes' principle through a demonstration involving the change in weight of a piece of lead when it is immersed in water. His understanding of the principle is then tested in a situation in which he has to explain why smoke rises in a chimney. Some students will be able to transfer the knowledge gained by studying the loss of weight of an object when immersed in water to the chimney problem. Some positive transfer will occur, but surely not because of any simple similarity between the task elements involved or the overt responses involved. The transfer, in this case, would appear to occur because the student is able to derive and understand a principle. Ausubel (1963) has taken the position that transfer in most academic learning situations is much more dependent on such verbal mediating processes than it is on objective task similarity and response similarity. What the pupil must do is first recognize that a solid body immersed in water has an upward force exerted on it by the water and that a body of hot gas also has an upward force exerted on it by the surrounding air. Both situations have to be coded as situations involving an upward thrust on a body exerted by a surrounding medium. In order for the pupil to be able to do this he must have learned in the first place not just that a body immersed in water loses weight, but that this is an example of a class of situations in which a body is surrounded by a gaseous or liquid medium. He has to learn to code such situations as belonging to a class. It is through learning to code situations as presenting or not presenting the essential features of Archimedes' principle that makes transfer possible. The application of a principle to different situations demands that the situations have some similarity, but the similarity may be at an abstract level, as it was in the case just examined.

A point to be noted is that when a student learns Archimedes' principle by observing the loss of weight of a piece of lead as it is immersed in water and then applies his knowledge to understanding why smoke rises in a chimney, any positive transfer that occurs can hardly be interpreted in terms of any simple concept of stimulus similarity. A body immersed in water and smoke in a chimney do not have stimulus similarity in any simple sense of the term. However, the physicist who examines the two situations can *abstract* certain similarities. He sees that water provides a certain buoyancy for the lead, and that the air around the chimney provides a buoyancy for the smoke in the chimney, sufficient to make it rise. Transfer from the one situation to the other occurs because the individual is able to *code* the information from the two situations in the same way. If a person were not able to code the information in the two situations in the same way, involving coding categories such as *buoyancy*, transfer would probably not occur.

It has long been suggested by knowledgeable teachers that it is much more economical to learn principles than facts. The argument is that principles enable the student to solve a whole range of problems; facts are much more limited in the uses to which they can be put. A classic demonstration of this was reported by Judd (1908). In the demonstration two groups of children were formed. One group was taught the principle of refraction. Both groups were then given practice in throwing darts at a target placed twelve inches under water. The darts had to be thrown obliquely, which made this a fairly difficult task to learn. The target was then raised until it was only four inches beneath the surface of the water, and the children were asked to continue their efforts to hit the target under the new conditions. The group that had been instructed in the principle of refraction adjusted much more readily than the other group to the new condition. The control group showed little transfer from the learning that had taken place under the initial condition. This experiment was later repeated by Hendrikson and Shroeder (1941), who substituted an air rifle and the shooting of a pellet for the dart. The results were closely similar to those reported by Judd. The principle taught represents in these studies a condition that facilitates transfer.

There are also other ways in which general principles may transfer to a range of new situations. In another classic experiment by Bagley (1905), different groups of children were taught neatness in two different ways. One group was taught neatness with respect to certain specific situations, such as in the way they did their schoolwork. The other group was taught neatness as a general principle of action to be pursued in daily life. In one group neatness was largely confined to the specific situation in which it was taught. In the other group there was some transfer of this characteristic to a range of situations. Although Bagley obtained this result, there is little evidence to show that most principles of conduct taught in school or home generalize to other situations. Sad to say, there is no known way, as yet, through which principles of conduct can be effectively taught with any guarantee that they will affect conduct in a wide range of situations.

One is tempted to generalize from the studies of Judd and Bagley and say that the learning of principles is a sound educational procedure because it facilitates transfer, but clearly this does not always happen. Not only do principles sometimes fail to generalize, but they may transfer to situations in which they are not appropriate. It is probable that the generalization of principles to new situations follows the same laws as other forms of transfer. If the student is faced with a situation in which the application of a previously learned principle is appropriate, he is most likely to apply the principle if the situation is similar to those in which he has made successful application of the principle in the past. As it becomes different from the previous situations, then it becomes less and less likely that the principle will be applied. Children who have learned Archimedes' principle can easily explain why the diver has to wear artificial weights. However, the same children are quite unlikely to see that the phenomenon of smoke rising in a chimney is also an illustration of the same principle. This is because Archimedes' principle is always learned by means if illustrations of bodies submerged in liquids, and to apply the same principles to the behavior of gases is quite a remote application.

The learning of principles represents the acquisition of mediating processes that facilitate related learning. The acquisition of a principle can be thought of as learning how to solve a whole class of problems; when examples of this class of problems are presented, they can readily be solved. The learning is closely related to the acquisition of verbal skills, though it is conceivable that something analogous to a principle could be learned without any verbal habits becoming involved.

The learning of principles also represents one way in which verbal processes can facilitate the transfer of what has been learned to a range of new situations. Other verbal processes also facilitate the solution of new problems.

Verbal associations may sometimes show transfer value in quite surprising ways. An interesting example of this is found in a study by Judson, Cofer, and Gelfand (1956). The central task for subjects that forms the focus of this study is known as the Maier two-string problem. In the original version of this problem, the subject is presented with two strings suspended from the ceiling of a room. The room is empty except for a pair of pliers, which appear to have been carelessly left on the floor. The subject is instructed that his task is to tie together the ends of the two pieces of string, a task that appears to be deceptively simple. Most subjects go about attempting to solve this problem in a direct fashion. They take hold of the end of one piece of string and then reach over to take hold of the other. They find that the two pieces of string are sufficiently far apart to make this impossible. They can be tied together, but the two ends are so far apart that it is impossible to reach one piece while holding the other. One solution to the problem is to use the pair of pliers lying on the floor. What the subject must do is to attach the pliers to one of the strings, which can then be swung as a pendulum. Once the string is swinging, it can be caught while the subject holds on to the other string, and the problem is solved. This is a rather difficult problem; not more than 50 per cent of college students can be expected to solve it.

In the Judson *et al.* study, subjects were asked during class hours on four consecutive days to learn word lists. One of these word lists included the sequence "rope, swing, pendulum"; this word list was administered to only one group. None of the other word lists included this sequence of words. On the fifth day all groups were given the Maier string problem and asked to solve it. The important result was that the group that had learned the word list containing the "rope, swing, pendulum" sequence were significantly more successful than the other groups in solving the problem. It may be noted that in this test the Maier problem was administered in a paper-and-pencil form, with an illustration of how the strings were suspended and the sketch of a person trying to reach one while holding the other.

This study clearly illustrates the way in which past associations between words or ideas can influence and facilitate problem-solving behavior. Many times in solving some kind of novel problem, the solution appears to come out of the blue. What probably happens in such cases is that some association built up in the past suddenly influences behavior.

Other techniques have been developed for studying in the laboratory the manner in which learned verbal associations can mediate behavior.

Like all laboratory approaches, these techniques involve gross simplifi-
cations of the problem. A common pattern for undertaking such studies
of verbal behavior is the following:

1. The subject learns to associate word A with word B.
2. The subject learns to associate word C with word B.
3. The subject is tested for the extent to which he associates word A
with word C.

The learning that occurs in steps 1 and 2 of this general plan is typically
found to also build an association between words A and C even though A
and C are never learned together. The learned associations of these two
words with word B provide the basis for a mediating process that relates
word A to word C. Although extensive research has been undertaken
following this general plan, the findings have not yet reached the point
of providing principles of value to education. Yet the approach offers
promise. Perhaps the technique offers some promise of discovering the
laws that describe the chaining of ideas in a typical train of thought.

An interesting problem of transfer is the extent to which responses
acquired to words are transferred to the objects that the words represent.
Much of classroom teaching involves the acquisition of information
related to words, but the hope is that this information will give meaning
to the objects represented by the words. This problem is not really studied
in a classroom setting, but can be studied in the laboratory. An example
of such a laboratory study is found in the work of Hartman (1963). His
study is dependent on the fact that one can condition a human subject
to blink every time a word appears on the screen. One can then find out
whether the appearance of the object will then also produce the eyeblink.
Hartman, for example, conditioned subjects to blink when the word
pink appeared, and sought to determine whether they would also blink,
after training, when a pink light appeared. Although this statement is a
gross oversimplification of the study, it presents the essential characteristics. He found that transfer did occur from the word to the object
to quite a striking extent. But before making any rash generalizations,
note that the subjects had all had extensive experience both with the
words and with the objects they represented. Too often in class, objects
are discussed that the pupil has never encountered. Under such conditions one would expect much less transfer from the training with the
words to responses to the objects.

A new technique has been developed for the experimental study of
problems of transfer related to those we are considering here. This new

approach involves what are known as reversal shifts and nonreversal shifts. The technique, as described by Kendler and Kendler (1962), involves the presentation of pairs of stimuli such as squares and circles that may be either white or black. The subject must decide which one of the two is "right." The experimenter arranges that only one of the dimensions (either the black-white or the circle-square) is to be the relevant one in the training series, and, perhaps, he decides that a black figure is to be considered "right" and a white figure "wrong." Then, after the subject has learned to choose the black figure, the rules are changed. The change can be made in either of two ways:

1. The experimenter can reverse the rules. In this case, the white figure is now the right one and the black figure is wrong. Learning the new rule involves what is called a reversal shift.

2. The experimenter may shift to the other dimension and call the square "right" and the circle "wrong." The learning of this new rule involves a nonreversal shift. (In later studies this has been referred to as an *extradimensional* shift.)

In this technique, all of the subjects are first trained to respond to one particular characteristic, such as the black figure; that is to say, they learn to discriminate on the dimension of brightness. Then half of the subjects have the rule changed so as to involve a reversal shift, and the other half have the rule changed by introducing a nonreversal shift.

The Kendlers report that older children and adults perform a reversal shift more readily than a nonreversal shift, but for very young children and subhuman animals the reverse is true. This is an interesting finding, for one would expect, in terms of the Osgood transfer surface, that strong negative transfer would take place in the reversal shift situation (the stimuli are the same but the responses are opposite). The fact that with older children and adults this does not occur is inconsistent with the model and suggests that the model holds only when complex mediating responses do not occur. (The data supporting the Osgood model generally involves situations in which one does not have to assume that complex mediating responses are occurring.) The Kendlers suggest that in older children and in adults a mediational mechanism is operating that permits a rapid change in response to occur in the reversal-shift situation. The Kendlers propose that the mediational mechanism is a language system, for such a system distinguishes the younger children from the older.

In a later experiment, Kendler (1964) attempted to find some more direct evidence that the mediational process involved in children is verbal. What she did was to force the children to verbalize what they were doing during the task and related this to what happened when the rules were changed. She believed that the evidence derived from the experiment supported the position that appropriate verbalization facilitated the reversal shift.

Level of Learning of the First Task in Relation to the Amount of Transfer

The relationship of level of learning on Task 1 to the amount of transfer to Task 2 is clearly an important and practical problem. If increased learning on Task 1 produces an increase in the amount of transfer, then there is strong argument in favor of thorough learning of whatever is learned in school, for much of such learning is offered because of its supposed transfer value.

Underwood (1951) found that with a verbal learning task the amount of transfer depended on the degree of learning of the initial task. This is to be expected where transfer is positive and where it depends on the generalization of the response involved. Atwater (1953) found a similar effect. Another and quite complex investigation by Mandler (1954) in general confirmed these results, but also indicated that the relation between the level of learning on Task 1 and the amount of transfer to Task 2 is not a simple one.

The results of these studies generally indicate that the amount of transfer from Task 1 to Task 2 is likely to increase with increases in practice on Task 1, and that if the transfer is negative with small amounts of practice, then the amount of negative transfer will also decline with increases in practice on Task 1.

An outstanding fact in the whole of the literature on transfer indicates that thorough learning is a desirable condition for efficient transfer. This fits well with many common observations made on behavior. The pupil who learns to speak a halting French in the classroom becomes unable to deliver a word of the language when faced by a visitor from France. The person who has recently learned to drive a car has the greatest difficulty in switching to a new car; the driver with many years of experience has no difficulty in switching to any new model that comes off the line. The experienced musician can switch from his customary instrument to another similar one with little difficulty, but the novice is upset by any change in his equipment.

Knowledge of this aspect of transfer suggests the tremendous importance of thorough learning of whatever is learned. This in turn suggests that learning should be so planned and scheduled that overlearning is the rule. Hasty and superficial treatment of subject matter in schools would appear to be a waste of time.

Task Difficulty and Transfer

An interesting problem of some educational significance is whether transfer occurs more readily from an easy task to a complex task or from a complex task to an easy one. A few years ago psychologists were inclined to take the position that transfer would take place more readily from the complex to the simple. The argument was that the complex task would include all the elements involved in the simple task, though including also some additional elements; but when the reverse procedure was adopted the simple task would not include all the elements involved in the complex task and, hence, much less transfer could occur. This is a persuasive argument, and a few early studies seemed to provide supporting evidence. However, when Holding (1963) reviewed all the studies he could locate, he found as many studies reporting more transfer in the easy-to-difficult situation as those reporting more transfer in the difficult-to-easy situation. This finding is particularly interesting in view of the fact that some of the studies reporting opposite results involved very similar tasks. If the review of the literature had found that transfer occurred best in, say, the easy-to-difficult task situation when certain tasks were used and that the reverse was true when certain other tasks were used, then the experimental evidence would have been easy to interpret; but this was not found to be the case.

Holding showed in an experiment of his own that, with a simple task, optimum transfer occurred from the easier to the more difficult problem; but with more complex tasks, optimum transfer occurred from the more difficult to the easier problems. His experiments indicate that there is a complex relationship between task difficulty and amount of transfer.

Implications of Knowledge of Transfer for Classroom Practice

Early experiments on transfer, such as those carried out by Thorndike, suggested that extreme caution must be exercised in assuming that transfer of training will occur. The work of Thorndike disposed of most of the doctrines related to transfer that had dominated educational practice during the nineteenth century. However, Thorndike's research provided little basis for newer practices, except to suggest that the goals of education should be achieved by the most direct means possible, for any other approach was likely to be met with failure. If the work of Thorndike on transfer did not produce an educational revolution, at least it did result in the development of a certain amount of modesty concerning what could and what could not be achieved through education.

As further work progressed, the research worker had more to say concerning ways in which teaching could be planned so that a maximum amount of transfer should result. From this subsequent research, there emerges, first, the concept that learning in the classroom should be such that it results in a thorough mastery of whatever is to be learned. In many activities, classroom learning may have to be planned so that skill is developed to a greater degree than that which the pupil feels is necessary.

Second, if transfer is to take place, there is considerable data to support the point of view that the pupil should have experience with a wide range of problems that differ somewhat from one another. This provides experience in dealing with the slightly unusual, and develops an expectation that each problem will have to be solved in a way that is somewhat different from that used in the solution of previous problems. In a sense, this may be called training for flexibility; but it is one of the keys to transfer of training.

Third, the teacher should emphasize principles and their application. Many teachers make the error of citing numerous facts without indicating that each is an example of the same underlying principle. But the statement of a principle is not enough. Pupils must also have the opportunity of practicing the use of the principle with a variety of problem situations.

As a final word concerning classroom practice, there is strong reason for reiterating what was said at the beginning of the chapter: much of the transfer that is implied in educational literature probably does not take place. The encouragement teachers may give to creative activities may have no effect on the creative behavior shown by the children in other situations. Practices of the teacher that reduce the tension of the child in the classroom may not reduce his tendency to manifest neurotic behavior outside the classroom. Even in such a matter as the use of good speech, habits in the classroom may not carry over into the school and neighborhood. Under many circumstances, transfer cannot yet be predicted.

Transfer Across Sense Modality

Another important problem for all educational planning is the extent to which material learned through one sense modality, such as hearing, transfers to learning through another sense modality, such as vision. For example, suppose a child learns to say French words, corresponding to common English nouns, as they are spoken by his teacher. When he has reached the point of being able to give the French equivalent of an

English word that he *hears,* will he be equally proficient at giving the French word when he sees the *printed* English word? A further problem is the extent to which learning involving spoken words will transfer to situations involving the actual objects named. The transfer from the printed word to the spoken word, or the reverse, is a problem of particular interest in the field of foreign language instruction.

An extensive study of this problem has been undertaken by Asher (1964), who provided different groups of undergraduates with training in vocabulary in Spanish, Japanese, Turkish, Persian, and Russian. None of the students had had any previous experience with the language in which they were given training. Asher's general procedure was to provide vocabulary training in one of these languages through one sense modality (hearing or vision) and then, later, he asked the same students to relearn the lists of words in the other modality. The experimenter could then determine the extent to which learning the list through one sense modality facilitated learning through the other. Since the study covered many facets of language learning, a comparison of the transfer from vision to hearing and from hearing to vision can be made only with respect to Spanish, Japanese, and Russian. In the case of Spanish and Japanese, the sequence of learning through vision and later relearning through hearing was found to be superior to the reverse; but there was no significant difference between the orders of sequences of learning for Russian. It should be noted that the Japanese was presented in the Romanized alphabet (similar to that used here), but the Russian was presented in Russian script.

Asher suggests that the problem of transfer is one of what he calls *phonetic fit.* What he means is that there will be good transfer of learning from hearing to seeing, or the reverse, in a language in which there is a close relationship between the spelling of words and the way they are pronounced. English is an example of a language with a poor phonetic fit. When the phonetic fit is poor, the transfer is reduced from the one modality to the other. Thus the study indicates that the extent to which there is transfer from spoken instruction in a foreign language to printed instruction, or the reverse, depends on the extent to which there is a straightforward and simple relationship between print and speech.

An interesting finding was that when intensive training in oral Russian was given first, then exposure to printed Russian produced *pronunciation shock,* characterized by a decrease in the quality of spoken Russian. However, the reverse effect was found with Japanese, in which the introduction of printed material improved the quality of pronunciation.

The Asher study was concerned with the transmission of only verbal material, either through the visual or auditory modalities; but an interesting problem is given by associating an English word with a foreign word, and when the learner on a later task has to name visually presented objects. One might expect that there would be less transfer across modalities when the transfer was from a task involving words to a task involving objects than when the transfer is between two verbal tasks. A direct study of this problem does not appear to have been undertaken.

A study by Kale, Grosslight, and McIntyre (1953) examined the related problem of the value of pictures, either still or in motion, in the teaching of Russian vocabulary. They found some evidence that the use of pictures, particularly motion pictures, appeared to facilitate learning. They also found that the simultaneous auditory presentation of the words displayed on the screen seemed to interfere with rather than facilitate learning. The study leads one to suspect that there may be good transfer from word-object associations to the corresponding word-word associations; but this is a matter requiring fuller investigation.

Summary

1. In the history of education the doctrine of formal discipline represents a theory of transfer that has had an important influence on educational practice. The doctrine of formal discipline proposed that education could best be brought about by training the mind through difficult mental exercises.

2. Transfer of training was defined through a statement from McGeogh and Irion: "Transfer of training occurs whenever the existence of a previously established habit has an influence upon the acquisition, performance, or relearning of a second habit."

3. Transfer may be positive or negative. The former is a facilitating process, the latter an interfering one. Transfer may occur in all kinds of perceptual and motor responses, as well as with higher mental processes.

4. Transfer must be distinguished from some other processes in which learning on a task influences performance on a subsequent task, such as the warm-up phenomenon or fatigue.

5. A number of different designs have been used to study the transfer process. The classical design has been replaced by two designs known as *proaction* design and *retroaction* design. Each has particular advantages in the study of certain transfer problems. A problem in the design of all transfer studies is what to assign to the control group while the experimental group is engaged in one of the tasks.

6. Edward L. Thorndike was one of the first psychologists to give

careful thought to the problem of transfer. His theory was that transfer from Task 1 to Task 2 would occur insofar as the two tasks included identical elements. The theory encountered difficulty when an attempt was made to specify what those identical elements might be. Later research workers distinguished two kinds of identical elements, one residing in the nature of the stimuli involved and the other in the nature of the responses. The laws of transfer may be expected to be different when Tasks 1 and 2 differ in the nature of the stimuli involved and when they differ in the responses.

7. Osgood developed a model that takes into account both the differences in the situations presented by two tasks and the differences in the responses called for by them. On the basis of the Osgood model, predictions of when positive transfer will occur can be made with considerable accuracy. The model is much less satisfactory for predicting when negative transfer will take place. An older model, developed by Robinson, fits some of the data on negative transfer somewhat better than does the Osgood model. The Osgood model takes into account transfer occurring through stimulus generalization and response generalization.

8. Research on the development of learning sets has provided valuable data concerning the conditions necessary for transfer in certain kinds of learning situations such as those that fall into the category of *learning how to learn*. The results of the learning-set studies appear to be particularly useful for understanding the development of highly transferable approaches to the solving of problems in young children and subhuman subjects. However, one may expect that in older children and adults the capability of using language may permit shortcuts in the learning process.

9. The role of mediating processes involving language has been stressed by Ausubel, who has suggested that the presence or absence of such processes is often much more significant for predicting the occurrence of transfer than are such factors as task similarity or response similarity. The key to much of the transfer that may occur in the application of a scientific principle appears to depend on the ability of the individual to code the properties of situations to which the principle may be applied. The possibility that verbal processes are the key to the understanding of transfer in older children and adults is brought out by Kendler and Kendler in a series of studies involving a problem-solving task.

10. The degree of learning of the first task appears to be related to the amount of transfer that occurs. The data also suggest that if there is to be expected negative transfer from Task 1 to Task 2, then the amount of such negative transfer will decline as Task 1 is more and more adequately learned.

11. The relationship of transfer to the relative difficulty of Task 1 to

Task 2 has not been clearly identified by research. The results of studies lack consistency and lead to no firm conclusion.

12. Transfer across sense modality is an important educational problem. Transfer from auditory training to visual training in a verbally taught foreign language will take place effectively if the written and spoken forms of the language display phonetic fit.

9

Developmental Processes in Relation to Learning

I**T IS ONLY** recently that studies of development have been oriented at all toward problems of learning; and although in the last two decades there has been a vast proliferation of studies of human development, only the more recent ones show that they have been influenced by the research methodology and concepts evolved by learning psychologists. Our purpose here, then, is to discuss some aspects of the historical trend of research on human development, indicate how the ideas that have evolved have influenced educational thought and the planning of classroom learning, and then try to sift out some of the obsolete concepts from the newer ones now emerging while suggesting the implications for human learning of these newer concepts.

A single chapter on problems of developmental psychology in relation to learning can only begin to cover a rapidly expanding field of research to which whole volumes are devoted.

Development and Learning

From the time of conception and throughout the life of the individual, changes occur in his structure that have a marked influence on the learning process. These changes are described partly as growth processes and partly as developmental processes. Although the words *growth* and *development* are often used loosely as if they referred to the same kind of change, they are used technically with two distinct meanings. Growth refers to the ordinary increase in bodily size that takes place through the division of cells and their increase in number. Development, on the other hand, refers to changes in the way the cells are organized and interrelated. A low-grade moron may grow to a full six feet, but may still be unable to exercise ordinary control over his bladder and bowel move-ments. His nervous system never *developed* to the point of providing the *organization* needed for the learning of this control. Mere size does not ensure that the parts of the body work efficiently together. More than size is needed, for the cells have to be organized in such a way that they function effectively as a team if the body is to show complex be-havior. Such organization is referred to as *development.*

Although there is generally some relationship between size and devel-opment, an increase in size does not always result in a corresponding increase in development. The example just cited illustrates an extreme in which an increase in size was not accompanied by a corresponding in-crease in development. Sometimes the reverse occurs. Many dwarfs show excellent mental development without the usual corresponding gain in size. As far as behavior is concerned, it is not just the number of cells in the body that determines how adequate behavior is in coping with the environment, but rather, it is the way in which these cells are organized.

The central component of the learning machinery of the body, the nervous system, develops early and is ready to provide the basis for learning before the child is born. Experimental evidence has been col-lected to indicate that learning of a simple conditioning type may occur before birth, but it is unlikely that learning plays any significant role in development at this stage. Since there is no direct connection between the nervous system of the mother and that of the developing embryo, there is no direct way in which the experience and learning of the mother can influence the developing child. However, the hormones in the mother's blood stream may diffuse through the placenta and have some influence on the embryo; but how this may influence the course of de-velopment has not yet been established. The influence of such changes in the hormone balance may be mild and temporary.

At birth the nervous system is well developed, and most of the sub-sequent increase in size will result from the laying down of insulating sheaths around some of the fibers. The cells that are to function later in the adult life of the individual are already in the system. However, the system functions very differently from that of the adult. This can be demonstrated partly in terms of the actual structure of the system, but also in terms of the way in which it functions. The brain at birth already shows certain electrical rhythms of its own, and these can be recorded; but they are quite different from those of the more mature individual. At birth, the electrical rhythms are more like those of the sleeping adult than of the waking adult, but we cannot infer from this that the newborn infant has experiences similar to those of a sleeping adult. Nobody knows what the experiences of the newborn infant are like, though many have speculated on this matter. Some of the early clinical psychologists speculated and even claimed that they were able to assist patients in remembering what happened at birth. The indications are that this is nonsense. The higher centers of the brain have not developed at birth to the point where they can retain such a memory trace at the conscious level. In addition, it is doubtful whether any events related to birth can form the kind of experience that is likely to be registered at this stage. It is reasonable to assume that the sensory experience of the newborn may be something like the visual experience of an adult who gains vision for the first time after a corneal-graft operation. The visual experiences are meaningless, and only when they are repeated a large number of times under appropriate conditions do they begin to build into the nervous system permanent traces needed for their interpretation.

The fertilized cell from which the mature organism grows has the potentiality of evolving complex structures, and some of these structures evolve and produce behavior without a marked period of learning. The classic demonstration of this occurs in the case of the developing fertilized frog's egg. This developing embryo can be subjected to a chemical treatment that will stop all movement but which will not stop the growth and maturation process. When the tadpole has reached a certain state of development, it is transferred to fresh water, where the effect of the chemical rapidly disappears. The tadpoles are then able to swim immediately. The nervous system has evolved structures that permit the animal to swim. This process by which structures develop and permit behavior is referred to as *maturation*. The nervous system has the capacity of developing an organization within itself that provides the necessary basis for certain limited behaviors, such as locomotion in the tadpole and parallel activities in man. The organization also provides a basis on which more complex behaviors may be built through learning.

An interesting form of behavior that clearly has an important central unlearned core is known as the avoidance of visual cliffs. The essential nature of the phenomenon is that a young animal that has had little or no direct experience at dealing with depth phenomena is placed on a flat surface bordered by a sharp drop; the creature typically avoids the drop and, in the case of the human infant, the drop is avoided even when a sheet of glass is placed over the chasm so that the infant could readily crawl over the glass. If the "cliff" formed by the drop is shallower at one end than the other, the infant will move to the shallow end before descending the cliff and crossing the chasm. Walk and Gibson (1961) reviewed studies of this phenomenon which had been undertaken by various research workers using, altogether, ten different species that ranged from turtles to humans. The phenomenon was shown to occur in all the species studied.

The phenomenon suggests that the nervous system may have built-in capabilities of interpreting the environment beyond what psychologists in the past have thought it to have. The repertoire of unlearned responses that may form the foundation for learning may be much larger than has commonly been assumed.

The Concept of Maturation and the Developmental-Stage Approach

The concept of maturation emerged early in the history of psychology and had a profound effect on the approaches used to study problems of animal development, including human development. A major influence is found in the extensive researches that characterized the early decades of the present century and were designed to provide a description of the developmental process as it "normally" occurs. Such studies had little to do with learning and, indeed, played down the role of learning. Some of the early studies, such as those undertaken by John B. Watson, were concerned with the identification of the reflex patterns that characterize the nervous system.

A number of reflexes, such as the reaction of the pupil of the eye to light, had been well identified as being independent of learning. Then, too, there were some more complex behaviors in the infant, such as sucking which can be elicited by tickling any part of the cheek or mouth. The main block that stood in the way of developing a complete list was that learning is generally so closely intertwined with the manifestation of the unlearned behavior that the two cannot be separated. Some behaviors that appear to be learned, from the point of view of the parent, are not primarily learned activities. For example, the mechanism necessary for walking seems to be largely one that appears as a result of the growth and development process independent of any special training. Its rudiments can be observed at an early stage. A six-month-old child who is held so that his feet press lightly on a firm surface will often show alternating movements of the legs very similar to walking. The mechanism is built into the spinal cord and lower brain centers, and such walking movements will occur in mammals that have had the higher centers of the brain removed. However, at six months the mechanism for walking has not yet reached the level of maturity necessary for the complete act to take place, and neither is the musculature developed to the necessary point. Later there will come a time when the child will walk, for the mechanism involved will be complete. Learning may enter into the refinement of the skill and develop it to the point where the child can walk and balance in difficult situations, and a few, through special training, may become tight-rope walkers; but the basic skill appears to be built into the body.

In one of the classical experiments in psychology Dennis and Dennis (1940) were able to demonstrate the built-in nature of the walking activity. These research workers had been engaged in the study of Hopi Indians, who bind their infants to cradle boards that prevent movements of most of the body. They were able to persuade some of the mothers to remove the boards at an early age so that the babies would be free to move their legs and obtain practice with some of the component skills that may go into walking. If walking were a learned activity, then those babies that remained bound to the cradle boards and who had no possibility for practice should learn to walk later than those who had freedom of movement and opportunity to practice. But in this study, both groups learned to walk at approximately the same time.

Somewhat similar results have been obtained by using the method known as the *co-twin control method.* In this method, one identical twin is typically given special training in some function such as walking, but the other is not. A study is then made to determine whether the one who receives training walks at an earlier age than the one who does not have the advantages of such training. In one such study by Hilgard (1933) on a pair of twins, one twin was given early training in a skill and three months later was given retraining in the skill at the time when the second twin was trained in it for the first time. The twins were aged fifty-four to sixty-six months during the period the experiment was in progress. The experiment included training in a number of different skills, including memory for digits, memory for objects, tossing a ring over a peg, and walking the length of a narrow board. The general conclusions from this study are that little was gained by providing the early practice period, for the twin who did not have this opportunity quickly caught up with the one who did. The fact was also brought out that both the twins returned to the same level in the skills despite their different attainments with practice, which suggested that level of skill was determined largely by general developmental level. Myrtle McGraw (1943) in a later study showed that a similar phenomenon was found in stair-climbing behavior in young children.

In such studies, similar results have generally been found: The twin who is given special training does not perform any earlier than the twin who does not receive special training. The results of such a study are shown in Figure 10. These experiments with identical twins represent excellent scientific designs, since one twin provides a control for the other. The method has proved to be one of the best for studying developmental problems with human subjects. With animals other methods

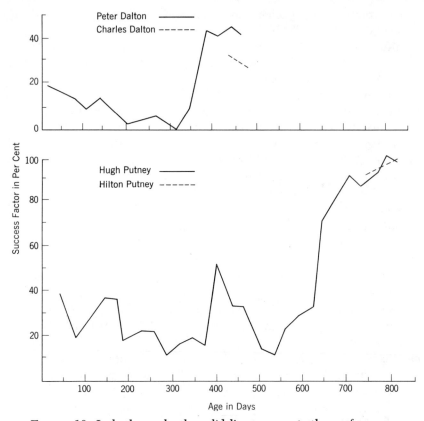

FIGURE 10. In both graphs the solid line represents the performance of the twin that was given special training in toilet habits. The dotted line represents the performance in toilet habits of the twin that received no special training and who was given no opportunities to learn until a later date. (From Myrtle B. McGraw, *The Neuromuscular Maturation of the Human Infant*. New York: Columbia University Press (1943), p. XIV. Reproduced by permission of Columbia University Press.)

can be used, but with the human there are limitations to what one can do in experimental situations.

Two unlearned patterns of facial expression have been established by long experimentation, though at one time psychologists considered that many different forms of facial expression were inborn. The two patterns of expression that have survived investigation as patterns readily identifiable and unlearned are the *startle pattern* and the smile. The startle pattern occurs after any sudden strong stimulation, such as the sounding of a loud gong or the loss of support, as when the person holding a baby allows him to fall a foot or so by suddenly lowering the supporting hands. The startle response is characterized by diffuse movement throughout the body, sometimes a stiffening of the arms and legs, and crying. The pattern can be fairly well identified in slow-motion films and can be distinguished from other patterns of response. It cannot be distinguished from fear responses or other strong responses. The startle response appears to be a reaction that occurs in a broad range of situations. It is a reaction that, because of its uniformity under varied conditions, indicates that the young baby has not yet reached the point of discriminating between broad classes of situations that it encounters.

In the early months of the life of the child, the smile is elicited by a number of different stimuli, including patting, tickling, pain, and other conditions. Later it is elicited by the appearance of the face of the mother or by any object that generally resembles that face. Although in early life it is aroused by unpleasant as well as pleasant stimuli, it ultimately comes to be associated only with pleasant stimuli and mainly those that are social in origin. The innate nature of smiling is seen in the fact that children who are blind from birth smile just like other children, although they have never seen this form of facial expression in other children. They also come to smile on much the same occasions as sighted children.

The studies of McGraw and Hilgard, which have been cited and which have been very influential, are studies of rather simple motor skills that have important components at the reflex level. One is hardly justified in generalizing from studies of the development of simple motor skills to problems of conceptual development. It seems probable that development in the conceptual area is dependent on the background of the child and does not follow a rigid pattern as some have assumed.

There is certainly substantial information to support the point of view that a rigid pattern of development, which cannot be modified through special training with any long-term results, is limited only to certain relatively simple motor skills; but more complex aspects of development can be influenced substantially through appropriate training procedures. A number of studies have been undertaken in which children at the four-year level have been trained to read, and the acquisition of this skill has not been dependent on particularly high general ability. There are also, of course, many authentic and well-documented cases of children who learned to read at even younger ages, including studies of J. S. Mill and Francis Galton. Musical prodigies all show the effects of concentrated and well-directed early training, and so forth. The overwhelming weight of the evidence indicates that conceptual development and the development of complex motor skills are highly dependent on training. Far from having to wait until the maturation process has produced a state of readiness, training in such skills appears to be a major determinant and can be begun with profit at a very early age, perhaps even as early as the second year of life. Evidence to support this position with respect to the value of training at an early age has been gathered together by Fowler (1962) from many sources. His array of information is impressive and should provide a powerful antidote for those whose ideas about the planning of education are derived largely from the maturationist viewpoint.

Attempts to Describe Rigid Developmental Patterns

The maturationist point of view, with its emphasis on the emergence of behavior at particular times in the life history, had great influence on the study of development during the first half of the present century. This point of view led to the assumption that the description of the pattern of development of a sample of children would provide a picture typical of all children. Those who sought to describe developmental patters were not particularly interested in problems of learning but in the patterns of behavior that emerged from the organism under conditions that were restricted only in that they did not involve excessive deprivation. The patterns of behavior thus described were believed to represent a background on which the effects of learning are imposed.

Among those who devoted a lifetime to the description of the sequences with which behavior emerged was Arnold Gesell. The extensive and detailed descriptions that were the products of his work are based largely on the rather dubious assumption that the behavior patterns described are not highly modified by the learning conditions to which the child is exposed. The tradition of such work is biological and is reminiscent of the vast work undertaken by zoologists on the life cycles of organisms. Because it is descriptive rather than experimental, it does not include the study of ways in which the pattern of development can be modified by circumstances. Experimentation rather than the mere description of what has been observed, is necessary to find out how to modify the course of development.

While Arnold Gesell was undertaking his studies at Yale, where emphasis was placed on motor and perceptual development, across the world in Geneva, Piaget was attempting to describe the intellectual development of the child. Piaget too must be considered as coming in the biological tradition that directed efforts to the description of the characteristics of organisms. Piaget refers to his "experiments" with children, but these would be considered as demonstrations rather than as experiments by American psychologists. Here again the approach seems to imply that the stages of intellectual development will occur or must occur and that gross modification of them as a result of exposure to appropriate learning conditions is unlikely.

The approach of Piaget and his associates is much more like that of a clinician than that of an experimentalist, so verification of his findings is a difficult matter. What one person may see in the behavior of a child solving a problem, another may not. The problems of scientific procedure in this area are far from being solved. Thus one can find studies undertaken outside of Piaget's laboratory, some of which provide descriptions of intellectual development similar to that provided by Piaget and some of which do not. Thus Deutsch (1943) conducted research to determine whether he could identify the stages in the development of ideas about cause and effect, which Piaget claimed to have observed but failed to find a similar pattern of development. A study by Estes (1956) did not find the pattern of development in numerical and logical thinking that Piaget had previously reported. The difference in the findings of Piaget and his critics may well be a result of the differences in the backgrounds of the children involved in the studies. More recently a study by Lovell (1961) claimed to have found evidence supporting the pattern of the development of thinking found by Inhelder and Piaget (1959); but all that one can find out from the Lovell article is that he believed he saw in the behavior of the children the same behaviors as those which Inhelder and Piaget had described. This is not supporting evidence; indeed, it is not evidence at all.

Although many of the reported findings of Piaget and his associates remain controversial, there can be no doubt that his work has been stimulating to research. As we learn more about the conditions under which his findings can be reproduced, the value of his contribution should be enhanced.

Research that will either support or refute a theory of intellectual development is difficult to undertake without introducing bias and prejudice into the results. A problem administered to children may show, say, type A thinking among the younger children and type B among the older; but this may well be a result of the nature of the problem itself. Other problems may not show such a sequence in the development of thinking. In addition, the data derived from giving children problems is often difficult to score objectively without introducing the personal biases of the scorer. All these problems are evident in the study by Lovell (1961), which attempted to determine whether the stage in the development of logical thinking described by Inhelder and Piaget (1958) could be reproduced. Lovell noted that the problems that Inhelder and Piaget had used were not described in sufficient detail to assure Lovell that he could reproduce them with any accuracy. In addition, the reader of the article has to accept on faith that the scoring of the problems did not involve the personal prejudices of the person who scored the performances of the pupils. Lovell concluded that his data reflected the same stages in logical thinking as Inhelder and Piaget had reported, but one cannot tell whether this "confirming" evidence is genuine or merely a reflection of prejudices involved in scoring. The design of an experiment that would eliminate such prejudice is a technically difficult problem.

Functional Age and Organismic Age

Attempts have been made to describe developmental level in terms of an age scale. The mental-age scale developed by Binet was of this kind, which has had a long and important influence on educational thought. In the system developed by Binet, the performance of a child on a set of tests of intelligence could be compared with that of average children at different age levels. Thus, the performance of a particular ten-year-old might be closely similar to that of an average eight-year-old. In this case the mental age of the child would be eight years. Later the intelligence quotient was introduced. Still later the concept of an age scale was applied to other aspects of development. These later applications have had considerable influence and for this reason must be considered here, despite the fact that age scales are no longer in good repute among psychologists.

A child may be said to have the same height as that of the average eight-year-old. If this is so, one may say that he has a "height age" of eight years. If this same child can solve mathematics problems with the same facility as the average nine-year-old, then he may be said to have a "mathematics age" of nine years. His height age may be quite different from his actual age, which in this case might be seven years. The development of the child may be measured along a number of different dimensions; and, if it is measured in terms of an age scale, then one may have measures of height age, weight age, dental age, reading age, arithmetic age, carpal age, and so forth. (Carpal age is the extent to which the carpal bones in the wrist are composed of fully developed bone rather than of cartilage, as they are in the very young child.) Olson (1959) studied the growth of a group of children over a period of years and claimed that all of these growth functions tended to be parallel—that is, a child did not suddenly show growth in one of these functions, moving ahead of the other functions. He concluded that the level of development of a child could be described in terms of a single index, which was the average of several of these age measures. He called this composite the "organismic age," which supposedly indicated the general level of development of the child. Olson further hypothesized that the measure called "organismic age," since it indicated the general level of development, could be used to predict over-all level of performance in academic work, for whatever might be expected to depress organismic age might also be expected to depress academic achievement. If all functions do develop together, as Olson suggests, then one should be able to predict reading development from the stage of development of the bones in the wrist. This follows logically from the theory. A number of studies have been undertaken to determine whether this is so.

Tyler (1953) has raised many questions concerning the utility of the concept of an organismic age. He doubts that any meaning can be given to the average of a series of scores of such diverse structures and functions as height, dentition, and skill in arithmetic. Organismic growth does show greater stability than the I.Q., but this is really a statistical artifact, because it involves a greater number of components. Fluctuation in one of the components may not produce much change in the total.

The data that has been collected does not support the conclusion that there is value in calculating the organismic age of a child. Klausmeier, et al. (1958) obtained developmental-age measures on children for height, weight, strength of grip, dentition, carpal development, mental development, reading, arithmetic, and language. The measures were made on boys and girls in the fourth, fifth, and sixth grades. The measures of physical development bore little relation to those of behavior development. A child who was advanced in dental development had no more chance of being advanced in reading or arithmetic than a child who was retarded in dental development. There is little tendency for a child to be generally advanced or for a child to be generally retarded. In the population studied by Klausmeier, all growth functions did not go together, nor did development proceed as a whole.

In the Klausmeier et al. data, organismic age did not show itself to be a particularly useful measure for predicting academic achievement, which is best predicted from measures of the capacity to undertake such learnings. Including physical measures in making the prediction of academic achievement merely contaminates good data with bad.

There are many reasons why Olson's findings and the theory of development he constructed out of them are not substantiated by the work of others. A major one is that the group of children on which Olson based his theory was sufficiently different from other groups to make generalization to these other groups unwarranted. Olson's population of children came almost entirely from a middle-class group in a university town. The children were derived from an environment favorable to all aspects of development. Under such conditions, a disease, for example, that depressed bodily development might well keep a child out of school long enough to depress academic learning. Effects such as this one may well account for the remarkable tendency for all growth functions to proceed together in the Olson data.

Where other conditions exist, such parallelism of growth functions may also not exist, and under these other conditions the concept of an organismic age may not be a useful one. There is certainly no basic law of development that says that all developmental functions must proceed together, or that the organism grows as a unity. Matters are much more complex, and one growth function may be depressed without a resulting depression in others.

Despite the fact that organismic age has not turned out to be a particularly useful idea, the concept of a developmental age in some function may have some value. There is a certain convenience in describing a twelve-year-old child's reading age as nine, for this clearly indicates that he will require different reading material from the average child in his age group. There are still better ways of describing a child's reading level that have greater precision and usefulness; but these are technically complicated, and for this reason they have not displaced the concept of a reading age.

What are the alternatives to age scales for describing the level of development? Alternative systems have been evolved because of the fairly obvious fact that a backward child of one age cannot be reasonably compared with an average child of another. A dull fifteen-year-old may have a mental age of ten, and yet he is likely to be very different from a ten-year-old. The average ten-year-old is likely to present himself as bright and alert, but the very dull fifteen-year-old is an obvious problem in his behavior and in his capacity to handle problems. It would be much more reasonable to compare the dull fifteen-year-old with other children of his own age and to come out with a statement such as that he is intellectually in the lowest one per cent of his age group. Comparison within an age group is a much better basis for description and appraisal than comparisons between age groups.

Early Learning

A considerable time ago Beach and Jaynes (1954) made an analysis of the various ways in which early experiences may influence adult life. The analysis grew out of a review of the research that had been completed up to that time; and, although much research has been done since, the Beach and Jaynes analysis has not been superseded. Beach and Jaynes point out that there are three ways in which early experiences can influence later life. First, the habits developed in infancy may persist into adult life—a matter that has long been recognized. Second, early perceptual learning may influence adult behavior—a matter that has recently become a focus of research. Third, there may be critical periods of development—that is to say, periods during which certain experiences may have to take place in order for the orderly sequence of developmental events to occur. The concept of a critical stage of development is still controversial, but what appear to be striking examples have been found in the area of imprinting in subhuman species.

The second of the influences mentioned by Beach and Jaynes has particularly important implications for education. If learning occurs in infancy merely by being exposed to a varied and complex environment, then much can be done to make the early years a rich educational experience.

Hebb (1949, 1958) believes that evidence indicates that learning, when considered over the life span, is a two-stage process. The first stage, referred to as early learning, involves certain fundamental processes that must be mastered before more complex learnings can be undertaken.

The concept of early learning is easily misunderstood; the layman thinks of the first steps in learning as consisting of such processes as the learning of words and certain manipulative skills such as are involved in feeding, washing, playing with toys, and so forth. However, from the point of view of the psychologist, these are quite complex skills, and presuppose that still earlier learning has taken place. The first steps in learning may involve such processes as recognizing two sounds as different, recognizing a line as a line and perhaps the meeting of two lines to form a corner as corner, and recognizing tactile sensations of roughness, smoothness, etc. Such recognitions and discriminations are taken so much for granted that it is hard to realize that they require any learning at all. As a matter of fact, some psychologists of the past have even supposed that complex shapes can be recognized and complex discriminations made without any learning. One group of psychologists, who became known as the Gestalt psychologists, took the view that the capacity to see simple shapes is inborn and requires no learning; but this does not seem to be the case.

Research on the influence of early perceptual learning began with informal studies involving case histories of animal behavior, but research has recently become more systematic with more adequate control over relevant conditions.

Many years ago a German opthalmologist, von Senden (tr. 1960), became interested in the perceptual abilities of adults who had gained their vision for the first time through an operation involving a corneal graft. One of the striking characteristics of these individuals was their inability to use their newly-acquired sense of vision; and, indeed, some never learned to use it, despite the fact that surgery had restored their eyes to the point where they were physiologically capable of providing information about the surrounding world. These patients had extreme difficulty in learning to make the simplest discriminations, such as that of distinguishing a triangle from a square. Although they could make this simple discrimination by touching cutouts of the two shapes, the visual discrimination could be made only after an almost unbelievable amount of practice involving many months of exercises. Hebb (1949) was the first to realize the importance of this phenomenon. He pointed out that the adult who gains vision for the first time has to undertake a tedious early learning process which, unlike later and more complex learning, is very slow indeed. The adult learning to use vision is similar to the infant slowly learning the simplest discriminations.

Certainly, the learning of the adult who gains vision is hard to understand unless one introduces the concept of an early stage of learning that is very slow. Such a position has important implications for child rearing, for the period of infancy then comes to be regarded as a period when crucially important learning is taking place. If this is so, then experiences in infancy may be expected to have important bearing on learning that takes place later.

Laboratory animals that are deprived of learning experiences early in life commonly demonstrate extraordinarily stupid behavior. Hebb (1958) describes the case of a dog that was raised in an environment in which it did not have opportunities for learning to avoid some of the common hazards of life. When this same dog was later let loose in a laboratory, it showed a striking inability to avoid bumping its head against a low pipe. Other dogs that had been raised in a typical dog environment were able to avoid this pipe almost at once, but the dog brought up in the restricted environment bumped its head a score or more times and without any indication that it had benefited at all from its experience. Presumably this dog was engaged in a process of early learning, which here again involved a simple function. The performance of the dog in this situation was similar to that of the man attempting to learn for the first time the visual discrimination of a square and a triangle. In both cases the rate of learning is very slow indeed, and the behavior in comparison with that of the normal adult seems unbelievably stupid.

Deprivation of opportunities to learn during the early period of development has also, in animals, many other interesting results. In another study by Melzack and Thompson (1956), twenty-one Scottish terriers were divided into two groups. One group was reared in a bleak environment—a laboratory cage from which the animals could not view other activities in the laboratory. The other group was provided with an "enriched curriculum"—they were raised in the homes of laboratory workers. Later, the behavior of these two groups of animals was compared, and with striking results. The animals in the group exposed to the enriched environment were generally superior in social and competitive situations, but the group that had been reared in the cage were the dogs that delighted visitors with their friendliness and spontaneity. Indeed, visitors to the McGill laboratory were often asked to identify the group that had been reared under conditions of psychological deprivation, and they were generally wrong in their choice. The typical dog that had been raised in a stimulating environment watched the visitor from a corner of the room, but did not approach him. On the other hand, the dog raised in a restricted environment was full of spontaneity and approached the visitor with friendliness. The dogs raised in the rich environment had little charm for the visitor. They gave the appearance of being thoroughly bored with the intrusion into the laboratory. They knew enough about the world to know that a visitor was an uninteresting event, as far as they were concerned, and they would not waste their energies inspecting a person of no value or interest to themselves. On the other hand, the dog from the restricted environment did not know what to attend to and what not to attend to. So he tended to investigate everything new.

These informal studies generally preceded a systematic laboratory approach to the study of the effect of early perceptual experience. In a later study, Melzack (1962) compared the problem-solving abilities of dogs raised under typical circumstances with dogs raised in cages that restricted their visual experiences. The problem on which the dogs were tested was one requiring a black-white discrimination, but it involved reversal training—that is, the dogs were first trained to react to a white area in contrast to a black area and then were retrained to respond to a black area in contrast to a white. This kind of laboratory testing provides vastly more objective results than come from the observations on the general behavior of dogs discussed in earlier paragraphs. Melzack found that on the task of learning the black-white discrimination, and also on the reversal training task, the dogs raised in a normal environment learned more rapidly than those raised in a restricted environment.

Another series of systematic experiments on the effects of early perceptual learning in chicks has been undertaken by Gibson and Walk (1956) and Gibson, Walk, Pick, and Tighe (1958, 1959a, 1959b). These studies provided evidence that chicks exposed to a circle and a triangle during the first 120 days of their lives showed superior performance on a form-discrimination problem involving these forms. However, some of the characteristics of the forms to which they were exposed appeared to be important, and particularly whether the forms were flat or three-dimensional.

In all of the cases we have studied up to this point in which there had been a deprivation of early learning experiences, the result was a certain stupidity of behavior that is not easily overcome. Prolonged learning is necessary if this deficiency is to be removed, and this fact suggests that the slowness with which the very young child learns may reflect the slowness with which early learning takes place. The term *early learning* refers to the learning of the fundamental ability to discriminate and identify stimuli; the evidence indicates that these learnings must precede more complex learnings. We do not know at this time whether deficiencies in early learning can ever be entirely made up later in life. This matter requires systematic investigation. A few pieces of evidence suggest that some of the deficiencies produced by a lack of early learning may be rather permanent.

Now that research has begun to determine the intellectual importance of early learning, attempts may be made to develop learning programs that reach right down into infancy. Although educators have long recognized the importance of early childhood in the development of a well-adjusted personality, a new appreciation of the importance of this period for intellectual development also suggests that the early years should be years of planned learning. At present, these years are little influenced by planning.

Early Learning, Maturation, and Curriculum Planning

One theory states that learning of complex skills should be postponed until the child has matured to the point where such learning is easily undertaken; however, this theory neglects to take into account the fact that extensive learning must take place before such skills can be acquired.

Why the average kindergarten child cannot read is a complex problem. A simple explanation in terms of maturation is not adequate to cover the situation. If early learning, or the lack of it, is a major factor, then we may be forced to discard the notion that the first grade is too early to begin reading—provided, of course, there has been a previous period of adequate and appropriate early learning. It may well be that a suitable and planned period of learning during the first few years of life might prepare a child to read at a much earlier age than most children learn to read at present. This is a possibility, not an established fact; but it opens up new horizons for the planning of early education.

However, there is another point to consider: Learning opportunities cannot be withheld until the time that learning can be undertaken with maximum efficiency. The age of maximum learning speed for most complex academic learning is probably the early twenties, but academic learning cannot be postponed until this time. Most academic learning, and most nonacademic learning too, must take place at a time when the child is far from having developed to the point of maximum learning efficiency. Judgment is involved in determining whether it is worth waiting until learning can be undertaken with greater efficiency. The importance of reading as a key to learning in most other areas requires that the skill be acquired at a relatively early age, even though it might be learned much more rapidly one or two years later. What the curriculum specialist aims to do is plan a program such that, by the time adulthood is reached, the maximum possible learning along particular lines has been achieved.

An attempt has been made by Havighurst (150) to provide a list of learning experiences that take into account both the maturational level of the child and the demands of the culture. Havighurst describes this attempt as representing a position midway between those who consider that the child should grow up with a minimum of constraints, and those who believe that the cultural heritage should be imposed firmly on the child. The tasks are described as *developmental tasks;* they include such varied activities as learning to walk, building attitudes, developing various concepts, acquiring moral values, and so forth. Some of the tasks arise mainly from physical maturation, some originate in the pressures of the culture, and some are a result of the personal values and aspirations of the learner. The system is an attempt to plan learning in terms of both environmental pressures and internal development.

The Bloom Hypotheses

Thinking in the last ten years has moved from the position that emphasizes maturational processes to the position that cognitive processes are trainable perhaps from birth. At the same time, some effort has been made to bring together the available data and to formulate a few general principles of development. One of the most careful and comprehensive of these efforts is that undertaken by Bloom (1964). The first point made by Bloom is that the relationship between two measures of the same function taken at differing points of time is to be understood in terms of what has been called the overlap hypothesis. Consider, for example, a characteristic such as height, which has been measured on the same group of individuals at age 3 and age 20. Now the height at age 20 may be considered to consist of two components: the height at age 3 plus the increment added to that height during the next 17 years. Thus the height at age 20 will be influenced by what the height was at age 3, because this height is included in the height at age 20. Thus, there will be a correlation between height at age 3 and height at age 20, merely because the one height is included in the other. Even if the growth after age 3 is unrelated to the growth that has taken place before age 3, a correlation may be expected in terms of the overlap hypothesis, and the amount of correlation may be predicted under these circumstances. Bloom points out that in growth studies the correlations between two measures taken with an intervening interval of time do not really represent predictions; they show how much growth has already taken place. If two measurements of height were made after all growth had taken place—say, at age 20 and age 30—a perfect correlation would be obtained. The less the one measure includes all the growth included in the other, the lower will be the correlation.

The conclusion to be drawn is that when any characteristic is measured at two points in time, they tend to be correlated merely because the one measure is included in the other.

Now let us consider what would happen if children were measured in height at age 3; and then some were later exposed to poor nutrition and some to good nutrition during the subsequent 17 years. Let us also assume that the children up to age 3 had received similar nutrition. What would be found under these circumstances is that the amount of growth between age 3 and age 20 would then be more closely related to the quality of nutrition than to the height at age 3. This leads to Bloom's second generalization: that changes in a measure from one age to another are highly related to relevant environmental conditions in which the individuals have lived during the period.

The third generalization is that a characteristic can be changed to the greatest extent during the period of most rapid growth. On the basis of this conclusion, he suggests that measured intelligence can be most dramatically changed by events that take place before age 4—generally, the period of most rapid growth. Bloom also estimates that during the period of most rapid growth, one year of growth may produce results equal to 8 or 10 years of growth at a later age.

Development in Relation to Child-Rearing Practices

The influences of child-rearing practices on later development has long been a matter of great interest to psychologists because of the possibility that therein lies the key to the establishment of a better society. Although this has long been a matter of speculation among both psychiatrists and clinical psychologists, only in relatively recent times have research techniques been developed that are capable of removing this problem from the field of speculation. The typical research approach has been either that of observing the effects of altering the maternal relationship and thus attempting to determine the effects of some form of deprivation, or that of studying the effect on animals of providing substitutes for the natural mother that have certain built-in characteristics.

A special case of maternal deprivation is found in children assigned to institutional care early in infancy. An early study by Spitz (1945) claimed to have found severe damage to personality resulting, it was alleged, from institutionalized children not receiving appropriate affection. The latter study had a profound effect on educational literature, where it has been widely cited, despite the fact that it is crude in approach and the conclusions are remote from the data. Spitz referred to the group of symptoms manifested by the children as *hospitalism.* These symptoms included either excessive crying or lethargy and lack of responsiveness as well as lack of normal cognitive development. However, Spitz's interpretation of his findings has been widely questioned, though his observations may well have been correct. Many reasons other than deprivation of affection may have been the cause; infants in institutions have typically suffered deprivations of all kinds. Many have also suffered deprivations before birth. For example, if the mother is feeble-minded, the infant may behave as feeble-minded children are to be expected to behave. When Dennis and Najarian (1957) studied young children in an institution in Lebanon where little mothering occurred, no evidence could be found of either the emotional disturbance or lack of development reported by Spitz. Some children in the Dennis and Najarian study were retarded, but the group as a whole showed a wide range of ability.

Yarrow (1961) has reviewed the literature involving deprivation studies in infants and has made a clear analysis of what maternal deprivation may involve. He points out that the mother provides sensory stimulation for the infant through the tactile, auditory, and visual senses. This stimulation is provided through the regular activities in which the mother engages with the infant such as feeding, cuddling, playing, and even merely by being present. In addition, the mother brings all kinds of objects to the child and functions as a mediator between the child and the environment. When the child is placed in an institution, all of these sources of stimulation are reduced in quantity; but the absence of the mother also has certain other effects. The mother typically anticipates the needs of the infant; but those who operate institutions may not be so solicitous, and there may be frustrating delays in gratification of the child's needs. The frequency with which needs are met in institutions may be less than when the mother cares for the child, and thus the child may be deprived of one of the conditions that leads to a sense of security.

Yarrow considers that the difference between institution-reared and mother-reared children may be largely a result of differences in the stimulation provided by these two sets of circumstances. Yarrow also comes to the conclusion that long-term deprivation of appropriate stimulation may result in a depression of intellectual functions. This does not exclude the possibility that some of the intellectual inferiority found in institution-raised children may be a result of inherited factors. Yarrow's conclusions are reinforced by those of Casler (1961), who made an independent review of the same literature.

Important studies of Harlow (1958) in this field have been undertaken with macaque monkeys, which, compared with the human infant, are relatively mature at birth and are sufficiently capable of coordinated movement to make experimentation possible within a few days of birth. The studies have special significance in the present context, since they throw some light on later problem-solving behavior and behavior related to the handling of novel situations. Studies of the affectional responses of these creatures were begun by Harlow as a result of observation made during a long period during which macaque infants had been bottle-fed and reared by humans rather than by monkeys, a procedure that cut down greatly on the mortality of the infants. Human mothers are not only less absent-minded than monkey mothers, but they are also equipped with antibiotics, vitamins, and other valuable items. During the course of this work it was noticed that the monkey infants formed strong attachments to the diapers that were used to cover the floors of the cages. The infants held on tightly to these pads and had violent temper tantrums when they were taken away. Such attachment of an infant to a soft object had already been noted in the baby chimpanzee and is referred to as *contact comfort*.

Furthermore, it was observed that the baby macaque monkey survives only with the greatest difficulty when it is placed on the bare wire mesh of the floor. It survives somewhat better when a wire-mesh cone is provided to which it can cling, and even better when the cone is covered with terry cloth. These observations suggest that various factors may be involved in survival. One of these may be the position of the monkey, a horizontal position being less favorable than a vertical position. Another possibility is that suitable tactile stimulation must be provided. There is also the hypothesis that, in addition to these factors, the milk-giving properties of the mother may also have important effects on affectional responses in some of the stages of development of the baby monkey. With these hypotheses in mind, Harlow began to build substitute mothers, the characteristics of which could be varied to determine how each characteristic affected development.

The first substitute mother was built from a block of wood covered with sponge rubber, and this in turn was covered with terry cloth. A light bulb in the back of the wood radiated heat. The result was (Harlow, 1958) a "mother, soft, warm and tender, a mother with infinite patience, a mother available 24 hours a day, a mother that never scolded her infant and never bit or struck her baby in anger." Another mother was built of wire mesh and given all of the valuable features of the other, except that it did not provide such adequate contact comfort. In the initial experiment with four newborn monkeys the cloth mother lactated—that is, it was equipped to produce milk—and the wire mother did not; and for four other monkeys the condition was reversed. In this experiment a record was kept of the amount of time the infants spent clinging to one or the other of the mothers. The results from the experiment were clear. The baby monkeys spent most of their time clinging to the mother that provided contact comfort. The fact that the substitute mother provided milk had little to do with the attraction it offered for the baby. This tendency to prefer the mother that provided the maximum amount of contact comfort persisted for over six months; and during that time the monkeys that had the opportunity to cling to the warm cloth-covered mother spent an average of nearly eighteen hours per day clinging to it. Those that had the wire mother spent an almost negligible time clinging to it.

These results indicate that the attachment an infant develops for its mother has very little to do with the feeding process, and that disposes of the theory that love and affection are derived from association with the satisfaction of hunger or thirst. Contact comfort overwhelms nursing as a basis for the affectional responses.

A common observation is that the child who is frightened runs to his mother and clings there as long as the frightening object is present. A similar characteristic behavior is manifested by macaque monkeys. Harlow (1958) and his colleagues have tested this response with the two types of substitute mothers previously discussed. A number of fear-producing stimuli were introduced in the presence of both the baby and the substitute mothers. The response of the baby monkeys to the cloth mother was much the same as that which occurs in the presence of the real mother; the fear-producing stimulus caused the monkey to run to the cloth mother and cling to it. The wire mother served very little purpose in this respect. There was also no difference between the responses toward the cloth mother that lactated and the one that did not.

In another study an investigation was made of the behavior of the infants toward the substitute mother in the presence of stimuli that arouse curiosity. In the human child, as in the macaque, the mother becomes a base of operations for exploring the world. The infant will explore new stimuli and then return to the mother after a brief spell. The cloth mother functions for the little macaque monkey in just this fashion. In the presence of new stimuli, the young animal makes brief exploratory sorties and then returns and clutches the substitute mother. In the absence of the substitute mother, the amount of emotional behavior is substantially increased.

Another point of real interest is that Harlow finds that the attachment that the monkey forms for its cloth mother is quite as strong as the attachment it would naturally form for its real mother. Again, it also appears that the security provided by the real mother is no greater than that provided by the cloth mother.

Some additional findings are also of interest. Harlow found that monkeys raised on wire mothers tended to have more fluid bowel movements than those raised on terry-cloth and rubber mothers. He suggests that this may signify a relationship between physiological functions and the method of rearing, a relationship that psychiatrists have long suggested exists. Harlow's data can be interpreted otherwise to indicate merely that the wire mother provides a form of support for the youngster that mechanically disturbs its intestinal function.

In a later study Harlow (1962) showed that normal adult sexual behavior in monkeys is dependent on the previous occurrence of adequate infant-infant interactions. Even monkeys raised on cloth monkeys would develop normal adult sexual patterns of behavior provided they had the opportunity of interacting with other infants. However, the monkeys raised on cloth mothers showed little interest in their offspring, a fact that bears out the idea of Freud that early experiences may be vastly important as determinants of adult behavior.

An extended series of studies has been undertaken with rats and mice on the effect of early stimulation on later emotionality and later learning. In these studies, reviewed by Denenberg (1964), animals were stimulated, during the first 20 days of life, by various means ranging from stroking from head to tail to violent shaking and electric shock. Emotionality was measured by a number of different techniques including counting the number of times the animals excreted or defecated when placed in an open space; the amount of water consumed after a period of deprivation; and the frequency with which the animals would "freeze" when engaged in a task in which they received an electric shock for incorrect responses. The data indicates that animals stimulated during the first twenty days of life, either violently or gently, show less emotionality in young adult life than those animals that were not administered the early stimulation. Violent and unpleasant stimulation in early infancy did not produce highly emotional rats, as perhaps one might have expected; the reverse was the case. At this point, these results should not be generalized to the human species, though the generalization may be valid.

The relationship of early stimulation, either violent or mild, to learning in the adult life of the organism is complex, as Denenberg (1964) points out. Emotionality, as defined in these experiments, seems to be related to motivation; but the extent to which motivation interferes with or facilitates learning and problem solving depends on the difficulty of the task. An old law in psychology, the Yerkes-Dodson law, states that the optimum level of motivation for a task decreases as the task becomes more difficult. Thus, rats that had been shocked in infancy, and that show a low level of emotionality as adults, might be insufficiently motivated to perform well on very easy tasks but might be working at their optimum on tasks a little more difficult. On the other hand, rats that had not been especially stimulated in infancy would be more emotional as adults and hence be most capable of performing effectively on simple tasks. Denenberg considers that the evidence, taken as a whole, supports this kind of relationship.

Social Aspects of Child Development in Relation to Learning

Two theories emphasize opposing elements concerning the basis of the commonly observed pattern of social behavior in children. These theories differ fundamentally, but one cannot say at this time which one is the soundest; and both may offer explanations that are partially true.

One theory emphasizes learning as the basis of the development of social behavior. It points out that the young infant learns that the presence of another human is associated with the satisfaction of all his needs, and hence the need for human company develops as a secondary or derived need. This theory is, on the surface, an attractive one; but it fails to take into account the fact, emphasized by the alternative theory, that in some species the young grow up with almost negligible social needs, despite the fact that the mother animal satisfies the needs of the young for food. The rat is an example of such an animal that is fed by its mother and yet that grows up with almost no social needs. Rats can be kept in cages isolated from other rats without showing any disturbances of behavior. In contrast, primates, including man, show marked effects when isolated from other members of their species. An adult rat deprived of the company of other rats does not show any particular changes in behavior as a result of this deprivation. A chimpanzee, on the other hand, once isolated, becomes neurotic and disturbed. He will gaze in the direction where he knows other chimpanzees to be. The social need, once established, continues to operate. Why the need develops in the case of primates and not in the case of the rat must represent a species difference. Species differ in the extent to which, given social stimulation early in life, they will develop a need for social stimulation. Man belongs to a species the members of which characteristically develop social needs. They may have an inborn disposition to acquire such a need. We are not saying that learning does not play an important part in the acquisition of this need, for it probably does. But the social species, such as man and the primates, learn in this direction; some other species do not.

Within any species, one may expect individual differences in the extent to which social needs are developed. This will depend partly on the learning situations presented. If the social situations the child encounters are not rewarding, then one may expect that social needs will develop only to a limited extent. Anne Roe (1957), as a result of a lifetime study of scientists, suggests that a physical scientist is a person whose attention has become directed toward the outside physical world because he does not find social relations particularly rewarding. This is an interesting hypothesis; and it suggests that a school that makes interpersonal relations highly rewarding is unlikely to turn out physical scientists.

There is also the possibility that a person who develops only very limited social needs may be one in his species whose disposition to learn in this direction is limited. This is just a supposition at this time, and no evidence is available, as far as the writer knows, to indicate whether this is correct or incorrect; but it is an idea to be kept in mind when the social behavior of man is interpreted. Teachers who attempt to develop social needs in children who show only minimal social needs may be sowing seed on barren ground. In children who have low social needs, any attempt to develop their social needs to a higher level may be forcing them to learn in areas in which they are not constitutionally suited to learn. Perhaps these speculations may serve as a note of caution to the teacher with high social needs herself, and who believes that all children should develop equally high social needs or that all children have equally high social needs that must be satisfied.

Although much that has been written about the development of social behaviors is speculative, there is a growing body of empirical research designed to explore relationships between adult behavior impinging on the child and the development of social behavior. An example of such a study is one by Peck (1958), in which four dimensions of parent-child interaction were related to six dimensions of child behavior. The four dimensions of parent-child interaction are consistency, democracy, trust, and severity. The dimensions of child behavior in this study were described as ego strength, superego strength, willing social conformity, spontaneity, friendliness, and hostility and guilt. Ego strength was found to be related to consistency, a position in keeping with current clinical knowledge. Friendliness is a product of a relaxed atmosphere, while hostility and guilt are generated by extreme severity. However, just how such findings are to be related to current knowledge of learning is not clear. No simple conception of learning accounts for the findings. Other findings of great interest derived from a study by Trapp and Kausler (1958) also point up the complexity of the relationship of learning conditions and the skills acquired. In the latter study, both large and small amounts of parental dominance tended to produce more adult avoidance than did an intermediate amount of dominance.

Perhaps the major difficulty in developing such research and relating it to a learning model is that, as yet, there is little standardization of terms in discussing many learning conditions. Each research worker develops his own concepts and labels them in his own way. However, one recent study has attempted to define a set of basic dimensions of parent behavior, and this study may pave the way for the systematic development of learning concepts in this important area. This study must now be considered.

In the last decade some information has been accumulated concerning the relationship of child-rearing practices and certain aspects of learning. The outstanding study in this area is one conducted by Sears, Maccoby, and Levin (1957), and involved the child-rearing practices of 379 mothers. Child-rearing practices are defined as dimensions of maternal behavior.

In the Sears *et al.* study, the group of mothers carefully studied came from two suburban towns in a large metropolitan area of New England. The group was derived from a complete range of social classes, and in this respect must be considered highly representative of a New England population of mothers. The median age of the group was 33.6 years. Both ends of the education continuum were well represented, with 22 per cent having completed college and 14 per cent never having completed high school. The group also represented a wide range of income.

Data were collected concerning the child-rearing practices of this group of mothers by means of extended interviews that had been carefully planned. The aspects of the mothers' behavior studied were those considered to be most influential with respect to the child. For this reason, careful inquiries were made into such matters as the disciplinary measures, permissiveness, severity of training, temperamental qualities of the mother, and attempts to develop more mature behavior. Much of the study is descriptive and provides a record of the child-rearing practices of a group of New England mothers at mid-century. Studies of child-rearing practices conducted fifty years from now will undoubtedly compare the data with that collected by Sears *et al.* The strictly descriptive aspects of this study are not related to the topic at hand, and therefore will not be reviewed here. What we are concerned with here are the ways in which these characteristics group themselves and the relationship of these groups of behavior to aspects of the learning process.

Sears *et al.* subjected their data to a factor analysis in order to determine the way in which the characteristics of child-rearing practices grouped themselves. Five major groupings were found, which are described as follows:

Permissiveness-strictness. This characteristic emerged from the study as the most all-pervasive of the ones studied. At one end of the scale are mothers who imposed strong restrictions on children with respect to play in the house and showed high demands for good table manners, quietness, orderliness, and neatness, low permissiveness with respect to aggression toward parents, siblings, and other children, as well as low permissiveness with respect to sex behavior. The relationship of this aspect of parental behavior to the behavior of the child brings out the interesting finding that permissiveness concerning aggression results in a high level of aggressive behavior on the part of the child. The implication is that such behavior is not learned by reinforcement but has to be controlled by some degree of suppression. This fits well the findings of Lebo and Lebo (1957), who found that children who expressed most aggression in their classrooms also expressed the most in a free-play situation conducted by a therapist. They did *not* find that those who failed to express aggression in daily life tended to show aggression in play therapy. Aggression, it appears, can be either generally expressed or generally absent. The same effect is not evidenced in the case of dependency relationships. A permissive attitude toward dependency does not seem to encourage dependency.

General family adjustment. This characteristic is the extent to which the mother manifested such attributes as high esteem for herself and her spouse, was happy about becoming pregnant, enjoyed interaction with her baby, and was satisfied with her present life situation. Although this has commonly been considered to represent one of the most important conditions related to the development of desirable attributes of personality, the study provides virtually no data concerning its relationship to the later characteristics of the child.

Warmth of mother-child relationship. The name for this characteristic provides a good description of the behavior to which it refers. This characteristic appeared to have an all-pervasive effect on the behavior of the child. Maternal coldness was associated with difficulties related to the negative functions such as feeding and bladder control, and emotional difficulties related to these functions. In addition, maternal coldness was associated with the slowness in the development of a conscience. The authors of the study suggest that the warm mother offers more reinforcements than the cold mother, and hence provides a more favorable condition for many of the learnings that must take place in the first few years of childhood.

Responsible child-training orientation. The high end of this scale describes a mother who takes her child-rearing duties with great seriousness and feels the weight of her responsibilities. Little information is given concerning the relationship of this factor to child behavior.

Aggressiveness and punitiveness. The mother who is high in this dimension expects the child to be aggressive toward other children, but administers severe punishment if the child should show aggression against the parent. The high end of this scale identifies a mother who has a high level of aggression, but who will not tolerate aggression toward herself. The researchers concluded that a high level of punitiveness is quite ineffective in child training, a conclusion that is consistent with data reported in other parts of this book. They also point out that their data supports the position that punishment does little to eliminate undesirable behavior. Severe physical punishment was associated with feeding problems and with aggression in the home. Nevertheless, some caution is necessary in drawing conclusions from this aspect of the study. Sears and his associates conclude that under certain conditions punishment may be effective, but the nature of these conditions has not yet been determined.

Other cultures provide different contrasts in child-rearing practices that may add to an understanding of the relationship of early training conditions to adult personality. A particularly striking contrast is presented in Israel, where the child-rearing practices with children raised in the Kibbutz can be contrasted with those of the more typical family situation. Rabin (1965) compared the behavior of children and young adults who had been raised in each of these two situations.

The Kibbutz is a voluntary organization of individuals who have come together to pool their energies and resources, to live in a state of economic collectivism, and to delegate to the group as a whole the main responsibilities of child-rearing. In such a collective, the mother has continuous contact with the infant only during the first four months; after that, the contacts are steadily reduced until daily contacts between parent and child are restricted to one or two hours, when the parents visit the child-raising houses and interact with the child. The typical child-rearing practices of the parents are taken over by the *metapelet,* a term that is translated as "one who takes care of." Thus, in infancy and early childhood, those raised in the Kibbutz come into contact with many adults who are responsible for their welfare, including the biological mother, the metapelet, the people who relieve the metapelet at various times during the day, the night watchwoman, and perhaps others too; and the child must compete with many other children of similar age for the services and attention of these adults. The Kibbutz child-rearing situation appears to provide a socially more complex environment than does the typical family situation; and, in the early years, the Kibbutz situation may be intellectually more deprived. There are also lessened opportunities for intense identification with single adult figures.

The complexity of the early environment in the Kibbutz appears to have a retarding effect during the first few years. The children are not only less intellectually developed than are the family-reared children, but they also show a greater frequency of emotional problems such as are reflected in tantrums. Nevertheless, such problems are short-lived, for the difficulties of early life are soon overcome and a benign educational environment produces accelerated educational development. The Kibbutz child with his relationships to many adults shows few strong attachments and also fewer conflicts with adult figures, particularly during adolescence. The conflicts of the teen-age period are largely absent because the youngster does not have to struggle for independence and for personal identity—he has already gained these at a much earlier age.

The study suggests that early emotional problems do not necessarily forewarn of subsequent emotional problems at a later age. Apparently, they do not represent learned patterns of responding, but rather they reflect states of disorganization, which are replaced later by more adequate patterns of responding. The data also suggest that an intellectually barren infancy does not do irreparable damage that a stimulating environment in the later years cannot remedy.

Development as a Learning and Relearning Process

Habits that are learned at one age are often inappropriate at another age and must be displaced by new and more appropriate habits. This greatly complicates the learning process and reduces it in efficiency. A two-year-old child is reinforced when he intrudes on adult company. The adults are likely to stop their conversation and direct their attention to the child, who finds the behavior of the adult highly rewarding. Over the next few years, the adults continue to reinforce this behavior until it is a well-established habit. However, around the time the child enters school, the adults suddenly change their attitude toward the child who intrudes and stops their conversation. A habit that was considered cute at the age of four suddenly becomes quite obnoxious at the age of six.

Another illustration of the way in which learning must often attempt to develop behaviors that are inconsistent with those previously learned is found in the case of speech. Early speech is often learned as baby language. Incorrect pronunciations are often deliberately encouraged in the very young by speaking to them in a language that reflects incorrect usage and incorrect pronunciation. Later, the language habits the child has thus acquired must be displaced by new language habits more appropriate for adult communication. Often the baby language is so well established that it continues to appear for years after efforts are begun to teach adult speech habits. The old established habits interfere with the development of new habits, and the learning of correct adult usage is a very difficult task.

The inconsistencies in values and attitudes that characterize the mature person are undoubtedly the result of inconsistent learning throughout the growing period. Here again, the point must be made that learning that produces such inconsistencies is wasteful and results in the development of individuals in whom there is conflict of motives and conflict of responses. Such individuals are ineffective insofar as there is such conflict.

Language Learning in the Developmental Process

The research literature on the development of language is vast, as is attested to by the fact that McCarthy's (1954) review of the subject in the *Manual of Child Psychology* covers close to a thousand references. At least one reason for this large research literature is that phenomena in language areas are so easily quantified. It is simple to count the number of words used, the length of sentences, or the number of different words used in an utterance as each year of childhood passes by; at least it is a beguilingly simple-appearing matter, though often unexpected complexities arise. For this reason, data collection on language development has been undertaken on a vast scale. But the richness of facts has not always been accompanied by a wealth of useful theory. Indeed, this is an area that has attracted the empirically oriented psychologist rather than the theoretician, and theory has often come from the linguist rather than the psychologist. The impact of the learning psychologist on conceptions of language development has been small until the last decade.

Many of the early theories of language were descriptions of language rather than attempts to indicate mechanisms that might be involved in its acquisition. For example, Gregoire (1937, 1947), after extensive studies of young children, took the position that the young child is endowed with a large repertoire of sounds which he must learn to use with discrimination. His theory involves the learning of appropriate sounds from this large repertoire for use on particular occasions. A large repertoire of sounds, of the kind postulated by Gregoire, provides a situation in which the learning of language can be described well as an instrumental conditioning process. Skinner (1958) has speculated at length on this possibility and has provided a psychological interpretation of linguistic behavior based on a learning theory.

Of substantial impact on education has been the work undertaken on language development by Jean Piaget and his associates. The voluminous work of this group can be given only passing reference here, because its relation to the study of learning still has to be worked out, but its long-term influence on the study of human learning may be great.

Summary

1. The distinction is made between growth and development: The term *growth* refers to an increase in size; the term *development* refers to a change in organization and resulting function.

2. Although simple conditioning may occur prior to birth, the state of the nervous system in the first few months of life is such that only limited learning can take place, and there is limited capacity for retention.

3. As development proceeds, some behaviors begin to emerge as a product of the maturation process. The dramatic discovery, half a century ago, that locomotion in some creatures is a product of the animal's native equipment, has had a strong influence on thinking in the area. Extensive work was later undertaken to determine what patterns of behavior might show a similar emergence with the maturation of the nervous system. Early studies of the emergence of a number of reflexes were followed by more extensive studies designed to discover the developmental patterns and stages of the child.

4. The importance of the maturation concept was also greatly enhanced by work with twins, in which one twin was given special training in a skill that the other did not receive. The extra training generally had only a transitory effect, and any special advantages were rapidly lost.

5. The concept of organismic age grew naturally out of the concept of maturation; and it has important influences on educational thought. It involves the idea that all growth functions go hand in hand, and that whatever depresses one function also depresses other developmental functions. This concept has not survived well the results of systematic research, which has demonstrated a far greater degree of independence of growth functions than Olson believed to exist.

6. Considerable evidence has been accumulated to show that learning occurs in two stages. This theory has been advanced by Hebb, who has also gathered together in his laboratory considerable evidence to support the position. Early learning is very slow and time-consuming. Late learn-

ing is relatively rapid. If early learning is prevented by replacing the developing organism in an environment that limits experience, the organism will show certain deficiencies in his behavior when he is placed in a more typical environment. The handicaps produced by the restricted environment take long to overcome because they involve an early learning process.

7. There is a possibility that some of the difficulties in learning that children may manifest in school may be the product of inadequate early-learning experiences. At present there is no way of discriminating between failure to learn that is the product of inadequate maturation, and failure to learn that results from inadequate early learning.

8. Bloom has advanced a series of hypotheses related to development. He points out that the period of maximum rate of development is the period when the environment can have maximum impact. He also finds data to support the position that the change in a measure from one age to another is a function of environmental events.

9. The relationship of child-rearing practices (and the stimulation that accompanies them) to the intellectual development of the child is a matter of considerable interest. Although Spitz claimed that children in foundling homes manifested a behavioral disturbance called *hospitalism*, which he considered to be a product of a lack of affection, there is little evidence to support his contention. On the other hand, Harlow has demonstrated that macaque monkeys require adequate *contact comfort*, or certain emotional disturbances result. Harlow also points out that the mother, or the substitute, represents an important place from which the young explore the world and to which they can return when this exploration builds up anxieties. Without such support in exploring the environment, emotional disturbances are likely to appear with increased frequency. The relationship between stimulation and development is an area in which important relationships are now being explored.

10. An important field of research that is opening up new ways of exploring learning in the young is the study of the relationship of child-rearing practices to child behavior. Several important studies have now been undertaken in this area, and they have served the purpose of identifying broad variables as well as beginning to relate these variables to child behavior. Research indicates that the relationship between adult behavior and learning in the child is complex.

11. Language development is an area in which there has been extensive research. Also there have been attempts to apply learning theory to the understanding of how language develops, the most comprehensive of which comes from B. F. Skinner, who has attempted to view language as the learning of a system of instrumental responses. Research resulting

in the description of language development as it occurs in relation to thought processes is beginning to produce findings of importance for the planning of education.

12. Research has been undertaken on the characteristics of events that reinforce at different ages. Perhaps the main conclusion to be drawn from such studies is that little is known as yet concerning the nature of reinforcing events in the case of human learners.

10

Some Acquisition and Retention Phenomena

THE LEARNING phenomena discussed up to this point have only touched on the general course of learning. That is because the course of learning depends, to a considerable extent, on the conditions under which learning occurs as well as on some of the conditions that occur prior to learning.

Suppose a pupil is acquiring vocabulary in French. At the end of each week the total size of his French vocabulary can be measured by giving him an objective test of his knowledge of French words. Let us assume that all of these tests are of equal difficulty and that each one tests the pupil's knowledge of the five thousand most common words in the French language. Each test might include a hundred words the pupil would have to translate, and his score would be based on the number of words he translated correctly. A graph showing the change in the status of his French vocabulary as the weeks passed could then be plotted. Such learning curves may be plotted for any area of learning, provided there is available some measure of the amount of learning that has occurred. The curve not only represents where the person started and where he finished in the particular period of time, but it also shows whether there were periods in which learning was more rapid than in other periods.

The learning curve representing acquisition of French vocabulary represents only one of many functions acquired during the learning of a foreign language. The curve is a record of a limited aspect of learning, and, even though it represents vocabulary learning, it does not represent every aspect of vocabulary. The curve indicates nothing about how well the vocabulary was learned. It does not indicate which classes of words were learned best. It provides no information about how much of the vocabulary will be retained six months hence. It does not indicate the extent to which the vocabulary is readily available. If the tests had required the student to fill in blanks rather than select correct answers, the curve produced would also have been different, because it would have measured a somewhat different learning function. Any single learning curve does not represent learning in its entirety. It represents only a limited aspect of learning.

Two learning curves based on data related to the acquisition of language skills are represented in Figure 11 and Figure 12. The one represents the acquisition of English vocabulary from the beginning of learning. The other represents the acquisition of one aspect of writing skill, but the graph begins at a stage where considerable skill has already been acquired. The graphs represent learning as it occurred under the particular conditions prevailing. The curve in Figure 11 is approximately S-shaped; but under other learning conditions, different forms of the curve might have been produced.

A learning curve is a way of representing the progress of learning. Generally it represents the cumulative *effect* of numerous conditions that

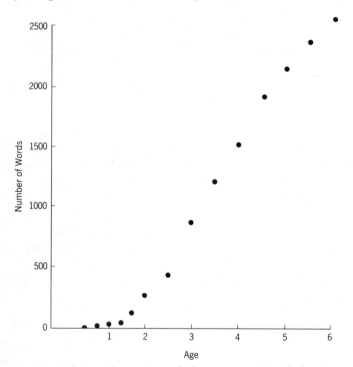

FIGURE 11. Relation of size of vocabulary to age. (Graph drawn from data by M. E. Smith, 1926.)

result in the acquisition of the skill. It is a *representation* of the acquisition of the skill, but it tells little about how the skill was acquired.

Whether one is concerned with the learning of a rat in the laboratory or the learning of a child in the classroom, there are advantages in keeping track of the learning process by making a continuous record of the acquisition of the skill. This may be done in many different ways. In a typing class the teacher may give a typing test after each period of training in the acquisition of a skill. A resulting score, commonly given in words per minute, may be recorded. A basketball coach may plot the *cumulative* number of points scored by each athlete during the season. Skinner, in working with pigeons, uses a similar score; his typical procedure is to record and plot the cumulative number of pecks given by the pigeon, which has been trained to peck at a disc on the wall of the training box.

The usual method of demonstrating progress in learning is to plot the scores on a graph. In the illustration given of the pupil learning French, the progress of learning is represented by a close approximation to a straight line, but this is not typical.

Until recently, the psychologist asked to present a curve representing the basic learning curve would likely have drawn one similar to that shown in Figure 13. A curve with this shape is commonly produced in

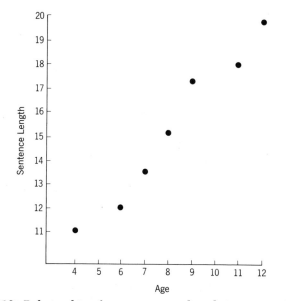

FIGURE 12. Relationship of mean sentence length in composition and school grade. (Graph drawn from data provided by Stormzand and O'Shea, 1924.)

the learning of complex skills. Learning in the early part is rapid; then the apparent rate of learning becomes less and less rapid. Skills such as that involved in the sending of Morse code typically demonstrate such a curve of learning, but this curve does not necessarily represent learning under all conditions.

Spence (1956) has brought together some interesting information concerning the shape of the learning curve. After reviewing the literature, he finds that classical-conditioning learning takes the form of an S-shaped curve. Learning curves that illustrate this position are shown in Figure 14. Spence also reviewed the data available concerning the shape of the learning curve for instrumental learning, and found that where the function measured is frequency of response, then the curve is also S-shaped. Where other characteristics of the response are recorded, then

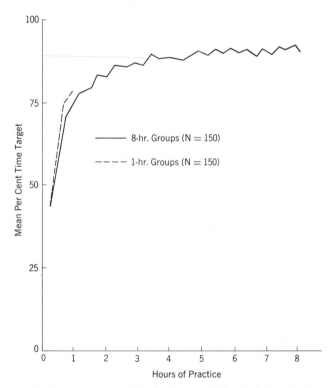

FIGURE 13. Curve representing learning of the skill involved in the control of the performance of a miniature plane, the movements of which are manipulated by means of a set of controls similar to those used in an aircraft. Data from Ammons *et al.*, 1958. (Reproduced by permission of the American Psychological Association.)

the S-shaped curve does not always appear. Learning curves from an instrumental-learning situation are shown in Figure 15. One is tempted to generalize that when a new habit or skill is learned from the beginning, the resulting curve is S-shaped, but caution makes it necessary to add the qualification that this seems to be true only when response frequency is involved. Later, when further studies have been undertaken, the latter qualification may be removed.

Why then is the typical learning curve found in most training studies (and presented in Figure 13) not found to be S-shaped? The answer

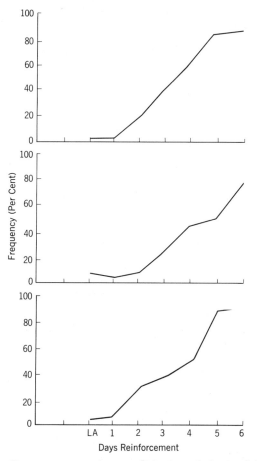

FIGURE 14. Curves representing conditioning of the eyelid response for three monkeys. The point marked L.A. (light adaptions) shows the frequency of response to the conditioned stimulus before conditioning. (After Hilgard and Marquis, 1936, p. 190. Reproduced by permission of the American Psychological Association.)

seems to be that the acquisition of most skills in a training or school situation involves component skills that have already been learned. The sending of Morse code involves the use of letters and manipulative activity, and these are not new to the learner. The learner also has a general conception of what the skill is about and what he has to do to acquire proficiency. Thus, some related learnings have already been accomplished. The learner is not in the position of a subject in a laboratory experiment in which the experimenter is attempting to condition the subject's pupillary reflex to the sound of a bell, a learning that is quite remote from anything he has ever previously learned. The writer suggests that the typical learning curve of school situations is one that is represented by the right-hand section of an S-shaped curve. This sec-

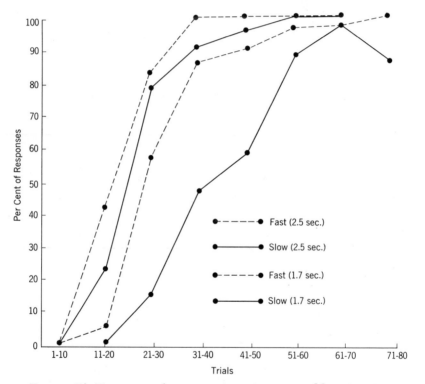

FIGURE 15. Frequency of responses in an instrumental learning situation of groups of rats. The requirement of the learning situation was that the rat touch the bar. The two curves showing learning involve different learning criteria from the other two curves. (The curves are presented by Spence and are based on unpublished data by Ramond.) (From K. W. Spence, *Behavior Theory and Conditioning*. New Haven: Yale University Press (1956). Reproduced by permission of the Yale University Press.)

tion of the S-shaped curve corresponds well to a curve that rises rapidly and then shows a typical negative acceleration as learning proceeds.

Some learning curves may show periods of learning followed by periods in which no recordable learning takes place. Such curves were first discovered in a study of Morse-code learning by Bryan and Harter (1897), but other illustrations of this phenomenon have been found in a number of different fields. In Figure 16, the flat portions of the graph

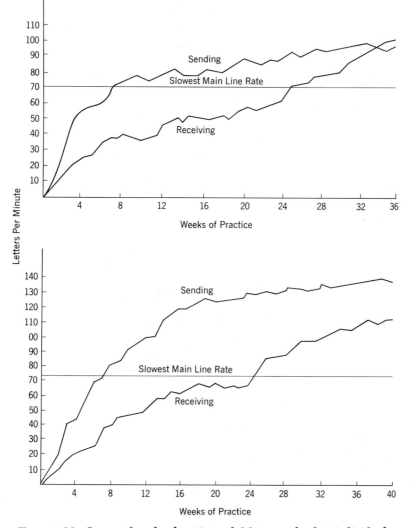

FIGURE 16. Curves for the learning of Morse code for individual subjects showing plateaus on the receiving curves. (From Bryan and Harter, 1897, p. 49.)

in which no progress is visible are named *plateaus,* and several plateaus are said to occur when learning extends over a long period of time. When and where plateaus may be expected to occur cannot be predicted at this time. There is even some controversy whether plateaus are genuine phenomena and typical of complex skill learning. The flattening out of a learning curve insofar as it is a genuine phenomenon does not necessarily indicate that a final limit of learning has been reached. It may be just a temporary limit resulting from the fact that the person cannot make further progress until he takes a new approach to the task. It is quite conceivable that a plateau might be eliminated in some cases if proper guidance could be given to the learning process. In the case of the plateaus that appear in the curve for learning Morse code, the common belief is that the plateau represents the time in learning when the learner has reached the limit of what he can achieve by working with the coding and decoding of individual letters. Before he can make further progress, he must learn to take letters in groups and code and decode entire groups as units. As soon as he realizes that he must cease working with individual letters and must start working with groups, then he begins to make progress again. In other tasks, plateaus may have different significance. Sometimes they may mean that the learner has acquired certain component skills and now must integrate the components he has learned. Thus, in learning to drive a sports car, a student may be able to steer adequately, and he may also be able to change gear adequately; but he may still have to learn to steer *while* he is changing gear. The experienced teacher learns to recognize the various stages of learning and the difficulties they may involve.

Families of learning curves produced in experiments involved in the development of learning sets are particularly instructive. In a typical learning-set development procedure, described by Harlow (1959), an animal is confronted with two food wells covered with different-shaped objects. In the particular trial, the food well that is covered with the barrel-shaped object contains food and the one covered with the cube does not. The animal is given six trials to learn which is correct and which incorrect. At the end of six trials the problem is changed to a new problem. After, say, eight such problems, each requiring six trials, the success on the first trials on each problem, taking all problems together, can be computed, and so too for the second trial, the third, and so forth. In this way a curve can be developed that will show the trend in learning over the six trials when the performance on all eight problems are combined. The same can be done with the next eight problems, and the next eight, and so forth. Each curve will represent problem-solving ability at a particular level of training in problem solving. The resulting family of curves will show changes in the form of the learning curve with the

development of sophistication in problem solving. Such a family of learning curves produced by Harlow (1959, p. 496) is shown in Figure 17.

This family of curves is particularly interesting in that there appears
to be a progressive change from an S-shaped curve in the case of the
lower curve with the naive subjects to a more conventional learning
curve with the highly trained problem-solvers. This is added evidence
that the shape of the learning curve, when a novel learning function is
involved, is likely to be roughly that of an S.

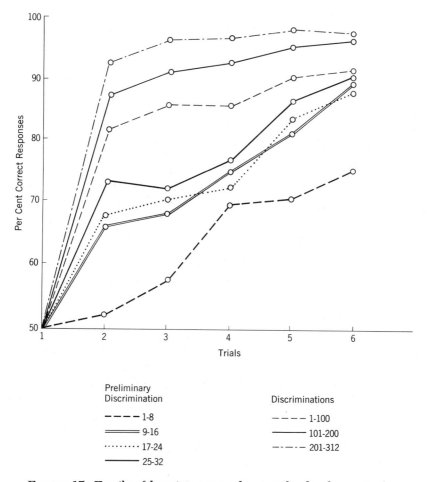

FIGURE 17. Family of learning curves showing the development of a
learning set. (From H. F. Harlow, "Learning Set and Error Factor
Theory," in S. Koch (ed.), *Psychology: A Study of a Science*, Vol. 2
(New York: McGraw-Hill Book Company, 1959). Used by permission of McGraw-Hill Book Company.)

Learning curves do not always show the smooth contour such as is presented by those that have been discussed. Variations in numerous conditions result in fluctuations in the learning process. These include fluctuations in motivation, the presence of distractions over which the experimenter has no control, and, perhaps too, periods when effort to master one part of the activity interferes with the mastery of the other parts. When the learning curves of a number of different individuals are combined, these ups and downs come at different parts of the learning curve and hence tend to be smoothed out.

Learning curves tend to level off after practice has been continued for a time. This leveling off is referred to as a *crude limit of learning*. It is not generally the absolute limit of learning, since further learning will occur if conditions are modified. There are occasions when the very best conditions for learning have been provided and the leveling-off represents a level of performance beyond which the person cannot go. In this case the limit of learning reached is commonly referred to as the *physiological limit*. One always has to be cautious in assuming that the maximum level of performance has been reached, and probably very rarely is it reached. What is considered at one time to be the physiological limit of performance often becomes later merely a landmark as new records are set. At one time it was considered physiologically impossible for the human to run a mile in less than four minutes, and the performance of a generation of athletes provided evidence to support this point of view. However, in recent years training techniques have changed, and the running of a mile in less than four minutes has become a fairly common event in athletics.

In the case of intellectual learning similar to that which occupies a large fraction of the school program, there is no study on record that gives any reason for believing that a physiological limit has been reached. From what is now known of the learning process, there are indications that most of the learning that occurs in the academic areas occurs under conditions that are far from optimal. It seems not too much to hope that during the next fifty years the amount that children are able to learn in school may double without any increased effort on their part. This seems to be a reasonable expectation at the present time.

Many advantages would accrue if one were able to predict in advance the course of learning for a particular individual—that is, if one could predict the exact form of the individual's learning curve. One would then be able to know the limit of learning for the particular individual and also the rate at which he might be expected to learn. If the teacher were equipped with such information, it would be possible for him to plan learning for each child, taking into account individual differences. At the present time only rough predictions are possible concerning the future course of learning, and hence many mistakes are made in planning individual learning programs.

Another important point about learning curves is that the crude limit of learning is usually what the guidance counselor wishes to predict when he administers an aptitude test to a pupil. The aptitude test is administered so that the counselor may obtain some indication of how far the pupil may be expected to go in a particular area, given the usual kind of learning program. The counselor knows that if more efficient methods of teaching were available, a pupil might go much farther than the test predicted. An aptitude test, say, to predict success in a future course in a foreign language, only predicts the kind of level the pupil may be expected to achieve under the kinds of learning conditions existing at present.

Mathematical Models and Learning Curves

During the last decade, considerable interest has been shown in attempts to derive a learning curve by mathematical methods from assumptions made about the learning process. For example, if the assumption is made that equal amounts of practice produce equal increments of correct responses, then learning would be represented by a straight line on a graph that related the percentage of correct responses to the amount of practice. Such an assumption would not be valid and would not produce a learning curve that corresponded, to any extent, with that produced by real data. The problem is to make assumptions that lead to curves that correspond closely with those produced through the analysis of real data. If a set of assumptions can be made about learning from which mathematical procedures can derive a learning curve that fits closely that derived from real data, one can then say that the mathematical model has validity. This procedure is roughly that followed by scientists in the physical sciences who frequently make assumptions concerning the nature of the phenomena they are studying and then derive mathematical equations from those assumptions. The next step is to find out whether experimental data fits the mathematical functions that have been thus derived. Elaborate computers are often used to calculate the results expected in terms of theory, which are later compared with those from actual data.

Psychologists have attempted to produce theoretical learning curves, starting with many different assumptions about the learning process. Some of the curves thus produced have shown a remarkable degree of correspondence with actual data. An example of such a theoretically derived curve is shown in Figure 18. In this figure the circles represent

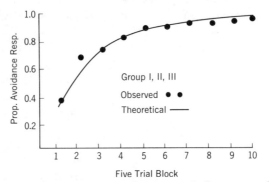

FIGURE 18. Graph showing the fit of actual data to a theoretical learning curve. (After Brody, 1957, p. 243. Reproduced by permission of the American Psychological Association.)

the points on the curve derived from experimental data. The continuous curve represents a theoretical curve. The data in this case fits well the theoretical learning curve. Indeed, the fit is exceptional. Other cases could be presented in which a much poorer fit was obtained. The Brody (1957) data are presented here to indicate that this approach may well have a bright future.

An extensive literature has grown up on the use of mathematical models in the behavioral sciences. A leader in this field has been W. K. Estes, who has prepared an excellent summary of his own and related work (1959). The model of learning on which Estes based his work is different from that used by many other psychologists also interested in exploring the use of mathematical models. An alternative model is found in the work of Bush and Mosteller (1955). The reader who may wish to explore more widely the use of mathematical models in the social sciences may consult a work by Kemeny and Snell (1961).

Retention

A discussion of recording the progress of learning is appropriately followed by a discussion of the related problem of recording the retention of what has been learned. Just as the learning curve is a record of only one aspect of learning measured in a particular way, so too is a curve of retention a record of a product of learning as it is measured at various intervals of time after the learning conditions have ceased to operate. Since retention can be measured in a number of different ways, a graph representing the degree of retention can be drawn for each way in which retention is measured. These graphs may show great differences one from another, according to the measure that is used. Indeed, differences may be so great that a skill learned may show zero amounts of retention by one method of measurement, but substantial retention by another. Methods of measuring retention vary greatly in sensitivity, and hence it is important for the student of education to have some familiarity with such methods, particularly if he wishes later to conduct studies of the long-term retention of some of his students of the subject-matter taught in class. The following methods have been widely used for measuring retention:

The recall method. This is the method most familiar to every teacher. It requires the pupil to recall whatever he can of the skill that has been acquired. The measurement of vocabulary in a foreign language can be measured by a recall test in which either the foreign words are presented and the pupil must give the English translation, or the English words are given to be translated into the foreign language. Essay tests typically call for recall skills. Motor skills involved in the operation of equipment may be measured by requiring the examinee to demonstrate his skills. Such a recall procedure is the least sensitive one available for the measurement of retention.

The recognition method. This method applies mainly to the measurement of cognitive skills such as are learned in academic classrooms. When this method is applied, the subject demonstrates retention by recognizing a correct response. The objective type of examination is the most widely used example of this method of measuring retention. Every pupil and teacher knows that it is much easier to recognize the right answer than it is to produce it with few cues. In the recognition method of measuring retention, many cues are provided; but in the recall method, there are very few cues present to elicit the response. The difference in the number of cues present accounts for the difference in sensitivity of the recognition method in comparison with the recall method.

The relearning, or saving, method. Some sensitive techniques have been developed that can demonstrate that there has been retention even though all of the ordinary tests of retention used in schools indicate that there has been none. A very sensitive technique widely used in laboratories is known as the saving method. In this method the subject learns the material to a certain standard of proficiency. If he is learning a list of words, then he may learn them to the point where he can repeat the list back perfectly on three *successive* trials. This would generally be done by presenting him with the list of words, permitting him to read it through once, and then asking him to recall the list he has read. This is repeated time after time until he reproduces the list perfectly on three successive occasions. After a period of time, the degree to which he has retained the list is measured by determining how much further learning must take place in order to relearn the list to the point where, once again, it can be repeated perfectly on another three successive occasions. If twenty-five repetitions were required in the original learning series to reach the point of perfect recall, only five repetitions might be required at a later time to reach the same point of learning. And since, on relearning, five instead of twenty-five repetitions were required, one might say that on relearning there was a "saving" of eighty per cent. This is how the method acquired its name. In some studies it has been the only method so far developed that is sensitive enough to provide evidence that there has been some retention of the original material learned.

There is a little evidence to show that occasionally experiences can be recalled in great detail even though the original experiences were transitory. A person may at times recall briefly earlier experiences in great detail, even though the details involved were not noted particularly at the time. There is also some evidence that under hypnosis a person's ability to recall material recently learned, such as poetry, may be heightened. Clinical psychologists and psychiatrists have also claimed that, during clinical treatment, recall may be greatly heightened. However, most psychologists would probably take the point of view that the claims of clinicians in this respect are grossly exaggerated. For example, the claim made by some of the early psychoanalysts that a person might recall the shock of birth is hardly credible in terms of our current knowledge.

Curves of Retention

Whatever is learned is retained to a greater or lesser degree depending on numerous factors operating in the learning situation. All teaching is undertaken on the assumption that retention will occur; but many teachers, unfortunately, are more concerned with immediate retention than with retention over longer periods. The practice of classroom recitation is based largely on the assumption that evidence of immediate retention is evidence that learning of a fairly permanent character has taken place. This assumption is not sound. Immediate retention is no evidence that retention over long periods of time will take place.

Retention is the continued capacity to behave in a particular way that has been learned. Retention implies the retention of a response. Forgetting is the gradual or rapid loss of a response in the repertoire of the individual. When a child forgets a poem, it means that he has lost the ability to recall the poem—that is, he has lost the capacity for making the responses involved in the recitation of the poem. The word *forgetting* is used here loosely. Although the pupil has forgotten the poem insofar as recitation is concerned, he has not forgotten everything about the poem. He would probably still recognize the poem as one he had learned previously. Even if he had so far forgotten the poem that he did not recognize it, he might still find it unusually easy to learn.

Forgetting is a normal everyday event, and a constant reminder of man's limitations. There are also certain kinds of forgetting that the clinician tries to produce in individuals in order to help them with their problems. To a great extent, the treatment of mental disorders is an attempt to rid the person of certain unwanted aspects of behavior. These unwanted aspects of behavior may vary from minor twitches of the muscles of the face to deep-seated anxiety responses that torture the soul. That such responses are generally very difficult to eliminate is attested to by the fact that therapy is a long and rather unsatisfactory process. Behavior is not eliminated easily. Sometimes there seems to be no method through which unwanted behavior can be eliminated. Oddly enough, fate seems to have decided that the things we want to retain most, such as intellectual knowledge, is not easily retained, but neurotic behavior of which we would like to rid ourselves remains remarkably persistent.

A typical curve of retention is shown in Figure 19. Although the curve is derived from data from this century of Cain and Willey (1939), the general form of the curve was known to Ebbinghaus and to other psychologists of the last century. The reader must realize that only in general features does the curve remain the same from one batch of

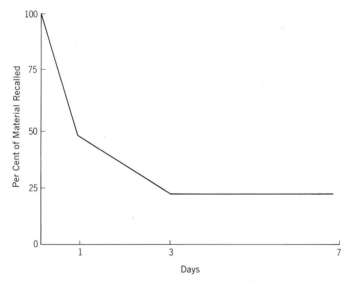

FIGURE 19. Curve of retention for nonsense syllables. (After Cain and Willey, 1939, p. 211. Reproduced by permission of the American Psychological Association.)

data to another, the most notable of these features being the rapid decline in the amount of material retained during the period that immediately follows learning, and then a declining loss as time progresses. Many different conditions determine the extent to which there is an initial rapid loss in what has been learned.

Ammons *et al.* (1958) studied long-term retention of two skills. One skill was referred to as a procedural skill. It involved the manipulation of a set of controls in the correct sequence by following a chart on the wall. The other task involved the control of the performance of a miniature plane by operating a set of controls similar to that found in an aircraft. Figure 20 shows the loss in skill in the procedural task over a period of two years. The two lines on the graph are for the subjects who had five training trials and those who had thirty training trials. The difference in the percentage of the acquired skill lost is markedly less for the group that had the most training. However, there is a sense in which this graph overestimates the loss, for a large part of the losses tend to be rapidly regained once practice trials are given. The greater the amount of previous training and the greater the time interval during which no practice took place, the greater was the amount of retraining required to regain the original skill. Figure 21 shows the retraining curves for the

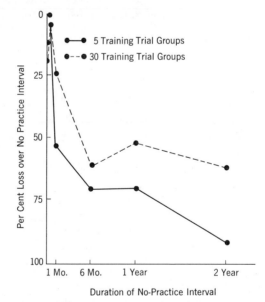

FIGURE 20. Loss of performance on sequential task over a period of no practice up to 2 years. The loss is shown for two groups, one of which had 5 training trials while the other had 30 training trials. (From Ammons *et al.*, 1958, p. 322. Reproduced by permission of the American Psychological Association.)

airplane-control task for those who had originally been given one hour of practice on the task.

Reminiscence

The first discussion of reminiscence comes from a paper by Ballard (1913) which became famous. Ballard worked for the London County Council school system and visited classrooms as an inspector for the system. On one such occasion he observed the children in a class memorizing a poem he had assigned to them. At the end of the class period he asked them to write out as much of the poem as they could remember, and he then collected and scored the papers. What the children did not know was that he was to return to the same class on the following day, when he asked the same children to write out again all that they could

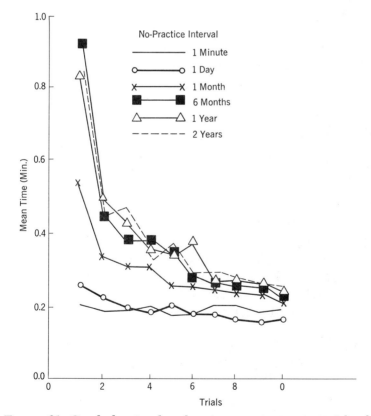

FIGURE 21. Graph showing the relearning curves on a sequential task for groups retrained after various intervals. (After Ammons *et al.*, 1958, p. 321. Reproduced by permission of the American Psychological Association.)

recall of the poem. Much to his surprise, he found that the children remembered more of the poem on the following day than they had immediately after learning. Sometime between the original learning of the poem and the period of recall on the following day some additional learning had occurred. The additional learning that apparently occurred after the end of the learning period was referred to as *reminiscence.* The same pattern of study was repeated with a variety of other materials, which ranged from nonsense syllables to meaningful material, and similar results were achieved. The curve of retention did not show a decline beginning immediately after learning, but rather, it first showed a rise before the typical fall began. For nearly half a century students of education were taught about the reminiscence phenomenon, until an experiment was undertaken that indicated that in all likelihood the phenomenon was nothing more than an artifact of the experimental situation. Perhaps one lesson to be learned from this is that the mere repetition of an experiment is not enough to demonstrate the soundness of the conclusions.

The demonstration that the phenomenon of reminiscence with verbal material is probably an artifact of experimentation and not a genuine phenomenon provides a worthwhile lesson in the problems of experimenting with learning. For this reason we may spend a little more time in discussing the matter than it would otherwise merit. Let us consider first the classical design that has been used in the supposed demonstration of reminiscence. In this design the following steps were taken:

1. A learning period
2. A test of retention
3. A period of unrelated activity
4. A test of retention

Ammons and Irion (1954) saw that there was a basic defect in this design. It is conceivable that the measurement of retention that occurs immediately after the learning period may function as an additional learning period and produce learning that does not show up until the next time retention is measured. Reminiscence may be nothing more than the learning produced by the situation in which learning is measured. What Ammons and Irion did was to test this hypothesis by the following experimental design, which used two groups rather than the one that had been typically used in previous experimentation:

Group A	Group B
1. A learning period	1. A learning period
2. A test of retention	2. A period of unrelated activity
3. A period of unrelated activity	3. A test of retention
4. A test of retention	

The only difference in the treatment of the two groups lies in the omission from Group B of the test of retention immediately after the learning period. The results of this experiment are interesting. What happens is that in Group B the final test of retention shows a rise in comparison with the test of retention given immediately after learning. However, Group B, on the final test of retention, shows a level of performance that is not at all comparable with that of Group A given at a similar period after the end of learning. Group B shows a performance similar to that of Group A immediately after learning. In other words, Group B does not show the reminiscence phenomenon, though it should if the phenomenon is a genuine one. Only Group A shows the reminiscence phenomenon, and only Group A had the advantage of the test of retention immediately after learning and the possibility of benefiting from the practice that this test of retention may have provided. The data strongly suggests that the reminiscence effect with verbal material is due to the practice provided by the test of retention given immediately after learning.

A few would dispute the position taken here and maintain that the reminiscence phenomenon as reported by Ballard is a genuine phenomenon. Ausubel (1963) still supports the latter position, but the studies he cites to back up his point of view hardly seem admissible. These include a study by Stevenson and Langford (1957) that found that a delayed retention group performed better than an immediate performance group on a perceptual task. However, this might be expected, for the children knew that they were to be retested on the following day and probably discussed the task among themselves. A study by Sharpe (1952) is also cited to support the notion that reminiscence genuinely occurs. In the Sharpe study, what is referred to as the reminiscence effect is, in fact, nothing more than an artifact of the way in which the statistical data were manipulated. Thus, one is led to the conclusion that there is no clear-cut effect of the kind described by Ballard; and the phenomena that have been described are not genuine, but products of poor experimentation or careless statistical analysis.

The reminiscence phenomenon and the way in which it is produced reflects some of the difficulties that are encountered in collecting data for plotting a curve of retention. One cannot plot a curve of retention by the simple procedure of measuring from time to time the amount retained; for each time one does this, additional learning opportunities are afforded. What one generally has to do is train a large group to a given point of proficiency, then divide the large group into a number of subgroups which are then tested, each at a separate and distinct interval of time. Thus Subgroup 1 might be tested after one day, Subgroup 2 after two days, and so forth. Each person would be tested only once after the end of the learning period.

Although the Ballard type of reminiscence phenomenon appears to be an artifact of the experimental situation, there is a related phenomenon. Reminiscence over a short period of time, of the order of several minutes, takes place with a task involving muscular coordination. This phenomenon has commonly been demonstrated with what are called *pursuit tasks*. In these tasks, the subject is required to turn or move levers in order to keep a movable sight on a moving target. The target moves and has to be followed by the sight through the appropriate manipulation of the levers or cranks. When practice is given on such a task, the level of skill continues to improve after practice has stopped. This has been shown by many research workers, including Bourne (1956), Ray (1959), and Eysenck (1956).

The interpretation generally given to this short-term type of reminiscence is that during the period of practice an inhibition process develops that has the effect of interfering with the performance of the skill. When the period of practice ends, then the state of inhibition slowly dissipates and the level of skill improves. This concept was originally developed by Hull (1943), and had a significant position in his theory of learning.

Meaningfulness and Retention

The opinion is commonly held that meaningful material is more easily retained than nonsense material. The early students of learning phenomena, such as Ebbinghaus, who conducted his classic experiments in the last century, were impressed with this difference in retainability, which appeared to be dramatized by the results of their experiments. However, the experimental results are not as clear-cut as they appear to be on the surface, for this happens to be a difficult area for experimentation.

Consider, for example, the problem of obtaining meaningful and meaningless material for the conduct of a study of retention. Suppose a poem is to be compared for retainability with a list of nonsense syllables. Immediately one is confronted with the problem that any poem is meaningful, because it has already entered into past learning. A child who is learning the lines

> Listen my children and you shall hear
> Of the midnight ride of Paul Revere

is not learning completely novel material. He is already familiar with the name of Paul Revere and the story associated with him. He has also learned something about the typical order in which words appear. When he encounters the word *you* in the first line, he knows that it is almost certainly followed by a verb. Thus, many of the associations between words that the learning of the poem requires have already been to some extent made. Meaningful material, because it is meaningful, is material that has already entered into some learning. To conclude, then, that meaningful material is more easily retained than meaningless material would be merely to conclude the obvious—that the material already partially learned is the more readily retained.

This does not answer the question of whether meaningful material would be retained less well than meaningless material learned to an equal level. The few studies that come close to the answering of this question do not, as a matter of fact, provide clear-cut results. Katona (1940, 1942) trained subjects to solve problems in two ways. One method involved an understanding of the method involved in the solution, and the other method taught the solution without understanding. He found that the solution learned with meaning was better retained than the one learned by a blind procedure. This fits well with commonly held notions about retention, but when the experiment was repeated by Hilgard *et al.* (1953) a corresponding difference was not found.

Overlearning and Retention

Material may be learned to the point where immediate recall is just possible, or it may be learned beyond this point. If practice occurs beyond the point where immediate and complete recall is first possible, then overlearning is said to have occurred. Typically in schools, learning is organized so that considerable overlearning is scheduled. There is little merit in a child's learning to spell only to the point where he can spell the particular words immediately after practice but is unable to recall the spelling at a later date. Teachers for centuries have been familiar with the fact that the best single way of preventing subsequent forgetting is to provide for overlearning.

Overlearning does not have to take the form of drill or rote learning. For example, once a child has acquired some minimal mastery of the number products used in multiplication, the utilization of these products in the solution of daily problems both within and outside of the classroom will provide extensive overlearning, so that the skill is ultimately retained for a lifetime. Similar overlearning occurs in reading, though many of the illiterates identified at induction stations during the Second World War had once learned to read but had not retained the skill.

Many skills are characteristically learned to the point where they are retained for life through extensive overlearning. Few persons ever forget how to ride a bicycle once they have learned, for there is extensive opportunity for overlearning. Much the same applies to skating; people who have learned to skate may spend years away from the sport and yet return to it with little loss of skill. Secretaries who leave the office for marriage do not forget how to type. Later, if they have to return to an office job, they regain their old skill in a matter of hours. Overlearning is generally a sound investment of the pupil's time, particularly if it is coupled with a meaningful activity, as when the pupil overlearns his multiplication tables by solving mathematical problems of consequence to him.

One cannot always count on unplanned opportunity to provide the needed overlearning. An interesting example of this is found in the teaching of music, where the learner must acquire technique before he can perform a composition adequately. Simple pieces of music have been found to be of limited value in developing technique, because they do not provide opportunity to practice particular skills that must be mastered. For this reason the great teachers of music have developed exercises, commonly known as études, which provide such practice. In learning the violin, the student will work on études whatever the level of his development. In the earlier stages he may work on études that provide him with extensive practice in such matters as rhythm, scales, and so forth. Later he will work on études by Paganini, which provide some of the most difficult aspects of violin performance. In violin playing there is an exercise to provide practice for whatever aspect of technique the person may be deficient in. Such exercises are the products of great teachers who had an intuitive understanding of the problems of learning we are now considering. In other areas of learning there has been much less done to provide such specialized opportunities to learn specific aspects of the skill involved. Although many teachers have worked on this problem, few of them leave behind a record of their experience or of the techniques of learning they have used. Musicians, in contrast, have handed down their systematic teaching skills.

The External and Internal Storage of Information

There has long been a controversy among educators concerning the extent to which the pupil should be expected to store information internally and how far he should become dependent on the use of reference works, such as encyclopedias, for the storage of information. This is a complicated problem. In order to take sides on the issue one would have to know the storage capacity of the human and also something about the time it takes to store particular bodies of information. If the human is a limited-capacity storage system, then it is clear that he must learn to use reference sources, where information is stored external to himself, for he would have no other choice. On the other hand, if his storage capacity is very large, then there are advantages in storing internally as much information as possible—unless disproportionally large amounts of time are needed to acquire and store the information.

The practices that have evolved in our society place emphasis on systems of storing knowledge external to the individual. Thus a machinist, operating a lathe, must have available a handbook that stores all the information he needs for setting up the tool. He consults the handbook to determine the cutting speed he should use on a particular piece of metal. He does not have to store within his brain the equivalent of several pages of detailed specifications for cutting speeds; all he has to store is the knowledge that the information can be found in the handbook. If he were to commit the material to memory, he would have to spend many hours of study distributed over several weeks. Even after devoting this much effort to the task, he would still not be able to reproduce the data from memory with the same accuracy with which he could find it in the handbook.

The occupation of the machinist is not unique in this respect. Workers in almost every occupation use extensive bodies of information stored externally. Most professional people have at hand a library of important sources of information they can consult. Even a source of twenty or thirty books can contain large quantities of information. Salesman do not have to remember the names of all of their customers; they have a file containing such information with the data placed in some order, such as alphabetical order, from which information can be readily retrieved. Modern civilization is highly dependent on the existence of information storage systems that vastly increase the human's capability of using available knowledge.

Although man has long used storage systems external to himself, in the form of scrolls and tablets and, later, books, no entirely satisfactory system has been devised for enabling him to obtain access to the information thus stored. The index to a book, the table of contents, the library catalog, and related devices are all designed to assist the individual to gain access to stored knowledge; but none of these are completely satisfactory, as any user knows. Extensive research is now being undertaken on this problem, mainly by people involved in library science.

The assumption generally made is that whatever is learned in elementary school should be stored internally so that the performance of the skills involved can take place without referring to a book or other source of information. At the secondary-school level, there are clear advantages in being able to add and multiply without having to consult a table. The same can be said for the learning of a foreign language. Unless a person can store internally the vocabulary and general rules of syntax of a foreign language, it is of little practical use to him. On the other hand, the fine details of geography might as well remain stored in a book, though the pupil should undoubtedly retain a broad general knowledge of the subject. Perhaps it is important to know that Paris is in France, but it is much less important to know exactly where in that country the city is located or on what river it is to be found. However, the pupil should know just where to find these details.

Short-Term and Long-Term Storage of Information

Psychologists have been inclined to take the view that there are two fairly distinct forms of storage of information. That information can be stored and retained for a long period is obvious from personal experience, but less obvious is the fact that some information is stored for only a short time and is then, as it were, discarded. One may look up an address and retain it long enough to write it down on the face of an envelope, but a minute later one may not be able to remember the address at all. If the address has to be remembered for as long as a minute, he may repeat it to himself a number of times during the minute and thus extend the period of retention. The remembering of an address for a period just long enough to permit writing it down is an example of short-term storage.

Hull (1943) was one of the first psychologists to note the existence of a short-term storage mechanism. He took the position that any stimulus produced an internal state referred to as the *stimulus* trace, which persisted for a short time. In his original version of the theory (1943), the stimulus trace might last as long as 30 seconds; but in the later versions (1952), the duration of the trace was cut to a matter of 2 to 3 seconds. The trace involved a continuation of those neural activities that were aroused by the original stimulus. A further development of the concept of a short-term storage system has been developed by Broadbent (1958), who has taken the position that the information thus stored fades within a period of 2 to 3 seconds. From the Broadbent point of view, one function served by the short-term storage is the temporary holding of information for processing by the higher centers during a period when the higher centers are processing other information. Thus, a businessman may finish listening to a statement of a client and hold in temporary storage the information given him by his secretary that his long-distance call is ready. Having listened to the end of his client's statement, he then turns to the matter of the long-distance call. However, note that the information concerning the long-distance call does not have to be remembered permanently; short-term retention of the information is sufficient.

Although the presentation here has implied that there is a clear-cut distinction between short-term and long-term storage, there is still controversy about whether there are two distinct mechanisms or only one.

What Is Retained

What is retained? This is an important question, but it cannot be fully answered at this time. One interpretation is that a particular stimulus produces activity in some nerve cells and not in others. When the stimulus is recalled, presumably a process takes place that leads to the activity of these nerve cells in which the stimulus originally produced activity. An internal image of a stimulus would be one consequence of the recurrence of activity in the nerve cells that had originally responded to the presence of the stimulus. In this case, memory involves the storage of information necessary for generating activity in particular groups of cells. The fact that one can conjure up an image of an object seen yesterday supports this position. But this concept of storage does not take into account many important facts related to retention. One fact it neglects is that experiences related to action are much more readily retained than those that are not action-related. Consider, for example, the task of remembering the features of a map of certain terrain. To stare at it and hope that the information will sink in, as many children are likely to do, is to provide a poor situation for the acquisition and retention of information about it. Somewhat better, in terms of retention, is the approach in which the person studying the map tries to find answers to some of the questions that might be asked about it. Such an approach is vastly superior to that of looking and hoping that some of the information will rub off. A still more effective way of learning the features of a map would be to use it to guide one in going from one place to another. Let us assume that, in each of these three cases, the time spent in perusing the actual map is the same. Just looking at the map alone would result in the storage of little information. The procedure that involved the greatest amount of action and decision-making in relation to the map would produce the most effective retention.

The important relation that exists between action and retention suggests that one can view much of the storage process as the storage of action tendencies. What a person is likely to remember about a particular building he frequently visits is how to find his way about in it; his stored action patterns enable him to do this. Even though he had visited the building frequently, he probably could recall little about such details as architectural features, color of walls, or the other items; but he could tell someone else just how to find a certain room he had visited.

Although the example given has involved action patterns requiring gross bodily movement, presumably actions related to problem solving could also be stored as action tendencies that would be evoked by particular classes of problems. The action systems thus evoked will not always be appropriate, but they will represent the influence of past problem solving on present problem solving. Thus, a teacher who has learned to handle disciplinary problems by administering punishment behaves as if she had stored this response tendency, which any disciplinary problem immediately releases.

Although both of the mechanisms considered here may have to be considered in a theory of memory, writers of the past have given particular attention to the one that emphasizes the storage of sensory data. This is a complex enough problem without considering the relationship of retention to action. The storage of sensory data must clearly involve some kind of consolidation of all previous experiences. Most of us have seen hundreds of oak trees in a lifetime; but our memory of an oak tree is not a memory of each one of these oaks, but rather it is a consolidation of all the experience we have had with oak trees. Henry Head (1920), an English neurologist, was the first to point out that memories of specific instances are combined into a single memory trace, which he referred to as a *schema*. This, in turn, led to a series of studies on how the schema, or trace, changed with the passage of time. Bartlett (1932) later wrote extensively on Head's concept of schema, and brought the concept to the attention of psychologists. The concept of a schema is something like this: If a person is asked to describe, say, a house built in a modernistic style, he is likely to describe the general characteristics of a modern house without reference to any particular house. His conception of a modern house—that is to say, the retained schema—represents a consolidation of a long series of encounters with modern houses. In reproducing this stored information, he is likely to relate the attributes that are characteristic of this style of house that are the essential items of information represented by the schema.

As far back as 1922, Wulf (tr., 1937) suggested that whatever is retained undergoes slow modification as time passes; and he believed he had experimental evidence to show that memory traces undergo such modification. Wulf claimed, for example, that in successive attempts to reproduce drawings resembling common objects, the subject made drawings that resembled more and more the real object.

The basic defect in the early experiments lay in the fact that each time a subject attempted to recall and reproduce a drawing to which he had been exposed, the reproduction process itself may have produced learning. Hence, a subject who is exposed to a diagram and is then asked to reproduce it on successive occasions may be involved in a learning process that interferes with the retention process itself and produces modifications in the memory trace. Later experiments have eliminated this possibility by dividing the subjects into groups. One group reproduces the diagram after a given interval of time, and other groups reproduce it at different intervals. In a study along these lines by Hanawalt (1937), no progressive changes in the memory trace could be found, which suggests that the changes found earlier were a function of the procedure involving successive reproduction. A still later study of the same problem by Hebb and Foord (1945) involved the use of a recognition technique for measuring retention, and here again the conclusion was that no progressive changes could be found in the memory trace.

The conclusion seems to be that so long as successive reproduction is not used, there will be no progressive changes in the memory trace other than those that characterize forgetting processes. On the other hand, in daily life repeated reproductions of a memory trace are the rule, and under such conditions one may well expect to find progressive changes produced by the learning effects involved in recall. These phenomena clearly show the great complexity of the process of retention, and indicate that it is much more complicated than a mental filing system from which the information can later be withdrawn with various degrees of completeness.

Some Problems of Information Storage in Memory

In an address to the American Educational Research Association in 1966, Donald Broadbent presented a psychological theory of information storage in human memory, using the analogy of a library storage system. In the latter system, books and other sources of information are received by a library, where they are first catalogued and then placed in storage in a suitable location on the shelves. Broadbent proposes that the human, who receives information through his senses, tags the incoming information as belonging in a certain category before assigning it to storage, much as the librarian catalogues a book. In this discussion, he talked of items of information being stored in a particular location in memory. (He does not mean that items are actually stored in some *physical* location; the term *location* is derived by analogy from the way in which information is stored in libraries in certain physical locations.) Experiments show that some items stored in memory can be readily retrieved together, and others cannot. Those that can be readily retrieved together are described as having been stored in the same location. Many techniques can be adopted to find out how information is categorized for storage in memory. One way is to study the errors made on recall. Why this provides a useful technique can be seen readily by looking at a simple analogy. Consider, for example, the task of pulling folders containing information from a file of such folders. If an error in pulling a folder is made, a folder near the one that should have been pulled is most likely to be pulled rather than one that is stored in a more remote place.

Through the use of such a technique, Broadbent has shown that, in the case of short-term storage, acoustical properties of words often determine how material is stored. He points out that if a person is presented with the letters *B, C,* and *D,* which he must immediately recall, he is likely to produce such errors as *V, G,* and *P.* The errors are like-sounding letters rather than letters closely related in alphabetical sequence. The suggestion is that the information pertaining to the letters of the alphabet is filed in terms of the sound of the letters. It is also clear that the information is also filed in other ways, for we have no difficulty in recalling the alphabet in terms of the usual ordering of the letters. In the case of long-term memory, the acoustical properties of words and symbols become much less important, for information appears to be categorized for storage much more in terms of conventional aspects of meaning. The concept of *tree* is much more likely to be associated in memory with the concept of *garden* than with the concept of *tea* to which it is acoustically similar. This leads to another important point that Broadbent makes, which is that much information stored in memory appears to have a multiple classification. Just as a book on Roman buildings stored in a library may be classified under a number of different categories such as, *architecture, history,* and *Rome,* so too may an input of information into human memory be categorized in a number of different ways.

In this way, ideas are cross-referenced much as an entry in the card catalog of a library is cross-referenced. To some extent the cross-referencing is represented by the associations one develops between words. Thus, when a person is asked to give all the words he associates with the word *light,* he is likely to come up with a series such as *electricity, read, sun, bulb, switch, bright.* These words, in a sense, represent the cross-referencing in the storage system of the word *light* with a host of other words.

Some Factors Related to Retention and Recall

Relationship of Recall to Cues Present During Learning

The extent to which recall can occur depends to some extent on the degree to which cues that can arouse the relevant responses are present. Many cues are provided in recognition tasks, but fewer cues are provided when the process involves recall. Furthermore, in some recall situations, adequate cues are provided; but in others, the cues may be so inadequate that incorrect responses are evoked. The poorly worded essay question may evoke an inappropriate response on the part of the examinee, who claims that he was misled by the question; and the well-worded question may evoke the appropriate response in every student who has profited from study. A related question is whether irrelevant cues present during learning should be present in the recall situation if recall is to be facilitated. If the student learns while the radio is tuned to his favorite music, does the absence of the sound of such music during the examination limit the student's recall of the material he has learned in its presence?

One of the few technical discussions of this problem is provided by Bugelski (1956). He points out that most studies of retention have attempted to keep the conditions of learning and the conditions of recall approximately the same. However, he points out that any serious change in these conditions is generally assumed to interfere with recall, and cites the common example of the child who in the privacy of his room learns a poem for recitation and then is quite unable to recall it when on the stage in front of an audience. Bugelski also points out that the one study that has some bearing in this kind of situation was designed to investigate a problem in retroactive inhibition. The study was conducted by Bilodeau and Schlosberg (1951). The task to be learned involved the memorization of pairs of adjectives. A part of the data of this research permits the comparison of material learned and recalled in one situation with material learned and recalled in another situation. The two situations involved differences in posture (standing versus sitting), differences in the room, and differences in the methods of presentation. The investigation showed that when such variations were introduced into the recall situation, there was much more serious interference with the recall process than when the conditions remained the same.

The Effect of Earlier and Later Learning on Retention

When retention is reduced because of some earlier learning of the individual that somehow interferes with the retention process, the phenomenon is designated as *proactive inhibition*. If the interference is produced by some subsequent learning, the phenomenon is known as *retroactive inhibition*. These phenomena are to some extent familiar to most school children. Their importance to retention was first emphasized by Melton over twenty-five years ago in a paper with Irwin (1940), and has been explored further in a series of papers by one of Melton's students, B. J. Underwood.

These phenomena can be considered to be, to a great extent, the same as those of negative transfer, and have already been discussed in the chapter on transfer. When one learning activity interferes at some other time with another learning activity, one may say that there has been a negative transfer from the one learning activity to the other. Our discussion here of the phenomena is primarily in relation to retention rather than to transfer effects.

The phenomena of proactive and retroactive inhibition raise questions concerning certain aspects of the curriculum. One might expect that a student who is studying two foreign languages would have greater difficulty in acquiring these foreign languages than if he had the opportunity of studying them separately. The retention of the one would be obstructed by the learning of the other, and the obstruction would be greatest when the languages were similar. Greater interference might be expected with French and Spanish learned simultaneously than with, say, French and German. A curriculum should be planned for a particular child so that these sources of inefficiency in the retention process are minimized.

Learning and Retention as a Function of the Time Schedule

Almost every educational program is planned so that it fits some kind of time schedule that is believed to be efficient for the purpose at hand. Often, of course, such time schedules have to fit into a system prescribed by the administration of an educational institution, as when particular courses at a university are planned to fit the quarter system. Most educators also acknowledge the fact that some schedules are more efficient than others for learning particular aspects of subject matter. Difficult mathematics courses are always spread out over a considerable time, never compressed into short periods of one or two weeks as are some language courses given by universities during the summer. As the saying goes, mathematics courses require a certain amount of time for the learning to be absorbed. Let us consider some of the problems involved in this matter of scheduling learning periods.

When learning is scheduled on a concentrated basis with a single long period of practice that is extended until the material to be learned has been learned, it is said that the practice is *massed*. When learning takes place in a number of learning periods separated either by other activities or by periods of rest, the practice is said to be *distributed* or *spaced*. The relative merits of spaced versus unspaced practice was one of the earliest problems studied by psychologists interested in the systematic investigation of problems of learning. Ebbinghaus (1885), who is commonly regarded as the father of modern learning psychology, published a classic work describing a series of experiments that he had conducted in the field of learning, and laying the foundation for the future experimental development of the scientific study of learning. In particular, he was the first to realize that the study of learning could not easily be undertaken through the learning of meaningful materials, because some people would come to these materials with more previous experience than would others. In order to eliminate this source of difficulty, Ebbinghaus asked his subjects to learn nonsense syllables, such as "gub," "zac," "ref," "kes," and so forth. These nonsense syllables have the advantage of being fairly unfamiliar, and hence all learners start at roughly the same point in their learning. But some initial differences may exist in familiarity with these materials, since at least some of them will be recognized as parts of words familiar to some of the subjects; and the person who is familiar with the greatest number of words is most likely to have the most familiarity with these syllables.

With such materials, Ebbinghaus was able to conduct experiments with massed and distributed practice. In the case of massed practice, he could provide his subjects with a list of twenty or more nonsense syllables to be learned at a single sitting. He could also give the same list to others who learned them with distributed-practice periods, which were separated by periods of rest or periods of other activity. When this is done, it is possible to determine the number of minutes of practice needed to master the list by the various methods involved. His conclusion, which has been well substantiated by other studies, is that distributed practice has a considerable advantage over massed practice—that is, it takes less time to learn material if learning is distributed over several spaced sessions than if all the work is done at a single session. At one time the advantage of distributed practice was ascribed to the effect of reminiscence, but this explanation does not hold today. A more likely explanation is that, with massed practice, inhibition builds up that interferes with learning. Spaced learning provides opportunity for the inhibition to dissipate. What is commonly referred to as *mental fatigue* is an inhibitory process similar to the one considered here.

It would be useful if we could now state how long a learning period should be, and how far apart the periods of practice should be spaced. But, although there have been many studies undertaken of the relative efficiency of learning when the intervals between trials are varied, there is no consistency in the results they have produced. The results of such studies are conflicting because it probably makes a difference what kind of task is to be learned. For example, in an early study by Warden (1923), subjects were required to learn to find a path through a maze. Different groups were given practice at intervals of six hours, twelve hours, and one-, three-, and five-day intervals. In this study the twelve-hour interval produced the most efficient learning. In another study by Lorge (1930), rather different results were obtained. Lorge used three tasks, as follows:

1. Mirror drawing. In this task the subject was required to make a line around a given pattern, being guided by what he could see in a mirror.

2. Mirror reading. The subject must read printed material appearing in a mirror.

3. Code substitution. The subject is required to substitute letters in printed material with new letters, according to a code given him.

In the Lorge study, the tasks were learned under three conditions. One of these was massed practice; the second was distributed practice, with one-minute intervals between trials; the third was distributed practice, with twenty-four-hour intervals between trials. With every task, the subjects performed more efficiently when practice was distributed than when it was massed. Surprisingly small differences were found between the distributed practice with one-minute rest intervals and twenty-four-hour intervals.

What are the practical implications of the work on distributed versus massed practice? The most obvious one has already been put into effect— namely, that the work in school should be divided into rather short sessions covering particular areas of content. The fact that distributed practice is generally (but not always) more efficient than massed practice may raise some problems about the efficiency of a core curriculum as it is commonly run. The breaking down of subject-matter lines and the assignment of rather long blocks of time to combinations of subjects such as English and social studies, which are not then taught as separate subjects, may sometimes tend to make for massed practice, but this does not have to be so. The forced division of time into periods has certain advantages in this respect. It does require the teachers to change regularly the learning activities involved.

The place in which there is least application of the principle of distributed practice is probably when the pupil studies in his own home. Such study tends to represent massed learning, and is consequently much less efficient than it should be. The high-school pupil who has to learn a speech from Julius Caesar is likely to sit down and attempt to learn it at a single session; and this practice is indirectly encouraged by teachers who give occasional large assignments of this kind and ask that they be completed in too short a time (or too long a time, which results in procrastination, with similar effects). In such an assignment the pupil should probably start by reading through the speech to be learned a few times, concentrating on the meaning and looking up any words that he does not understand. He should then plan several short learning sessions distributed over several days. There are also some advantages in planning these sessions for just before going to bed, so that the learning period is not followed by any activity that could interfere with the learning of the speech.

The educational psychologist can never be content just to know that one method of learning requires a shorter total time in the capacity to repeat the material than does some other method. Quite as important as the matter of speed of learning is the extent to which material is retained. What would be the use of a speedy method of learning if it were found that retention was poor? Our immediate question is whether learning by distributed practice produces as satisfactory retention as does learning by massed practice. This is a question that numerous studies have been designed to answer with a great range of different materials.

Cain and Willey (1939), who compared retention curves of massed and distributed practice for meaningless material, found that after seven days those who had had distributed practice retained almost three times as much material as those who had had massed practice. Much the same results hold for meaningful material, although the results are not always quite so dramatic. The results hold for a variety of materials. In one relatively unique study by T. W. Cook (1936), the finding was that the solutions to puzzles were retained better over a considerable period when the problems had been solved by distributed-practice sessions than by massed-practice sessions. The nature of the materials learned is also a factor in determining what is retained.

Theories of Forgetting

Learning theories have characteristically maintained that what is learned is probably learned permanently, unless some specific activity is undertaken that in some way disposes of the response that has been learned. This viewpoint is in sharp contrast with that of the layman who generally takes the position that once the active process of learning has ceased, forgetting rapidly sets in, until, after a time, whatever has been learned ceases to exist as a habit or a skill. The learning theorist accounts for most forgetting by some process other than that of fading. He has to account for forgetting, because forgetting is an incontrovertible fact. Let us consider at this point some of the processes that may account for forgetting, and, at the same time, bring together some of the evidence that supports the existence of the particular process.

Forgetting as a fading process. The theory of forgetting that is most widely held by the public at large is the theory that whatever is learned slowly fades, much as the pattern on a pair of draperies fades from prolonged exposure to the sun. This theory is derived from the common experience that, as time goes by, a memory becomes less and less accessible and the details become more and more obscure. One piece of evidence that is quite embarrassing to this theory is that memories that appear to have completely faded may sometimes return with remarkable vividness under special conditions such as hypnosis or clinical treatment. So striking is this phenomenon to the clinician that many have suggested the possibility that whatever is learned is never lost but merely becomes unavailable under most circumstances. This is an extreme point of view and represents a generalization that goes way beyond the facts. Few psychologists today, if any, would go along with such an extreme position. Most would take the view that a theory of forgetting that is just a theory of fading through disuse is largely unacceptable. If this kind of a process occurs at all, then it is a minor one. Forgetting occurs mainly for reasons other than fading.

Forgetting as a repression process. The theory of forgetting as a repression process is a clinical view of forgetting based on the observation that some anxiety-producing experiences may be forgotten by a patient and yet still continue to affect his behavior. Also, under clinical treatment the individual may sometimes regain the memory he has lost. There can be no doubt that repression is a genuine phenomenon, but most of the cases reported manifest dramatic losses of experiences. In the most dramatic cases the loss of the ability to recall covers a wide range of experience, and, in such instances, the phenomenon is referred to as amnesia. Few, if any, modern psychologists would be willing to take the position that all forgetting is repression; but it probably does represent one of the mechanisms involved in forgetting, at least in some cases. It may account for common slips of memory, as when one cannot recall the name of a dentist with whom one has had a painful experience, or when one forgets to keep any appointment that may be painful in character. It does not account very well for the kind of forgetting that occurs as time separates the learner from his school days—the kind of forgetting that is commonly described as a fading process (although it is not).

Although clinical psychologists are convinced that repression is an important factor in at least some aspects of the retention process, experimental evidence of this phenomenon has not been obtained. There are serious difficulties involved in the design of an experiment that might demonstrate repression. Intensely unpleasant experiences may appear to be repressed because they did not result in effective learning in the first place. It is not sufficient to design an experiment in which, say, two lists of words are learned but the one list is learned while the subject is given intermittent electric shocks. The one procedure may result in less efficient learning than the other, which shows up in long-term retention. Failure of the shocked group to recall the words associated with shock would not demonstrate the operation of repression. It could mean that the unpleasant effects of shock reduce the efficiency of the original learning process.

In a study by Krugman (1958), a group of psychiatric patients and a group of normals were given a learning task, an interpolated activity, and then a task to measure retention. The interpolated task involved either failure or success, or was neutral with respect to such matters. The failure experience generally had a significant depressing effect on retention, which suggests that the anxiety involved may have resulted in some degree of repression of the learnings with which it had been associated. The psychotic patients showed a greater effect of the failure experience on retention than did the normal group.

Forgetting as an interference process. There is a considerable amount of evidence that forgetting can be considered to some degree a process in which one learning interferes with another. The processes involved are named *proactive* and *retroactive* inhibition. Scheduling one learning session, followed closely by a second, different learning session, can be shown to interfere with the retention of what was learned at the first session. This is evidence that interference phenomena exist and can be introduced so as to reduce retention. We also know that a period of inactivity or a period of sleep is most beneficial to the retention process. Indeed, more can be done to improve retention by controlling subsequent activities than by almost any other process. This already has been pointed out.

Forgetting and extinction. Extinction is *not* a forgetting process as the term *forgetting* is used here. Extinction does not so much eradicate a response as it does inhibit a response. However, extinction may lead to forgetting. If the learner does not practice a response, then forgetting is likely to occur.

Summary

1. The progress of learning is commonly represented by a graph known as a learning curve. Such a curve represents only one aspect of learning. Each one of a number of separate curves may represent several distinct aspects of the learning involved in the acquisition of a complex skill.

2. Learning curves may have many different shapes, depending on the conditions of learning and the degree to which the skill or component skills have been previously mastered. Although the typical form of learning curve that has been presented in textbooks of educational psychology for the last fifty years shows a rapid early rise followed by a period of less rapid learning, such a curve is not necessarily found. Many learning

curves are found that are shaped approximately like an S. Such curves are found in cases in which the skill is learned right from the beginning. They are found in both classical conditioning and in instrumental learning. Typical school learning may be considered to represent the upper portion of such a curve.

3. Some curves representing learning show a flattened-out portion followed by a rise. Such a flattened-out portion is referred to as a *plateau.* The conditions under which such plateaus occur are obscure, and there is even some doubt whether they are genuine phenomena. There is the possibility that they may be produced by some uncontrolled factor in the learning situation, and would not occur if such a factor were controlled. If plateaus are genuine phenomena, many explanations may be offered for their existence.

4. Families of curves produced in studies of learning sets may show progressive changes in the shape of the learning curve as the learner becomes more sophisticated. In the illustration given, the learning curves showed a progressive change from a S-shaped curve to the typical learning curves that have long been given in textbooks.

5. The typical flattening-out of the learning curve represents a crude limit of learning. This is not the absolute limit of learning but the limit under the particular conditions operating. If conditions are changed, the learner may achieve higher levels of skill.

6. Attempts have been made to derive theoretical learning curves from assumptions about the nature of learning. This represents a new avenue to the study of the learning process, one that offers considerable promise.

7. The degree to which acquired skills are retained can be studied by many different techniques. Some are much more sensitive than others for indicating that some skill has been retained.

8. Methods for measuring retention differ in the extent to which they provide cues that can elicit the skill originally learned. The recall method provides the fewest cues; the recognition method provides a greater number. The most sensitive of all methods is the relearning, or saving, method, which may measure retention even when the recognition method fails to do so. The extinction method has been widely used. This latter method is used in typical experiments involving both classical and instrumental conditioning, particularly when simple skills are involved.

9. The curve representing retention generally shows a sharp decline after training ceases. This is followed by a much less marked decline as additional time passes by. The development of any theory of forgetting is handicapped by the lack of knowledge concerning the mechanism involved in the retention process.

10. The phenomenon of reminiscence has long been investigated and

discussed in educational literature. The research at the time of writing indicates that reminiscence occurs over short periods in the case of motor skills, but that it is not a genuine phenomenon in the case of verbal learning. In the latter case, what was considered to be the phenomenon of reminiscence is almost certainly an artifact resulting from the design of the experiments.

11. Overlearning is one of the best ways of ensuring that learning will continue to have a marked and permanent effect.

12. Information may be stored either internally or externally. Beyond the elementary school, teaching devices should provide external storage sources that the student should learn to use.

13. Some evidence suggests that there are two storage systems, one a short-term system and the other for relatively permanent storage. The value of a short-term storage system would be that it would permit the storage of much information needed for brief periods of time without placing demands on the more permanent storage system.

14. Remembering can be studied in relation to the retention of traces of the inputs or in terms of the retention of the action systems that are learned in relation to the inputs. Although effective retention appears to be highly related to the extent to which response learning is involved, studies of retention have typically investigated the perceptual aspects of what is retained.

15. Although some of the early research workers believed that they had found evidence that memory traces underwent systematic changes with the passage of time, more careful experimentation indicates that this is not so. However, the process of recall may result in changes in the memory trace.

16. The learning of one skill shows more or less interaction with the retention of other skills that have been learned. This interference process is known as either retroactive or proactive inhibition.

17. The extent to which learning should be distributed or massed is not a question that can be definitely and finally answered by research. Although the weight of the evidence is in favor of distributed practice, this advantage does not occur under all conditions.

18. A number of theories of forgetting have been advanced. The oldest is that forgetting is a matter of fading, but there is little evidence to support such a theory. Repression has also been advanced by clinicians as a major mechanism involved in retention, but there is little experimental evidence to support the concept that repression is involved in forgetting. Theories of forgetting that are based on the concept that interference is produced by other learning have much experimental evidence to support them.

11

Problem Solving and Decision Making

THE TERM *Problem solving* is a generic term that includes within its scope a great many different forms of complex behavior. Problem-solving behavior occurs in the presence of a task, a goal to be achieved in relation to the task, and a problem solver who is not equipped with the appropriate response required for solving the task. The solution to the problem is learned through the occurrence of a complex mediating process sometimes referred to as thinking.

Problem solving is considered to be a form of learning because a successful attempt to solve a problem results in a fairly permanent modification of behavior. Problem solving may be undertaken at the same time as instruction is given, or it may take place outside of an instructional setting. In either case, one may expect learning. Gagné (1964) has suggested that all learning phenomena may be arranged from the most simple to the most complex. At one end of this scale he places classical conditioning, and at the other end, problem solving. In between these extremes he places simple verbal learning, concept learning, and other learning phenomena.

Situations in Which Problem Solving Has Been Studied

Research on problem solving is still at the stage in which scientists are attempting to find suitable techniques. To a great extent this is a matter of finding problems that can be administered to subjects and that will yield research results of significance for the development of a theory of problem solving. At this stage of knowledge, the selection of problems cannot be based on the proven superiority for research purposes of one class of problems over another. The problems that have been chosen have been considerably varied, and a brief review of some that have been used will indicate the range of research in this area. Since problem solving is an activity commonly undertaken and frequently observed in daily life, it is hardly surprising that much of the early research in the area has been closely tied to practical problems.

Problem solving at its simplest level has generally been referred to as decision making or choice behavior, though some psychologists would prefer to exclude these behaviors from the category. The earliest research in this area was undertaken by economists who became concerned with decision making on the part of consumers. Economists have long studied such questions as when does a consumer decide to spend three thousand dollars on a car and when does the same consumer decide to keep the money in the bank? Economists have generally assumed that the consumer, in making his choice, is fully aware of the consequence of each decision he has to make—that is to say, he knows what he will gain by having the car and what he will gain by keeping the money in the bank. Classical economic theory took the position that the result of the consumer's choice was to give him as much pleasure as possible. An excellent review of these classical economic approaches to decision making and choice has been prepared by Edwards (1954), whose article also provides an introduction to some of the more modern approaches to the same problem. In the hands of psychologists, similar problems have led to extensive research. In the psychological laboratory, studies have been made of decision making in economic situations. For example, studies have been made of situations in which the person has to decide between making a choice involving a definite gain of one dollar and a choice involving only a ten per cent chance of gaining ten dollars. In choices of this kind, subjects seem to prefer one set of probabilities to another. Generally, subjects prefer low probabilities of losing large amounts of money to high probabilities of losing small amounts of money. There are also presumably large individual differences in the risks that will be taken.

A number of different positions can be taken concerning what is maximized by the choice in such situations. Some have argued that choices are made to maximize expected gain, others that the choices minimize regret; but what actually happens is obscure.

The simple decision-making situation can be elaborated so that two persons are involved and the decisions of the one influence the decisions of the other. Such problem situations are referred to as games and are illustrated by the familiar tic-tack-toe. When the loss of one player is equal to the gain of the other, the game is referred to as a zero-sum game. Extensive mathematical theory has been developed in this area as well as in the more general area of decision and choice. Despite its mathematical sophistication there is controversy concerning the contribution this research has made to the development of psychology as a science.

During the last twenty years, research on problem solving has also been focused on the task of the maintenance man faced with the problem of diagnosing the cause of a malfunction in a piece of complex equipment. Efficient methods of problem solving become particularly crucial where electronic devices are involved and in which there may be thousands of components, each one of which may be a potential source of trouble. The testing of each component is impractical and would take too long. Methods have had to be found for training trouble shooters that will permit them to narrow down the source of a malfunction through the efficient collection of information.

Those who have considered this problem have pointed out that the most efficient procedure would be one that eliminated at each step half the components as potential sources of trouble. Thus, a radio technician examining a receiver can apply a single test that will tell him whether the trouble is in the high-frequency or the low-frequency end of the receiver. If he finds that it is in the low-frequency end, then he can apply a second test that will determine whether the trouble is in the first stage or the second stage. Thus, by applying a few tests he can narrow it down to the component that has to be changed or adjusted. This procedure is derived not so much from psychology as from information theory that has contributed substantially to our understanding of how problems can be most efficiently solved.

One can devise the most effective routine for the solution of problems, but this is no guarantee that the problem solver will follow the prescribed procedure. Training in the problem-solving aspects of trouble shooting is to some extent a matter of training the trouble shooter so that he will not only know the most efficient procedures to follow but will actually follow them. It is also a matter of attempting to ensure that he will continue to use the same efficient procedures over long periods of time. Trouble shooters readily fall into sloppy ways. It is always a temptation for a trouble shooter to fall back on hunches that this component or that is the source of the difficulty. Well-trained trouble shooters tend to fall back upon these inefficient methods of problem solving.

One may well ask why the trouble shooter gives up effective methods in favor of a method of hunches and guesses. The reason seems to be that a few of these hunches work out and are successful. Such successes reinforce the guessing procedure and happen sufficiently often to establish it as the habitual approach. A lucky hunch provides rewards more rapidly than does a systematic approach.

Some research workers have selected problems much more remote from the practical affairs of men. The German school of psychologists that included Wertheimer, Koffka, Kohler, and Duncker, tended to study problems involving visual perception. From such studies they optimistically hoped that principles true of all problem-solving behavior could be found.

Studies of problem solving have already been considered in the section on concept learning. A person attempting to discover the defining attributes of a concept is faced with a problem to solve. The advantage of studying problem solving within this context is that concept learning is a well-defined phenomenon and much is already known about it. The study of concept learning also has appeal to those concerned with educational problems in that the phenomenon is closely tied to school learning. In Geneva, Piaget and his associates have devised sets of problems that can be administered for probing the thinking processes of children of all ages. So far, no standard sets of problems have emerged that appear to be of indispensable value for investigating problem solving though some have been widely used over a period of twenty or more years.

The Classification of Problems

A major difficulty encountered in bringing order into the field of problem-solving research stems from the fact that there is not, as yet, any satisfactory classification of problems. A satisfactory classification of problems would have to be such that knowledge available about, say, class X problems would be applicable to all members of that class. At present, research undertaken using a particular problem is not necessarily applicable to other problem-solving situations. The needed classification system has to be developed on the basis of extensive knowledge, and perhaps sufficient knowledge is not available at this time.

One broad classification of problems does receive support from a number of different directions. This classification separates problems into those that have a fixed solution and those that are open ended—that is, those for which many different solutions are possible. The problem of finding the correct tube to replace in a malfunctioning television receiver is a fixed-solution type of problem. On the other hand, the problem of finding a material for surfacing roads that is better than those available can have many solutions. This classification of problems has been proposed independently by Marx (1958) and by Bartlett (1959). It is similar to one of the classifications of problems proposed by Guilford (1956) on the basis of research on tests. Guilford refers to the fixed-solution problems as involving *convergent* thinking, in that the thinking processes involved have to converge on the one and only correct solution. In contrast, problems that do not have unique solutions are said to involve *divergent* thinking, in that the thought processes involved must move out into unexplored territory.

Guilford's classification is not just speculative but is based on some evidence. He finds that data from the use of psychological tests indicate that the abilities involved in convergent thinking are somewhat different from those involved in divergent thinking.

Descriptive Theories of Problem Solving

Of all the theories of problem-solving that have emerged over the years, the one that has been most influential in educational circles is that of Dewey (1910), which he outlined in a book entitled *How We Think*.

Let us consider Dewey's theory of problem solving at greater length, because it will provide some understanding of what constitutes a good theory for educational purposes. The essence of the theory is that problem solving involves five stages, described as follows:

1. A state of perplexity, doubt, frustration, or the like.
2. The identification of what is believed to be the problem.
3. A search for facts and a formulation of possible solutions.
4. The testing of successive solutions and, when necessary, the reformulation of the problem.
5. The application of the correct solution.

It is claimed that all successful problem solving requires that the problem solver pass successfully through each one of these stages. Failure in problem solving is due to failure in one of these stages. Some of Dewey's followers have gone a step further in applying the theory and have taken the position that practice in each one of these steps results in the production of a successful problem solver. For example, a few years ago the writer paid a visit to the Air University, the highest school of the United States Air Force, in which officers are trained to fill important command positions. There he found placards on the walls of the classrooms outlining the five steps in the Dewey description of the problem solving process. He was told that this theory of problem solving was one of the major bases of the high-level education provided by the school, and that exercise was given in the practice of this problem-solving procedure through work on the solution of high-level military problems.

The theory of Dewey, although it has merit for designing a curriculum, also has weaknesses. One major weakness is that much of what is termed problem solving does not take place always according to this type of sequence of events. If it did, it would be a simple kind of phenomenon to study. A primary source of information that provides considerable knowledge concerning how some people solve problems is found in the reports of scientists concerning the way in which *they* solve problems, and the picture is somewhat different from that described by Dewey. Wertheimer (1945) tells how he discussed this matter with Einstein and how Einstein described the problem-solving process, a description that corresponds rather closely with reports given by other scientists, as, for example, Helmholz and Poincaré. Einstein noted that when he had a problem to solve, he would make considerable effort to solve it, but that often this was of no avail. He would then leave the problem and perhaps move on to the consideration of other matters. At a later time a solution to the problem would come, as the saying goes, "out of the clear sky." When the solution came, he would be able to recognize it as the solution but, oddly enough, would not always understand why it was the solution, nor could he necessarily demonstrate that this was the correct solution. Formal demonstration that a particular solution was a solution often came at a much later date and only after considerable further struggle. Note that in this account of problem solving the solution did not come after the "testing of successive solutions" at the conscious level, as Dewey would have us believe; but it was somehow generated by the operation of some process over which the problem solver had little or no control.

Scientific studies by the great French psychologist Binet (1922) had led to a similar conclusion at the turn of the century. Binet conducted experimental studies of the nature of intelligence and arrived at the conclusion that the essential elements of problem solving were not observable to the problem solver himself and could not be included among the inner mental processes he could observe. Much the same conclusion had been arrived at before the turn of the century by the experimental psychologists of the Wurzburg University, who, after the most painstaking studies, found that the study of the field of a person's consciousness provided little help in the understanding of the problem-solving process. Thus, in scientific language, it can be said that the solution of a problem, in some persons at least, depends on the existence of mediating processes over which the individual has no conscious awareness or control.

A final criticism of descriptive theories of problem solving of the type considered is that they are prescientific theories. A scientific theory of problem solving would indicate characteristics of the problem solver or of the problem which can be measured and which show something about the success that may be expected if a particular individual is given a particular problem to solve, or which will indicate how conditions must be changed if a particular individual is to learn to solve a particular kind of problem. The latter question is one that the educator wishes to answer almost as a part of his daily routine.

Descriptive Theories Based on Research on Problem Solving by Simulating Thinking

An entirely new approach to many scientific problems has been developed in recent years through the availability of high-speed computers. The chemist can now hypothesize the nature of the mechanism underlying a particular chemical process and can then set up a computer to calculate the experimental results to be expected if the mechanism actually operates. The "data" produced by the computer can then be checked against real data collected in actual experiments. The comparison permits an evaluation of the reasonableness of the underlying mechanism that the experimenter hypothesized. Much of the time, computers, when they are used by physical scientists, are used to "generate" data, which is later compared with actual data.

The psychologist has attempted to adopt much the same approach to problems of behavior. Brief mention has already been made of the way in which some learning theorists have attempted to build mathematical models which in turn can be applied to the production of theoretical learning curves. Insofar as the theoretical learning curves approximate real learning curves based on actual data, support is provided for the theory of learning on which the theoretical curves are based. Psychologists have also attempted to study other complex behavior by similar procedures, and especially those behaviors designated as thinking or problem-solving behaviors. An early review of research in this area by Hovland (1960) provides a stimulating and imaginative account of the direction in which work is going in this new approach to complex intellectual behavior. A broad general discussion of this problem in this section will be followed in the next section by a more detailed discussion of its application.

Hovland pointed out that the public widely recognizes that the operations that computers perform bear a resemblance to the operations performed by the human. They are, in fact, commonly called giant brains, and the storage unit is widely referred to as a memory unit. The use of such terms reflects an intuitive understanding that the computers perform operations analogous to those performed by humans. This is a little different from what the scientist does, for he is more concerned with hypothesizing certain operations that the human performs and then making the machine perform the same operations to see if it achieves the same results. This parallels closely the work of the physical scientist.

Before further discussion of this problem, the student should know that computers that perform the operations considered here must be provided with (1) information to be used in solving the problems, and

(2) a program, or set of procedures, that tells the computer how to behave. The program may instruct the machine to look for certain elements in a problem, make comparisons, and so forth. In the study of thinking and problem-solving processes, the program includes operations that the human thinker or problem solver is believed to perform.

Hovland presents a number of different attempts to make machines simulate human behavior. These include the following:

1. Computers have been programmed to develop proofs of some of the theorems of Euclid. The machine is given a set of basic axioms and propositions and a set of rules concerning the possible ways of using them to prove a new theorem. These are stored in the machine either as information or as programs of procedures to follow. The machine is also programmed to use short cuts and various cues. It goes about developing a proof of a new theorem much as a human would. It tries out various "hunches" and, if these do not work, sets up subgoals representing steps in the desired proof. The machine can also be arranged to make use of knowledge that it acquires as it proves new theorems. Once such a machine is working, one can compare the difficulties encountered by the machine with the difficulties encountered by human learners. If the two sets of difficulties match, then support is given to the model of thinking on which the operation of the machine is based.

2. A second type of simulation involves the very evident human capacity to improve performance as a result of experience. An attempt to develop a general problem solver by Newell *et al.* (1959) is designed to

FIGURE 22. The IBM 709 data processing system at System Development Corporation in Santa Monica, was used in the studies of Newell *et al.*, 1958, on the simulation of problem-solving behavior.

perform in this way. The most advanced devices of this kind are checkers-playing machines. Here again, one can set up rules so that the machine can determine whether an item of information acquired is or is not worth storing, and then one can make a comparison of the behavior of the machine with that of the human organism.

3. Another striking example of simulation is the attempt to simulate concept formation. A machine may be fed certain designs, some of which are labeled as positive instances and some as negative instances. The task of the machine is to determine what are the defining attributes of the positive instances that differentiate them from the negative instances. This may involve, as was mentioned in a previous section on concept formation, the determination of whether the concept is conjunctive, disjunctive, or relational. The machine may also be programmed to try out a number of strategies in the formulation of the concept.

Perhaps the most striking result of the work that has been undertaken on the simulation of higher mental processes is that even when scientists have thought that the processes were understood, attempts to simulate them have revealed that they must be much more complex than they were originally believed to be. This in turn has led to a more precise description of what the processes involve. Hovland, in the final paragraph of his article, suggested that studies of simulation may lead to an understanding of the inadequacies of present ways of solving problems. This, in turn, may lead to the development of machines that will be more effective for problem solving. Perhaps, too, it may lead to methods of training human problem solvers that may result in superior performance.

THEORY OF HUMAN PROBLEM SOLVING
BASED ON SIMULATION

The previous section has implied that a theory of problem solving may emerge from attempts to simulate human problem solving with modern electronic equipment. The theories that emerge are descriptive but vastly more precise than, say, the descriptive theory of problem solving of Dewey. The operations involved in problem solving must be precisely specified, for a computer requires such precise specification. There can be nothing vague about it. The problem-solving procedure is an attempt to simulate the behavior of a particular organism, with a particular history, faced with a particular class of problems.

Newell *et al.* (1958) described, in a paper entitled "Elements of a Theory of Human Problem Solving," an attempt to develop and state such a theory. The theory is stated in a form that a computer can carry out. In addition, it makes certain predictions about human behavior that can be tested. For example, it predicts how much difficulty a human problem solver may be expected to have with particular classes of problems, and how long it will take to solve certain problems in relation to others. A descriptive theory of problem solving that has these advantages is a great advance over earlier descriptive theories, which tended to be so vague that no definite predictions could be made from them.

The theory of human problem solving developed by Newell and his associates is in the field of elementary symbolic logic. It assumes that problem solvers in this field discover proofs of theorems by four methods, which are:

1. Substitution, which involves an attempt to find a proof by generating it from a known theorem by substitution of terms.

2. Detachment, which involves working backwards to obtain a new expression whose proof implies the proof of the desired expression.

3. Forward chaining, a syllogistic form of reasoning.

4. Backward chaining, also a syllogistic reasoning process, but the reverse of forward chaining.

The assumption is made that the human problem solver makes use of these four basic processes. The assumption is also made that when these processes, or combinations of them, fail, the problem solver breaks down the problem into subproblems, which are then first solved before the total over-all problem is attacked.

In order to test out this theory of problem solving, a digital computer is provided with a program that permits it to perform these operations for finding proofs, and also a set of axioms and previously proved theorems. The machine is then ready to find the proof for a new expression submitted to it.

Newell and his associates state that the evidence points in the direction of indicating that the performance of the machine is qualitatively like that of the human problem solver. First, the machine does actually succeed in developing proofs of propositions, which it prints out on a paper tape together with all of the unsuccessful attempts. Second, many of the behaviors of the machine are similar to those of the human problem solver. The machine may utilize hints. For example, if the problem involves certain kinds of propositions, the machine may attempt to solve the problem by utilizing theorems that involve similar propositions. Third, the behavior of the machine shows tendencies similar to the sets of human problem solvers. Fourth, the machine shows a process similar to insight, in that it may arrive with suddenness at the solution of problems.

Other Descriptive Theories of Problem Solving

A comprehensive review of descriptive theories of problem solving could well fill a book, let alone a single chapter. A brief comment is in order here to indicate why some of the classical descriptive theories of problem solving are not discussed at greater length. Since the major historical conflict has been between associationistic theories of problem solving and Gestalt theories, a brief comment on these two theories is given to indicate why further discussion of them adds little at this time.

Associationistic theories of problem solving assumed that problems consisted of component stimuli that led to responses. The responses occurred because they had been associated in the past with particular stimuli. Some psychologists believed that these associations were represented by connections in the nervous system between the sensory inputs and the nerve mechanisms that produce movements. The associationist attempted to break down problem-solving behavior into elements, but, since he tended to be vague as to what those elements were, demonstration of the soundness of the theory was lacking.

The Gestalt psychologists took exception to the atomistic approach of the associationist and connectionist psychologists and suggested that the problem solver did not respond to stimulus elements, but to systems of relationships. Several mechanisms for problem solving were proposed by the Gestalt psychologists, including that which involves the reorganization of the relationships perceived in the problem situation. Here again, while the theory has much about it that is convincing, the difficulty has been to describe the problem-solving processes with the precision needed for testing whether they can account for the production of problem solutions.

The Study of Mediating Processes and Intervening Variables in Problem Solving

Three main approaches to the study of mediating processes in problem solving have been developed. The first of these is the experimental approach in which factors believed to be involved in the solution of a particular problem are in some way either facilitated or interfered with. The effect of this facilitation or interference on the solution of the problem can then be studied. The second, the psychometric approach, focuses on measuring the abilities of the individual to perform certain mediating processes, such as the ability to make inferences from data and then to determine whether this ability is related to problem-solving performance. The third, represented by the work of Piaget and his associates, involves an attempt to identify and describe the development of intellectual processes that form the foundation for problem solving. This third approach resembles closely the work of the biologist engaged in describing the development of an organism.

The experimental psychologist who pursues the first of these approaches has typically attempted to formulate a theory of problem solving, generally in stimulus-response terms, and then has designed experiments to test aspects of the theory. Maltzman has proposed a theory of problem solving that attempts to relate problem-solving behavior to the simpler processes of habit learning and habit organization. An external stimulus may become associated with an organization of habits known as a habit-family hierarchy. Habit families are also associated with one another through mediating mechanisms. If one habit family is tried and fails, it becomes temporarily inhibited and another habit family takes its place. The fractional anticipatory goal response is important to the Maltzman theory because, when goal anticipation related to a particular response is aroused, the response is more likely to occur. Such arousal occurs through the presence of cues or instructions indicating the general nature of the response needed to attain a solution.

Another example of the approach of the experimentalist undertaken within the framework of stimulus-response theory is shown in the work of the Kendlers (1962). This work has already been discussed in connection with the chapter on transfer of training, but the Kendlers have also been concerned with research on problem solving. Their work on reversal shifts and nonreversal shifts emerges as an attempt to identify some of the internal mediating processes involved in problem solving. In a sense, it is the experimental counterpart of the work of Piaget, and it provides experimental evidence that substantiates some of Piaget's observations.

The Kendlers argue, much as Hebb (1958) has, that problem solving involves a series of mediating processes occurring one after another until a successful one is reached. Whether these are referred to as parallel chains, as the Kendlers do, or as phase sequences, as Hebb does, or as sequences of hypotheses, as Dewey did, makes a difference in the kind of research pursued. It is too early to say that one of these approaches will be more productive of knowledge than the others.

Reese (1962) has reviewed a number of studies similar to the Kendlers' in which an attempt has been made to determine the mediating processes operating in children of different ages as they solve problems. The data suggest that in preschool children, mediating processes do not occur to the same extent to which they occur in children aged 12 or older. This may be a result of the fact that mediating processes may be dependent on the existence of well-developed concepts that young children do not have.

The experimental psychologists have typically studied rather simple problems, and their work may be overlooked in education because it seems remote from classroom problem solving. Yet the fact is that such studies are throwing considerable light on problem-solving processes. Consider, for example, a series of studies by Weir (1964) that use one of the simplest problem-solving tasks ever used in an extended program of research. The subjects were faced with a panel on which there were three knobs. On certain trials, one of the knobs would release a marble into a trough, and only this particular knob would release a marble; the other two knobs would not. The task of the subject was to press the knobs in such a way that he would obtain the maximum number of marbles. Perhaps one might expect that such a problem would be readily solved; and the subject would soon learn that only one of the knobs ever released a marble, and he would continue to press only that particular knob. What actually happens is that subjects generally press all three knobs to some extent, despite the fact that the pressing of only the one ever yields a reinforcement. The baffling part of the situation, for many subjects, is that the knob that yields a marble does this only on certain occasions. Some subjects assume that this is due to the fact that the particular knob will produce a marble only if it has been preceded by a particular sequence of pressing the other knobs, and hence they continue to press these knobs. Such a belief results in a certain "strategy" of knob pressing. Other strategies follow from other beliefs. Now Weir turned up the interesting finding that those who performed best on this task in the later trials of the series were the 3-year olds and the young adults. They were the ones who tended to press most often the knob that sometimes produced the marble. This raises the interesting problem of why the very young and the grown-up came nearer to a solution than those in the middle of the age range. Weir has some interesting suggestions.

He interprets the behavior of the very young children as representing the direct consequences of reinforcement and suggests that it lacks any complex thinking component. The child learns to press most frequently that knob for which he is reinforced, and this leads to the one knob being pressed most frequently. The adult, on the other hand, is likely to try out various strategies and finally arrive at the decision that pressing the one knob alone yields the best return, and this also results in an effective solution. In the middle age groups, the children have many ideas (strategies) which they try out, but they have difficulty in keeping track of how effective these ideas are in producing marbles. The result is that they continue to try out sequences of knob pressings in the hope that one will produce a marble every time. They never hit on the idea that the best course to pursue is that of pressing only one of the knobs on every trial.

This ingenious series of studies involving a problem with simple characteristics indicates the rich findings concerning thinking processes that such a procedure may yield.

In the second approach to problem solving, the psychometric approach, the scientist seeks to measure the ability to perform certain psychological processes related to problem solving and then determines whether his measure predicts the ability to solve problems that involve these processes. Thus, measures of the ability to perform some of the processes related to deductive reasoning have been developed, and studies have been conducted to determine whether such measures do predict problem-solving ability in complex situations involving deductive reasoning. Tests that measure the ability to perform a particular class of mediating processes are commonly referred to as aptitude tests. Chapter 15 discusses at length the relationship of aptitudes to the ability to perform various tasks, including that of problem solving.

The third approach stands out in strong contrast to that of the experimentalist and the specialist is psychometrics. It is basically the traditional approach of the biologist studying the development of organisms and is illustrated by the work of Piaget with children at Geneva. In his early work, Piaget viewed the developing intelligence of the child in much the same way that a biologist would view the developing organs of an embryo. The essential nature of the approach was that of observation and description. Externally the child could be seen adapting to the environment, but these external adaptations were assumed to result in changes in internal organization and the development of new internal structures. The interaction of the organism with the environment produces structures of ever-increasing complexity, which in turn can cope with progressively more complex problems presented by the environment.

Because the writings of Piaget and his associates run into more than 20 volumes, a summary would constitute a book in itself. Here we can only consider a few of the important points he makes that have particular relevance to a broad understanding of problem solving. The central task that Piaget set for himself as his lifetime work is that of describing the development of the human intellect, and he saw the central function of the intellect as that of coping with the problems presented by the environment. The description of the development of the intellect is the description of the development of problem-solving ability. Although the monument of research that Piaget has built over a lifetime includes a vast mass of detail, there are certain cornerstones within this monument that stand out because of their important implications for education and because they conform to the findings of other research workers.

First, Piaget affirms that, at the infantile level, exposure to a variety of experiences whets the infant's appetite for exploration. By coping with new objects and situations, internal structures are developed that result in an expanding capacity for handling a still greater variety of new situations. This position conforms well with the findings of Hebb (1958) and those who have studied the effects of environmental deprivation in animals.

Second, although the child in the elementary-school years has some capacity for thought independent of the immediate situation at hand, his thinking still has to have concrete events for its initiation and guidance. The child's thinking is still highly oriented toward the concrete situation at hand and is controlled by it. At this level, too, exposure to a variety of experiences increases the repertoire of the child's behavior and develops in him a greater variety of approaches to new problems that may arise. He becomes able to ask more significant and penetrating questions about problems presented to him. Hunt (1961) has reviewed related studies as a part of his review of the work of Piaget, and indicates that a substantial amount of evidence supporting the latter position is available from other independent sources. Throughout this stage, thought becomes progressively more independent of immediate events and becomes, as Piaget describes it, "decentered." In terms of the current concepts of experimental psychology, one would say that at this stage thought, internal verbal behavior, comes to play a role as a central mediating process in behavior. Thus, problem-solving behavior becomes more and more an internal process and progressively less a matter of manipulating the external situation. Much of the internal process appears to be verbal behavior, a position supported by the work of Kendler and Kendler (1962), Kendler (1964), and by a study of Gagné and Smith (1962) that showed that adolescents required to verbalize (speak out aloud) a principle involved in problem solving were more easily able to solve the problem. The latter research generally endorses the position taken by Piaget. It is interesting to reflect on the fact that leadership in this field has come mainly from those who pursue research in the tradition of the biologist, and that the role of the experimenter has been only that of confirming findings.

Third, in the final stage of intellectual development, during the teens, thought achieves real independence from the immediate situation and the child becomes capable of formal operations such as are involved in long trains of reasoning.

In recent years Piaget has been influenced considerably in his point of view by modern writings on logic. He sees logic as a reflection of the way central processes operate rather than being just a model that thinkers may try to follow. Piaget sees intelligent behavior as being logical behavior, and intelligent behavior occurs in a human because the nervous system interacting with the environment acquires the capacity for performing logical operations.

Although the work of Piaget reflects the tradition of the biologist who observes organisms, it has sparked the undertaking of much experimental research. Just as the biological sciences went through a long period during which scientific activity was confined to observing organisms without experimenting with them, so too, perhaps, are the behavioral sciences undertaking, through the work of men like Piaget, a similar period of collecting observational data. This period of observing behavior as it naturally occurs will undoubtedly pave the way for the experimentalists that follow.

Motivation and Problem Solving

Both laymen and psychologists have long held the opinion that problem-solving behavior is likely to be most effective when motivation is at a high level. Common observation seems to support this point of view. The scientist, whose job consists of solving problems, is generally reputed to be highly motivated in his work, often to the point where he devotes all of his waking hours to the pursuit of knowledge. The phrase describing the doctrine on which many children are raised, "If at first you don't succeed, try, and try again," is also a statement of the doctrine that motivation counts in the solving of life's problems.

Although this doctrine is held with strong conviction, very little scientific evidence can be mustered to give it support. Some of the most obvious experiments have not yet been made. It might be interesting to find out whether a person who was hungry showed greater problem-solving skill in opening puzzle boxes containing food than would a person who was not hungry. Probably it is only under exceptional circumstances that a person is motivated to solve problems when the drive operating is one of hunger. Lack of interest in any experiment of this kind is attributable to the belief that the motives that operate in most human problem solving are quite different from the drive resulting from food deprivation.

Two approaches have been made to the study of the relationship of motivation to problem-solving behavior. One of these is based on the assumption that anxiety often operates as the driving force in much problem solving. The other assumes that an important driving force is achievement motivation.

Travers *et al.* (1955) attempted to relate drive, as measured by the Taylor Manifest Anxiety Scale, to performance on complex verbal problems of a practical nature. The relationships between these variables appear to be complex. The anxiety factor appears to have more influence in making performance consistent with aptitude than in contributing directly to success or failure. High-anxiety problem solvers did just about as well as low-anxiety performers, but their performance was much less predictable, as shown in Table 1. This does not fit in well with the hypotheses advanced by Janet Taylor, whose general theory would lead one to expect a negative relationship between anxiety level and performance on very complex tasks.

A second approach to the study of the relationship of motivation to problem solving is through the measurement of achievement motivation. In an interesting study of this matter by French and Thomas (1958), subjects who were presented with a fairly complex problem to solve were measured with respect to achievement motivation. These investigators found that the more highly motivated subjects were more successful than the poorly motivated subjects in solving the problem. There was also a tendency for the better motivated to spend a longer time with the

TABLE 1*

Correlation Between Scores on Aptitude Tests and Scores on a Complex Problem for Groups Divided According to Scores on a Test of Anxiety (Taylor Manifest Anxiety Scale)

Condition of Testing	Predictor Variable	SCORE ON ANXIETY TEST			
		Low	Low Middle	High Middle	High
Relaxed Conditions		N = 83	N = 140	N = 40	N = 25
	General Intelligence	.27	.19	.27	.37
	Arithmetic Reasoning	.02	.26	.27	.46
	Word Knowledge	.33	.19	.26	.24
Anxiety-Arousing Directions		N = 115	N = 180	N = 49	N = 26
	General Intelligence	.22	.46	.48	.52
	Arithmetic Reasoning	.30	.38	.48	.47
	Word Knowledge	.19	.43	.39	.60

* Data from R. M. W. Travers, J. E. Marron, and A. J. Post, "Some Conditions Affecting Quality, Consistency, and Predictability of Performance in Solving Complex Problems." Air Force Personnel and Training Research Center, Research Report, 55–27, 1955.

problem, though this alone did not seem to contribute much to success. The study fits well the common conception that success in problem solving is partly a function of motivation, and that high motivation can contribute to success in high-level problem solving.

Attitudes in Relation to Thinking Processes

Thinking processes are extremely complex. Rarely are they strictly logical and rational. More often are they influenced by irrelevant psychological events that should have little bearing on the process if it is to be effective. Scientists are only beginning to explore these problems connected with thinking. An interesting study related to these phenomena is one by McKillop (1952), who studied the relationship between a reader's attitude and certain types of responses to reading materials.

In the McKillop study, reading passages were prepared relating to three topics. These topics were Negroes, communism, and Israel, and all were clearly topics about which considerable differences in attitude exist. All of the children also took an attitude test related to these three topics in order that the relationship between attitude and responses to the passages could be determined. As in other studies, very little relationship was found between the amount of information extracted from the passage and the attitude of the reader with respect to the content of the passage. Youngsters could read the passage and then answer multiple-choice questions related to the passage, regardless of whether their own attitudes were positive or negative toward the material. When the questions were so worded that they required the reader to make an inference on the basis of the passages, a tendency became apparent for the readers to be biased by their own attitudes. Finally, when the reader was asked to make some judgment with respect to the passage, such as whether an argument is reasonable, the influence of the reader's attitude on his responses became very apparent indeed. The choice of a title for the passage proved to be a task in which the reader's attitude became particularly apparent. Often the choice of a title was quite inappropriate and one that did not fit the spirit of the passage. Only as long as the situation was clearly structured was the student able to keep his feelings out of the picture; but as soon as there was an element of looseness in the situation, the feelings of the reader came to the surface. Of particular interest was the tendency for pupils to dub as stupid a passage that did not fit in with their own attitudes. The implications of this study are that instruction in reading should be something more than instruction in mechanics and information gathering. In addition, instruction should be training in thinking. McKillop implies that perhaps a good point at which to start training might be in finding evidence to support one's belief. Later this search for, and examination of, evidence might be extended to cover points of view incompatible with the person's belief. This suggestion is a highly controversial one. Should a person ever go out to look for evidence to support his point of view? Would it not be much better for him to examine all of the evidence available, regardless of the position it endorses?

Numerous later studies of the same phenomena have been undertaken by psychologists. These studies have been reviewed by Feather (1964). They generally lead to the conclusion that the information retained from a particular communication depends on the attitudes of the person receiving the information.

Experience as a Generator of Problem-Solving Variables

Common observation indicates that problem-solving ability is highly dependent on experience. The specialist in any field is one who has become effective in solving a limited range of problems through extensive experience with those problems. The specialist exists in our civilization because the public believes that extensive experience in solving a limited range of problems results in a facility for solving those problems. To some extent, this is a consequence of the fact that problems tend to repeat themselves, with minor variations, but, as will become evident later, there are factors other than this operating. Experience with a particular class of problems is clearly considered to be advantageous for solving similar problems. Let us pause here to consider an item of vocabulary. The layman talks about "background experience" to indicate the various events that have happened to an individual that account for his present behavior, but the modern behavioral scientist uses a different term. The latter uses *antecedent conditions* rather than "background experience" to refer to what has happened to the individual. The term *antecedent condition* is much more scientifically acceptable. The word *experience* refers to some kind of internal event inside the individual of which he has personal knowledge. It is something that is inferred from the events that have happened to him, though it is sometimes inferred from his behavior. The scientist prefers to stay with what is observable, and in the study of a person's past history the antecedent conditions (meaning the past conditions) are the observable factors, not the personal experience of the individual who was exposed to these conditions. Experience is something inferred from conditions, and the scientist prefers to deal with conditions rather than with inferences from these conditions.

An earlier chapter pointed out that the early learning process involves the development in us of the ability to recognize such basic elements in the surrounding stimuli as those of shape and form, differences in pitch and tonal quality and the like, perceptions related to the localization of the individual with respect to his environment, and so forth. If early learning does not occur, either because of the biological inability of the individual to learn or because of lack of opportunity, then the individual becomes quite incapable of mastering a whole class of problems. Examples of this kind from daily life are quite easy to find. The person who has never learned the basic discriminations that have to be learned if the individual is to locate himself in space shows himself to be extraordinarily stupid in this respect. Some of these people can become lost even when they are but a few blocks from their home. The apparent stupidity which even bright women may show when confronted with a simple mechanical problem would appear also to be an illustration of the extraordinary handicap that can be placed on behavior by the absence of early learning. In the absence of early learning, even the simplest problem that is dependent on it becomes one of extreme difficulty. The ineptness is often such that it stands out in marked contrast to the other skills of the individual. Sometimes the apparent stupidity involved is such that others who have the skill simply cannot believe that the ineptness is anything other than a pose, but this it certainly is not.

What has been termed late learning leads to at least three classes of variables related to problem solving. These are variables related to concept formation and the development of coding systems, to response tendencies, and to the development of problem-solving techniques, which have been named *learning sets*. Each one of these will be given brief consideration.

The development of concepts and coding systems. The general conditions under which concepts are formed and the nature of a concept as a classification scheme have already been discussed, but certain additional characteristics of the classifying tendency of living organisms must be considered. Bruner, who has done much to develop ideas in this area, has introduced the term *coding system* (1957) to describe the results of this form of behavior. The organism learns to code situations that are encountered, and this may lead to appropriate behavior in relation to them. Problem situations may be coded in many ways. They may be coded in terms of the kinds of solutions that are likely to be successful. If an automobile engine fails to function, a simple test will indicate whether the problem is to be coded as an electrical problem or a fuel problem. Problems may be coded as solvable or unsolvable, among many other ways. All problem-solving behavior implies that the problem has been in some way coded, even if the code involves no more than the notion that "this problem is solved maybe by hitting the gadget with a hammer." A simple case of the teaching of a coding system that will help the pupil solve new problems is the teaching of phonics. Through the teaching of phonics the pupil is able to decipher new words he encounters in his reading and, with a little luck, pronounce them correctly. Bruner proposes that those coding systems should be taught that permit the greatest application to the solving of new problems. This may prove to be a difficult matter requiring decades if not centuries of research.

The development of response tendencies. The reinforcement of particular classes of solutions to problems results in the tendency for those response categories to become established as trends in behavior. The establishment of a habit hierarchy is presumably a phenomenon of this type. The responses that have had the highest frequency of success in the past are those that emerge first in a problem-solving situation. If these fail, they may still be repeated until extinguished. Most problem solvers display the phenomenon of trying again and again their favorite solutions, even though they result in failure. As responses in the system of habit hierarchies result in failure, more and more complex mediating responses are called into play.

The development of problem-solving techniques. Although unguided experience results in the development of problem-solving techniques through the development of learning sets, at least some techniques of problem solving can be taught directly. This is a matter that has been the subject of considerable research in the armed services, which have sought to develop teachable methods of problem solving to those engaged in trouble shooting on complex electronic equipment.

The design of systematic trouble-shooting procedures has been based on not only psychology, but also related areas such as information theory. One can demonstrate that the most efficient method of problem solving under some conditions is that in which each decision eliminates half of the possible solutions. In trouble shooting a fire-control mechanism for a fighter aircraft, each step in finding the faulty component should rule out half of the components. If a step rules out less than half of the components, then it is less efficient than is theoretically possible. Training procedures for trouble-shooting equipment should be such that the trained trouble shooter performs in this way. How to *keep* him behaving in this way is another matter, but enough is known about training in problem solving to at least turn out a man from the training program in some areas with efficient problem-solving procedures.

Models and Thinking

Another approach to the study of thinking is the study of the models that are used as a crutch to thought. Before proceeding to this matter, let us consider what is meant by a model. While the term *model* is widely used to refer to such matters as a miniature of the real thing, or a perfect example, or a person who displays clothes in a store, the technical use of the term in the psychology of thinking refers to a very different phenomenon. A model, in the latter connection, is simply an analogy or a representation of a phenomenon or set of events. This definition has become widely accepted through an article by Chapanis (1961), which discusses the function of models in the solving of problems.

In the article cited, Chapanis points out that models are widely used in teaching. A teacher who uses a globe in the discussion of world geography is using a model. The globe is a representation of the world, not just a miniature. Some countries are painted red, though the corresponding geographical regions may be green with vegetation. Large cities are indicated by tiny black square areas, though the metropolitan areas may be nearer to being round. Lines of latitude and longitude are drawn on the globe, though these are not real lines on the surface of the earth. Most wall charts represent models in the sense that the globe is a model.

Models may be of two types: replica models and symbolic models. A replica model bears a close resemblance to the object represented. The globe used by the teacher as a model of the earth is a replica model in most respects. Symbolic models, on the other hand, do not look like the objects they represent. An example of a symbolic model is a table of organization for a school district showing the relationship between the various persons and bodies that operate the system.

The history of education provides numerous examples of the introduction of models for facilitating thought about problems. A famous example of such a model is the notion of an apperceptive mass proposed by Herbart. The basic idea involved in this model is that ideas are organized in the mind and form an organized mass to which related concepts can be attached. New elements could be added to the mass if they had some compatibility with what was already there. The model is an attempt to describe a physical mass to which new objects can be attached if they have certain properties.

The use of models in thinking and problem solving has advantages and disadvantages. On the positive side, models help describe and develop understanding of phenomena. Sometimes they suggest experiments that might be done. For example, the model of Herbart suggests that new concepts unrelated to concepts previously acquired will not be retained easily because they will not adhere to the apperceptive mass, and this hypothesis could be checked by experiment. Models also sometimes help one to see new relationships, as when a globe is used to demonstrate that the polar route is the shortest route between San Francisco and Leningrad. Models, if they are good models, can also be used to predict which solutions to a problem are most likely to be successful. Clearly, models may play an important role in problem solving and thinking, but this fact has so far had little impact on education.

Models also involve dangers and may, at times, prevent the solution of a problem from being reached. Chapanis points out that it is all too easy to assume that a model is a good model and that it does provide a sound analogy. In order to prevent this from happening, a model to be used for solving problems and for other purposes should be validated. This means that evidence should be collected to demonstrate that the model is a sound analogy and behaves in ways similar to the phenomenon it represents. Perhaps the latter is a thoroughly teachable aspect of the use of models in the solving of problems.

Problem Solving and Discovery Methods of Learning

During the present century, dissatisfaction has been expressed with methods of teaching that emphasize the direct presentation of subject matter to children with the expectation that they will learn and retain it. This dissatisfaction has led to the development of problem solving and discovery methods of teaching and learning. The Progressive Education Association, through a series of publications during the nineteen thirties, took the position derived from John Dewey that education should consist of a sequence of meaningful experiences each of which should involve, in essence, the solution of a problem by the pupil. Subject matter was to be acquired as it was needed for the solution of problems. The movement did not deny the importance of subject matter, but the traditional methods of acquiring it were questioned. The new methods of instruction were thus distinguished from the older methods, which had emphasized the presentation of subject matter in an organized way to students. The traditional methods will be referred to here as *expository methods*.

While the Progressive Education Movement emphasized problem solving and inquiry on the part of the pupil as the essential processes involved in acquiring an education, the radical movement in education today emphasizes *learning by discovery*. Just as the Progressive Education Movement of two or more decades ago found support in psychoanalysis, so today do the advocates of learning by discovery find some support from a fringe of reform-minded psychologists. Bruner (1961), for example, has taken the extreme position that the school should be a place where children *discover* truths and not a place where they *learn* truths. It is easy to accept such arguments when they are preached with sincerity; but the mysticism, emotionalism, and the fervor manifested by so many of those engaged in the movement does not compensate for an extraordinary lack of data with which to back up the claims.

Ausubel (1963) has summarized the arguments commonly put forth to support discovery processes as the basis of teaching in schools and has provided an adequate refutation of them. He has pointed out that the proposition that man should discover for himself the knowledge he wishes to possess is nonsense except perhaps in very young children. Man does not have time to do this; and there are often far more efficient ways of acquiring knowledge than by discovery. Discovery methods of acquiring knowledge are time consuming, and any proposal to adopt them in schools as a method of learning would require justification. Perhaps the pupil's most valuable asset is time, and time must be used wisely. Those who advocate discovery methods of learning imply that discovery is the only way of achieving true understanding. This is another unsubstantiated claim. Certainly, understanding can be acquired by many different educational processes. Then there is the argument advanced by Gertrude Hendrix (1961) that basic understanding does not involve the use of words and that children acquire essential nonverbal understanding through a discovery process. This concept of nonverbal understanding is based largely on a study Hendrix undertook in the field of teaching mathematics, but the conclusions she has drawn from this study are of questionable validity. The argument is also advanced that discovery methods of learning will not only teach the child how to discover knowledge but will also teach him the subject matter of the particular discipline involved. This is similar to the unsubstantiated claim of the Progressive Education Movement that organized subject matter would be learned while the children were engaged in meaningful projects, or problem solving. The argument fails to recognize the fact that knowledge has structure and that the pupil may never become aware of nor understand the structure of particular fields of subject matter by solving problems that utilize first one fragment and then another. Bruner (1960) has also been a leader of those who have taken the position that the difference between the schoolboy learning physics and the physicist working in his laboratory is one of degree, for both should be engaged in discovery activity. The argument seems to be that the best way for a child to acquire an understanding of physics is for him to behave like a physicist and to discover the laws of physics. To Ausubel and to most psychologists such arguments are absolutely incredible. The best that can be said of them is they are based on faith; but critical reviewers are likely to demand that which they lack most—evidence.

Ausubel has made an excellent review of the evidence pertaining to the value of discovery methods of learning; and he comes to three conclusions. First, he concludes that most of the articles that are cited as supporting the use of discovery methods of learning provide absolutely no data, but give only opinions. Second, those studies that have been undertaken, and that can be considered to be reasonably well controlled, report negative findings. Third, the few studies that report positive findings include gross flaws in their design that invalidate their reported findings.

The issue considered here does not involve a choice between discovery learning and rote learning. The issue is the relative effectiveness of discovery learning compared with other kinds of meaningful learning including learning by problem solving, learning through engaging in projects of various kinds, and learning through many other situations that call for understanding on the part of the learner. Ausubel points out that psychological theory suggests that there are certain situations in which the discovery method might be used to advantage despite its time-consuming nature. When a learner approaches a field that is new to him and in which he has little previously acquired knowledge on which he can build, then the time taken to engage in discovery may be well spent. Under such conditions, discovery activity may bring him into close contact with the new area of knowledge. However, once he has acquired the basic concepts, expository teaching methods involving the presentation and demonstration of knowledge may then rapidly build upon what he has learned; and such methods may, at that stage, provide highly meaningful experiences.

Summary

1. *Problem solving* is a generic term that includes within its scope a multitude of different complex behaviors. Different forms of behavior may be classified on a scale that varies from simple conditioning to complex problem solving.

2. Problem-solving behavior has been studied in many different situations. Simple types of problem-solving situations, involving choice have long been studied by economists. Other practical problems have been more recently studied in the psychological laboratory. Situations involving games have also been studied and have been the basis for much theorizing by psychologists, mathematicians, and others. The party puzzle has also been widely used for problem-solving research. In recent years, some research has been done involving trouble shooting with complex equipment, because this form of problem solving is of particular importance to the armed services.

3. Problems are often classified into fixed-solution problems and

variable-solution problems. These two classes of problems are said to involve convergent and divergent thinking processes.

4. Many approaches have been adopted for the purpose of identifying the mediating processes and intervening variables operating in the solving of problems. The approach of experimental psychology, the approach of psychometrics, and the approach of the biologist (as seen in the work of Piaget) have all made contributions.

5. Early theories of problem solving were descriptive. The most notable of these was that developed by John Dewey who suggested that problem-solving could be considered to involve five basic phases. Such a theory of problem solving, like other descriptive theories, is prescientific in the sense that it does not specify the conditions that must be measured to predict problem-solving behavior.

6. Attempts have been made to develop descriptive theories of problem solving and then to stimulate the various processes involved on a computer. The behavior of the computer resembles that of the human problem solver in many important respects: it actually produces solutions to problems, utilizes hints and cues, and shows *sets*.

7. Other descriptive theories of problem solving include those developed by associationist psychologists and Gestalt psychologists. Although these theories have much about them that is convincing at the descriptive level, they have not led to any powerful ideas about how problems are solved.

8. Mediating processes and intervening variables have been studied through two approaches. On the one hand, there have been contributions made by experimental psychologists and, on the other, there have been important discoveries made by psychologists engaged in the development of tests. Both approaches appear to be making contributions.

9. The relationship of motivation to problem solving is clearly important, from both the theoretical and practical points of view. Research in this area has been limited by lack of devices that can make any claim to measure motivation. The main candidates for the title of measures of motivation in recent years have been the Taylor Manifest Anxiety Scale and instruments for measuring achievement need. The relationship between manifest anxiety and problem-solving performance is complex. Achievement motivation has a more direct relationship to problem-solving behavior.

10. Antecedent conditions operate in many ways on the problem-solving process. Background knowledge has obvious relevance to the process. Experience may also generate coding systems that permit the classification of problems in categories, which may facilitate the discovery of the solution. In addition, background experience generates re-

sponse tendencies and problem-solving techniques. The latter have been studied in research on learning sets.

11. A new approach to the study of thinking is the study of the models that are used by thinkers as devices for the solution of problems. The study of model building has also the further function of discovering ways through which problem-solving behavior can become more effective.

12. Discovery methods of learning involve a problem-solving approach. These have been widely advocated as providing an efficient learning situation for the acquisition of subject matter in schools. So far, the evidence is lacking to indicate that the procedure is efficient.

12

Social Factors Influencing Learning

EARNING occurs in a social context except for the hermit investigating some small aspect of the universe from the confines of his
cave. The child who is captive in the classroom is exposed con-
tinually to social events that may well slowly shape aspects of his
behavior and even have an influence on academic learning. Although the
claim has long been made that the social climate and social events in the
classroom are important conditions related to achievement, there has not
been any abundance of evidence to support that position. A review of
research on social interaction in the classroom by Withall and Lewis
(1963) comments on over one hundred research studies but fails to
produce any convincing or overwhelming evidence to support the position that scholastic achievement is highly influenced by social events
occurring within the school. The evidence reviewed by the latter writers
shows that the interest of research workers has been largely focused on
the relationship of social events to personality development, personal
adjustment and mental hygiene, anxiety, hostility, expressive behavior,
social skills, and so forth.

Social psychologists have not been particularly concerned with problems of intellectual development. Yet, it is clear that some social events
have an impact on learning. The teacher's intellectual interaction with
the child must obviously be one factor related to the child's achievement.
Under the old Lancastrian plan, in which pupils taught pupils, these
daily interactions were of central importance in the promotion of
academic learning. But the issue is not whether social interactions do or
do not facilitate learning, for obviously they do. The crucial problem is
whether it makes a difference in learning to have one kind of social
interaction rather than another—for example, a warm social interaction
in contrast to a cold intellectual approach.

A Classification of Groups

The particular social interactions engaged in by a child depend on the groups to which he happens to belong. The classification of groups considered here is one discussed by Lorge (1958), but it is also similar to that provided by a more recent writer, Golembiewski (1962).

Groups may meet in a face-to-face situation, or the members may never encounter one another. For example, a teacher who runs a home-study program for a group of crippled children has pupils that, in a sense, constitute a group, but they never meet together. Groups identified for surveys are of this character. An organization running a public-opinion poll may select a group of insurance brokers, distributed across the country; this type of group is called a *nominal group,* because the members are identified and are considered to belong to a named group. Such a group is a non-face-to-face group.

Even groups that are face-to-face may show no positive amount of interaction. For example, pupils in a very traditional classroom may show no interaction even though they represent a face-to-face group.

A face-to-face group may be assembled for a particular purpose and then dismissed. Such a group is referred to as an *ad hoc* group. It is illustrated by a committee set up to run a particular school function or by a group of people assembled to take part in an experiment. Such *ad hoc* groups are to be contrasted with groups who have a tradition and history and whose procedures have been established by a long period of interaction. A school faculty is such a traditioned group.

The distinction between *ad hoc* and traditioned groups is not so clear as it seems on the surface. An *ad hoc* committee established by the Congress for a particular purpose meets with a knowledge of how such committees undertake business; in a sense, it is a traditioned group.

Groups assembled for a particular purpose and then abandoned probably behave rather differently from traditioned groups that meet over long periods. This is an important point, because most research on behavior of groups has been undertaken with *ad hoc* groups assembled for the purposes of the research and then dismissed. The results of such research may not apply to the behavior of traditioned groups, though they are often applied in this way. Often training in group work is given in groups assembled for this purpose. The training given by such enterprises probably helps the participants to work better with similar *ad hoc* groups, such as committees; but many who have been through such training have had disastrous experiences when they have tried to apply the techniques they have learned to groups differently traditioned. A technique of group leadership may not apply to a traditioned group because it runs counter to the customs and practices of the group. An interesting example of this is seen in a study of various techniques of training that have been used in the armed services for attempting to ensure that men will eat the unfamiliar emergency rations when required. In one such study (Torrance, 1958) a number of different techniques were tried out, including one that involved the explanation of the purposes of the special ration and why it should be consumed. In another approach the leader consumed the ration in front of the men to show that, despite appearances, it was quite palatable. In a third approach the men were ordered in a typical military manner to consume the ration. The latter technique was found to be quite the most effective in the military situation. This is hardly surprising, since this is the technique the men expect to be used and which is accepted by them as an appropriate one to follow. Much the same problem arises when a teacher who has come from a very informal school program takes over a classroom in a school run along traditional lines. The group in this new school is very unlikely to accept the permissiveness which the new teacher attempts to introduce. A group that has developed traditions is limited in what it will accept outside of this framework of tradition.

The Pupil as a Member of a Traditioned Group

The fact that the pupil is a member of a group within the school, which interacts in a face-to-face situation and which has been traditioned, has important consequences for the learning process, particularly at certain stages in his development. Although there is some pressure at all ages to conform to standards of the group, these pressures become particularly effective during adolescence, when any infringement of the customs of the group becomes a serious breach of etiquette. The psychology of adolescence is to a great extent the study of the relationship of the adolescent to his peer group and the effect of this relationship on his behavior.

Membership in a traditioned group of adolescents may have many consequences on the learning process in the classroom. During the period of adolescence the youngster shows an increasing interest in members of the opposite sex, and this interest and the activities that go along with it may become serious competitors for the youngster's time. During the college years this competition for the student's time may become so serious that it interferes with achievement. The sixth-grader may be concerned only with the friendship of children of the same sex, but the physical development that occurs during the teens results in a curiosity about the opposite sex and related behaviors that become quite time-consuming. Occasionally this competition of interests between the academic and the social is solved by happy compromises, as when a boy finds a congenial companion of the opposite sex with whom he can do his homework. The development of heterosexual interests may also interfere with learning in other ways. One common source of interference is the interest displayed between a boy and a girl during classwork, to the exclusion of activities ordinarily associated with academic learning.

Interactions in classrooms are commonly between pupils and teachers, and less commonly are there pupil-pupil interactions. The relative effectiveness for learning of these two interaction situations is a matter of real interest, as is the comparison of learning involving interaction with learning involving no interaction. Although some research has been undertaken on these problems, much of the literature on the subject is befogged by the use of an inappropriate vocabulary. For example, some writers refer to discussion methods of teaching as pupil-centered or student-centered, and lecture methods are referred to as teacher-centered. The terms are both nonsensical and misleading. A teacher who carefully prepares a presentation to the class with attention to what he knows about pupil interests and the pupil's level of knowledge can hardly be described as behaving in a teacher-centered way. The pupil who is intent on obtaining a good grade through apple polishing may use classroom discussion to flatter the teacher. Can this be appropriately referred to as pupil-centered learning? The terms *teacher-centered* and *pupil-centered* make implications about the teaching situation that go far beyond the data available; and they are also used to imply falsely that so-called pupil-centered discussion methods must have virtues that so-called teacher-centered lecture methods do not have.

The virtues attributed to discussion methods and the lack of virtues attributed to lectures through labeling them student-centered and teacher-centered stimulated considerable research during the period 1945–1955, but little of the research approached the problem by making an analysis of the nature of the learning to be expected from discussion and the learning to be expected from lecture. On the contrary, the typical research procedure involved the teaching of one or more sections of a course by one method and one or more sections by another method, and making a comparison of the effectiveness of the two methods by means of scores on the final examination. This procedure makes the assumption that a single measuring device, the final examination, is adequate for appraising the merits of the two approaches; but the fact is that they may be achieving rather different objectives.

Lorge and his associates (1958), who have reviewed such studies (of which there are now many), point out that there are no consistent differences found between the two techniques in the amount learned during a semester or other specified period. Differences in the achievement of the pupils' learning under the two conditions are small. Sometimes they favor the discussion group and sometimes the lecture method. One reason for this is that the groups involved in the various experiments vary from rather small classroom groups to large lecture sections in colleges. It is possible that when large numbers of students are involved, the lecture method may be superior simply because it is not feasible to organize such numbers into efficient discussion groups. With smaller groups, organization for discussion may be much more feasible. There is also the possibility that much depends on the nature of the subject matter to be learned. What may be an efficient way of learning in one content field may be inefficient in another.

Differences between a face-to-face interacting group and a face-to-face noninteracting group have been extensively studied in relation to the speed and adequacy with which the members learn. The usual context of such studies has been the classroom, where the noninteracting group is taking a course by lecture and the other is learning by a discussion method. Unfortunately, in such studies the term *discussion* is generally rather loosely used, and it may refer to a whole range of activities, from one that is not too different from traditional recitation to one in which a teacher has only a small part to play and the interaction is between pupils. Interest in this comparison came into being with the rise of the progressive-education movement as an organized influence in American education, and represented one of the fundamental differences between the so-called progressive classroom and the traditional classroom. By the early thirties, when the progressive-education movement was at its peak of influence, a number of studies had already been carried out that compared pupil-centered discussion learning with teacher-centered lecture learning.

Smith and Dunbar (1951) studied 118 college students in a course of general psychology. They found virtually no relationship between class participation in discussion and increase in test scores over the semester. Participants tended to be nonconformists in other phases of college life, and the authors of the study suggest that participation is an example of nonconformist behavior. Participants were no more interested in the course than were nonparticipants.

McKeachie (1962), who also reviewed studies comparing lecture and discussion methods of instruction, came to much the same conclusion as Lorge *et al.*,—namely, that on achievement tests the two methods do not generally produce different results. McKeachie argues, on the basis of some rather weak evidence, that discussion methods may produce learning in areas other than those measured by achievement tests and, specifically, that they are more effective than lecture methods in developing attitudes and motives and a changing behavior. This has been suggested by the authors of a number of studies in the area, although the evidence presented to support the proposal is slight. One study by Thie (1925), two by Zeleny (1927, 1940), and one by Asch (1951) take this position.

Thie (1925), who used high-school English classes for his study, found that the group that was taught by a discussion method showed a greater tendency to undertake both voluntary work and individual activity. Another important finding was that the students learning through discussion reported greater enjoyment in their work and were very much more likely to enroll in additional English courses in subsequent semesters. In the studies by Zeleny, the results suggested that pupil-pupil discussion and traditional recitation procedures produced roughly the same amount of growth in knowledge and understanding of subject matter.

The study by Asch (1951) is of later vintage than those by Thie and Zeleny (1927). By that time a new emphasis had appeared on the educational scene—namely, the influence of certain groups in the mental-health field who had put forward the idea that certain kinds of mental patients could be helped most by providing an atmosphere in which they could work out their problems by themselves. The function of the person administering treatment was to provide the right atmosphere and never direct the patient as to what he should do. This kind of treatment was called nondirective therapy. Enthusiasts for this approach to mental-health problems soon proposed that the same methods might be used in the classroom and that the teacher should only set the stage for learning. According to this view, the pupils should direct their own learning, and the role of the teacher should be nondirective.

In the period of enthusiasm for the application of nondirective techniques to the classroom, which began around 1945 (although the same tendency had been seen earlier under the name of progressive education, and still earlier under the Rousseau theory of education), experiments began to be conducted that compared the learning achieved in nondirective classrooms with the learning achieved in classrooms in which the teacher assumed a directive role. The study by Asch is one of many that made this comparison. In the Asch research, the group that had directed study involving both lecture and discussion was superior in subject-matter knowledge to the group that was not directed by the teacher. However, the students in the nondirective sections felt that their approach to learning was more helpful than was that in the directive approach. There was also some indication in this study that pupils in the nondirective group made some improvement in emotional adjustment as a result of the experience, and the other group did not.

The establishment of *ad hoc* interacting groups within a classroom is a common teaching procedure. In the elementary school, teachers will almost routinely, divide the children into groups for particular learning activities such as reading, mathematical problem solving, and so forth. This is commonly regarded as an effective procedure, though most people cannot tell why it should be particularly effective. One would expect many learnings to occur much better in group situations than when the same learning is attempted under isolated conditions. The fact has been pointed out many times in this book that the teacher has difficulty in providing one of the most important conditions for learning—namely, reinforcement. When a child is learning to read, there is no way in which the teacher can reinforce each right response for each individual child. She can reinforce the responses of a particular child by working with that child individually; but when she does this, reinforcements are not provided for the behavior of other children in the class who are also learning to read. In traditional educational methods, recitation was considered to be a procedure in which some process analogous to reinforcement functioned for the whole class—that is, when Jimmy was asked a question and gave the right answer, the whole class supposedly learned the correct answer. Van Wagenen and Travers (1963) found that in a recitation-type of situation, pupils who observed another pupil being reinforced learned considerably less than the pupil who made the response and at whom the reinforcement was directed. Learning procedures involving small groups of pupils have been designed to permit a greater number of pupil responses and, hence, a greater number of reinforcing events. Reinforcements may have been expected to function mainly for the specific child involved in the recitation. Teachers of the last twenty years have recognized the weakness of this procedure, and procedures that involve the splitting of a class into small learning groups are designed to remedy some of the weaknesses in the traditional learning situation. The most typical of such groups is the reading group found in the lower grades, where the children are just learning to read. The reading group is basically a way of increasing the number of reinforcements a child receives during learning. Through the group, children can pool their knowledge and provide much more frequent reinforcements for one another than can be provided by the teacher. Too often the value of learning in groups is discussed as though there were some particular magic in the presence of a group. The group may be no more effective in the teaching of reading than some well-designed piece of mechanical equipment that rapidly and systematically reinforced correct responses.

Some higher educational institutions have used small discussion groups as an integral part of the instructional process. One common procedure is for the large classes to divide into small groups for discussion of the topic at hand, and then a representative of each small group reports to the full class. The procedure is largely based on certain common prejudices. Watson (1953) investigated this procedure and was surprised to find that many of these prejudices, which he himself held, were unsound. For example, he suspected that some groups had good discussions from which all profited, and that others did not. Such was not the case. Within single groups there were likely to be individuals who thought the discussion good and those who thought it profitless. Other surprising findings were that the best discussion groups were large (ten to fifteen members). Students who rejected authoritarian points of view also tended to reject group work. Men with little professional work in the field tended to rate group work high.

The behavior of groups during problem solving and the relative merits of group problem solving versus individual problem solving will be considered in another section, but some discussion is appropriate at this point pertaining to differences in behavior and consequent learning that may occur in interacting groups of different size. Carter and his associates (1951) compared the behavior of individuals participating in groups of different size. In groups as small as four, considerable opportunities were provided for the individual to behave and to demonstrate his capacity for making a contribution. However, as the group increased in size, there was a certain tendency for the more aggressive members of the group to take over and dominate the situation. Under the latter circumstances, the individual member of the group had a greatly reduced opportunity to participate and to contribute ideas.

The discrepancy between the Watson study and the Carter study should be noted. Watson found that the best discussion occurred in the larger groups, but the finding of Carter et al., was the reverse. This discrepancy is possibly a result of the fact that the two sets of groups were convened for different purposes. The Watson students were convened in groups to discuss the classroom presentation they had heard. On the other hand, in the Carter study the groups were engaged in group problem solving. What may be an optimum size of group for one activity may not be optimum for another. The data suggest that large groups of a dozen or more may be unwieldy for engaging in problem solving requiring systematic effort, but that a more discursive exploratory activity may be engaged in effectively by groups of the latter size.

A particularly interesting example of *ad hoc* groups constituted for training purposes is found in programs developed by social psychologists for the development of sensitivity to the processes that go on in groups. Such procedures stem from the work of the late Kurt Lewin. They are best exemplified today in the work of the National Training Laboratories conducted under the auspices of the National Education Association. In such programs, students participate in certain group processes under the guidance of a skilled trainer, and through this experience attempt to achieve some understanding of the dynamics of group activity. The reader interested in studying further the use of the *ad hoc* group for this specialized form of training is referred to a volume by Thielen (1954). Although the attempt to provide training in the very complex skills involved in working with groups is notable, great difficulties have been encountered in collecting evidence to demonstrate that social learning does actually occur. The problem of developing scientific techniques for studying learning in such a situation is challenging.

Group Processes in Relation to Problem Solving

Problem-solving learning takes place in social situations—in schools—that is, in situations in which other students are present. The effect of the presence of other people on the problem-solving process is of considerable interest to teachers, particularly insofar as social conditions can be arranged to facilitate the learning of problem-solving techniques. Another problem is the matter of the extent to which a person should learn to solve problems alone, or whether social problem-solving situations provide such advantages that they should be adopted. These are matters that research workers are just beginning to study.

One important reason for assembling children in groups in the classroom is for them to participate in problem activities that often require the work of more than one person in order to bring the activity to a successful conclusion. For example, the writer has often divided his class into several groups of four or five students each, so that each group can undertake a small psychological research project during the semester. The groups are then able to undertake much more significant projects than the individuals alone would be willing to undertake. This is one advantage of group problem solving, but there are supposedly others that are less well identified and less obvious—if they are real advantages at all. One of the supposed advantages is that a group is a more efficient device for the solution of a problem than is an individual. Some of the evidence concerning this point will be discussed in the paragraphs that follow. Another possibility is that the group may solve problems more rapidly than would an individual solving the same problems alone, and hence the group situation may provide for each member a more varied experience than he could obtain for himself.

An additional claim for the value of group process as a means of solving problems has appeared in the writings of an advertising executive, Alex Osborn (1957). In these writings the claim is made that groups can solve problems more effectively than individuals, provided a technique known as *brainstorming* is adopted. This technique originally arose in the advertising world, but it has since become fashionable in many areas, including education. The effective use of the brainstorming technique calls for a group chairman who is well trained in the skill. The chairman establishes the rules for conducting a brainstorming session and sees that the rules are rigidly adhered to by all of the participants. The session takes place in two parts, often with a coffee break or rest period between the first part and the second. In the first part the participants are informed about the nature of the problem to be solved and are asked for ideas that might solve the problem or at least contribute to its solution. Participants are encouraged to put forth *any* ideas that come to mind, even wild ones. It is against the rules to criticize any ideas that are suggested, and every attempt is made by the chairman of the session to make the atmosphere a relaxed one in which no person is ever criticized for any idea he produces. The chairman encourages individuals who produce ideas, and perhaps even gives particular encouragement to those whose ideas some members of the group might receive with coldness. In this part of the sessions, ideas are listed; but the names of those who produced the ideas are not listed. In the second part of the session the rules are changed. In this part the group is no longer asked to produce ideas, but the ideas that have been produced are critically examined. The most promising ones are then thought through and often modified or converted into a form in which they can be practically applied. Osborn claims that his technique of brainstorming produces highly original solutions, better ones than are produced by more conventional ways of solving problems. He also claims that it is the group process and the way in which it is conducted that accounts for the effectiveness of the solutions produced.

The literature on problem solving does throw some light on the value of the group process for solving problems. One of the earliest studies of the relative effectiveness of groups and individuals in solving problems was conducted by Watson (1929), who studied the performance of both individuals and groups in performing the task of making as many words as possible out of the letters included in a given word, which was always a long word. Watson first asked his subjects to work individually on the task. Then he formed them into groups of twenty and asked the groups to undertake the same task with a new word. The task was then repeated in the group situation and was finally repeated in the individual situation. He found that the number of words produced by the group was larger than that produced by any individual. However, many who have read this study have concluded that this is evidence to show that the group is superior in its problem-solving capacity than is the individual. This conclusion is not justified, because Watson also discovered another important fact, which was that the individuals working alone produced a greater number of different and distinct solutions than did the group. The data suggests that the group does not have any remarkable effect on the production of solutions, but rather, its effect is inhibiting. Individuals who would have produced original solutions alone do not produce them in the group situation. In the brainstorming techniques, fewer solutions may be produced by the individuals working in a brainstorming session than would be produced by the same individuals working alone. The group does not appear to facilitate thinking, but rather, in this particular instance, it is restricting. Similar results were found in a subsequent study by Watson in which many different tasks were used. However, in the subsequent study there were many cases in which the problem-solving performance of the group was less than the individual problem-solving performance of many members of the group.

Somewhat similar results have been found by later investigators such as Shaw (1932) and Husband (1940). The total work output of groups is superior to that of the typical individual, regardless of whether the task is a problem-solving task or a more routine assignment. However, the *sum* of the work of individuals alone is invariably greater or of better quality than that of the same individuals assembled into a group.

In another study by Taylor, Berry, and Block (1957), performances by four-man groups and by individuals were compared on problems that permitted creative solutions. The number of ideas produced by the groups was less than the number produced by the individuals working separately. The groups were also inferior in terms of the quality of the solution produced, compared with the best of the solutions produced by individuals.

The reader has to be on guard when he sees the statement that groups produce better solutions to problems than do individuals. That statement is likely to mislead, because it is generally intended to mean that the performance of the group is superior to the *average* performance of the individuals working alone and isolated from the others. The *average* performance of individuals working independently may be poorer than that of the individuals working as a group, but this does not exclude the possibility that some of the individual solutions may be superior to that of the group. Some commonly are.

The experiments discussed do not lend any great support to the idea that problems can be most effectively solved by a brainstorming technique. If problems are to be most efficiently solved, then the advantages of individual effort as well as group effort need to be mobilized. The fact that the group does tend to inhibit the individual means that there should also be some opportunity given to the individual to develop ideas independently. Of course, at this time we do not know whether some individuals are more inhibited than others by the presence of a group, and this is a matter to be considered. Some individuals prefer to work alone and apart from others when problems are to be solved, and others prefer to work in a group situation. The present writer has great difficulty in thinking carefully and systematically in a group situation, and requires the peace and quiet of isolation in order to do his best work. He looks back in horror at the times when some well-intentioned conference chairman assigned him to a group to solve, or try to solve, some problem that had arisen. Possibly the group situation does not provide him with the stimuli that are necessary to maintain his thinking behavior.

Lorge et al. (1955), as a result of a study in which both individuals and groups solved problems of a realistic and practical nature, suggested that when groups produce solutions that are superior to those produced by individuals, certain conditions are likely to exist. One of these is that the group has information, and pools information, that the individuals separately would not have. In this particular experiment, the subjects, working either individually or in groups, were permitted to ask questions of the examiner. The groups asked for more information than did the individuals, and hence were better able to solve the problems. Here again, it is probable that the individual members would have asked more questions when working alone than they did when working in the group, but in the group situation there was some possibility of pooling their resources. There is also another factor that sometimes makes for group superiority, and that is discussion. Thorndike pointed out (1938) that discussion in itself may sometimes improve the judgment of a group, but this is not always so. If the majority of a group is misinformed, there is a real possibility that the group decision after discussion may be even worse than it was before discussion.

The matter is also complicated by some evidence that in a group problem-solving situation a permissive atmosphere is more advantageous than a highly structured atmosphere for the more intelligent groups only. Calvin et al. (1957), who published the latter result, also found that people of average intelligence were handicapped by a permissive atmosphere.

The belief is commonly voiced that groups may sometimes provide opportunities for learning that individual work does not. For example, children working on arithmetic problems in groups may find that they are teaching one another. At least those who could not solve the problems by themselves might perhaps learn to solve the problems by observing other members of a group with whom they are working. Hudgins (1960) studied group problem solving as a teaching situation. He provided children with practice in problem solving (in arithmetic), some in a group situation and some working individually. Then all subjects were tested on their ability to solve similar problems. His conclusion was that group problem solving had no particular value in teaching children to solve arithmetic problems.

Communication Networks and Problem Solving

A key to the understanding of the conditions under which a group is an effective problem-solving agent is found in research on communication networks. Groups differ considerably in the way in which information is transmitted. In some groups there is two-way communication among all members. In others there is two-way communication only between the leader and the other members of the group. There are many additional communication systems that might develop within groups. The relationship of the communication system to problem-solving effectiveness can be studied through techniques that control the communication channels through which information is passed. One technique is to have the members of the problem-solving group in different rooms, but with telephonic communication established in a prearranged pattern. Another procedure is for the members of the group to communicate in writing with one another, but only in the directions indicated by the experimenter.

One such study is by Heise and Miller (1951). In this study the investigators found that two-way communication between all members of a three-man group was most effective in solving a dull and commonplace problem. On the other hand, a problem that required the coordinated work of the members was undertaken most effectively in a group in which communication was limited between members of the group and the leader. These research workers concluded that "the performance of a small group depends upon the channels of communication open to its members, the task the group must handle, and the stress under which they work."

Social Facilitation

A long history of work in experimental psychology has shown that individuals working in a noninteracting group—that is, in a group in which they are not communicating with one another—are nevertheless influenced in their work by the presence of one another. The fact that there is generally a tendency for persons working in groups to work more rapidly than when the same individuals are performing the same tasks alone has given the phenomenon the name of *social facilitation*. Most of the early work on this phenomenon was undertaken with adults performing relatively meaningless tasks, such as producing as many words as possible beginning with the letter *B*, or canceling all of the *A*'s in a page of print. A later study was performed with children by Mukerji (1940), also with meaningless tasks, and similar results were found. Mukerji found that nearly 90 per cent of the children worked more rapidly in a group situation than alone. Almost all of the work on social facilitation has been done with repetitive tasks that provided little challenge to the individual. Just what would happen if the same experiments were to be repeated with tasks requiring problem-solving abilities is not clear at this time. The writer's hunch is that a similar social-facilitation phenomenon would occur; but the matter needs to be settled by careful experimentation.

What is the basis for social facilitation? The phenomenon is a complex one; and although it has been clearly demonstrated to exist, the factors involved have not been clearly identified. There is some reason for believing that the group situation elicits competitive striving and also imitative behavior. This is suggested in a research undertaken many years ago by Wyatt, Frost, and Stock (1934), which indicated that workers sitting near one another tended to have a similar output. This was not due to a tendency for persons with similar work habits to sit near each other, for the relationship disappeared when the same individuals were required to work in isolation.

Imitative Behavior

An important aspect of behavior in the educational process is imitative behavior. The stress that communities place on having teachers of fine character partly stems from the concept that the commendable attributes may rub off on the pupils by some kind of imitative process. In addition, a considerable part of what the teacher does in the classroom is a process of demonstrating in such a way that the pupils can effectively imitate the performance. The importance of imitation varies with the subject matter. The teaching of surgery, for example, would be hardly feasible if it did not lean heavily on an imitative process. On the other hand, work in creative writing should avoid any imitative process, for it would clearly defeat the purposes of the course. (This is not to say that a course in creative writing does not depend on certain language skills of which some have been learned by an imitative process.) In some other areas of learning, the value or limitations of imitation in the learning process is much less clear. If the teacher in the first grade were concerned with a project involving the modeling of clay, should she demonstrate techniques for modeling or will this stereotype and inhibit the creative behavior of the children? One suspects that the answer depends largely on what is to be achieved immediately. If some creative product is sought, then imitation is not to be encouraged, for it may prevent the achievement of the goal. On the other hand, the teacher may be concerned with developing *techniques* in clay modeling, believing that when the pupils have mastered these techniques, they will be better able to perform creatively. In still other areas the uses of imitation are obviously limited. One does not learn to use a typewriter by observing another person type. One must perform the typing act oneself and slowly learn to improve it. Nevertheless, one may sometimes learn specific aspects of the skill by having those aspects demonstrated. The writer remembers a youngster in a typing class who had developed the habit of pushing the keys. A demonstration by the instructor of striking the keys helped to remedy the faulty technique.

Until quite recently the idea was held that man has a built-in natural tendency to imitate and that this tendency accounts for the way in which children copy adults. One cannot entirely dispose of this theory, because many species do show a capacity for imitation that is difficult to account for except by postulating such a tendency. Birds will grow up to give a reasonable reproduction of the song of the birds with which they have been raised. If they have been reared by a bird of a different variety, then they will learn to sing the song of the bird by whom they have been raised—not the song that is characteristic of its own breed. Such facts that have been well established in experimental studies give support to the idea that in at least some species the young may have a built-in mechanism that leads to imitation in certain spheres of activity. Species may differ in this respect. Our problem here is the nature of imitation in man.

Miller and Dollard (1941), who have studied both theoretically and experimentally the phenomenon of imitation in man, differentiate between two aspects of imitation. These are described as *matched dependent behavior* and *copying*. Let us consider first the matched dependent behavior. This behavior is well illustrated by the tendency for pupils to reflect many of the aspects of the behavior of the teachers. It is not that the pupils set out deliberately to copy the behavior of the teacher, for they do not. Without being aware of what they are doing, they nevertheless manage to reflect aspects of the teacher's behavior; but they are not particularly concerned about the fact that some of their behaviors do not match very well. This tendency to match behavior is typically found in situations in which persons have to relate to figures of prestige, much as the pupils relate to the prestigeful figure of the teacher. Followers acquire some of the behaviors of their leader. The gang shows much of this phenomenon, and the followers in the gang may even go so far as to choose clothes that emulate those of the leader. This is not the result of any complicated thinking process, but just a tendency for the follower to *match* the behavior of the leader.

An important aspect of matched dependent behavior, when it has occurred over a long period, is the phenomenon known as *identification*. When this happens, one person comes to behave in a way very similar to that of the person whose behavior he partially matches. When such a matching of behavior is accomplished, the observer may infer that the behavior may have similar underlying causes. For example, a child is in close contact with an adult who is violently anti-Russia. After some years of this association the child also becomes anti-Russia and frequently makes statements expressing disapproval of things Russian. The behavior of both the child and the adult would be attributed in each case to the presence of an underlying attitude that found expression in statements of hostility toward Russia. Not only is superficial behavior acquired by this process, but underlying characteristics also develop through which behavior is organized and becomes consistent.

Many evidences indicate that matched dependent behavior and its consequence, identification, represent one of the major elements in the development of personality; and it is particularly influential as a generator of attitude. For this reason, the attitudes of children tend to show a considerable resemblance to those of their parents. Children tend to vote in the same way as their parents, and they also tend to show a considerable resemblance to them in their religious attitudes.

How far can the teacher influence behavior through identification? Probably much less than is commonly supposed. The child comes into contact with many teachers with many different attitudes and personality characteristics. This great variety is to be contrasted with the fact that children have only one set of parents, with whom they have daily and extensive contacts over many years. Identification with the parents must necessarily play a greater role in the molding of personality than can contacts with teachers.

In contrast to matched dependent behavior, copying behavior is a much more complex process. Let us consider a simple example of copying behavior. A first-grade teacher is teaching children to write their names. She sits down with one child and writes out his name on a piece of paper. The child then makes an attempt to copy the pencil lines made by the teacher. After writing out half of his name, he realizes that some of the letters are wrong in shape, so he begins again, paying greater attention to the shape of the individual letters. What the pupil is doing in this instance is *discriminating* between the model and his own efforts to reproduce the model. He recognizes similarities and differences, and takes action to correct the differences. Perhaps the distinction may be expressed in this way: Matched dependent behavior is stupid behavior, whole copying behavior has to be to some degree intelligent.

Miller and Dollard (1941) have conducted experiments with both animals and children that indicate that this aspect of imitation can be considered to be a learned form of behavior. The fact that one can demonstrate that imitative behavior can be learned does not permit one to generalize and conclude that all imitative behavior is learned or that learning is the only factor involved.

The Miller and Dollard experiments were quite simple in design. A child was brought into a room in which he could see two chairs with a box on each chair. He was told that one of the boxes contained a gum drop. Before he was allowed to go to one of the chairs and make a choice, he witnessed another child perform in this situation. When his own chance came to make a choice, the experimenter either reinforced him for doing the same thing as the other child had done or he reinforced him equally often for not following him as for following him. In the one case, the experimenter would be reinforcing matched dependent behavior; in the other case, there would be no reinforcement for such behavior. Miller and Dollard found that the children who were reinforced for manifesting matched dependent behavior showed an increasing tendency to display this behavior. The implication is that this form of behavior is highly susceptible to learning.

The behavior described by Miller and Dollard can also be interpreted as involving a process other than the observer child matching his behavior to that of an observed child. The performance watched by the observer child may serve the purpose of giving him a cue that he can use in later solving the problem himself. The cue would be just as effective if it did not involve the behavior of another child, but involved a mechanical lever lifting the lid off the correct box. If the child learned that the box that had the lid lifted by mechanical means contained the gum drop, one would hardly say that he was imitating the mechanical lever. The essential feature of the learning situation is really not the presence of a child whose behavior is observed. Nevertheless, there are situations in which a person matches his behavior with that of another person and the learning mechanism suggested by Miller and Dollard may be the mechanism through which such matching behavior is made possible.

Miller and Dollard have shown that copying behavior may have disadvantages as well as advantages in the learning process. Copying may teach a person to perform certain essential acts related to the solution of a particular problem but may leave him with an inability to solve the problem for himself. A fifth-grader may be baffled by a problem of long division but eventually completes it to the teacher's satisfaction by copying the procedure from the paper of another. This copying behavior does nothing to help him solve future problems of long division, because it does not permit the copying of certain internal behaviors that form an essential part of the process. Copying behavior, if it is to be effective, must permit the learner to copy most of the essential processes of the skill to be learned. When imitation is incomplete, learning is generally ineffective.

One can give numerous illustrations from school situations where learning is thoroughly ineffective because the imitation is incomplete. Pupils who learn to do their mathematics by formula are the commonest examples of this phenomenon. True, they are able to produce right answers, but only so long as all of the problems remain in exactly the same format. Give the problem a new twist, and the pupil is completely lost. Incomplete imitation makes for a situation in which there is little transfer of training.

There is another aspect of imitative behavior that is of immediate practical importance to the beginning teacher. This is the tendency for the pupils to imitate the general characteristics of the teacher. Anybody who has spent time visiting schools will probably have noted that in the quiet rooms the teacher is typically a quiet person who rarely if ever raises his voice. On the other hand, a noisy classroom is typically run by a noisy teacher, who talks in a loud voice and who commonly raises his voice to recover control of the class. Some systematic studies support this common observation. In the studies conducted by Anderson and his associates (1945, 1946) at Michigan State University, the finding was that aggressive teachers had many pupils manifesting aggressive behavior. Low aggression on the part of the teacher was accompanied by little aggression among the pupils. When further research has been undertaken, one suspects that there will be justification for the generalization that pupil behavior is to a great extent an imitation of teacher behavior. Some teachers may find it hard to accept the idea that a class out of control usually indicates a teacher out of control.

Early childhood behavior is filled with incidents in which the young child is reinforced for imitating the adult. The mother of the eighteen-month-old child holds out a cookie and says "cookie." After making various attempts to obtain the cookie, the child eventually says the word the mother is saying and immediately is given the cookie. The cookie functions not only as a reinforcement for the use of the word, but also reinforces imitative behavior. From the earliest contact with adults there are numerous reinforcements that function indirectly to reinforce imitative behavior, though their primary purpose is to reinforce some other aspect of behavior.

Research of a quarter century ago attempted to demonstrate that imitative behavior reflects a learned tendency to imitate; more recent research has been designed to achieve the more modest goal of identifying some of the conditions under which matching behavior occurs. This research has been reviewed by Bandura and Walters (1963), both of whom have contributed extensively to the research literature. The review covers a number of studies in which children of preschool age have been exposed to "models" that display aggression to an object such as a doll. The studies demonstrate that after such exposure the children show an increased display of aggression. The children could be exposed to either the real-life model behaving in front of them or to a movie or a cartoon showing the same aggression.

Such simple demonstrations are oversimplifications of the problem, for other studies also reviewed by Bandura and Walters (1963) clearly show that the mere watching of a model is generally not enough to produce matching behavior. A crucial factor in determining whether matching behavior does or does not occur is what happens to the model as a result of the performance that is observed. If the model's performance can be observed to result in punishment, then matching behavior is unlikely; but if the behavior is rewarded, then matching is much more likely to occur. Bandura and Walters point out that the punishment or the reward does not actually have to be observed by the watching child for it to influence the extent to which matching behavior will occur. It is sufficient for the reward or punishment to be implied, or for the observing child to know that the kind of behavior which is being observed is, in fact, commonly punished or commonly rewarded.

Some Research on Control and Leadership with Implications for Teaching

Direct research on teacher-controlled and permissive classrooms has not been particularly productive. This fact was discussed at considerable length in an earlier chapter, in which it was pointed out that such research involves a vast complexity of variables the effects of which cannot be sorted out in the classroom situation. Other approaches are possible. Leadership in its relationship to learning can be studied through laboratory experiments. Such research may provide an avenue to the study of problems of learning in the classroom that is more productive than the direct approach.

A central issue in the conflict among the advocates of different teaching methods is the matter of the leadership pattern considered to be most effective in promoting learning. Arguments about such matters have been largely polemic, and generally centered about the relative merits of a traditional versus a progressive curriculum. Some laboratory research has been undertaken in this area, and includes a study that has had widespread influence on educational thought. The reference here is to the famous study by Lewin, Lippitt, and White (1939) entitled "Patterns of Aggressive Behavior in Experimentally Created 'Social Climates.'" As the title indicates, the focus of the study was not on leadership in relation to learning, but leadership in relation to the incidence of aggressive behavior.

In the study of Lewin, Lippitt, and White, boys aged ten and eleven were assigned to three types of groups, each type having a characteristic leadership that distinguished it from the other types. The three leadership patterns were (1) an authoritarian leader who directed the group in what to do, (2) a democratic leader who encouraged group-decision processes and who functioned as a member of the group, and (3) laissez-faire leadership that left the children to their own devices. The activities involved were those that would be considered hobbies: the building of model boats and planes, painting, and other manual arts and crafts. The incidence of aggressive behavior showed marked differences in relation to the three types of leadership involved. Laissez-faire leadership was accompanied by the highest incidence of aggressive behavior, and somewhat lower was the democratically led group. The groups with the authoritarian leaders showed either a very high incidence of aggressive behavior or a very low one. Although these results are of interest in connection with problems of discipline, so many of which are problems of aggression, they do not throw any direct light on problems of learning except insofar as aggressive behavior may interfere with learning. However, the research workers involved in this study also collected some additional data concerning the amount of time spent in work under the three leadership situations, and these results have more direct bearing on the problem of learning. Output of work was related to type of leadership. As long as the authoritarian leader was present, there tended to be a high output of work; but the output declined rapidly when this type of leader left the room. In the groups exposed to democratic leadership, there was less output in the presence of the democratic leader; but the output of work continued in the absence of the leader. Under laissez-faire leadership, the presence of the leader seemed to be a disadvantage to the work of the group.

The results of this study have been widely applied to the planning of leadership roles for teachers, but many psychologists would doubt whether such application is justified. Rarely are the results of a single psychological experiment so sound and so secure that one can be certain they would be reproduced in other experiments. As far as this writer can determine, there has been no real attempt in America to replicate the experiment, a first step that should be taken before any extensive applications of the results are made. Similar experiments have been conducted by Japanese psychologists working with Japanese children. White and Lippitt (1960) report two studies conducted by Misumi and his colleagues, and cite the following conclusions:

> . . . the group morale was higher in the democratic groups than in the other two. They frequently exchanged friendly remarks and showed more concern and satisfaction with the work and more willingness to continue it. . . . As to the quantity of work, the democratic groups obtained the highest rating; the autocratic groups the next, and the laissez-faire groups last. As to the quality, the autocratic groups did the best work, the democratic groups were next, and the laissez-faire groups last.

In a second experiment by Misumi and his colleagues (see White and Lippitt, 1960) some complicating results were found. On the more interesting of two tasks, the work done in the democratic group was superior; in the less interesting task, the autocratic groups performed best.

Anyone tempted to apply the results of the studies of Lippitt, White, Lewin, and others to a classroom situation should also read a study by Guetzkow et al., (1954) which virtually tried to apply the findings at the college level. The latter investigators were in charge of a seminar for graduate teaching assistants, the members of which decided to study the effects of different teaching methods in a course in general psychology. The teaching methods involved (a) a *recitation-drill* method, which was run on strictly authoritarian lines with the instructor each day giving a short lecture and asking the class prepared questions, (b) a *group-discussion* method, in which interactions with the instructor at meetings of the class were initiated largely by the students themselves and where the instructor played the role of chairman of the session, and, (c) a *tutorial-study* method, in which the instructor was available for helping the students find answers to the questions that came up in their independent study. These methods were selected because they represent different degrees of self-directed versus teacher directed work, and because they also permitted a contrast between an emphasis on group work and an emphasis on individual work. The learning of the students was evaluated on the basis of a number of tests and other devices at the end of the course. The performance of the three groups in terms of measures in the course was strikingly similar; the only significant differences were on those measures on which the *recitation-drill* group did best—namely, the final examination, and the choice to go on and take more work in psychology. In terms of the usual measures of academic success, the classes run along authoritarian lines appeared to be the most successful.

One cannot tell at this time whether the differences between the results of the various experiments reflect differences in the backgrounds of the subjects, or whether other factors are involved. The differences are sufficient to be noteworthy, and again reflect the need for the replication of the original experiment. Many aspects of the study are far from clear. A movie made of the three different groups operating under the three different sets of leadership conditions showed that there were other important variables operating in terms of which the results might be interpreted. For example, the authoritarian leaders played a role that was, to say the least, unfriendly, if not hostile. The fact that under this condition children tended to be either unduly subdued or overtly aggressive is hardly surprising. But authoritarian leaders do not have to be that way. They can be subtle in their approach, even friendly. They may use all kinds of devices to obtain cooperation, which is then reinforced. One can even conceive of an authoritarian leadership that might operate in such a way that the work of the group would continue in the absence of the leader.

Some of the data more recently published about the original experiment by White and Lippitt (1960) suggests that the autocratic leadership may have been so contaminated by an unpleasant element that the results produced were quite inevitable. White and Lippitt state that the autocratic leaders gave disrupting commands in 11 per cent of their verbal behavior; that of the democratic leaders was only 1 per cent. Twenty-four per cent of the verbal behavior of the democratic leader represented guiding suggestions; but only 6 per cent of that of the autocratic leader did. Little praise was given in any of the leader roles; but the autocratic leaders devoted 5 per cent of their remarks to praise and the democratic leaders 2 per cent, a slight margin in favor of the practices of the autocratic leaders. The general trend of the evidence indicates to this writer that autocratic leadership was accompanied by certain irrelevant and unpleasant elements that may have seriously stacked the deck. An experimenter who had read Machiavelli's *Prince* might have designed a style of autocratic leadership that produced quite different outcomes. The writer is not arguing in favor of autocratic leadership in education; he is merely curious about the relationships that really exist between leadership and performance.

One is tempted to speculate at this point that the main difference between judicious autocratic leadership and judicious democratic leadership in a classroom may not be found in the quality or the quantity of learning produced, but in other factors. Learning under democratic conditions may be more pleasant. In addition, democratic practices may encourage decision making and other activities that can have important later consequences. In addition, of course, democratic practices in teaching may well contribute to the development of democratic values.

Summary

1. Learning occurs in a social context. The effects of the social conditions of learning need to be understood, since they may constitute important conditions related to learning.

2. Various social conditions may exist in teaching situations. A classification of social groups developed by Lorge and his associates represents a convenient framework within which to discuss social conditions existing in learning situations. This classification includes four categories of groups: (1) face-to-face, interacting, traditioned groups; (2) face-to-face, interacting, *ad hoc* groups; (3) face-to-face, noninteracting groups; (4) non-face-to-face, noninteracting groups. In each category, certain learning conditions are operating.

3. Pupils must be considered as members of traditioned groups with certain expectancies about the behavior of school personnel and the behavior of teachers.

4. Relationships between the teacher's method of conducting the class and the effectiveness with which learning takes place are not particularly consistent from one research to another. Whatever differences exist appear to be largely in side effects, such as the amount of voluntary work undertaken, rather than in the level achieved in the particular skill that is to be learned.

5. Group procedures for problem solving have long been considered as situations that might provide particularly effective solutions, but experiments have not generally confirmed this position. Individuals working alone produce a greater number of distinct solutions than individuals solving problems in group situations. The effect of the group tends to be inhibiting. However, a distinction must be made between a group as a producer of a solution to a problem and a group as an instructional situation for its members.

6. The establishment of small *ad hoc* groups within the classroom may provide a condition favorable to one child's reinforcing the responses of another.

7. The phenomenon of social facilitation has been well established. Although not all children manifest social facilitation, the majority do.

8. The layman has generally considered that imitation plays an important role in the learning of the child, and the psychologist has produced evidence to indicate that this is so. Miller and Dollard have made

the distinction between two types of imitative behavior, which they refer to as matched dependent behavior and copying behavior.

9. Much of imitative behavior appears to be learned; at least, research workers have demonstrated that animals that do not normally imitate other members of their species can learn to do so. In addition, the learning of imitative behavior has been demonstrated in children.

10. Many studies have been conducted in which a child has the opportunity to observe the performance of another and the effect of this observation on behavior is determined. A particularly important factor in determining whether matching behavior will or will not occur is whether the observed behavior is rewarded or punished.

11. Although direct research on the relative effectiveness of different teaching methods has been extensive, it has not yielded a comparable quantity of significant results. Another approach to the problem of discovering relationships between teacher role and learning is to conduct laboratory experiments. One of the most famous of these experiments contrasted three roles: the autocratic, the democratic, and the laissez-faire. Although the results of this experiment have been widely applied to educational problems, there is doubt whether such wholesale application is justified. The experiment has never been adequately replicated with the addition of proper controls; and until this happens, the results must be considered highly tentative. Similar experiments conducted in Japan with Japanese children have produced somewhat similar, but not entirely identical, results. Other studies conducted on the teaching of college students produced very different results.

13

The Learning of Attitudes

M OST OF this volume has been devoted to problems related to the learning of skills, concepts, and other mediational processes, but another large class of important learnings have hardly been touched upon. These are learnings related to approach and avoidance tendencies. These are first seen early in childhood, when certain objects become attractive and are approached, and others initiate a negative reaction. Approach and avoidance tendencies, which are so clearly seen in the manifest behavior of the child, later become internalized, and the child shows an acceptance or rejection of ideas or values.

Some of the early approach and withdrawal reactions appear to involve little learning, if they involve learning at all. The newborn monkey clings to warm, soft objects. Later it shows tendencies to avoid certain objects, such as a mask representing a monkey's face. Some of the avoidance reactions may be violent. The typical reaction of a young parakeet to the sight of a snake is that of sheer terror and panic. There is real difficulty in determining the extent to which such responses are learned, and, as in the case of imprinting, learning factors cannot be ruled out. In many such withdrawal or approach responses, what appears to occur without learning may well involve learning. Fear of the dark, which is a common manifestation of children, may involve learning in this way. The child learns a certain dependency on visual stimuli and, so long as these stimuli are present, maintains a state of adjustment to his environment. In darkness these cues are absent, and the child's behavior becomes disturbed. Although such an interpretation is reasonable, there are immense difficulties in demonstrating that it is a sound one.

Approach and avoidance responses become more numerous as age advances. Some of these come to be referred to as attitudes, others as interests, and still others as values. Distinctions among these terms are not clear. A distinction commonly made is that interests refer to matters of preference for activities; and attitudes refer to a positive approach or negative avoidance of ideas and objects. Both interest and attitude involve the concept of rejection or acceptance, and both involve some kind of affective (feeling) response to the object involved. Attitudes and interests have much more specific objects of reference than do values. The latter relate to broad goals, but attitudes and interests are related to narrow channels into which activity is funneled—either toward or away from an object or idea. Interests and attitudes may determine the choice of means through which the value system and the goals implied by it may be achieved. A person's life may be dominated by religious values and religious goals, but he may have positive and negative attitudes to various religious practices and to the means of achieving religious ends.

Although the origin of attitudes is seen in simple responses of approach or withdrawal, in their more mature form attitudes represent highly complex aspects of behavior. The failure of early researchers to recognize the complexity of the phenomena involved resulted in some despair when research produced so many inconsistent results. Indeed, so unsatisfactory did the term seem to be that, in the years following World War II, many scientists, for example, Doob (1958), took the position that the concept of attitude should be abandoned. Despite such recommendations, the concept has remained, and psychologists have slowly managed to tease out some of the components it involves. A recent attempt to do this by Katz and Stotland (1960) suggests that attitudes include several components. The latter writers reject the idea that attitudes are simply approach or withdrawal tendencies, and suggest that they include to some degree each one of the following elements:

Affective components. These consist of primarily positive or negative affects (feelings). Attitudes may differ in the extent to which they involve such affective components. Some attitudes are quite irrational and involve little except this affective component. Political attitudes, in their most primitive form, may be primarily of this character. The person who likes one set of political ideas and dislikes another, but cannot tell why, reflects an attitude that has a major affective component but very little else. Many attitudes are of this nature, and common observation suggests that they are quite easily learned; most people are characterized by many attitudes that are primarily of this character.

Cognitive components. Attitudes differ in the extent to which they involve knowledge. Some attitudes are highly intellectualized. A person may take a particular position on a certain political issue because he has thought through the problem and, after considering all the available evidence, decides that the position he takes is the most acceptable one. He may have no strong feelings about the matter—that is, the affective component may be minor. On the other hand, his attitudes may not only be highly intellectualized, but may also have a strong affective component. The intellectual component and the affective component work hand in hand, but they are still independent components. The intellectual component of attitude discussed here is sometimes referred to as the cognitive component. The word *cognitive* implies knowing. Hence, the cognitive component of an attitude is that aspect which is based on knowledge or derived from it in some way.

Action components. Every student of the psychology of attitudes is impressed with the fact that many expressed attitudes bear little relation to behavior. A person may express strong religious attitudes, and yet his membership in his church involves little more than paying a pledge. In such a case the religious attitudes lack any substantial action component. The fact that the action component can be independent of the other components is important for planning education. Much of what goes on in the name of attitude education is the education of the affective and the cognitive components of attitudes, and these components may never be carried over into action systems. Thus, one finds that the American public, probably the best-informed public in the world, has a deplorably poor record at the polls; the percentage is small compared with that of most other democratically run countries. How relationships are established between the cognitive components of attitudes and action systems is not clear at this time. This is really a problem of transfer of training. Though there is some evidence that transfer can take place from cognitive systems to action systems, the conditions that make this possible have not yet been established. Clearly, teachers cannot remain content with educating only the cognitive aspects of attitudes, for education must involve something more than preparation for an armchair approach to life. The action system of an attitude may have little support from the cognitive system, which may be almost entirely lacking. A person may have a well-developed action system with respect to religion, but have few beliefs about religious matters that he can state clearly. A person may fight and die for his country, and yet have only the vaguest idea of the values for which his country stands.

Attitudes as Intervening Variables

Attitudes are not directly observable phenomena, but are constructs introduced to account for behavior as it is observed. A pupil is said to have a favorable attitude toward school, but the attitude itself is not observed. What is observed is the presence of many behaviors on the part of the pupil indicating acceptance of the school situation, and the absence of rejecting behaviors, such as are involved in playing truant. From these behaviors an attitude is inferred that accounts for the consistent trend in behavior. The attitude thus inferred represents an intervening variable that operates on behavior and has the same relation to it as any other intervening variable discussed in this book. Often a degree of complexity is involved in predicting behavior from attitude, because these may be complex in character. Prediction may be possible only when separate measures are available of the affective, cognitive, and action components.

Attitudes represent learned characteristics of the human organism. The laws that describe the conditions under which they are learned are presumed to be similar to the laws involved in the learning of other characteristics. Reinforcement, imitation, and other processes that have already been discussed are considered to represent the processes involved in the learning of attitudes; but experimental work attempting to isolate and evaluate the effects of each process separately has not been undertaken. The reason for this may well be that psychologists undertaking research on learning have avoided the study of such complicated variables as are involved in the representation of attitudes.

Measurement of Attitudes

Although attitudes may be reflected in a variety of behaviors, the typical method of measurement is confined to the use of verbal behavior. So well set is this pattern that the textbook by Edwards (1957), entitled *Techniques of Attitudes Scale Construction*, confines its discussion almost entirely to the measurement of attitudes through verbal behavior. In that book an attitude is defined as "the degree of positive or negative affect associated with some psychological object," a definition originally proposed by L. L. Thurstone. The term *psychological object*, as used in this definition, is broad in scope and might refer to a religion, political system, type of work or vocation, literary work, a nation, a minority group, a law, and so forth. The measures of attitude implied by this definition are also primarily measures of affect, and hence do not attempt to measure either the cognitive component or the action component of attitude. The fact that an important book on the measurement of attitude should place this limitation on what is to be measured in the attitudinal field reflects well what has been typically measured and the kinds of measures that have been used in attitude research.

Verbal behavior may be used in many ways in the determination of underlying attitudes. The remarks that people make are used everyday as a basis for guessing the underlying attitudes. A special case that has been extensively studied is the expression of opinion. Any expression of opinion provides a small amount of evidence concerning attitude. A similar small amount of evidence can be obtained by asking a person whether he agrees or disagrees with a particular statement of opinion. An example of this would be to ask a person whether he agrees or disagrees with the statement, "Federal legislation should be introduced to socialize medicine." Agreement with this statement indicates a favorable attitude toward socialized medicine, and disagreement an unfavorable one.

Considerable effort has been devoted to ordering into scales series of opinions with respect to particular issues. Such ordered sets of statements are referred to as attitude scales. They are used to appraise attitudes by asking subjects to examine each statement and to indicate agreement or disagreement. An examination of these responses can then be used to provide a measure of attitude. It is clear that endorsement of extreme statements would indicate an extreme attitude. On the other hand, the endorsement of statements nearer a middle position indicates a corresponding scale position of the attitude.

Techniques for selecting statements for inclusion in attitude scales and for assigning them to positions along a scale are numerous, and many are highly complex. Edwards (1957) describes some of the more straightforward of these techniques and discusses their applications. However, there are many others that have been developed and that represent a complete area of technology in itself. There would be little point in discussing at length in this chapter the highly refined psychometric methods that have been produced for the construction of attitude scales, but it is important to point out that the products of such techniques are scales that measure mainly expressions of affect toward psychological objects. Such measures of attitude do not imply that the attitude has any appreciable cognitive component—that is, they do not indicate whether a person can justify his attitude by giving reasons for his position or can dispose of other positions by relevant arguments. Such measures of attitude also do not imply that the particular attitudinal position has any action component attached to it. On a typical verbal-attitude scale a person might appear to be strongly opposed to socialized medicine, but this would be no basis for assuming that this same person would be willing to devote his energies to opposing legislation related to socialized medicine. Many of the difficulties of research on attitudes would have been overcome if it had been realized at a much earlier stage that the measures derived from verbal-attitude scales may not be expected to necessarily predict action.

Early Studies of Attitude Change

The verbal-attitude scale was an important development of the thirties that has played a major role in research in social psychology over several decades. This invention also had impact on educational research and resulted in numerous studies of the effect of various classroom procedures on attitude change, as measured by these verbal devices. Procedures for the measurement of attitudes emerged at the time when the motion picture was attracting attention as a teaching medium, so it is hardly surprising that considerable effort should have been devoted to the study of the motion picture as an instrument for changing attitudes. A classic study by Peterson and Thurstone (1933) demonstrated that exposure to silent motion pictures did result in changes in attitude as measured by verbal scales, and that such changes had some permanence. The films used in these studies were selected because the topic and the treatment was such that they offered promise of producing attitude changes. The films were selected to change attitudes toward such varied subjects as national groups, such as the Chinese, and present methods of treating criminals. Many studies of this general nature have been undertaken since the original Peterson and Thurstone studies and with comparable results. A film well designed for changing attitudes as measured by verbal-attitude scales does produce measurable changes in the attitudes expressed on these scales. Some of these studies, such as those conducted by Hovland et al. (1949) during the war years, have also shown that films that are not well designed to produce attitude change do not produce well-depicted attitude change.

Such studies were considered, at the time they were made, to be demonstrations of the direct influence of movies on attitudes, but time and the development of more sophisticated concepts of attitude have raised questions concerning what such studies demonstrate. Although it is clear that the movies provide a learning situation, just what is learned remains an open question. Is the situation simply a matter of verbal learning—that is, does the learner merely change his verbal habits and his way of speaking about the particular object? Are changes in verbal habits also accompanied by changes in affective responses— that is, does the person "feel" differently about the object as a result of viewing the film? Such studies also do not reveal the relationship between whatever learning takes place as a result of the learning conditions and action systems related to the particular attitude. Although the early studies, demonstrating that silent films could influence attitudes as measured by attitude scales, raised hopes that such changes might be accompanied by changes in other aspects of behavior, many subsequent studies were very disappointing. These later studies showed a lack of relationship between attitudes as measured by such scales and attitudes as measured through other aspects of behavior.

Education and the Learning of Attitudes

A large number of studies have been undertaken to determine whether formal educational programs, as they are typically pursued in schools and colleges, result in changes in attitudes and value systems. Such studies can tell little about the mechanisms involved in the learning of attitudes or the conditions under which they are most readily changed. Even if one can demonstrate that a four-year college curriculum results in the changing of attitudes, one cannot know from this data alone the particular aspects of the curriculum that were effective and those that were not.

Although such studies contribute little to our knowledge of the processes involved in the learning of attitudes, they may nonetheless provide pointers indicating some areas in which research might profitably be undertaken. For this reason, a brief review of research of this character seems to be appropriate here.

A comprehensive summary of research on attitude change resulting from college programs has been prepared by Jacob (1957). This study is rather broader than a study of attitudes, for its general theme is the relationship of the individual's personal system of values to a college education and how this education influences his value system. The general finding of the report is that a college education results in greater homogeneity of values and attitudes. Those who enter college with extreme views tend to move in toward the center as their college education progresses. This is to be expected. The typical college professor is likely to express middle-of-the-road views, and these are likely to exert some influence on the attitudes and values of the students. This will lead to a modification of views in the direction of a middle-of-the-road course. Furthermore, interaction with a diversity of students the majority of whom do not represent extreme viewpoints is likely to result in the modification of students' attitudes away from the extremes.

Studies during the period following the Great Depression showed that college education had a liberalizing effect on the attitudes of college students, but more recent studies do not show the same trend. Perhaps this is to be expected. During the economically hard years of the thirties, liberal views were widely held by academicians, and extensively expressed. In more recent years there have been pressures exerted on the academician to keep his political opinions to himself. This, in turn, would have the effect of limiting the liberalizing effect of a college education. Nevertheless, studies by Newcomb at Bennington College and at Catholic University of America (1943, 1946) showed that when an institution promoted a particular point of view and system of values, the students over the four years in that institution showed a change in attitude consistent with the institutional point of view. Whether these changes are transitory or relatively permanent, nobody knows at this time.

Despite the fact that Jacob finds that the modern American college has no great liberalizing effect on student attitude, he does conclude that the graduates are characterized by a particular set of values and opinions.

Although these opinions and attitudes are the product of many influences, Jacobs considers them to be, to some extent, a product of the college influence. He also believes that the great majority of college graduates are self-centered and aspire to material goals; and they expect to be able to gratify their material wants without too much effort on their part. They also value the traditional moral virtues of honesty, sincerity, and loyalty. They subscribe to religion in a traditional but somewhat apathetic way. They are also more tolerant than the rest of the population of radical ideas and unconventional people. Tolerance for others is one of their important virtues. They are less suspicious than many persons in our society who view college professors as subversive or godless.

The numerous studies reviewed in the Jacobs report are of interest for evaluating college education as it exists in America today. But they provide little information concerning the way in which education should be organized in order to produce particular attitude changes. From such studies there is no way of discovering the laws of learning that produce attitude changes. Other studies are needed in order to determine the conditions favorable or unfavorable for attitude formation and change. Some of these studies must now be considered.

Attitude Formation and Change as a Learning Phenomenon

In the early thirties Edward L. Thorndike had begun to speculate that interests and attitudes were learned by the same laws that apply to the learning of verbal habits and intellectual and other skills. The law of effect was considered to represent the central mechanism operating, and experiments were undertaken by Thorndike and his associates (1935) that demonstrated that certain aspects of these phenomena—namely, aesthetic preferences—could be modified by appropriate conditions of reward. This work did not attract the attention it merited, and not until the years following the Second World War was any extensive interest displayed to this approach to the study of attitudes.

Reinforcement-learning theorists would predict that the most effective way to change attitudes would be to arrange in some way for behavior related to the new attitude to be elicited and then to reinforce that behavior. Of course, the difficulty in following such a procedure is that usually there is no method of eliciting the desired behavior. Every teacher knows that if one reinforces studiousness, improved scholarship results; but there are many children who never manifest studiousness with sufficient frequency for reinforcement to have a measurable effect. Nevertheless, the matter is one of great theoretical interest, and psychologists have attempted to design experiments to test this theory of attitude change.

Scott (1957) designed a study to determine whether a situation in which a person was required to make a statement with which he did not agree, but which was reinforced, resulted in a change of attitude in the direction of the reinforced statement. The situation was an ingenious one. Students were required to engage in debates on various issues and were assigned the task of presenting speeches representing points of view with which they did not agree. In some cases the speech was followed by a reinforcement, which consisted of a purported vote indicating that they had won the debate. Post-tests of the attitudes of the students indicated that those who were named winners of the debates showed a significant change of opinion toward the position they had presented in the debate, but the so-called losers had not changed significantly. The interpretation of these results in terms of reinforcement theory would be that the presentations at the debates were reinforced and that this generalized to related expressions of opinion.

Festinger and Carlsmith (1959) conducted another study that demonstrated a similar phenomenon. In this latter study, the hypothesis was that "if a person is induced to do or say something which is contrary to his private opinion, there will be a tendency for him to change his opinion so as to bring it into correspondence with what he has said or done. The greater the pressure used to elicit the overt behavior, the weaker will be the tendency." In this study, subjects were exposed to a boring set of tasks and were then paid to tell other subjects that the experience had been interesting and enjoyable. On a subsequent test of their enjoyment of the tasks, a change was found in the direction of increased expressed enjoyment. But, when the reward offered was high and far beyond that necessary to elicit the behavior, the change in attitude was relatively small.

The two studies cited in the previous paragraphs were based on an instrumental-learning model. Others have considered that classical conditioning, interpreted as a case of contiguity learning, presents a satisfactory model of attitude formation. Staats and Staats (1958) designed an experiment to test the hypothesis that attitude responses could be conditioned to a simultaneously presented verbal stimulus. The procedure involved the presentation of a name, such as "Dutch," which was presented a number of times and accompanied each time by the auditory presentation of a different word. The words accompanying each name were all different, but they all had a common evaluative meaning. For example, the words paired with "Dutch" included *gift, sacred,* and *happy;* the words paired with "Swedish" included *bitter, ugly,* and *failure.* As a result of this pairing of the names with words, all of which had the same evaluative component, the meaning attached to the names was demonstrated to change.

A similar point of view is stressed in a study by Kimbrough (1956), who proposed that attitudes consist of implicit verbal responses. By this Kimbrough means that when it is said that a person has a favorable attitude toward the law, he has many associations between the concept of law and positive verbal statements about the law and related matters. If, on the contrary, the concept is associated with negative rejecting statements, then he is said to have a negative attitude. Kimbrough presented some evidence to show how the development of associations might accompany the development of attitudes.

Another approach to the study of the development of attitudes as learning phenomena has been to find parallels between the learning of attitudes and the learning of concepts. Rhine and Silun (1958) developed the theme that concepts often have values as defining attributes, and that these defining attributes are learned just like any other set of defining attributes. For example, the concept of a criminal involves such defining attributes as a person who breaks the law, a person who performs acts that violate the rights of others, and so forth. The concept of a criminal also generally includes the defining attributes of being wicked, bad, or morally reprehensible. Although the concept of a criminal can be defined strictly in terms of behavior, moral evaluations generally form an integral part of the concept. In the study by Rhine and Silum, the investigators demonstrated that such values can be learned as aspects of concepts. Subjects were told that anthropologists had visited a little-known tribe, and that the experimenter wanted to know whether the subjects could predict the characteristics of that tribe. Certain tendencies on the part of the subjects to name particular characteristics were reinforced. Reinforcement was found to influence attribute development and the strength and resistance to change of the value judgments made about the imaginary tribe. The approach is an interesting one. For a more extended discussion of concept formation as a model describing the formation of attitudes, the reader is referred to an article by Rhine (1958).

The conditioning and learning studies considered in this section are mainly concerned with the learning of cognitive components of attitudes. The typical conditioning study makes no attempt to discover how the affective components of attitudes are developed, though sometimes there is the implication that the affective components are learned in exactly the same way as the cognitive components. Some psychologists might even take the position that the conditioning studies considered evade the central problem of attitude development and change by focusing on the learning of verbal responses. However, some promise is offered for the study of the development of affective components of attitude in such studies as those of Staats and Staats (1958) and the study by Kimbrough (1956). However, none of the studies that have been considered is concerned with the development of action systems in relation to attitudes.

Dissonance Theories of Attitude Change

Although a simple concept of attitude change through reinforcement finds support in much of the data that have been discussed, more complicated explanations have to be introduced in order to understand the results of some studies. For example, Rosenberg (1960) conducted a study in which subjects were hypnotized and then given a posthypnotic suggestion to become very favorable in their attitude toward such matters as Negroes moving into white neighborhoods, comprehensive Federal medical insurance, and other controversial issues. In other words, the subjects were commanded to feel differently from the way they had felt prior to hypnosis, but they were not reinforced for manifesting particular behaviors. The interesting result was that although the subjects did express different feelings toward the various issues, under posthypnotic suggestion, they also showed a tendency to change their beliefs with respect to these issues in a manner that tended to make them consistent with their newly acquired way of feeling.

The data derived from the Rosenberg study, like that from many other studies, does not fit the reinforcement model of learning. In order to understand such data, the concept is usually introduced that man cannot tolerate any inconsistencies that he perceives in himself, and also that he will change in a direction that tends to reduce internal inconsistency. Thus, a person who believes in an isolationist position on foreign policy and who feels strongly and positively about the isolationist position has almost certainly a system of beliefs consistent with the way he feels. He will tend to acquire further information consistent with the way he feels and consistent with the information previously acquired. He is likely to forget information presented to him that does support his beliefs and feelings.

This concept of man that emphasizes striving toward unity has had a long history and a substantial impact on education. The great Prussian educator Froebel was one of the first to view man in this light, though he derived this conception from the theological doctrine that the soul is characterized by unity. Psychologists later came to observe that people do not readily tolerate inconsistency within themselves and that many psychological mechanisms have the function of minimizing inconsistency in what the individual perceives in himself. Freud long ago observed that people commonly fail to recognize in themselves those characteristics that do not fit their own self concept. A wealthy man, who regards himself as a philanthropist, may fail to recognize a streak of stinginess in his day-to-day dealings. A man of generally kindly disposition may fail to recognize the numerous small hostile acts he directs toward his mother-in-law. Later research workers noted that a reader tends to assimilate information consistent with his own personal viewpoint much more readily than information that is inconsistent. The most ambitious attempt to bring together relevant knowledge in this area is found in a book by Festinger (1957) entitled *A Theory of Dissonance.*

Although the theme of Festinger's book is that man strives toward consistency, he prefers to use the term *dissonance* to that of *inconsistency.* The entire book is concerned with four propositions. First, the presence of dissonance is "psychologically uncomfortable" (p. 3) and, hence, dissonance motivates the person to reduce it. Second, the person actively avoids situations likely to increase any dissonance already present. Third, an inconsistent environment tends to continuously produce dissonance within the individual. Fourth, individuals differ in the extent to which they will tolerate dissonance within themselves. Festinger also suggests a number of mechanisms that commonly come into play when dissonance occurs. Some of these can be illustrated by an example. Suppose that a person, strongly opposed to the United States program of foreign aid, were exposed to a lecture in which the arguments in favor of foreign aid were clearly presented and evidence was given to support the arguments. Such a lecture presents a situation producing dissonance in our listener. He may reduce this dissonance in a number of different ways. First, he may pass off the arguments and evidence as "nonsense" and forget about the whole affair. Second, he may retain the information provided in the lecture but take the stand that it involves assumptions he does not accept. Third, he may change his attitude toward the foreign aid issue. The latter he is most likely to do when the arguments are only moderately different from his present position. If the arguments are highly inconsistent with his present position then he is more likely to behave in terms of the first two alternatives.

Many of the studies previously cited, which can be interpreted in terms of reinforcement theory, can also be interpreted in terms of dissonance theory. The type of study in which a person is placed in a situation, such as a debate, in which he makes statements inconsistent with his attitude but for which he is reinforced, can be readily understood in terms of dissonance theory. In the Scott study (1957), it will be recalled, the subjects whose debate speeches were reinforced with applause showed changed affective components of their attitudes. Dissonance theory would take the position that applause increased the acceptability of the position the subject had been required to take in his speech. Once the subject had accepted to some degree a new set of beliefs, then the affective component of his attitude would have to be changed in order to reduce the dissonance thus produced.

A systematic attempt to interpret research on attitude change in terms of dissonance theory can be found in a volume by Rosenberg and others (1960).

However, although cognitive dissonance theory has now been under investigation for nearly a decade, there is still no substantial evidence to support it. This does not mean that the theory should be rejected, because negative evidence is also lacking. Chapanis and Chapanis (1964), who reviewed many of the studies that have been cited as supporting dissonance theory, came to the conclusion that most of them involved technical difficulties and flaws that made it impossible to draw any valid conclusions from them.

Characteristics of the Social Situation in Relation to Attitude Change

Theory of dissonance identifies some of the internal conditions that result in attitude change, but it has very little to say about the external events over which control can be exercised and which, in turn, influence attitudes. There is certainly no question that some social situations are much more effective than others in changing attitudes and that some speakers influence their audience and others do not. Consideration should be given at this point to these social factors.

Group Pressures and Changes in Attitude

Some of the early research on social psychology demonstrated that the opinion of an individual might be modified by knowledge of the opinion of the group to which he is assigned. In a typical experiment of this kind, the opinion of individuals with respect to some issue is measured before and after they are exposed to the opinion of the group. There are many ways in which this experiment can be carried out. One technique is for each to express his opinion by checking on a list the statement that best corresponds to his belief. The statements of opinion are then taken to a back room where they are supposedly tallied. Each person in the group is then given a slip of paper on which is indicated the majority position of the group with respect to the issue. Each member then has a further opportunity to indicate his own position. In the typical experiment, the second assessment of the opinions of the individuals shows a drift in the direction of whatever was indicated to be the opinion of the group. Numerous experiments of this general character have been undertaken. Sometimes groups of stooges were used who expressed opinions uniformly different from those of the experimental subjects. At other times the information passed back to each member of the group concerning the opinion of the group was faked information. The results from such studies were quite clear, though there were individual differences in susceptibility to influence by the group.

The early research discussed in broad, general terms in the previous paragraph revealed an important phenomenon, but it did little to reveal the mechanisms involved in the modification of behavior. Neither did it contribute to our knowledge of how attitudes are learned. Nevertheless, it provided a foundation on which other research relevant to the understanding of the phenomena have been undertaken.

Raven (1959) found that individuals would alter their opinion to conform to the group norm even though that opinion was not to be divulged to the group. This indicates that the tendency to conform to the group norm is not just a result of a fear of immediate group disapproval. Of course, there is the possibility that such fear of disapproval in the past, and perhaps even actual disapproval, may have built up inhibitions that operate in further situations even when direct disapproval cannot be a consequence. However, other results reported by the same research worker indicate that, under some conditions, fear of rejection may provide a motive for attitude change.

The relationship of a person to a group may vary, as was brought out in an earlier chapter on social factors related to learning. This in turn may determine the influence the group may have on the modification of attitude. In a study by Siegel et al. (1957) the effect on attitudes of two different kinds of group membership was studied. This study draws a distinction between a person's membership group—the group to which he belongs—and his "reference" group, which is the one to which he aspires to belong. The Siegel study involved a group of college students who lived in dormitories during their freshman year. During this year the dormitory group constituted the membership group. These students also expected to be assigned to a different type of lodging during their sophomore year, and several different accommodations were available that differed considerably in status. The lodgings of highest status were those that were intermingled with the fraternities. The study showed that the attitudes of the students were influenced both by their membership in the freshman dormitory group and also by the housing group, or reference group, to which they aspired to belong.

Mere contact with a group does not necessarily change attitudes or make the person more accepting of the group. Campbell (1958) gave a questionnaire to 746 pupils in the seventh, ninth, and eleventh grades both before and after desegregation. He could find no change in the attitudes of white toward colored students as a result of their contact with colored students. He concluded that parental position was a much more important determinant of attitude toward the Negro than was actual experience with members of that group.

Finally, although attitudes and opinions may be both changed and maintained as a result of membership in appropriate groups, so too may attitudes be disintegrated by depriving the individual of his ordinary relationships to groups. A striking example of this was presented by the North Korean prisoner-of-war camps, where concerted efforts were made to change the attitudes of the United Nations prisoners. Biderman (1956) interviewed 220 of these prisoners on their return to the United States and attempted to discover the techniques that had been used. Those in charge of the prison camps did all they could to break down the usual group relationships. The prisoners were rewarded for spying on one another and giving away their comrades for minor breaches of discipline. Any man who assumed a leadership role and attempted to hold the group together was immediately separated from the group. Prisoners were often isolated prior to indoctrination sessions. Rewards and punishments were administered without any rhyme or reason. Anxiety and despair were deliberately cultivated. Incidents were staged to demonstrate to the prisoners that their captors were both omnipotent and omniscient. Trivial and meaningless regulations were rigidly enforced. The entire effort on the part of the captors was to place the prisoner in a world governed by wholly different rules from the one to which he was accustomed, and lacking in any of the supportive effects of group membership. Under such conditions, it appears that the attitudes the prisoner brings to the situation become readily modified, perhaps because there is little incentive for maintaining them in a situation in which they cease to have value as ego defenses.

Communication as a Means of Changing Attitudes

Many studies have been conducted that have demonstrated that attitudes can be changed by providing information with respect to the issues involved. The common procedure in the changing of attitudes by this method is to measure the affective component of attitude before and after providing selected items of information designed to produce change. The general trend of the results of these studies is that a communication is most effective in changing attitude when it represents a position not too different from that of the recipient. It has also been shown by Weiss

(1958) that the mere labeling of a communication by the recipient as extreme may sometimes inhibit the change that it might otherwise produce. Another related phenomenon was found by Hovland *et al.* (1957), who conducted a study of the effects of communications on changes in attitudes toward the use of alcohol as a beverage. In the latter study, those whose attitudes changed most as a result of the communication were those with moderate positions relatively close to that of the communication. Research also indicates that change in the structure of information given is not always reflected in a change in attitude, as one might expect it to be.

The conclusion that a person's attitude is most likely to be influenced if there is only a small discrepancy between his attitude and that of the communication holds up only when there are few social pressures operating. In a social situation in which the group exerts pressure on the individual, very different phenomena may be seen. Helson *et al.* (1956) conducted an experiment in which the attitude of a person toward war as an instrument for achieving goals was influenced through his participation in a social situation. The social situation was an artificial one. The subject was placed in a booth and was told that there were four others in other similar booths. He was also told that he could listen in to the interaction of these four people through a system of telephonic communication. The discussion that the subject heard about issues related to war was a recording on tape that permitted the standardization of the social situation. The degree of shift from private opinions was found to be a function of the discrepancy between the opinion held by the listener and the opinion expressed by the four people whose communication could be heard through the telephonic system. The greater the discrepancy, the greater the shift in attitude.

Helson *et al.* account for the results of their experiment by suggesting that attitudes are not generally firmly anchored phenomena, and hence the immediate social situation provides anchorage. Certainly there are powerful motives for conforming to the group in such matters, for the penalties for not conforming often involve rejection and ridicule.

A related problem in providing communications designed to change attitudes is whether such a communication should begin by taking a position close to that of the person whose attitude is to be changed and then slowly move away from that position in the direction of the change to be made, or whether the initial position of the communicator should diverge greatly from that to be changed. The question is important from the point of view of the teacher. An attempt to provide an answer to this question is found in a research by Harvey and Rutherford (1958). Since their research represents an indirect attack on the problem, some explanation of their procedure is necessary. Their basic technique involved what is known as the autokinetic effect. The phenomenon is illustrated by the projection of a small spot of light onto the wall of a darkened room. When this spot of light is observed, it *may* appear to move, and different observers will report different amounts of movement. The amount of movement reported is altered by suggestion and by group pressure. A person in a group of people who state that they see the light move one to two feet is likely to report a similar movement, and if the group reports a movement of only a few inches, then the observer is likely to report a movement of only a few inches. By repeated exposure to such a situation, a person may develop a *strong* concept of how much movement takes place. Fewer exposures will produce a *weaker* concept. Once such a concept has been formed, it may be changed either by gradual degrees through exposure to groups that make gradually more divergent judgments concerning the amount of movement, or by exposure to groups that, from the start, show markedly divergent judgments from the person involved.

The results of the experiment generally do *not* favor the approach to attitude change whereby the communicator begins with a position similar to that of the person whose attitude is to be changed and then gradually shifts. Within the limits of the experiment, the best approach required that the communicator take a position divergent from that of the person whose attitude was to be changed. This was true with both weak and strong attitudes. However, the special nature of the experimental situation limits the generalizations that can be made from it. The experiment needs to be repeated in different contexts. At this time the results can be considered only suggestive.

Peak and Morrison (1958) conducted a study on the relationship of attitude to information. The study incorporates an important distinction between "information known" and "information accepted." Information known, with respect to an issue, is information of which the person is aware but does not know whether it is true or relevant. Information accepted is information the person accepts and, presumably, considers to be true. These two classes of information bear different relationships to attitudes. In a group on which no effort had been made to influence attitudes (control group), the amount of information accepted was related to attitude position—i.e., those most in favor of segregation of the Negro indicated more accepted information with respect to this position than those who assumed the opposite position. On the other hand, the number of items known is unrelated to the attitude position of the person involved. This means that the relationship of knowledge, or the cognitive component of attitude, to other aspects is complex. This study also revealed a complicated relationship between attitude position, the amount of information known and accepted related to the segregation issue, and scores on the F-scale (a device designed to measure authoritarian trends in personality). The relationship of these three variables was of such a complicated nature that it cannot be described here briefly.

Osgood and Tannenbaum (1955) have attempted to formulate a theory to describe what happens when a listener is exposed to a speaker expounding a particular point of view. The core concept of the theory is that when a listener is exposed to a speaker propounding a proposition, the listener comes under pressure to change his attitude to conform to that of the speaker and the proposition. The amount of change depends on many factors, including the congruity of the speaker and the point of view he is propounding. If the speaker's point of view is inconsistent with what is known about his other beliefs, then little attitude change may be expected on the part of the listener. Thus, a speaker who unexpectedly embraces an unpopular cause is unlikely to change the attitudes of listeners either with respect to himself or with respect to his cause. A Southern congressman, up for re-election, who made a speech favoring integration to a Southern white audience would be very unlikely to gain popularity either for himself or his cause. The successful leader typically stands as a champion of causes that the public is already willing to accept.

Berlo and Gulley (1957) attempted to conduct an experimental study to test the hypothesis of Osgood and Tannenbaum. From a knowledge of the attitudes of subjects prior to exposure to speakers, and from a knowledge of the proposition advocated by the speakers as well as the expected attitudinal position of the speakers, predictions were made of the expected attitude changes of the listeners. The predictions thus made on the basis of theory were found to be far more accurate than would be expected on the basis of chance.

In another study of Tannenbaum (1956), a more elaborate test was made of the relationship of attitude toward source and the amount of attitude shift produced by a communication from the source. The finding was that the more the source was favorably regarded, the greater was the shift in attitude in a favorable direction. The more the source was unfavorably regarded, the greater was the shift in attitude in an unfavorable direction. This statement of the findings is probably a gross oversimplification of what is occurring. There is some evidence that there is an interaction of a complicated kind between the attitude toward the source and the attitude toward the object. Also, a communication may change attitude toward the source as well as attitude toward the object.

Although many studies have demonstrated that *attitude toward the communicator* is a vital condition for attitude change, the concept is a very vague one. No major attempt has been made to discover the components of this condition. One that has been investigated is the prestige of the communicator. In a study by Scollon (1957), films designed to change attitudes were shown with commentators who varied from one another in prestige. One conclusion from the study was that some of the films using a prestigeful commentator produced significantly more attitude change than the same films when they were anonymously narrated. The more clearly the prestige of the narrator was defined, the more the attitudes were changed. In addition, the closer the prestige communicator was related to the audience group, the greater the change in attitudes produced. The group consisted of Army basic trainees whose attitude toward field rations was to be changed by indoctrination with movies. The prestige figure was a Korean War veteran, a figure obviously related to the group whose attitude was to be changed.

Perceptual research discussed in the chapter on the subject has brought out evidence that what is observed or attended to in the environment is partly a product of personality structure. Research in the specific area of attitudes indicates that personality structure may determine, to some extent, what is learned.

Jones and Kohler (1958) conducted experiments to test the following hypotheses:

1. Prosegregation subjects learn plausible prosegregation and implausible antisegregation statements with less difficulty than they learn plausible antisegregation statements and implausible prosegregation statements.

2. The reverse is true for antisegregation subjects.

3. Those with neutral or intermediate beliefs learn all types of statements equally well.

The data from the experiments was consistent with these hypotheses, and particularly striking in the case of the second experiment.

Jones and Kohler interpret the results of their experiments in terms of the theory that behavior tends to promote consistency of attitude or belief. Thus, a person is inhibited in the learning of statements that run counter to his beliefs, because this inhibition protects his beliefs. The principle, for which there appears to be evidence from many sources, has important educational implications, one of which is that there are many occasions when it is important for a pupil to keep an open mind. Once a position has been taken and an attitude begins to form, any subsequent change may be difficult to produce. Attitudes once formed call forth psychological mechanisms that prevent them from being changed. However, not all research in this area produces results that are equally clear. Thus, Carlson (1956) found that a particular attitude may not necessarily influence what related information is retained from a relevant communication, but sometimes it may.

What are the implications of this body of research for education? Clearly this is an area of emerging knowledge, but many of the discoveries are not yet so definite that straightforward application is possible. The fact that a communication cannot be relied on to change attitudes is an important outcome. Simple communication sometimes changes attitude and sometimes does not, depending on the presence or absence of other circumstances.

Another important finding is the crucial importance of the status of the person making the communication, or the attitude of the person toward the communicator. Whether teachers have the necessary prestige or status or are regarded with sufficient favor by pupils to be communicators with high potential for changing the attitudes of pupils is an unanswered question. One may, perhaps, hazard the guess that most teachers do have this potential. Teacher training may have little capability to produce in teachers those personal characteristics that enable them to influence the attitudes of pupils.

A serious problem for the educator is raised by the discovery that what is learned depends, to some degree, on the attitudes of the learner. An open mind is an abstraction that probably does not exist. Information-learning processes and cognitive processes are selective in their operations and result in the conservation of current attitudes. This tendency to preserve the present system of beliefs and opinions and to defend them by ignoring information that runs counter to them is a serious impediment to education, especially since the child comes to school with all kinds of attitudes that he has already formed in his neighborhood and in his home. When undesirable attitudes have already been formed in out-of-school situations, the task of the school in changing such attitudes is great.

The school can be expected to function most effectively in the development of attitudes in those areas in which attitudes have not already been formed. Under such conditions, attitude formation can be expected to occur readily, and the results may be expected to have considerable permanence.

Ego Defense Mechanisms and Resistance to Attitude Change

Sarnoff and Katz (1954) have advanced the point of view that attitudes may function as protectors of the ego of the individual. Resistance to attitude change may arise from the possibility that a change would deprive the individual of an important defense mechanism. Thus, a person may have anti-Negro attitudes because they enable him to feel superior to at least a section of the community and help to compensate for feelings of inadequacy. If his negative attitude toward the Negro were to be destroyed, he would then be deprived of some of the foundation on which his feelings of adequacy were based. In order to prevent such a mishap, his attitude is likely to be rigidly maintained.

A paper by Katz *et al.* (1957) presents an experiment designed to test the hypothesis that the giving of insight into defense mechanisms will produce more attitude change in medium ego-defensive persons than in high and low ego-defensive persons. The low ego-defensive person is not likely to change his attitudes by this procedure since his attitudes are not primarily defense mechanisms. The high ego-defensive person, on the other hand, is so defensive and has such a need to maintain his attitudes as defense mechanisms that he is unlikely to be influenced by procedures designed to provide personal insight. The procedure involved in this study was to measure attitude toward the Negro before and after exposure to experiences designed to provide insight into the mechanisms of defensiveness and repression. The sessions were part of a regularly scheduled college course. The results of this experiment were consistent with the hypothesis: The middle ego-defensive group showed the greatest attitude change. In this study, ego defensiveness was measured by means of the F-scale designed to measure authoritarian trends in personality, and also a scale from the Minnesota Multiphasic Personality Inventory designed to measure paranoid trends.

Results similar to those reported in the latter study were found in a research by Irvine (1956), who reported that individuals moderately defensive on the F-scale were more likely to change in attitude as a result of reaching appropriate materials than those who were high or low in defensiveness.

In another study by Katz *et al.*, which also involved the changing of attitudes toward the Negro, the research workers found that the development of insight into self was a more important condition for attitude change than was the providing of information selected to influence the attitude. This is an important finding and reflects the basically irrational nature of attitudes.

Culbertson (1955) found that role playing was a powerful technique for changing of attitudes, which again suggests that behavior related to a new attitude will result in some change of the underlying attitude so as to make it consistent with the behavior.

Authoritarian personalities, as measured by the F-scale, may show modifiability of attitudes under certain conditions. Wagman (1955) hypothesized and found some evidence for the idea that authoritarian personalities would show the greatest modifiability of attitudes under authoritarian pressure, and least when a nonauthoritarian information-giving approach was employed. In this case the procedure to produce attitude change involved a class in general psychology that was conducted in two different ways, to correspond to the two different conditions of the experiment.

A common ego defense that may sometimes make a course of action consistent with existing attitudes is the attaching of a label to a situation. A parent who chastises a child and then has guilt feelings may partly resolve his own anxieties by saying that it was all for the good of the child. Several studies have been undertaken that show that the labeling of a situation in this way may alter behavior with respect to it. DiVesta and Bossart (1958) showed that the labeling of a decision as "economic" or "ethical" made a difference in the attitudes reflected in relation to it. In DiVesta and Bossart's study a man is described as living in a low-cost housing development, where he can live so long as his annual income is less than $2,900. In order to send a son through college, he considers taking on another job to bring in additional income. However, if he undertook the additional job, he would be required to tell the housing authority, and he would have to move to a more expensive residence, the increased rent of which would absorb the additional income. A situation such as this can be labeled as an economic problem, or it can be labeled as primarily an ethical problem. If this problem is presented to a person as an economic problem, he is likely to suggest that the man should not tell the housing authority: but if the problem is presented as an ethical one, he is more likely to propose that the man report his changed financial status.

McClintock (1958) presented his subjects with an interesting situation involving conflict of motives, and demonstrated that the label applied to the situation influenced the judgments of subjects concerning how they should act in this situation. McClintock showed that the label applied made a difference to the course of action recommended by subjects.

I. L. Janis has conducted a series of researches to determine the extent to which the attitudes of a person are generally modifiable or generally resistant to change. In one of the later articles in this series (Janis and Field, 1956) considerable evidence is presented that there is a general factor of persuadability—that is, over the whole range of attitudes there is a tendency for the attitudes of a person to be modifiable by persuasion or to be rigid and uninfluenced by persuasion. The nature of the general persuadability factor involved is not clear. It could be, at least partly, a general ego-defensiveness factor. It could also represent a submissiveness factor. The latter hypothesis is suggested by a study conducted by Helson et al. (1956), in which it was found that those who showed the greatest amount of shift and also the most frequent shifts, as a result of knowing the opinion of a membership group, were individuals shown to have a high degree of submissiveness, as measured by the Allport Ascendancy-Submission Scale.

The upshot of this discussion is that just as cognitive learning does not take place with equal facility in all individuals, so too does the learning of attitudes present individual differences. However, in the two cases the variables involved are different. In the case of cognitive learning, the individual differences are mainly attributable to differences in the ability to perform certain mediating processes. In the case of attitudes, there are conditions of the organism that result in resistance to change. Ego defense appears to be the main mechanism that interferes with the learning process of attitude modification, but there may be others that have not been identified at this time. Such mechanisms may be called into play or inhibited by labeling the attitude-learning situation in some appropriate way.

Little is known at this time concerning the extent to which children of different ages manifest ego-defense mechanisms that interfere with the education of attitudes. Until further knowledge is available, attitude education must remain relatively inefficient.

An Overview: Attitude Formation and Change as a Learning Problem

Few studies of attitude have been undertaken as studies of learning phenomena. Most of the research undertaken represents the efforts of social psychologists to understand social phenomena. Interest in attitudes as the products of learning represents a new emphasis in this research field, though a few initial studies were made over a quarter of a century earlier. The greater emphasis on attitude change than on attitude formation in contemporary research also reflects the fact that research workers as well as teachers are confronted with subjects in whom attitudes have already been formed, and both experimenters and educators have more opportunity for changing these attitudes than for forming entirely new attitudes in areas in which none exist. The learning problem that has been studied is, then, much more similar to the problem of modifying a skill already acquired than it is to the problem of developing a skill from its initial stages. Some problems of attitude change are also more closely related to the problem of extinction than they are to the problem of acquisition.

A primary mechanism involved in the initial formation of attitudes is probably positive reinforcement. This would account well for the fact that parents appear to be the prime determiners of attitudes (at least there is a high relationship between the measured attitudes of parents and the measured attitudes of their children). Daily approval and disapproval, much of it of a very mild character, might well result over a period of years in firmly established attitudes. Although positive reinforcements probably play an important part, anxiety reduction may also function in the formative stages. Expression of attitudes contrary to those of the other members of the family group might well arouse anxiety. Hence, the expression of accepted attitudes may have anxiety-avoiding and anxiety-reducing effects.

Once the child has acquired tendencies to imitate, this may become a factor involved in the acquisition of attitudes. The tendency for attitudes to be modified to conform to those of a group could be explained in terms of imitative tendencies, and so too can be the tendency to accept attitudes expressed by authority figures. One cannot, of course, rule out entirely the operation of rational processes, as when a person carefully considers an argument and decides to change his attitude. However, most research has little to say about rational reasoning processes in this respect, and is based on the assumption that attitude formation and change is largely an irrational process.

Presumably, attitude responses show generalization to new stimuli just like any other responses. Attitude toward a particular political group, say Communists, could well generalize to socialists and liberal democrats, and might come to elicit the same responses. This fits well with common observation, and could explain the irrationality of many of the attitudes that all persons manifest. In the same way, the responses associated with attitudes toward a particular member of a particular group, say a Negro, might well generalize not only to all other members of the same group, but also to groups who showed even a remote relationship of color. Such generalization could well explain many irrational likes, dislikes, and preferences.

Ego-defense mechanisms are ill understood with reference to their role in learning. One may hypothesize that ego-defense mechanisms operate to reduce anxiety. Hence, when an attitude is modified as an ego-defense mechanism, the new attitude is learned through the anxiety reduction that occurs. This suggestion is highly speculative and needs to be studied.

Although the learner strives for unity within his system of attitudes and cognitive structures, since inconsistency produces anxiety, there is still some possibility for inconsistent structures to exist within the same person and at the same time. When this happens, the phenomenon of compartmentalization is generally found. The most commonly cited case of this phenomenon is that of a man who subscribes to orthodox religious values each Sunday, but who then casts them to the winds each Monday in order to pursue his business. Of course, there is no implication here that the majority of businessmen are unethical. It is just that there are some who hold different ethical standards on Sunday than they hold on other days of the week. They can do this because they have two different sets of ethical standards linked to different action systems. Such an inconsistency may exist without troubling the individual, but in some cases it may lead to serious conflict. The latter occurs when the separation between the compartments is broken down in some way.

Compartmentalization is an important ego-defense mechanism of which clinicians have been aware for a long time. The nearest learning situation that has been studied is the formation of systems of inconsistent skills tied to different situations, yet not interfering with one another. A person who learns to drive cars both with automatic shifts and with standard shifts may have these separate skills so well compartmentalized that they always occur on appropriate occasions and do not interfere one with another. Effective compartmentalization of these skills occurs if they are effectively tied to different stimuli. Perhaps the effective compartmentalization of attitudes also depends on the two sets of attitudes being effectively tied to different stimuli.

Summary

1. Attitudes evolve from approach and avoidance tendencies. Some of these approach and avoidance responses become internalized as the child grows. Attitudes toward particular objects and ideas may involve not only acceptance or rejection but also affective elements, or feeling elements.

2. Although values involve broad goals of life, attitudes are much more specific elements in the personality. Values may guide the selection of the goals of life, but attitudes may influence the selection of particular means for achieving the goals.

3. The concept of attitude has often been considered as unsatisfactory. Certainly, an attitude is a complex phenomenon and has a number of separate and distinct components.

4. One component of attitude is the affective component. In everyday language this component represents how the individual *feels* about an idea or object. Such feelings are often quite irrational.

5. Another component is the cognitive component, which involves the structure of knowledge related to the attitude. Some attitudes have an important intellectual component; others involve little more than the affective component.

6. Still an additional component of attitude is that represented by action systems. Some attitudes may have no action systems related to

them; but others, when aroused, lead to strong and immediate action. Little is known at this time about ways of developing attitudes so that they will have a strong action component, yet education cannot be satisfied with the development of attitudes that never lead to action. The problem of developing attitude systems with strong action components is partly a problem of transfer of training.

7. Attitudes are generally considered to be intervening variables that in many situations must be measured before behavior can be predicted. However, the complex nature of attitudes means that they represent complex systems of variables. Simple verbal-attitude scales, of the type that have been widely used for research, represent a gross oversimplification of the structure of attitudes.

8. Early studies of the effects of educational and other experiences on attitudes, as measured by verbal scales, demonstrated that changes could be fairly readily produced. Such studies did little to indicate the nature of the process involved in attitude change. Studies of the college curriculum in relation to attitude change have demonstrated that, under some circumstances, exposure to college may result in attitude change. An overview of college graduates shows that they are characterized by certain attitudes that distinguish them from other groups, even though they manifest wide individual differences.

9. In recent years a number of studies have been undertaken to discover the learning processes involved in attitude formation and attitude change. A common pattern for these studies is to arrange a situation in which a particular attitude is expressed and then reinforced to determine whether reinforcement-learning theory can be applied to this area.

10. Reinforcement conceptions of learning are limited in the understanding they provide of attitude change. Dissonance theory has been introduced to help account for some of the phenomena observed in studies of attitude change. According to this theory, the internal behaviors of the individual are such that dissonant or inconsistent elements tend to be eliminated and the individual is protected from elements in the environment that might produce dissonance.

11. Considerable evidence has been accumulated to demonstrate that persons tend to modify their attitudes to conform to those of the group with which they are identified. Many factors enter into this relationship, and it is not simply a matter of fear of rejection or desire for acceptance by the group.

12. Education is commonly based on the assumption that attitudes can be changed by communications, such as are provided by lectures and printed materials. Considerable research has been undertaken to test this hypothesis. These studies have generally produced positive results, but the effectiveness of a communication in building or changing attitudes

depends on a multiplicity of factors. The extent to which the attitude of the communicator differs from that of the person to whom the communication is made is an important factor in determining the amount of change to be expected.

13. Although research generally favors a technique of attitude change in which the communication represents a position slightly different from that of the receiver, it does not favor a technique in which the communicator begins by taking the *same* position as that of the receiver and then shifts away from that position. Generalization from the latter research must be treated with caution, since it was based on an experimental situation substantially different from that generally involved in attitude change.

14. Models that attempt to describe the changes in attitude that occur as a result of a communication generally involve at least two factors. One of these is attitude toward the source, and the other is attitude toward the particular object involved. An additional factor is the attitude expressed by the communication.

15. A relationship exists between the information acquired and the attitudes of the person acquiring the information. In general, information consistent with a person's attitudes is more readily acquired than inconsistent information.

16. Attitudes have an important relationship to ego-defense mechanisms, and may actually function as ego-defense mechanisms themselves. Considerable research has been undertaken in which an attempt has been made to produce conditions favorable to attitude change by breaking down the defense mechanisms that are operating and preventing change. The results indicate that ego-defense mechanisms are deeply involved in attitudes, and that a planned program of attitude change must take this relationship into account. The defensiveness with which a person accepts or rejects a communication may be altered by the label attached to it. Related to this whole problem is the finding that some people are more persuadable than others, regardless of what may be the issue involved.

14

Perceptual and Phenomenological Approaches to Learning

ERCEPTUAL processes are mediating processes within the individual about which he is sometimes able to give reports. An external stimulus (S) produces an internal trace (s), which may last for several seconds. Several lines of evidence point to the existence of such a trace. When food is placed before an animal and is then covered up, the animal typically continues to respond as though the food were still there. There is some physiological evidence that after a significant stimulus is removed that the central nervous system continues to remain in a state of excitation. So far, one can represent what has happened by the following simple diagram:

$$S \longrightarrow s$$

However, this represents only the first stage of a typical train of events. The hunter who has a fleeting glance of a moving animal may, as he thinks back over what he has seen, ask himself, "Was it a deer?" Such internal behavior following the occurrence of a stimulus and its trace is generally represented by the symbol (r). These internal responses may then be followed by some readily observable response (R), such as when the hunter turns to his companion and says, "I think I saw a deer." This sequence of events may be represented in the following way:

$$S \longrightarrow s \longrightarrow r \longrightarrow R$$

The traditional approach to the study of (s) and (r) has been through asking a person to report what is going on inside himself, but this approach has been so unsatisfactory and has yielded so little knowledge that other methods of exploring these internal phenomena have had to be evolved. Psychologists have not readily found alternative avenues to the study of sensory processes, which is why the study of aspects of perception related to learning has been so much slower in developing than the study of aspects of response. The change in emphasis from merely asking the person what is going on inside of him to an emphasis on experimental procedures that help to make such inferences has also resulted in a change in the kind of theory that has evolved. Studies based on personal reports of internal happenings tended to produce theories based on personal experience; but newer experimental approaches have tended to draw more from physiology in their theoretical developments. The earlier chapter on the information-handling processes in the nervous system gave some indication of the impact that physiologists have had on our present understanding of certain elementary aspects of perception. This chapter will be concerned with some of the more complex aspects of information-handling processes in relation to learning.

The research on learning that has been discussed up to this point has emphasized response processes and procedures related to the control of responses by reinforcement. Now we will consider the study of perception, which emphasizes the input end of the learning process (S and s). It includes studies of how the organism acquires information about the world around it and the conditions that facilitate and interfere with the acquisition of information. It also investigates the internal utilization of information by the organism and the storage of this information. Perceptual theory has much to contribute to the understanding of learning, for it indicates ways in which the acquisition of skills and knowledge can be facilitated by controlling the information supplied and the form in which it is supplied.

Associationism

The earliest theories of learning were perceptual theories. They were concerned with the way in which perceived objects or events became associated with one another, and from this point it was easy to extend the theory to cover the learning of relationships among ideas.

Books on learning still make extensive reference to learning by association, an approach that is somewhat different from any that have been presented up to this point in this book. The word *association* has had a long history of over two thousand years in psychology and philosophy, and is still retained in the discussion of learning because it has become a part of the layman's vocabulary with which he discusses problems of learning. The doctrine of association was first drawn up in a systematic form by Aristotle, who used it as a basis for describing mental life. According to Aristotle, ideas are somehow connected in the mind. Thus, when a person has forgotten the name of an acquaintance, he may begin by saying to himself, "I seem to remember his name was something like Field." Then he begins to think of names that sound like *field*, or are *associated* with it. *Farmer* comes to mind, but is rejected. Then he tries names that are similar in sound, such as *Wield, Neild, Neil,* and so forth. When this does not work, he begins to think of words that are closely associated with the first one. He thinks of *Orchard,* and immediately knows that he has found the right name. Aristotle placed great emphasis on the process of searching for related ideas as a central part of the process of recall. He believed that association between ideas was not an arbitrary matter, but followed definite laws, which have come to be known as the laws of association. Of course, most psychologists would not agree that the process of thinking goes on in this way at all, but Aristotle considered that this was a reasonable description of how his own mind worked and assumed that the minds of everybody else worked in much the same way.

Aristotle also observed that some ideas became associated with other ideas because of the existence of certain conditions. He observed, for example, that objects and events became associated with one another because they occurred together. This became a law of association. We may associate grapefruit with the breakfast table because in our house grapefruit is served primarily at breakfast. Sometimes this is referred to as association by contiguity. Another of the laws of association was that events or objects became associated with one another because they were similar. One remembers the features of a house in which a friend lives because it is similar to one's own. A third of these laws was the law of association by contrast. We remember the lady in the unusual dress because she was so different from the others at the party, and we also associate her with the particular party.

For nearly two thousand years, philosophers tried to revise the laws of association to make them, as far as possible, the laws of thinking. So impressed were some philosophers with this possibility that one of them, David Hume, who lived about 200 years ago, believed that the laws of association had the same importance for psychology that the law of gravitation has for physics. Other laws, subsidiary to those that Aristotle had stated, were slowly added. One of these, for example, was the law of frequency, which stated that two ideas tend to become more strongly associated the more frequently they have been aroused together. Then vividness was introduced as a factor to account for the strong association of some ideas that are associated together only once.

The theory of association of ideas provided some limited possibilities for making predictions that could be verified. Certainly, a child who is learning to read must associate the sight of the word with the sound a sufficient number of times before the connection will become firmly established. The capacity of the theory to make this and other predictions is one reason why it survived. Some data went against the theory, as, for example, the fact that sometimes ideas were aroused together that had not apparently occurred together previously. However, theories are rarely upset by the existence of facts that run counter to them. Theories are abandoned only because they are replaced by better theories that take into account more facts and make better predictions than the theories they displace.

The growth of experimental science in the nineteenth century had its impact on thought related to psychological problems, as it has on thought in all other areas. Fechner, an experimental physicist who became impressed with psychological factors in observation, began to conduct experiments on the process of making simple judgments. The associationist approach to problems of learning was given an experimental foundation by Hermann Ebbinghaus, who began a series of studies that have had considerable influence on teaching procedures. Consider, for example, the fact pointed out by Ebbinghaus that, in learning, effort should be spent on the building of useful associations and not on associations that must later be broken down. Let us consider this point further in order to indicate some of the useful products of associationistic approaches.

Considerable energy is often expended, during learning, in building wrong associations, which later must be broken down. A young child is trying to learn "Mary had a little lamb," and repeats the first line over and over to himself. What he is doing is more than learning the correct sequence of words. Each time he reaches the word "lamb," he goes back to the start of the line again and says the word "Mary." In doing this, he is building an association between the last word in the line and the first word, an association that may often be disastrous when the time comes to recite. When the latter occasion occurs, he recites the first line and then, after a brief hesitation, goes back and recites the same line again, because this is what he learned to do. The last word of the first line has to become associated with the first word of the *second* line if he is to go through the poem, and he may have failed to build this latter association.

In learning by parts, many associations are built that later have to be broken down. In addition, the individual, having learned each part, must then learn to connect the parts. Thus, any advantage that the learning-by-part system might provide is canceled by these other learning activities that have to go on in order that the individual may be able finally to produce a smooth performance. The part method of learning, when it is found to be inferior, owes its inferiority very largely to the unnecessary associations that are built up by the method and which later have to be replaced by other associations connecting the parts.

During the nineteenth century, the theory of association found a scientific ally in the science of physiology which was then emerging. The nervous system was found to consist of cells and long connecting fibers down which impulses were transmitted. All this fitted well the associationist doctrine. Could not the cells correspond to ideas, and the connecting fibers to associations with them? History was to show that the analogy was actually a poor one, and that no such simple relationship could possibly exist.

The emergence of physiology as a science had another important influence on the development of psychology, which resulted in the development of a new kind of associationism. The study of the structure and function of the nervous system soon led to the understanding that some nerves conducted information into the central system, and others transmitted impulses that led to responses. Mental life appeared to be related to the flow of inputs and outputs. According to this conception of the behavior, the main associations developed were those between stimuli and responses rather than between responses and responses, such as are represented by one set of ideas and another set of ideas. In order to distinguish this new concept from that of classical associationism, the term *connectionism* was coined to effectively describe a learning theory in which learning involved the establishment of connections between stimuli and responses.

The development of the new objective science of psychology during the period following World War I inevitably placed emphasis on those aspects of behavior that were observable, and particularly on those that were easily observed—namely, muscular movement and speech. Inner processes, and especially those related to perception, became neglected because of the difficulty of linking them to observable events. A few psychologists during this period did continue to investigate perceptual processes, but only in the last two decades has this work produced techniques that have permitted a genuine scientific approach to problems involving perception.

Research on word association has recently taken on a new lease of life. The vigor of the field is well exemplified by a book by Goss and Nodine (1965) which places heavy emphasis on research related to the role of meaningfulness in verbal learning.

Perception and Information Processing

Theory of perception has a particularly important impact on education, in that the area is concerned with those processes by which the organism obtains information about its environment. The central characteristic of all perception is that it involves some input of information from the environment; indeed, one cannot talk of a perceptual process except insofar as there is some input of information from the external world.

Evidence indicates that the human has only a limited capacity for processing and utilizing information from the environment. At least, the environment provides sources of information vastly greater than the higher centers of the nervous system are able to process. In the first place, the sense organs receive a limited sample of information from the external world; but the sample provided through the sense organs must be whittled down to quantities that the higher centers are able to utilize. The organism is not arbitrary in the information that it receives, but rather it is highly selective. This is the only way that it can develop a working relationship with the environment.

Three general aspects of the information-handling aspects of perception must now be considered; these are the selective nature of the intake process, the compression of information, and the information structuring itself that results in the full development of a meaningful perception.

The Selection of Information Sources

Before the turn of the present century, psychologists had noted that perception was preceded by certain preparatory activities that facilitated the occurrence of the anticipated perception. A person looking for a lost object in the house moves around and scans the various areas where the object might be. The person waiting the arrival of a plane at an airport strains his eyes toward the horizon to catch the first glimpse of the incoming aircraft. These preparatory activities consist, at least partly, of muscular adjustments that facilitate the perception that is anticipated. Other activities within the nervous system may also be involved. Similar behaviors and adjustments appear to take place without any awareness on the part of the person, and result in a sensitivity to perceive certain objects and events rather than others. These conditions that favor some perceptions over others are known as *sets*. The presence of a set is demonstrated by a heightened tendency to perceive certain objects or events, an increased speed with which these are perceived, or by an added vividness of the perception itself.

What are referred to here as *sets* were referred to by earlier writers as *determining tendencies*. Some modern writers, such as Solley and Murphy (1960), refer to them as *expectancies*. The meaning of all three of these terms is approximately the same; but the term *set* will be used here.

The phenomena that are frequently discussed under the heading of "attention" are manifestations of the phenomenon of set. Teachers generally agree that a child has to attend to his work, and perhaps also to the teacher, if he is to learn effectively; and the attention process represents the same readiness to perceive to which the term *set* is applied. The process of a child attending to his work is clearly one that involves such muscular adjustments as the focusing and direction of his eyes, as well as certain processes within his nervous system that facilitate the assimilation of information transmitted through his senses.

Sets are generally classified into the two broad categories of *humoral* and *neural*. A humoral set is one that arises as a consequence of a chemical change in the body. The teenager who suddenly comes to notice and attend to members of the opposite sex is manifesting the effects of a humoral set resulting from the generation of sex hormones within the body. The thirsty traveler in the wilds is sensitive to the slightest sound that might indicate the flow of water. Neural sets, on the other hand, are more of an immediate product of events within the nervous system. Of course, humoral sets are a product of events in the nervous system; but the primary activators of the sets are chemical constituents of the body fluids. In the case of neural sets, the activating conditions lie within the nervous system and may be the product either of previous conditions or of the way in which the nervous system is built in the particular species. A connoisseur of old violins will catch sight of an instrument in a window across the street, even though his companion can hardly see it. This is clearly a learned set. But some sets may be a product of the particular way in which the nervous system of the particular species tends to be built. In species that are social by nature, the tendency is for one member of the species to pay attention to other members of the same species, regardless of sex. Species that lack such social tendencies may attend only to members of the opposite sex, and attention may be confined to certain times in their life cycles.

Since a set represents a readiness to attend to objects or events of a certain class, a knowledge of the conditions that produce them has important implications for educators. Certainly, some teachers claim that some children lack a disposition to attend to matters presented through the school curriculum. A knowledge of some of the factors that influence disposition to attend could be an important step toward solving the educational problems these children represent.

Research on factors that facilitate perception is extensive, but the results are not as clear-cut as one might hope them to be. A thorough analysis of the results has been made by Allport (1955), whose analysis and conclusions will be followed here. A brief discussion of the questions asked and the answers provided by empirical studies follows:

To what extent do physiological needs determine what is perceived? In a well-known investigation by Levine, Chein, and Murphy (1942), subjects who had been deprived of food for various lengths of time were presented with pictures and asked to give associations with the pictures.

As deprivation of food increased to several hours, there was an increase in the number of associations related to food; but this was followed by a decline as deprivation was prolonged further. On the other hand, when Guetzkow and Baldwin (1950–51) presented subjects with Rorschach cards after various periods of food deprivation, no change was found in the number of food responses. Some research indicates that complex functions related to the interpretation of the environment are influenced by need. Atkinson and McClelland (1948) found that the interpretation that subjects gave to pictures depended on the length of time they had been deprived; as hunger increased, the stories told about the pictures showed increases in the frequency of themes related to food deprivation. The picture that best differentiated the most hungry from the least hungry subjects, in terms of the interpretation given, was one that showed food, but in an unstructured relationship to a person. The weight of the evidence seems to be in the direction of answering the question with a qualified yes. Just why the effect is sometimes evident and sometimes not is far from clear. How far one can generalize to physiological needs other than hunger is also not clear. One certainly suspects that activity of the sex glands has much to do with the tendency of boys and girls in adolescence to perceive and to pay attention to members of the opposite sex. Every horseback rider knows that a stallion becomes difficult to control in the presence of a mare, but a gelding will pass by a mare without even pricking up its ears.

If particular objects have been associated with reward or punishment, does this influence the later perception of those objects? This is also a problem about which there has been a long history of research. The classic investigation was conducted by Schafer and Murphy (1943); it used a complex design in which ambiguous figures were presented. Those figures that were associated with reward were more readily recognized in later parts of the experiment. However, when the experiment was repeated by Rock and Fleck (1950), negative results were found. Nevertheless, when Smith and Hochberg (1954) repeated the essential design of the Schafer and Murphy experiment, the punishing effect of a shock was found to decrease the tendency to perceive the figure with which it was associated, a finding that supported the conclusions of the original experiment. In a later experiment by Rigby and Rigby (1952), children were positively reinforced with candy when certain capital letters turned up in a game. When other letters turned up, the children were negatively reinforced by the taking away of candy. The letters that had been positively reinforced were later shown to be more easily recognized on short exposure (with a device known as a tachistoscope) than letters that had either not been reinforced or had been negatively reinforced. In another experiment by Proshansky and Murphy (1942), rewards and punishments were shown to influence the judgments made of the length of lines. In this experiment, long lines were associated with reward and short lines with punishment. The result was a tendency for the subjects to over-estimate the length of lines in later situations in which there was neither reward nor punishment. The results of research generally point in the direction that events or objects associated with reward tend to be more readily perceived than those that have not been thus associated.

The effects of punishment are not so clear. Solley and Murphy (1960), who have reviewed the research on the effect of punishment on the sensitivity of a subject to a stimulus, point out that the studies involve two kinds of experimental situations. In the one situation, the stimulus is a signal that a punishment is to occur from which there is no escape. In the other situation, the stimulus is a signal that punishment will occur unless the subject takes some appropriate action. In the first situation, no escape is possible; but in the other, the attentive subject can escape the incidence of the aversive stimulus. In these two situations the presence of an aversive stimulus has entirely different effects on perception. If the subject can escape, then the effect of the aversive stimulus is to heighten the sensitivity of the subject to the stimulus, which is more readily perceived. If, on the contrary, the stimulus is a signal for the occurrence of an aversive stimulus from which there is no escape, then the sensitivity of the subject is decreased. This interpretation of available studies makes much sense. An organism has an obvious survival advantage if it is particularly sensitive to those stimuli that are signals of the incidence of a potentially harmful event.

To what extent is the nervous system constructed to give priority to certain information for reasons other than those considered in the previous subsections? Strong stimuli generally command the attention of most complex organisms, a fact that is familiar to the teacher who shouts at children; but the effect of such stimuli is often disorganizing rather than conducive to clear perception. Such stimuli also commonly produce avoidance rather than approach behavior. Even more important, from the teacher's point of view, is the fact that stimuli that are either novel or complex will also command attention, but generally they do not have a disorganizing effect.

The effects of novelty have been extensively investigated by Berlyne, who has summarized his own research and the research of others in a book entitled *Conflict, Arousal and Curiosity* (1960). The results of such research generally show that creatures with complex nervous systems spend more time attending to and exploring novel stimuli than they spend with the familiar. Such behavior clearly has survival value, for an animal that did not attend to novel stimuli would not have very long to live. Wild animals attend to novel stimuli without showing much exploration of them; domestic species show both attention and exploration. Children, belonging as they do to a domestic species, show exploration of these stimuli as well as attention to them.

Children, like the members of many other mammalian species, tend to select for exploration those aspects of their environment that are the most complex (though complexity is often difficult to separate from novelty). In terms of designing teaching situations, this finding is awkward, for although complexity commands attention, effective teaching situations are likely to be simple.

Although there is considerable conflict of conclusions within the entire area of perception that has just been considered, the weight of the evidence indicates that perception is influenced by the needs and personality characteristics of the subject, as well as previous experience with respect to reward or punishment with the object of perception. The effect is not an overwhelming one. Indeed, it is generally small and difficult to measure, and it has remained a controversial issue because the results of experiments are rarely clear-cut.

What implications do these perceptual phenomena have for education? Although one might expect children to more readily perceive material related in some way to their need structure, the advantage gained would be so slight that one would hardly expect it to have a significant effect on the learning process. The influence of the personality structure on retention is a much more marked phenomenon than the influence of personality on the learning process itself.

Information Transmission and Compression

In the chapter on the nervous system, the point was made that the peripheral nerves and nuclei, as well as some more centrally located portions of the nervous system, serve the function of compressing the information supplied to the senses. The compression of information results in those aspects of the source of stimulation that carry the most information being emphasized, and those that carry the least being suppressed—at least, that is the way it is in the case of visual transmissions. The compression process is necessary since the higher centers are capable of handling only a limited amount of information within a given time span.

Although the compression produced by the process known as lateral inhibition occurs in the peripheral regions of the nervous system and at some distance from the main mass of brain material, other processes, with similar simplifying effects, occur at higher levels. Those processes that involve the use of concepts also serve this purpose, for they simplify

the information provided by the environment. Concepts permit the classification of inputs into broad categories; and thus the environment is
perceived as containing objects in the general class of chair, table, floor,
and so on. At these higher levels one has difficulty in distinguishing between processes that are involved in the transmission of information and
processes involved in the interpretation of the information provided.
One could as well consider the process of categorizing the incoming information as a process involving the structuring of information, which
is considered in the next section. There is a complete continuity of the
processing of information from the time it reaches the sense organ to
the time when it has reached the higher centers and has led to some
kind of action. No clear separation can be made between information
transmission and information processing.

Structuring Information

The incoming information, when it reaches the higher centers, becomes
structured; and the emergence of structure is closely associated with using
the information effectively. The process of structuring is so rapid in
typical perceptions that one has to find situations in which it is slowed
up in order to study the phenomenon in the laboratory. However, daily
life does provide some illustrations of cases in which the normal rapid
structuring of the incoming information is slowed to a pace at which
it can be studied. For example, present a person with an ink blot from
the Rorschach series and ask him what he sees in it. As he concentrates
on it, the meaningless mass of ink begins to take form. Soon he sees in
it, perhaps, an insect or the outline of a tree or a leaf. This process occurs
through the matching of the incoming information with stored information. The process of structuring the information is slow, in this case, because the situation presented is ambiguous.

The process of structuring information became the central phenomenon
to be studied by a group of psychologists who developed what they
referred to as *Gestalt* psychology. The Gestalt psychologists stressed the
inborn nature of the perceptual structuring process. Certainly, the infant
in his first few weeks of life shows some capacity for seeing structure
in his surroundings. For example, he can fixate a light with his eyes and
can follow it as it is moved. Such a fixation of the eyes on the light
suggests that the infant is able to distinguish between the light and the
rest of his environment, and can thus structure the environment into
light and *other-than-light*. Although the infant can do this, it is clear that
the light is meaningless to him; for meaning has to be acquired through
long experience with lights and other phenomena.

Meaningless structurings can also be undertaken by adults under some unusual circumstances. Many years ago, von Senden observed the behavior of adult patients who, through corneal grafts, were able to see for the first time. Such a patient could tell that there was something drawn on a white sheet of paper in front of him, but could not tell that it was the outline of a square. The evidence indicates that the nervous system has some capacity to give the incoming information structure, but that extensive experience is required to give meaning to the form and structure that is perceived. In addition, much complex structuring of the environment has to be based on extensive experience. To be able to perceive the form of an oak tree in a Rorschach ink blot requires extensive previous experience with oak trees. There is no innate property of the nervous system that could provide such a complicated structuring of an ink blot without extensive experience. At the present time, nobody knows what are the limits of the innate capacity of the nervous system to structure information coming from the senses; but its clear that, at some point, experience becomes necessary.

The word *Gestalt* means a structure of pattern, and Gestalt psychologists emphasized the tendency for people to perceive patterns even when none really existed in the material perceived. Although many of the theories of the Gestalt psychologists have been shown to be unsound, they were responsible for the discovery of many phenomena of considerable significance. Some of the important concepts they evolved will be considered in the following paragraphs:

Phenomena that are experienced manifest form. This is a fairly well-established phenomenon. Consider, for example, the following diagram:

If the reader will stare at this collection of dots, he will soon observe that he is seeing them as having some organization and form. He may see the dots as an outer row bounding a square with a dot in the center. He may perceive them as five vertical rows, five horizontal rows, or a set of diagonal rows. He will not just perceive them as dots on a page, but as an organization of dots. As he watches them, the organization may undergo change from one pattern to another; but there is always pattern and form in the way in which the dots are perceived.

The form or pattern is not inherent in the dots themselves. One can no more say that they consist of five vertical rows than one can say that they consist of five horizontal rows. The person looking at the dots is the one who imposes the pattern on them. Organization is a function of the process of perceiving the dots and of the entire process of perception.

Sensory experiences are not just little bits of experience that have an additive effect; but rather, they have organization, in experience, which gives them their unique characteristic.

The Gestalt psychologists did drive home the point that perception occurs within a frame of reference. The printed symbol "1" can stand for either the letter "l" (as in "let") or the numeral one. In context it is always correctly interpreted; sometimes it is perceived as the letter and sometimes as the digit. Stimuli are always perceived and judged with reference to other stimuli.

Sensory experiences tend to be organized in a way that provides the greatest simplicity, regularity, and completeness. This was called the Law of Pragnanz, and means that perception results in simple organizations rather than complex ones. In the case of the rows of dots presented previously, we are more likely to see dots organized as rows rather than as a square within a square. The simpler organization takes precedence over the more complex organization. If a person is shown for one-tenth of a second a drawing of a square from which a corner has been cut off, he is quite likely to reproduce it as a perfect square. This may be a result of the Law of Pragnanz, but it may also be a result of the fact that we have seen numerous squares in our life and can expect to see a square rather than some odd and unusual shape. The effect of expectancy may override the actual information presented. Figures that are roughly circular tend to be reproduced as circles. The stimulation presented to the senses may be complex, but the resulting perception tends to appear in a form which represents a simple and unified figure. A corollary of this is that figures that represent an incomplete structure may often be perceived as a complete structure.

Perception is organized into a figure and a ground. When one regards an ordinary scene such as the family sitting around the table eating, one is bombarded by numerous stimuli. Some of these stimuli are responded to very actively, but others are not. One member of the family is talking intently, and we are attending closely to him. At this time our attention is directed toward him, and most of the other events around us fade into the background. In terms of the language used to describe perceptual phenomena, one would say that the person attended to stands out from the ground as a figure. Later, when attention is switched to the food, the food becomes the figure and stands out from the ground. Attention is a process through which one becomes responsive to certain stimuli and organizes these stimuli into meaningful patterns that stand out from the mass of other stimuli that are not attended to (collectively referred to as the ground). The organization of the perceptual field into a figure and ground results in the selection of certain information for further use and the discarding of the rest of the information into the background. This permits the organism to behave effectively in a complex world without becoming overwhelmed by the vast sources of information available.

Learning may involve the development of the capacity to differentiate various objects as figures against a background of all other objects. Vetter (1965) has shown that giving a person experience with a particular aspect of the environment results in that part of the environment being seen more readily as figure rather than as ground. What one is familiar with tends to stand out as ground. A person with no knowledge of machinery who is shown a complex mechanism sees little except a complex mass of metal. As he learns about the nature of the equipment, he learns to recognize the significance of certain parts and can point to these. These parts now stand out as a figure against the general background of the mechanism. Ultimately, attention may be turned to any part, and the part emerges from the rest as a figure. In terms of typical S——→R learning theory, one would say that each of the parts that can so emerge from the rest in the perceptual field is a *discriminated stimulus* —that is, it can be discriminated from the rest and responded to separately from the rest. Whether one discusses the phenomena in terms of perception and what happens in the person's conscious field of experience, or whether one discusses it in terms of learning theory, the same end result is implied. In both cases, the implication is that the person can respond to the particular machine part as a meaningful set of stimuli.

In any teaching process that involves demonstration, the teacher must be sure that the pupil perceives as a figure the element that is central to the demonstration. In demonstrations of technical equipment, such as the differential of a car, the student often sees nothing more than a mass of meaningless moving parts, which do not become more meaningful as the teacher singles out each one. In teaching a foreign language, an instructor may begin by talking the language in class, but to the student this may provide nothing more than a background jumble of sounds. This is not too profitable an experience, for nothing becomes discriminated from anything else by this process. In effective learning, the teacher must be sure that the proper figure–ground relationships are established. Learning may involve the establishment of such relationships.

The Value System and the Structuring of Information

The knowledge concerning structuring that has been discussed up to this point has involved to a great extent the structuring of boundaries of objects. This is an important matter, for it is the boundaries that carry the most significant information about objects. Much of the information reaching the higher centers does not pertain to boundaries. For example, verbal information has to be structured in terms of characteristics other than boundaries, except insofar as one considers the beginning and the end of a sentence as involving some kind of psychological boundary. Knowledge is limited concerning the factors that influence the structuring of these other aspects of information; but the best explored of these is the influence of values.

A highly controversial study by Postman, Bruner, and McGinnies (1948) has been the foundation for a long list of studies of this problem. In the latter study a personality-measuring device known as the *Allport-Vernon Study of Values* was administered to groups of subjects. This instrument gives scores that supposedly indicate the extent to which the life of the person is dominated by each of six values: the theoretical, economic, aesthetic, social, political, and religious. The speed with which the subjects were able to recognize words flashed for a very brief time on a screen was also measured. The finding was that the higher the score of an individual in any one of the six value categories, the greater was his capacity to recognize words related to that category. Capacity to recognize words was measured by the shortness of the exposure of the word that permitted recognition. The results of this well-known experiment are, nevertheless, controversial, because the experimenters failed to control one important variable that was brought to light by a later experiment by Howes and Soloman (1951). In the latter study, the data demonstrated that the duration of exposure required for the recognition of a particular word depended on the extent to which the person had been previously exposed to that word. Frequency of previous exposure was measured by obtaining from a word count an index of the frequency with which the word occurs in common reading materials. When the frequency of previous exposure was controlled by selecting words of uniform occurrence in printed English, most of the relationship between the value system of the individual and the ease with which he recognized words disappeared. Some small residual relationship did appear to remain; but the effect was small, if not negligible, in comparison with the effect of previous frequency of occurrence of the words.

Another question is the extent to which the value placed on an object modifies the appearance of the object. In this area, as in many others, the initial work was conducted by Bruner, who has done much to develop the entire area. His research paper was published under the authorship of himself and Goodman (1947). It covered two experiments. In the one, ten-year-old children were asked to adjust the size of a circular spot of light to match the size of either coins or cardboard discs. The children showed a tendency to overestimate the size of the coins, but not the size of the discs. In the second experiment, the data supported the hypothesis that poor children showed a greater tendency than rich children to overestimate the size of the coins. The study was repeated with one important variation by Ashley, Harper, and Runyon (1951), who hypnotized the subjects and suggested to some that they were rich and to others that they were poor. In this experiment the "poor" subjects showed a greater tendency to overestimate the size of the coins than did the "rich" ones. When the same subjects were given metal slugs and told that they were made of either lead, silver, white gold, or platinum, the tendency to overestimate the size of the slug varied with the "value" of the metal involved. In another study by Lambert, Soloman, and Watson (1949), children in a nursery school earned chips, which they could later cash in for a reward. The children tended to overestimate the size of the tokens, and this overestimation of size tended to increase as the chips were used over a longer time as a part of a reward system. Beams and Thompson (1952) showed children food objects for which they had expressed a preference. The children were then asked to estimate the size of the object by adjusting the size of a projected image of the object. Once again, overestimation of size was found to occur. However, not all results fall so neatly into line. When Carter and Schooler (1949) attempted to repeat the Bruner and Goodman experiment with certain minor refinements, they failed to confirm the original results. Klein, Schlesinger, and Meister (1951) conducted an experiment in which subjects had to estimate the size of discs bearing symbols having both strong positive and strong negative value. No consistent relationships were found between tendencies to overestimate the size of the disc and the symbol involved. Some subjects consistently overestimate the size of the discs, and others consistently underestimated them.

These inconsistencies seem to have been resolved by Tajfel (1957), who re-examined all the evidence. He noted that a tendency to overestimate the size of a valued object occurred only when the object belonged to a series, with the larger members of the series having greater values. Thus, coins belong to a series, and, in general, the larger the coin the more it is worth. With such a series of objects one would expect the overestimation-of-size effect to occur. Even the finding of Bouwhuis et al. (1965) that smokers tended to overestimate the size of cigarettes fits well, for an unsmoked cigarette has greater value than a small smoked stub. On the other hand, if the objects were such that the smaller members were the most highly valued, then there would be a tendency to underestimate the size of a valued object. In a later study, Stayton and Wiener (1961) found just that. The object, the size of which had to be estimated, was a small compact car, which was highly popular at the time the study was undertaken. It was generally preferred over the large car, which was then out of fashion. Stayton and Wiener found a tendency for the subjects to underestimate the size of the small car. A general theory related to this phenomenon has been outlined by Stayton (1964).

The personality characteristics of an individual may produce in him a tendency to perceive his environment in a way consistent with those characteristics. Projective tests, such as the Rorschach, are based on the assumption that the perceptions involved in looking at ink blots are indicative of the personal characteristics of the person. The argument is that if it can be shown that the structuring of an ink blot is related to personality, then it may be presumed that other perceptual structuring processes are also related to personality characteristics.

Studies of the Rorschach test and other well-known projective devices do not produce highly consistent results. Some of the studies provide a positive answer to the above question, but others have yielded negative results. Such inconsistent results of studies lead one to suggest that only under certain conditions will there be a tendency for personality characteristics to influence perceptions. Just what those conditions are has not yet been determined. Insofar as the answer to the above question is in the affirmative, one may suspect that the way in which the child sees the classroom is a function of his own characteristics. Most teachers are familiar with a few children who perceive the teacher as a hostile figure, despite every effort on the part of the teacher to appear otherwise. How children perceive the school is a matter in which investigations have only begun. Some preliminary studies by Hughes (1959) indicate that the perceptions of many children of the classroom are very different from what adults commonly assume them to be.

Moulton *et al.* (1958) found that measures of need for achievement were related to the speed with which subjects recognized achievement-oriented words. However, this relationship occurred only after subjects had experienced the frustration of achievement in a problem-solving situation in which they attempted to solve a complex problem in a time that was purposely set much too short for the task. The latter procedure was designed to arouse achievement need.

Another related problem is the extent to which emotionally disturbing stimuli are difficult or easy to structure. This is an area in which the results of early research were seriously contaminated with a variable that has already been discussed in connection with other studies of perception. It is not enough to demonstrate that anxiety-producing words or words that produce a high emotional response (words such as *bitch, guilty, illegitimate,* etc.) are more difficult to recognize when they are exposed briefly than are words that are not thus colored. Unfortunately, the emotionally toned words are less frequently seen in print than are neutral words and hence, for this reason alone, are more difficult to recognize. This was the basic defect in an early study by McGinnies (1949), who thought that he had demonstrated that words that produce emotional responses were more difficult to recognize on brief exposure than neutral words. The basic defect of the McGinnies study was overcome in later studies by Nothman (1963) and by Cowen and Beier (1952, 1954). The latter employed the technique of requiring the subject to recognize words from fuzzily typed copy. The words were retyped on successive pages of booklets, and each page turned brought a more clearly typed version into view. The experimenters determined the number of pages that had to be turned before a word was correctly recognized. Evidence was forthcoming that anxiety-producing words were more difficult to recognize than were neutral words. The data supports the general hypothesis that words that are emotionally disturbing arouse defense mechanisms that prevent them from being recognized. Another interesting feature of the latter study was that the experimenters could demonstrate that emotional responses to the critical words occurred even before the subjects were able to recognize them.

A study by Fulkerson (1957) indicates that the phenomenon is one of considerable complexity. He found that words that are taboo in our society are more difficult to recognize than non-taboo words, but only if the taboo words are fairly common ones. He also found, as have previous research workers, that the most important factor determining the ease with which words are recognized is the frequency with which they have been seen in print.

The evidence, taken as a whole, indicates that needs and values bias the interpretation given to information about the environment and that emotional factors may interfere with or facilitate the perception of certain events. Thus, one may well expect that children from different backgrounds, and with different sets of values, will differ markedly in the interpretation given to such familiar school materials as stories and other pieces of literature and perhaps even historical materials.

The Contributions of Internally and Externally Supplied Information to the Structuring Process

The structuring process involves a complex bringing together of information from the outside world and information stored internally. All the evidence points in the direction that only a small fraction of the information available to the sense organs ever reaches the higher centers, and yet each person has the experience of perceiving the environment in the greatest of detail. A theory of perception has to reconcile these two apparently inconsistent facts.

The reconciliation is brought about by the theory that whenever a small amount of information about the environment reaches the higher centers of the brain, then this information is used to provide an elaborate internal reconstruction of the environment. This reconstruction is so automatic and effortless in a familiar environment that the individual is not aware of its occurrence, and he assumes that the wealth of detail he appears to perceive is all derived from the immediate input of information from his senses. This position is consistent with a vast amount of information. It accounts for the frequent misperceptions that plague our lives. It leads one to expect that, when several people witness the same incident, they will give radically different accounts of what has happened, for they use different internally stored information in constructing their perceptions. Much reading behavior can be understood in such terms, particularly when it involves rapid reading. The person familiar with the subject of a book can skim over the pages and then report what the book is about. In doing this, he is not demonstrating fantastic reading skill, but is showing skill in the reconstruction of the knowledge contained in the book by combining the fragmentary evidence derived from scanning the pages with the knowledge he has previously stored about the subject matter.

The position taken here also provides an understanding of the frequent misperceptions of children. The child's stored information about his environment is limited and, hence, insufficient to provide realistic reconstructions of his environment or of what is happening there. For this reason, perception comes to have a closer correspondence to reality as the child grows older and as he has more information available with which to develop internal reconstructions that correspond closely to the environment.

Adaptation-Level Theory: A Systematic Approach to the Problem of Structuring Perceptions

Gestalt psychologists were content with discovering broad relationships; and, despite the ingenuity they displayed in demonstrating the phenomena previously discussed, few of them carried out systematic experiments. Contemporary psychologists in the field of perception, such as Helson (1964), have been highly critical of the lack of systematic research on the part of those who sponsored the Gestalt approach and have attempted to fill the vacuum. Helson has also gone far toward clarifying the meaning of such terms as *frame of reference*. He has also introduced the term *adaptation level,* which has come to assume a position of considerable importance in contemporary psychology.

In introducing the concept of adaptation level, Helson points out that we tend to judge experiences in terms of opposites (or bipolarities, as he calls them). For example, we judge weights to be light or heavy, colors are described as bright or dull, a room is described as being light or dark, acquaintances are described as friendly or hostile, and so forth. A person who goes out to move some rocks in his garden may point to some as being light and some heavy. However, after he has spent the afternoon lifting 100-pound rocks, then 50-pound rocks, which he originally thought of as heavy, no longer seem so. After the prolonged lifting of the heavy rocks, the 50-pound ones now seem light. What has happened here is that his adaptation level has changed through the lifting of the heavy rocks.

The adaptation level is a sort of neutral point. In the rocks example, it is the point between weights that are judged as heavy and weights that are judged as light. In the case of judgments about the level of lighting of a room, it is a level of illumination that is judged to be between the level judged to be bright and the level judged to be dark. Helson also carries over the concept to human relations and would, for example, say that there is a neutral point between behavior that is judged to be friendly and behavior that is judged to be hostile. The concept is not restricted in its application to simple sensory inputs.

Adaptation level, with respect to any particular phenomenon, whether it be level of illumination or a more complex environmental characteristic, is always a product of three sets of conditions: (1) the immediate stimuli on which attention is focused, (2) the context or the background against which the objects commanding attention are presented, and (3) previous experience. Helson has attempted to show that a certain mathematical relationship exists among these three classes of events and adaptation level.

Perceptual Approaches to Problems of Learning

Much of this book has been concerned with the shaping of responses, an approach that has resulted in an emphasis on the response end of the learning process. Many psychologists have taken the position that the most important events in learning occur at the stimulus end rather than at the response end of the chain of events. A quarter of a century ago, a central issue in most controversies concerning the nature of learning was whether one could best understand learning by studying changes in responses as they occurred during acquisition or whether the learning process could only be understood in terms of the perceptual processes that accompanied it. Today such controversies represent dead issues, for psychologists have abandoned any narrow approach that claims that the key to the understanding of learning lies in one area rather than another. Perceptual aspects of learning are recognized to have importance as well as other aspects of the entire process.

Despite the broad outlook taken by contemporary psychologists in this matter, the approach taken to problems in learning in typical schools of education is narrow, and represents, to a great extent, the position of those psychologists of a quarter of a century ago who took the extreme stand that learning could be understood only in terms of a personal (or phenomenological) point of view. Of special far-reaching influence have been the ideas of Kurt Lewin. A brief review of some of the more important of these ideas is given here because of the impact they have had on thinking about problems of education. The reader should keep in mind that although these ideas have been influential, they have not been demonstrated to have extensive value for the effective planning and controlling of the learning process, and have proved unattractive to research workers. Outside of education, Lewin's approach is today only of historical interest.

Lewin's Field Theory

One cannot say at this time that the concepts that Lewin introduced have led to more effective ways of organizing and planning learning, but they have had an influence on the way in which learning problems are discussed in educational circles. They also provide a language for discussing many of the events that occur in the phenomenal field. Some of his more important concepts are the following:

Life space. Lewin (1936, 1948, 1951) thought of the universe of personal experience as a space in which a person moves. This space, which is referred to as a *life space* to distinguish it from the physical space in which a person moves, is psychological, not physical. Two students in a class may be surrounded by two closely similar sections of physical space, but they may be living in two very different life spaces. Goals and evaluations are all a part of the immediate life space of the person. Included in the life space of the individual are ideas and perceptions of objects of significance to him, and also ideas and conceptions of future events in his life. The person is also a region within life space, which thus consists of the person plus his psychological environment.

The life space does have some correspondence with the physical space in which the individual lives, but the degree of correspondence varies from one person to another. In the psychotic individual there may be almost no correspondence between the life space and the physical space.

Just as physical movement occurs in physical space, as when a person walks down the street, so too does psychological movement occur in the psychological life space. A person may *move* toward certain goals or, in making a decision, may *move* away from one alternative and toward another. Such movements in the psychological life space may not correspond with any physical movement. As the person moves from one region to another in his life space, his behavior may show corresponding changes.

Although we have introduced the concept of life space by referring it to a universe of experience, the concept does not have to be considered in this light. One can consider it strictly as an inference from behavior, which includes verbal behavior. In other words, it can be considered as a construct introduced in order to understand events as they occur. It does not necessarily have to be identified with the idea of a field of consciousness, but can be considered as a complicated internal mechanism the components of which produce behavior as it is observed.

Valences in life space.   Certain regions of life space or objects in those regions attract the individual so that he moves toward them. Such regions are said to have positive *valence*. Other regions are said to have negative valence and to repel locomotion toward them. Thus, regions containing facts that have anxiety attached to them are generally repelling.

This concept of Lewin has proved fruitful as a basis for research, particularly research on the analysis of conflict. Conflict arises when the valences in life space provide two courses of action only one of which can be taken. Particularly serious are those conflicts in which the individual must move into one of two regions, both of which have negative valences. A child knows that he will have deep guilt feelings if he lies, but that to confess what he has done will bring down on him severe punishment. In whichever of these two regions of life space he moves, he will have unpleasant consequences; but no escape is offered. He must move into one of them. One response in such a situation is a state of inaction. Another is vacillation. First there is a tendency to go one way; but as anxiety builds up, the individual changes his mind and goes in the other direction. Much research undertaken since Lewin's death in 1947 has involved his analysis of conflict.

The valences of objects or regions in the life space produce tensions that have to be resolved. Movement in the life space represents an attempt to resolve these tensions.

Regions within life space manifest differentiation.   Learning, as life progresses, results to a great degree in the differentiation of regions of life space. The objects within these differentiated regions become more meaningful and acquire valences. For a young child, the region involved in his vocational future may be quite undifferentiated; but as he grows and learns, this area becomes progressively more differentiated. Certain objects, such as the achievement of a college degree, not only become meaningful goals, but also may acquire positive valence. Some of the objects in other regions, which do not initially trigger behavior, come to do so much as discriminated stimuli do.

The change that learning involves is, in Lewin's terms, a change in cognitive structure. Just how does the teacher produce changes in cognitive structure? Lewin and his followers tend to be vague on this important point, though they have some suggestions. One is that the region in which restructing is to occur should be one that provides rewarding experiences. If it has this characteristic, then the individual is likely to seek out this region and remain there. Apparently, by being there, some restructuring is likely to occur. They suggest that school should be a place that provides many sources of stimulation and yields satisfaction, so that the child moves into that region of his life space that is occupied by the ideas and objects derived from the school environment. To a great extent, this is what many modern schools attempt to do. The idea is an interesting one, but it is based almost entirely on a highly speculative theory.

Behavior is determined by conditions in the life space. This is a concept that some later psychologists attempted to use and develop, and that has been a central one in the thinking of those associated with the Rogerian school of counseling psychology. According to the Lewinian viewpoint, as well as the viewpoint of a few modern psychologists, all of the factors that determine the direction behavior is to take lie in the life space of the individual as it is at present. Some psychologists, such as Snygg (1959), state almost the same proposition by saying that all determinants of behavior lie in the phenomenal field. In terms of Lewin's theory of behavior, all one has to do in order to predict behavior is to know the phenomenal field of the person at the time when behavior is to be predicted. This is the kind of theorizing that is very difficult, if not impossible, to demonstrate to be false. It is also equally difficult to demonstrate that it is sound and useful for making predictions. The problem lies in the fact that there are difficulties in exploring the life space of an individual, and there is no way of determining the content of the life space of an individual at a particular time. Suppose that I am confronted with some personal problem and go to a psychologist for advice. The psychologist may wish to obtain information about my life space, but this he cannot do without changing it; for he himself becomes an object in my life space as soon as he starts his exploration. One cannot determine the content of the life space of another without changing it. Hence, one cannot know the conditions existing at a particular time in the life space of another. This is one of many serious difficulties involved in this approach to the study of learning that has made it virtually impossible to approach the problems experimentally. Other theoretical approaches to learning have become preferred simply because they do not involve such insurmountable barriers. As an exercise, the reader may well go back over the brief materials covering Lewin and ask how the ideas involved could ever be related to scientific observations. The difficulties of doing this have discouraged scientists from attempting to extend this approach.

The points that Lewin made with respect to learning are not particularly helpful in the matter of planning learning in schools. They provide absolutely no information about the characteristics of the learning situation that are likely to be most conducive to learning except for saying that the learning situation itself should have positive valence and that the pupil should want to move *into* that region of his life space involving learning rather than *out* of it. The theory tells nothing about the way in which learning materials should be organized and presented, and it makes no contribution to understanding of the structure of human abilities in relation to school learning. Its contribution to the control of the learning process and the prediction of what learning will occur was of only the most limited character. Its attractiveness to people connected with education is difficult to understand. Perhaps its main contribution has been to draw the attention of psychologists to the fact that, in some learning tasks, important events take place at the perceptual end. Certainly this is true. An artist learning to draw the human body is not simply learning a motor skill. He is learning above all to *perceive* the human form with a clarity and precision and with an understanding of the interrelationship of the parts. This perception is far different from the crude way in which the human form is typically perceived. Learning to draw the human form is basically the learning of a perceptual skill, and the mere practicing of the motor components will do little to help it develop. Such perceptual learning needs to find a more significant place in research, but progress is hampered by a lack of research techniques.

THE SELF CONCEPT AND LEARNING

An important theoretical development of those who have approached behavior from the viewpoint of Lewin is that of the *self concept*. In the terminology of Lewin, the self concept is represented by a region of the life space that handles beliefs about the self. The behaviorist would define the self concept in terms of the statements that the person makes about himself. These statements can be said to represent a system of beliefs. If this definition is accepted, then the set of beliefs represented by the self concept may be expected to have the same properties as any other set of beliefs.

The reason for including a discussion of the self concept in a volume on learning is that current educational literature makes frequent reference to it as a condition related to learning. The implication is that a learner who has a suitable self concept will learn more easily in a school situation than one who has an inappropriate self concept. For example, the statement is commonly made that a person who thinks of himself as stupid is likely to be more poorly motivated in an academic learning situation than a person who thinks of himself as bright. The assumption underlying such a position is that there is a causal relation between the self concept and the rate of learning, though the alternative is also possible—that high achievement may produce a positive and constructive concept of the self.

When educators state that the self concept influences learning behavior, they are saying that the concept is more than a set of beliefs. They are ascribing to it many of the properties commonly ascribed to motives, such as those of energizing and giving direction to behavior. This is an assumption that goes way beyond the facts.

Present emphasis on the self concept as a factor in learning comes from the school of counseling associated with the name of Carl Rogers (1954). At least a part of the problems presented by people who seek counseling stems from the fact that the concept they have of themselves is inappropriate. Freud had stressed this fact much earlier when he pointed out that the disturbed patient was often afflicted with deep-seated and inappropriate feelings of guilt, which plagued his life. In a sense, such feelings of guilt might be considered an aspect of the self concept in that they imply such beliefs as "I am wicked" or "I am a wrongdoer." Carl Rogers, who has made extensive use of the notion of a self concept in developing his theory of counseling, had contact at the University of Chicago with William Stephenson, who suggested a research technique that might be applied to the study of changes in the self concept that occurred during counseling (1953). The result was a long series of studies of the effect of counseling on changes in the self concept, which have been published in many sources. The general trend of this research was to demonstrate that self concepts did change during counseling, and that counseling was effective insofar as its purpose was to change the self concept. Research in which measures of self concept are repeatedly applied to people not counseled (Taylor, 1955) shows increased consistency of the measures as they are repeated, but less over-all change than in those who receive counseling. The data fit well the position that the learning occurring during counseling of the Rogerian type can be represented by changes in the self concept.

Some evidence has been collected to show that if children with poor self concepts are matched on intelligence-test scores with others having good self concepts, the ones with good self concepts tend to achieve better in school (Sears, 1959; Spaulding, 1960). This data cannot be interpreted to mean that the self concept influences achievement. Another possible interpretation is that members of the high-achieving group have superior self concepts because they are superior achievers. From the data alone, one cannot tell whether a superior self concept produces high achievement or whether high achievement produces a superior self concept. The latter hypothesis is given some plausibility in a study by Stevens (1956), which demonstrated that successful students described themselves more accurately than did failing students, who, perhaps as a defense mechanism, did not appear willing to think of themselves in realistic terms.

A single unique study by Bieri and Trieschman (1956) suggests that the self concept may influence certain aspects of social learning. These investigators found evidence that learning to associate an adjective with the name of a person was more easily accomplished when the adjectives could apply to the self concept of the learner. The argument is that when it is possible to project one's own self concept onto other people, this provides a situation favorable for learning related to those people.

That there may exist complex and indirect relationships between the self concept and motivation is shown in a study by Martire (1956). In this study, subjects rated themselves with respect to how they would *like* to be (self ideal) and how they *thought* they were (self concept). Ratings were undertaken on a set of traits commonly believed to be related to achievement. The finding was that those subjects who had high need-achievement scores showed a greater discrepancy between self ideal and self concept than other subjects who showed a lesser degree of achievement motivation. Why high need-achievement subjects should show a discrepancy between self ideal and self concept is difficult to say. The main purpose of mentioning the study here is to indicate that the self concept may be indirectly related to motivation and hence, indirectly, to learning. More research is needed before definitive statements about this matter can be made.

The establishment of a direct causal relationship between the self concept and achievement would be a very difficult matter. It would be necessary to establish that changes in the self concept, such as are produced by counseling, resulted in changes in the level of achievement. Even this would not be clear-cut evidence, for changes in achievement might be a result of other aspects of the counseling process. The idea that the self concept may influence achievement does not have any sound theoretical support. The most convincing evidence available at this time to support this hypothesis is anecdotal, which is hardly enough to give any strong support.

Research on matters related to the self concept has been extensive, as Wylie (1961) shows in her excellent review of the research literature, which covers over four hundred references. However, the latter review also points out that much of the research has little to do with learning, and that most of it is inadequate in terms of research methodology. The review also points out that research on the self concept has not generally led to the development of useful psychological concepts, although there are a few that show a little promise. Wylie thinks that ideas such as self-acceptance and self-esteem offer some promise, but that the majority of constructs do not.

The Nature of Perceptual Theories of Learning

Throughout this book the theoretical framework used to present much of the available knowledge of learning is one in which stimuli or patterns of stimuli become linked with response systems, though often through complex mediating processes. This way of organizing our thinking about learning problems follows what is referred to as a stimulus-organism-response pattern, because emphasis is placed on a chain of events that links the stimuli and the corresponding responses of the organism. We have also indicated that, through reinforcement, some control may be exercised over emitted behavior and that certain stimuli may become the occasions calling forth such emitted behavior. But here, in the perceptual approach to learning, is quite a different approach. When the assumption is made that learning takes place when there is some kind of reorganization of the perceptual field, what is said is that learning involves the building of new relationships among stimuli. In other words, in perceptual theories of learning, account has to be taken of the establishing of relationships between one stimulus and another stimulus. In brief, these may be termed "S⟶S" theories, to contrast them with "S⟶R" theories.

In the past S⟶R and S⟶S theories have tended to deal with different learning phenomena. S⟶S theorists have tended to specialize in problems related to how the person comes to perceive the world as he does. They have dealt with learning in which the learner reports marked and often dramatic changes in the phenomenal field. They have also studied problem solving, but again in situations in which the problem is solved with a flash of insight and the sudden appearance of a new way of perceiving the elements of a problem in their relation to one another, problems that *require* the individual to reorient his thinking.

Summary

1. Perceptual processes are mediating processes within the individual about which he is able to give some report. The universe as perceived by the individual himself is sometimes referred to as the phenomenal field.

2. Although the study of reinforcement emphasizes the output end of the system, the emphasis in studies of perception is on the input end.

3. The earliest theories of learning were perceptual theories that maintained that the essential process in learning was the association of one idea with another. Modern forms of association theory are not basically perceptual theories, though some psychologists continue to study the manner in which percepts of some events or objects in the environment come to be associated with other objects or events. Attempts have been made to link the theory of associationism with the physiology and neurology of the nervous system, but such efforts have not been particularly successful.

4. Theory of perception has a particularly important impact on education in that it focuses on the problem of how the organism obtains and utilizes information about the environment. For convenience, three phases of the information intake process are considered; (1) the selective nature of the intake process, (2) the information transmission process itself, and (3) the structuring of the incoming information.

5. Perception is preceded by certain preparatory activities that determine the information that is received. These are referred to as sets, or determining tendencies or expectancies. At any particular time, an organism is more readily triggered to perceive one object or event than another.

6. The transmission of information involves the compression of the information before it reaches the higher centers. The general result of compression is that it simplifies the information and facilitates the transactions that the organism undertakes with a complex environment.

7. The information that is received is structured. Considerable information was acquired by the Gestalt psychologists concerning the conditions that lead to the structuring of information. The latter psychologists were particularly interested in the structuring of visual information, and that part of the information involved in boundaries and edges. Another area that has been explored is the extent to which needs and values influence the structuring process.

8. The structuring process involves the utilization of the incoming information and also the drawing on the information that is stored and that has been derived from previous experience. The perceptual process is, in a sense, a process that reconstructs external events from small

quantities of incoming information. The reconstruction aspect of the perceptual process accounts for many of the misperceptions that occur.

9. Although Gestalt psychologists were content to discover broad relationships, they have been criticized for having failed to introduce measurement into their system. In this respect, the most notable critic of these psychologists has been Helson, who has tried to introduce concepts of measurement and quantity into the psychology of perception. An important concept introduced by him is that of *adaptation level*.

10. The psychologists of a quarter of a century ago tended to stress the study of the responses involved in learning, but many modern psychologists are more concerned with the role of inputs of information and perceptual processes. There is widespread agreement that the understanding of the learning process calls for an understanding of perceptual aspects of learning as well as response aspects.

11. Although there are few contemporary psychologists who take the position that the only important aspects of learning are the perceptual aspects, the past generation of psychologists had some outstanding men who took this position. Notable among these was Kurt Lewin.

12. Lewin introduced many ideas that have had an influence on ways of thinking about learning phenomena. One of the most important of these concepts is that of *life space,* a concept that is psychological rather than physical. The events occuring in life space must have some relationship to events in physical space if the individual is to function effectively in a real world. Events and phenomena in life space have valencies which determine the trend of behavior. Behavior is assumed to be determined by conditions in the life space.

13. Although the system of Lewin placed emphasis on the perceptual aspects of the learning process, it has relatively little to suggest concerning the way in which the learning situation should be organized in order to produce effective learning.

14. The role of the self concept in learning is a matter of controversy. Although some clinical psychologists have taken the position that a healthy self concept has a positive effect on learning, there is little direct evidence to support that position.

15

The Measurement of Some
Mediating Processes Involved
in Learning: Aptitudes

DESPITE the use of modern methods, a number of children are slow in the development of even a rudimentary skill in reading, and some may even reach college with so little skill that they are not able to perform the reading required to earn passing grades. Differences in of learning occur despite uniform learning conditions. Learners differ in their capacity to learn. Such differences in learning capacity are a result of differences which lie within the individual. They are a result of differences in the way in which the mediating processes operate. The internal workings of one child are built differently from those of others, partly because his experiences built different characteristics into him as he developed.

Variables that result from individual differences in function and structure are referred to as *intervening variables*. This term implies that variables intervene between the stimulus and the response, and account for the fact that differences in response occur even when individuals are all exposed to the same stimulus.

Motives represent one class of intervening variables. In a previous chapter, some of the research related to motivation was discussed. In order to predict the course of learning, information must be available concerning the level of motivation of the individual; but motives are not the only intervening variables operating. In order that the course of learning may be predicted, information must also be made available concerning the capacity of the individual to perform the mediating processes that the learning requires. The latter variables are referred to as *aptitudes*. Our purpose here is to consider aptitudes in relation to the learning process. Sometimes measures of aptitude are referred to as measures of individual differences.

The problem of discovering individual differences that are intellectual in character has had a long history. Two problems are really involved in this: One is that of determining what the variables are; the other is how they are generated. If, for example, one can demonstrate that there is operating a variable related to what is popularly called intelligence, and that measures of this variable can be used to predict the learning of certain skills, then one can say that one has a variable useful for making such predictions. This does not imply in any way that a person's level of intelligence is determined by the genes he inherited. Indeed, the established relationship in this case between a measure of intelligence and a measure of learning implies nothing about how intelligence is generated.

The problem of measuring the capacity of the child to achieve, and hence of predicting his achievement, has often been treated at a rather simple-minded level. Ferguson (1954), who was one of the first to define the nature of the problem, discussed it along the following lines:

Learning can be represented graphically by a learning curve that represents the progress of learning. The problem of predicting achievement is that of predicting some characteristic or characteristics of the learning curve. One characteristic one may wish to predict is the slope of the curve—that is, does the person learn relatively rapidly or relatively slowly? However, one may wish to predict another characteristic of the learning curve, which is the point at which the learning curve tends to flatten out. The prediction of where this will take place is the prediction of how far the child can go in a particular area of learning. Typically, a learning curve will ultimately show that further learning is not taking place; when this point is reached, one may say that learning has reached a *crude limit*. This is the limit under the given circumstances, but it might not be the limit under other circumstances. For this reason the term *crude limit* is applied, rather than saying that the limit of learning has been reached. Often one may wish to predict this crude limit of learning—for example, whether the crude limit of learning in mathematics for a particular child is long division or differential equations. One may wish to predict whether the crude limit of learning for typing in the case of another child is forty or eighty words per minute. The prediction of the crude limits of learning in particular learning situations from the intervening variables involved is a very important matter to the educator.

The history of the development of standardized tests is to a marked extent the history of research on the discovery of variables related to school achievement. The original work of Binet (1905), which is familiar to every student of education, was an attempt to develop an instrument capable of predicting achievement under conditions of good motivation. Binet sought to measure with some precision a central and important variable in the achievement described by the word *intelligence.* It was defined as the capacity to perform certain mental operations, such as remembering digits, recognizing differences and similarities between ideas, and so forth. One assumption underlying the test that Binet produced was that the capacity to perform the mental operations called for by the test represented an intervening variable related to academic learning—that is, academic learning called for similar operations. A second assumption was that a single, central variable was involved, which he referred to as intelligence. Although his test called for the performance of many different mental operations, they were all presumed to·reflect a general capacity to perform intellectually. A third assumption was that the ability defined by his test was not only a unitary central ability but also a stable and enduring one. Binet needed a test that would identify the mentally handicapped who were likely to remain so throughout their lives.

There has long been controversy in popular magazines concerning what is meant by *intelligence.* From the point of view of the psychologist, intelligence is simply whatever is measured by intelligence tests. Many questions may be asked about measures of intelligence, such as to what extent a high score is dependent on having had a good education, a high cultural level in the home, and rich preschool experiences, or is it more dependent on the genes received from the parents. In asking these questions, the psychologist is asking how the variable intelligence is generated —that is to say, the influences that result in different individuals achieving different scores. A point of departure for seeking an answer to such questions is the study of the emergence of differences in intelligence among very young children.

Infant Intelligence Scales

At one time it was thought that it would be possible to develop ways of predicting the learning capacity of a child from his performance in infancy. The hypothesis was advanced that superiority of performance in childhood was the result of a superior physical constitution, and that this superiority would be manifested in infancy. The high stability of the intelligence quotient derived from the Binet instrument suggested that the same stability might exist down through lower ages. The central difficulty in the development of such a device is that it is not possible to ask the infant to solve problems. Even with a one-year-old one can do little more than see whether he has mastered certain motor skills, such as the use of a spoon or the grasping and manipulating of objects that are a part of his play activities. In the development of infant scales, the assumption is made that intellectually more capable infants are those who develop most rapidly during infancy and whose motor skills develop early. Two of the scales developed along these lines are those by Gilliland (1949) and Gesell and Amatruda (1941). These scales include observations of such matters as the ability of the infant to fixate an object with his eyes, his capacity to turn his head in the direction of a sound, his ability to reach and grasp for objects, and so forth.

These tests measure rather different functions than are measured by typical intelligence tests for later childhood. The latter emphasize problem-solving skills; the former emphasize motor skills. Skills in the making of movements—that is, motor skills—are quite unrelated to problem-solving skills. A person who is a good problem solver may or may not be good in the various motor skills. A person who is intellectually dull may or may not be good in motor skills. Superiority in motor skill is no guarantee of superiority in behavior involving language. It is hardly surprising, then, that the measures of infants based on the measurement of motor skills do not predict scores on intelligence tests given later in childhood. It would be much more likely that they would predict athletic performance than intellectual level. The fact is, however, that they do not predict anything of consequence. Table 2 shows the relationship between scores on a developmental scale and scores on an intelligence test individually administered at the age of five.

Thus, the evidence of the early emergence and development of a central intervening variable related to learning is lacking. There seems

TABLE 2*

Correlation Between Scores on the Stanford-Binet Test Administered at the Age of Five and Infant Scale Scores. For Each Group There Were Ninety-one Cases

Age of Administration of Interest Scales	Correlation with Total Score on Infant Scale	Correlation with Motor Items Only	Correlation with Adaptive Items Only	Correlation with Social Items Only	Correlation with Language Items Only
3 months	.008	.012	.042	.050	.066
6 months	—.065	—.060	—.029	—.140	.046
9 months	—.001	.100	—.022	—.043	—.017
12 months	.055	.112	—.017	.074	—.002
18 months	.231	.071	.246	.065	.224
24 months	.450	.133	.331	.214	.453

* Data from L. D. Anderson, "The Predictive Value of Infancy Tests in Relation to Intelligence at Five Years," *Child Development,* 10 (1939), pp. 203–212. Reproduced by permission of the Society for Research in Child Development.

to be no way, at this time, of measuring the capacity of the very young child to perform the internal operations analogous to those measured by the tests of intelligence given to older children. Infants may be characterized by a single, major intervening variable related to learning which reflects the general effectiveness of their nervous system, but there is no way at present of obtaining evidence to demonstrate the presence or absence of such a variable.

The Generation of the Variable Intelligence

It is common to say that those characteristics that are inherited are a product of *nature* and those that are acquired are a product of *nurture*, but the influence of nature and nurture are inextricably interwoven in the case of most psychological characteristics. The fact that a particular characteristic is inherited does not mean that it cannot be changed, either favorably or adversely, through the influence of the environment. Clubfoot is an example of a characteristic that is inherited as a recessive characteristic, but this no longer condemns the individual to a life in a wheel chair. Today, through modern surgery, deformed feet can be altered to the point where the cripple can learn to walk almost as well as a person born with normal feet. The original defect places some limitations on what he can do, but they are minor. Other inherited characteristics are a result of abnormal chemical processes in the body. Muscular distrophy is presumably in this category and is characterized by a growing weakness of the muscles, which ultimately progresses to the point where the muscles are so weak that the individual ceases to be able to care for himself. In the later stages of the disease, the muscles involved in breathing become so weak that the individual may literally suffocate. Such an inherited condition is very obscure in its causes, but one may expect that ultimately it may be possible to correct the defect in the chemistry of the body that produces the condition.

Other defects may be much more difficult to remedy, if they can be remedied at all. Some persons manifest very unintelligent behavior because they have very inadequate brains. At the present time there seems to be little hope that such a deficiency can be remedied by surgical or medical means. However, by suitable training, such an individual may learn to do many things that he would not normally learn with ordinary training. If some deficiency exists within the nervous system, there are limits placed on what can be done to remedy it. If a child suffers from a high and prolonged fever so that many of the cells in the brain are destroyed, there is no way in which other cells of the body can assume the functions of the destroyed cells; neither is there any way in which new cells can be provided. Much the same is true of a person who is born with a nervous system of limited capacity. Cells cannot be added to his nervous system, and neither can other cells of the body make up for the deficiencies of the system. Nevertheless, differences in training can produce great differences in the capacity of the individual to function. Such a statement within an educational context is really a truism, for all education is predicated on the assumption that the training to which a person is exposed does make a difference. There are many reasons for believing that the cave man was just as well endowed intellectually as modern man, but his limited capacity for problem solving was a result of his limited education. Were it possible to take a cave man's infant and raise him in a modern environment with all of the advantages that education provides, one would expect that he would grow up to be a person similar in all respects to modern man. We cannot deny that great variations in behavior can be produced by differences in the environment. Educators, since they are so deeply concerned with the role that learning can play in the development of man, have tended to emphasize the importance of the learning process in determining what the adult can and cannot do. This emphasis has often been to the neglect of the fact that the accomplishments of any particular member of the human race may be limited by the characteristics that he has inherited.

What kind of evidence is there that heredity plays some part in determining the individual's level of intellectual capacity? The most direct evidence available is that children who are raised from birth in foundling homes differ from one another very markedly in intellectual ability. These children are exposed from the earliest stages of their life to a uniform environment, and whatever differences appear must be due to differences in inherited abilities. Such children do differ very markedly from one another in their performance of intellectual problems. The only alternative to the hypothesis that such differences are inherited is the possibility that the children were exposed to different conditions before they were born. This hypothesis is unlikely to be sound, for it is well established that depriving the mother of important foods does not deprive the baby of these substances. The embryo has the capacity to draw on the reserves of the mother. If the intake of calcium of the mother is insufficient, the embryo will draw on the calcium in the bones of the mother, and this may go on to the point where the bones of the mother actually become brittle or soft. Much more likely is the hypothesis that the differences among the foundling children in intellectual performance are due to inherited characteristics.

The type of study just discussed is one in which the environment is held constant, but the heredity factor differs from child to child. An alternative procedure is to conduct studies in which the inherited ability is constant but the environment differs. Only a very exceptional kind of situation permits this; but before it is discussed, certain common misconceptions related to this matter must be cleared up. First, it is incorrect to assume that all children in the same family inherit the same characteristics. Each child receives from his two parents a batch of genes, but the sample that one child receives will almost certainly differ from any sample that his brother receives. A child does not receive through the heredity mechanism all of the genes his parents possess, but only a sample of them. Thus, brothers in the same family differ from one

FIGURE 23. In some situations, long-term predictions from test scores must take into account the cultural factors that may influence the intervening variables involved. In the illustration, Professor Malouf, of the University of Utah, is seen engaged in a project concerned with the counseling and guidance of Ute Indians and with the adaptation of tests to make them suitable for predicting learning within this group. Tests as they are ordinarily given in schools did not measure appropriate intervening variables related to learning among Ute Indians, and hence the project was developed in order to provide suitable instruments and services.

another in the genes they receive. If this were not so, brothers or sisters within the same family would show a much higher degree of resemblance than they do.

So far as is known at the present time, the only children who receive identical genes from their parents are identical twins, who are believed to be derived from a single fertilized egg cell. This cell splits into two cells, as a fertilized egg cell normally does in the process of development, but at this point the normal pattern of development ceases. The usual next step in the development would be for the pair of cells to divide again to form a four-celled body, and then an eight-celled body. In the case of identical twins, it is believed that the two cells that are first formed separate, for some unknown reason, and each one independently grows to be a complete embryo. These two embryos inherit identical genes from the parents, and whatever differences later emerge must be due to environmental influences. Of course, the environment may start its work early, and already by birth some differences may appear. It is generally found that one of the developing twin embryos has a more favorable place in the uterus than does the other, so at birth the one will be rather heavier than the other. Such minor disadvantages suffered early in life may later disappear, for such environmental deficiences tend to have only a minor depressing effect on the general pattern of development.

Identical twins reared together in the household in which they are born have not only identical inherited characteristics but closely similar environments. The environments cannot be identical, for accidental circumstances will favor one more than the other; and chance, too, will bring the one valuable experiences that the other may never encounter. Such environmental differences as occur by chance do not seem to have any great consequences in the development and life of most identical twins reared together. The twins tend to resemble one another highly not only in physical features but also in ability, achievement, and interest pattern. Some identical twins struggle hard to appear different and make every effort to dress differently and to groom themselves in different ways; but, despite this struggle for difference, there is still such a striking resemblance that associates often make fun of this effort to be different. Similar physical structure generates similar behavior, particularly when the environments are similar. One can hardly expect the twins' own efforts at achieving separate recognition to be too successful.

Our main interest in identical twins in the present context lies not in the fact that those reared within the same household show a close resemblance to one another (even to the point where they develop similar cavities in the teeth), but in those who have been reared in different environments from an early age. Identical twins occur rather rarely. The incidence of twins in the population of the United States is approximately one birth in eighty-six, but only a small fraction of these twins are identical; and of these identical twins, only a small fraction are separated soon after birth and reared in different environments. It is this latter group in which we are interested, for it is in this group that we can find pairs of individuals in which the inherited factors remain constant but the environment varies.

Great difficulty has been experienced by scientists in finding such pairs of twins. Often the one twin does not even know about the existence of the other. Cases can be identified only through widespread publicity campaigns; and, even so, such extensive campaigns within a country such as the United States are unlikely to yield more than a score of cases.

Some rough estimation of the relative strength of the influence of heredity and environment as factors determining test scores *within our culture* can be made by examining the relationship between identical twins on scores on particular tests. We would expect that such twins reared together in the same household would have closely related scores on, say, a test of intelligence, because both the inherited and the environmental factors are the same for both twins. If the twins were separated shortly after birth and placed in very different environments, one might expect them to differ somewhat in their scores. If environment rather than heredity is the main factor that determines a child's intelligence test scores, then little relationship would be expected between the scores of the identical twins. The data provided by Burt (1958), which is shown in Table 3, indicates that the intelligence test scores of identical twins tend to be related even though the twins are raised in different environments. The data suggests, but does not unequivocally prove, that the scores on the particular intelligence test used are determined both by the inherited characteristics of the individual as well as by environmental conditions. It is certainly conceivable that if the twins who were separated had been placed in environments that differed more widely for each pair, the relationships between the pairs that were separated might have been reduced even further. However, the data also indicates that when unrelated children are reared together, they show only slight resemblance in their intellectual background, despite exposure to the same environment. Apparently the pressures of the environment are not sufficient to produce a high degree of resemblance.

In the study of nineteen pairs of twins reared apart, which was reported some years back by Newman, Freeman, and Holzinger (1937), the twins were classified according to the differences in the education to which each member of a pair had been exposed. The most pronounced

TABLE 3*

Correlation Between Scores on Intelligence Tests of Pairs of Children

	Identical Twins Reared Together	Identical Twins Reared Apart	Nonidentical Twins Reared Together	Unrelated Children Reared Together
Group Intelligence Tests	.944	.771	.542	.281
Individual Intelligence Tests	.921	.843	.526	.252

* Data from Burt, who reports that the correlations are based on at least thirty pairs of identical twins. C. Burt., "The Inheritance of Mental Ability," *American Psychologist,* **13** (1958), pp. 1–15.

differences were seen in three pairs in which members of a pair differed on an Intelligence Quotient Scale by twenty-four, nineteen, and twelve points. The greatest of these three differences was between a pair of twins known as Gladys and Helen. Gladys had received only three years of grade school, while Helen had received a college degree and had become a teacher. The intelligence quotients of these two youngsters were 92 and 116 respectively. The pair whose intelligence quotients differed by nineteen points were James and Reece, whose measured intelligence quotients were 96 and 77 respectively. James had lived with a good small-town family and had completed high school; Reece had lived with a primitive mountain family and had gone to school part-time through the eighth grade. The third pair, Eleanore and Georgiana, had intelligence quotients of 66 and 78. Eleanore had gone through five grades of schooling; her sister had received a full high-school education and an additional three years of normal school.

The data suggests that the difference in intelligence quotients to be expected between children raised with the poorest educational opportunities that our culture has to offer and those that are exposed to the best would be about twenty points. This allows considerable latitude for the operation of both heredity and environment in producing differences between people. It means that effective education can make a person intellectually more effective in solving problems, for this is what an intelligence test measures; but it also means that there is probably a limit to what the educator can do. Thus, a child who, in one community with grossly inadequate educational facilities, would grow up to be a person classified as mentally handicapped would, in another and better community, grow up to be a dull but adequate person. Such a person would never come close to the problem-solving ability of the average person, but he would have gained enough to enable him to take care of himself through life, and this would have been an important educational accomplishment.

Such extremes as we have considered are relatively rare except in certain well-identified groups. The Southern Negro is generally known to have been exposed to an educational background that is very inferior to that of the Northern white, so it is hardly surprising that his scores on intelligence tests tend, on the average, to be lower than that of whites. That much of this difference, if not all of it, is a product of the inferior background of the Southern Negro is seen by the fact, unearthed many years ago by Klineberg (1935), that the children of Southern Negroes who migrate north to New York City show a progressive rise as the children are exposed to the Northern educational system. Over a period of five or six years, the gap found by Klineberg between the intelligence-test scores of the whites and the migrant Negroes steadily declined, despite the fact that when Klineberg made his study much of the Northern education provided for Negroes was inferior to that provided for whites. The difference between the intelligence quotients of the white and the Negro in America is much what one would expect it to be if the white and the Negro had the potential of being intellectually equal, but one of the groups was afforded inferior schooling. Equal intellectual potential does not mean that all members of each group have equal potential. Within each group there are the most extensive differences, but the average of the two groups, given equal educational opportunity, might be expected to be equal in terms of what we know at the present time. Although this latter statement is an inference and not a directly established fact, it fits so well the various sources of data that it cannot be easily brushed aside.

Relationship of Measures of Intelligence to Measures of Learning

The measurement of intelligence had its origins in a need to identify children incapable of learning in ordinary school programs. This was the context of the work of Alfred Binet when he was called by the French Ministry of Education to undertake work that led to the development of his famous testing instrument. The thought that formed the foundation of the Binet scale was based on the assumption that a measure of intelligence would generally predict the level of achievement of a child, and that it would thus be able to differentiate the mentally handicapped child from the child who scored high on a scale of intelligence but who was a poor achiever for other reasons. A scale of intelligence conceived in this manner would be expected to show some relationship to school achievement, though not a perfect relationship. A test of intelligence that was perfectly related to achievement would be of little value, for it would provide no information about a child other than what was already available. The numerous studies undertaken during the last half century or more have shown consistent correlations of approximately 0.6 between measures of intelligence derived from various versions of the Binet scale and standardized measures of achievement. Somewhat lower correlations are found with teachers' grades. Certainly there can be no question that the Binet type of intelligence test can be used to predict current level of learning in school children, though in some academic areas more accurate predictions can be made than in others. Predictions of achievement in quantitative subjects, such as mathematics, are less accurate than predictions in more verbally oriented subjects, such as social studies.

Measures of general intelligence predict with considerable accuracy the current status of achievement of the pupil, but they have had much less success in predicting how much school progress a pupil will make over a given period of time, such as a semester or a school year. This may appear to be a contradiction, but it is not. Gain scores on achievement tests are not so meaningful as one might suppose them to be. Consider, for example, a group of pupils in the sixth grade who are given an achievement test in mathematics at the beginning and end of the school year. The difference between their scores at these two testings represent gain scores, but these gain scores are not comparable one with another. One pupil starts out the year with a score that is not much better than chance but makes a gain of, say, 20 points during the year. Another pupil starts out with a very high score and shows a gain of only 5 points; but he could not show a greater gain since he answered every question correctly on the final test. This is just one reason why two gain scores are often not comparable. Another reason is that gain scores in different ranges of the scale may not be comparable. A pupil may be able to move his score very easily from, say 20 to 40; but to make a gain from 50 to 70 may require a tremendous amount of work and diligent effort. Since these difficulties of scaling have not been solved, scientists have not been able to establish at this time whether there is or is not any substantial relationship between gain in knowledge over periods of time such as a semester and measures such as are provided by intelligence tests.

Another approach to the study of the relationship of measures of individual differences to learning is found in studies in which they are compared with performance on laboratory learning tasks. A common pattern for such studies has been to administer a battery of tests to those serving as subjects, and then to subject them to a series of learning tasks. Such tasks often involve simple operations such as adding together two numbers, maze learning, writing numbers backwards, decoding, and so forth. The scores on the measures of individual differences can then be compared with measures of how much is learned or other measures derived from the learning tasks. In some studies, the comparison has been with gain scores on the learning tasks—that is, with scores derived from subtracting the initial level of performance on the learning task from the final level of performance. Other scores may also be derived from the learning tasks. The learning curve for each subject can be plotted and the mathematical properties of each curve determined. The mathematical properties of the curves can then be compared with the measures of individual differences.

The classic article on the problem was published by Woodrow (1946). This article reviewed research on the problem up to the time when it was published, much of which had been undertaken by Woodrow himself. His conclusion was that very little relationship had been demonstrated between measures of learning and measures of individual differences. The correlations rarely departed significantly from zero. However, one is not justified in concluding from the data reviewed by Woodrow that measures of general intelligence and other measures of individual differences are unrelated to learning, for the learning tasks studied were not particularly promising for that purpose. The problems included in intelligence tests have all been very carefully selected; but the learning tasks were not selected with corresponding care. Surely one would not expect much relationship between learning to add two numbers accurately and rapidly and performance on an intelligence test, but there are verbal learning tasks that appear to require the performer to undertake operations in his brain similar to those called for by intelligence tests. In a more recent study by Duncanson (1964), in which much greater care was exercised in the selection of learning tasks, relationships were found between measures of general intelligence and learning.

Experimental psychologists are now making substantial progress in the analysis of verbal learning tasks such as are involved in paired-associate learning and serial learning, and this analysis should make it possible to identify aspects of the verbal learning process that may be expected to be related to aspects of intelligence as it is commonly measured. Small adjustments of a learning task may change the relationship to measures of intelligence. For example, in a series of studies conducted at the University of Utah, we have typically found a substantial correlation between grade-point average and a serial learning task involving nonsense syllables when the presentation rate is one syllable per second and the task is of a particular length. However, very similar tasks involving different rates of presentation of information have not shown a similar relationship. The possibility exists that both grade-point average and serial learning tasks given under particular conditions may both measure the individual's ability to process information; but if the speed of presentation of the serial learning task is slowed up, then it ceases to measure this kind of variable. This illustration points out some of the difficulties that are encountered in comparing measures of individual differences with measures derived from learning in the laboratory.

The outcome of the research reviewed here on the relationship between measures of intelligence and gain scores on learning tasks is that the technical difficulties involved in such research have not yet been resolved, and the nature of the relationship involved remains a matter for speculation.

Measured Intelligence as a Predictor of Academic Learning in the Culturally Deprived

How does the fact that intelligence-test scores reflect both inherited and environmental influences affect the value of intelligence tests for making predictions of academic learning? This is an important matter, partly because the hue and cry has been raised from time to time that intelligence tests are "unfair" to children from a lower socioeconomic group. This argument has been repeatedly raised by Eells *et al.* (1954) and others who have attempted to devise tests that would be "fair" to all classes. Much of this criticism and effort is a consequence of a misunderstanding concerning the way in which intelligence-test scores are influenced by the environment. The argument is that, for example, a person who comes from a depressed environment who achieves an intelligence-quotient score of 90 and whose score, if he were raised in a favorable environment, would have been 110 is likely to behave more like a person with an intelligence quotient of 110 than like one with an intelligence quotient of 90. The argument goes on to the effect that the test is "unfair" to him and does not reflect his "true" level of intelligence, and that what is needed is a test that will show his "true" intelligence quotient to be 110. The argument is fallacious and misleading and does not fit many of the important facts that have been discovered in recent years.

Research at the present time indicates that whatever depresses the scores on intelligence tests produces a general depression on the person's capacity to perform. In the hypothetical example one would expect, on the basis of evidence at present available, that the person involved would behave in educational situations like a person with an intelligence quotient of 90 rather than like one with an intelligence quotient of 110. Therefore, the score on the intelligence test, depressed though it is, will provide a better predictor of educational achievement than will a score based on some kind of test that takes into account differences in background. Some interesting research on this problem has come from the armed services, where this problem is one of central importance (see Gordon, 1955). Suppose a man enters the armed services and obtains a classification-test score equivalent to an intelligence quotient of 80; but it is found that, given a superior environment, he might well have had one equivalent to an intelligence quotient of 100. The question is, will he learn at the 80 level or the 100 level? The evidence indicates that, despite equal opportunities to learn with those from a superior environment, he will still learn at the 80 level rather than the 100 level. The depression of scores on a test of intelligence represents in such cases a prolonged period of deprivation from satisfactory learning opportunities. Such prolonged periods of deprivation have considerable effects on the general pattern of behavior, and may prevent the development of learning sets that play such an important part in late learning.

These and similar results seem to indicate that intelligence tests, although they provide scores that are influenced considerably by differences in environmental conditions, make fair predictions. The fear has often been expressed by educators that such a test will reflect a depressed score even though the youngster may be able to learn at a level far above that indicated by the test. Such will generally not be the case, for, as we have said before, whatever depresses intelligence-test scores is likely to depress performance in learning situations. Attempts to build tests in which such depressing influences in the background do not affect scores result in devices that are rather poor predictors of school performance.

When intellectual performance is depressed through inadequacies in the environment, the permanence of the depression can be well understood in terms of the concept of early learning described by Hebb and discussed at greater length in other parts of this volume. Some intellectual deficiencies can be, presumably, accounted for in terms of inadequate opportunities for early learning to take place. It is certainly conceivable that a child may, through an impoverished environment, fail to develop certain basic intellectual skills. Just as the dog brought up in a protective, yet deprived, environment may not develop the fundamental skill of avoiding bumping into objects, it is possible that the human may present a similar intellectual clumsiness through lack of intellectual stimulation during long years of childhood. We know, too, that such deficiencies in early learning may not only result in gross deficiencies of behavior, but that these deficiencies may be permanent.

Depression in intellectual performance due to a deprived environment bears all of the marks of deficiencies in early learning. Particularly striking is the relatively permanent effect of such deficiencies and the difficulties encountered in trying to overcome them. Intellectual level, when it has been depressed through a poor environment, can be slowly raised through *many years* of exposure to a superior environment. Children of Negroes in the Klineberg study (1935) who came north to live in Harlem showed a slow and steady rise in measured intellectual level; but the rise even after a year in the superior environment was very small. However, the effect of the superior environment was marked only after a period of many years, a fact consistent with the hypothesis that a process similar to that of early learning was involved. Just what the early learning process involves is quite obscure. Can it be speeded up through a suitable educational program? This is a possibility about which nothing is known at this time.

Stability of Individual Measures of Intelligence

Even if intelligence-test scores, such as are provided by an intelligence quotient, varied considerably over the years, they still might be very useful measures if they were capable of predicting the pupil's immediate level of performance in his academic work. Nevertheless, if they showed substantial variation over periods of one or two years, their value would be limited; for there are many advantages in planning pupil programs well ahead if the level of performance of the pupil can be predicted for several years into the future. The reader can understand, then, why it is that educational psychologists have been interested in discovering the extent to which the intelligence quotients of children at a particular level are predictable from the intelligence quotients measured at an earlier time. The stability of mental test performance is a matter of practical importance, as well as one with theoretical implications.

It is difficult to obtain data that will indicate the extent to which there is stability in intelligence quotients, because many children who are tested today did not take any test five to ten years ago. Another difficulty that arises is that many children who have been tested and then retested after an intervening period of several years have unfortunately been given tests that are so different in the abilities they measure that the scores cannot be compared. The best that one can usually hope to find is a group of children who have been given tests that are closely similar and of which the measures obtained by the two methods are roughly comparable. A part of the difficulty is due to the fact that the tests also change as the years go by, and children may not be retested on the same test because during the intervening years it has become obsolete. In some of the best data available on this problem of the consistency of test scores, namely, that of Honzik, MacFarlane, and Allen (1948), the children were tested at age six to seven with the 1916 Stanford-Binet Test; then, in the age bracket of eight to fifteen, they were tested with the Stanford Revision of this test. Finally, at the age of eighteen they were tested with the Wechsler-Bellevue Test. All of these tests provide scores that measure approximately the same characteristics, and hence it is possible to make a table that converts the score on the one into a comparable score on the other.

Changes in intelligence quotients over the twelve-year period from six to eighteen years of age are shown in Table 4. Roughly two-fifths of the cases change by less than fifteen points over this period, and three-fifths of the cases change by less than twenty points. From the writer's point of view, this represents surprising stability, particularly in view of the fact that the intelligence-quotient scale ordinarily used covers a range of more than sixty points. The stability is sufficient to be able to determine, during the elementary-school years, the broad intellectual range that one may expect the person to fall into during his early adult life. On the other hand, one can expect a few surprises. A few children will make quite dramatic changes in their test scores. One child in the sample made a change of more than fifty points.

At the present time relatively little is known about the reasons for

TABLE 4*

Changes in Intelligence Quotient Between the Ages of Six and
Eighteen for 222 Children

Change in Intelligence Quotient	Per Cent of Children
50 or more points	0.5
30 to 49 points	8.5
20 to 29 points	25.0
15 to 19 points	24.0
10 to 14 points	27.0
0 to 9 points	15.0

* Data from Honzik *et al.*, "The Stability of Mental Test Performance Between Two and Eighteen Years," *Journal of Experimental Education*, **17** (1948), pp. 309–324.

the marked changes that occur over long periods of time in the intelligence quotients of some of these children. Honzik *et al.* state that there
is a tendency for the children who do change to come more and more in
line with the ability level of their parents. This could be because heredi-
tary factors will ultimately show through. The alternative explanation,
equally plausible, is that the level of intellectual stimulation of the home
is the one that ultimately determines the level of intelligence of the
individual concerned. Neither learning theory, nor any other theory,
indicates at this time which one of these two explanations is the sounder,
nor whether both contain an element of truth. One conclusion of Honzik
and his associates offers some clue concerning the causes of these fluctuations. They state that children whose scores showed large fluctuations
were children who had life histories that showed marked variations in
disturbing and stabilizing factors. The idea is plausible that such children
may at times have been so emotionally disturbed by events in their
home that they were not able to demonstrate their true capacity on the
test. The writers of the article also report that there were some children
who, despite gross fluctuations in the emotional atmosphere of the home,
showed little change. This also makes sense. For reasons that are not
understood at this time, some children do not become as much disturbed
as others by turmoil in their social environment.

A second point that is brought out by the data considered is that
as the child grows older, the accuracy with which his intelligence
quotient at the age of eighteen can be predicted is materially increased.
This is shown in Table 5, which indicates the relationships as they were
found by Honzik and his associates. In this table, the column at the left
indicates the age of the child at the earlier of the two testings that are
being compared. The line of ages along the top of the table indicates the
age of the child at the second of the two testings. As an example of the
way in which this table is read, consider the bottom line. This line indicates that the first of the two testings took place at age twelve and that
ninety-two children were involved. These same children were retested
with the same test at the age of fourteen, and a correlation of 0.92 was
found between the first set of scores and the second set. This same group
was also retested at the age of eighteen on the Wechsler-Bellevue Test.
The correlation between the scores obtained at the age of twelve on the
Stanford Revision and the scores on the Wechsler-Bellevue was found to
be 0.76.

Because a different test was used at the age of eighteen from the one
used in previous years, this would tend to lower the correlation between
the first testing and the second testing. Different tests always measure
somewhat different combinations of ability.

TABLE 5*

Correlation Between Individual Measures of Intelligence Obtained
on the Same Group of Children at Different Ages

Test Administered	Age	N	AGE OF SUBSEQUENT TESTING STANFORD REVISION FORM L (Age 12)	(Age 14)	WECHSLER-BELLEVUE (Age 18)
Stanford-Binet (1916 Revision)	6	214	.71	.67	.61
Stanford Revision (Form L)	8		.85	.85	.70
Stanford Revision (Form L)	10	107	.87	.85	.70
Stanford Revision (Form L)	12	92		.92	.76

* Data from Honzik *et al.,* "The Stability of Mental Test Performance Between Two and Eighteen Years," *Journal of Experimental Education,* 17 (1948), pp. 309–324.

Substantial evidence indicates that measures derived from individual tests of intelligence can be considered to operate as intervening variables in many learning situations. In some learning situations, they do not operate as intervening variables. In general, they are fairly good predictors of academic performance in the upper grades of the elementary school and at higher levels. They are particularly effective in predicting performance in typical academic work, but have little success in predicting that of art or music. They are not equally effective in predicting the performance of the child in all subject-matter fields.

In those areas in which intelligence tests have proved to be useful for predicting academic performance, predictions are still made with a rather large margin of error. When it is said that they are good predictors, the implication is that they are better predictors than the judgment of adults would be. Indeed, the justification of a test of intelligence is that it provides a better indication of the level of accomplishment to be expected than can be derived from other sources. Nevertheless, correlations between intelligence-test scores and measures of achievement are unlikely to be even as high as 0.7. Generally they will be found to be in the region of 0.5, if a reasonably reliable measure of achievement is available. Although intelligence tests measure an important intervening variable (or variables), there are clearly others that are not measured by such an instrument.

Intelligence or Intelligences

The intelligence tests that have been considered are based on a number of assumptions. One of these is that intelligence is a central, sovereign trait, a single characteristic that can be measured and that determines the adequacy of a person's performance in all of the intellectual activities in which he engages. The typical way of measuring this intellectual capability is to present the individual with a range of problems and to obtain the average of his performance on these problems. With a knowledge of this performance, the inference is made that he will perform at a similar level on intellectual problems he encounters elsewhere. This is roughly right. The Binet-type test of intelligence does predict adequacy of performance in a great range of situations, although its adequacy in this respect is much less at the lower age levels than at the higher ones. We cannot expect an intelligence test to be of much use in this respect in the age range of three to six; but above that range, predictions of considerable accuracy can be made concerning the performance of the child in academic work and in other situations where performance is related to intellectual capacity.

Above the age of about six years, the scores on a test of the Binet type show considerable stability from year to year and over periods of several years. It represents a stable characteristic within the cultural conditions that generally prevail. It shows considerable relationship with performance in the academic subjects, but little relationship with performance in such skills as typing.

The score on a test such as the Binet represents the average of the performance of a number of different abilities represented by different items on the test. The fact that a number of different abilities is involved in the test is clear to anybody who has administered the test a large number of times. For example, some children excel on the memory items, but not on other items. Other children do well on the reasoning items and the vocabulary, but poorly on the memory items. The different problems in the scale seem to tap a number of fairly distinct abilities. Shortly after Binet completed his classic work, many psychologists had already begun to ask whether it might not be better to measure the separate and distinct abilities involved, rather than to throw them together and obtain an average of performance on all of them. Separate measures of the distinct abilities involved might provide a system of intervening variables capable of predicting learning in a great range of skills. Different skills might have to be predicted with different combinations of these aptitudes or measures of intervening variables. This problem was a good one to pose but a difficult one to solve, for there seemed to be no agreement concerning the number of aptitudes that were involved, and no techniques were readily available for finding out how many of them there were and what they could be. One possibility is that every single type of test problem measures a different ability, and that each one of these abilities ought to be measured separately; but this would result in the proliferation of vast numbers of tests. In the early days of psychological testing, this is exactly what happened. Anyone who developed a new test marketed the instrument as one measuring a new ability that other tests did not measure. To this process there appeared to be no end, and the market became cluttered with innumerable testing devices.

While this process of test proliferation was proceeding, scientists were developing techniques for determining how many distinct and separate variables were being measured by any particular collection of tests. These techniques were known as *factor analysis* and were designed to determine how many distinct abilities have to be measured in order to cover the various abilities measured by a battery of tests. A large group of tests is generally found to represent only a few distinct abilities of any real importance, but each test represents its own special combination of these abilities. Thus, although a battery may consist of twenty tests, it may measure only four or five major abilities, because each one of the tests consists of a different combination of these abilities.

Unfortunately, at this time there is no theory available concerning the pattern of emergence of specialized aspects of aptitude. Many have been tempted to speculate that first there emerges an ability that one may call general intelligence, and that later specialized aspects of aptitude emerge. This would make a nice theory if one could demonstrate that this were so and if one could show the pattern of emergence of specific aptitudes. In one of the few researches on the subject, Hagen (1952) studied the aptitudes measured by the Wechsler Intelligence Scale for Children in order to determine whether, as the child grows older, the various subtests measure less a general factor called general intelligence and more a set of fairly specific aptitudes. Her data did not support this idea. The test measured just as much a general factor at the beginning of elementary school as it did early in high school. No evidence could be found for the gradual emergence of a set of specific aptitudes and a declining importance of a general intelligence factor. The emergence of special aptitudes is a complex problem, as is the matter of their generation.

On the other hand, historical data indicates that at least some aptitudes emerge at an early age. Great musicians have commonly shown their talent in the preschool years. Some great artists show a similar precociousness. A few mathematicians have manifested a similar pattern. However, one can also point to late-bloomers, whose talents did not manifest themselves until the middle adult years.

The specialized aptitudes that are measured in various test batteries vary, to some extent, according to the purpose for which they are built; but they nevertheless are closely similar. Table 6 illustrates some of the kinds of test problems that are used and the predictions that are commonly made from tests that include the particular type of item. The table also indicates the names commonly given to the aptitudes that are measured by the types of test item listed. Some of the items imply the existence of illustrations that are not included in the table.

An inspection of Table 6, which describes some of the aptitude tests commonly included in batteries given at the high-school and junior-high-school level reveals that they reflect two trends. The one trend comes down from Binet and represents the attempt to build test items that provide problems quite unrelated to areas in which some children have had

TABLE 6

Some of the Aptitude Factors Commonly Measured by Tests Included in Aptitude Test Batteries

Illustration of Test Problem	Name Given to Factor Measured	Predictions Commonly Made with This Type of Test
What is the meaning of the word "ascend"? 1. go up 2. lift 3. elevate 4. rain	Verbal factor	Predicts grades in academic work, particularly in those fields where the content is largely verbal. Sometimes used for diagnosing difficulties in reading if the difficulty is believed to be due to a deficiency in knowledge of the meaning of words.
Multiply the numbers as indicated. $\begin{array}{cc} 16 & 39 \\ \times\ 6 & \times\ 4 \end{array}$	Numerical computation	Used for the prediction in the learning of skills which require numerical operations of a simple character, as, for example, many trades and skills such as those of the machinist and the bookkeeper.
What is the next number in the series? 2 4 8 16 ———	Numerical reasoning	Used for predicting grades in academic work involving reasoning with numbers. Physics is an example of such academic work, and so too would be work in engineering. Tests of this kind are used for predicting success in such areas at the college level.
Which object can be made by folding the paper along the dotted lines?	Space-relations factor or perceptual factor. (There are several perceptual factors.)	Used for predicting the ability to learn engineering drawing, sheet-metal work, and other skills involving space relations.

TABLE 6—Continued

Illustration of Test Problem	Name Given to Factor Measured	Predictions Commonly Made with This Type of Test
In the following list of pairs of names, place a check in the parentheses after a pair if the two names are identical. Chamberlin Chamberlin ( ) Jeremiah Jeremiah ( ) Gleason Gleeson ( ) Learned Learned ( )	*Perceptual-Speed Factor*	Has had a long history of predicting success in simple clerical jobs.
Which jug of water is most likely to tip over?	*Mechanical-Aptitude Factor*	Predicts learning of a great range of mechanical skills.
Place a check mark in the parentheses after each word which is correctly spelled. Perscription ( ) Opportunity ( ) Fundermental ( ) Demonstrate ( ) *In the following sentence choose the correct version.* Each one of the students were was } allowed to correct are } his own examination.	*Language usage*	Used for predicting performance in learning higher-level clerical tasks such as involve stenographic and secretarial skills.

special opportunities to learn. The early factor-analytic studies reflected this trend and emphasized the development of rather novel test problems that the pupil was unlikely to have encountered previously. L. L. Thurstone (1947), who played a central role in the development of factor analysis, expressed the hope that the aptitudes discovered by his methods might represent quite basic and inherited abilities. He even went so far as to anticipate the possibility that the study of genetics might ultimately reveal the relationship between the genes that a person inherited and his scores on aptitude tests. For this reason Thurstone's aptitude tests were always composed of items that, at least on the surface, were unrelated to the training given in schools.

The second trend in aptitude testing is illustrated by the last two tests in the table. Such tests represent abilities that reflect long periods of learning. In the mechanical area, prolonged exposure to mechanical problems develops a facility in solving such problems; and this facility, measured by a test, can be used to predict future level of achievement in the mechanical area. Inherited factors may play a part, but there is no attempt, in the measurement of mechanical ability, to develop test problems in which previous experience plays only a minimum part. Indeed, it is well established that scores on a test of mechanical aptitude are highly related to the kind of learning experiences to which the individual has been exposed. This concept of aptitude fits well with what is known of learning. Prolonged exposure to certain categories of problems may be expected to build up structures within the individual that will determine the course of subsequent learning. A high score on a test of mechanical aptitude may be presumed to indicate that the individual has had extensive experience with mechanical problems, and that early learning has taken place in this area to the extent that will facilitate subsequent learning. Differences between boys and girls on such tests probably reflect differences in exposure to mechanical learning situations. A difference that is probably similar in origin is found between city-reared boys and country-reared boys. The city group generally tends to have lower scores on tests of mechanical aptitude than does the country group, which has had superior mechanical experience on farms.

It is presumed here that tests of language usage, usually tests of knowledge of expression in English, function in much the same way as do tests of mechanical aptitude. They are highly useful for predicting academic performance. Such tests represent the extent to which the individual has had prolonged training that makes him sensitive to problems of English expression. Here again, one cannot doubt that limitations are placed on the level of skill that a person can reach by the nervous system that he has inherited. A mentally handicapped person cannot be expected to acquire much skill in the use of language, despite prolonged training. However, the skill does appear to be trainable within limits, though the training process is a very slow one. If a person has the capacity to learn, but through an accident of education does not, many years of effort may be required to make up for this deficiency. The slowness of the learning process in this field suggests that it is similar in many respects to the early-learning process rather than to the rapid process of later learning.

There are, beyond doubt, other areas in which prolonged learning over the early years of life develops capacities to learn further which should be measured in aptitude batteries. The emphasis has often been placed on the development of aptitude tests that do not measure specifically learned skills; this has resulted in the neglect of aptitudes that training in the early years may develop.

What is already known about early learning leads one to assume that if an aptitude that is mainly a product of early learning does not develop because of lack of opportunity, it is not likely that it can be developed rapidly by concentrated training over short periods. General observations support the view that the incapacity that results from inadequate experiences in the mechanical field is rather permanent. The adult who lacks any kind of "mechanical sense," as the saying goes, may make very little progress in this area for the rest of his life. Another factor also comes into play, and that is the satisfaction that many individuals derive from being quite helpless. Once the adult community recognizes that a person is mechanically inadequate, he is rescued quickly from any mechanical problem situation in which he is floundering. In this way, the other members of the adult community deprive him of the possibility of making up for his previous lack of experience. The mechanically inept manage to lean on the good will of the rest of the community in solving the mechanical problems they encounter. It is socially acceptable for women to behave in this way. Men have greater difficulty in playing a role of helplessness and in being accepted in that role in the community.

A large number of different test variables related to intellectual performance have been identified by those working in the psychometric field, but rather few of these have been of demonstrated value in predicting the course of learning. Although factor studies have shown the existence of fifty or more test variables, not many more than half a dozen have been shown to be useful as predictors of achievement. As a matter of fact, the remainder not only fail to predict achievement, but also fail to predict performance on the job. Many psychologists are inclined to believe that the remainder are only test variables—that is, they measure performance in a test situation, but this measure has little relationship to performance in other situations. At the time of writing, some of the variables described by Guilford as measures of creativity are assumed by many to measure aptitudes related to the performance of creative acts; but there is little evidence to support this contention. The test variables may have little relevance for predicting the occurrence of creative acts or the capacity to learn creative behavior. When it is said that man is characterized by as many as fifty aptitudes, one must remember that most of these aptitudes have little to do with the learning of anything the individual is likely to learn in any school situation. In addition, most of the aptitudes that have been demonstrated have been demonstrated only in the case of adults. The pattern of emergence is not known. Indeed, little is known about the existence of special aptitudes in children of elementary-school age.

The aptitudes discussed in this section have proved to be important variables for the prediction of achievement in academic situations in the adolescent and the adult. For this reason, they are included in most batteries of aptitude tests administered at the high-school level. Such tests predict well the capacity of the student to learn in different subject-matter fields. Tests of a number aptitude and numerical-reasoning aptitude have good predictive value for courses that are mathematical in nature. Verbal-factor tests predict in the verbal-learning areas. Space-perception aptitudes are useful for predicting performance in engineering drawing and in subjects in which space perception plays an important role.

Although these aptitude variables have proved to be successful predictors of achievement in learning situations, they have not shown themselves to be of much value for predicting performance of a job situation. Presumably, this is because they represent intervening variables related to learning and function as such. When a learning function is not involved, as it may not be on a job, then they lose their predictive value.

Measures of Motor Skill

Up to this point we have considered the measurement of various thinking and problem-solving skills that are indicative of future levels of learning mainly in academic areas. This does not exhaust, by a large measure, the aptitudes that must be taken into account in making an inventory of the strengths and weaknesses of the individual. There are, in addition, certain perceptual and motor skills that determine to some extent the capability of the individual for further learning.

Skills involved in the manipulation of objects and materials and the skills involved in gross muscular movement and in coordinated movements are referred to as *motor skills*. In the learning of some trades and professions, capacity for acquiring such skills is a factor in the learning process. In dentistry, for example, the student must have the capacity for learning the finger dexterity necessary for performing fine cutting operations on objects, usually teeth. The toolmaker requires similar skills. The baseball player, on the other hand, must be able to learn rapid, but precise, gross bodily movements. In the last half century, the development of machinery has eliminated the need for many motor skills that formerly played a very important part in the success of craftsmen. The maker of fine furniture today uses power tools for many operations, and he no longer has to use great manual skill in whittling his wood down to size by painstaking hand manipulation. A machinist today may need very little hand dexterity to produce an object that is accurate to within a ten-thousandth part of an inch. All he has to do is to set up a machine tool in an appropriate way, and the rest is done for him. What used to require manual dexterity requires more and more brainwork; and this means that persons who formerly might have been barred from an occupation because of lack of dexterity in manipulating objects and materials may now, with the use of modern machine tools, produce something approaching fine craftsmanship. With the advance of the machine age, motor skills are becoming less and less significant assets for those who possess them.

Intellectual skills are thus becoming more and more the primary asset that may help a person in life. This is in many ways unfortunate, for there are many whose outstanding aptitudes lie in the motor-skill areas.

Tests of motor skills have had a long history, and their development preceded the developments of tests of intellectual skills. Some of the earliest were developed by Galton, who administered his battery to many thousands of subjects of all ages. By the turn of the century, American psychologists had become interested in the area; and most of the work undertaken was prompted by the idea that tests of simple motor skills could be used to predict performance in complex activities that involved these skills. Thus, it might be assumed that tests of hand steadiness might predict rifle marksmanship, since steadiness is a component in the total skill of rifle marksmanship. Another example is the possibility that finger dexterity might be used to predict success in watch-repair work. Here again, the skill that is measured, finger dexterity, is a component of the total skill involved in repairing watches. Sometimes such predictions were found to work out rather well; but sometimes, for unaccountable reasons, the expected relationships did not materialize.

The advancement of knowledge in this area has been handicapped greatly by the difficulties of undertaking research. Tests of motor skills generally require apparatus, which is expensive to build and maintain. Unlike most paper-and-pencil tests of intellectual skills, students taking the tests show great improvement with practice; and the question has to be raised whether the most useful measure is a person's initial performance or his performance after he has had some practice. All of these problems have added greatly to the difficulty of the task faced by the research worker interested in the area. Some meager knowledge is, however, available concerning the number of different motor skills that may be involved in complex tasks, and these must now be considered.

At the present time there appears to be a limited number of distinct abilities in the motor area. Measurement of these abilities may be used at a future time for the purpose of predicting the ability of individuals to learn skills which involve these motor abilities. The abilities as identified by Fleishman (1956) are as follows:

Reaction time is the speed with which an individual can make a response to a stimulus he is expecting. One measure of this ability is that of raising a finger at a predetermined signal, such as a click or when a light is turned on.

Tapping ability is the speed with which an individual can perform a rapid movement, such as tapping a table top.

Psychomotor coordination is represented by such skills as require the coordination of the eye and the hand. It is involved in both fine and gross movements.

Manual dexterity is a popular term with a technical meaning. It refers to the ability to make skillful, controlled arm or hand movements at a rapid rate. In one test of this ability, the subject must turn over blocks as rapidly as possible.

Finger dexterity involves the rapid manipulation of objects with the fingers. It does not include arm motion, as does manual dexterity. In one test of this ability, the subject is required to manipulate small pegs with tweezers.

Psychomotor precision, although very little is known about it, appears to involve speed as well as precision. It is similar to finger dexterity, but seems to involve more eye-hand coordination.

Steadiness is measured by tests in which a steady hand yields a high test score.

Motor kinesthesis is measured by placing the individual in some unstable piece of equipment, such as the simulated cockpit of a plane. The cockpit is so arranged that it may tip to one side or the other, but can be righted by the movement of a rudder. The person must maintain the cockpit in an upright position by the control of the rudder.

Aiming or psychomotor speed is skill in performing at a high speed a simple task such as making dots in circles or making marks on standard answer sheets.

Ambidexterity is measured by asking right-handed subjects to perform simple tests, such as tapping tests, with the left hand and vice versa.

Many of these abilities require equipment for their measurement, although some of the others can be measured through paper-and-pencil tests. There is little possibility that reaction time can be measured through a paper-and-pencil test, but such tests have been devised to measure tapping and aiming.

We cannot think of these motor skills as being aptitudes in the same way as the intellectual abilities previously discussed are aptitudes. What we refer to as an aptitude is generally a stable and enduring trait that can be used to make predictions about the course of learning. The motor skills that we have considered here do not represent, as far as is known, stable and enduring traits, and should not be used, at least not at this time, for making any long-term predictions concerning what trade or skill a person can or cannot learn.

Change in Pattern of Aptitudes Required at Different Levels of Practice

Procedures for selecting those persons most likely to succeed in a particular learning program have generally made the assumption that the same single patterns of aptitudes is required throughout the program.

Thus, in selecting students for college, the assumption is made that those who are most likely to succeed in the first year of college are also those most likely to succeed in the subsequent three years. Generally, this is a reasonable assumption. Data has empirically demonstrated that those who do well in their freshman year are also the best prospects for the full degree program. However, there are some learning conditions in which the aptitudes required for the early stages of learning are considerably different from those required for the later stages. A research by Fleishman (1954) points up this phenomenon rather clearly.

In the Fleishman study, subjects were required to learn a complex coordination task known as the Complex Coordination Test, Model E. In this task the subject has to manipulate a set of controls similar to those used in a small aircraft. The responses may depend on the pattern appearing on the display board. This is a task in which extensive learning may take place, and the subject rapidly improves his pattern of performance. As a task it is quite complex. Fleishman also administered to his subjects a battery of aptitude tests involving performance on much simpler tasks. He then determined the extent to which each aptitude involved in his battery predicted performance on the complex task at each level of learning. Thus, he could determine whether advanced levels of learning called for different combinations of aptitudes from those called for by the earlier stages of learning.

The results of his study are shown in a graph presented in Figure 24. In this graph, the horizontal axis represents stages of learning on the complex task. The vertical axis represents the percentage of each aptitude involved in the task. Thus, one can see from the graph that as practice progresses, the complex-coordination factor increases as a learning factor, and the other factors assume less importance. With increasing practice, the visualization factor and spatial-relations factor show a marked decline in significance.

An implication from the research that has just been considered is that the tests that predict best in the early stages of learning of the complex task may not be those that predict best in the later stages.

The Trainability of Abilities

When it is said that an ability exists, the speaker is saying that an instrument for measuring it has been developed and that the measure thus derived is reliable. Sometimes there is also the added implication that the measure appraises some distinct aspect of behavior. Although psychologists have sought to discover abilities that can be used for the prediction of behavior, people involved in education have tended to look at

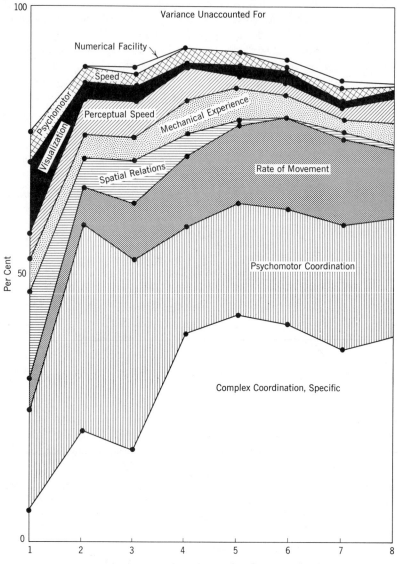

FIGURE 24. Graph showing the relationship between level of practice on a psychomotor task and the aptitudes required. (From Fleishman, 1954, p. 248. Reproduced by permission of *Psychometrika*.)

the lists of abilities thus developed and to think of them as aspects of behavior on which education should focus. The educator's line of thinking in this respect is attractive, for it appears to provide a systematic approach to the development of the individual: Maximum development would be achieved by giving training in each of the basic abilities that psychologists have identified. The fact that abilities, as measured by aptitude tests, reflect the effects of training does not lead to the conclusion that education should be organized around them.

The theory is superficially attractive; but, at a scientific level, it finds no support. First, many of the abilities that have been identified do not seem to represent particularly significant aspects of behavior. Second, the evidence seems clear that at least some of the abilities that have been identified can be trained only very indirectly. For example, abilities involving speed are important in many occupations. Clerical workers are commonly selected on the basis of their ability to perform certain perceptual operations at a fast pace; and motor speed factors, such as are measured by the Minnesota Rate of Manipulation Test, have also been used for the selection of factory workers. Now, how would the teacher train a speeded function?

The answer to this question, given by experienced teachers, is that one does not train speed directly. Consider the problem of teaching the pupil of piano to play a scale at high speed. This is done by practicing the scale *slowly*, but with flawless accuracy. Speed comes when the pupil has learned the exact sequence of operations that have to be performed and has learned them to the extent that each operation triggers the next. This is done by *slow* practice. Fast practice, on the other hand, does not accomplish this; forced speed, before the pupil is ready, results in errors, and errors involve practicing what is wrong. On this basis, slow practice would establish the necessary chain of associations between one movement and the next, and hence establish all the conditions necessary for rapid performance. The purpose here is to point out that an ability, the core of which is speed, cannot be and should not be trained directly. This is a far cry from the notion of training each separate ability by some direct means.

Another but more controversial example of an ability that is probably not directly trainable is the ability to produce original ideas—an ability measured by a number of tests currently available. Many educational programs have been described that give children practice in the production of original ideas. In a recent review of research related to the trainability of this ability, Travers *et al.* (1965) came to the conclusion that the various attempts to train it directly had either failed to show any effects from training or had been so ill-designed that an apparent training effect could not be considered as genuine.

However, the research has uncovered some interesting findings. Both Cline and Richards (1963) and Travers *et. al.* (1965) have found substantial correlations between the ability to make original responses and measures of knowledge in children. This relationship is hardly surprising. Anyone who examines the original responses on any test designed to measure originality is impressed by the extraordinary knowledge shown by those children who produce large numbers of original responses. If a child is asked to suggest an original use for the "lead" in a pencil, and he suggests that it might be used in an atomic pile, he is demonstrating unusual knowledge. First, this child knows that the "lead" is not lead at all, but carbon. Second, the child also knows that carbon is used in atomic piles. The response shows not only originality but also substantial knowledge, and it would not have been possible without such knowledge. Clearly, the child who has extensive knowledge has vastly greater possibilities of producing original ideas than the child who is relatively ignorant. The inference from such a position is that training to produce original responses might well involve the acquisition of knowledge. Although knowledge may not be a *sufficient* condition for producing original responses, it would appear to be a *necessary* condition.

Aptitude tests have been designed to predict trainability in various areas, but this does not mean that they represent categories of behavior in which specific training should be given. Classifications of aptitude tests (such as P. J. Guifford has proposed) have nothing to do with identifying areas of behavior that the school should attempt to develop.

A Classification of Aptitude Variables Postulated as Determinants of Achievement

As a first step toward the development of a theoretical structure for use in the development of research on aptitudes, it seems desirable to attempt to classify and inventory the variables that must be considered in the prediction of achievement. The following tentative categorization is suggested because it permits some integration of aptitude-measurement theory with the stimulus-response type of learning theory.

Classes of Variables

The intervening variables related to human achievement that must be postulated in order to predict level of achievement at the end of training are numerous, but the following categories seem to include most of those that it seems necessary to postulate in a reasonably parsimonious system, except for those that fall into the "motivation" category.

Category I variables relate to the extent to which the individual has already acquired the responses to be acquired in training. Measures of the extent to which the individual begins training with a repertoire of responses identical with those to be learned are usually referred to as measures of previous achievement. These variables, in some situations, are an extremely important determinant of final achievement. It seems probable that, in the armed forces, variables in this category are likely to be more important than in civilian training situations. A school for clerks in the armed forces is likely to seek out for training those who have had some civilian experience as clerks rather than those who have had experiences as farmhands or as equipment operators. On the other hand, a civilian school that provides training in clerical fields is likely to have much less experienced novices entering its classes.

Certain aptitude tests of motor skills fall into this category. The high specificity in motor skills and the lack of relationship between measures of even apparently similar motor skills classify them clearly in this grouping. Most tests of motor skills are designed to determine whether the individual has, in his repertoire of responses, certain motor responses that constitute part of those to be learned.

Category II variables measure the extent to which the individual has acquired responses that are prerequisites for learning the responses to be acquired in training. This category of variable has probably little relevance as a determinant of achievement in most training programs, because they do not attempt to build in an orderly manner on knowledge previously acquired. This class of variable is, beyond doubt, an immensely important determinant of achievement in courses in those few fields in which the subject matter forms a logically structured system of ideas. Mathematics approximates the ideal of orderly structure, and in that field it is clear that success in each course depends on the extent to which the individual has acquired certain prerequisite knowledge. However, in most learning programs, including those provided in many liberal-arts areas, there are no clearly identifiable prerequisites.

Category III variables represent the extent to which the individual has, through extensive experience in a particular area of activity, acquired rules that can be applied to the solution of broad classes of problems. Thus, the boy who has had many years of experience with mechanical toys shows what may be termed rule-regulated behavior in approaching mechanical problems. When faced with a novel mechanical device that does not work, he is unlikely to bang it at random in the hope that this will make it go; he is more likely to explore the problem systematically. He will attempt to solve the problem by applying rules derived from past experience. At a very simple level, these rules are a little like learning sets with which Harlow (1960) and others have experimented. Another obvious and common type of interference of this nature is found in the amateur typist, who has, as a result, immense difficulty in learning a more orthodox method. Relatively little has been done to develop measures of these negative learning sets because of the wide range of antecedent conditions which may produce them.

It seems reasonable to hypothesize that learning-set variables are more important determinants of achievement in short training programs than in long ones. In the longer programs the early part of training amy provide conditions which affect sets and produce sets more influential on later training than the sets acquired before the program began.

Category IV variables measure the ability to make the discriminations necessary to profit from training. These variables are commonly referred to as *process variables,* in accordance with the phenomenological type of construct that is most widely pursued in the field of aptitude measurement. The argument is that they measure the extent to which the individual can undertake certain *mental processes* necessary for success in training. For example, if the training of the sheet-metal worker requires that he be able to visualize how objects made of sheet metal would appear if opened up and laid out on a plane, then an aptitude test might be developed that would measure the ability to perform this mental operation. It is, of course, quite unnecessary to consider these variables from such a mentalistic viewpoint. They can be considered strictly as response variables that define the ability to make certain stimulus discriminations necessary for training. There are advantages in considering them as measures of the ability to make discriminations. One is that it is a desirable step away from the introspective approach, which has dominated the field, and a step toward the description of objective measures in objective terms.

The vast number of different stimulus discriminations that must be made in order to acquire skill in all of the training situations in which individuals are placed is such that it seems almost impossible to include, in a comprehensive aptitude-test battery, instruments that measure the ability to make each and every one of these discriminations. The problem of reducing these discriminations to a more convenient and parsimonious number does not seem to have been successfully solved at the present time.

The relationship between the stimulus discriminations required by tests and those required in the learning situations in which they are designed to predict performance are usually assumed to be relationships of identity. It is usual for aptitude tests to be based on some kind of analysis of the discriminations required for learning a particular task. The usefulness of this technique seems to be well accepted, and gives support to the assumption that the discriminations involved in the test situation and the learning situation may be successfully matched with one another.

Some of these complex stimulus-discrimination variables are often, according to the current custom, described as personality variables. Discriminations related to various aspects of social situations are examples of variables that fall into this category. However, the nature of the social discriminations necessary for performing a particular type of work are usually extremely difficult to identify and even more difficult to reproduce in miniature testing situations. The classification of variables into intellectual variables and personality variables has never been used within the framework of S——→R psychology. Perhaps a more useful classification is that of unipolar and bipolar variables.

Ferguson (1956) attempted to develop the concept that abilities of the kind that are revealed through factor analysis represent attributes that have achieved some stability and that manifest a transfer function. Measures of verbal abilities show a relationship to performance in many situations. Vocabulary tests, for example, predict achievement in many different college courses; and this reflects the fact that the abilities involved are highly transferable. Some abilities show greater transfer than do others. Verbal ability, as measured by a vocabulary test, shows transfer to an amazing range of situations. On the other hand, reaction time is an ability that has relatively little transfer to other performances.

Summary

1. Individuals differ in the extent to which they can perform the internal operations necessary for learning. Measures of these individual differences are referred to as aptitudes. There is not only the problem of identifying and measuring these variables, but also there is the problem of identifying the conditions that produce them.

2. Learning can be represented graphically in the form of a typical learning curve. Aptitude tests are commonly used for predicting the crude limit of learning in particular areas of study.

3. The original work of Binet was an attempt to measure a major variable related to learning in school. Although half a century has passed since Binet developed his famous test, there is still considerable speculation concerning the origin of the characteristic measured by the test. This characteristic is either not present or has not been measured by infants, which suggests that it emerges as the nervous system matures. Infant scales tend to measure motor and perceptual skills rather than those skills measured by intelligence tests.

4. The history of psychology has provided a wealth of studies related to the problem of the genesis of the characteristic measured by intelligence tests. This is an important problem in the planning of learning situations. If this intervening variable can be changed in magnitude through suitable training, then the curriculum must take this into account. Studies of identical twins reared together and reared apart indicate considerable stability of measures of intelligence despite large differences in the environment. Nevertheless, the changes that can be made fit the

idea that a change from a poor to a highly favorable environment may make an appreciable difference, after many years, in the intellectual effectiveness with which a person functions. Whatever changes can be made are slow to be produced, and may well reflect a process of learning similar to that which Hebb calls early learning.

5. Studies that have attempted to relate scores on measures of intelligence to measures related to learning have not produced a clear picture. Scores derived from intelligence tests are related to achievement in school subjects, but very little is known about their relationship to amount of improvement in a given period of time. Lack of knowledge is due to the fact that present research techniques involve difficulties that have to be overcome. Studies of the relationship of measures of intelligence to measures derived from learning in simple laboratory situations have also failed to provide a clear picture of the relationship. Evidence indicates that, under certain conditions and with suitable tasks, positive relationships will be found.

6. Evidence indicates that cultural deprivation will produce both a depression of measured intelligence and also a depression in school achievement. Intellectual depressions thus produced are not rapidly remedied by improving environmental conditions, but any improvement represents a very slow change.

7. Within the American culture, intelligence quotients, as measured by individually administered tests of intelligence, show considerable stability after the age of six; and later measures can be predicted well from earlier measures even when several years separate the two testings. This stability is partly a reflection of the fact that the cultural environment of most growing children remains a relatively constant factor. Few children are exposed to striking changes in their cultural environment.

8. A number of distinct aptitudes have been measured in young adolescents. These variables have been used successfully for predicting achievement in related fields. The earlier aptitude batteries tended to include tests the content of which was not closely related to formal schooling; but the more recent aptitude batteries include many tests that might well be described as achievement tests. Scientists have not yet been able to discover any clear-cut pattern of emergence of aptitudes. All one can say is that they appear to depend on both native endowment and experience. The aptitude variables that have been most successful for making predictions in learning situations are those designed to be measures of achievement.

9. Considerable work has been undertaken on the aptitudes related to the acquisition of motor skills. Fleishman has identified ten such factors, but these have only limited predictive value in learning situations. Indeed, some appear to represent variables that are highly restricted in

the situations in which they operate. Our culture is probably one in which these variables will play a declining role.

10. Much learning has to be undertaken by very indirect means.

11. Aptitudes represent many different classes of variables. A classification is provided which is related to how they may function in a learning situation.

16

Learning Theory and the Mechanization of the Classroom

THE INTRODUCTION of mechanical equipment into the classroom has been a slow process. Indeed, many would say that far too little attention has been paid to the development of educational inventions that might facilitate learning in the classroom. Yet, in a sense, few aspects of our culture have ever been so profoundly influenced by a single invention as education was by the development of the printing press. Perhaps it is the overwhelming influence on education of the invention of printing that makes one inclined to overlook the significance of other inventions.

Most of the early inventions that had an impact on education facilitated in some way the presentation of stimuli. The blackboard, in addition to printing, was a device that had this characteristic. At the response end of the learning process, the response medium remained that of the spoken word. Cheap materials on which responses could be recorded for further study and examination were relatively late in development. Expensive materials, such as parchment and brush and ink, were kept for sophisticated scholars rather than for learners. The small hand slate was one of the first devices introduced on an extensive scale that influenced the form of the response in the educational process.

In the early part of the present century, substantial efforts were made to improve education through the improvement of the methods used for the presentation of stimuli. The development of methods of projection and photographic film gave considerable impetus to this movement. The assumption continued to be that all that had to be done to upgrade education was to improve the techniques for stimulus presentation. The development of visual and auditory aids emerged as a field of specialization, and bureaus for the dissemination of visual and auditory aids showed a mushroom development in schools and universities. The impact of this approach on educational reform is still strong, and even in the last decade millions of dollars have been spent on the development of films designed to provide complete courses in certain areas of the physical sciences.

Although the approach to the improvement of education through improvements at the stimulus end of the process has its merits—and who would deny the vast importance of the introduction of printed materials, —there are limits to what can be done. Education involves much more than the mere presentation of stimuli. It also involves mediating processes and responses. Major improvements in the educational process must involve changes at both the stimulus end and the response end. A dawning awareness that such is the case first appeared in the period between the two world wars. Developments during this period must now be considered.

Early Attempts to Produce an Industrial Revolution in Education

The title for this section is taken from a farsighted article by Sidney Pressey, published over a quarter of a century ago (1932). In this article Pressey pointed out that nearly every field of human endeavor had been influenced by mechanization except education, and that it was time for educators to give up their medieval practices and begin to utilize mechanical equipment in the classroom. Many conditions were to make this industrial revolution in education slow in coming, not the least of which is, oddly enough, one of the admirable personal qualities of educators— namely, the personal enjoyment they derive from their interaction with pupils. The emphasis on the socialization of learning in the classroom stems from the observation that the teacher is limited in what he can do to promote learning, and that influences other than the teacher must be brought to play if learning is to be an efficient process. Social activity represents one way in which it may be possible to facilitate the learning process; but the preoccupation with social activities as a means of promoting learning has resulted in educators overlooking other techniques that might be used, particularly those that involve mechanical devices. The interests of teachers lead them to the development of social inventions rather than mechanical ones.

Pressey saw that mechanical devices could perform many functions that teachers do not have time to perform and that probably are not produced satisfactorily by social interaction. Pressey, in the development of his work, saw that the road to educational reform involved much more than changes at the stimulus end of the learning process. If the efficiency of school learning were to be improved, then there must be changes at the response end as well as at the stimulus end. It is for this reason that the pioneer work of Pressey must be considered a radical departure in its approach to educational problems.

Pressey began his pioneer work in teaching machines with the idea that intelligence testing and testing for information could well be undertaken with automatic devices. He had the foresight to see that the development of the objective test, which had come into prominence during World War I, would place burdens on teachers and others unless mechanical scoring procedures were developed. In his first article on the subject (1926), he described a self-scoring testing device which he had developed. In this early article there was little mention, except in the title, of the possibility that the device might facilitate learning as well as facilitate testing.

The early teaching machines were nothing more than testing devices that provided the learner with immediate opportunities for finding out whether the answer he selected was right or wrong. In a machine of this type the learner was given questions followed by several suggested answers, only one of which was right. In the early Pressey machines, the questions and suggested answers appeared in a slot in the machine. In later devices, the question and suggested answers were printed on a separate sheet. The learner would look at question number one, and then select what he thought to be the right answer. He then pressed the key on the machine that bore the same number as the answer he had chosen. If it was the wrong answer, nothing happened. If it was the right answer, the machine moved on to the next question to be answered. The machine kept a record of the number of wrong answers chosen. Once the series of questions had been completed, the machine was set again on question number one, and the student worked through the problems a second time, attempting to lower his score on the basis of what he had learned the first time he had gone through the series. The machine was not based on any particularly complicated learning theory, but only on the assumption that if the student knew when he was right or when he was wrong, learning would occur. Knowledge of results was the one essential principle on which such machines were based. This is a point of merit, for too much work in the classroom is undertaken without any knowledge of results or with knowledge of results that are so far postponed that the student does not benefit from it.

The type of learning machines that Pressey tried to develop and did develop was also evolved in a number of simplified forms. One of these was manufactured by Science Research Associates. In the latter version of the testing-learning device, an answer sheet was inserted in a frame, and the student recorded his answers by punching a hole in the answer sheet. If his answer was correct, he found a solid surface behind the place where he had made his punch. If his answer was incorrect, he found a hole.

Not only were simplified versions of Pressey's tester-trainer developed, but the United States Navy build a rather elaborate version which disposed of the need of a separate booklet of questions. In the Navy version, the questions and the alternative possible answers appeared in a window in the apparatus. When the correct answer was selected, the next question moved into position; and the process was repeated until the entire series of questions had been exposed. The learner could then run through the entire series again, and repeat the process until he knew all of the answers.

The Navy device was an expensive piece of equipment and, like all complicated pieces of equipment, involved problems of maintenance. Although the ideas underlying it had some merit, it never became widely used; but at least part of the problem in introducing it to organizations was that the organization had to find the money for the purchase of the equipment, and such money was often difficult to obtain.

These early pieces of equipment were never widely used. Indeed, Science Research Associates withdrew their simple punchboard device from the market, presumably for reasons of lack of support, although it was an ingenious device. Why this equipment never became widely adopted is a matter of speculation, but the chief reason seems to have been that it was ahead of its time. A body of teachers, imbued with the traditional notions that a teacher can teach only through direct interaction with the pupils, has difficulty in considering the notion that there are other ways of promoting learning, ways that have never yet been seen in the classroom.

The early teaching devices that emerged through the influence of Pressey were not considered to be replacements for the teacher in the classroom, but rather, they were regarded as additives to the typical on-going business of the classroom. They represented one more way through which learning could be promoted and, at the same time, provided a check on how well the student was progressing. Some of the later developers of teaching machines conceived of them as playing a much more central role in education, perhaps even that of taking over most instructional functions.

The Beginnings of the Impact of Learning Theory on the Design of Classroom Equipment

The equipment that has been considered up to this point was based on common-sense conceptions of learning. Perhaps the nearest that any of it came to being based on a scientific principle was the emphasis given by Pressey to the importance of immediate knowledge of results. His early pieces of equipment could not represent any high level of psychological sophistication, because knowledge available was limited. The same cannot be said of the position today, for during the last twenty years psychology has shown great advances in the field of learning, advances that make it possible to write a volume of this kind.

Although research on learning has been largely oriented toward the theoretical rather than the practical during the last few decades, many of the research workers who have been involved in these advances consider that the time has come for the application of some of the knowledge that has been accumulated.

Increased knowledge of the conditions that influence the course of learning now makes it clear that the machines developed by Pressey do not satisfy some of the requirements that a good teaching machine should meet. An outstanding scientist to be attracted to the study of problems of classroom teaching in the postwar period was B. F. Skinner, who, it is said, became interested in the problem after he visited the first-grade room in which his child had been placed. Legend has it that he was horrified to see the conditions for learning that existed, and set himself the task of bringing some measure of reform into educational practice, much as Pressey had attempted twenty years previously. His classroom observations led him to the opinion that one cannot rely on the busy teacher to function as a reinforcing agency in the classroom any more than one can rely on the experimenter in the laboratory. Both need equipment for this purpose. The classroom version of the equipment was to be referred to as a teaching machine.

Skinner must certainly have made a comparison between learning conditions as they occur in the classroom and learning conditions in his laboratory. As a leading proponent of reinforcement-learning theory, he understood the importance of reinforcement in the shaping of behavior, and while his laboratory was well designed for providing reinforcements to organisms, the school was not. The laboratory provided adequate reinforcements because it had been equipped with suitable electronic and mechanical equipment to perform this task. Indeed, without such equipment the effective reinforcement of subhuman organisms would be impossible. Skinner sought to build equipment that would provide in the classroom the same efficient reinforcing system that existed in his laboratory.

He saw that classroom equipment would have to be constructed to include certain important characteristics. A teaching machine would have to control the stimuli provided and permit the learner to produce the complete response to be reinforced. The lack of this feature was a central weakness of the machines designed by Pressey, which required only that the student *select* the correct response. In teaching, one does not want to teach only the skill of judging; one wants to develop the capacity for appropriate action. It is desirable that pupils learn to recall rather than recognize, and the multiple-choice machine does not teach them to do this. Skinner believed that the multiple-choice machine may actually teach wrong responses, but there is doubt whether this is so. There is at least some evidence to show that students taking multiple-choice tests do not learn wrong responses. The mere making of wrong response, even when the examinee believes it is a right response, does not seem to increase the strength of the wrong response measurably.

A second important requirement of a teaching machine is that it must lead the student through a carefully designed series of steps in acquiring any particular skill. This is how living creatures in the laboratory are taught to perform complex acts. They are taken through a series of steps each one of which leads to a closer approximation to the complex performance that the experimenter is attempting to produce. Sometimes these steps involve the development of component skills. Sometimes they involve the closer and closer approximation to the final behavior desired. The steps that the learner must go through to achieve a particular objective is referred to as a *program*. A program consists of a set of *frames*. Each frame constitutes a specific learning experience. A single frame may provide information and also pose a problem to solve; or it may only pose a problem. In the case of learning in animals, the program must be carefully designed by an experimenter who is aware of the behavior patterns of the creature involved. In the case of a human learner, the program must be designed with as full a knowledge as possible of the laws of behavior of the human organism. After a teaching machine has been developed, a large amount of work is required for the development of programs of learning to be inserted into the machine. The development of such programs is a technology in itself.

Two early types of machines were produced by Skinner for the teaching of children. One of these was designed for the teaching of arithmetic and spelling in the lower grades. The problems to be presented by the machine were printed in a set of frames, either on cards or on a disc. Only one frame with one problem printed on it was exposed to the learner at one time. The learner gave an answer by moving a set of printed letters or figures into appropriate positions either to spell a word or to provide a numerical answer. If the answer was correct, the machine moved on to the next problem by presenting a new frame. If the answer was wrong, the learner tried again to produce a correct solution until the correct one was found. The pupil could not go on to a new step until he had mastered the previous steps.

Such a machine may have merit in the lower grades, but one that provides for more complex responses is needed for the junior-high-school or high-school level. Among the machines at present under experimental trial for the higher grades are several in which the student writes in his response to the question. When he is ready to determine whether it is correct or not, he pulls a lever that moves what he has written under a piece of glass, where it cannot be changed. The same lever exposes the correct answer, which he must now compare with his own answer. If the two answers match, he moves a lever that brings up the next question and also punches a hole in the frame of the question that has been correctly answered; this prevents the question from coming up again. When he has gone through all of the frames, the machine starts again and takes him through those that he missed the previous time around. When he has mastered all of the problems, he is ready for the next program to be inserted into the machine. A picture of an advanced teaching machine is shown in Figure 25.

FIGURE 25. The illustration shows an advanced type of teaching machine developed by the Learning Research and Development Center at the University of Pittsburgh. The part of the equipment shown is the computer-controlled tutorial carrel. The student hears questions through the earphones and types his answers on the keyboard. His typed answers are displayed on the oscilloscope screen immediately above the keyboard. (Photograph provided by courtesy of the Learning Research and Development Center, University of Pittsburgh.)

Skinner has pointed out that such a machine does not really teach. It merely brings the pupil into contact with the teacher who composed the program through the mediation of the piece of equipment. If the teacher has done a poor job in preparing the program, then little learning is likely to occur. The machine makes it possible for many students to have this contact with the thought of an experienced teacher who has substantial knowledge about the programming of learning.

The renewed interest in the development of teaching machines stimulated by the work of Skinner has in turn stimulated many commercial concerns to consider the production of such devices. There is not space here to evaluate each of the products currently available, and, in any case, such an attempted evaluation would be inappropriate. The lack of data concerning the merit of the various teaching machines available is striking and quite inadequate to provide a basis for an evaluation. However, a general overview of some of the equipment that is becoming available is in order, though any evaluative comments must be considered to be highly speculative.

The equipment that is appearing on the market varies from very simple devices costing less than twenty dollars to complex pieces of machinery priced at several thousand dollars. Some of it is mechanically well designed, but some is not. Manufacturers are faced with the problem of developing pieces of equipment that are mechanically highly reliable and yet within the price range that school boards are likely to consider to be attractive. One suspects that the history of teaching machines will be the same as the history of most other types of mechanical inventions— namely, that most of the early models will fail to satisfy the consumer and disappear, and that ultimately a few satisfactory models will emerge.

Theoretical Requirements for a Teaching Machine

The machines discussed up to this point are all devices that have been designed in terms of *some* of the principles of learning that should be applied if learning is to move forward at a maximum speed. For example, devices so far built take into account individual differences only to a limited extent. The learner sets his own pace of work, but does not have the opportunity to work additional problems in areas where he shows deficiencies. Fast learners may also have to work more problems than are necessary for effective learning. An ideal machine should be able to adjust itself to the performance of the student, much as the expert teacher would if assigned the task of helping a single pupil. Technology has reached the point where a machine could be designed that would be much more adaptable to circumstances than the machines currently available. Why are available machines so restricted in what they can do and in the learning factors that they can take into account? The answer is that those that are to be sold to schools must be cheap and, therefore, simplified versions of ideal machines. Selling price is the major factor that restricts such machines in the functions they are capable of performing.

A diagram of an idealized teaching machine is shown in Figure 26. Each box represents an essential function of this machine. First, there would have to be a device that stored both problems and information. The problems and information stored would represent the several learning programs that the machine was capable of providing. There would

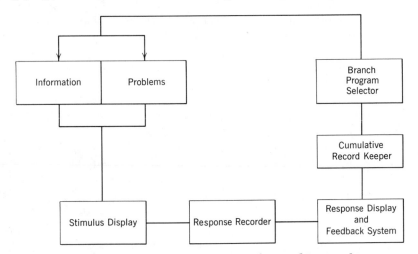

FIGURE 26. Diagrammatic representation of a teaching machine.

have to be included a program selector by means of which the learner would choose the program to which he was to be exposed.

A second component is the stimulus display panel, which would have to be some device, perhaps like a television screen, that would display the problem to be solved or the information to be given to the learner. Third, there would have to be a device through which the learner could record his response. If Skinner's plan is to be followed, the response recorder must be such that the student generates and records his response and does not merely record his choice from a number of responses suggested to him. In many ways this is the most difficult component to design.

As soon as the response is made, the machine must evaluate the response and provide the learner with immediate information about it. The component that does this is the response evaluator, which also incorporates a feedback system so that the learner may obtain knowledge of results. Teaching machines available at present always include a component of this kind, though it is often primitive. The learner may be shown the correct response and be required to make the comparison with his own. In the ideal machine, the comparison would be made automatically.

The equipment also includes a component that is not included in any machine available at present. This is the cumulative record keeper. The functioning of this component may be described as follows. Some learners are likely to require fewer problem-solving experiences than others in order to achieve mastery of a particular area. The cumulative record keeper would keep a cumulative record of the learner's progress and, when the learner began to miss many problems in a sequence, would provide additional practice in that area by switching to a special program. Such special programs, designed to be switched in whenever the learner's progress called for them, might be called branching programs. The latter term is derived from computer work in which an analogous operation is sometimes performed. When the learner was progressing well, the machine might also arrange to cut down on the number of problems provided. Some problems might be automatically skipped.

The cumulative record keeper would feed its information into the branch program selector, which in turn would determine the material that was fed from the main information and problem library.

Computer-Based Teaching Machines

Stolurow (1961) has used the word *adaptivity* to describe the extent to which a teaching machine can "adjust to the specific needs of the individual learner" (p. 14). Minimally adaptive devices are found among the familiar equipment of the elementary school in the form of flash cards and very simple teaching aids. Typical teaching machines are described by Stolurow as partially adaptive machines. According to Stolurow, a machine with high adaptivity is able to perform all of the functions of the effective teacher, such as providing materials needed by the pupil at the most advantageous times in the learning sequence, backtracking when the pupil encounters difficulties, keeping track of progress, pacing the student so that he neither dawdles nor has to hurry to an unnecessary degree, and so forth. Only those teaching machines that have a computer system built into them are completely adaptive machines.

The general requirements for a teaching machine have been known for some time, but the difficulties of building one that satisfies all the requirements have been financial rather than technical. Modern computing equipment can perform most of the tasks that such a machine has to perform; but a modern computer, together with the auxiliary devices necessary for the construction of a teaching machine, form a very expensive package. At the time of writing, two computing devices have been adapted for teaching at the University of Illinois, a computer-based teaching laboratory is in the process of being developed at the University of Pittsburgh, and others are in various stages of development. Interest in this approach to teaching is developing so rapidly that what is said here, by the time it is published, will probably no longer represent the frontier of knowledge.

The teaching machine illustrated in Figure 25 provides both visual and auditory information to the learner who can also communicate with the machine by means of a teletype keyboard. The machine can be programmed in a number of different ways. The machine may ask the learner to spell *house*. The learner then begins to attempt to type out the word on the keyboard. As he types, the letters appear on a screen. If he makes an error, the machine will stop him and say "try again." If he spells the word correctly, then the machine will tell him that he is right and can give other words of encouragement. If he fails twice to spell the word, the machine will give him the correct spelling. The machine gives the pupil personal and undivided attention. Instruction is completely individualized, and the patience of the mechanical teacher never wanes.

One of the modern teaching devices, developed at the University of Illinois, was appropriately named "Plato" by its creators. Those who write about the device refer to the set of rules governing the teaching as the *teaching logic*. Various models of Plato have been built around a number of different computer systems. Two fundamentally different sets of rules have been used in the operation of Plato. One of these is referred to as *tutoridl logic* and the other as *inquiry logic*. In the former case the machine is set to teach the student particular subject matter. In the latter case the machine performs a task similar to that of engaging in dialogue with the student. In teaching subject matter, the learner works through a program by being presented with information and then being given questions to answer. Where the student encounters particular difficulty in solving a problem, he is given additional practice in related areas through the introduction of what are called branching programs.

From the point of view of the student, the essential elements of Plato are: (1) a keyboard, much like that on a typewriter, which is used for answering or for asking questions; (2) a television screen, which is used for transmitting the information to the student; and (3) a "help" button, which the student pushes when he fails to answer a question and gives up. The result of pushing the button is to take the student into a sequence of presentations designed to help him achieve the understanding necessary for solving the problem. At the end of the help sequence, the learner is presented again with the original problem that led him to push the "help" button. The learner does not have to go through all the material in the help sequence. If at any point during that sequence he feels that he can solve the original problem, he can return to the problem by pushing a button marked "aha."

The information for such a device can be stored in a number of ways. One device that has been used as a part of Plato is a bank of slides, any one of which can be selected and projected on the television screen.

When the student undertakes a dialogue form of tuition, the procedure involved is less simple and straightforward. Complications are immediately introduced by the fact that the machine has limited capacity for interpreting questions typed on the keyboard. Although it is conceivable to design a machine that would correctly interpret a vast range of questions, present models of teaching machines are much more limited in what they can do. Sometimes the device is used to provide the student with a list of questions, in a particular subject-matter area, that he can answer. The student then types the code number of the question he wants to ask. Sometimes he may be permitted to ask very short questions or give very short answers in a clipped form of English. The term *pidgin English* seems appropriate in more than one way for such a language. Machines could be built that have far greater capacity for handling inputs of language, but the cost exceeds that which is likely to receive support.

In terms of actual applications, the cost factor is not so overwhelming as it might seem to be. A single computer could well provide teaching for a thousand pupils simultaneously, and the pupils would not all have to be working through the same lessons. One could conceive of a situation in which a single computer was providing material for perhaps as many as a hundred different lessons at the same time. The very high speed of operation of such machines would ensure that, even with many, many pupils and many different teaching programs, the delay in answering questions would be a matter of milleseconds rather than seconds.

In a society in which machines occupy positions of high status, one can readily attach more importance to such technical developments than they really merit. The education provided by such devices is a far cry from the kind of classroom pictured by John Dewey. In such a classroom, pupils would be struggling with problems in the way in which they would have to struggle with them as adults. They would have to go to sources of information available to them, including books and journals, and at times would be expected to collect their own data. The exercise in problem solving would not be complete unless the student brought together his materials in a well-documented report in which the values of the various sources of evidence were carefully weighed. The problem itself would provide a contact with the real world and its problems, and the inquiry would provide an example of how rational man should live. Real life provides no "help" button to push. The computer-based teaching machine has much more in common with traditional education procedures than it has with what has been termed progressive education.

The Characteristics of the Program

The early teaching programs of Pressey were nothing more than tests used in connection with a machine that indicated whether the answers given were correct or incorrect. Later programs developed by Skinner involved giving the student very small amounts of information followed by a problem. In the early Skinner-type program, the small doses of information were carefully sequenced. This procedure was derived from his observations on animals that behavior generally had to be shaped little by little. The Crowder type of program, in contrast, gives the learner large chunks of information that take some time to digest and, only then, is a problem solved. There are also a number of other variations that may be made in the design of teaching materials for programmed learning.

A distinction is commonly made between linear programs and branching programs. In a linear program, every learner responds to the same set of frames. In such a program, sufficient cues are given so that the learner makes few or no mistakes. On the other hand, in using a branching program, some learners are exposed to frames that other learners never even see. For example, in the use of a branching program one learner may reach a point where further experience is necessary with a particular class of problem. This he is given in a branch program, while another learner moves ahead into a new area of knowledge. Much the same purpose is achieved in a linear program when some students, who have had sufficient practice with a particular class of item, are allowed to skip ahead.

Glaser (1965) has reviewed research that has attempted to study the advantages, if any, of a branching type of program. So far, the evidence indicates no very striking advantage.

GRADES AND TEACHING MACHINES

The use of teaching machines may make it possible to provide a new and more rational basis for the assignment of grades. Since the Skinner type of teaching machine is so arranged that the learner passes on to a new program only after he has mastered the previous program, then a grade might indicate the number of programs that had been mastered.

On this basis, grades become much more meaningful than they are under typical learning conditions. If the student completes only 80 per cent of the programmed material included in a course, then he could be given a grade of 80. The grade would indicate the percentage of the material that had been mastered, and hence is much more readily interpreted than a grade of C or B.

How far the ideal of requiring complete mastery of a program is a feasible one to follow in practice remains to be seen. In a field such as mathematics, in which each step in thinking follows on the previous step, this requirement seems reasonable. No teacher would expect a child to begin to work on multiplication until he had already mastered addition. On the other hand, most fields of knowledge, outside of perhaps mathematics and physics, are not structured in this way. A pupil may well move on to the study of the geography of South America even if he has not properly mastered the previous unit on, say, the geography of North America. Geography does not have to be learned in a rigidly ordered sequence, as does mathematics.

The Design of Teaching Programs

The success of a teaching machine depends on the skill with which the learning program is designed. The art of program writing is relatively new, and hence definite rules to follow cannot be given at this time. Program writing has much more resemblance to the problem of designing a typical grade-school workbook than it has to that of writing a textbook. In order to understand some of the difficulties and problems encountered in writing programs for machine teaching, consider a brief spelling program cited by Skinner (1958), reproduced in Table 7. In the first frame, the pupil is told the meaning of the word *manufacture*, and then is told to spell out the word. In the second frame the pupil is told that the syllable *fact* in the word *manufacture* came from the same source as the same letters in the word *factory*. The pupil then writes out the word *fact* as a part of the word *manufacture*. Subsequent frames relate other parts of the word to other words. Thus, the pupil, in learning the word, learns not only how to spell it but also the relationship of parts of the word to other words.

One technique used is to slowly reduce the cues provided, which is to some extent the one used in the program under consideration. In this program, the first frame involves only a copying operation. In the four following frames, the pupil must do more than just copy. He must find

TABLE 7*

A Set of Frames Designed to Teach a Third- or Fourth-Grade
Pupil to Spell the Word *Manufacture*

---

1. Manufacture means to make or build. *Chair factories manufacture chairs.*
   Copy the word here:

2. Part of the word is like part of the word *factory*. Both parts come from an
   old word meaning make or build.

   m a n u — — — — u r e

3. Part of the word is like part of the word *manual*. Both parts come from an
   old word for hand. Many things used to be made by hand.

   — — — — f a c t u r e

4. The same letter goes in both spaces:

   m — n u f — c t u r e

5. The same letter goes in both spaces:

   m a n — f a c t — r e

6. Chair factories — — — — — — — — — — — chairs.

---

* Reproduced from B. F. Skinner, "Teaching Machines." (*Science,* Vol. 28, 24 October
  1958, p. 972) Reprinted from *Science* by permission.

within himself the letters to be inserted. Finally he has to spell out the
entire word without any cues concerning the way it is spelled. Most
learning is of this character. The learner is slowly able to perform with
fewer and fewer crutches.

Skinner has numerous suggestions concerning the use of techniques in
which cues are steadily reduced. He suggests that in learning geography,
the teacher may first provide the student with a fully labeled map and
ask him to find distances and relationships between the various features
of the map. In later frames, some of the names on the map may be withdrawn or some of the letters may be missing from the names, and further
questions are asked. In the final frames, the pupil may be asked questions
without any map present.

Although cue reduction is an important concept applied in the writing of learning programs, there is another aspect of program design in
which the selection of proper cues is also important. In the planning of
all learning conditions, care must be taken to ensure that correct re-

sponses are made. The performance of an incorrect response rarely serves any purpose. Correct responses will be made by the learner if he is given adequate cues, and hence a frame should always contain sufficient cues to ensure a correct response. If, for example, the answer to a particular question in a program for teaching general psychology is the word *reflex*, then this response can be almost assured by including in the frame a brief discussion of reflexes relevant to the question. A less complete cue would be the case in which the number of letters in the word was specified.

Some program writers emphasize the importance of using very small steps in passing from frame to frame. This means that a program is likely to involve a great number of frames. Skinner has suggested that a learning program in spelling for a single grade might involve as many as eight to ten thousand frames. A teacher cannot personally supervise and reinforce ten thousand responses a year in the development of a single limited skill, but a machine can easily perform such a function. In order to complete this program, the pupil would probably have to spend only as little as fifteen minutes a day working through the program.

Although the advantage of using a small step from frame to frame lies in the fact that this will reduce the number of incorrect responses, there must surely be some lower limit of the efficient size of the step. One suspects that the abler learners will require a much larger step than will the slow learners. Problems related to the size of step are many—and almost entirely unsolved.

The Programmed Textbook

An outcome of thinking related to the development and design of learning machines is the programmed textbook. The concept seems to have been developed by Robert Glaser. One does not have to examine many textbooks to see that they do not generally conform to the concept of a program of learning as it has emerged in recent times. Textbooks present a series of ideas and leave the student pretty much on his own in making use of the material presented. Sometimes a workbook accompanies a textbook; and the student, at the end of each section in the text, solves a series of problems in the workbook. The problems may serve the purpose of facilitating retention by providing additional practice, or they may provide skill in the application of the ideas that have been studied, and hence ultimately contribute to the student's ability to transfer what he has learned to new situations. The textbook-workbook relationship is particularly important at the elementary-school level, where it constitutes a typical part of the classroom procedure. The modern concept of a programmed textbook differs from the concept of a textbook-workbook combination in many important respects that must be considered.

First, the programmed textbook emphasizes the role of problem solving in learning. New material is fed to the learner in quite small quantities; and with each new idea introduced, the learner is given problems to solve that require the use of this new idea. In traditional study procedures, most of the time of the learner is devoted to reading; but in the programmed textbook, most of his time is spent in problem solving. In a sense, a programmed textbook is much like a textbook and a workbook combined, in which the reading is frequently interrupted with problem-solving activities. It is not feasible to skip quickly through such a book. Some mathematics books approximate closely the programmed textbook in that they place emphasis on problem solving as an essential element of efficient learning in the area.

Second, in the programmed textbook there is some opportunity provided for feedback, which in turn may provide for reinforcement. The student has, at each stage, some indication of how he is doing and where his deficiencies and difficulties lie. He can obtain immediate knowledge of results, and does not have to wait until the teacher corrects his paper or places the answers on the board. In some versions of the programmed textbook, he may be given information concerning why he is wrong in making a certain answer. The latter type of programmed textbook has been developed by Norman Crowder, who refers to it as the *scrambled textbook*. One example of the scrambled textbook is designed to provide instruction in the playing of contract bridge. In this book the student is presented with a bridge problem such as might be involved in bidding. Certain bids have been made, and the player holds certain cards. What should be bid now? The various possible bids are listed; and when he chooses one, he finds opposite it a page number to which he is instructed to turn. On this new page he may find an explanation of why the bid was a poor one and instruction to turn back to the original page and make another bid. The process is repeated until he comes up with the bid which is considered to be the most advantageous in the particular situation.

Third, programmed textbooks offer some possibility of adjusting the amount of problem solving performed by a student to his particular requirements. The student may, at a certain point in his work, count up the number of problems he has solved. If he has solved more than a certain proportion correctly on the first attempt, then he may skip the problems that follow. If he has solved less than the required proportion, then he must go on and solve additional problems until he has demonstrated that he has mastered the concept involved. There are also extensive possibilities for providing cues for the student who is unable to solve the problems unaided. Thus, the problem-solving process can provide additional instruction for those who need it.

Learning programs designed for machine use may often be used as programmed textbooks. If such a program is printed in booklet form, the student may answer each question while covering up the answer printed in the space below; and thus work through the entire set of questions, checking his answers as he goes. The only advantage of passing the same material through a machine is that the machine does not permit the student to cheat by looking at the answer before he has attempted to answer the question himself; but cheating does not appear to be an important factor.

Teaching machines have been stimulating in leading educators to think more carefully about the problem of presenting subject matter. The resulting emphasis on the planning of learning may be the most important contribution that the entire movement may make to education.

Adapting the Scrambled Textbook to Machine Presentation

Just as the Skinner-type learning program, originally designed for machine, may be adapted for use in book form, so too may the scrambled book and other forms of programmed textbooks be adapted for machine use. Western Design produced a machine called the Autotutor which presents material in the scrambled-book form. A picture of such a machine is shown in Figure 27. In this machine the material to be presented to the student is projected from a film onto a ground-glass screen. Each frame includes a substantial quantity of information, much more than is presented in a Skinner-type program. The student reads and studies the material and then solves the problem that follows the material. He then chooses the solution given at the bottom of the frame that corresponds best with his own. Following the suggested solution is a number, which the student then presses in the selector panel. Once this number has been punched in the panel, a new frame is shown on the screen. This new frame will either tell him why his answer was wrong and refer him back to the original problem for another try, or tell him that he was right and present new material and a new problem.

There is no basis at this time for evaluating such a device. Although some may look at it and say that it is merely a device for turning pages— and in a sense it is—this evaluation may grossly undervalue the device. There is the distinct possibility that the mechanical device may force upon the learner a systematic procedure. The programmed text alone

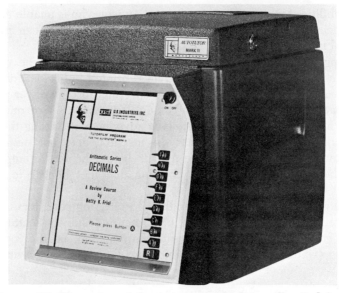

FIGURE 27. Illustration of the Autotutor, which is well suited for the presentation of the scrambled textbook type of program. (Photograph by courtesy of U.S. Industries Inc.)

may tempt the learner to skip, to look ahead, and to be unsystematic. The Autotutor type of device makes it difficult for the learner to behave in this scatterbrained way. These are questions that future experimentation will have to resolve.

Research on the Value of Teaching Machines and Programmed Learning

Although substantial effort has been devoted to the development of new teaching machines, much less effort appears to have been directed to research on problems related to the value of such devices. This is partly a result of the fact that it is much easier to change educational procedures than it is to determine the consequences of these changes. There are also a number of difficulties involved in research in this area that are only slowly coming to be recognized. Consider, for example, the problem of comparing the effectiveness of teaching by machine with the teaching of the same subject matter by more typical classroom procedures. What appears to be an obvious way of doing this is to find a machine-taught program, administer it to a number of classrooms, and then to compare the resulting achievement of the pupils with that of the pupils in other classrooms in which the same subject matter was taught by conventional means. Such a comparison appears to be a fair test of the relative worth of the old and the new procedures, but it actually does not answer any questions. Suppose, for example, that the teaching-machine group learns more on the average than the other groups combined. Can one then conclude that teaching-machine presentation of the particular subject matter is superior to that of traditional teaching? Such a conclusion cannot be drawn, for undoubtedly some of the teacher-taught groups will have higher average scores than the machine-taught group, even if most do not. Some teachers might be found who could produce more learning in pupils than was produced by the particular program taught by machine.

In contrast, if the traditional methods had turned out to be superior, somebody might be able to rewrite the teaching-machine program so that it would provide results superior to that produced by traditional teaching. G. Della-Piana (in personal communication) has made the interesting observation that one can take any teaching program designed for machines and prepare a better conventional teaching procedure, and that one can also take any conventional teaching procedure and design a better machine-teaching program.

Such difficulties have led research workers to undertake such activities as those of determining whether teaching machines do, in fact, teach, or of determining which of several forms of program are most effective. Stolurow (1961), who has summarized research up to about 1960, points out that it shows that teaching machines can be used for teaching persons who vary from retardates to gifted. He might have added that similar machines can also be used to teach pigeons, so the results of research are hardly surprising. Stolurow points out an interesting finding that appears in much of the research, which is that one cannot predict learning in a teaching-machine situation from aptitude tests as well as one can the outcomes of conventional teaching. The lower-ability pupils appear to achieve more. This is certainly consistent with the well-known fact that the duller pupils need a more highly structured learning situation than do the more gifted. Perhaps one might also expect that the more gifted would learn less in a highly structured situation than in one in which there was less control over their activity. Finally, some knowledge has been achieved concerning the value of various techniques for the construction of teaching programs. For example, Coulson and Silberman (1959) investigated the first section of a program developed for teaching the elementary psychology course at Harvard. They prepared various forms of this program, including one that had multiple-choice answers which was compared with one in which the student had to write out his own answers. One form of the program involved small steps in knowledge, and another large steps. A third involved a branching program (like that involved in pushing the "help" button on Plato) and another provided no such branching program.

In this particular study, the results favored the small step rather than the large, but the small-step program was more time-consuming—a fact that may account for the effect. This outcome may be the result of the subject matter involved. One can reasonably suspect that if a program involves the learning of definitions, then small steps would be superior to large ones. However, if the program were teaching the understanding of principles, the reverse might be the case. Multiple-choice responses were found to be as effective as responses that the student had to construct—a rather puzzling finding. Finally, no particular advantages were found with branching programs except when the time in learning was taken into account. Branching programs required less training time. In this research, the variables studied had insignificant effects.

The research indicates that this is an area where vigorous efforts are being made to produce educational advance; but there are no signs, as yet, that a great revolution of educational practice is in the making.

Information Storage and Retrieval

Teaching machines and programmed learning, as it has developed over the last two decades, seems to have been unduly influenced by certain prejudices about how and what children learn in school. Undue emphasis seems to have been given to the notion that the teacher is the main reinforcer of pupil behavior, and, since teacher reinforcements cannot be provided for individual pupils very frequently, machine methods of reinforcement need to be introduced. However, anyone who observes a class in session in the elementary school comes to realize that, in a well-run class, most of the reinforcements are provided by the work materials; and the role of the teacher is that of bringing the pupil into contact with appropriate learning situations. Typical work materials have built-in systems of reinforcement. A child reading a second-grade book knows when he is reading correctly, for then the pictures correspond to the text. Most workbooks provide reinforcements in one form or another. In addition, children working in pairs may reinforce one another's behavior when the materials have been properly designed for group work. The classroom is not the bleak reinforcement-scarce situation that some psychologists have described it as being.

Another misconception is that learning in school is always for permanent retention of all that is to be learned. In some areas, the objective may well be mastery to the point where what is learned can be applied or reproduced. In the lower grades, thorough mastery is obviously important. At the high-school level, there is certainly justification for learning foreign languages to a point where there has been sufficient retention so that the person can communicate in the language. On the other hand, it is probably much less important to retain the details of the geography of a foreign country than to know where such information can be obtained and how to read a map that will give the geographical features. Much knowledge should be acquired in the form of knowing where to look for it. Programmed learning fails to bring the student into contact with reference sources or to provide him with knowledge of where information is to be found. Learning in the higher grades of elementary school and through high school must become progressively more concerned with teaching pupils how to retrieve information from the vast amount stored in various sources. A person who knew only the information he has learned and is unable to find new information as he needs it, would be a sorry product of the educational system.

Simulators and Trainers

A simulator is a training device that simulates all or most of the requirements of the situation that the learner must ultimately handle. One of the early simulators was a device for training a person to drive a car. It involved the usual front-seat arrangement found in a car, but through the windshield was seen a picture of a road ahead projected from a movie film. The operator could change the speed of the car by manipulating the gas pedal and could keep the car on the road by steering. In this simulator, as in other simulators, an attempt was made to build a thoroughly realistic situation in which the skill to be acquired is learned under circumstances that approach the real thing.

In contrast, a trainer, unlike a simulator, does not generally simulate as far as is feasible the circumstances under which the skill is ultimately performed. For example, a film strip may be used to demonstrate to a mechanic the various mechanical operations he must perform; and as each frame is presented, he may attempt the operation it portrays. Here the device is used to prompt and to provide cues, rather than to encourage the performance of the skill under the same conditions to be found in the real-life situation. One cannot draw a sharp line between trainers and simulators; but some devices do attempt to simulate actual conditions as their central feature, and others place emphasis on providing cues for the learning process.

After the outbreak of World War II, interest in simulators and trainers was greatly increased through the military need to train large numbers of young men in new skills, many of which involved complicated pieces of equipment. World War II was mainly responsible for the establishment of simulators as a permanent part of training procedures. An area of particular importance in this connection was pilot training. The grandfather of all simulators for the training of pilots was the Link Trainer, a highly successful device for learning many flying skills, which probably accomplished more than any other device to establish the simulator as a worthwhile piece of training equipment. The Link Trainer was basically an airplane cockpit, complete with controls, which could be tipped at all angles. The cockpit was mounted about six feet above the floor level and was surrounded by scenery that showed clouds and a horizon. The Link Trainer behaved like a very unstable aircraft. Although a typical plane will practically fly itself and remain fairly stable once in level flight, the Link Trainer requires a continuous adjustment of the controls in order to maintain a level on-course flight. The pilot of the Link Trainer must continuously use his flying skills in order to maintain a particular flight plan. The device was so successful that for many years qualified pilots in the United States Air Force were required to spend a certain amount of their time each month in flight trainers in order to maintain their skills. An example of a modern simulator trainer used for training jet pilots is shown in Figure 28.

The advantages of the simulator are well seen in the Link device and in more advanced flight simulators. It permits practice without any of the hazards that accompany real flight. It is much cheaper than an aircraft to produce, maintain, and "fly." It can be built so that actual flying may be simple in comparison to "flying" the simulator. It can be used to give the beginner confidence that he might not attain if learning occurred under conditions of real hazard. It can provide the experienced pilot with the opportunity to fly under Instrument Flying Regulations, with the cockpit covered to eliminate visual cues. The simulator has immense training advantages over actual aircraft.

Because the flying of large modern aircraft is much less a problem of learning fine muscular coordination, and much more a matter of learning complicated intellectual skills, a simulator can be built that can provide training in nearly all of the skills required for flying the actual aircraft. In addition, certain "emergency" situations can be made to occur during a "flight" of a simulator: the instrument panel can show a fire in an engine, engine failure, a defect in the landing gear, and so forth. Thus, through the use of the simulator, training can be given in the handling of emergencies, which are made to occur when the pilot does not expect them. The simulator can also provide training for the entire crew in the coordination of their work, a skill essential for proper flight operations. A final advantage of the flight simulator is that it can be so

FIGURE 28. Flight crews of United Air Lines, in training for DC-8 Jet Mainliner operations at the company's Denver Pilot Training Center, "fly" the great plane by means of the electronic simulator shown. It was installed by United in September, 1958—first in the airline industry. In the cockpit are (from left) Flight Instructor Wood, Captain Craine, First Officer Meyer, and Second Officer Monroe.

constructed that a record can be kept of the performance of the flight crew, and errors can be corrected immediately.

Many trainers that have been developed may be very efficient as trainers, even though they do not simulate very well the actual situation in which the skills are to be applied. Consider, for example, the problem of training men to service and maintain a complicated piece of electronic equipment used for helping planes to make blind landings. One of the important skills involved in the maintenance of such equipment is trouble shooting, a skill that can be acquired by long experience with the actual equipment. Another way to learn the trouble-shooting skill is for the trainee to work on a trainer especially devised for the learning of this skill. Trainers have been built that consist of panels on which diagrams of the various parts of the equipment have been drawn. On each drawing of a part there is a button that can be pressed. The learner is told that there is something wrong with the equipment, and that the symptom is that no "blips" appear on the scope although the scope is lit. The learner then makes a decision concerning which of the various components to test first. When he has made this decision, he presses the button on the diagram of the component. If a red light appears, then he knows that the component is defective. A green light indicates that the component is in working order. Apart from the fact that the trainer is much cheaper than the actual equipment, it has other advantages. One of these is that the student does not have to spend time removing components in order to test them. Some training panels of this type may permit the student to work and solve ten times as many problems as he would have time for on the actual equipment. Thus, this type of trainer is effective by emphasizing the *frequency* factor in learning.

Various trainers have been developed to improve speed of perception with the object of improving reading speed. One of these devices is the tachistoscope, which can be used to flash words or short sentences on a screen for very brief periods. Such a device was evaluated by Smith and Tate (1953), who were interested in the effect of tachistoscopic training on reading speed. In this study, tachistoscopic training did produce an increase in reading speed. However, the subjects in the experiment believed that they had made tremendous gains in speed by the use of the device, although only moderate gains were objectively demonstrable.

A particularly notable attempt to develop trainers is found in the foreign language area, where both universities and military schools have tried out new ways of teaching languages. In one installation, which the writer visited some years ago, the students were seen working in a classroom divided into separate booths. In each booth was a tape recorder, headsets, and a microphone. The student checked out the tape that was appropriate to his particular level of learning, and set to work to learn the lesson; but this did not involve merely listening to the recording on the tape. The equipment was so arranged that the recorded lesson was on one of the channels of the tape, while the other channel was a blank. As a part of the lesson, the recorded voice would ask the student to answer certain questions, and this he would do by talking into the microphone. The student's voice was recorded on the blank channel on the tape. He could then go back and replay both his answer and the model answer already recorded on the tape. Any part of the lesson he found difficult he could also play back, and attempt again to make the required responses in the foreign language.

At the time this installation was seen, plans were underway to build a mechanism that would permit the instructor to monitor the work of the student. This would involve the building of a number of circuits to allow the instructor to switch his receiving equipment to any of the booths and listen to the performance of each student. Such monitorship seems to be most desirable, since the student is not always a good judge of his own product. Any incentive value that such monitorship may have is probably quite unnecessary, because the learning conditions are such that the students work extremely hard at their lessons and do not engage in distracting activities. In such a classroom one does not observe, as one does in a typical adult classroom, many of the students engaging in such activities as doodling, whispering, daydreaming, and so forth. An illustration of such a classroom, developed by Rheem Califone Corporation, is shown in Figure 29. A close-up of a booth is shown in Figure 30.

Language installations of this type reflect well the main principles that should guide the mechanization of the classroom. The student plays an

FIGURE 29. Illustration of a mechanized language learning laboratory developed by Rheem Califone Corporation and installed at the John Burroughs High School in California. The learning laboratory provides a situation in which the pupil learns at his own individual pace. He may repeat a tape until he has achieved mastery. (Photograph by courtesy of the Rheem Califone Corporation.)

FIGURE 30. Photograph shows a booth in a language learning laboratory. The booth includes a tape recorder operated by the student which may record the responses he makes which he can then compare with the recording of the correct response. (Photograph by courtesy of the Rheem Califone Corporation.)

active part in the learning process. He sets the pace of learning. He can repeat work with which he has difficulty. He is given regular reinforcement and knowledge of what is right and wrong about his performance. He does not have to be doing roughly the same work as the other students in the room, and may be several tapes ahead or behind them.

In such a classroom, the instructor is a busy person. First, he has the responsibility of building the curriculum and of constructing the tapes based on the curriculum plan. Lesson planning, which is undertaken by most teachers at a perfunctory level, now becomes a central and time-consuming activity. Once a certain lesson has been produced and recorded on tape, the task is not completed, for the instructor must then listen to the performances of students to determine whether some parts are too difficult or too easy. The lesson must then be reworked and prepared in a form in which it will be used until new improvements can be introduced into it. Additional practice tapes must also be available for some students who are slower than others and who need additional practice.

Besides the preparation of a curriculum and the materials that are used in it, many additional duties are a part of the task of the instructor. He must keep records of the individual progress of each student, and monitor his work so that he can help him. Sometimes individual instruction becomes important, as in the case of a student who has special difficulties in pronouncing particular words. Some students must be kept from pushing forward at too fast a rate; they may need additional practice at levels that they have just completed. Methods of testing the students must be established to provide checks at the various stages of learning. Then, of course, new students entering the school must be given an orientation to the procedures. Within such a setting, the teacher is a busy person, but the tasks undertaken are very different from those undertaken in the traditional classroom. The teacher spends very little time going over material found in textbooks, but spends a much larger amount of time planning learning experiences and helping the students with their difficulties.

The development of trainers during the war period was not based on any sudden and rapid advance in learning theory; rather, such devices were common-sense applications of engineering knowledge to problems of instruction. Perhaps their importance may be considered to lie in the fact that they represented a bridge between technologists and teachers, and pointed the way to a *rapprochement* of these two groups.

Summary

1. Most of the inventions that have had an important impact on education are those involving the presentation of stimuli. The introduction of printed materials was probably the most important of all these. Equipment that in some way modifies not only events at the stimulus end, but also events at the response end, has been slow in being developed.

2. In the mid-twenties, Sidney Pressey attempted to bring about what he called the industrial revolution in education. Pressey designed a number of testing machines which offered possibilities also of serving the role of teaching machines. The educational culture was not ready at that time

to give serious consideration to such devices, and by the mid-thirties Pressey gave up his attempt to produce an educational revolution single-handedly.

3. The World War II period and the years that followed showed great developments in theoretically oriented knowledge of learning. In recent years some of this knowledge has been applied mainly through the efforts of B. F. Skinner. The latter was particularly impressed with the difficulties encountered by teachers attempting to shape the behavior of many children through the application of reinforcements. The teaching machines he designed were to shape behavior in much the same way that the behavior of animals was shaped in his laboratory. Positive reinforcements were to be applied through the operation of the teaching machine, and behavior was to be shaped by small steps. Skinner also insisted that the learner be able to make the complete response to be learned, not merely select a response.

4. Numerous pieces of equipment, described as teaching machines, are now on the market or have been described in the technical literature. These vary from machines costing less than twenty dollars to complicated pieces of electronic equipment. The value of these devices is still a matter for speculation.

5. An area of research on educational problems has been opened up through the incorporation of computers into teaching machines. At present, this is an interesting field of enquiry, but much more must be found out before it can be said that the computer is a useful device for research on teaching and whether it has practical merits for use in the school teaching situation.

6. The suggestion has been made that a student learning through use of a teaching machine might be graded in terms of the percentage of a program that he masters.

7. Crucial to the use of teaching machines is the availability of suitable programs. At present, the design of a program is more of an art than a science, but principles of design are beginning to emerge. Each frame of the program must produce sufficient cues so that there is a very high probability that the correct response will occur. The program should also use small steps from frame to frame, though there are probably individual differences in the size of step that is most efficient.

8. The programmed textbook is similar to the program used in a teaching machine, but it is so arranged that it can be used without any mechanical equipment. The scrambled textbook is a form of the programmed textbook with a special system of built-in cues.

9. Theoretical requirements of teaching machines may be laid out. The more complicated pieces of equipment will come near to matching these

requirements. The simpler devices sacrifice some characteristics for the sake of economy.

10. The late thirties and the war period that followed resulted in the production of many trainers and simulators, many of which involved the application of highly novel concepts of instruction. These were devices that involved modifications not only in the method of presenting the stimuli, but also in the way in which responses were made and shaped. They manifested the application of engineering to problems of instruction, but were not based on any particularly sophisticated theory of learning. Simulators attempt to reproduce the actual situation for which the person is being trained; but trainers may have only a relatively remote relationship to that situation, but they have other advantages. Trainers may make it possible to provide more training in a given time than would be possible with the actual equipment. In the academic areas, one of the most notable developments of trainers is in foreign-language teaching, where large mechanized teaching installations are now functioning. The development of trainers and simulators gives the instructor a role different from that which he has conventionally assumed. Where trainers are used, the instructor has more time to diagnose learning difficulties, to plan, to revise curricula, and to perform similar activities.

17

Epilogue

T HE PREVIOUS chapters of the book have given an overview of the results of research on learning. It is clear that this is a vigorous area of inquiry which occupies the time and energies of numerous dedicated research workers. The results achieved have been substantial. It is also clear that scientists are still far from the development of a set of precisely stated laws that can have direct bearing on classroom practice. Some might even doubt whether the aim of developing such a set of laws is a reasonable goal for research, and might say that the most that can be achieved is a set of general statements that may serve as a guide to action in the planning and management of learning situations. Time will reveal what are and what are not realistic goals for research on learning.

That some progress has been made in discovering important generalizations that may be used in the management of learning cannot be denied. An appropriate function of a final chapter may be, then, to gather together what the author considers to be the most significant of these generalizations in terms of their applicability to understanding and guiding classroom practice. The generalizations that follow represent an attempt to assemble such a list, but the reader must bear in mind that it represents only the judgment of one man. Others who may draw up such a list may consider that different generalizations are more defensible or that some of the generalizations listed are not fully justified at this time. The writer was curious to see such a compilation, and thought that the reader might share in his curiosity. The contents of this volume were then scanned for the purpose of drawing from it those generalizations that seemed to be the most significant. The list thus prepared must, therefore, be considered in context; each summarizing statement cannot include all of the qualifications for it that are included in the text. While realizing the intellectual hazards that are involved, the following list of generalizations has been prepared:

POSITIVE REINFORCEMENT

1. A reinforcer is a condition that follows a response and results in an increase in the strength of that response. Good planning of reinforcing contingencies is one of the most effective ways of shaping behavior.

2. Reinforcements are most likely to be effective if they follow performance immediately. However, under suitable conditions they may be delayed and still be effective, provided the subject reinforced maintains an orientation toward the task.

3. Most reinforcers, but not all, that operate on human behavior have acquired their reinforcing properties through learning. Since learning experiences differ from child to child, the conditions that reinforce also vary from child to child.

4. Individuals differ in the events that are reinforcing, and teaching should be arranged to provide those reinforcing contingencies that are most effective for particular pupils.

5. Well-established habits are best maintained through the use of a schedule of reinforcement that is less than 100 per cent. Reinforcements for maintaining such habits should not be at regular intervals or after fixed amounts of work; they will be more effective if distributed at random.

6. Any novel or unusual event may function as a reinforcer.

7. The successful completion of a task or the discovery of the solution to a problem may be reinforcing for those behaviors that led up to these events.

8. Many reinforcers are conditions that satisfy needs. For this reason, effective learning commonly takes place when the task involved is related to the satisfaction of a need.

9. The magnitude of the reinforcement provided is not necessarily related to the amount of learning produced. In education, a safe rule, probably, is to use small reinforcements. However, there are advantages in setting the reinforcement so that it is related to the quality of the response reinforced.

10. The magnitude of a reinforcement is likely to be of much less significance than the fact that a reinforcement will or will not occur.

11. Experience without active participation and without reinforcement can conceivably produce learning, but the learning process involved is inefficient compared with that which occurs when performance is directly reinforced.

12. Reinforcement may involve the transmission of information, or change in affect. In human learning, the informational aspects of reinforcement appear to be of paramount importance. (The information provided by reinforcing events is commonly called feedback.)

13. Reinforcement is commonly given in the form of information. In some learning situations, this information may be given prior to a response and be as effective as when it is given after a response.

NEGATIVE REINFORCEMENT AND PUNISHMENT

14. The punishment of incorrect responses may increase the rate at which learning occurs. However, this use of punishment is not recommended because it may have other harmful effects, such as the development of an aversion for the entire learning situation.

15. Punishment and threat operate by producing inhibitions. These inhibitions may generalize to other stimuli and responses. Severe punishment may produce inhibitions of responses that have considerable permanence. Hence, if punishment is used, it should be mild and directed primarily at the inhibition of responses that are incompatible with the response to be learned.

16. Failure depresses those intellectual activities closely associated with school learning. Failure experiences are likely to result in relatively inefficient learning in the period that follows them.

GENERALIZATION, INHIBITION, AND TRANSFER

17. Stimulus generalization represents one of the most important means whereby the skills learned can be applied to new and similar situations.

18. Most learning involves the learning of inhibitions. The learning of inhibitions with respect to social behavior is of particular importance. Inhibitions may be learned by various means, such as punishment or preventing a response in a situation in which the individual is motivated to so respond.

19. Extinction is one effective way of eliminating an unwanted behavior if it is possible to arrange for the manifestation of the behavior without reinforcement. Often this cannot be accomplished, because the reinforcer may be internal to the learner or caused by conditions that cannot be controlled.

20. Negative transfer is most likely to occur in those situations in which the stimuli are the same as those previously encountered but the responses required are different.

21. Transfer of training is most likely to occur with well-practiced skills rather than with those in which a lesser level of skill has been acquired.

22. Since the learner is an active organism who naturally emits large amounts of behavior, restlessness is to be expected in children. Extreme restlessness and distractibility is, however, a part of the brain-damage syndrome.

PERCEPTION AND COGNITIVE LEARNING

23. The perceptual system is a system with a limited capacity for handling information. Mechanisms exist that limit the amount of information received by the system.

24. Information reaching the receptors is compressed during the process of transmission to the higher centers.

25. The perceptual system, when working to capacity, handles information from only one source.

26. Knowledge as it exists in books and other documents reflects many structures; knowledge as it is stored in the individual also reflects structure. This internal organization of knowledge is referred to as a cognitive structure.

27. Individuals are characterized by a large number of different abilities, but only some of these abilities appear to serve a useful function in a civilized community.

28. Gains in intelligence-test scores are partly a function of the social and educational conditions to which a child is exposed.

29. The structure of aptitudes is such that pupils grouped in terms of scores on one aptitude will not be well-grouped with respect to other aptitudes.

30. The aptitudes involved in learning a task may differ at different levels of achievement with respect to the task.

31. Time devoted to the learning of principles may provide superior possibilities for the transfer of what has been learned to new situations—more so than the same amount of time devoted to the learning of facts.

32. Certain skills may be taught that have extensive applicability to the solution of new problems. The learning of these skills is referred to as "the acquisition of learning sets."

33. Bodies of content that have general value for developing problem-solving ability have not been developed.

34. Meaningful material is more easily learned than meaningless material, because it represents material that has already been partly learned.

35. Information is better retained if it is consistent with the learner's own values than if it is inconsistent.

36. Concepts represent classifications of experiences. Such classifications are formed through opportunities to classify exemplars under conditions that provide the learner with information concerning the acceptability of his classification.

37. The learning of concepts involves the identification of the defining attributes of the class of phenomena included in the concept. Learning a concept may be shortened by providing cues concerning the nature of the defining attributes.

38. Sudden insight into the solution of a problem occurs in those situations in which the learner has had extensive previous experience with related problems and with transferring what he has learned to new, but related, problems.

LEARNING AND RETENTION

39. The characteristics of the learning curve depend partly on the conditions under which learning occurs and the amount and nature of previous learning. In the acquisition of highly novel learnings in which previous experience can play little part, an S-shaped learning curve is commonly found.

40. Learning from printed material is improved by practicing recall as a part of the learning process.

41. Overlearned skills are better retained than skills learned to a lesser degree.

42. Periodical review and reinforcement are necessary for permanent retention. Reviews should be at increasing intervals of time.

43. Forgetting is largely a result of the interference of other learning activities with what is to be retained.

44. The typical curve for the retention of a skill shows a relatively sharp initial decline and then a gradually less rapid decline.

45. Reminiscence is probably not a genuine phenomenon in the case of verbal learning, but the result of an experimental artifact. However, genuine reminiscence appears to occur in the learning of motor skills.

46. Individuals fail to make proper use of information that is inconsistent with the position they themselves hold.

MOTIVATION

47. Needs are aroused by deprivation and also by stimuli related to their satisfaction.

48. Failure to provide sufficient stimuli impinging on the organism may produce a deterioration of intellectual skills as well as emotional disturbances.

49. A person's level of aspiration is related to his history of experiences of success and failure.

50. The self-selection of the means of satisfying needs does not necessarily lead to a healthy life. A person may learn through self-selection to satisfy needs in ways antithetical to his own well-being.

51. Measured interests bear little relation to achievement. So far there is little evidence to show that interests, as they are commonly measured, reflect important motives.

52. Achievement motivation develops during the school years, and its development is related particularly to the characteristics of the home.

Particularly important are the attitudes of the parents with respect to the child being independent.

53. Positive and negative affect and changes in affect may have influence on the level of motivation. However, one cannot say that men are motivated by pleasure seeking and pain avoidance alone.

54. Rate of learning is related to the arousal level of the individual. Learning may be inefficient because the arousal level is either too high or too low. The arousal level may be changed by changing the amount of stimulation provided by the environment.

55. Learning situations involving approach-avoidance conflicts should be avoided since they are typically met with vacillating and ineffective behavior.

SOCIAL CONDITIONS OF LEARNING AND ATTITUDES

56. The activity and productivity of a group depends upon the characteristics of the leadership provided. However, there is no clear superiority of one kind of leadership over another for all purposes. The main advantage of a leadership in which pupils participate in setting their own goals is that it encourages the continuation of activity when the designated leader is absent.

57. Group work involving the interaction of group members may provide sources of reinforcement that would not otherwise exist.

58. Human subjects tend to be more productive when they work in group situations than when they work in isolation, even when there is no interaction between the members of the group.

59. The tendency to imitate appears to be learned through reinforcement, and hence there may be differences among children in the ability to learn through imitation.

60. A strong case can be made for the position that permanent and enduring changes in attitudes require changes in the underlying need system that they satisfy.

61. Attitudes expressed in the form of opinions may be changed by the use of reinforcement. However, such changes are primarily related to the cognitive component of attitudes, and may not change related action systems.

DEVELOPMENT

62. Only to a limited degree does human development manifest a regular and well-identified pattern. Studies that attempt to identify such a uniform pattern have not generally been reproduced under other cultural conditions.

63. Evidence is accumulating that learning occurs in two stages. Early

learning is slow and involves the acquisition of basic discriminations. Late learning builds rapidly on the foundation of early learning.

64. Failure to learn at a particular age may be the result of the fact that the nervous system did not develop to the point where such learning is possible; an alternative reason may be lack of early learning (as described by Hebb).

65. The ability to learn increases up to the early adult years.

66. Ability to learn at any particular stage of development is a product of the individual's inherited characteristics and the previous learning situations to which he has been exposed.

The generalizations presented in the above list are far from the precisely formulated equations that might constitute the product of a mature science of educational psychology; but despite their looseness, they are not without worth. First, they are of value in understanding many of the phenomena that occur in the teaching of children. Such understanding may not lead immediately to improved ways of managing the·learning process; but the hope is that, in time, understanding leads to more effective ways of control. For the teacher to know that forgetting is not so much a matter of the fading of the memory trace but an interference process, does not help too much at this time in the improvement of teaching practices, except insofar as one can plan learning so that activities that are likely to provide psychological interference do not follow closely on one another in the school program. The interference theory of forgetting also suggests that periodical review is essential for permanent retention.

Knowledge of natural phenomena typically proceeds from the stage in which it provides only understanding to the stage in which it provides a means of control in addition to understanding. Early work on genetics carried out by Mendel provided understanding of the general nature of the mechanism involved in heredity. Later workers found means of modifying the genes involved in the heredity mechanism, and hence of finding ways of controlling changes. The science of genetics has proceeded from a state in which it involves understanding alone, to one in which it can also exercise some degree of control over the phenomena with which it is concerned. Educational psychology is emerging from the stage in which it can provide limited understanding of some learning phenomena, to the stage where it can also provide control over learning.

Although the traditional purposes of educational psychology have been to provide some help for the teacher and to improve the design of the materials of instruction, the ultimate purposes of the discipline must be to provide a basis for the design of efficient teaching methods. At this time such a goal is remote, but a brief consideration of how such a goal is to be reached will indicate the developments that the discipline of educational psychology should look forward to in the future.

Some Problems in the Design of Teaching Methods

A teaching method is a set of learning conditions. A teaching method is commonly thought of as being defined by a set of actions on the part of the teacher or by a prescribed pattern of interaction between the teacher and the pupil, but the present definition is much broader in scope. The characteristics of the textbooks and other teaching equipment are just as much a part of a teaching method as is the behavior of the teacher. If learning conditions are ever to be systematically planned, then the most effective planning will be that which involves all aspects of learning conditions. In order to facilitate further discussion of this matter, the term *learning conditions*, rather than the term *teaching methods*, will be used. Our concern, then, is that of indicating the role that educational psychology must play in the systematic and comprehensive design of learning conditions in educational programs.

The design of human learning conditions is generally considered to be a two-stage operation. First, the goals of learning must be specified; and second, procedures, materials, and equipment related to the achievement of those goals must be specified. With respect to the first of these two stages, psychologists have already played an important role by providing means through which the goals of learning can be accurately specified. The outcome of this influence is the position widely accepted by educators that there is little point in setting up broad, vague goals such as "citizenship." Such goals must be defined in terms of the behavior manifested by those in whom the goal has been achieved if they are to serve as a basis for the planning of learning. Various attempts have been made to classify and define behaviors related to particular goals, the most notable of the various attempts being the taxonomy of problem-solving behavior by Bloom (circa 1955) and his associates.

The systematic design of learning conditions involves the planning of the child's environment in such a way that the impact of stimuli has the maximum effect in promoting learning in the directions that are specified by the objectives. Let us assume that the latter have been adequately defined in terms of measuring instruments. All objects and events that exert control over the learning of the pupil must be incorporated into the design. The main events that exert control over the learning of the pupil are the behaviors of the teacher, and the main objects that exert such control are the pieces of educational equipment provided. Progress has already been made in designing educational equipment in accordance with the research findings of psychologists; particularly notable has been the attempt to design textbooks in such a way that a suitable level of vocabulary and reading difficulty is used. The latter development was first introduced by Thorndike over a quarter of a century ago, and has had far-reaching effects. Much still needs to be done in the improvement of the design of educational equipment. The chief obstacle in the path of the further systematic and scientific improvement of such equipment is that psychologists have not studied to any great extent the effect of environmental conditions on learning except in the case of the study of reinforcers.

The design of teacher behavior is a much more complex matter than the design of the objects in the educational environment, and yet the matter is a crucial one. Most educational reformers have directed their efforts toward the problem of changing teacher behavior in such a way that it provides effective conditions for learning. Few have been concerned with changing other aspects of the educational environment. This is because reformers have clearly recognized that the behavior of the teacher is probably the most crucial determinant of the amount of learning that takes place. The problem of the design of teacher behavior is twofold. The first is that of deciding which teacher behaviors are to characterize the teacher in relation to his work. The second is that of developing teacher-training methods or otherwise arranging conditions so that the desired teacher behaviors occur. A brief consideration of each of these is instructive.

The generalizations derived from research on learning already provide some basis for the design of teacher behavior. There is perhaps little point in discussing at greater length the various concepts and generalizations about learning that have been presented in this book and that find application in the design of teacher behavior. The reader might undertake such a task as an exercise that will serve the purpose of bringing together some of the knowledge acquired in the study of this book.

A plan for teacher behavior is still a far step from arranging for teachers in the classroom to perform according to the plan. A plan for teacher behavior might well be such that many teachers could not perform in accordance with it. Just as composers have been known to write pieces of music that no musician can possibly play, so too can educational planners produce blueprints for education that require the actors on the educational scene to play parts that are incompatible with their personalities. Although a design for teaching may specify that only positive reinforcements are to be used, a teacher who has considerable hostility in his personality may be able to generate only limited amounts of positive reinforcements but large amounts of negative reinforcements. A design for teaching may specify that the teacher is to permit considerable free movement of the pupils within the classroom, but the need of the teacher to control others may be such that he cannot tolerate freedom on the part of the pupils.

An important function of teacher education is to see that teachers enter schools manifesting a pattern of behavior that provides a condition for effective learning. The faculty of schools and colleges of education are fully aware of the difficulty of this task, though their colleagues in other academic areas often are not. Two general approaches to the problem of producing teachers who will manage learning effectively are generally pursued. One of these is to select for teacher education those students whose behavior is compatible with the pattern of teacher behavior desired. For example, if the pattern of behavior desired included that of encouraging the pupil to make a decision for himself, then people with a high need to control others would not be selected for teacher education.

The second approach to the problem is that of training teachers in the pattern of behavior that it is desired they manifest in the classroom. This training may involve the observation of the classroom behavior of teachers already trained, with the anticipation that imitation and copying behavior will transfer the pattern of behavior from the trained teacher to the untrained. In addition, the teacher trainee will learn principles of learning and effective teaching that may become guides to action. The latter procedures probably lack the effectiveness needed. The verbal learnings that take place in colleges of education are only to a limited extent converted later into appropriate actions in the classroom. This is one of many reasons why education is far from the point where a teaching method can be systematically designed and immediately tried out in the classroom.

References

ALLPORT, F. H. *Theories of Perception and the Concept of Structure.* New York: Wiley, 1955.

ALLPORT, G. W. *Personality: A Psychological Interpretation.* New York: Holt, 1937.

AMMONS, H., and A. L. IRION. "A Note on the Ballard Reminiscence Phenomenon," *Journal of Experimental Psychology,* 48 (1954), pp. 184–186.

AMMONS, R. B., R. G. FARR, E. BLOCH, E. NEWMAN. M. DEY, R. MARION, and C. H. AMMONS. "Long Term Retention of Perceptual Motor Skills," *Journal of Experimental Psychology,* 55 (1958), pp. 318–328.

AMSEL, A., and I. MALTZMAN. "The Effect upon Generalized Drive Strength of Emotionality As Inferred from the Level of Consummatory Response," *Journal of Experimental Psychology,* 40 (1950), pp. 563–569.

ANDERSON, H. H., and J. E. BREWER. "Studies of Teachers' Classroom Personalities: I. Dominative and Socially Integrative Behavior of Kindergarten Teachers," *Applied Psychology Monographs,* No. 6, 1945.

ANDERSON, H. H., and J. E. BREWER. "Studies of Teachers' Classroom Personalities: II. Effects of Teachers' Dominative and Integrative Contacts on Children's Classroom Behavior," *Applied Psychology Monographs,* No. 8, 1946.

ANDERSON, L. D. "The Predictive Value of Infancy Tests in Relation to Intelligence at Five Years," *Child Development,* 10 (1939), pp. 203–212.

ANNETT, J. "The role of Knowledge of Results in Learning: A Survey," *Technical Report: NAVTRADEVCEN 342-3,* U.S. Naval Training Device Center, Port Washington, New York.

ANNETT, J. *Some Aspects of the Acquisition of Simple Sensori-motor Skills.* Unpublished D. Phil. thesis, Oxford University, 1959b.

ARCHER, E. J. "Concept Identification as a Function of Obviousness of Relevant and Irrelevant Information," *Journal of Experimental Psychology,* 63 (1962), pp. 616–620.

ASCH, M. J. "Nondirective Teaching in Psychology: An Experimental Study," *Psychological Monographs,* 65, No. 4 (1951).

ASHER, J. J. "Vision and Audition in Language Learning," *Perceptual and Motor Skills,* 19 (1964), pp. 255–300. (Monograph Supplement No. 1, 19, 1964)

ASHLEY, W. R., R. S. HARPER, and D. L. RUNYON. "The Perceived Size of Coins in Normal and Hypnotically Induced Economic States," *American Journal of Psychology,* 64 (1951), pp. 564–572.

ATKINSON, J. W., and D. C. MCCLELLAND. "The Projective Expression of

Needs: The Effect of Different Intensities of the Hunger Drive on Thematic Apperception," *Journal of Experimental Psychology*, **38** (1948), pp. 643–658.

ATWATER, S. K. "Proactive Inhibition and Associative Facilitation as Affected by Degree of Prior Learning," *Journal of Experimental Psychology*, **46** (1953), pp. 400–404.

AUBLE, D., and E. MECH. "Response Strength in a Classroom Task Related to a Forward Delay in Reinforcement," *Journal of Educational Psychology*, **45** (1954), pp. 175–181.

AUSUBEL, D. P. *Psychology of Meaningful Verbal Learning.* New York: Grune and Stratton, 1963.

BAGLEY, W. C. *The Educative Process.* New York: Macmillan, 1905.

BAILEY, C. J. "The Effectiveness of Drives as Cues," *Journal of Comparative and Physiological Psychology*, **48** (1955), pp. 183–187.

BALLARD, P. B. "Obliviscence and Reminiscence," *British Journal of Psychology, Monograph Supplement*, **1**, No. 2, 1913.

BANDURA, A., and A. C. HUSTON. "Identification as a Process of Incidental Learning," *Journal of Abnormal and Social Psychology*, **63** (1961), pp. 311–318.

BANDURA, A., and R. WALTERS. *Social Learning and Personality Development.* New York: Holt, Rinehart & Winston, 1963.

BARE, J. K. "The Specific Hunger for Sodium Chloride in Normal and Adrenalectomized Rats," *Journal of Comparative and Physiological Psychology*, **42** (1944), pp. 242–253.

BARNETT, S. A. "Experiments on 'Neophobia' in Wild and Laboratory Rats," *British Journal of Psychology*, **49** (1958), pp. 195–201.

BARTLETT, F. C. *Remembering.* Cambridge: Cambridge University Press, 1932.

BARTLETT, F. C. *Thinking: An Experimental and Social Study.* New York: Basic Books, 1958.

BEACH, F. A., and J. JAYNES. "Effects of Early Experience upon the Behavior of Animals," *Psychological Bulletin*, **51** (1954), pp. 239–263.

BEAMS, H. L., and G. G. THOMPSON. "Affectivity as a Factor in the Perception of the Magnitude of Food Object" (abstract), *American Psychologists*, **7** (1957), p. 323.

BERDIE, R. F. "Scores on the Strong Vocational Interest Blank and the Kuder Preference Record in Relation to Self Ratings," *Journal of Applied Psychology*, **34** (1950), pp. 42–44.

BERDIE, R. F. "Aptitude, Achievement, Interest, and Personality Tests: A Longitudinal Comparison," *Journal of Applied Psychology*, **39** (1955), pp. 103–114.

BERLO, D. K., and H. E. GULLEY. "Some Determinants of the Effects of Oral Communication in Producing Attitude Change and Learning," *Speech Monographs*, **24** (1957), pp. 10–20.

BERLYNE, D. E. *Conflict, Arousal, and Curiosity.* New York: McGraw-Hill, 1960.

BERLYNE, D. E. "Novelty and Curiosity as Determinants of Exploratory Behavior," *British Journal of Psychology*, 41 (1950), pp. 68–80.

BEXTON, W. H., W. HERON, and T. H. SCOTT. "Effects of Decreased Variation in the Sensory Environment," *Canadian Journal of Psychology*, 88 (1954), pp. 70–76.

BIDERMAN, A. D. "Communist Techniques of Coercive Interrogation," *USAF Personnel and Training Research Center Development Report*, No. 56–132 (1956), 33 pp.

BIERI, J., and A. TRIESCHMAN. "Learning as a Function of Perceived Similarity to Self," *Journal of Personality*, 25 (1956), pp. 213–223.

BILODEAU, I. M., and H. SCHLOSBERG. "Similarity in Stimulating Conditions as a Variable in Retroactive Inhibition," *Journal of Experimental Psychology*, 41 (1951), pp. 199–204.

BINDRA, D. *Motivation, A Systematic Reinterpretation*. New York: Ronald, 1959.

BINET, A. *L'Etude Experimentale de l'Intelligence*. Paris: A. Costes, 1922 (reprinted).

BINET, A., and T. SIMON. "Methodes Nouvelles Pour le Diagnositic du Niveau Intellectuel des Anormaux," *Année Psychologique*, 11 (1905), pp. 191–244.

BLOOM, B. S. *Stability and Change in Human Characteristics*. New York: Wiley, 1964.

BLOOM, B. S. (ed.), *Taxonomy of Educational Objectives: The Classification of Educational Goals*. New York: Longmans, Green, c. 1956.

BLOOMERS, P., L. M. KNIEF, and J. B. STROUD. "The Organismic Age Concept," *Journal of Educational Psychology*, 46 (1955), pp. 142–150.

BOURNE, L. E., JR., and E. J. ARCHER. "Time Continuously on Target as a Function of Distribution of Practice," *Journal of Experimental Psychology*, 51 (1956), pp. 25–33.

BOURNE, L. E., and C. V. BUNDERSON. "Effects of Delay in Information Feedback and Length of Postfeedback Interval on Concept Identification," *Journal of Experimental Psychology*, 65 (1963), pp. 1–5.

BOUWHUIS, D., and J. C. VAN HAMM. "Need and Stimulus Pattern as Variables of Perception," (abstract) *Psychological Abstracts*, 39, No. 11118, 1965.

BROADBENT, D. E. *Perception and Communication*. New York: Pergamon, 1958.

BROADBENT, D. E. *The Well-Ordered Mind*. Address given before the 1966 annual meeting of the American Educational Research Association.

BRODY, A. L. "Statistical Learning Theory Applied to an Instrumental Avoidance Situation," *Journal of Experimental Psychology* 54 (1957), pp. 240–245.

BROKAW, L. D. "Technical School Validity of the Airman Activity Inventory," *USAF Personnel and Training Research Center, Technical Report* No. 56–109 (1956).

BROZEK, J., H. GUETZKOW, and M. V. BALDWIN. "A Quantitative Study of

Perception and Association in Experimental Semistarvation," *Journal of Personality*, **19** (1950–51), pp. 245–264.

BRUNER, J. S. "The Act of Discovery," *Harvard Educational Review*, **31** (1961), pp. 21–32.

BRUNER, J. S. *The Process of Education*. Cambridge: Harvard University Press, 1960.

BRUNER, J. S. "Going Beyond the Information Given," pp. 41–69, in Bruner, J. S., *et al.*, *Contemporary Approaches to Cognition*. Cambridge: Harvard University Press, 1957.

BRUNER, J. S., J. J. GOODNOW, and G. A. AUSTIN. *A Study of Thinking*. New York: Wiley, 1956.

BRUNER, J. S., and C. D. GOODMAN. "Value and Need as Organizing Factors in Perception," *Journal of Abnormal and Social Psychology*, **42** (1947), pp. 33–44.

BRUNER, J. S., and L. POSTMAN. "Symbolic Value as an Organizing Factor in Perception," *Journal of Social Psychology*, **27** (1948), pp. 203–208.

BRYAN, W. L., and N. HARTER. "Studies in the Physiology and Psychology of the Telegraphic Language," *Psychological Review*, **4** (1897), pp. 27–53.

BUGELSKI, B. R. "Presentation Time, Total Time, and Mediation in Paired-Associate Learning," *Journal of Experimental Psychology*, **63** (1962), pp. 409–412.

BUGELSKI, B. R. *The Psychology of Learning*. New York: Holt, 1956.

BUGELSKI, B. R., and T. C. CADWALLADER. "A Reappraisal of the Transfer and Retroaction Surface," *Journal of Experimental Psychology*, **52** (1956), pp. 360–370.

BUGELSKI, B. R., and J. RICKWOOD. "Presentation Time, Total Time, and Mediation in Paired-Associate Learning: Self-Pacing," *Journal of Experimental Psychology*, Vol. 65, No. 6 (1963), pp. 616–617.

BURT, C. "The Gifted Child," *British Journal of Statistical Psychology*, **14** (1961), pp. 123–139.

BURT, C. "The Inheritance of Mental Ability," *American Psychologist*, **13** (1958), pp. 1–15.

BUSH, R. R., and F. MOSTELLER. *Stochastic Models for Learning*. New York: Wiley, 1955.

BUTLER, T. A. "Discrimination Learning by Rhesus Monkeys to Visual-Exploration Motivation," *Journal of Comparative and Physiological Psychology*, **46** (1953), pp. 95–98.

CAIN, L. F., and R. DE V. WILLEY. "The Effect of Spaced Learning on the Curve of Retention," *Journal of Experimental Psychology*, **25** (1939), pp. 209–214.

CALVIN, A. D., F. K. HOFFMAN, and E. L. HARDEN. "The Effect of Intelligence and Social Atmosphere on Group Problem Solving Behavior," *Journal of Social Psychology*, **45** (1957), pp. 61–74.

CAMPBELL, B. A., and F. D. SHEFFIELD. "Relation of Random Activity to Food Deprivation," *Journal of Comparative and Physiological Psychology*, **46** (1953), pp. 320–322.

CAMPBELL, E. Q. "Some Social Psychological Correlates of Direction in Attitude Change," *Social Forces,* **36** (1958), pp. 335–340.

CARLSON, E. R. "Attitude Change through Modification of Attitude Structure," *Journal of Abnormal and Social Psychology,* **52** (1956), pp. 256–261.

CARLTON, P. L. *Response Strength as a Function of Delay in Reward and Physical Confinement.* Unpublished master's thesis, University of Iowa, 1954.

CARTER, L. F., and K. SCHOOLER. "Value, Need, and Other Factors in Perception," *Psychological Review,* **56** (1949), pp. 200–207.

CARTER, L., W. HAYTHORN, J. LANZETTA, and B. MAIROWITZ. "The Relation of Categorizations and Ratings in the Observation of Group Behavior," *Human Relations,* **4** (1951), pp. 239–254.

CASLER, L. "Maternal Deprivation: A Critical Review of the Literature," *Monograph, Society for Research on Child Development,* **26** (2) (1961), 64 pp.

CASTANEDA, A., B. R. McCANDLESS, and D. S. PALMERO. "The Children's Form of the Manifest Anxiety Scale," *Child Development,* **27** (1956), pp. 317–326.

CASTENEDA, A., D. S. PALMERO, and B. R. McCANDLESS. "Complex Learning and Performance as a Function of Anxiety in Children and Task Difficulty," *Child Development,* **27** (1956), pp. 327–332.

CATTELL, R. B. *Prediction and Understanding of the Effect of Children's Interest upon School Performance.* Urbana: University of Illinois, 1961.

CHAMBERLIN, D., E. CHAMBERLIN, E. N. DROUGHT, and W. E. SCOTT. *Did They Succeed in College?* New York: Harper, 1942.

CHAN, A., and R. M. W. TRAVERS. "Effect on Retention of Labeling Visual Displays," *American Educational Research Journal* (in press).

CHAPANIS, A. "Men, Machines, and Models," *American Psychologist,* **16** (1961), pp. 113–131.

CHAPANIS, NATALIA P., and A. CHAPANIS. "Cognitive Dissonance: Five Years Later," *Psychological Bulletin,* **61** (1964), pp. 1–22.

CHERRY, E. C. "Some Experiments on the Recognition of Speech with One and Two Ears," *Journal of the Acoustical Society of America,* **25** (1963), pp. 975–979.

CHILD, I. L., and J. W. M. WHITING. "Determinants of Level of Aspiration: Evidence from Everyday Life," *Journal of Abnormal and Social Psychology,* **44** (1949), pp. 303–314.

CLARK, R. A., R. TEEVAN, and H. N. RICCIUTI. "Hope of Success and Fear of Failure as Aspects of Need for Achievement," *Journal of Abnormal and Social Psychology,* **53** (1956), pp. 182–186.

CLINE, V. B., and J. M. RICHARDS. "Creativity Tests and Achievement in High School Science," *Journal of Applied Psychology,* **47** (1963), pp. 184–189.

COFER, C. N., and M. H. APPLEY. *Motivation: Theory and Research.* New York: Wiley, 1964.

COLEMAN, E. B. "Improving Comprehensibility by Shortening Sentences," *Journal of Applied Psychology,* **46** (1962), pp. 131–134.

COLLINS, C. C. "The Relationship of Breadth of Academic Interests to Academic Achievement and Academic Aptitude," *Dissertation Abstracts,* **15** (1955), pp. 1782–1783.

COOK, T. W. "Distribution of Practice and Size of Maze Pattern," *British Journal of Psychology,* **27** (1936–37), pp. 303–312.

COULSON, J. E., and H. F. SILBERMAN. "Effects of Three Variables in a Teaching Machine," *Journal of Educational Psychology,* **51** (1960), pp. 135–143.

COWEN, E. L., and E. G. BEIER. "A Further Study of 'Threat Expectancy' Variable on Perception," *American Psychologist,* **7** (1952), pp. 320–321 (abstract).

COWEN, E. L., and E. G. BEIER. "Threat Expectancy, Word Frequencies, and Perceptual Precognitive Hypotheses," *Journal of Abnormal and Social Psychology,* **49** (1954), pp. 178–182.

COWLES, J. T. "Food Tokens as Incentives for Learning in Chimpanzees," *Comparative Psychology Monographs,* **14,** No. 5 (Serial No. 71) (1937), p. 78.

CRESPI, L. P. "Quantitative Variation of Incentive and Performance in a White Rat," *American Journal of Psychology,* **55** (1942), pp. 467–517.

CRESPI, L. P. "Amount of Reinforcement and Level of Performance," *Psychological Review,* **51** (1944), pp. 341–357.

CULBERTSON, F. M. "The Modification of Emotionally Held Attitudes through Role Playing," unpublished doctoral dissertation, University of Michigan, 1955.

DALE, E., and J. S. CHALL. "A Formula for Predicting Readability," *Educational Research Bulletin,* **28** (1948), pp. 11–20 and 37–54.

DAVIS, C. M. "Results of the Self-Selection of Diets by Young Children," *Canadian Medical Association Journal,* **41** (1939), pp. 257–261.

DEESE, J. *The Psychology of Learning.* New York: McGraw-Hill, 1958. de Montmollin, G. "Les Problems *du Commandement,* Etudes Anglo-Saxonnes Recentes," *Année Psychologique,* **54** (1954), pp. 459–478.

DELLA-PIANA, G. M., and N. GAGE. "Pupil's Values and the Validity of the MTAI," *Journal of Educational Psychology,* **46** (1955), 167–178.

DEMBO, T. "Der Ärger als Dynamisches Problem," *Psychologiche Forschung,* **15** (1931), pp. 1–144.

DENENBERG, V. H. "Critical Periods, Stimulus Input, and Emotional Reactivity," *Psychological Review,* **71** (1964), pp. 335–351.

DENNIS, W., and P. NAJARIAN. "Infant Development under Environmental Handicap," *Psychological Monographs,* **71,** No. 7 (1957).

DENNIS, W., and M. G. DENNIS. "The Effects of Cradling Practices upon the Onset of Walking in Hopi Children," *Journal of Genetic Psychology,* **56** (1940), pp. 77–86.

DEUTSCH, J. M. "The Development of Children's Concepts of Causal Relationships," pp. 129–145 in BARKER, R. G., J. S. KOUNIN, and H. F. WRIGHT (eds.), *Child Behavior and Development.* New York: McGraw-Hill, 1943.

DEWEY, J. *How We Think.* Boston: Heath, 1910.

DIAMOND, S. *Personality and Temperament.* New York: Harper, 1957.

DIAMOND, S., R. S. BALVIN, and F. R. DIAMOND. *Inhibition and Choice*. New York: Harper & Row, 1963.

DI VESTA, F. J. *Process Concepts in the Social and Personal Adjustments of Adolescents*. Memoir No. 287 (1948). Cornell University Agricultural Experiment Station, Ithaca, New York.

DI VESTA, F. J., and P. BOSSART. "The Effect of Sets Induced by Labelling on the Modification of Attitudes," *Journal of Personality*, **26** (1958), pp. 379–387.

DOMAS, S. J., and D. V. TIEDMAN. "Teacher Competence: An Annotated Bibliography," *Journal of Experimental Education*, **19** (1950), pp. 101–218.

DOOB, L. W. "The Behavior of Attitudes," *Psychological Review*, **54** (1947), pp. 135–156.

DOUGLASS, H. R., and C. KITTELSON. "The Transfer of Training in High School Latin to English Grammar, Spelling, and Vocabulary," *Journal of Experimental Education*, **4** (1935), pp. 26–33.

DOUVAN, E. "Social Status and Success Striving," *Journal of Abnormal and Social Psychology*, **52** (1956), pp. 219–223.

DUNCAN, C. P. "Transfer of Motor Learning as a Function of Degree of First-Task Learning and Inter-Task Similarity," *Journal of Experimental Psychology*, **45** (1953), pp. 1–11.

DUNCAN, C. P. "Transfer after Training with Single versus Multiple Tasks," *Journal of Experimental Psychology*, **55** (1958), pp. 63–72.

DUNCANSON, J. P. *Intelligence and the Ability to Learn*, unpublished doctoral dissertation, Princeton University, 1964.

EBBINGHAUS, H. *Über das Gedächtnis*. Leipzig: Duncker und Hambolt, 1885.

EDWARDS, A. L. *Techniques of Attitude Scale Construction*. New York: Appleton-Century-Crofts, 1957.

EELLS, K., A. DAVIS, R. J. HAVIGHURST, and R. W. TYLER. *Intelligence and Cultural Differences*. Chicago: University of Chicago Press, 1951.

EKMAN, P. *A Comparison of Verbal and Nonverbal Behavior as Reinforcing Stimuli of Opinion Responses*, unpublished doctoral dissertation, Adelphi College, 1958.

EPPS, H. O., G. B. MCCAMMON, and Q. D. SIMMONS. *Teaching Devices for Children with Impaired Learning*. Columbus, Ohio: Parents' Volunteer Association, 1958.

EPSTEIN, A. N., and E. STELLER. "The Control of Salt Preference in the Adrenalectomized Rat," *Journal of Comparative and Physiological Psychology*, **48** (1955), pp. 167–172.

ESTES, B. W. "Some Mathematical and Logical Concepts in Children," *Journal of Genetic Psychology*, **88** (1956), pp. 219–222.

ESTES, W. K. "An Experimental Study of Punishment," Psychological Monographs, **57**, No. 263, 1944.

ESTES, W. K., pp. 380–491, "The Statistical Approach to Learning Theory," in Kochs, S. (ed.), *Psychology: The Study of a Science*, Vol. 2. New York: McGraw-Hill, 1959.

EYSENCK, H. J. "Reminiscence, Drive, and Personality Theory," *Journal of Abnormal and Social Psychology*, 53 (1956), pp. 328–333.

FARBER, I. E., and K. W. SPENCE. "Complex Learning and Conditioning as a Function of Anxiety," *Journal of Experimental Psychology*, 45 (1953), pp. 120–125.

FEATHER, N. T. "A Structural Balance Model of Communication Effects," *Psychological Review*, 71 (1964), pp. 291–313.

FEIGENBAUM, E. A., and H. A. SIMON. "Brief Notes on the EPAM Theory of Verbal Learning," pp. 333–335 in *Verbal Behavior and Learning*, Cofer, C. N. (ed.). New York: McGraw-Hill, 1963.

FERGUSON, G. A. "On Learning and Human Ability," *Canadian Journal of Psychology*, 8 (1954), pp. 95–112.

FERSTER, C. B., and B. F. SKINNER. *Schedules of Reinforcement.* New York: Appleton-Century-Crofts, 1957.

FESTINGER, L. *A Theory of Cognitive Dissonance.* Evanston, Ill.: Row, Peterson, 1957.

FESTINGER, L. "A Theory of Social Comparison Processes," *Human Relations*, 7 (1954), pp. 117–140.

FESTINGER, L., and J. M. CARLSMITH. "Cognitive Consequences of Forced Compliance," *Journal of Abnormal and Social Psychology*, 58 (1959), pp. 203–210.

FISCHER, G. J., and M. B. COOK. "Influence of Distribution of Practice and Varying Speeds of Stimulus Presentation on Incidental Learning," *Psychological Reports*, 10 (1962), pp. 539–545.

FLEISHMAN, E. A., and W. E. HEMPEL. "Changes in Factor Structure of a Complex Psychomotor Test as a Function of Practice," *Psychometrika*, 19 (1954), pp. 239–252.

FLEISHMAN, E. A., and W. HEMPEL. "The Relation between Abilities and Improvement with Practice in a Visual Discrimination Reaction Task," *Journal of Experimental Psychology*, 49 (1955), pp. 301–312.

FLEISHMAN, E. A., and W. E. HEMPEL. "Factorial Analysis of Complex Psychomotor Performance and Related Skills," *Journal of Applied Psychology*, 40 (1956), pp. 96–104.

FORLANO, G. *School Learning with Various Methods of Practice and Rewards.* New York: Teachers College, Columbia University, Teachers College Contributions to Education, No. 688, 1936.

FOWLER, W. "Cognitive Learning in Infancy and Early Childhood," *Psychological Bulletin*, 59 (1962), pp. 116–152.

FRANDSEN, A. N., and A. D. SESSIONS. "Interests and School Achievement," *Educational and Psychological Measurement*, 13 (1953), pp. 94–101.

FRANK, J. D. "Recent Studies of Level of Aspiration," *Psychological Bulletin*, 38 (1941), pp. 218–225.

FRENCH, E. G. "Some Characteristics of Achievement Motivation," *Journal of Experimental Psychology*, 50 (1955), pp. 232–236.

FRENCH, E. G. "Motivation as a Variable in Work-Partner Selection," *Journal of Abnormal and Social Psychology*, 53 (1956), pp. 96–99.

FRENCH, E. G., and F. H. THOMAS. "The Relation of Achievement Motivation to Problem Solving Effectiveness," *Journal of Abnormal and Social Psychology*, **56** (1958), pp. 45–48.

FULKERSON, S. C. "The Interaction of Frequency, Emotional Tone and Set in Visual Recognition," *Journal of Experimental Psychology*, **54** (1957), pp. 188–194.

FURST, E. J. "Effects of the Organization of Learning Outcomes: II: Study of the Problem by Means of Factor Analysis," *Journal of Experimental Education*, **18** (1950a), pp. 343–353.

FURST, E. J. "Effect of the Organization of Learning Experiences upon the Organization of Learning Outcomes: I: Study of the Problem by Means of Correlation Analysis," *Journal of Experimental Education*, **18** (1950b), pp. 215–228.

GAGNÉ, R. M. "Problem Solving," pp. 293–317 in MELTON, A. W. (ed.) *Categories of Human Learning*. New York: Academic Press, 1964.

GAGNÉ, R. M. *The Conditions of Learning*. New York: Holt, Rhinehart & Winston, 1964.

GAGNÉ, R. M., and E. C. SMITH. "A Study of the Effects of Verbalization on Problem Solving," *Journal of Experimental Psychology*, **63** (1962), pp. 12–18.

GAGNÉ, R. M., K. E. BAKER, and H. FORSET. "On the Relation Between Similarity and Transfer of Training in the Learning of Discriminative Motor Tasks," *Psychological Review*, **57** (1950), pp. 67–79.

GARDNER, E. F., and G. G. THOMPSON. *Social Relations and Morale in Small Groups*. New York: Appleton-Century-Crofts, 1956.

GATES, A. I. "Recitation as a Factor in Memorizing," *Archives of Psychology*, **6**, No. 40, 1917.

GERALL, A. A., P. B. SAMPSON, and G. L. BOSLOV. "Classical Conditioning of Human Pupillary Dilation," *Journal of Experimental Psychology*, **54** (1957), pp. 467–474.

GESELL, A., and C. S. AMATRUDA. *Developmental Diagnosis: Normal and Abnormal Child Development*. New York: Hoeber, 1941.

GEWIRTZ, J. L., and D. M. BAER. "Deprivation and Satiation of Social Reinforcers as Drive Conditions," *Journal of Abnormal and Social Psychology*, **57** (1958), 165–172.

GIBSON, E. J. "Retroactive Inhibition as a Function of Degree of Generalization between Tasks," *Journal of Experimental Psychology*, **28** (1941), pp. 93–115.

GIBSON, E. J., and R. D. WALK. "The Effect of Prolonged Exposure to Visually Presented Patterns on Learning to Discriminate Them," *Journal of Comparative and Physiological Psychology*, **49** (1956), pp. 239–242.

GIBSON, E. J., R. D. WALK, and T. J. TIGHE. "Enhancement and Deprivation of Visual Stimulation during Rearing as Factors in Visual Discrimination," *Journal of Comparative and Physiological Psychology*, **52** (1959a), pp. 74–81.

GIBSON, E. J., R. D. WALK, H. L. DICK, and T. J. TIGHE. "The Effect of Prolonged Exposure to Visually Presented Patterns on Learning to Discriminate Similar and Different Patterns," *Journal of Comparative and Physiological Psychology*, **57** (1958), pp. 584–587.

GILBERT, L. C. "Speed of Processing Visual Stimuli and Its Relation to Reading," *Journal of Educational Psychology*, **55** (1959), pp. 8–14.

GILLILAND, A. R. *Test for Infants 4–12 Weeks Old.* Boston: Houghton-Mifflin, 1949.

GLASER, R. (Ed.) *Teaching Machines and Programmed Learning* II. Washington, D.C.: National Education Association, 1965.

GLAZE, J. A. "The Association Value of Nonsense Syllables," *Journal of Genetic Psychology*, **35** (1928), pp. 255–269.

GOLEMBIEWSKI, R. T. *The Small Group: An Analysis of Research Concepts and Operations.* Chicago: University of Chicago Press, 1962.

GORDON, L. V., and E. F. ALF. "The Predictive Validity of Measured Interest for Navy Vocational Training," *Journal of Applied Psychology*, **46** (1962), pp. 212–219.

GORDON, M. "The Influence of Background Factors upon the Prediction of Success in Air Force Training School," *USAF Personnel Training, Res. Center Res. Pub.* 1955, AFPTRC–TN–55–4, V, 14 pp.

GOSS, A. E., and C. F. NODINE. *Paired Associate Learning.* New York: Academic Press, 1965.

GOWAN, J. C. "Intelligence, Interests, and Reading Ability in Relation to Scholastic Achievement," *Psychological Newsletter*, N.Y.U. **8** (1957), pp. 85–87.

GREGOIRE, A. *"L'Apprentissage du Langage: Les Deux Premieres Annees."* Paris: Droz, 1937.

GREGOIRE, A. *"L'Apprentissage du Langage:* II. *La Troisieme Annee et les Annees Suivantes."* Paris: Droz, 1947.

GRIMES, J. W., and W. ALLINSMITH. "Compulsivity, Anxiety, School Achievement," *Merrill-Palmer Quarterly*, **7** (1961), pp. 247–271.

GUESTZKOW, H., E. L. KELLEY, and W. J. McKEACHIE. "An Experimental Comparison of Recitation, Discussion, and Tutorial Methods in College Teaching," *Journal of Educational Psychology*, **45** (1954), pp. 193–209.

GUILFORD, J. P. "The Structure of Intellect," *Psychological Bulletin*, **53** (1956), pp. 267–293.

GURNEE, H. "The Effect of Collective Learning upon the Individual Participants," *Journal of Abnormal and Social Psychology*, **34** (1939), pp. 529–532.

GUTHRIE, E. R. *The Psychology of Learning* (rev. ed.). New York: Harper, 1952.

HAGEN, E. P. "A Factor Analysis of the Wechsler Intelligence Scale for Children," *Dissertation Abstracts*, **12** (1952), pp. 722–723.

HAMBLEN, A. A. *An Investigation to Determine the Extent to Which the Effect of the Study of Latin upon a Knowledge of English Derivations Can Be Measured by Conscious Adaptation of Content and Methods to the Attain-*

ment of This Objective, unpublished doctoral dissertation, University of Pennsylvania, 1925.

HANAWALT, N. G. "Memory Trace for Figures in Recall and Recognition," *Archives of Psychology,* **31**, No. 216 (1937).

HARKER, G. S. *An Experimental Investigation of the Effects of Changes in the Delay of Reinforcement upon Level of Performance on an Instrumental Response,* unpublished doctoral dissertation, State University of Iowa, 1950.

HARLOW, H. F. "The Formation of Learning Sets," *Psychological Review,* **56** (1949), pp. 51–65.

HARLOW, H. F. "The Nature of Love," *American Psychologist,* **13** (1958), pp. 673–685.

HARLOW, H. F. "Learning Set and Error Factor Theory," 492–537, in *Psychology: A Study of a Science,* Vol. 2, Koch, S. (ed.). New York: McGraw-Hill, 1959.

HARLOW, H. F. "The Heterosexual Affectional System in Monkeys," *American Psychologist,* **17** (1962), pp. 1–9.

HARTLINE, H. K., and F. RATLIFF. "Inhibitory Interaction of Receptor Units in the Eye of Limulus," *Journal of General Physiology,* **40** (1956–57), pp. 357–376.

HARTMAN, T. J. "Semantic Transfer of the Differential Conditioned Eyelid Response from Words to Objects," *Journal of Experimental Psychology,* **65** (1963), pp. 194–200.

HARVEY, O. J., and J. RUTHERFORD. "Gradual and Absolute Approaches to Attitude Change," *Sociometry,* **21** (1958), pp. 61–68.

HAUTY, G. T. "Response Similarity-Dissimilarity and Differential Motor Transfer Effect," *Journal of Psychology,* **36** (1953), pp. 363–379.

HAVIGHURST, R. J. *Developmental Tasks and Education.* New York: Longmans, Green, 1953.

HAYWARD, S. C. "Modification of Sexual Behavior of the Male Albino Rat," *Journal of Comparative and Physiological Psychology,* **50** (1957), pp. 70–73.

HEAD, H. *Studies in Neurology.* Oxford: Oxford University Press, 1920.

HEBB, D. O. *The Organization of Behavior.* New York: Wiley, 1948.

HEBB, D. O. *Textbook of Psychology.* Philadelphia: Saunders, 1958.

HEBB, D. O., and E. N. FOORD. "Errors of Visual Recognition and the Nature of the Trace," *Journal of Experimental Psychology,* **35** (1945), pp. 335–348.

HEISE, G. A., and G. A. MILLER. "Problem Solving by Small Groups Using Various Communication Nets," *Journal of Abnormal and Social Psychology,* **46** (1951), pp. 327–335.

HELSON, H. "Adaptation Level as a Basis for a Quantitative Theory of Frames of Reference," *Psychological Review,* **55** (1948), pp. 297–313.

HELSON, H. "Adaptation Level as a Frame of Reference for Prediction of Psychophysical Data," *American Journal of Psychology,* **40** (1947), pp. 1–29.

HELSON, H. *Adaptation-level Theory.* New York: Harper & Row, 1964.

HELSON, H. "Perception," Chapter 8 in Helson, H. (ed.), *Theoretical Foundation of Psychology.* New York: Van Nostrand, 1951.

HELSON, H., R. R. BLAKE, and J. S. MOUTON. "An Experimental Investigation of the 'Big Lie' in Shifting Attitudes," *Journal of Social Psychology,* **48** (1958), pp. 51–60.

HELSON, H., R. R. BLAKE, J. S. MOUTON, and J. A. OLMSTEAD. "Attitudes as Adjustments to Stimulus Background and Residual Factors," *Journal of Abnormal and Social Psychology,* **52** (1956), pp. 314–322.

HENDRICKSEN, G., and W. H. SCHROEDER. "Transfer of Training in Learning to Hit a Submerged Target," *Journal of Educational Psychology,* **32** (1941), pp. 205–213.

HENDRIX, G. "Learning by Discovery," *Mathematics Teacher,* **54** (1961), pp. 290–299.

HERNANDEZ-PEON, R., and H. SCHERRER. "Habituation to Acoustic Stimuli in the Cochlear Nucleus," *Federation Proceedings,* **14** (1955), p. 71.

HERNANDEZ-PEON, R., H. SCHERRER, and M. JOUVET. "Modification of Electrical Activity in Cochlear Nucleus during Attention in Unanesthetized Cats," *Science,* **123** (1956), pp. 331–332.

HERON, W. T. "Internal Stimuli and Learning," *Journal of Comparative and Physiological Psychology,* **42** (1949), pp. 486–492.

HILGARD, E. R., and D. G. MARQUIS. "Conditioned Eyelid Responses in Monkeys, with a Comparison of Dog, Monkey, and Man," *Psychological Monographs,* **47**, No. 212 (1936), pp. 186–198.

HILGARD, E. R., R. P. IRVINE, and J. E. WHIPPLE. "Rote Memorization, Understanding, and Transfer; An Extension of Katona's Card Trick Experiments," *Journal of Experimental Psychology,* **46** (1953), pp. 288–292.

HILGARD, J. R. "The Effect of Early and Delayed Practice on Memory and Motor Performances Studied by the Method of Co-twin Control," *Genetic Psychology Monographs,* **14**, No. 6 (1933).

HINDE, R. A. "Factors Governing the Changes in Strength of a Partially Inborn Response by the Mobbing Behavior of the Chaffinch: I. The Nature of the Response and an Examination of Its Course," *Proceedings of the Royal Society,* B., **142** (1954), pp. 306–331.

HOLDING, D. H. "Transfer between Difficult and Easy Tasks," *British Journal of Psychology,* **53** (1962), pp. 397–407.

HONZIK, M. P., J. W. MACFARLANE, and L. ALLEN. "The Stability of Mental Test Performance between Two and Eighteen Years," *Journal of Experimental Education,* **17** (1948), pp. 309–324.

HOVLAND, C. I. "Computer Simulation of Thinking," *American Psychologist,* **15** (1960), 687–693.

HOVLAND, C. I., and W. WEISS. "Transmission of Information Concerning Concepts through Positive and Negative Instances," *Journal of Experimental Psychology,* **45** (1953), pp. 175–182.

HOVLAND, C. I., O. J. HARVEY, and M. SHERIF. "Assimilation and Contrast

Effects in Reaction to Communication and Attitude Change," *Journal of Abnormal and Social Psychology,* **55** (1957), pp. 244–252.

HOVLAND, C. I., A. A. LUMSDAINE, and F. D. SHEFFIELD. *Experiments on Mass Communication,* Vol. III. Princeton, N.J.: Princeton University Press, 1949.

HOWES, D. H., and R. L. SOLOMAN. "Visual Duration Threshold as a Function of Word-Probability," *Journal of Experimental Psychology,* **41** (1951), pp. 401–410.

HUDGINS, B. B. "Effects of Group Experience on Individual Problem Solving," *Journal of Educational Psychology,* **51** (1960), pp. 37–42.

HUGHES, M. M. *Development of the Means for the Assessment of the Quality of Teaching in Elementary Schools.* Salt Lake City: University of Utah, 1959.

HULL, C. L. *Essentials of Behavior.* New Haven: Yale University Press, 1951.

HULL, C. L. "The Meaningfulness of 320 Selected Nonsense Syllables," *American Journal of Psychology,* **45** (1933), pp. 730–734.

HULL, C. L. *Mathematico–Deductive Theory of Rote Learning.* New Haven: Yale University Press, 1940.

HULL, C. L. *Principles of Behavior.* New York: Appleton-Century-Crofts, 1943.

HULL, C. L. *Essentials of Behavior.* New Haven: Yale University Press, 1951.

HULL, C. L. *A Behavior System.* New Haven: Yale University Press, 1952.

HUNT, E. B. *Concept Learning.* New York: Wiley, 1962.

HUNT, J. McV. *Intelligence and Experience.* New York: Ronald, 1961.

HUSBAND, R. W. "Cooperative versus Solitary Problem Solution," *Journal of Social Psychology,* **11** (1940), pp. 405–409.

HUTTENLOCKER, J. "Some Effects of Negative Instances on the Formation of Simple Concepts," *Psychological Reports,* **11** (1962), pp. 35–42.

INHELDER, B., and J. PIAGET. *The Growth of Logical Thinking from Childhood to Adolescence.* New York: Basic Books, 1959.

IRVINE, LA V. F., "Intensity of Attitude, Personality Variables and Attitude Change," *Dissertation Abstracts,* **16** (1956), p. 1519.

JACOB, P. E. *Changing Values in College.* New York: Harper, 1957.

JANIS, I. L., and P. B. FIELD. "A Behavioral Assessment of Persuasibility: Consistency of Individual Differences," *Sociometry,* **19** (1956), pp. 241–259.

JOHNSON, R., and C. THOMSON. "Incidental and Intentional Learning under Three Conditions of Motivation," *American Journal of Psychology,* **75** (1962), pp. 284–288.

JONES, E. E., and R. KOHLER. "The Effects of Plausibility on the Learning of Controversial Statements," *Journal of Abnormal and Social Psychology,* **57** (1958), pp. 315–20.

JORGENSON, G. Q. *Predicting Academic Achievement of College of Education Females Using a Motivational Device,* unpublished master's thesis, University of Utah, 1960.

JUDD, C. H. "The Relation of Special Training to General Intelligence," *Educational Review,* **36** (1908), pp. 28–42.

JUDSON, A. J., C. N. COFER, and S. GELFAND. "Reasoning as an Associative

Process; II. Direction in Problem Solving as a Function of Prior Reinforcement of Relevant Responses." *Psychological Reports,* **2** (1956), pp. 501–507.

KALE, S. V., J. H. GROSSLIGHT, and L. J. McINTYRE. "Exploratory Studies in the Use of Pictures and Sound for Teaching Foreign Language," *Technical Report,* Special Devices Center, U. S. Navy SPECDEVCEN pp. 269–7–53.

KATONA, G. *Organizing and Memorizing.* New York: Columbia University Press, 1940.

KATONA, G. "Organizing and Memorizing: A Reply to Dr. Melton," *American Journal of Psychology,* **55** (1942), pp. 273–275.

KATZ, D., and E. STOTLAND. "A Preliminary Statement to a Theory of Attitude Structure and Change," pp. 423–447 in Koch, S. (ed.), *Psychology: A Study of a Science,* Vol. 3. New York: McGraw-Hill, 1959.

KATZ, D., C. McCLINTOCK, and I. SARNOFF. "The Measurement of Ego Defense as Related to Attitude Change," *Journal of Personality,* **25** (1957), pp. 465–474.

KATZ, D., I. SARNOFF, and C. McCLINTOCK. "Ego Defense and Attitude Change," *Human Relations,* **9** (1956), pp. 27–45.

KAUFMAN, A. E. "The Mediating Role of Need-Related Cues in Problem Solving," *Dissertation Abstracts,* **18** (1958), pp. 1106–1107.

KEARNEY, N. C., and P. D. ROCCHIO. "The Relation between the MTAI and Subject Matter Taught by Elementary Teachers," *Educational Administration and Supervision,* **41** (1955a), pp. 358–360.

KEARNEY, N. C., and P. D. ROCCHIO. "Using the MTAI in Counseling Prospective Teachers," *Personnel Guidance Journal,* **34** (1955b), pp. 159–160.

KEARNEY, N. C., and P. D. ROCCHIO. "Relation between a Teacher Attitude Inventory and Pupils' Ratings of Teachers," *School Review,* **63** (1955c), pp. 443–445.

KELLEY, E. L., and D. W. FISKE. *The Prediction of Performance in Clinical Psychology.* Ann Arbor: University of Michigan Press, 1951.

KEMENY, J. G., and L. J. SNELL. *Mathematical Models in the Social Sciences.* New York: Ginn, 1962.

KENDLER, H. H., and T. S. KENDLER. "Vertical and Horizontal Processes in Problem Solving," *Psychological Review,* **69** (1962), pp. 1–16.

KENDLER, T. S. "Verbalization and Optional Reversal Shifts among Kindergarten Children," *Journal of Verbal Learning and Verbal Behavior,* **3** (1964), pp. 428–436.

KIMBROUGH, W. W. "A Study of Certain Implications of a Conception of Attitudes as Implicit Verbal Responses," *Dissertation Abstracts,* **16** (1956), pp. 1183–1184.

KLARE, G. R. *The Measurement of Readability.* Ames, Iowa: Iowa University Press, 1963.

KLAUSMEIER, H. J., A. BEEMAN, and I. J. LEHMAN. "Comparison of Organismic Age and Regression Equation in Predicting Achievements in Elementary School," *Journal of Educational Psychology,* **49** (1958), pp. 182–186.

KLEIN, G. S., H. J. SCHLESINGER, and D. E. MEISTER. "The Effect of Personal Values on Perception: An Experimental Critique," *Psychological Review,* 58 (1951), pp. 96–112.

KLINEBERG, O. *Negro Intelligence and Selective Migration.* New York: Columbia University Press, 1935.

KNIGHT, H. C. *A Comparison of the Reliability of Group and Individual Judgments,* unpublished master's thesis, Columbia University, 1921.

KORONACKOS, C. "Inferential Learning in Rats; the Problem Solving Assembly of Behavior Segments," *Dissertation Abstracts,* 17 (1957), pp. 682–683.

KOUNIN, J. S., P. V. GUMP, and J. J. RYAN. "Explorations in Classroom Management," *Journal of Teacher Education,* 12 (1961), pp. 235–246.

KRASNER, L. "Studies of the Conditioning of Verbal Behavior," *Psychological Bulletin,* 55 (1958), pp. 148–170.

KRUGMAN, A. D. "A Comparative Study of the Effect of Induced Failure, Induced Success, and a Neutral Task upon the Retentive Process of Anxiety and Normal Subjects," *Dissertation Abstracts,* 18 (1958), p. 662.

LAMBERT, W. W., R. L. SOLOMAN, and P. D. WATSON. "Reinforcement and Extinction as Factors in Size Estimation," *Journal of Experimental Psychology,* 39 (1949), pp. 637–641.

LAZARUS, R. S., J. DEESE, and S. F. OSLER. "The Effects of Psychological Stress upon Performance," *Psychological Bulletin,* 49 (1952), pp. 293–317.

LEBO, D., and E. LEBO. "Aggression and Age in Relation to Verbal Expression in Nondirective Play Therapy," *Psychological Monographs,* 71, No. 20 (1957).

LEVINE, R., I. CHEIN, and G. MURPHY. "The Relation of the Intensity of a Need to the Amount of Perceptual Distortion," *Journal of Psychology,* 13 (1942), pp. 283–293.

LEWIN, K. *Principles of Topological Psychology.* New York: McGraw-Hill, 1936.

LEWIN, K. *Resolving Social Conflicts.* New York: Harper, 1948.

LEWIN, K. *Field Theory in Social Science, Selected Theoretical Papers.* New York: Harper, 1951.

LEWIN, K., R. LIPPITT, and R. K. WHITE. "Patterns of Aggressive Behavior in Experimentally Created 'Social Climates,'" *Journal of Social Psychology,* 10 (1939), pp. 271–299.

LEWIN, K., T. DEMBO, L. FESTINGER, and P. S. SEARS. "Level of Aspiration," pp. 333–378, in HUNT, J. McV. (ed.) *Personality and Behavior Disorders.* New York: Ronald, 1944.

LIU, I. M. "A Theory of Classical Conditioning," *Psychological Review,* 71 (1964), pp. 408–411.

LORENZ, K. "Der Kumpan in der Umwelt des Vogels," *Journal Für Ornithologie,* 83 (1935), pp. 137–213, 289–413.

LORGE, I. L. *The Influence of Regularly Interpolated Time Intervals upon Subsequent Learning.* New York: Columbia University, Teachers College Contributions to Education, No. 438 (1930).

LORGE, I. "Groupness of the Group," *Journal of Educational Psychology,* **46** (1955), 449–456.

LORGE, I., and H. SOLOMAN. "Two Models of Group Behavior in the Solution of Eureka-type Problems," *Psychometrika,* **20** (1955), pp. 139–148.

LORGE, I., D. FOX, J. DAVITZ, and M. BRENNER. "A Survey of Studies Contrasting the Quality of Group Performance and Individual Performance, 1920–1957," *Psychological Bulletin,* **55** (1958), pp. 337–372.

LOVELL, K. "A Follow-up Study of Inhelder and Piaget's The Growth of Logical Thinking," *British Journal of Psychology,* **52** (1961), pp. 145–153.

LUCE, R. D., and H. RAIFFA. *Games and Decisions: Introduction and Critical Survey.* New York: Wiley, 1957.

LUH, C. W. "The Conditions of Retention," *Psychological Monographs,* **31,** No. 142 (1922).

LYON, D. O. "The Relation of Length of Material to Time Taken for Learning and the Optimum Distribution of Time," *Journal of Educational Psychology,* **5** (1914), pp. 1–9; 85–91; 155–163.

McCARTHY, D. "Language Development in Children," in *Manual of Child Psychology,* CARMICHAEL, L. (ed.). New York: Wiley, 1954.

McCLEARY, R. A., and R. S. LAZARUS. "Autonomic Discrimination without Awareness," *Journal of Personality,* **18** (1949), pp. 171–179.

McCLELLAND, D. C., J. W. ATKINSON, R. A. CLARK, and E. L. LOWELL. *The Achievement Motive,* New York: Appleton-Century-Crofts, 1953.

McCLINTOCK, C. G. "Personality Syndromes and Attitude Change," *Journal of Personality,* **26** (1958), pp. 479–493.

McFANN, H. H. "Effects of Response Alteration and Deficient Instructions on Proactive and Retroactive Facilitation and Interference," *Journal of Experimental Psychology,* **46** (1953), pp. 405–410.

McGEOCH, J. A., and A. L. IRION. *The Psychology of Human Learning.* New York: Longmans, Green, 1950.

McGINNIES, E. "Emotionality and Perceptual Defense," *Psychological Review,* **56** (1949), pp. 244–251.

McGRAW, M. B. *Growth, A Study of Johnny and Jimmy.* New York: Appleton-Century, 1935.

McGRAW, M. B. *The Neuromuscular Maturation of the Human Infant.* New York: Columbia University Press, 1943.

McKEACHIE, W. J. "Procedures and Techniques of Teaching: A Survey of Experimental Studies," Chapter 8 in Sanford, N. (ed.), *The American College.* New York: Wiley, 1962.

McKILLOP, A. S. *The Relationship between the Reader's Attitudes and Certain Types of Reading Response.* New York: Teachers College, Columbia University, 1952.

MALTZMAN, I. "Thinking: From a Behavioristic Point of View," *Psychological Review,* **62** (1955), pp. 275–286.

MANDLER, G. "Transfer of Training as a Function of Degree of Response Overlearning," *Journal of Experimental Psychology,* **47** (1954), pp. 411–417.

MARION, A. J. "The Influence of Experimenter Status upon Verbal Conditions," unpublished doctoral dissertation, University of California, Los Angeles, 1956.

MARTIRE, J. G. "Relationships between the Self Concept and Differences in the Strength and Generality of Achievement Motivation," *Journal of Personality*, **24** (1956), pp. 364–375.

MARX, M. H. "Some Suggestions for the Conceptual and Theoretical Analysis of Complex Intervening Variables in Problem-Solving Behavior," *Journal of General Psychology*, **58** (1958), pp. 115–128.

MASLOW, A. H. "A Theory of Human Motivation," *Psychological Review*, **50** (1943), pp. 370–396.

MELTON, A. W., and J. McQ. IRWIN. "The Influence of the Degree of Interpolated Learning on Retroactive Inhibition and the Overt Transfer of Specific Responses," *American Journal of Psychology*, **53** (1940), pp. 173–203.

MELTON, A. W., and W. J. VON LACKUM. "Retroactive and Proactive Inhibition in Retention: Evidence for a Two-Factor Theory of Retroactive Inhibition," *American Journal of Psychology*, **54** (1941), pp. 157–173:

MELZACK, R. "Effects of Early Perceptual Restriction on Simple Verbal Discrimination," *Science*, **137** (1962), pp. 978–979.

MELZACK, R., and T. H. SCOTT. "The Effects of Early Experience on the Response to Pain," *Journal of Comparative and Physiological Psychology*, **50** (1957), pp. 155–161.

MELZACK, R., and W. R. THOMPSON. "Effects of Early Experience on Social Behavior," *Canadian Journal of Psychology*, **10** (1956), pp. 82–90.

MERRITT, C. B. "The Relationship between Interest Level and the Discrepancy between Scholastic Aptitude and Academic Achievement," *Microfilm Abstract*, University of Michigan, 10(1), 63 (1950).

MILLER, D. R., and G. E. SWANSON. *The Changing American Parent*. New York: Wiley, 1958.

MILLER, N. E., and D. DOLLARD. *Social Learning and Imitation*. New Haven: Yale University Press, 1941.

MILLER, N. E. "Studies of Fear as an Acquirable Drive: I. Fear as Motivation and Fear-Retention as Reinforcement in the Learning of New Responses," *Journal of Experimental Psychology*, **38** (1948), pp. 89–101.

MILLER, N. E. "Extensions of Liberalized S-R Theory," pp. 196–292 in *Psychology: A Study of a Science*, Volume 2, Koch, S. (ed.). New York: McGraw-Hill, 1959.

MITZEL, H. W., and W. RABINOWITZ. "Assessing Social Emotional Climate in the Classroom by Whithall's Technique," *Psychological Monographs*, **67**, No. 18 (1953).

MITZEL, H. W., and W. RABINOWITZ. *Reliability of Teacher's Verbal Behavior: A Study of Whithall's Technique for Assessing Social-Emotional Climate in the Classroom*. New York: Office of Research and Evaluation, College of the City of New York, 1953.

MONTAGUE, E. K. "The Role of Anxiety in Serial Rote Learning," *Journal of Experimental Psychology*, **45** (1954), pp. 91–96.

MONTGOMERY, K. C., and M. SEGALL. "Discrimination Learning Based upon the Exploratory Drive," *Journal of Comparative and Physiological Psychology,* 48 (1955), pp. 225–228.

MOULTON, R. W., C. RALPHELSON, A. B. KRISTOFFERSON, and J. W. ATKINSON. "The Achievement Motive and Perceptual Sensitivity under Two Conditions of Motive Arousal," Chapter 24 in *Motives in Fantasy, Action, and Society,* ATKINSON, J. W. (ed.). New York: Van Nostrand, 1958.

MOWRER, O. H. *Learning Theory and Behavior.* New York: Wiley, 1960(a).

MOWRER, O. H. *Learning Theory and the Symbolic Processes.* New York: Wiley, 1960(b).

MUKERJI, N. P. "An Investigation of Ability in Work in Groups and in Isolation," *British Journal of Psychology,* 30 (1940), pp. 352–356.

MURDOCK, B. B., JR. "The Immediate Retention of Unrelated Words," *Journal of Experimental Psychology,* Vol. 60, No. 4 (1960), pp. 222–234.

MURRAY, H. A. *Explorations in Personality.* New York: Oxford University Press, 1938.

MYERS, K. E., R. M. W. TRAVERS, and M. E. SANFORD. "Learning and Reinforcement in Student Pairs," *Journal of Educational Psychology,* 56 (1965), pp. 67–72.

NELSON, F., I. REID, and R. M. W. TRAVERS. "Effects of Different Reinforcing Conditions on Paired-Associate Learning," *Psychological Reports,* 16 (1956), pp. 123–126.

NEWCOMB, T. M. *Personality and Social Change: Attitude Formulation in a Student Community,* New York: Dryden, 1943.

NEWCOMB, T. M. "The Influence of Attitude Climates upon Some Determinants of Information," *Journal of Abnormal and Social Psychology,* 41 (1946), pp. 291–302.

NEWELL, A., J. C. SHAW, and H. A. SIMON. "Elements of a Theory of Human Problem Solving," *Psychological Review,* 65 (1958), pp. 151–166.

NEWMAN, H. H., F. N. FREEMAN, and K. J. HOLZINGER. *Twins: A Study of Heredity and Environment.* Chicago: University of Chicago Press, 1937.

NICKELL, MADGE, and R. M. W. TRAVERS. "Effects of Different Reinforcers: A Comparison across Age Levels," *Psychological Reports,* 13 (1963), 739–746.

NOTHMAN, F. H. "The Influence of Response Conditions on Recognition Thresholds for Tabu Words," *Journal of Abnormal and Social Psychology,* 65 (1962), pp. 154–161.

OLDS, J. "Self-Stimulation of the Brain," *Science,* 127 (1958a), pp. 315–324.

OLDS, J. "Adaptive Functions of Paleocortical and Related Structures," pp. 237–262, in *Biological and Biochemical Bases of Behavior,* HARLOW, H. F., and C. W. WODSEY (eds.). Madison: University of Wisconsin Press (1958b), 476 pp.

OLSON, W. *Child Development.* Boston: Heath, 1959.

OSBORN, A. F. *Applied Imagination: Principles and Procedures of Creative Thinking.* New York: Scribner, 1957.

OSGOOD, C. E. "Psycholinguistics," pp. 244–316 in *Psychology: A Study of a Science*, Vol. 6, KOCH, S. (ed.). New York: McGraw-Hill, 1963.

OSGOOD, C. E. "The Similarity Paradox in Human Learning: A Resolution," *Psychological Review*, **56** (1949), pp. 132–143.

OSGOOD, C. E., and P. H. TANNENBAUM. "The Principle of Congruity in the Prediction of Attitude Change," *Psychological Review*, **62** (1955), pp. 42–55.

OSGOOD, C. E., G. J. SUCI, and P. H. TANNENBAUM. *The Measurement of Meaning*. Urbana: University of Illinois Press, 1957.

PAVLOV, I. P. *Conditioned Reflexes*. London: Oxford University Press, 1927.

PAVLOV, I. P. *Lectures on Conditioned Reflexes*. New York: International Publishers, 1928.

PEAK, H., and H. W. MORRISON. "The Acceptance of Information into Attitude Structure," *Journal of Abnormal and Social Psychology*, **57** (1958), pp. 127–135.

PECK, R. F. "Family Patterns Correlated with Adolescent Personality Structure," *Journal of Abnormal and Social Psychology*, **57** (1958), pp. 347–350.

PERLMOTTER, H. V. and G. DE MONTMOLLIN. "Group Learning of Nonsense Syllables," *Journal of Abnormal and Social Psychology*, **47** (1952), pp. 762–769.

PETERSON, R. C., and L. L. THURSTONE. *Motion Pictures and the Social Attitudes of Children*. New York: Macmillan, 1933.

POND, F. L. "Influence of the Study of Latin on Word Knowledge," *School Review*, **46** (1938), pp. 611–618.

POSTMAN, L., and L. W. PHILLIPS. "Studies in Incidental Learning: I, the Effects of Crowding and Isolation," *Journal of Experimental Psychology*, **48** (1954), pp. 48–56.

POSTMAN, L., P. A. ADAMS, and A. M. BOHM. "Studies in Incidental Learning: V. Recall for Order and Associative Clustering," *Journal of Experimental Psychology*, **51** (1956), pp. 334–342.

POSTMAN, L., J. S. BRUNER, and E. McGINNIES. "Personal Values as Selective Factors in Perception," *Journal of Abnormal and Social Psychology*, **43** (1948), pp. 142–154.

PRESSEY, S. L. "A Simple Apparatus Which Gives Tests and Scores—and Teaches," *School and Society*, **23** (1926), pp. 373–376.

PRESSEY, S. L. "A Third and Fourth Contribution Toward the Coming 'Industrial Revolution' in Education," *School and Society*, **36** (1932), pp. 668–672.

PRINCE, A. I. "The Effect of Punishment on Visual Discrimination Learning," *Journal of Experimental Psychology*, **52** (1956), pp. 381–385.

PROKASY, W. F. JR., and F. L. WHALEY. "Manifest Anxiety Scale Score and the Ready Signal in Classical Conditioning," *Journal of Experimental Psychology*, **63** (1962), pp. 119–123.

RABIN, A. I. *Growing up in the Kibbutz*. New York: Springer, 1965.

RAMOND, C. K. "Performance in Instrumental Learning as a Joint Function of

Delay in Reinforcement and Time of Deprivation," *Journal of Experimental Psychology*, **47** (1954), pp. 248–250.

RATLIFF, M. M. "The Varying Function of Affectively Toned Olfactory, Visual and Auditory Cues in Recall," *American Journal of Psychology*, **51** (1938), pp. 695–701.

RAVEN, B. H. "Social Influence on Opinion and the Communication of Related Content," *Journal of Abnormal and Social Psychology*, **58** (1959), pp. 119–128.

RAZRAN, G. "Experimental Semantics," *Transaction of the New York Academy of Sciences*, **14** (1951–52), pp. 171–177.

RAY, O. S. "Personality Factors in Motor Learning and Reminiscence," *Journal of Abnormal and Social Psychology*, **58** (1959), pp. 199–203.

REESE, H. W. "Verbal Mediation as a Result of Age Level," *Psychological Bulletin*, **59** (1962), pp. 502–509.

REID, I. *Sense Modality Switching in Relation to Learning*. Doctoral dissertation, University of Utah, 1964.

RHINE, R. J. "A Concept Formation Approach to Attitude Acquisition," *Psychological Review*, **65** (1958), pp. 362–370.

RHINE, R. J., and B. A. SILUN. "Acquisition and Change of a Concept Attitude as a Function of Consistency of Reinforcement," *Journal of Experimental Psychology*, **55** (1958), pp. 524–529.

RICE, J. M. *The Public School System of the United States*. New York: Century, 1893.

RIGBY, M. K., and W. K. RIGBY. "Perceptual Thresholds as a Function of Reinforcement and Frequency," *American Psychologist* (abstract), **7** (1952), p. 321.

ROBINSON, E. S. "The 'Similarity' Factor in Retroaction," *American Journal of Psychology*, **39** (1927), pp. 297–312.

ROCK, I., and F. S. FLECK. "A Re-examination of the Effect of Monetary Reward and Punishment on Figure-Ground Perception," *Journal of Experimental Psychology*, **40** (1950), pp. 766–776.

ROCK, R. T. *The Influence upon Learning of the Quantitative Variation of After-Effects*. Teachers College Contribution to Education, No. 650. New York: Teachers College, Columbia University, 1935.

ROE, A. "Early Differentiation of Interest," pp. 98–108 in *The Second University of Utah Research Conferences on the Identification of Creative Scientific Talent*. Salt Lake City: University of Utah Press, 1957.

ROGERS, C. R. *Client-Centered Therapy*. Boston: Houghton Mifflin, 1951.

ROSENBERG, M. J. "Cognitive Reorganization in Response to the Hypnotic Reversal of Attitudinal Affect," *Journal of Personality*, **28** (1960), pp. 39–63.

ROSENBERG, M. J., C. I. HOVLAND, W. J. McGUIRE, R. P. ABELSON, and J. W. BREHM. *Attitude Organization and Change*. New Haven: Yale University Press, 1960.

RYAN, G. *An Experiment in Class Instruction Versus Individual Study at the College Level*. Unpublished doctoral dissertation, Johns Hopkins University, 1932.

SAMUELSON, C. O., and D. T. PEARSON. "Interest Scores in Identifying the Potential Trade School Dropout," *Journal of Applied Psychology,* **40** (1956), pp. 386–388.

SARNOFF, I., and D. KATZ. "The Motivational Bases of Attitude Change," *Journal of Abnormal and Social Psychology,* **49** (1954), pp. 115–124.

SCHAFER, R., and G. MURPHY. "The Role of Autism in Visual Figure-Ground Relationship," *Journal of Experimental Psychology,* **32** (1943), pp. 335–343.

SCHWIEKER, R. F. *Stability of Interest Measures and Their Validation for Selection and Classification.* No. 59–36. USAF Wright Air Development Center, 1959.

SCOLLON, R. W., JR. "A Study of Some Communicator Variables Related to Attitude Restructuring through Motion Picture Films," *Dissertation Abstracts,* **17** (1957), p. 400.

SCOTT, W. A. "Attitude Change through Reward of Verbal Behavior," *Journal of Abnormal and Social Psychology,* **55** (1957), pp. 72–75.

SEARS, P. S. "Developmental Psychology," pp. 119–156 in FARNSWORTH, P., and Q. McNEMAR (eds.), *Annual Review of Psychology.* Palo Alto, Calif.: Annual Reviews, 1958.

SEARS, P. S. *Accuracy of Self Perceptions in Elementary School Children,* paper presented at California Educational Research Association meeting, 1959.

SEARS, R. R., E. E. MACCOBY, and H. LEVIN. *Patterns of Child Rearing.* Evanston, Ill.: Row, Peterson, 1957.

SHARPE, J. F. "Retention of Meaningful Material," *Catholic University of America Educational Research Monograph,* **16,** No. 8, 1952.

SHAW, M. E. "A Comparison of Individuals and Small Groups in the Rational Solution of Complex Problems," *American Journal of Psychology,* **44** (1932), pp. 491–504.

SHEFFIELD, F. D., and W. O. JENKINS. "Level of Repetition in the Spread of Effect," *Journal of Experimental Psychology,* **44** (1952), pp. 101–107.

SHEFFIELD, F. D., and T. B. ROBY. "Reward Value of Nonnutritive Sweet Taste," *Journal of Comparative and Physiological Psychology,* **43** (1950), pp. 471–481.

SHEFFIELD, F. D., T. B. ROBY, and B. A. CAMPBELL. "Drive Reduction versus Consummatory Behavior as Determinants of Reinforcement," *Journal of Comparative and Physiological Psychology,* **47** (1954), pp. 349–354.

SHERRINGTON, C. S. *The Integrative Action of the Nervous System.* Cambridge: Yale University Press, 1906.

SHILLING, M. *An Experimental Investigation of the Effect of a Decrease in the Delay of Reinforcement upon Instrumental Response Performance.* Unpublished master's thesis, University of Iowa, 1951.

SHIPLEY, T. E., and J. VEROFF. "A Projective Measure of Need for Affiliation," *Journel of Experimental Psychology,* **43** (1952), pp. 349–356.

SIEGEL, A. F., and S. SIEGEL. "Reference Groups, Membership Groups, and Attitude Change," *Journal of Abnormal and Social Psychology,* **55** (1957), pp. 360–364.

SILBERMAN, H. F. "Effects of Praise and Reproof on Reading Growth in a Nonlaboratory Classroom Setting," *Journal of Educational Psychology,* **48** (1957), pp. 199–206.

SKINNER, B. F. *The Behavior of Organisms.* New York: Appleton-Century-Crofts, 1938.

SKINNER, B. F. *Science and Human Behavior.* New York: Macmillan, 1953.

SKINNER, B. F. *Verbal Behavior.* New York: Appleton-Century-Crofts, 1957.

SKINNER, B. F. "Teaching Machines," *Science,* **128** (1958), pp. 969–977.

SMITH, D. E., and J. E. HOCHBERG. "The Effect of Punishment (Electric Shock) on Figure-Ground Perception," *Journal of Psychology,* **38** (1954), pp. 83–87.

SMITH, E. R., and R. W. TYLER. *Appraising and Recording Pupil Progress.* New York: Harper, 1942.

SMITH, H. C., and D. S. DUNBAR. "The Personality and Achievement of the Classroom Participant," *Journal of Educational Psychology,* **42** (1951), pp. 65–84.

SMITH, H. P., and T. R. TATE. "Improvements in Reading Rate and Comprehension of Subjects Training with the Tachistoscope," *Journal of Educational Psychology,* **44** (1953), pp. 176–184.

SMITH, M. "Group Judgments in the Field of Personality Traits," *Journal of Experimental Psychology,* **14** (1931), pp. 562–565.

SMITH, M. E. *An Investigation of the Study of the Development of the Sentence and the Extent of the Vocabulary in Young Children,* University of Iowa Studies of Child Welfare, **3,** No. 5, 1926.

SNYGG, D "The Need for a Phenomenological System of Psychology," pp. 3–27, in *The Phenomenological Problem,* KUENZLI, A. E. (ed.). New York: Harper, 1959.

SOLLEY, C. M., and G. MURPHY. *Development of the Perceptual World.* New York: Basic Books, 1960.

SPAULDING, R. L. *Differential Effects of High and Low Self Concepts Regarding Mental Ability upon Academic Achievement,* paper presented at California Educational Research Association, 1960.

SPENCE, KENNETH, W. *Behavior Theory and Conditioning.* New Haven: Yale University Press, 1956.

SPENCE, R. B. "Lecture and Class Discussion in Teaching Educational Psychology," *Journal of Educational Psychology,* **19** (1928), pp. 454–462.

SPITZ, R. A. "Hospitalism, an Inquiry into the Genesis of Psychiatric Conditions in Early Childhood," *Psychoanalytic Study of the Child,* 1945, 1, 53–74.

STAATS, A. W., and C. K. STAATS. "Attitudes Established by Classical Conditioning," *Journal of Abnormal and Social Psychology,* **57** (1958), pp. 37–40.

STARCH, D. "A Demonstration of the Trial and Error Method of Learning." *Psychological Bulletin,* **7** (1910), pp. 20–23.

STAYTON, S. E. "Value, Magnitude and Accentuation," *Journal of Abnormal and Social Psychology,* **62** (1961), pp. 145–147.

STAYTON, S. E. "Judgmental Bias in Perception as a Function of Learned Relationships between Attributes," *Perceptual and Motor Skills,* **19** (1964), pp. 351–361.

STEPHENSON, W. *The Study of Behavior.* Chicago: University of Chicago Press, 1953.

STEVENS, P. H. "An Investigation of the Relationship between Certain Aspects of Self-Concept Behavior and Student's Academic Achievements," *Dissertation Abstracts,* **16** (1956), pp. 2531–2532.

STOLUROW, L. M. "Teaching by Machine," *Cooperative Research Monograph* No. 6, U.S. Department of Health, Education, and Welfare, 1961.

STONE, L. J., "A Critique of Studies of Infant Isolation," *Child Development,* **25** (1954), pp. 9–20.

STORMZAND, M. J., and M. V. O'SHEA. *How Much English Grammar?* Baltimore: Warwick and York, 1924.

STROOP. J. R. "Is the Judgment of the Group Better Than That of the Average Member of the Group?" *Journal of Experimental Psychology,* **15** (1932), pp. 550–562.

SWIFT, E. J. "Studies in the Psychology and Physiology of Learning." *American Journal of Psychology,* **14** (1903), pp. 201–251.

TAJFEL, H. "Value and Perception of Magnitude," *Psychological Review,* **64** (1957), pp. 192–204.

TANNENBAUM, P. H. "Initial Attitude toward Source and Concept as Factors in Attitude Change through Communication," *Public Opinion Quarterly,* **20** (1956), pp. 413–425.

TAYLOR, D. M. "Changes in the Self Concept without Psychotherapy," *Journal of Consulting Psychology,* **19** (1955), pp. 205–209.

TAYLOR, D. W., and W. L. FAUST. "Twenty Questions: Efficiency in Problem Solving as a Function of Size of Group," *Journal of Experimental Psychology,* **44** (1952), pp. 360–368.

TAYLOR, D. W., P. C. BERRY, and C. H. BLOCK. "Does Group Participation When Using Brainstorming Facilitate or Inhibit Creative Thinking?" *Administrative Quarterly,* **3** (1958). pp. 23–47.

TAYLOR, J. A. "The Relation of Anxiety to the Conditioned Eyelid Response," *Journal of Experimental Psychology,* **41** (1951), pp. 81–92.

TAYLOR, J. A., and K. W. SPENCE. "The Relationship of Anxiety to Level of Performance in Serial Learning," *Journal of Experimental Psychology,* **44** (1952), pp. 61–64.

TERMAN, L. M., and M. A. MERRILL. *Measuring Intelligence.* Boston: Houghton Mifflin, 1937.

THELEN, H. A. *Dynamics of Groups at Work.* Chicago: University of Chicago, 1954.

THIE, T. M. "Testing the Efficiency of the Group Method," *English Journal,* **14** (1925), pp. 134–137.

THORNDIKE, E. L. *Animal Intelligence.* New York: Macmillan, 1911.

THORNDIKE, E. L. *Educational Psychology, Vol. II, The Psychology of Learning.* New York: Teachers College, Columbia University, 1923.

THORNDIKE, E. L. *Fundamentals of Learning*. New York: Teachers College, Columbia University, 1932.

THORNDIKE, E. L. *An Experimental Study of Rewards*, New York: Teachers College, Contributions to Education, No. 580, 1933.

THORNDIKE, E. L. *The Psychology of Wants, Interests, and Attitudes*. New York: Appleton-Century-Crofts, 1935.

THORNDIKE, E. L. *Human Nature and the Social Order*. New York: Macmillan, 1940.

THORNDIKE, E. L. "Interests and Abilities," *School and Society*, 5 (1917), pp. 178–179.

THORNDIKE, E. L., and R. S. WOODWORTH. "The Influence of Improvement of One Mental Function upon the Efficiency of Other Functions," *Psychological Review*, 8 (1901), pp. 247–261, 384–395, 553–564.

THORNDIKE, R. L. "On What Type of Task Will a Group Do Well?" *Journal of Abnormal and Social Psychology*, 33 (1938), pp. 408–413.

THURSTONE, L. L. *Multiple-Factor Analysis*. Chicago: University of Chicago Press, 1947.

TORRANCE, E. P., and R. MASON. "Instructor Effort to Influence: An Experimental Evaluation of Six Approaches," *Journal of Educational Psychology*, 49 (1958), pp. 211–218.

TRAPP, E. P., and D. H. KAUSLER. "Dominance Attitudes in Parents and Adult Avoidance Behavior in Young Children," *Child Development*, 29 (1958), pp. 507–513.

TRAVERS, R. M. W. (in collaboration with others) *Reinforcement in Classroom Learning*. Salt Lake City: Bureau of Educational Research, University of Utah, 1964.

TRAVERS, R. M. W., J. E. MARRON, and A. J. POST. *Some Conditions Affecting Quality, Consistency, and Predictability of Performance in Solving Complex Problems*, Air Force Personnel and Training Research Center, Research Report (1955), pp. 55–27.

TYLER, F. T. "Concepts of Organismic Growth," *Journal of Educational Psychology*, 44 (1953), pp. 321–342.

ULRICH, R. E. "Conversation Control," *Psychological Record*, 12 (1962), pp. 327–330.

ULRICH, R. E., R. R. HUTCHINSON, and N. H. AZRIN. "Pain-Elicited Aggression." *Psychological Record*, 15 (1965), pp. 111–126.

UNDERWOOD, B. J. "Associative Transfer in Verbal Learning as a Function of Response Similarity and Degree of First List Learning," *Journal of Experimental Psychology*, 42 (1951), pp. 44–53.

UNDERWOOD, B. J. "Verbal Learning in the Educative Process," *Harvard Educational Review*, 29 (1959), pp. 107–117.

UNDERWOOD, B. J., and R. W. SCHULTZ. *Meaningfulness and Verbal Learning*. Philadelphia: Lippincott, 1960.

VAN MONDFRANS, A., and R. M. W. TRAVERS. "Learning of Redundant Material Presented through Two Sensory Modalities," *Perceptual and Motor Skills*, 19 (1964), pp. 743–751.

VAN WAGENEN, R. K., and R. M. W. TRAVERS. "Learning under Conditions of Direct and Vicarious Reinforcement," *Journal of Educational Psychology,* **54** (1963), pp. 356–362.

VERPLANCK, W. S. "The Control of the Content of Conversation; Reinforcement of Statements of Opinion," *Journal of Abnormal and Social Psychology,* **51** (1955a), pp. 666–676.

VERPLANCK, W. S. "The Operant from Rat to Man: An Introduction to Some Recent Experiments on Human Behavior," *Transactions of the New York Academy of Sciences,* Vol. 17, No. 8 (June, 1955b), pp. 594–601.

VETTER, R. J. Perception of Ambiguous Figure-Ground Patterns as a Function of Past Experience," *Perceptual and Motor Skills,* **20** (1965), pp. 183–188.

VON SENDEN, M. *Space and Sight* (Tr. by Peter Heath). Glencoe: Free Press, 1960.

WAGMAN, M. "Attitude Change and Authoritarian Personality," *Journal of Psychology,* **40** (1955), pp. 3–24.

WALK, R. D., and E. J. GIBSON. "A Comparative and Analytical Study of Visual Depth Perception," *Psychological Monographs,* **75,** (15, Whole No. 519), 1961.

WALK, R. D., E. J. GIBSON, H. L. PICK, and T. J. TIGHE. "The Effectiveness of Prolonged Exposure to Cutouts vs. Painted Patterns for Facilitation of Discrimination," *Journal of Comparative and Physiological Psychology,* **52** (1959b), pp. 519–552.

WALLEN, N., and R. M. W. TRAVERS. "Analysis and Investigation of Testing Methods," pp. 448–505, in *A Handbook of Research on Teaching,* N. L. Gage, (ed.), Chicago: Rand McNally, 1963.

WALTER, L. M., and S. S. MARZOLF. "The Relation of Sex, Age, and School Achievement to Levels of Aspiration," *Journal of Educational Psychology,* **42** (1951), pp. 285–292.

WARD, L. B. "Reminiscence and Rote Learning," *Psychological Monographs,* **49,** No. 220, 1937.

WARDEN, C. J. "The Distribution of Practice in Animal Learning," *Comparative Psychological Monographs,* **1,** No. 3, 1923.

WARDEN, C. J., and M. AYLESWORTH. "The Relative Value of Reward and Punishment in the Formation of a Visual Discrimination Habit in the White Rat," *Journal of Comparative Psychology,* **7** (1927), pp. 117–127.

WATSON, G. "An Evaluation of Small Group Work in a Large Class," *Journal of Educational Psychology,* **44** (1953), pp. 385–408.

WATSON, G. B. "Do Groups Think More Efficiently Than Individuals?" *Journal of Abnormal and Social Psychology,* **23** (1928), pp. 328–336.

WATSON, G. B. "A Comparison of Group and Individual Performances at Certain Intellectual Tasks," *Proceedings of the Ninth International Congress of Psychology,* 1929.

WATSON, J. B. *Behaviorism.* New York: People's Institute, 1924.

WATSON, J. B., and R. RAYNOR. "Conditioned Emotional Reactions," *Journal of Experimental Psychology,* **3** (1920), pp. 1–14.

WEIR, M. W. "Developmental Changes in Problem-Solving Strategies," *Psychological Review*, **71** (1964), pp. 473–490.

WEISS, W. "The Relationship between Judgments of a Communicator's Position and Extent of Opinion Change," *Journal of Abnormal and Social Psychology*, **56** (1958:, pp. 380–384.

WERTHEIMER, M. *Productive Thinking*. New York: Harper, 1945.

WHITE, R. K., and R. LIPPITT. *Autocracy and Democracy*. New York: Harper, 1960.

WILSON, W. C., and W. S. VERPLANCK. "Some Observations on the Reinforcement of Verbal Operants," *American Journal of Psychology*, **69** (1956), pp. 448–451.

WITHALL, J., and W. W. LEWIS. "Social Interaction in the Classroom," Chapter 13 in *Handbook of Research on Teaching*, N. L. GAGE (ed.). Chicago: Rand McNally, 1963.

WOHLWILL, J. F. "Developmental Studies of Perception," *Psychological Bulletin*, **57** (1960), pp. 269–288.

WOLFE, J. B. "Effectiveness of Token Rewards for Chimpanzees," *Comparative Psychological Monographs*, **12**, No. 5 (Serial No. 60), (1936), p. 78.

WOOD, B. D., and F. W. FREEMAN. *An Experimental Study of the Educational Influence of the Typewriter in the Elementary School Classroom*. New York: Macmillan, 1932.

WOODROW, H. "Effect of Type of Training upon Transference," *Journal of Educational Psychology*, **18** (1927), pp. 159–172.

WOODROW, H. "The Ability to Learn," *Psychological Review*, **53** (1946), pp. 147–158.

WOODRUFF, A. D. "The Use of Concepts in Teaching and Learning," *Journal of Teacher Education*, **15** (1964), pp. 81–99.

WOODWORTH, R. S. *Dynamic Psychology*. New York: Columbia University Press, 1918.

WOODWORTH, R. S. *Dynamics of Behavior*. New York: Holt, 1958.

WORELL, L. "Level of Aspiration and Academic Success," *Journal of Educational Psychology*, **50** (1959), pp. 47–54.

WRIGHT, J. M. VON. *An Experimental Study of Human Serial Learning*. D. Phil. thesis, Oxford University, 1955.

WRIGHT, J. M. VON. "A Note on the Role of Guidance in Learning," *British Journal of Psychology*, **48** (1957), pp. 133–137.

WULF, F. "Tendencies in Figural Variation," pp. 136–148 in Ellis, A. (ed.), *A Source Book of Gestalt Psychology*. New York: Harcourt, Brace, 1938.

WYLIE, R. C. *The Self Concept*. Lincoln: University of Nebraska Press, 1961.

YARROW, L. J. "Material Deprivation: Towards an Empirical and Conceptual Re-evaluation," *Psychological Bulletin*, **58** (1961), pp. 459–490.

YOUNG, P. T. *Motivation and Emotion: A Survey of the Determinants of Human and Animal Activity*. New York: Wiley, 1961.

YOUNG, P. T. "Studies of Food Preference, Appetite and Dietary Habit: I. Running Activity and Dietary Habit of the Rat in Relation to Food Preference," *Journal of Comparative Psychology*, **37** (1944), pp. 327–370.

YOUNG, P. T., and J. P. CHAPLIN. "Studies of Food Preference, Appetite and Dietary Habit: III. Palatability and Appetite in Relation to Bodily Need," *Comparative Psychological Monographs*, 18, No. 3, 1945.

YOUNG, P. T., and E. H. SHUFORD. "Quantitative Control of Motivation through Sucrose Solutions of Different Concentrations," *Journal of Comparative and Physiological Psychology*, 48 (1955), pp. 114–118.

YUM, K. S. "An Experimental Test of the Law of Assimilation," *Journal of Experimental Psychology*, 14 (1931), pp. 68–82.

ZEAMAN, D. "Response Latency as a Function of the Amount of Reinforcement," *Journal of Experimental Psychology*, 39 (1949), pp. 466–483.

ZELANY, L. D. "Experimental Appraisal of a Group Learning Plan," *Journal of Educational Research*, 34 (1940–41), pp. 37–42.

ZELANY, L. D. "Teaching Sociology by a Discussion Group Method," *Sociological and Social Research* (1927), pp. 162–172.

Index of Names

Index of Subjects